STERLING
Education

Homeschool
Environmental Science

Comprehensive Content

4th edition

Copyright © Sterling Education

Customer Satisfaction Guarantee

Your feedback is important because we strive to provide the highest quality educational materials. Email us comments or suggestions.

info@sterling-prep.com

We reply to emails – check your spam folder

All rights reserved. This publication's content, including the text and graphic images or part thereof, may not be reproduced, downloaded, disseminated, published, converted to electronic media, or distributed by any means without prior written consent from the publisher. Copyright infringement violates federal law and is subject to criminal and civil penalties.

4 3 2 1

ISBN-13: 979-8-8855733-6-8

Sterling Education materials are available at quantity discounts.
Contact info@sterling–prep.com

Sterling Education
6 Liberty Square #11
Boston, MA 02109

©2026 Sterling Education

Published by Sterling Education

Printed in the U.S.A.

STERLING
Education

Thousands of students use our educational products to achieve academic success!

Many students find environmental science fascinating but challenging discipline. To do well in the subject, they need to understand core material, be able to extract and analyze information, and distinguish between related concepts rather than memorizing terms. With this book, students master environmental science content and develop the ability to apply their knowledge on quizzes and tests.

This book provides thorough coverage of environmental science topics, teaching the foundational theories and concepts necessary to master the core content. The material is clearly presented and systematically organized for learning important principles and relationships, providing comprehensive preparation.

From the foundations of Earth systems to the present-day climate challenges, students will develop a better understanding of ecosystems, population dynamics, use of natural resources, as well as the political and social landscape of environmental challenges. They will learn about Earth's biochemical cycles, land and water use, energy resources and their consumption, the significance of the various environmental movements and global initiatives, as well as how different human actions affect the overall balance within ecosystems.

Experienced science teachers prepared this learning material to build knowledge and skills crucial for understanding facts and events that shape the natural world. Our editorial team reviewed and systematized the content for targeted and effective learning, so students can significantly improve their understanding of the subject.

We wish you great success in mastering environmental science!

250614akp

Featured on

> If you benefited from this book, please leave a review on Amazon so others can learn from your input. Reviews help us understand our customers' needs and experiences while keeping our commitment to quality.

Homeschool study aids

STEM

Physics

Chemistry

Organismal Biology

Cell and Molecular Biology

Anatomy & Physiology

Environmental Science

Psychology

Social Studies

American History

U.S. Government & Politics

Comparative Government & Politics

World History

European History

Human Geography

Sociology

Visit our Amazon store

Page intentionally left blank

Table of Contents

CHAPTER 1: Earth Systems & Resources 23

    Earth Science 25
        Earth's landforms 25
        Sedimentary layers 26
        Uniform frequency and magnitude 26
        Faunal succession 28

    Geological Timeline 29
        Plate boundaries 29
        Geologic time scale 29
        Eons and Eras 30
        Periods and Epochs 31
        Plant and animal domination 31
        Geological history time scales 33

    Plate Tectonics 37
        Plate boundaries 37
        Divergent boundaries 37
        Convergent boundaries 39
        Transform plate boundaries 40

    Earthquakes 43
        Stratified Earth 43
        Earthquake terminology 43
        Seismic waves 44
        P and S waves 45
        Surface waves 45
        Seismograms 46
        Richter scale 47

    Volcanism 49
        Mountain building 49
        Magma and gases 49
        Magmatic volcanism 49
        Non-magmatic volcanism 50

Table of Contents (*continued*)

CHAPTER 1: Earth Systems & Resources (*continued*)

Earth's Planetary Movement ... 51
- Earth's rotation and revolution ... 51
- Solstices ... 51
- Equinoxes ... 53
- Earth's seasons ... 54

Solar Intensity and Latitude ... 55
- Solar irradiance ... 55
- Peak radiation ... 55
- Latitude and illumination angle ... 56
- Solar heat transfer ... 57
- Reflection and albedo ... 58
- Auroras ... 59

Atmosphere ... 61
- Earth's atmosphere ... 61
- Atmospheric composition ... 61
- Altitude, density, temperature and pressure ... 62
- Rayleigh scattering ... 64
- Atmospheric layers ... 65
- Atmospheric research ... 67

Questions: Earth Systems & Resources ... 69

CHAPTER 2: Weather & Climate ... 73

Weather Patterns ... 75
- Weather phenomena ... 75
- Relative humidity and dewpoint ... 76
- Precipitation ... 77
- Precipitation formation ... 78

Table of Contents (*continued*)

CHAPTER 2: Weather & Climate (*continued*)

Global Atmospheric Circulation 79
- Earth's rotation and tilt 79
- Coriolis effect 80
- Hadley cells 81
- Ferrel cells 82
- Polar cells 83

Pressure Systems and Winds 85
- Atmospheric pressure 85
- Cold and warm fronts 87
- Wave patterns 91
- Positive and negative tilt patterns 93
- Dips and ridges 94
- Wind rotation 95
- Geostrophic wind 96
- Jet streams 97
- Beaufort Wind Scale 98

Oceanic Influences 101
- Atmosphere-ocean interactions 101
- Thermocline 101
- Hurricanes 103
- Saffron-Simpson Hurricane Wind Scale 104
- Tides 105
- ENSO 106
- La Niña 106
- El Niño, temperature anomaly 107

Oceanic Circulations 109
- Surface ocean currents 109
- Gyres 109
- Surface currents of subtropical gyres 109
- Subsurface currents 111

Questions: Weather & Climate 113

Table of Contents (*continued*)

CHAPTER 3: The Living World 117

- **Ecosystem Structure** 119
    - Ecosystems 119
    - Terrestrial biomes 120
    - Aquatic biomes 121
    - Biological populations and communities 123
    - Biotic potential 124
    - Ecological niches 124
    - Fundamental niches 125

- **Interactions Among Populations** 127
    - Species diversity 127
    - Keystone species 127
    - Species interactions 128
    - Symbiosis 129
    - Trophic interactions 130
    - Edge effects 130

- **Ecosystem Diversity** 131
    - Evolution and origin of species 131
    - Natural selection 133
    - Positive and negative selection 133
    - Diversity 134
    - Ecosystem services 135

- **Energy Flow** 137
    - Ecological energy flow 137
    - Secondary consumers 137
    - Energy transfer 137
    - Photosynthesis 138
    - Cellular respiration 138
    - Food webs and trophic levels 139
    - Biomass 141
    - Ecological pyramids 141
    - Energy pyramids of biomass 142

Table of Contents (*continued*)

CHAPTER 3: The Living World (*continued*)

Natural Biochemical Cycles 143
    Conservation of matter 143
    Biochemical cycles 144
    Carbon cycle 144
    Nitrogen cycle 145
    Phosphorus cycle 147
    Sulfur cycle 148
    Water cycle 149

Ecosystem Change 151
    Climate shifts 151
    Species movement 151
    Environmental disruptions 152
    Ecological succession 152

Questions: The Living World 155

CHAPTER 4: Population 159

Population Biology and Ecology 161
    Ecological hierarchy 161
    Habitats and community 161
    Population biology and ecology 161
    Physiological stressors 162
    Environmental resistance 163

Population Dynamics 165
    Population cycle 165
    Population growth 165
    Growth curves 166
    Carrying capacity 168

Table of Contents (*continued*)

CHAPTER 4: Population (*continued*)

Reproductive Strategies and Survivorship Models 169
- Reproductive strategies 169
- r-selection 169
- K-selection 169
- Mortality patterns 170
- Survivorship curves 171

Human Population Dynamics 173
- Historical population sizes 173
- Family planning 173
- Distribution 174

Human Population Growth 177
- Fertility rates 177
- Net reproduction rate 178
- Replacement fertility rate 178
- Birth rates 179
- Net reproduction rate 179
- Populations doubling times 180
- Population estimates 181

Population Demographics 183
- Demographic transition model 183
- Demographic transition stages 183
- Age-structure diagrams 185

Population Policies 187
- Sustainability 187
- Environmentally sustainable trajectory 188
- India's population 190
- China's population 190

Table of Contents (*continued*)

CHAPTER 4: Population (*continued*)

Population and Environment..191
- Planetary boundaries..191
- Hunger...192
- Income..192
- Disease..193
- Human interactions..194
- Overpopulation..194

Questions: Population 197

CHAPTER 5: Land & Water Use 201

Human Impact on Global Resources 203
- Resource consumption rate...203
- Environmental impacts..204
- Extinction events...204
- Habitat destruction..205

Water Resources 207
- Global water resources..207
- Freshwater and saltwater...208
- Ecosystem changes..209
- Agricultural, industrial and domestic uses of water................209
- Global water shortages..211
- Water conservation...212

Table of Contents (*continued*)

CHAPTER 5: Land & Water Use (*continued*)

Forests 213
    Importance of forests in the ecosystem 213
    Old-growth forests 213
    Public lands 215
    National Forests 215
    Forest management 216
    Production forests 217
    Planted trees 218
    American Tree Farm System 218
    Forest fires 219
    Types of forest fires 221
    Deforestation 222

Rangelands 225
    Crop cultivation 225
    Overgrazing 226
    Desertification 226
    Rangeland management 227
    Federal rangelands 228

Agriculture 229
    Nutritional requirements of growing population 229
    Types of agriculture 230
    Industrial agriculture and Green Revolution 230
    Genetic engineering 231
    Agricultural pests 231
    Types of pesticides 232
    Benefits and harms of pesticide use 232
    Pesticide contamination 233
    Integrated pest management 234
    Public awareness and relevant laws 234

Table of Contents (*continued*)

CHAPTER 5: Land & Water Use (*continued*)

Land Conservation 237
    Public and federal lands 237
    National Parks 238
    Land conservation and preservation 240
    Restoration 242

Land Use 243
    Land use categories 243
    Urban land development 245
    Heat islands 245
    Suburban sprawl 246
    Urbanization 247

Transportation Infrastructure 249
    Transportation 249
    Federal highway system 249
    Waterways 250
    Roadless areas 251

Mineral Resources and Mining 253
    Mineral resources 253
    Mineral formation 254
    Mining of minerals 255
    Underground mining 256
    Surface mining 257
    Depletion of global mineral reserves 257
    Mining disasters 259
    Relevant laws and treaties 260

Fishing 263
    Commercial fishing 263
    Fishing methods 265
    Overfishing 268
    Aquaculture 269
    Relevant laws and treaties 272

Table of Contents (*continued*)

CHAPTER 5: Land & Water Use (*continued*)

Global Economics 273

    Global economy rankings 273

    Organization for Economic Cooperation and Development 274

    Global economy metrics 275

Globalization 277

    Integration and assimilation 277

    Environmental impacts 277

    World Bank 278

    International Monetary Fund 279

    Shared obligations and *Tragedy of the Commons* 280

    Relevant laws and treaties 281

Questions: Land Use 283

CHAPTER 6: Pollution 289

Air Pollution 291

    Air pollution sources 291

    Primary and secondary air pollutants 292

    Volatile organic compounds 293

    Acid deposition 295

    Smog and particulate matter 297

    Indoor air pollution 298

    Air pollution remediation 299

    Air quality regulations 300

Water Pollution 303

    Pollution of aquatic environments 303

    Surface water pollution 304

    Groundwater pollution 306

    Water quality and purification 307

    Sewage treatment 309

    Groundwater regulations 310

    Surface water regulations 311

Table of Contents (*continued*)

CHAPTER 6: Pollution (*continued*)

Waste Management 313
    Solid and hazardous waste 313
    Landfills 314
    Incineration 315
    Composting 316
    Transport of hazardous waste 316
    Treatment and disposal of hazardous waste 317
    Bioremediation 318
    Cleanup of contaminated sites 319

Pollution and Human Health 321
    Waste-related health hazards 321
    Water pollution and health hazards 322
    Air pollutants' impact on human health 323
    Smoking and its risks 324
    Noise pollution effects 325
    Dose-response relationships 326
    Biomagnification 327
    Hazardous environmental chemicals 328
    Dioxins 328
    Organochlorines 329
    Cadmium 329
    Toxic Substances Control Act (TSCA) 330

Economic Impacts 331
    Pollution costs 331
    Remediation and mitigation 332
    Externalities 333
    Cost-benefit analysis 334
    Economic, social and environmental costs 335
    Marginal costs 337
    Sustainability 338
    Waste reduction strategies 339

Questions: Pollution 341

Table of Contents (*continued*)

CHAPTER 7: Energy Resources & Consumption 345

    Foundational Concepts of Energy 347
- Organisms require sunlight 347
- Energy forms 347
- Power 348
- Basic SI units 349
- Derived SI units 349
- Non-standard international units 350
- Laws of thermodynamics 350

    Energy Consumption 351
- Mastery of fire 351
- Industrial Revolution 351
- Global energy consumption 352
- Future energy needs and global energy crisis 356

    Fossil Fuel Reserves and Use 359
- Fossil fuels 359
- Coal, oil and natural gas formation 359
- Extraction methods 360
- Processing 360
- Global demand 361
- Proven reserves 363
- Synfuels 365
- Environmental advantages and disadvantages of fossil fuels 365

    Nuclear Energy 367
- Atomic nuclei 367
- Fission reactions 368
- Nuclear fuel 369
- Electricity-producing nuclear reactors 370
- Advantages of nuclear power 373
- Disadvantages of nuclear power 373
- Ionizing radiation and human health 374
- Radioactive waste 375

Table of Contents (*continued*)

CHAPTER 7: Energy Resources & Consumption (*continued*)

Hydroelectric Power 377
    Hydroelectricity 377
    Dams and flood control 378
    Habitat loss 379
    Silting 380
    Small-scale hydroelectricity 380
    Ocean waves and tidal energy 381

Energy Conservation and Renewable Energy 383
    Consumption 383
    Energy efficiency 384
    CAFE standards 384
    Electric vehicles 384
    Mass transit 386
    Clean energy 387
    Solar energy 388
    Hydrogen fuel cells 389
    Biofuels 390
    Wind energy 391
    Geothermal energy 392

Questions: Energy Resources & Consumption 393

CHAPTER 8: Global Change 399

Stratospheric Ozone 401
    Stratospheric ozone formation 401
    Ultraviolet radiation 402
    Ozone depletion causes 403
    Effects of ozone depletion 403
    Strategies for reducing ozone depletion 404
    Relevant laws and treaties 405

Table of Contents (*continued*)

CHAPTER 8: Global Change (*continued*)

Atmospheric Greenhouse Gases 407
    Greenhouse effect 407
    Fluorinated gases 408
    Nitrous oxide 410
    Carbon dioxide 411
    Methane 412

Global Climate Change 415
    Anthropogenic causes 415
    Average temperature 415
    Impacts and consequences of global warming 416
    Efforts to reduce climate change 417
    Relevant laws and treaties 418

Loss of Biodiversity 419
    Marine life 419
    Habitat loss 419
    Overuse of species 421
    Pollution 422
    Exogenous species 422
    Endangered and extinct species 423
    Maintenance through conservation 425
    Seed banks 426
    Laws and treaties 427

Questions: Global Change 429

APPENDIX 433

Answer Keys 435

Annotated Glossary of Environmental Science Terms 437

Page intentionally left blank

Page intentionally left blank

CHAPTER 1

Earth Systems & Resources

Earth Science

Geological Timeline

Plate Tectonics

Earthquakes

Volcanism

Earth's Planetary Movement

Solar Intensity and Latitude

Atmosphere

Page intentionally left blank

Earth Science

Earth's landforms

Earth science attracts many people who love the outdoors, and scientists are studying the processes that create and modify Earth's landforms.

Some scientists research what drives surface features and processes, for example, why earthquakes occur, or volcanoes erupt. They are interested in understanding the layers of material beneath the surface, mantle and core, and the processes below the surface.

Oceans cover over 70% of Earth, and many ponder what lies within them. More may be known about the far side of the Moon than about deep oceans.

However, much is known, considering how hostile the ocean is for land-dwelling species.

Earth scientists study Earth as a complex intersecting and interdependent subset of systems. They collaborate to answer narrowly defined interconnected questions.

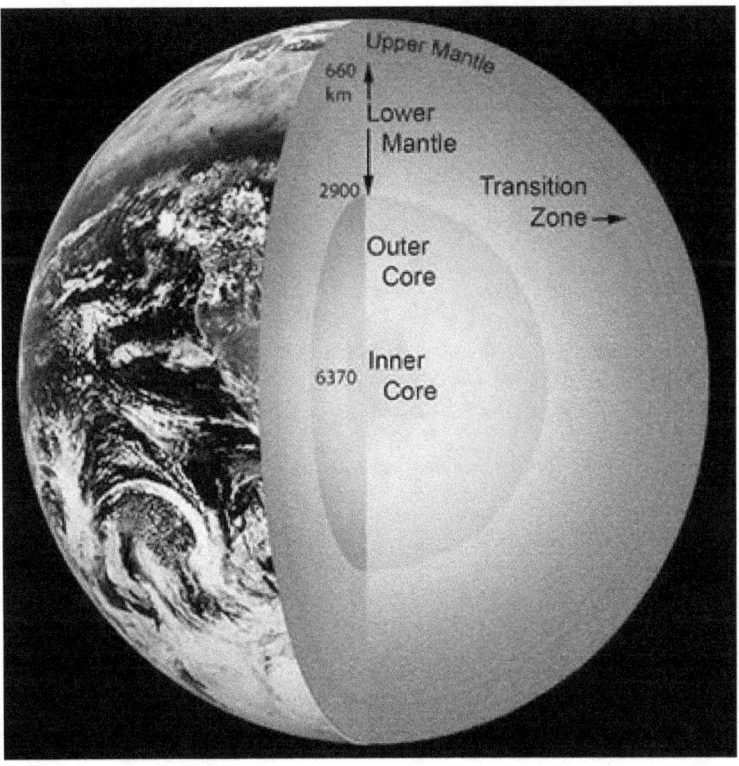

Earth's mantle and core shown schematically

Sedimentary layers

Mining has been of commercial interest since ancient civilizations, but it was not until the 1500s and 1600s that mining became a revenue-generating industry. Men who worked in the mines were among the first to understand the geological relationships between soil and rock types.

In 1669, Nicolaus Steno described two geologic principles from rock layer relationships. Steno's principles stated that 1) sedimentary rocks are *laid horizontally,* and 2) younger rock layers are *deposited on top* of older rock layers.

Hundreds of sedimentary layers formed over several million years, with sediment settling and being compressed into sections on top of the older layers, occurring in drylands and at the bottom of the oceans.

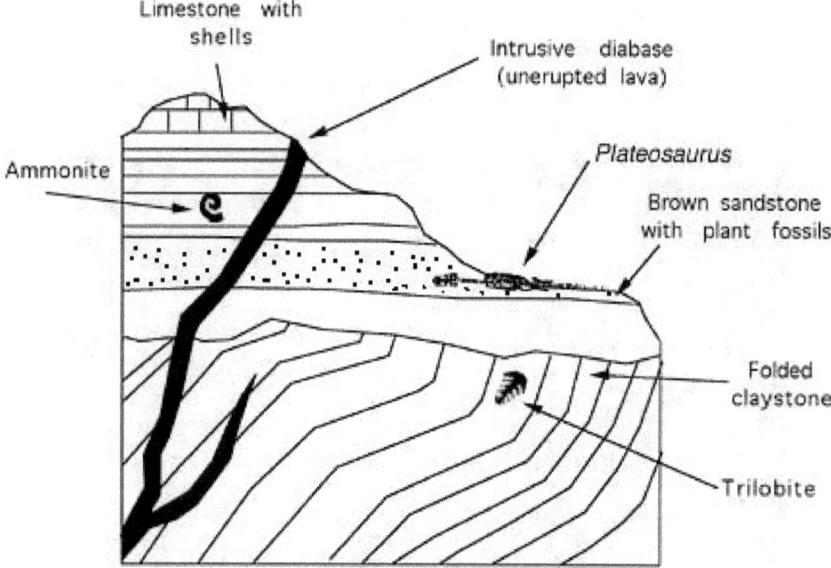

Topography and subsurface variations of sedimentary deposits

Uniform frequency and magnitude

James Hutton (1795) articulated the *principle of uniformitarianism* with the idea that natural geologic processes were *uniform in frequency* and *magnitude* over time. These principles allowed miners and scientists to recognize distinct rock successions within Earth's layers.

However, comparing rock sequences of distinct areas was often impossible because they categorized rocks by color, texture, or smell.

Fossils correlated geographically distinct areas over vast regions of Earth's crust.

Principle of superposition is that younger layers are deposited on top of older layers and build on the principle of original horizontality.

Principle of cross-cutting relationships is that layers that cut across other layers are younger than those they cut through.

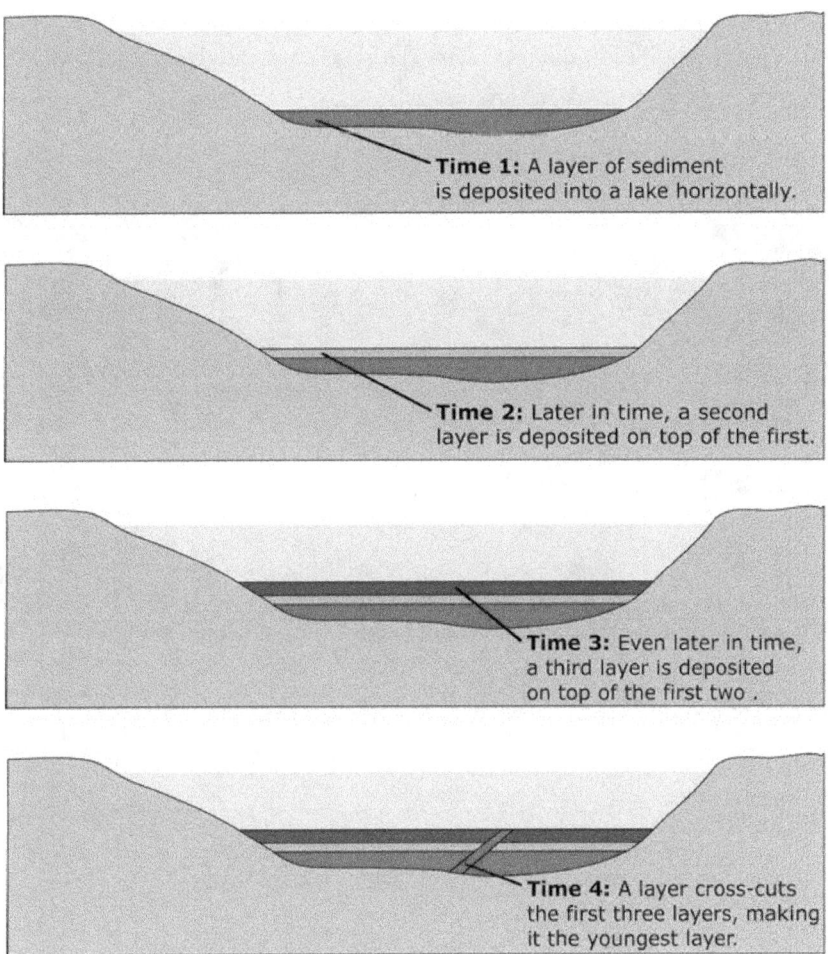

Superposition and sedimentary rock formation

Faunal succession

Another significant contribution to the geologic time scale came from a canal builder, surveyor, and amateur English geologist, William Smith. In 1815, Smith produced a geologic map of England and validated *faunal succession*, fossils arranged in rocks in a precise order.

Faunal succession (or *law of faunal succession*) is based on the observation that sedimentary rock strata contain fossilized flora and fauna that succeed each other vertically in a specific, reliable order consistent over vast horizontal distances.

Faunal succession uses fossils to define large increments within a relative timescale.

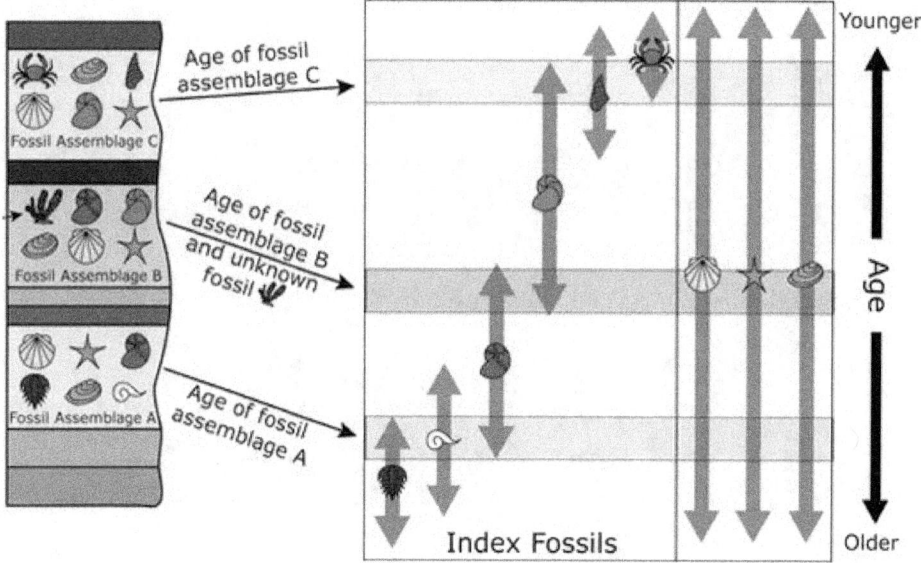

Faunal succession uses fossils to arrange known fossil species

Geological Time

Boundary events

Geologists divide Earth's geologic history into a series of time intervals. However, these time intervals are not equal in length, such as the hours in one Earth Day.

Instead, geologic intervals are variable because scientists divide time using significant events in the history of Earth, called *boundary events*.

Permian Period ended with the *Marine Realm* and *End-Permian Extinction* boundary event. Notably, it was the greatest mass extinction in the last 600 million years, during which 90% of marine animal species and 70% of land species disappeared. Theoretical causes of this mass extinction range from creating the Pangaea supercontinent to volcanism.

Cretaceous–Paleogene Extinction around 66 million years ago is a boundary event marking the ends of the *Cretaceous Period* and *Mesozoic Era*, beginning the current *Cenozoic Era*. It was a mass extinction of three-quarters of plant and animal species, including non-avian dinosaurs, and occurred over a geologically short period.

Geologic time scale

Geologic time scale shows the duration of Earth's history with linear timelines; thicker sections were more prolonged than thinner sections.

Phanerozoic Eon represents when most macroscopic organisms (e.g., algae, fungi, plants, and animals) lived and when animals evolved external skeletons (i.e., *exoskeletons*).

Phanerozoic Eon is subdivided into *Cenozoic*, *Mesozoic*, and *Paleozoic Eras*.

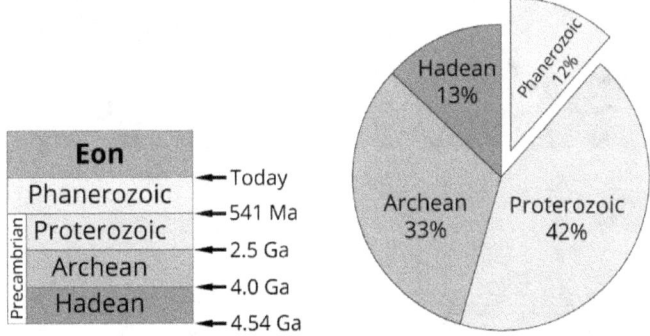

Eons with boundary events (on the left) and relative proportion of each Eon (on the right)

Eons and Eras

Geologic time scale is categorized into *Eons* with subdivisions. From largest:

Eon, Era, Period, Epoch, and *Age*.

Eons are the largest intervals of geological time and last hundreds of millions of years.

Phanerozoic Eon is recent and began 541 million years ago.

Eons divide into *Eras* as smaller intervals, defined by significant events.

For example, *Phanerozoic Eon* has the *Cenozoic, Mesozoic*, and *Paleozoic Eras*.

Eon	Era	Period	Epoch	
Phanerozoic	Cenozoic	Quaternary	Holocene	← Today
			Pleistocene	← 11.8 Ka
		Neogene	Pliocene	
			Miocene	
		Paleogene	Oligocene	
			Eocene	
			Paleocene	
	Mesozoic	Cretaceous	~	← 66 Ma
		Jurassic	~	
		Triassic	~	
	Paleozoic	Permian	~	← 252 Ma
		Carboniferous — Pennsylvanian	~	
		Carboniferous — Mississippian	~	
		Devonian	~	
		Silurian	~	
		Ordovician	~	
		Cambrian	~	
Proterozoic	~	~	~	← 541 Ma
Archean	~	~	~	← 2.5 Ga
Hadean	~	~	~	← 4.0 Ga
				← 4.54 Ga

← Younger / Older →

Eons, Eras, Periods, and Epochs for current Phanerozoic Eon

For example,

Eon	Era	Period	Epoch	Age
Phanerozoic	Cenozoic	Paleogene	Oligocene	Chattian
				Rupelian

Periods and Epochs

Eras are divided into *Periods* by events that are not as significant as those dividing them.

Paleozoic Era is divided into Periods:

      Permian, Pennsylvanian, Mississippian, Devonian, Silurian, Ordovician, Cambrian.

Periods are divided into *Epochs*.

Epochs exist only for recent geological time because older rocks are deeply buried, intensely deformed, and severely modified by long-term processes. Therefore, the geologic history of older rocks cannot be reliably interpreted.

Plant and animal domination

Eras are characterized by specific animal or plant domination.

      Cenozoic Era is the *Age of Mammals*

      Mesozoic Era is the *Age of Dinosaur*

      Paleozoic Era is the *Age of Fishes*

Zoic is Greek for *life; Cen- recent; Meso- middle; Paleo- ancient.*

Three divisions reflect significant changes in the composition of ancient life. However, this is overly simplified and has some significance, but it can be misleading.

For example, other animals (e.g., mammals, turtles, frogs, crocodiles, and insects) lived on land during the *Mesozoic Era* (i.e., *Age of Dinosaurs*).

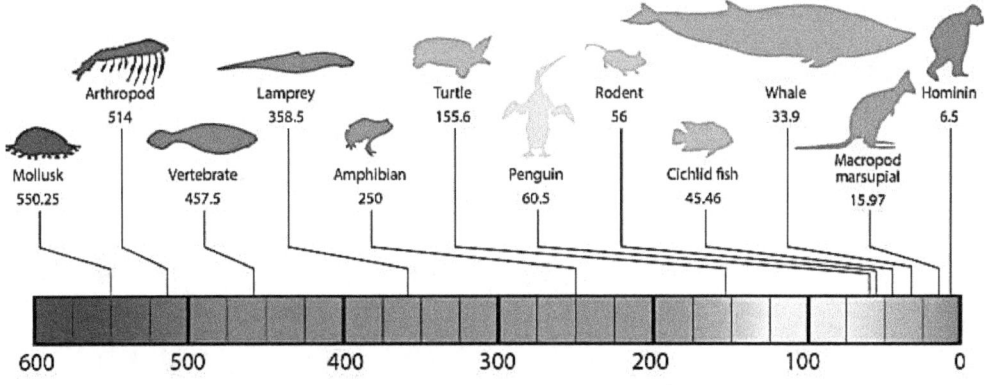

Species evolution noted in millions of years

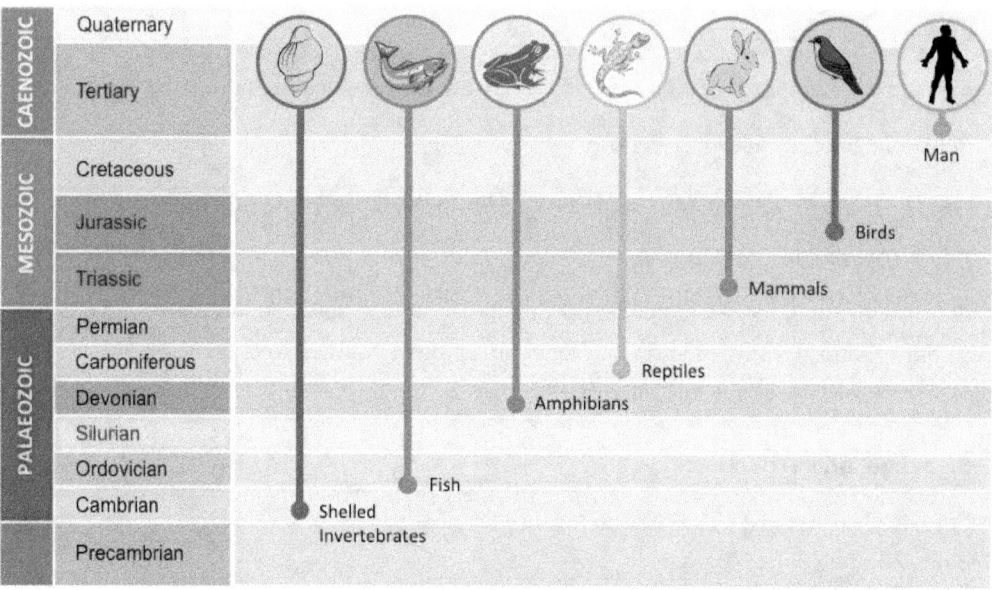

Fossil sequences during Phanerozoic Eon with three Eras, beginning in the Cambrian Period

Geological history time scales (*descending order*)

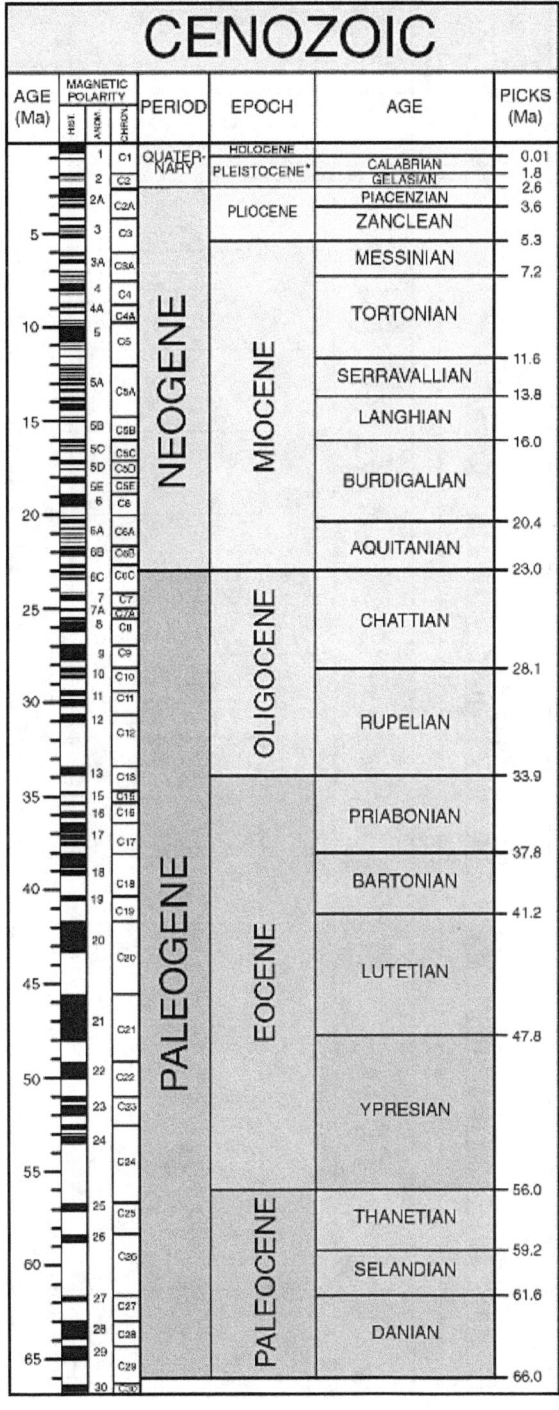

Cenozoic Era includes 66 Ma to present

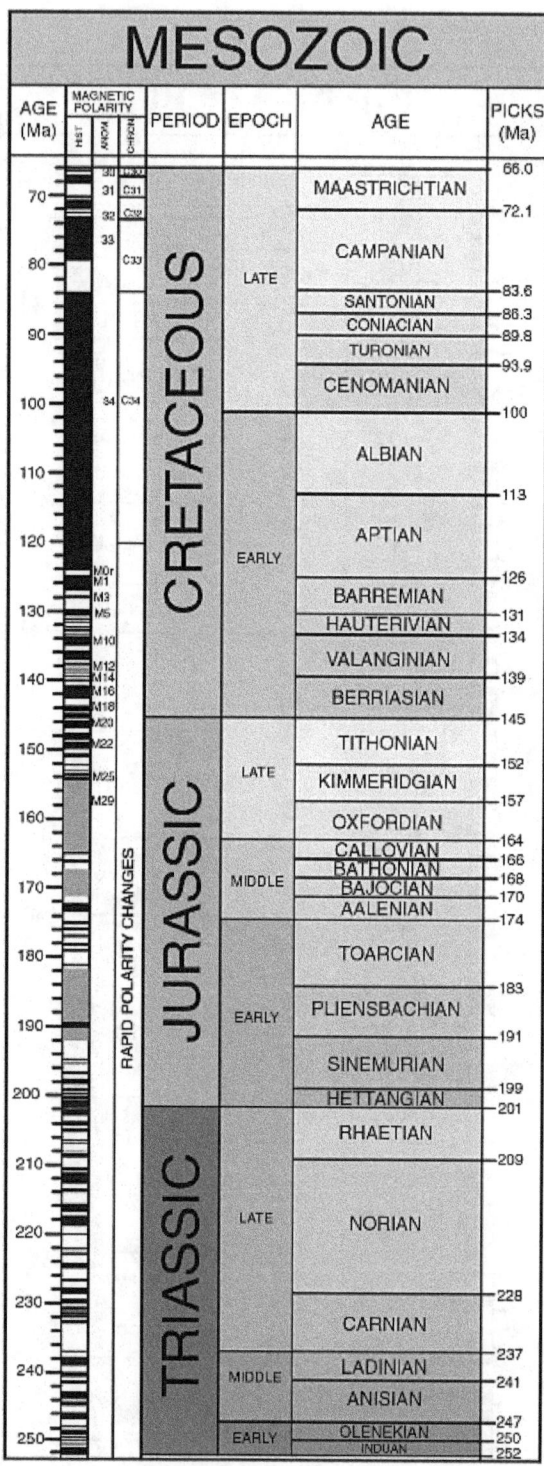

Mesozoic Era includes 252 Ma to 66 Ma

PALEOZOIC

AGE (Ma)	PERIOD	EPOCH	AGE	PICKS (Ma)
260	PERMIAN	Lopingian	CHANGHSINGIAN	252
			WUCHIAPINGIAN	254
				260
		Guadalupian	CAPITANIAN	265
			WORDIAN	269
			ROADIAN	272
280		Cisuralian	KUNGURIAN	279
			ARTINSKIAN	
			SAKMARIAN	290
			ASSELIAN	296
300	CARBONIFEROUS — PENNSYLVANIAN	LATE	GZHELIAN	299
			KASIMOVIAN	304
		MIDDLE	MOSCOVIAN	307
320		EARLY	BASHKIRIAN	315
				323
	CARBONIFEROUS — MISSISSIPPIAN	LATE	SERPUKHOVIAN	331
340		MIDDLE	VISEAN	
		EARLY	TOURNAISIAN	347
360				359
	DEVONIAN	LATE	FAMENNIAN	
380			FRASNIAN	372
		MIDDLE	GIVETIAN	383
			EIFELIAN	388
400		EARLY	EMSIAN	393
			PRAGIAN	408
			LOCHKOVIAN	411
420	SILURIAN	PRIDOLI		419
		LUDLOW	LUDFORDIAN	423
			GORSTIAN	426
		WENLOCK	HOMERIAN	427
			SHEINWOODIAN	430/433
440		LLANDOVERY	TELYCHIAN	439
			AERONIAN	441
			RHUDDANIAN	444/445
			HIRNANTIAN	
	ORDOVICIAN	LATE	KATIAN	453
460			SANDBIAN	458
		MIDDLE	DARRIWILIAN	467
			DAPINGIAN	470
480		EARLY	FLOIAN	478
			TREMADOCIAN	485
	CAMBRIAN	FURONGIAN	AGE 10	490
			JIANGSHANIAN	494
500			PAIBIAN	497
		Epoch 3	GUZHANGIAN	501
			DRUMIAN	505
			AGE 5	509
		Epoch 2	AGE 4	514
520			AGE 3	521
		TERRENEUVIAN	AGE 2	529
540			FORTUNIAN	541

Paleozoic Era includes 541 Ma to 252 Ma

PRECAMBRIAN

AGE (Ma)	EON	ERA	PERIOD	BDY. AGES (Ma)
	PROTEROZOIC	NEOPROTEROZOIC	EDIACARAN	541
				635
750			CRYOGENIAN	
				850
			TONIAN	
1000				1000
		MESOPROTEROZOIC	STENIAN	
				1200
1250			ECTASIAN	
				1400
1500			CALYMMIAN	
				1600
		PALEOPROTEROZOIC	STATHERIAN	
1750				1800
			OROSIRIAN	
2000				2050
			RHYACIAN	
2250				2300
			SIDERIAN	
2500				2500
	ARCHEAN	NEOARCHEAN		
2750				2800
3000		MESOARCHEAN		
				3200
3250		PALEOARCHEAN		
3500				
				3600
3750		EOARCHEAN		
4000				4000
	HADEAN			

Proterozoic Eon, Archean Eon, and Hadean Eon include 4.54 Ga to 541 Ma

Plate Tectonics

Plate boundaries

Surface layers occur sporadically and cover much of Earth's surface. These are tectonic plates with *plate boundary edges* (like puzzle pieces roughly fitting).

Plate boundaries have many faults, which are the prime locations for earthquake activity. Plate boundary edges are rough and often get caught on the boundary of another plate. When the fault slides, the edge is caught while the block moves. The energy typically expended in plate movement becomes stored as *potential energy* from the opposing plates.

Earth has three types of *plate boundaries* and *plate boundary zones,* which are broad belts without defined boundaries, and the effects of plate interaction are unclear.

Divergent boundaries

Divergent boundaries are boundaries between two tectonic plates that move away from each other, and the movement of plates retracting creates *basalt* oceanic crust.

First, lava spews from long fissures on the ocean floor, geysers spurt superheated water alongside these boundaries, and frequent earthquakes occur along the boundary rift.

Magma (or *molten rock*) rises from the *mantle* beneath the *rift*. Magma exudes and hardens into solid rock, forming a crust on torn edges of tectonic plates.

Magma from the mantle solidifies into *basalt* – a dark, dense rock beneath the ocean floor.

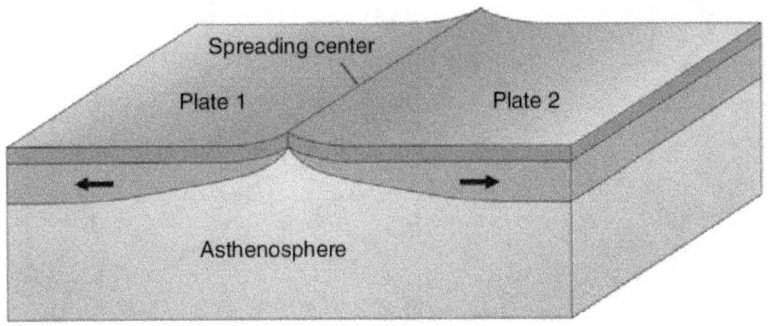

Divergent plate boundaries exude magma

Consequently, *oceanic basalt crust* is created at *divergent boundaries.*

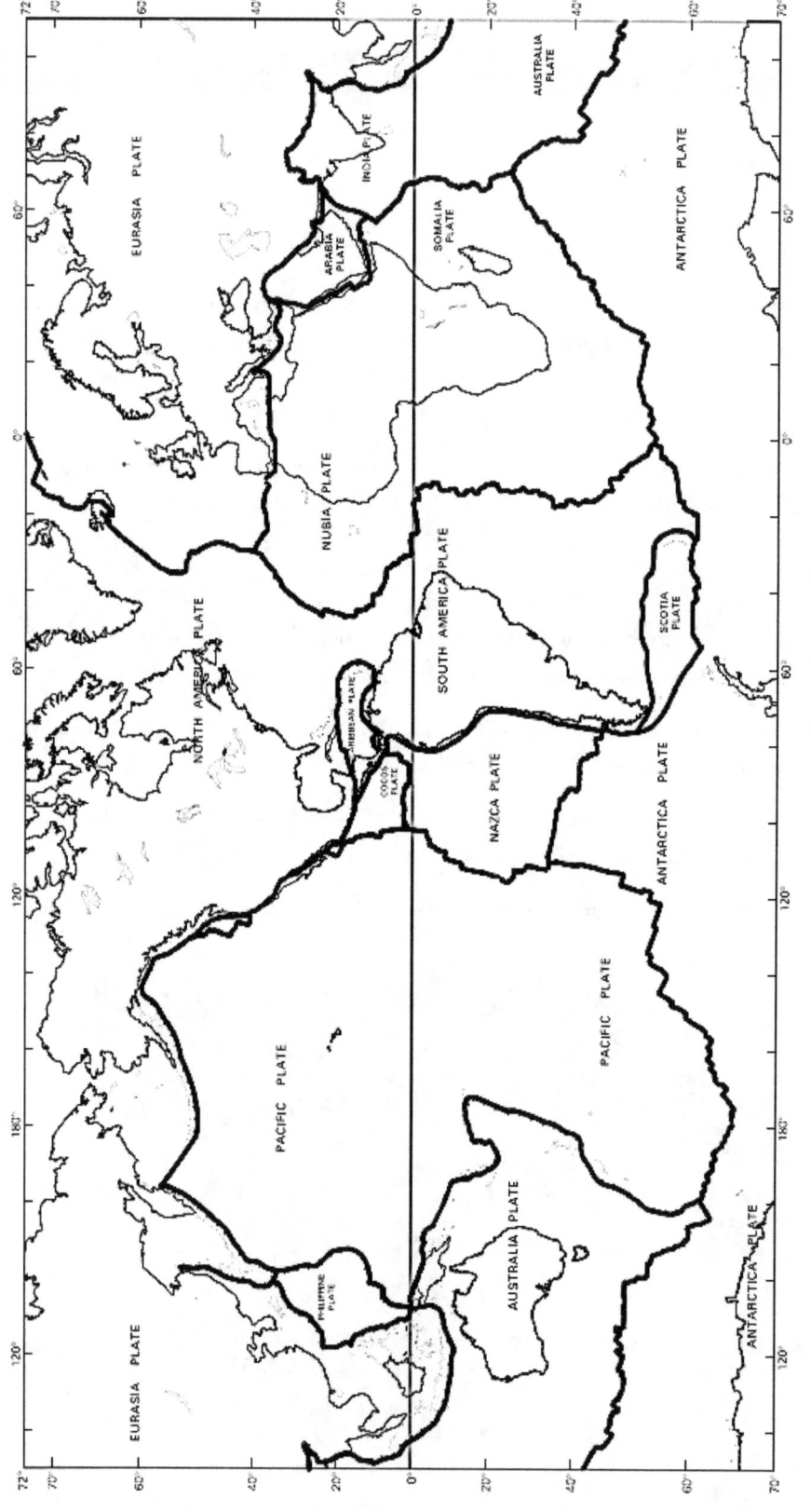

Tectonic plates spanning Earth

Convergent boundaries

Convergent boundary occurs when two plates come together, and the impact of two tectonic plates causes the edge of one plate to buckle under the other, destroying the crust.

Buckled plates push one or both edges up, forming a *rugged mountain range*.

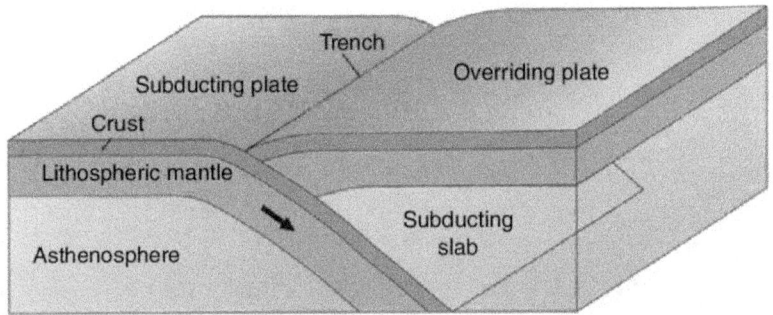

Convergent plate boundaries with subduction zones form rugged mountain ranges

One buckled plate sometimes forces the other *deep into a seafloor trench*.

Subduction is when one tectonic plate moves under another and plunges into the mantle at a convergent plate boundary.

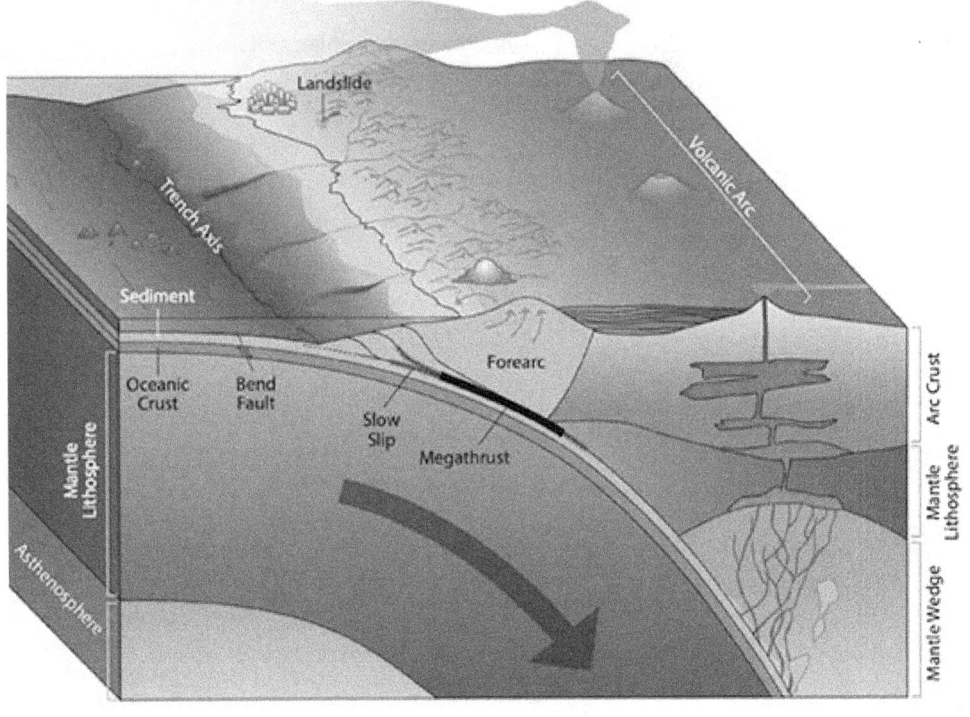

Subduction zone

Often, a chain of volcanoes forms parallel to the boundary, the mountain range, or the trench.

When this occurs, powerful *earthquakes* shake a wide area on both sides of the boundary.

One colliding tectonic plate may be topped with oceanic crust as the tectonic plate is forced into the mantle and melts. Magma rises through the other plate, hardening into the crust.

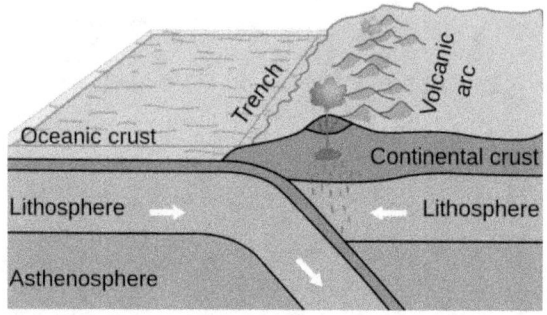

Convergent boundary zone with subduction of oceanic crust and volcano formation

Magma formed from the melting tectonic plates hardens into *granite* — a light-colored, low-density rock — and forms Earth's continents.

Continental crust (granite) is created, and oceanic crust is destroyed at convergent boundaries.

Transform plate boundaries

Transform plate boundaries form when two abutting tectonic plates slide horizontally past each other, and the crust is neither produced nor destroyed. This tectonic plate boundary splits and carries natural or human-made structures in opposite directions.

Plates grind against each other, and rocks lining the boundary are crushed, creating a *linear fault valley* or *undersea canyon*. *Earthquakes* rattle through a wide boundary zone.

Compared to convergent and divergent boundaries, magma *does not* form. Consequently, the crust is neither created nor destroyed but is cracked and broken at transform margins.

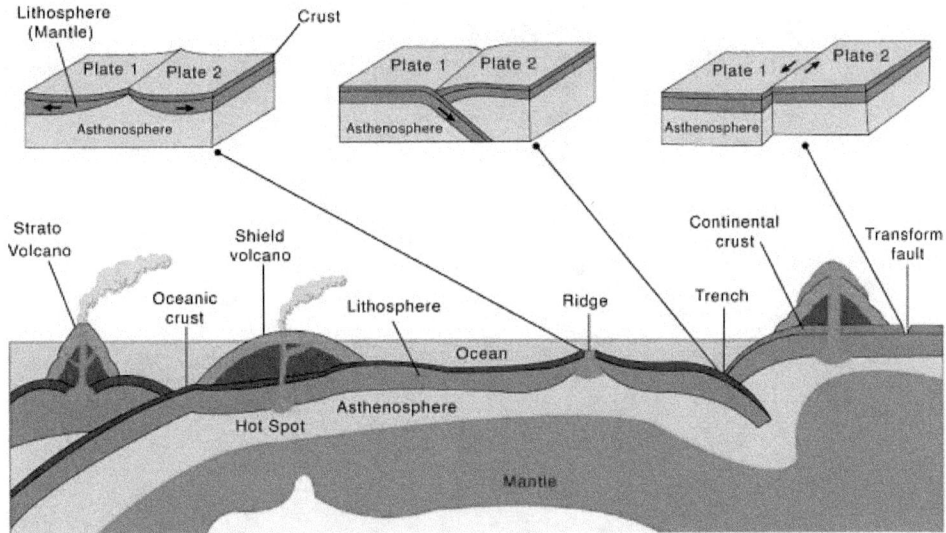

Divergent (left), convergent (middle), and transform plate (on the right)

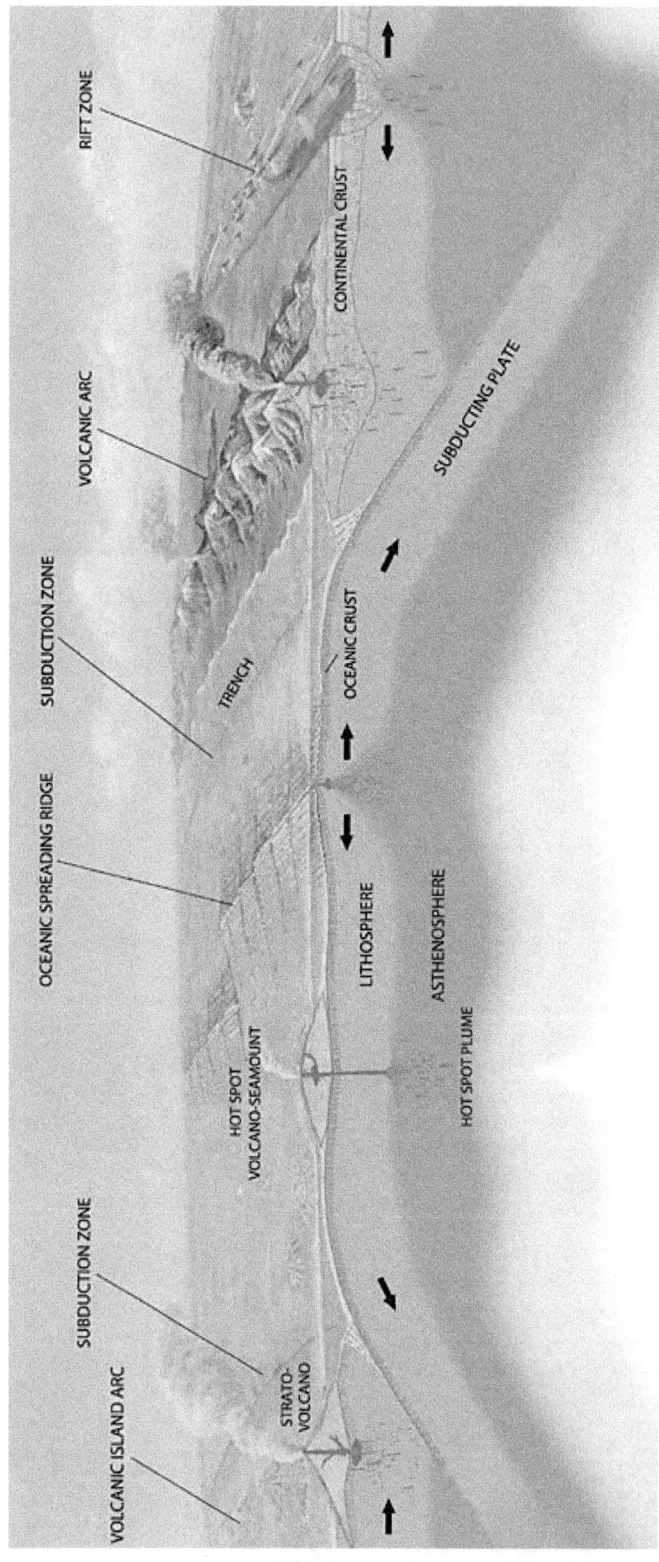

Convergent and divergent boundaries with subduction zones, volcanism, and crust formation

Earthquakes

Stratified Earth

Earth has four layers: the *inner core, outer core, mantle,* and *crust.*

Mantle and crust comprise a relatively thin *surface layer*.

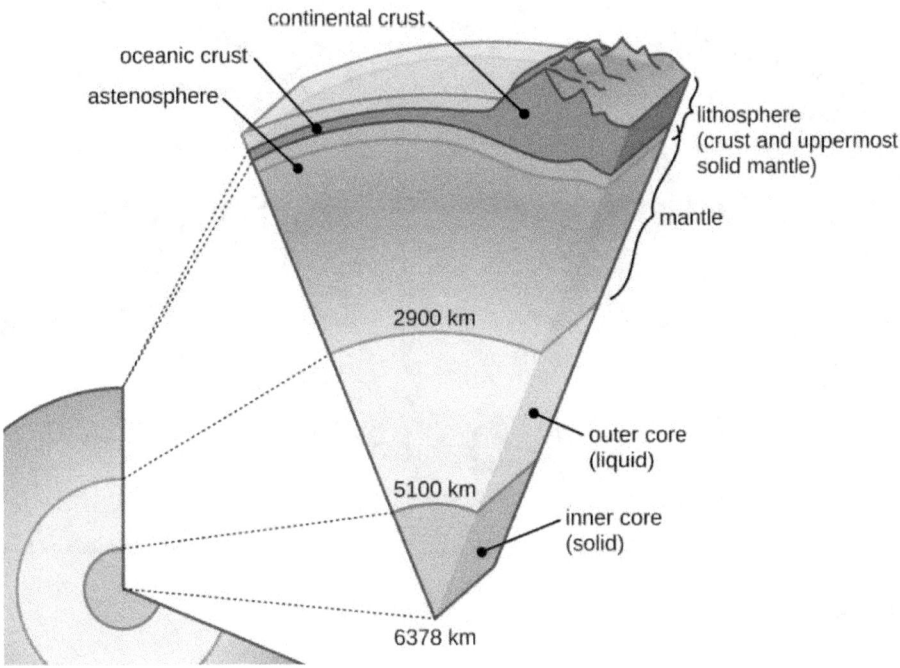

Crust, mantle, and core cross-sectional of Earth

Earthquake terminology

Fault plane (or *fault*) is the area of the tectonic plate that slips, causing an earthquake.

Hypocenter is the area below the Earth's surface where an earthquake originates.

Epicenter is the earthquake's origin on the Earth's surface (directly above the hypocenter).

Foreshocks are minor earthquakes in the same area before a large earthquake. It is unclear if foreshocks are precursors to larger earthquakes or small, independent earthquakes.

Mainshocks are large earthquakes, often causing the most destruction.

Aftershocks are minor earthquakes after mainshocks and may continue for years following powerful mainshocks.

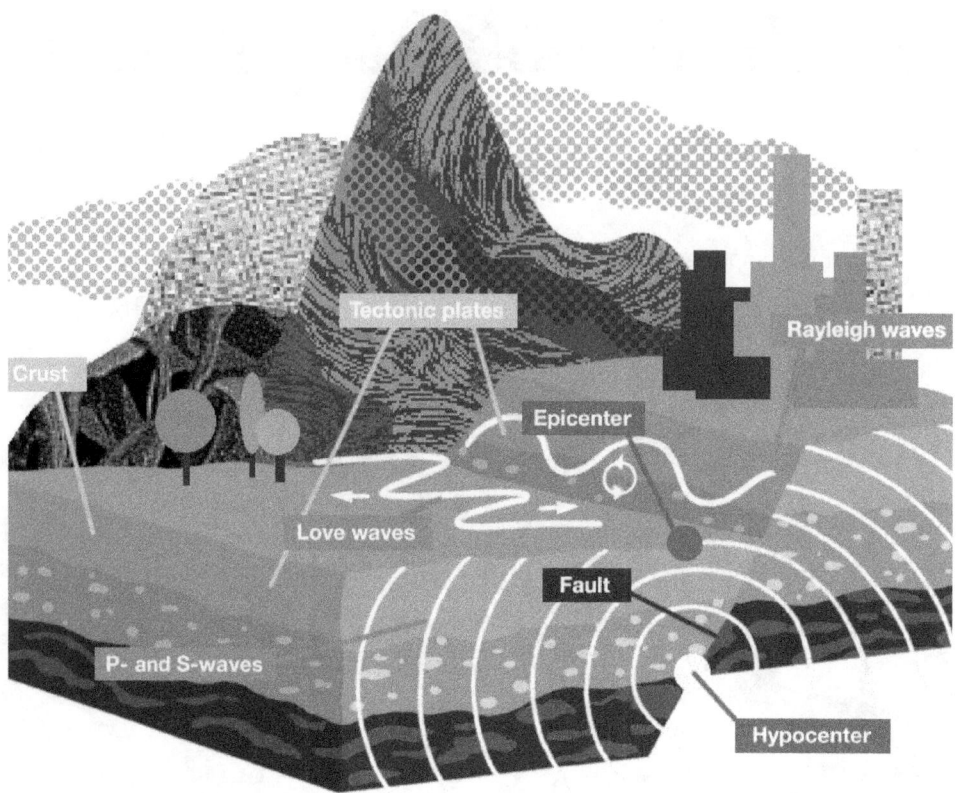

Raleigh and Love surface waves emanating from the hypocenter, Caltech Science Exchange

Seismic waves

When the force of the plates becomes larger than the friction that caused them to stop, the edges unstick, and the stored potential energy is released. Energy radiates outward from the hypocenter in all directions as *seismic waves* (like ripples in a pond) radiate outwards.

Seismic waves shake above and below the surface when moving in the crust, causing damage.

Most earthquake shaking is due to Rayleigh waves, which are much larger than other waves.

Love waves are surface waves named after British mathematician A. Love, who modeled the wave type in 1911. Love waves produce entirely horizontal motion; the amplitude is largest at the surface and diminishes with greater depth.

Quakes happen more frequently along specific faults, but earthquakes cannot be predicted. Some claim that specific weather patterns may exist or that animals can sense a change before an earthquake occurs. However, these events are inconsistent and given little credibility by the scientific community.

Three major seismic waves are *P waves*, *S waves*, and *surface waves*.

P and S waves

P and S waves are *body waves* because they travel through the body of the Earth and are not trapped near the surface.

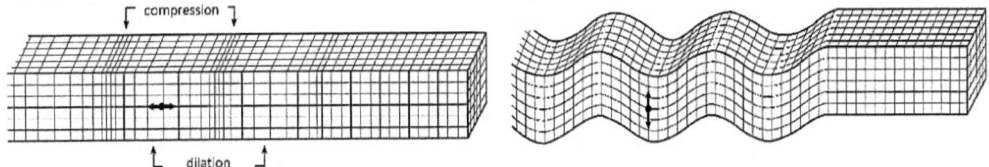

Body waves with P wave (left) and S wave (right) with direction of propagation →

Arrival times of P and S waves at seismometers determine the earthquake's location.

P waves travel fast and are the first to arrive from the earthquake.

In S (or shear) waves, rock oscillates perpendicular to the direction of wave propagation.

S waves travel about 60% of P wave speeds in rock and always arrive after P waves. *S waves are more dangerous than P waves because they have greater amplitude and produce vertical and horizontal ground surface motion.*

Surface waves

Surface waves travel slowly through Earth's material at the planet's surface, predominantly at lower frequencies and distinguished on a seismogram.

Shallow earthquakes produce stronger surface waves; the strength of surface waves is reduced in deeper earthquakes.

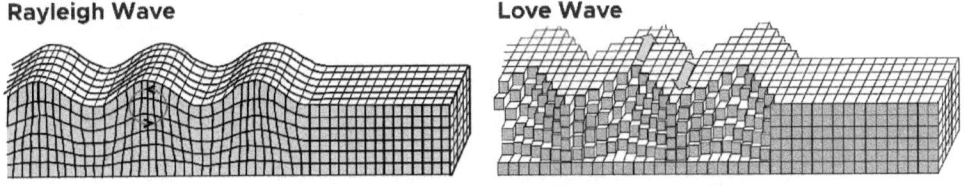

Surface waves with direction of propagation →

Rayleigh waves are surface waves named for Lord Rayleigh, who mathematically predicted them in 1885. They roll along the ground in a more complex motion than love waves.

Like Love waves, the amplitude of the Rayleigh waves decreases dramatically with depth.

Rayleigh waves roll like ocean waves, but particle motion is opposite to ocean waves. Because it rolls, a Rayleigh wave moves the ground up and down, forward and backward in the direction of wave movement.

Seismograms

Seismographs record earthquakes. The seismograph's base rests on the ground while a heavy weight hangs free. When the Earth shakes, the base and the coil or string holding the weight absorb movements, and a *seismogram* records the event.

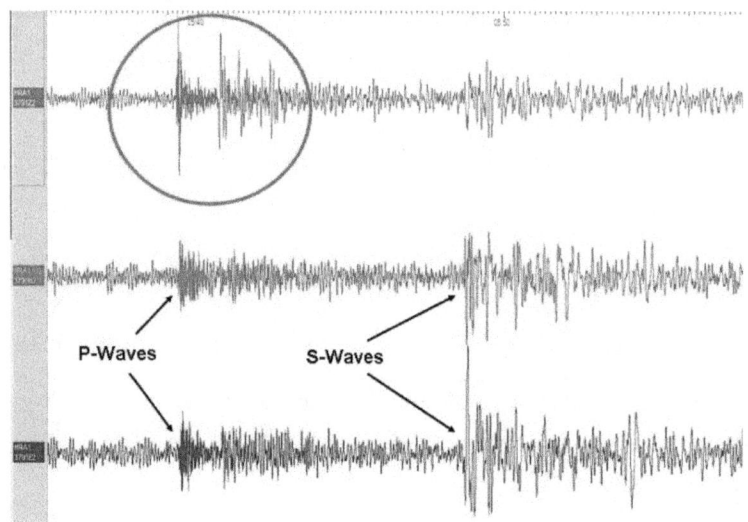

Seismogram readings differentiate waveforms

Seismograms locate the origin of earthquakes by triangulation, requiring three seismograph readings. A circle is drawn around the station with a seismograph, with the radius of each circle the distance from the station to the area where the earthquake occurred.

Epicenter is the location where the three circles intersect.

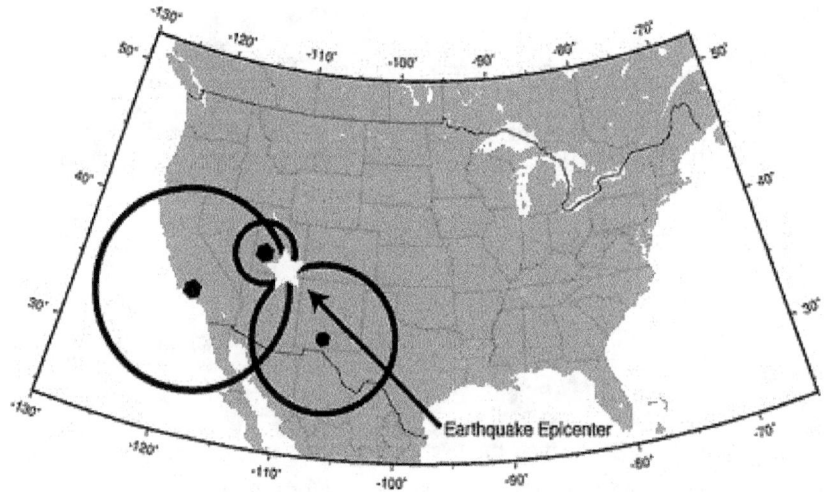

Triangulation method to determine the epicenter of an earthquake.

Richter scale

Earthquake strength depends on the fault's size and the amount of tectonic plate slippage.

Macroscopic measurements cannot record tectonic plate slippage; seismograms measure magnitude (or severity).

Magnitude is represented by a Richter Scale value using a base-10 logarithmic scale created by Charles F. Richter in 1935 for earthquake magnitudes.

Earthquake magnitude is measured by the logarithm of the wave amplitude (recorded by seismographs) and expressed in whole numbers and decimals.

Logarithmic scale represents force with each whole number increase in magnitude (e.g., 5.3 to 6.3) corresponding to a *tenfold* increase.

Increasing *one whole number* on the Richter Scale releases almost *31 times the energy*.

San Francisco Earthquake (and Fire) of 1906

On April 18, 1906, a 7.9 earthquake struck the coast of Northern California in San Francisco. Shortly after that, several fires broke out that devastated the city for days, destroying 80 percent of San Francisco and amplifying the death toll to more than 3,000 casualties.

As traumatic as the earthquake was, the subsequent fires were even more destructive. Fires from ruptured gas mains destroyed 25,000 buildings in the Mission District and its surrounding area. Some commentators maintain that the fires caused at least 90 percent of the destruction. Widespread looting and riots among evacuees also contributed to the chaos and damage.

The catastrophe resulted in property loss of $235 to $400 million ($6.7 to $11.5 billion in 2020 dollars) and loss of museums, laboratories, and other significant facilities. To this day, the *San Francisco Earthquake* remains the deadliest in U.S. history.

Notes for active learning

Volcanism

Mountain building

Subduction is when one tectonic plate moves under another.

Orogenesis (or *mountain building*) is when large pieces of Earth on top of subducting plates are pressed into the above plate.

Orogeny is a mountain-building process occurring at a convergent plate margin when plate motion compresses the margin. An orogenic belt (or *orogen*) develops as the compressed plate crumples and is uplifted to form one or more mountain ranges.

Volcanism is the eruption of lava and other material deep within the Earth.

Eruptions of material form a mountainous *volcano* structure.

Volcanoes are a type of volcanic eruption, but most eruptions do not form volcanoes.

Volcanism recycles plate tectonics material with material subducted below the crust, returning to the surface as *molten magma*.

Magma and gases

Magma erupts as *lava* (expelled molten rock) with gases, fluids, and solids at Earth's surface.

Solids include *igneous rock*, which can become sedimentary and metamorphic rocks.

Fluid products of erupted magma release water and contain silica, metals, and other elements. Magmatic fluid can change the composition of rocks, ore deposits, and sulfate minerals.

Gaseous elements (e.g., sulfur gases, water vapor, and carbon dioxide) cause the lava to erupt. Gases cause magma to expand, sending it to the surface quickly.

Volcanic gases enter the atmosphere, affecting atmospheric composition and global climate.

Magmatic volcanism

Magmatic volcanoes have *subduction zones, composite cones, hotspots,* and *flood volcanoes*.

Most volcanic eruptions occur underwater along mid-ocean ridges called *divergent margins*.

Ocean crust is pulled apart via plate divergence, causing the hot rock in the mantle layer below to melt due to the decreased pressure. Rock that melts is *magma*, composed of basalt.

Peridotite remains part of the mantle, a heavier rock composed mainly of olivine. This common volcanism occurs as a quiet oozing of basalt lava from ocean floor cracks.

There are few examples of divergent volcanism on land; they appear and act differently than divergent oceanic margins.

Subduction zone volcanism occurs along (convergent margins) where oceanic plates, saturated with sediment and water, plunge into the hot mantle layer.

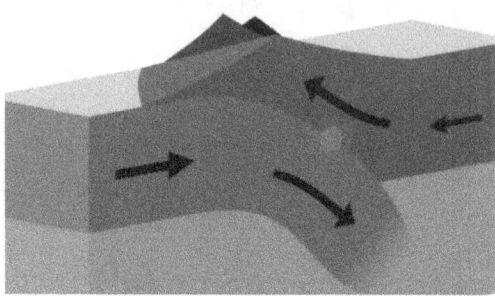

Subduction zone volcanism

Composite cone volcanoes (or *stratovolcanoes*) are cone-shaped volcanoes made of hundreds of layers of lava, rock, ash, and debris and produce most volcanoes. Magma is not created by releasing pressure on the mantle but instead by adding water to it. Subduction-created magma rises into the lower crust, collecting and occasionally producing a violent eruption. *Mount St. Helens* (Washington State) is a composite cone volcano.

Hotspot volcanism includes 10% of volcanoes. Divergent or convergent plate boundaries do not form these. Geologists thought hotspots arose deep within the mantle, but a new theory is that *lithospheric plates fracture*, causing pressure release of magma, like divergent volcanos.

Flood volcanism is the fourth magmatic volcanism, but it no longer occurs. In this instance, copious amounts of basalt lava poured out of breaks and fissures, covering thousands of square miles underwater and on land. Flood volcanism is an active research topic.

Non-magmatic volcanism

Non-magmatic volcanism is uncommon, but *mud volcanism* occurs on land and in the sea.

For example, hundreds of mud volcanoes occur on land in areas with abundant hydrocarbons (e.g., petroleum reserves), such as Azerbaijan and Trinidad.

Underwater mud volcanoes form near subduction trenches with *serpentinite mud*.

Mud diapirs and *mud volcanoes* are caused by the upward migration of high-pressure deep fluid penetrating the overlying strata.

Mud volcanoes form with mud fluid ejected from the surface or seafloor.

Mud diapirs form without mud fluid.

Earth's Planetary Movement

Earth's rotation and revolution

Earth has two planetary movements: *rotation* and *revolution*. Rotation describes the Earth's spinning on its axis, while revolution refers to its orbiting around the Sun.

Earth *spins along its polar axis*, making one rotation every 24 hours.

Earth's mass produces a gyroscopic effect (i.e., maintaining a fixed orientation in space due to angular momentum) that keeps its poles pointing in the same direction. However, a large earthquake may cause the Earth to wobble slightly on its axis.

Earth's rotation around its polar axis from west to east

Celestial equator is a reference line dividing Earth into Northern and Southern Hemispheres.

Earth moves with *constant motion* around the Sun, completing its orbit every 365.25 days. Earth's orbit around the Sun is not circular because the gravitational pull by our solar system's two largest gas planets (i.e., Jupiter and Saturn) distorts Earth's orbit into slightly *elliptical*.

Solstices

A solstice occurs twice a year when Earth's tilt is at its maximum, and the Sun is at its farthest point south or north of the Earth's equator. Due to the Earth's axis being tilted the most toward or away from the Sun, the Sun's apparent path reaches its farthest point north or south of the equator.

Summer solstice typically occurs around June 20th or 21st, when the Earth's tilt towards the Sun is greatest, and the Sun's rays reach the Tropic of Cancer (approximately 23.5° north of the equator) most directly.

Winter solstice occurs around December 21st or 22nd, when the Earth's tilt away from the Sun is at its maximum, and the Sun's rays reach the Tropic of Capricorn (approximately 23.5° south of the equator) most directly.

Depending on the hemisphere, a solstice marks the longest or shortest day of the year. In the Northern Hemisphere, the summer solstice defines the shortest night and the longest day of the year; the winter solstice marks the longest and shortest night. For the Southern Hemisphere, it is the opposite.

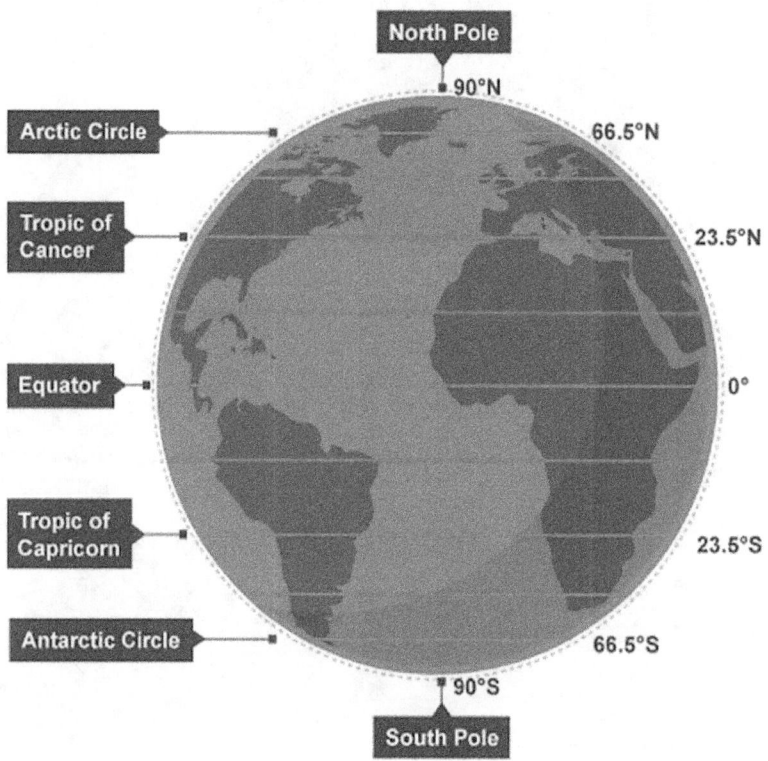

Earth's major lines of latitude

Equinoxes

Equinoxes are marked by the Sun's position relative to the Earth's poles. Like solstices, they occur twice a year and mark the day when day and night are equal (12 hours each). This happens because the Sun crosses the celestial equator as it moves north or south while the Earth's axis is neither tilted towards nor away from the Sun.

When the Sun is positioned directly above the equator, sunlight is evenly distributed between the two hemispheres, resulting in equal daylight and nighttime at all latitudes.

The vernal (spring) equinox occurs around March 20th when the Sun crosses the celestial equator, moving from the Southern to the Northern Hemisphere. It marks the beginning of spring in the Northern Hemisphere and autumn in the Southern Hemisphere.

The autumnal equinox occurs around September 22nd when the Sun moves from the Northern to the Southern Hemisphere. This equinox marks the beginning of autumn in the Northern Hemisphere and spring in the Southern Hemisphere.

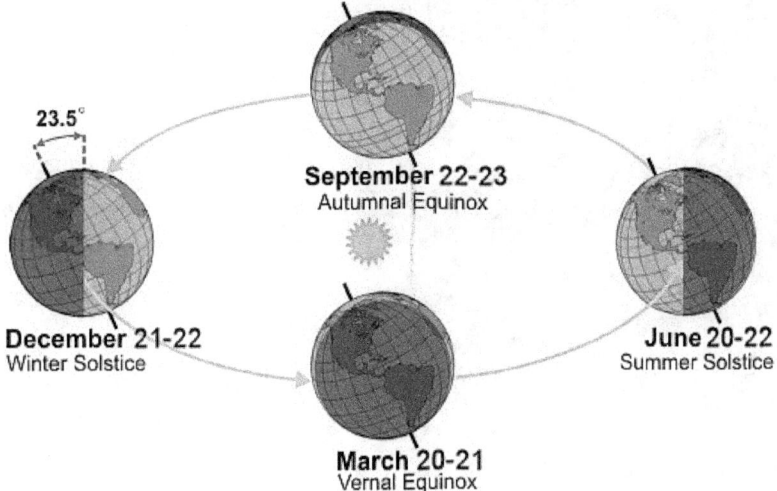

Equinoxes and solstices and their time frames

Earth's seasons

A common misconception is that Earth is closest to the Sun during summer, causing hot weather, and further during winter, therefore experiencing colder temperatures. Although sensible, this distance relationship does *not* dictate seasons.

In Northern Hemisphere, Earth is farthest from the Sun during summer and closest in winter. The extreme distance of Earth from the Sun means that solar heat minimally impacts seasons.

Seasons on Earth depend on the *axis*, an imaginary line connecting North to South Poles. Earth has seasons because its axis is not aligned precisely vertically and is tilted. Earth rotates on its axis as it orbits the Sun, but the axis always points in the same direction.

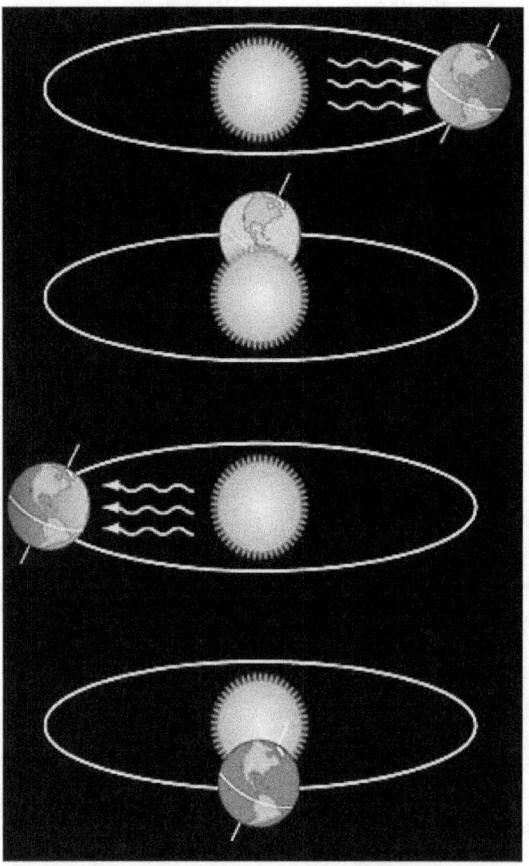

December:
Summer is south of the equator; winter is north of the equator. Sun shines directly on the Southern Hemisphere and indirectly on the Northern Hemisphere.

March:
Fall is south of the equator; spring is north of the equator. Sun shines equally on Southern and Northern Hemispheres.

June:
Winter is south of the equator; summer is north of the equator. Sun is directly in the Northern Hemisphere and indirectly in the Southern Hemisphere.

September:
Spring south of the equator; fall north of the equator. Sun shines equally on the Southern and Northern Hemispheres.

Earth's tilted axis and orbital path cause seasons

Solar Intensity and Latitude

Solar irradiance

Total solar irradiance is the maximum power the Sun delivers to Earth at its average distance. The average amount of solar energy Earth receives at the top of its atmosphere is approximately 1,361 Watts per square meter (W/m²).

Only half of Earth is irradiated at once; the total solar irradiance is halved.

Earth is in radiative equilibrium if incoming solar energy equals heat flow back into space, and the global temperature remains relatively stable.

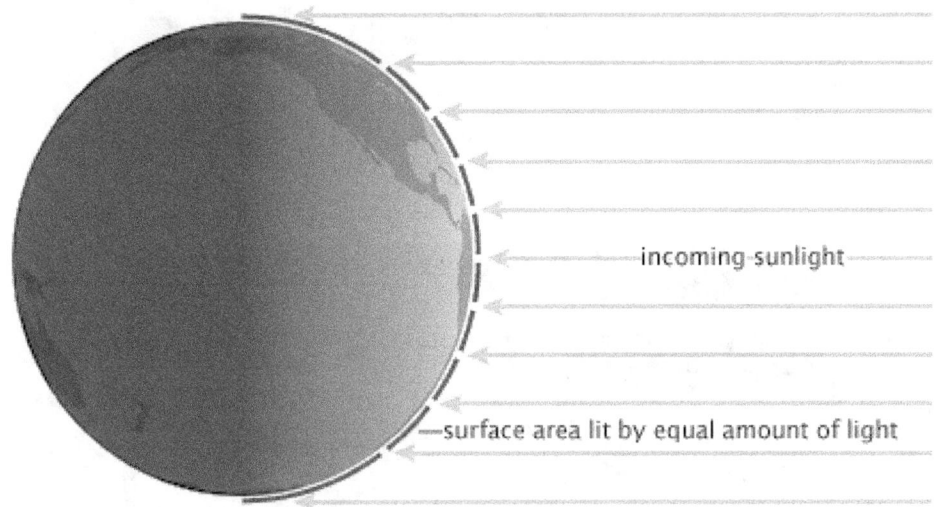

Total solar irradiance is the maximum power the Sun delivers with perpendicular light rays

Peak radiation

Matter with temperatures above absolute zero radiates energy in the electromagnetic spectrum.

Hotter objects have shorter wavelengths of radiated energy, while the hottest objects in the universe (e.g., some stars) radiate mainly x-rays and gamma rays.

Cooler objects emit longer-wavelength radiation, including microwaves, thermal infrared waves, radio waves, and visible light.

Sun's peak radiation is in the visible light spectrum, and its temperature is over 5,500 °C. Though solar radiation is often considered harmful, some forms are beneficial and vital parts of everyday life. Infrared radiation is the energy Earth releases to cool.

Average sunlight at the top of Earth's atmosphere is *one-fourth* of the total solar irradiance or about 340 watts per square meter.

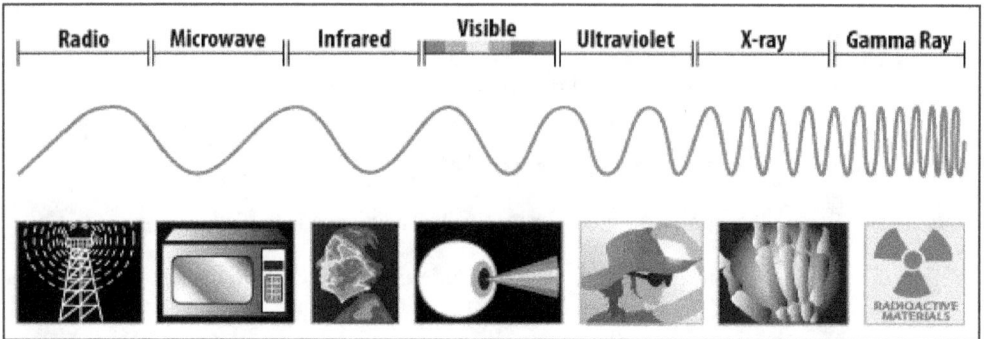

Types of radiation that compose the electromagnetic spectrum

Latitude and illumination angle

Latitude is a coordinate specifying a point's north-south position on the surface of Earth.

Latitude is –90° at the South Pole, 90° at the North Pole, and 0° at the Equator.

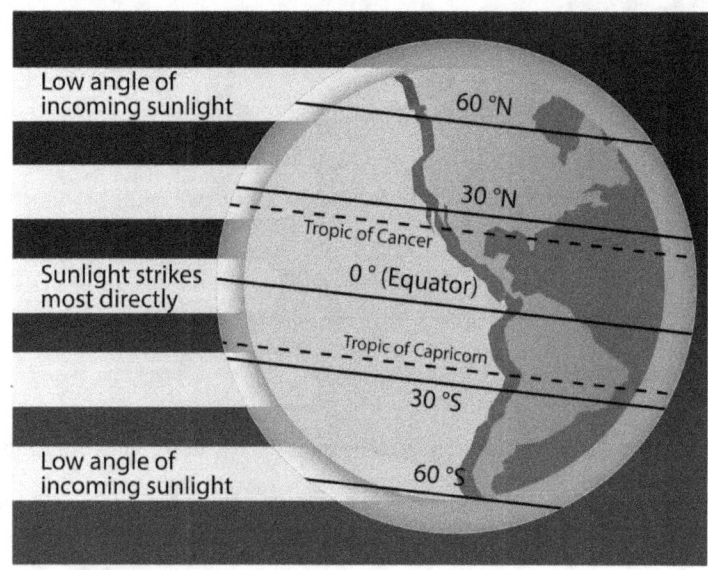

Illumination angles of sunlight striking the Earth's regions

Earth is a sphere, and the equator at midday is perpendicular to Sun's incoming light. Other locations receive the Sun's rays at an angle.

Progressive solar *illumination angle* decreases, and *latitude* increase reduces the average solar irradiance by 50%. Two equinoxes are when the Sun rises at 6 a.m. in all locations.

Sunlight intensity increases from sunrise until noon when the Sun is directly over the equator and casts no shadows (image C).

After noon, the intensity of sunlight decreases until the Sun sets.

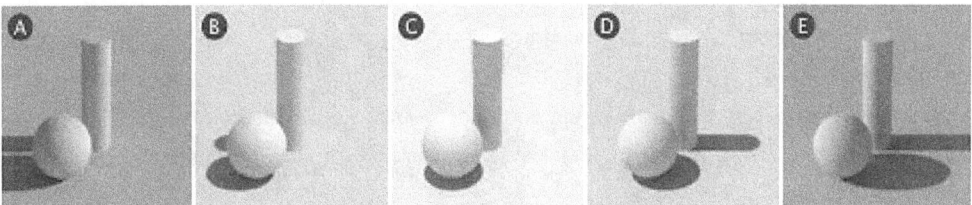

Hour affects the angle of incoming sunlight (indicated by shadow length) and light intensity

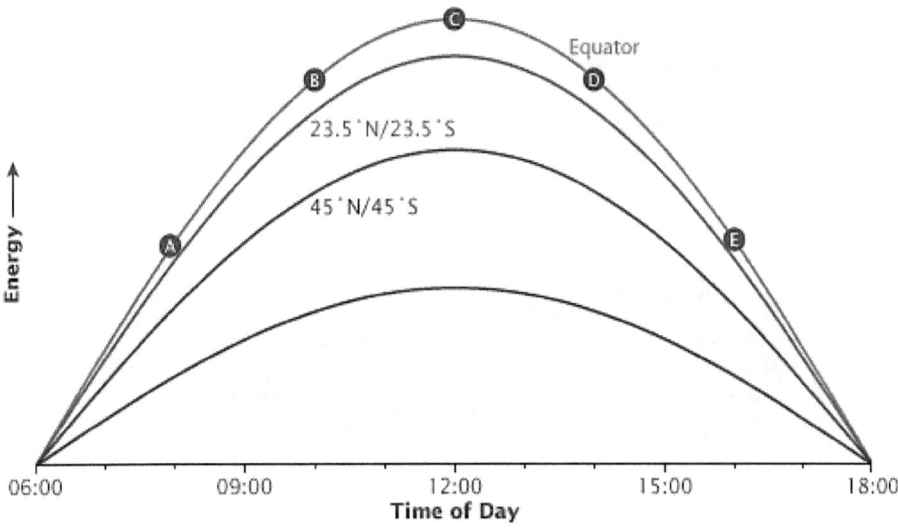

Solar radiation depends on time, latitude, and solar energy of vernal and autumnal equinoxes

Solar heat transfer

There are three primary ways of solar heat transfer: *radiation, conduction,* and *convection.*

While *radiation* transfers energy from the Sun to the Earth, *conduction* and *convection* are essential for distributing solar heat on and within the Earth's surface.

Radiation is when the Sun's electromagnetic radiation travels through space and heats Earth's surface. The radiation includes visible light, infrared radiation, and ultraviolet radiation.

When this radiation hits Earth's surface, it is *absorbed, reflected,* or *transmitted.*

Absorption of solar radiation by Earth's surface, atmosphere, and other objects leads to heating.

Conduction is when ground heat is transferred to the air. In the context of solar heat distribution, conduction occurs when solar heat absorbed by a body of water is then transferred to other parts of a system through direct contact.

Convection is the process where warm air rises. This movement is vital for creating a cycle of circulation. When air is heated, it becomes less dense compared to the surrounding cooler air. This less dense air rises, and as it rises, it starts to cool and becomes denser again. The rising warm air is replaced by the surrounding cooler air, which gets heated and rises. This cycle is what creates *convection currents*, which are crucial for mixing air and transferring heat.

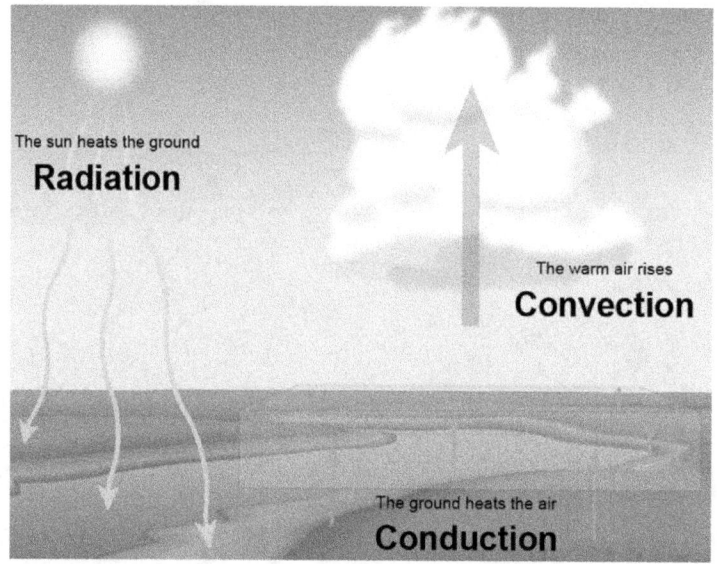

Solar radiation heats the ground, which causes air temperature to increase by conduction, and convection moves the warmer air upwards

Reflection and albedo

Some solar radiation that reaches the Earth's atmosphere and surface is reflected into space. This unabsorbed energy contributes to Earth's overall energy budget and affects climate.

The amount of reflected solar radiation depends on the different types of surfaces. For example, clouds, snow, ice, and other reflective surfaces have a higher capacity to reflect solar radiation.

Clouds reflect significant incoming solar radiation, especially low, thick clouds. Atmospheric gases and other air particles also reflect a portion of solar radiation.

The specific fraction of solar radiation reflected by a surface is *albedo*. Different surfaces have different albedos. Surfaces like ice and snow reflect much radiation and, therefore, have high albedos; asphalt surfaces and forests absorb most of the sunlight and have low albedos.

On average, approximately 29% of the incoming solar radiation is reflected into space, meaning the Earth's average albedo is around 0.29.

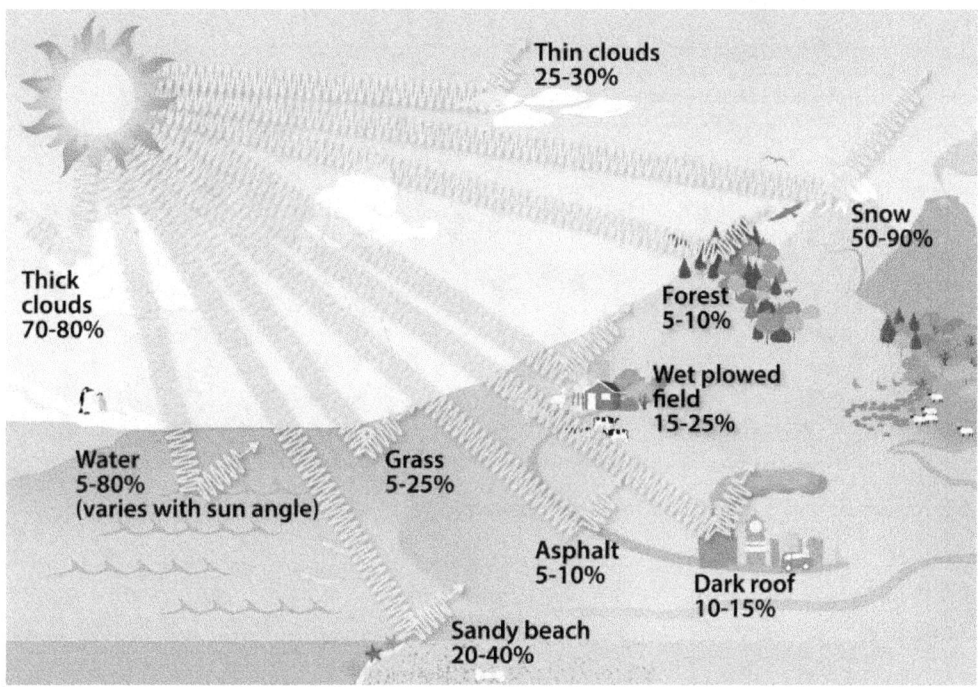

Albedos of different types of Earth's surface

Auroras

Aurora is a natural light display phenomenon observed in the skies near Earth's poles. Auroras are caused by the interaction of charged Sun's particles with Earth's *magnetosphere*. A *magnetosphere* is a region of space around the Earth dominated by its magnetic field, which acts as a shield, protecting the planet from harmful cosmic radiation.

The particles (i.e., electrons, protons, and alpha particles) are released by the Sun in what's called a *solar wind* (often during solar flares), and are captured by Earth's magnetic field. The magnetic field directs the particles towards the poles where they collide with atmospheric gases causing them to emit light of various intensity and colors. Green color is the most common but it depends on the type of gas and altitude.

While auroras are known for their beautiful display of lights, they can also produce sounds that could be described as crackling, whooshing, or whistling. These sounds are caused by the same processes that create the light.

Aurora Borealis is also known as Northern Lights and occurs in the Northern Hemisphere.

Aurora Australis is known as Southern Lights and can be observed in the Southern Hemisphere.

Alaska Aurora was a geomagnetic storm caused by a coronal mass ejection from the Sun

Atmosphere

Earth's atmosphere

Earth's atmosphere is crucial for creating and maintaining a habitable environment for life because it shields the planet from harmful radiation, regulates temperature, and provides breathable air.

Earth's atmosphere acts like an insulating layer to regulate Earth's climate and prevent extreme temperature fluctuations. Atmospheric gases, such as carbon dioxide (CO_2) and water (H_2O) vapor, prevent heat from escaping the Earth without facing the Sun. They also absorb the Sun's UV radiation, which is harmful to life on Earth.

The movement of the atmosphere, driven by the transfer of solar heat, creates weather patterns and distributes heat around the globe. The atmosphere also creates a pressure column, which is essential for the existence of liquid water on Earth's surface.

Atmospheric composition

Earth's atmosphere is composed of a mixture of gases, with nitrogen and oxygen the primary components, making up approximately 78% and 21%, respectively. The other 1% are argon and trace amounts of carbon dioxide, neon, methane, hydrogen, ozone, helium, krypton, and xenon.

The chart shown here provides a more detailed breakdown.

Water vapor (H_2O) is a variable component ranging from 0% in deserts to 4% in humid regions.

While trace gases are present in minuscule amounts, they play an important role in atmospheric processes, including the greenhouse effect. Aerosols and ozone layers affect weather, climate, and air quality.

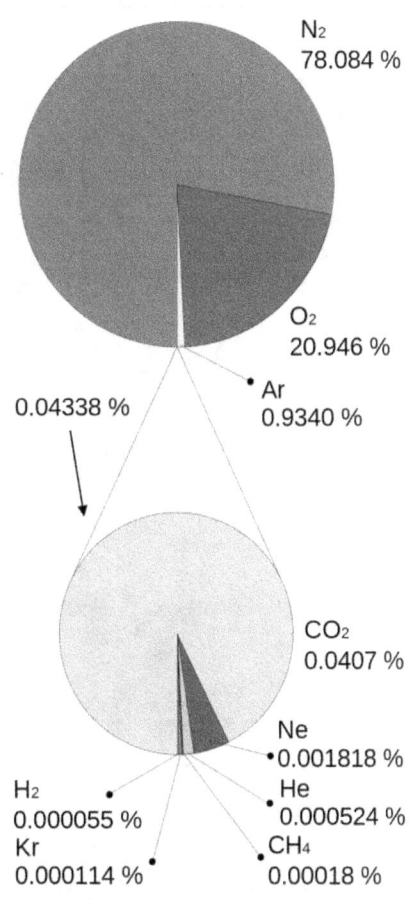

Altitude, density, temperature and pressure

Gas molecules are concentrated near the Earth's surface. This dense cloud of atmospheric gas absorbs solar high-energy X-rays and ultraviolet radiation, which warms the molecules.

Warmer molecules have greater kinetic energy (i.e., increased temperature).

Denser layers have greater heat-retaining capacity. Therefore, layers closest to Earth are warmer, and furthest away are colder.

The top layer is generally warmer, as *warm air rises* above cooler air.

Despite the warmer temperatures of layers closer to Earth, they feel cold for humans.

Molecules in the layer are too far apart to interact appropriately and heat the skin.

Altitude is inversely related to air pressure and density.

Higher altitude air experiences *less gravity* and has *lower pressure* and *lower density*. It has a low concentration with more distance between gas molecules.

Low-altitude air experiences *greater gravity* than molecules higher in the atmosphere.

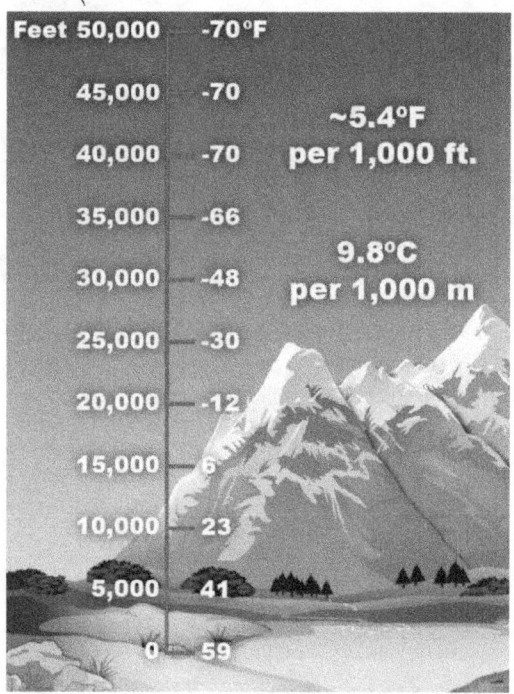

Temperature is greatest at sea level and decreases with elevation by 5.4 °F per 1,000 ft

Density is greatest at sea level and *decreases with elevation*.

Gravity has a greater effect near the surface, with molecules experiencing a downward pull.

Air density is greatest at sea level and decreases with increased elevation.

Gravitational force pulls gas molecules closer to the Earth's surface

Pressure at sea level is 1,000 millibars (mb) or hectopascals (hPa)

The vertical halfway point in the atmosphere is 500 millibars and occurs at ~18,000 feet.

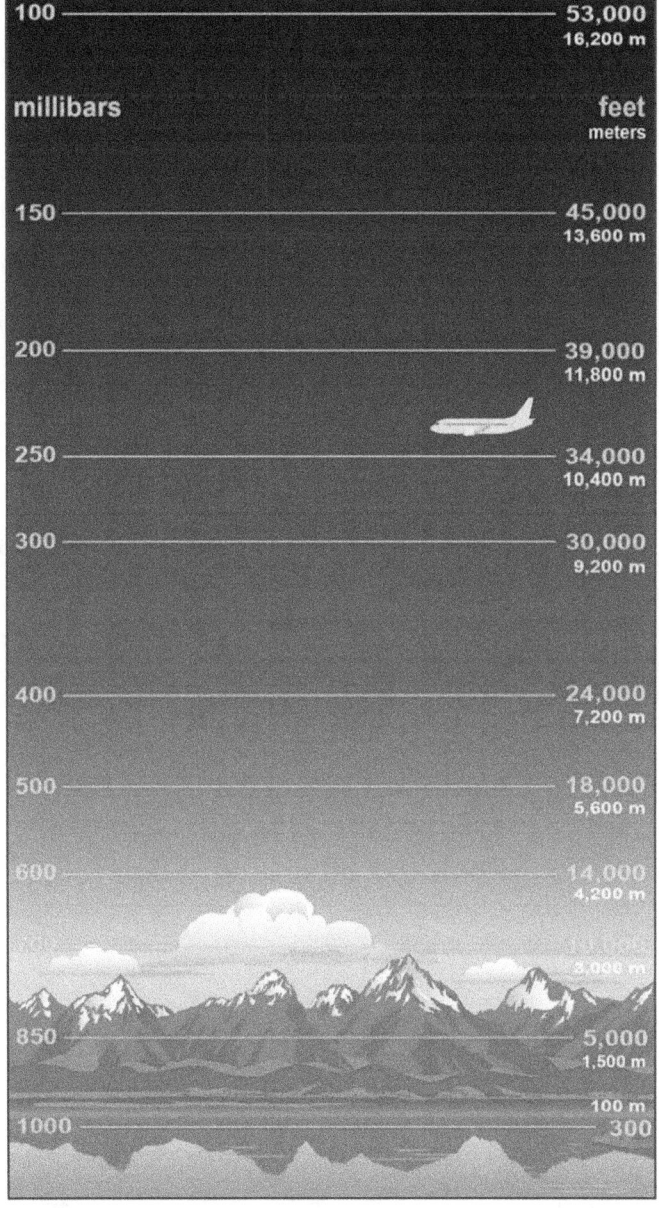

Pressure is inversely related to altitude

Winds result from a complex interplay between temperature, pressure, density gradients, and Earth's rotation.

Density gradients created by gravity are essential for creating and sustaining winds. As gravity compresses Earth's atmosphere, it creates air pressure as the driving force of wind.

Without gravity, there would be no atmosphere or air pressure and, thus, no wind.

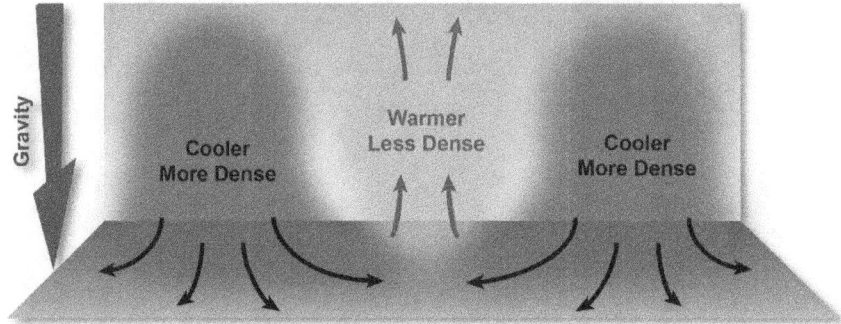

Gravity creates wind, National Weather Service

Rayleigh scattering

Rayleigh scattering is what causes the sky to appear blue. When sunlight passes through Earth's atmosphere, it interacts with air molecules, dust particles, and small particles in the atmosphere, causing light to scatter.

Rayleigh scattering is due to the electric polarizability of particles. Light waves have oscillating electric fields that interact with particle charges, allowing them to move at the same frequency. The particles become small radiating dipoles whose radiation scatters light.

During Rayleigh scattering, shorter wavelength light, such as blue and violet, are scattered more by molecules and particles than longer wavelengths (e.g., red and orange). **Most longer wavelengths (e.g., orange, red, and yellow) pass toward Earth.**

Shorter wavelengths are similar in size to atmospheric molecules and particles, so sunlight scatters more blue light in all directions than other colors passing through the atmosphere. **Blue light interacts with atmospheric gas molecules and radiates in all directions,** making the sky appear blue when **observed from the ground.**

Rayleigh scattering of light by particles and molecules in the atmosphere

Atmospheric layers

Atmosphere has five layers as boundaries where temperature, density, movement, and chemical composition changes occur. From the Earth's surface, layers are troposphere, stratosphere, mesosphere, thermosphere, and exosphere.

Exosphere is the outermost edge of our atmosphere and the layer separating the atmosphere from outer space. It is located above the thermosphere and extends from about 500 km to 10,000 km above the Earth's surface. With its extremely low density of hydrogen, helium, and other gases, the exosphere is a transition zone where gas molecules are still gravitationally bound but can escape into outer space.

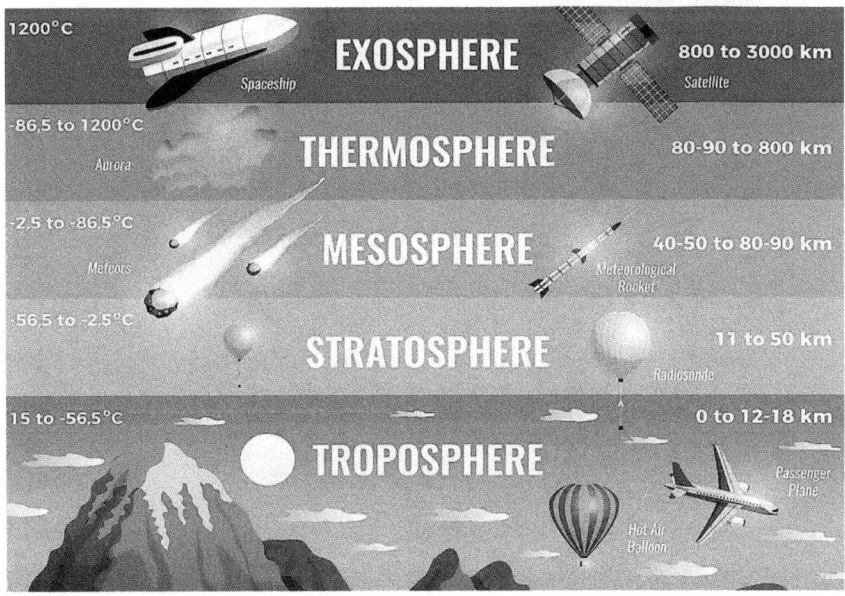

Atmospheric stratification

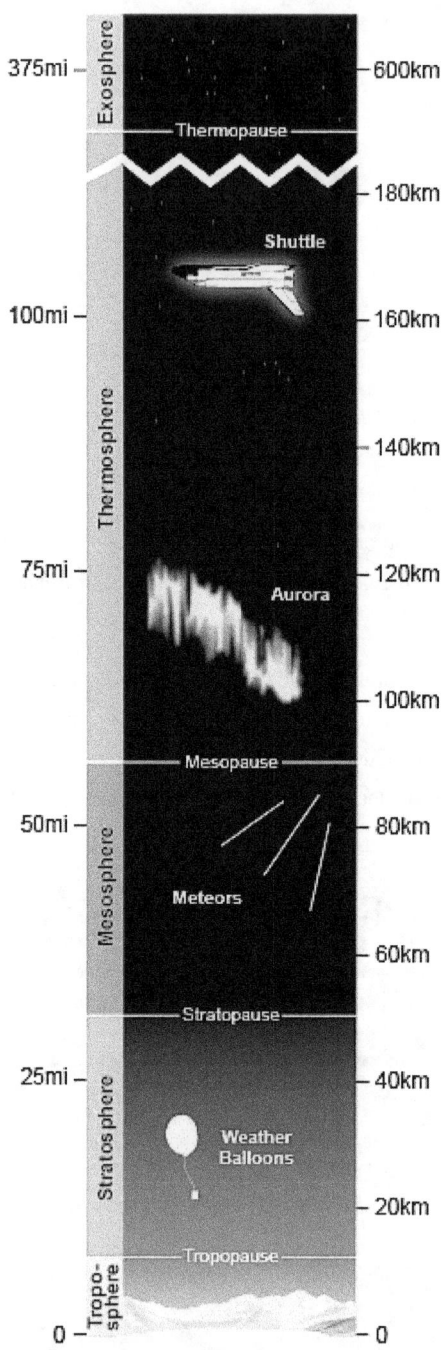

Exosphere is the coldest and outermost layer of the atmosphere; atoms and molecules escape into outer space; where satellites orbit Earth, 600 km above the surface.

Thermosphere is the upper atmosphere and is 85 to 600 kilometers above Earth.

Space shuttles travel in the thermosphere; auroras form and are seen from Earth's surface (bright lights seem so close but are more than 96.5 km away). The thermosphere is the thickest layer.

Mesosphere extends from 50 to 85 km above the Earth's surface with a temperature of –15 °C at the bottom of the layer.

Mesosphere gases are close and dense, slowing meteors entering the atmosphere; meteors burn and produce fiery streaks in the night sky (popularly called *shooting stars*).

Mesosphere and *stratosphere* (i.e., lower layer) compose the middle atmosphere.

Stratosphere is 50 km above Earth and 6.5 to 19.3 km thick. It has 19% of atmospheric gases and where weather balloons take readings. Warm air is at the top, preventing convection, as warm air has no upward movement.

Troposphere is the lower atmosphere where weather occurs. The layer begins at Earth and extends 6.5 to 19.3 km upward, varying with location. For example, it is 19.3 km at the equator, but at the poles, 6.5 km high.

Atmosphere layers with phenomena

Karman line is about 62 miles (100 km) and is the boundary between the atmosphere and outer space. Past this point, the atmosphere is so rarified that aircraft cannot generate enough lift, so orbital mechanics have become more applicable than aerodynamics.

Atmospheric research

Atmospheric research programs address:

- How is the composition of the atmosphere changing?
- How do atmospheric changes affect solar radiation and temperature?
- How does atmospheric composition affect air quality and climate?

Research programs addressing these environmental issues include:

Upper Atmosphere Research Program (UARP), which studies the processes controlling ozone concentration in the upper troposphere and stratosphere. Typical studies record reaction kinetics that directly and indirectly create and destroy ozone.

Radiation Sciences Program (RSP) uses satellite measurements of tropospheric aerosols, ozone, and their precursors for atmospheric transformations.

Tropospheric Chemistry Program (TCP) focuses on radiatively active gases, aerosols, cloud scatter, solar, and emitted radiation.

Atmospheric Composition Modeling and Analysis Program (ACMAP) studies oxidation efficiency and troposphere air quality, including how polluting aerosols affect clouds' properties and ozone's increasing depletion, focusing on long-term atmospheric composition trends based on weather satellite data and ground-based measurements.

Relationship matrix

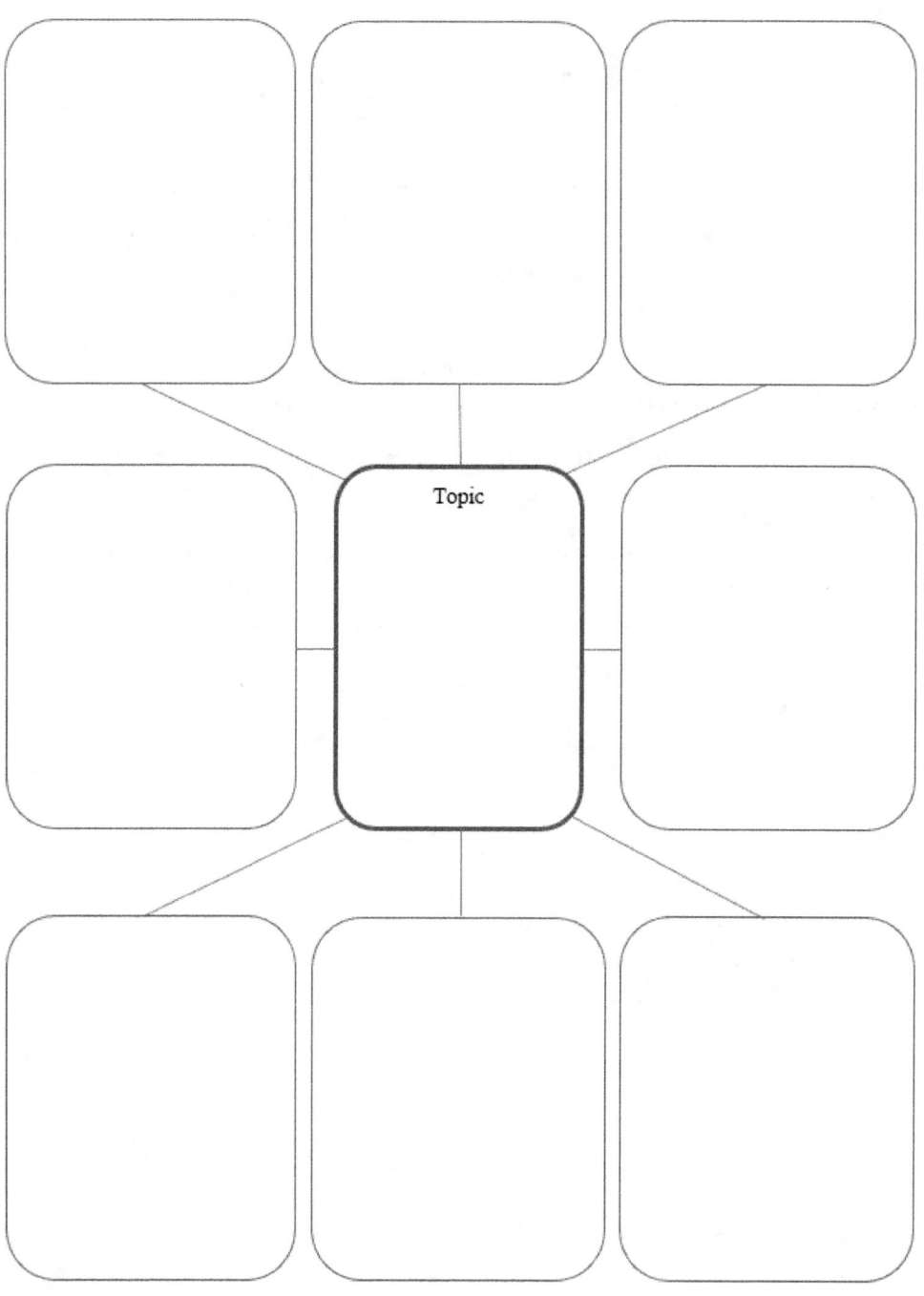

Questions: Earth Systems & Resources

1. Correlation and relative dating using index fossils is limited because:

   A. index fossils are extremely rare
   B. many sedimentary layers do not contain index fossils at all
   C. index fossils appeared for too short a time in the geologic record to be very helpful
   D. index fossils are rarely found in other than sedimentary rocks

2. According to the plate tectonics theory, seafloor spreading occurs at a:

   A. subduction zone
   B. convergent boundary
   C. divergent boundary
   D. transform boundary

3. The process that has yielded the most accurate estimate of the age of the Earth is a measurement of:

   A. rate of sedimentation
   B. radioactive decay of elements in minerals
   C. rate of increase of salinity of the oceans
   D. the rate of the cooling of the Earth from a molten mass

4. With all the Sun's energy striking the Earth every second of every day, why doesn't the Earth overheat and kill us all?

   A. Earth is so large and dense that it absorbs all this heat
   B. Earth is overheating regionally, melting rocks into the lava of volcanoes
   C. Earth maintains a balance by radiating this heat back into space
   D. Earth's atmosphere prevents solar radiation from reaching Earth's surface

5. Geologic Time Scale defines eras in terms of:

   A. major worldwide extinctions of life on Earth
   B. reversals in the Earth's magnetic field
   C. the beginning of the radioactive decay of elements in minerals
   D. major plate tectonic events

6. A helium balloon from the Earth's surface to the top of the stratosphere would notice that the temperatures:

    A. dropped steadily with increased altitude
    B. increased steadily with increased altitude
    C. dropped and then started to rise in the stratosphere about halfway
    D. rose and then started to drop in the mesosphere about halfway up

7. After a winter storm, bright sunlight returns, and the snow and ice on the road melt into liquid water. This is an example of:

    A. light energy converted to heat energy changing the state of water
    B. movement changing the position of snow and ice
    C. matter changing the heat of the atmosphere
    D. movement generating heat changes the position of ice and snow

8. The fluid core of the Earth:

    A. is mostly water that has leaked in from the oceans
    B. remains fluid because of heat generated by radioactive decay
    C. results from heat generated by the friction of the tectonic plates moving over each other
    D. is a watery substance that lubricates the movement of the tectonic plates

9. Which of the following statements about seismic waves is not true?

    A. In a P-wave, the material vibrates back and forth in the same direction as the direction of wave motion.
    B. P-waves travel more rapidly than S-waves.
    C. Both P-waves and S-waves travel readily through molten rock.
    D. Seismic waves are reflected at boundaries between rock layers with different densities.

10. How much of the Sun's radiation would strike the Earth if it did not have its atmosphere?

    A. about 10 times more
    B. about twice as much
    C. it would be about the same
    D. about half as much

11. The spreading of the sea floor along the Mid-Atlantic ridge is supported by:

   A. changes in the orientation of magnetized rocks as one moves away from the ridge.
   B. the sediment layer's thickness increases as one moves toward the continents.
   C. a large amount of heat escaping from the rift along the ridge.
   D. All these support the seafloor spreading hypothesis.

12. The two highest levels of the atmosphere contain only small amounts of oxygen, nitrogen, and ozone. These layers are the:

   A. mesosphere and thermosphere
   B. thermosphere and stratosphere
   C. stratosphere and troposphere
   D. thermosphere and troposphere

13. Which of the following has the highest albedo?

   A. a green tent
   B. a blacktop road
   C. a healthy oak tree
   D. snow on top of ice on a pond

14. The fact that there are seasons on the Earth is due primarily to:

   A. the tilt of the Earth's axis
   B. the changing distance of the Earth from the Sun during its orbit
   C. the precession of the Earth's axis of rotation
   D. the Coriolis effect

15. Volcanoes are triggered by:

   A. changes in solar radiation
   B. movement of tectonic plates
   C. human mining activities
   D. major changes in climate

Notes for active learning

CHAPTER 2

Weather & Climate

Weather Patterns

Global Atmospheric Circulation

Pressure Systems and Winds

Oceanic Influences

Oceanic Circulations

Page intentionally left blank

Weather Patterns

Weather phenomena

Weather is the degree to which it is cold or warm, calm or stormy, dry or wet, and so on.

Weather phenomena occur primarily in the *troposphere*, the atmosphere's lowest layer.

The troposphere contains significant water vapor, and temperature decreases with altitude. This contributes to the formation of clouds and precipitation. The troposphere is where the water cycle occurs, which involves evaporation, condensation, and precipitation. The temperature variations result in turbulence, which produces various weather phenomena.

Typical weather phenomena include rain, wind, clouds, snow, fog, dust storms, and thunderstorms. Less common are hurricanes, typhoons, and tornadoes, each of which originate from intersecting differences in air pressure.

Climate is a concept of expected atmospheric conditions over time. While weather is a short-term condition at a specific location and time, climate is the long-term characteristic of weather patterns in a given region over a long period, generally 30 years or more.

Aerial view of weather pattern

Relative humidity and dewpoint

Relative humidity is a ratio (as a %) of atmospheric moisture when saturated.

Humidity ratio is how much "air" is in the air *vs.* the amount of water.

Relative humidity uses the humidity ratio, which includes air temperature and the maximum amount of water the air can hold, displayed as a percentage. Relative humidity measures water vapor but *relative* to the temperature of the air. Given the temperature, it measures the amount of water vapor in the air compared to the maximum amount of vapor.

Relative humidity of 100% (i.e., dewpoint temperature equals air temperature) does not mean precipitation will occur. It is the maximum moisture in the air at that temperature.

Warm air has more water vapor (moisture) than cold air. Therefore, with the same absolute specific humidity, air has a higher relative humidity if the air is cooler.

Air has a lower relative humidity if the air is warmer and an observer *feels* the moisture (i.e., *absolute humidity*).

Meteorologists routinely consider the *dewpoint temperature* (instead of absolute humidity) to evaluate moisture, especially in the spring and summer.

Dewpoint temperature measures the amount of water vapor in the air and the temperature at which the air must be cooled for that air to be saturated.

Although weather conditions affect people differently, spring and summer surface dewpoint temperatures in the 50s are comfortable.

Dewpoint temperatures in the 60s are somewhat uncomfortable (i.e., humid).

Dewpoint temperatures in the 70s are quite uncomfortable (i.e., very humid).

For example, in the Ohio Valley (including Kentucky), common dewpoints during the summer range from the middle 60s to the middle 70s. Dewpoints as high as 80 or the lower 80s have been recorded, which is oppressive but relatively rare.

Dewpoint gives a quick reference for moisture content in air; relative humidity does not since the humidity is relative to air temperature.

Relative humidity cannot be determined by knowing the dewpoint alone; air temperature must also be known. If the air is saturated at a particular level (e.g., the surface), then the dewpoint temperature is the same as the air temperature, and the relative humidity is 100%.

The atmosphere is more moist with a dew point of 70 °F than a dew point of 30 °F.

Temp (°F)	Dew Point (°F)	Humidity
30	30	100%
40	40	100%
50	50	100%
60	60	100%
70	70	100%

Relative humidity vs. dew point

Precipitation

Precipitation is a water particle, either liquid or solid, that falls as rain, snow, sleet, and hail.

Drizzle, snow pellets, and snow grains are less common.

Rain is familiar with raindrops larger than 0.0508 cm in diameter. Smaller drops are drizzle, precipitation with uniform drops close together.

Drizzle appears to float while following air currents. Unlike fog, drizzle has sufficient mass to fall to the ground. Both drizzle and fog often occur together.

Ice pellets (or *sleet*) are translucent or transparent, typically round ice grains. These are formed by frozen raindrops or snowflakes that have melted and refrozen.

Hail is precipitation with small pieces (or balls) of ice that fall separately or freeze in large, irregular clumps. It is associated with thunderstorms and a 0.25 in. or larger hailstone.

Larger-sized hailstones (1.0 inch or larger) indicate a severe thunderstorm.

Small hail (or snow pellets) are opaque, white grains that are round (or cone-shaped) and not considered true hail because they are smaller than 0.25 inches.

Snow is composed of branched ice crystals that form six-pointed stars.

Snow grains are essentially frozen drizzles and are tiny, opaque, white ice grains.

Precipitation formation

When the relative humidity is 100 percent (i.e., dewpoint and air temperatures are the same), the maximum moisture is in the air at that temperature, and precipitation is likely to occur.

Saturation may result in surface fog and clouds (with tiny water droplets suspended in the air).

However, for precipitation to occur, the air must rise sufficiently to enhance condensation of water vapor into liquid water droplets or ice crystals (depending on air temperature) and promote the growth of water droplets, supercooled droplets, or ice crystals in clouds.

Droplets grow through *collision coalescence,* whereby droplets of varying sizes collide and fuse (i.e., *coalesce*).

Ice crystal processes (deposition and aggregation) are essential for particle growth. In thunderstorms, hail also can develop.

Once the suspended precipitation particles grow sufficiently, the air cannot support their weight, and precipitation falls from clouds.

In humid climates, thunderstorms often cause heavier rain than typical winter rainfall since air moisture content is higher in the spring and summer, and air usually rises more rapidly within developing thunderstorms.

Cloud microphysics studies droplets and ice crystals within clouds and related precipitation.

Global Atmospheric Circulation

Earth's rotation and tilt

Global atmospheric circulation is the movement of air around the planet. It explains how thermal energy and storm systems move over the Earth's surface.

Earth's rotation creates *angular momentum*; it is conserved and the product of mass, velocity, and distance from reference. Hence, velocity increases when the spin radius decreases (i.e., low to high latitude).

Global circulation would be simple without the Earth's rotation, tilt relative to the Sun, and surface water. With the Sun directly over the equator, the ground and atmosphere would heat up more than the rest of the planet. This region would become very hot, with hot air rising into the upper atmosphere.

This would create a constant belt of low pressure around the equator. That warm air would then move directly north toward the poles, becoming very cold and sinking, creating a large area of high pressure. The temperature and pressure difference would return the now-cold air south to the equator (above right), creating a simple global circulation.

Atmospheric circulation is created by masses moving in:

    1) *vertical motion* of warm air rising and becoming buoyant and

    2) *horizontal motion* (air flowing from high-pressure areas of dense compression to low-pressure areas of less density, creating wind.

Sea breezes are an example of both forces interacting with one another.

The global atmospheric circulation is made up of three primary convection cells:

    Hadley, Ferrel, and Polar cells

Hadley cells are closest to the equator, Ferrel cells are in the mid-latitudes, and Polar cells are near the Earth's poles. Together with the Coriolis effect, these three types of convection cells drive the global atmospheric circulation.

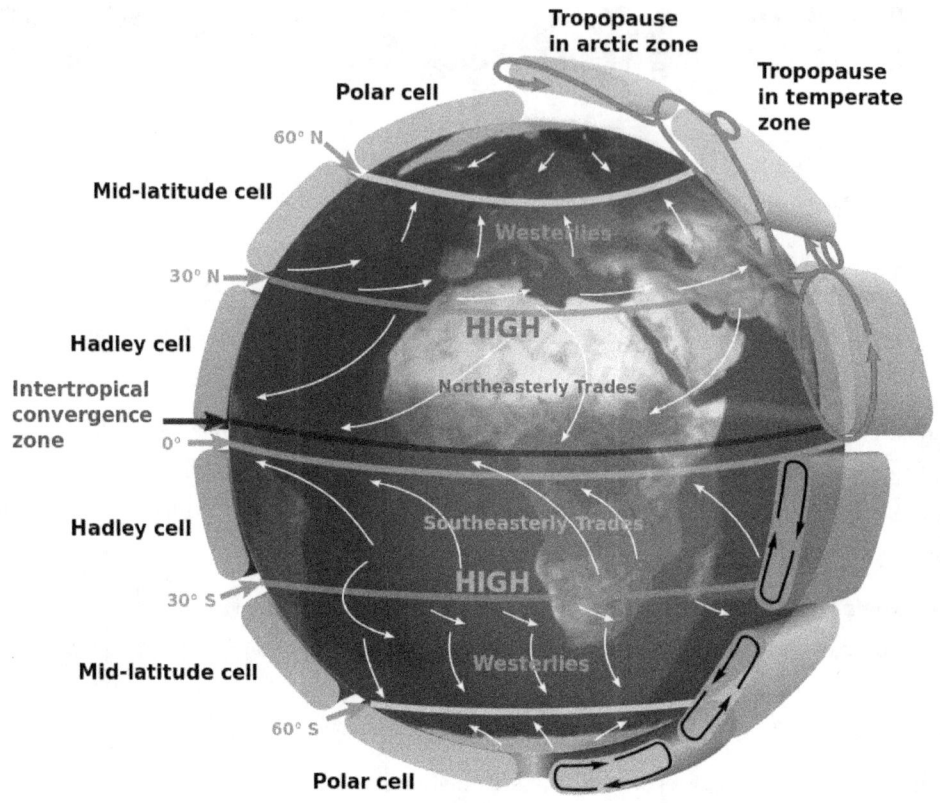

Hadley, Ferrel (mid-latitude)l, and Polar Cell circulation pressure gradients

Coriolis effect

Coriolis force causes long distances winds to curve due to Earth's rotation. Every point on Earth rotates around the axis once every 24 hours at varying speeds.

Air on the equator moves at 1,700 kph, while at 60° latitude, it moves at 850 kph since it is closer to Earth's spinning axis.

If Earth did not rotate on an angled axis, air would circulate between the equator and poles.

Earth rotates on an axis, so circulating air is deflected left toward the Southern Hemisphere and right toward the Northern Hemisphere. This deflection is the *Coriolis Effect*.

French scientist Gustave-Gaspard Coriolis discovered the *Coriolis force* while studying why shots from long-range cannons repeatedly fell to the right of the target. Since the Coriolis force only affects long-range masses, it is not apparent in local weather patterns. It does not make water drain in different directions in each hemisphere.

Coriolis force causes winds in *low-pressure* systems (hurricanes) to *rotate and spiral*.

Air starts moving in the typical *high-pressure to a low-pressure gradient.*

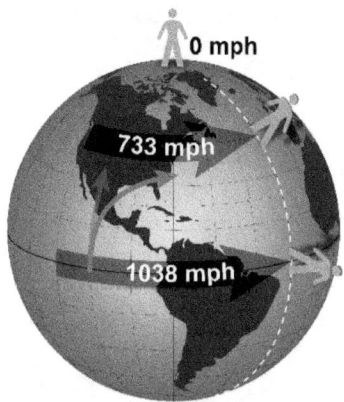

Coriolis effect from wind moving faster than Earth's rotation moves west to east (relative to surface).

As it travels, the Coriolis force causes it to bend and create a state of geotropic flow where the pressure gradient force and Coriolis force balance. When this occurs, the air no longer moves from high-pressure zones to low-pressure zones but instead travels a course parallel to isobars (notations on weather maps show changes in pressure).

Coriolis effect impacts wind direction.

> Northern Hemisphere has wind deflected to the *right.*

> Southern Hemisphere has wind deflected to the *left.*

Hadley cells

Hadley cells are the low latitude overturning circulations with air rising at the equator and sinking at roughly 30° latitude.

Moist, warm air rising at the equator causes considerable rainfall. The same air, drier and cooler when it falls, contributes to arid (or dry) conditions near 30° north and south.

Hadley cell circulation occurs from tropical atmospheric circulation in which air rising near the equator flows toward the poles 10–15 km above the surface, producing trade winds, tropical rain belts, hurricanes, tropical cyclones, jet streams, and subtropical deserts.

Hadley Cell Circulation controls Tropical trade winds and low-latitude weather patterns, producing general weather patterns for rainforests, grasslands, and deserts.

English meteorologist George Hadley (1735) studied weather patterns producing atmospheric circulation. He proposed that global-scale circulation was a larger version of local systems.

Hadley's model is accurate because Earth is differentially heated, buoyancy develops at low latitudes, and mass moves towards the poles, creating pressure gradients.

Hadley's circulation pattern terminates at 30 degrees (or 30°) latitude.

Atmospheric circulation strength is based on the dynamic balance between motions caused by differential heating and friction slowing winds.

Hadley cells operate between 0° and 30° to 40° North and South and are mainly responsible for equatorial region weather.

Without rotation, Earth would have two large Hadley cells; Earth's rotation produces the Coriolis effect.

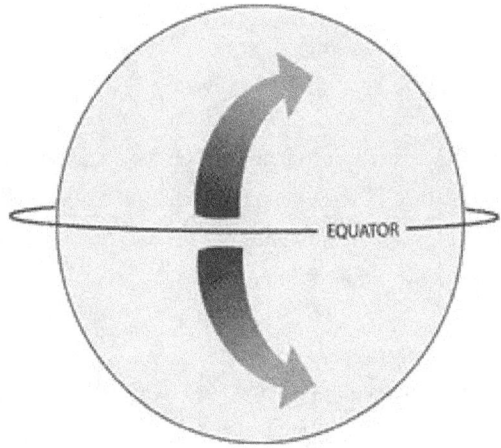

Haley's model of atmospheric circulation

Ferrel cells

*Ferrel cell*s are mid-latitude atmospheric circulation cells with air near the surface flowing poleward and eastward, while air higher in the atmosphere moves equatorward and westward.

Ferrel cell occurs at higher latitudes (between 30° and 60° N and 30° and 60° S): Air on the surface is pulled towards the poles, forming the warm south-westerly winds in the northern hemisphere and north-westerly winds in the southern hemisphere.

Air in Ferrell cells moves opposite to the air in Hadley cells, with warm air moving toward the polar regions. The warm air that has traveled up from the equator converges with the cold air at 60° latitude that has traveled down from the polar regions.

Ferrel cells are a secondary circulation feature, dependent upon the Hadley and polar cells. It is sometimes known as the 'zone of mixing.' At its southern extent (in the northern hemisphere), it overrides the Hadley cell; at its northern extent, it overrides the polar cell.

Hadley and Ferrel cells meet to produce unique wind systems. For example, at 30° N and S of the equator—where the Ferrel and Hadley cells meet—there is a high-pressure zone, which creates an area where the winds are often weak. This area is known as *horse latitudes*.

Polar cells

Polar cells are the smallest and weakest circulation cells, which extend from between 60° and 70° N and S to the poles.

Air in these cells sinks over the highest latitudes and flows towards lower surface latitudes.

Polar cells, at higher latitudes, air rises and travels toward the poles. Once over the poles, the air sinks, forming areas of high atmospheric pressure called polar highs.

At the surface, air moves outward from polar highs, creating east-blowing surface winds called *polar easterlies*.

At the poles, air is cooled and sinks towards the ground, forming high pressure, known as the *Polar high*. It then flows towards the lower latitudes.

At about 60° N and S, the cold polar air mixes with warmer tropical air and rises upwards, creating a zone of low pressure called the subpolar low.

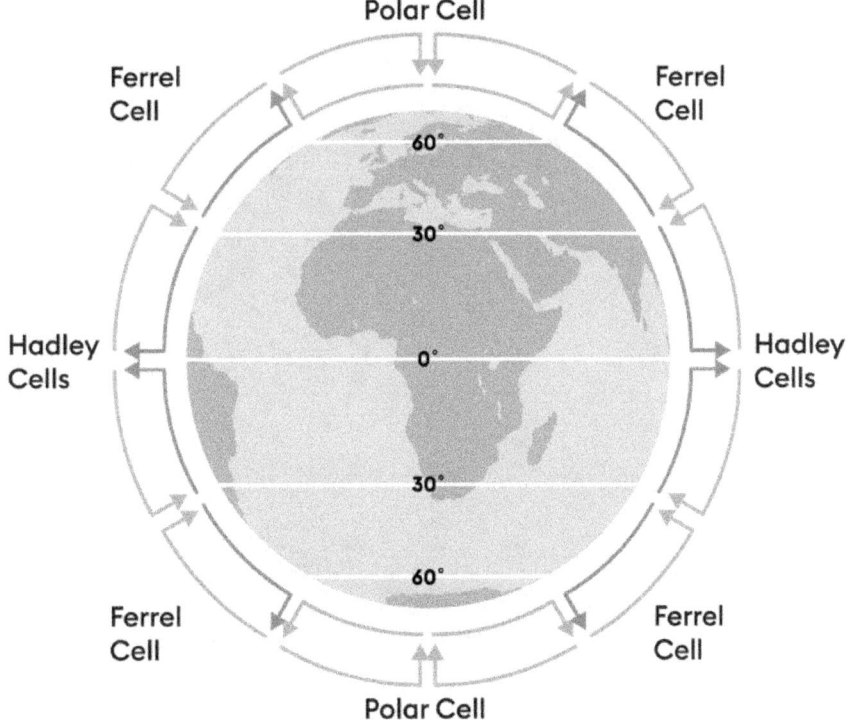

Hadley Cells, Ferrel Cells, and Polar Cells are global convection cells

Notes for active learning

Pressure Systems and Winds

Atmospheric pressure

Pressure gradient is the difference between two pressure centers.

A pressure gradient describes the difference in pressure between two points. It often describes how pressure changes over a distance in the atmosphere, particularly between high and low-pressure areas. The pressure gradient force is the force that results from this pressure difference, driving air from areas of high pressure to areas of low pressure.

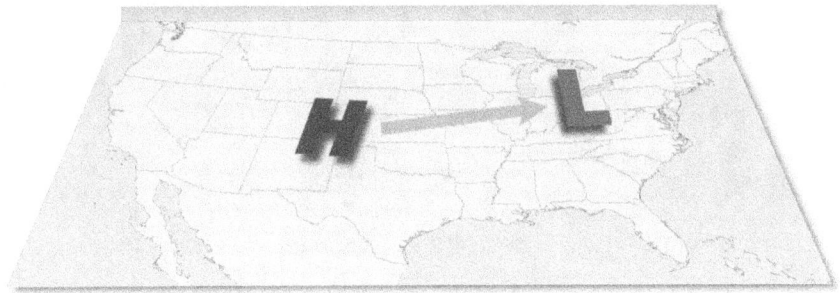

Pressure gradient moves air (wind) from high pressure to low pressure

Greatest *vertical motion* of air impacts air pressure at the surface.

Greatest *downward motion increases* surface air pressure.

Greatest *upward motion decreases* air pressure at the surface.

On a surface weather map, the closeness of isobars (lines of constant pressure) generally indicates the pressure gradient.

Isobars represent equal pressure on a surface weather map and indicate where the greatest *upward and downward motion* is occurring.

Isobars are lines of equal pressure

Wind generally flows along isobars, not directly across them. While the pressure gradient force initially drives wind from high to low pressure, the Coriolis effect, especially in the Northern Hemisphere, causes the wind to shift and move roughly parallel to the isobars; deflection is most pronounced at higher altitudes where friction is less.

Friction causes the wind to slow slightly; therefore, the wind flows out of high pressure and into low pressure across isobars at a shallow angle.

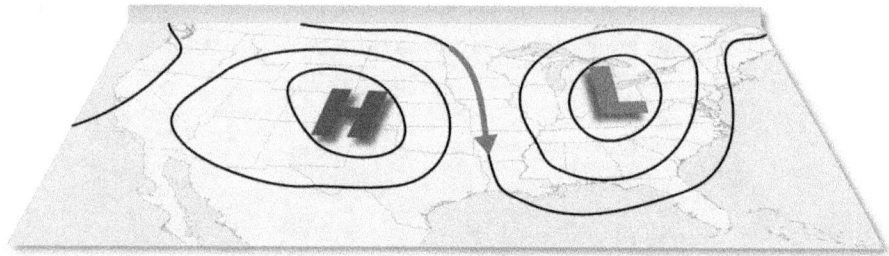

Wind flows along isobars

The *vertical motion* of jet streams creates high and low *surface pressure centers.*

Vertical air motion directly impacts surface air pressure, whether rising (upward) or sinking (downward). Sinking air, as seen under high-pressure systems, compresses the air and increases surface pressure. As seen with low-pressure systems, rising air expands the air and decreases surface pressure.

Divergence aloft, caused by jet streams, leads to sinking air and high pressure, while convergence aloft results in rising air and low pressure.

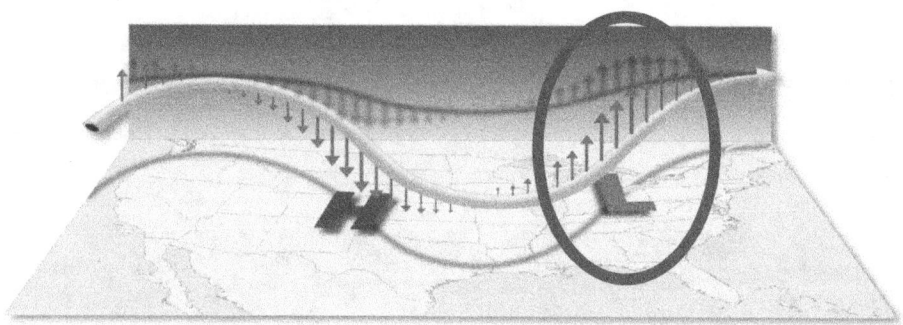

Low-pressure areas are where the rise in height is greatest

The greatest decrease in height of a specific pressure level typically occurs where the air is warmer, as warmer air is less dense and, therefore, has higher pressure at a given altitude.

As the areas of cooler air towards areas of warmer air, the height of a particular pressure level increases. Conversely, the smallest decrease in height, or even an increase, can be expected near areas of colder, more dense air.

Jet streams with the greatest *rise in height* are typically at surface *low pressure*.

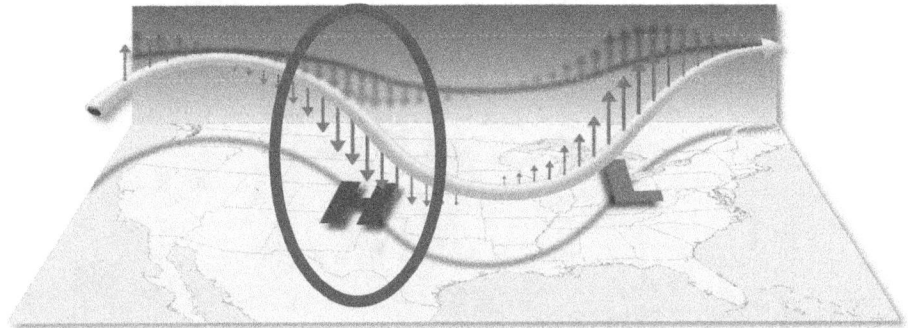

Greatest decrease in height is typically where surface high pressure is located

Cold and warm fronts

Cold and warm fronts are boundaries between air masses of different temperatures and properties, often associated with low-pressure systems.

Cold fronts mark the leading edge of a cold air mass displacing warmer air, while *warm fronts* indicate where warm air replaces colder air.

High and low-pressure systems can also create sharp boundaries, but these are not always directly associated with fronts. High and low pressure creates sharp boundaries.

Cold fronts have denser air than warm air, forcing the warm air to rise abruptly, leading to the rapid development of clouds and potentially severe weather (e.g., thunderstorms).

Occluded fronts occur when a cold front overtakes a warm front; the warm air is lifted entirely off the ground, creating a complex weather pattern.

Cold front is when cooler air replaces warm air (regardless of temperature difference)

Warm front is when warmer air replaces cold air. Warm fronts have warm air gently slide over cold air, causing a gradual rise of air and more widespread precipitation, like rain or snow.

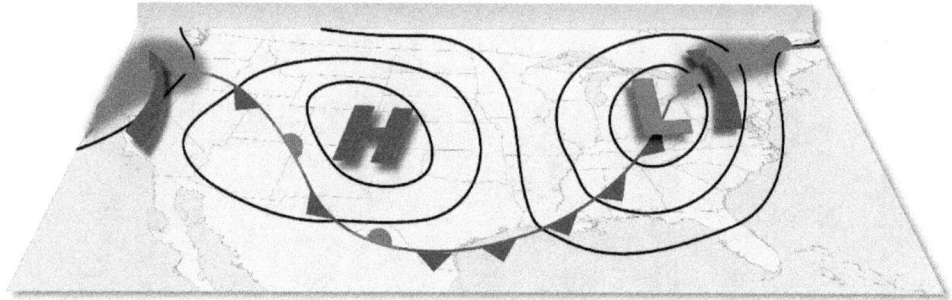

Warm front boundaries are not as well defined as cold fronts

Stationary front is the boundary between two air masses with no frontal movement. This stalled condition often leads to prolonged periods of similar weather conditions in the area where the stationary front is located.

Stationary front becomes a warm or cold front if the boundary moves

As a cold front advances, the colder, denser air pushes underneath the warmer, less dense air, forcing the warmer air upwards. This uplift of warm air can lead to cloud formation and precipitation.

Warmer air is less dense than colder air because the molecules in warmer air move faster and are farther apart.

When a cold air mass moves into an area occupied by warmer air, the colder, denser air slides underneath the warmer, less dense air. This interaction causes the warm air to be lifted abruptly. As the warm air rises, it expands and cools, leading to cloud formation and potentially precipitation.

Cold front movements can bring sudden temperature drops, gusty winds, and precipitation.

As the cold front advances, its cooler (denser) air undercuts the warmer (less dense) air, forcing it up over the front.

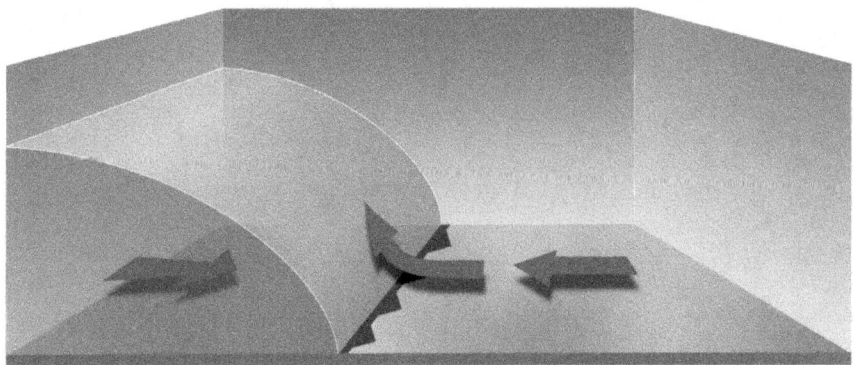

Cold fronts have cooler and denser air, undercutting warmer and less dense air

The rapid, forceful rise of warm air creates thunderstorms at cold fronts.

As a cold front moves in, the cold, denser air pushes under the warm, lighter air, forcing it to rise abruptly. This rising warm air then cools and condenses, forming clouds and potentially thunderstorms, especially if the air is also moist and unstable.

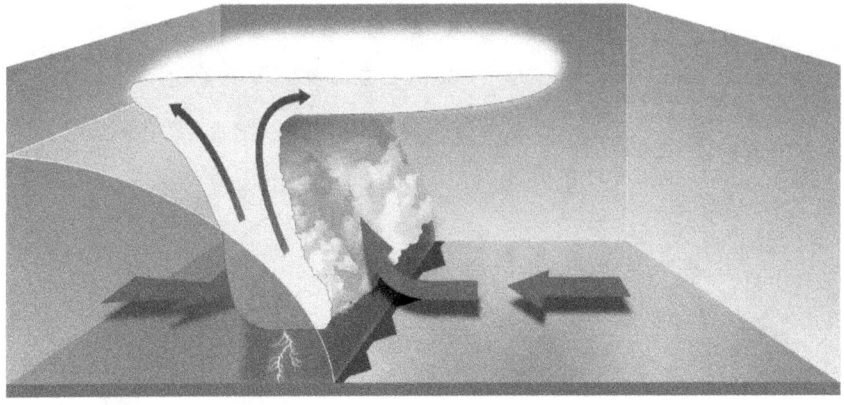

Cold fronts with forceful rising of warm air create thunderstorms

Warm air slides over the colder air, not displacing it like for cold fronts. The gradual rise of warm air along the frontal boundary creates a long, gentle slope, sometimes extending hundreds of miles ahead of the surface position of the front.

Warm fronts are lighter, denser warm air faster than retreating warm front, causing it to rise.

Lighter warm air moves faster than the retreating warm front, forcing air to rise

Occasionally, warm air lifted over the front is unstable and forms thunderstorms.

An unstable air mass is characterized by warm, moist air near the surface and cooler air aloft. If this air is lifted, it will continue to rise independently due to buoyancy, leading to cloud formation and potentially thunderstorms.

Thunderstorms require moisture, and the warm, moist air lifted over the front provides the necessary ingredients. As the air rises, it cools and condenses, forming clouds and precipitation.

If the air is both unstable and moist enough, thunderstorms can develop along or ahead of the front. These thunderstorms can bring heavy rain, lightning, and even strong winds.

Clouds and rain develop ahead of warm front

Inclement weather, such as thunderstorms, heavy rain, and snow, is often associated with lifting air at frontal boundaries.

Lifting occurs when one air mass forces another to rise, creating conditions that lead to cloud formation and precipitation.

A weather front is the boundary between two different air masses. When these air masses collide, one air mass is forced to rise over the other, a process called frontal lifting.

As air rises, it cools, and the moisture in the air condenses, forming clouds. If the air is moist and unstable, these clouds can develop into thunderstorms or other precipitation.

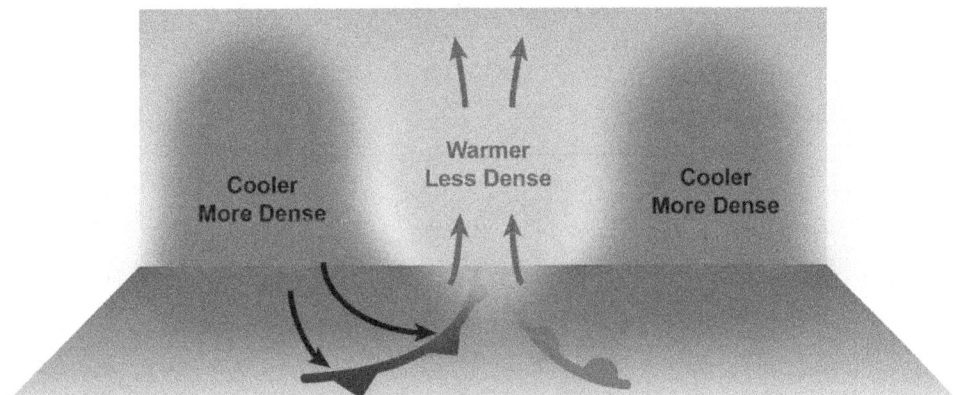

Inclement weather occurs near fronts where air is most readily lifted

Inclement weather, including thunderstorms, heavy rainfall, and even snowstorms, is often associated with weather fronts, particularly cold fronts. Fronts are the boundaries between different air masses, and the interaction between these air masses, which often involves air being lifted, can lead to cloud formation and precipitation.

Fronts create areas where one air mass is forced to rise over another. This lifting can be abrupt with cold fronts, where cold air wedges under warm air, causing it to rise rapidly.

As air rises, it cools, and if the air is moist, it can reach its saturation point, leading to condensation and the formation of clouds. If enough water condenses, it can fall as precipitation, such as light rain, heavy rain, snow, or hail.

When unstable air is lifted, it can lead to thunderstorms. The rapid rise of air, condensation, and latent heat release can create strong updrafts and the potential for severe weather.

Cold fronts are particularly known for bringing inclement weather because they often involve the rapid lifting of warm, moist air, which can lead to the formation of thunderstorms and heavy precipitation.

Wave patterns

Upper air maps (also called synoptic charts or constant-pressure charts) are maps of the atmosphere's upper layers. They are usually at a fixed-pressure level (e.g., 500 or 200 millibar) and show weather conditions, such as wind, temperature, and humidity at different altitudes. These charts help meteorologists understand the overall atmospheric structure and forecast weather.

Contours are drawn at 60 m intervals, with closer contours indicating faster wind speed.

Rate of change is more important than absolute values (in meteorology).

Gradients show a greater change with more intense weather.

Common wave patterns provide reliable weather predictions. Wave patterns occur at any point, not just in the locations depicted.

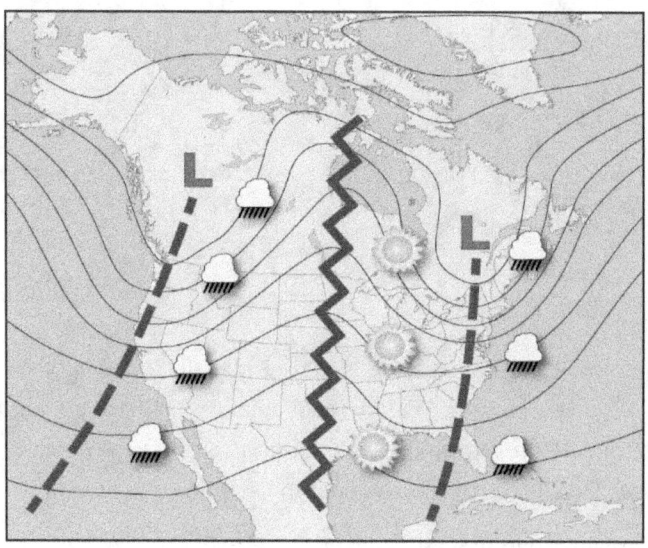

Wave patterns predict weather

Wave patterns in the atmosphere, like longwaves and shortwaves, can influence weather systems. In contrast, ocean wave patterns, like swell and wave period, are crucial for coastal weather conditions and surf forecasting.

Longwaves (or Rossby and planetary waves) are large, slow-moving waves in the upper atmosphere that can cause long-lasting weather patterns. They can lead to extended periods of rain or snow in certain areas while others experience dry conditions.

Shortwaves are smaller, faster-moving waves that can introduce changes in weather, such as thunderstorms, particularly when they interact with troughs (low-pressure areas).

Troughs, which are low-pressure areas, can be associated with storms and precipitation.

Ridges, which are high-pressure areas, tend to bring fair weather.

Jet stream is a fast-flowing band of air in the upper atmosphere, influencing the direction of storms and weather patterns.

Unsettled weather typically occurs between *troughs and downstream ridges.*

Fairweather typically occurs between *ridges and downstream troughs.*

Positive and negative tilt wave patterns

Positively tilted troughs are an upper-level system where the axis of the trough (a low-pressure area) tilts from southwest to northeast in the Northern Hemisphere and southeast to northwest in the Southern Hemisphere. This tilt is typically associated with less severe weather than negatively tilted troughs.

The trough's axis extends northeast to southwest in the Northern Hemisphere and southeast to northwest in the Southern Hemisphere.

While less likely to produce severe weather, positively tilted troughs can contribute to extended periods of rainy weather on the eastern side of the trough axis.

Positively tilted troughs are generally associated with more stable conditions at the surface. They are more common in spring and fall. They can form when a strong shortwave trough moves south on the west side of a trough that extends towards the equator.

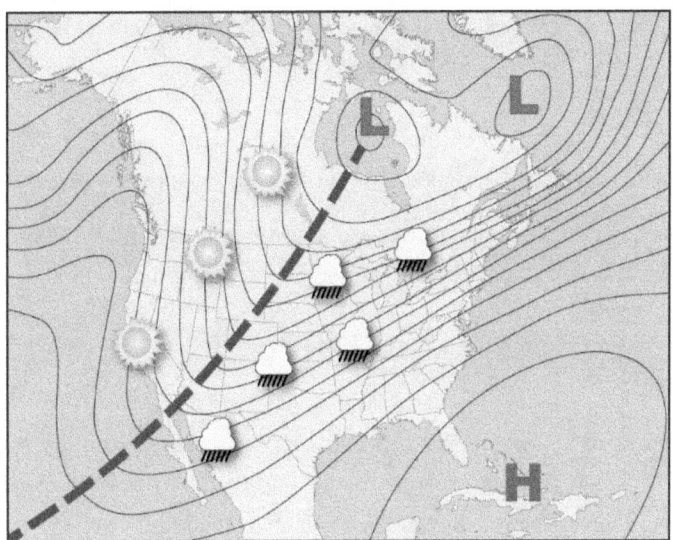

Positive tilt wave patterns – trough is orientated NE-SW from low pressure, creating large areas of unsettled weather east of a trough.

By contrast, negatively tilted troughs are associated with stronger weather systems.

Negatively tilted troughs have their axis tilted northwest to southeast in both hemispheres.

Negatively tilted troughs are more likely to produce severe weather.

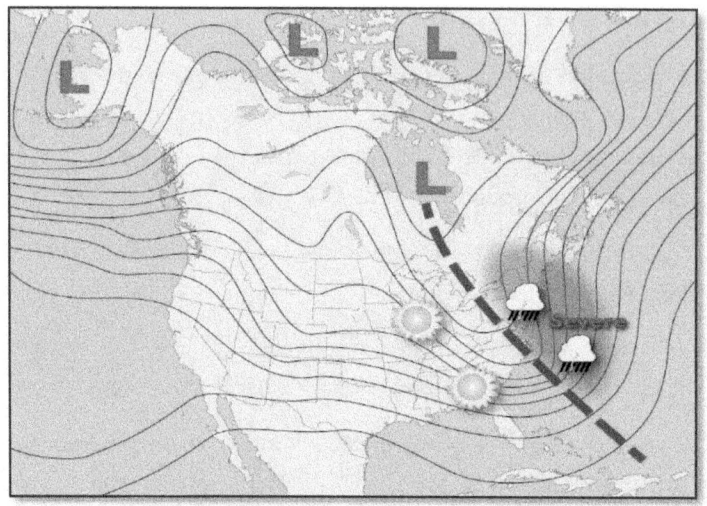

Negative tilt wave patterns – trough is orientated NW-SE from low pressure, creating a smaller area of unsettled weather east of the trough. However, this wave pattern produces severe weather.

Cooler, denser air is colder, with its molecules packed closer together, making it denser. Denser air exerts more pressure, causing lower atmospheric pressure.

Warmer, less dense air has warmer air molecules moving faster and spreading out, making it less dense. This less dense air exerts less pressure, resulting in higher atmospheric pressure levels.

Dips and ridges

Cooler, denser air tends to have pressure levels closer to the Earth's surface, while warmer, less dense air results in higher atmospheric pressure levels. This density difference leads to dips (troughs) and ridges in upper air charts, which are essentially contours of equal height at a specific pressure.

Dips and ridges use upper air charts to show the height of specific pressure levels, revealing patterns of dips (troughs) and ridges.

Dips indicate lower altitude areas for a given pressure, associated with colder, denser air.

Ridges represent higher altitude areas for the same pressure, often associated with warmer, less dense air.

Dips and ridges are significant because they drive weather patterns at the surface.

Height of pressure levels influences wind patterns, and the difference in height between a ridge and a trough (i.e., a gradient) can create areas of *convergence* (i.e., air flowing together) and *divergence* (i.e., air flowing apart), impacting weather systems like storms and high or low-pressure areas.

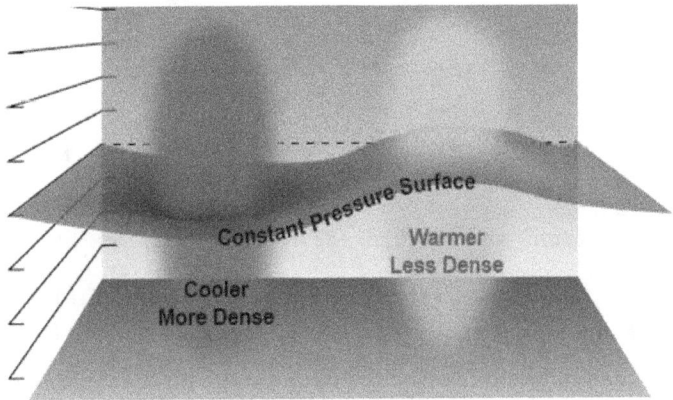

Dips and ridges. Cooler, more dense air means pressure levels occur closer to the Earth's surface. Warmer, less dense air pressure levels occur higher in the atmosphere.

Wind rotation

Air around low-pressure regions in the Northern Hemisphere is directed to the right and rotates *counterclockwise* around the system.

Air around high pressure in the Northern Hemisphere is directed away from the high-pressure force, producing a *clockwise* rotation.

However, winds within one kilometer of the ground are deflected toward low-pressure gradients because the friction with objects on the ground slows them down. As air spirals into low-pressure areas, it rises to the center of the convergence and begins to cool, creating condensation, clouds, and rain.

Some air parcels spiral away from the high-pressure areas, and rather than rise, they flow toward low-pressure areas, causing air to descend from above to maintain barometric balance, producing warm, sunny weather.

Coriolis effect impacts wind direction. Wind spirals away from high pressure in a clockwise direction and toward low pressure in a counterclockwise direction.

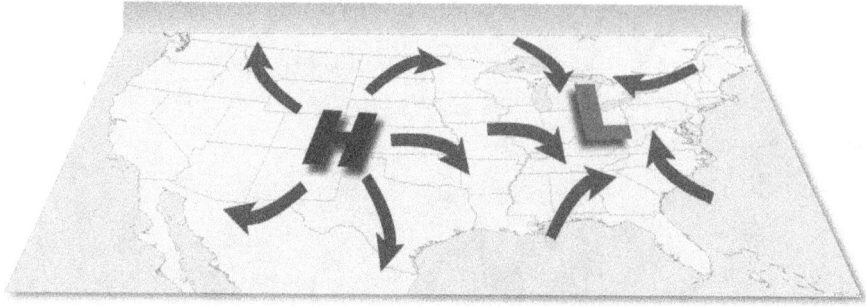

Coriolis effect impacts wind direction

However, the wind constantly wants to turn to the right because of the Coriolis effect.

Opposed to that is the pressure gradient force, which wants to take air from high pressure to low pressure. These two opposing forces balance.

Geostrophic wind

Geostrophic wind results from the balancing of the Coriolis effect and pressure gradient.

Coriolis effect (i.e., turning the wind to the right) and the pressure gradient force (i.e., wind flowing from high to low pressure) are balanced, and wind parallels isobars.

Geostrophic wind (or *geostrophic balance*) is the theoretical wind resulting from an exact balance between the Coriolis force and the pressure gradient force. Actual wind differs from geostrophic wind due to the influence of other forces, such as friction from the ground.

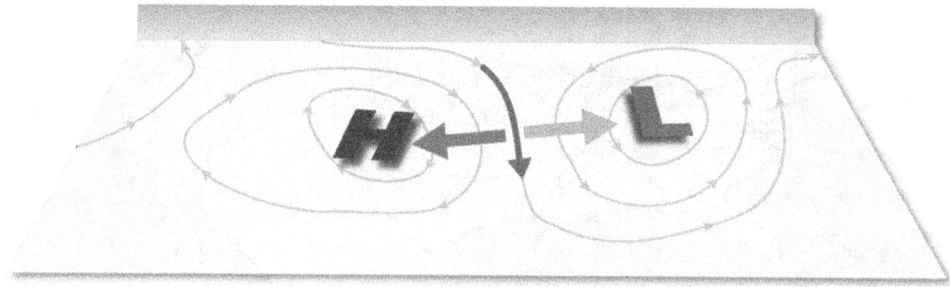

Geostrophic wind resolves the Coriolis effect with pressure gradients

Jet streams

Jet streams are responses to strong temperature gradients (i.e., greatest density change) with wind speeds of 50 kt (maybe> 200 kt).

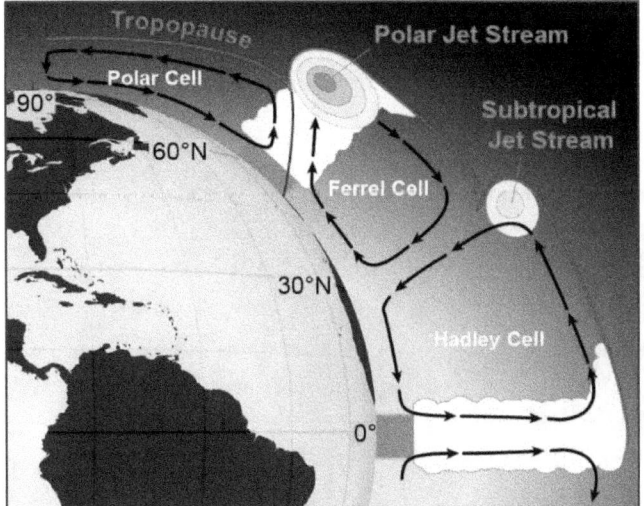

Heat transport to the poles and cold air toward the equator

Jet stream circulation follows the Sun, north and south, as the Sun's zenith changes seasonally.

At equator, air converges and is forced to rise, forming the *Intertropical Convergence Zone*.

At 30° N, air descends and the latitude of most deserts.

At 60° N, rising air leads to much rainfall in many of the world's forests.

At poles, descending air leads to desert-like conditions.

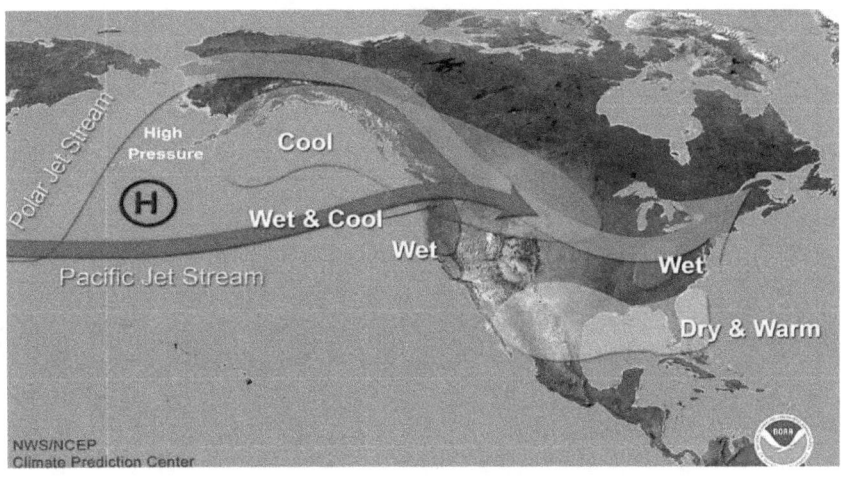

Pacific jet stream produces wet, cool, dry, and warm regions

Beaufort Wind Scale

Beaufort Wind Scale was initially developed for maritime use but has been extended for wind observations on land. It is used to estimate wind speed based on visual cues exhibited by the sea and land. The scale ranges from force 0 (calm) to force 12 (hurricane), with each number indicating a different wind speed and corresponding observable effects.

Force	Speed	Description	Observable effects
0	0 – 1 mph 0 – 1 knots	Calm	Calm; smoke rises vertically. Sea like a mirror.
1	1 – 3 mph 1 – 3 knots	Light air	Wind direction is shown by smoke drift but not by wind vanes. Ripples appear as scales form but without foam crests.
2	4 – 7 mph 4 – 6 knots	Light breeze	Wind felt on face; leaves rustle, ordinary vanes moved by wind. Small wavelets, still short but pronounced. Crests have a glassy appearance and do not break.
3	8 – 12 mph 7 – 10 knots	Gentle breeze	Leaves and small twigs constantly move; the wind extends a light flag. Large wavelets with crests breaking and foam of glassy appearance. Perhaps scattered white horses.
4	13 – 18 mph 11 – 16 knots	Moderate breeze	Raises dust and loose paper; small branches move. Small waves become larger; white horses start forming.
5	19 – 24 mph 17 – 21 knots	Fresh breeze	Small tree leaves sway; crested wavelets form on inland waters. Moderate waves, with pronounced long form; many white horses.
6	25 – 31 mph 22 – 27 knots	Strong breeze	Large branches move; wires whistle; umbrellas are used with difficulty. Large waves form; white foam crests are more extensive.

Force	Speed	Description	Observable effects
7	32 – 38 mph 28 – 33 knots	Near gale	Whole trees move; it is inconvenient to walk against the wind. Sea heaps up, and white foam from breaking waves blows in streaks along the wind's direction.
8	39 – 46 mph 34 – 40 knots	Gale	Twigs break off trees; generally, it impedes progress. Moderately high waves of greater length; edges of crests break into spindrift. Foam is blown in well-marked streaks along the wind direction.
9	47 – 54 mph 41 – 47 knots	Severe gale	Slight structural damage (roof shingles removed). High waves with dense foam streaks along the direction of the wind. Crests of waves topple, tumble, and roll over. Spray affects visibility.
10	55 – 63 mph 48 – 55 knots	Storm	Seldom experienced inland; trees are uprooted; considerable structural damage occurs. Very high waves with long overhanging crests; great foam patches blow in dense white streaks along the direction of the wind. The sea surface appears white, and the tumbling is heavy and shock-like.
11	64 – 72 mph 56 – 63 knots	Violent storm	Rarely experienced; accompanied by widespread damage. Exceptionally high waves (small and medium-size ships might be lost to view behind waves). The sea is covered with long white foam patches along the wind direction. Wave crest edges are blown into a froth. Visibility affected.
12	72 – 83 mph 64 – 71 knots	Hurricane	Air is filled with foam and spray. The sea is white with driving spray; visibility is seriously affected.

Beaufort Wind Scale, National Weather Service

Notes for active learning

Oceanic Influences

Atmosphere-ocean interactions

The atmosphere and oceans exchange and store energy through heat, momentum, and moisture. Oceans absorb heat more effectively than ice and land surfaces and store heat much more efficiently than land.

Coastal regions can remain more temperate, as oceanic heat is released slower than terrestrial heat. Changes in the energy balance between the atmosphere and the oceans are critical to the Earth's climate change.

Ocean currents are affected by variations in the circulation of the atmosphere. The force of the wind drives currents along the surface of the ocean. The frictional drag of the wind moving across the ocean's surface creates a current. This wind movement churns the water within a few meters below the surface.

Thermocline

Thermocline is a thin area of rapidly decreasing temperatures below the mixed layer.

Temperature decreases rapidly from *epipelagic* (upper layer) to colder *mesopelagic zone*.

Ocean water temperature remains constant below 3,300 feet to a depth of about 13,100 feet.

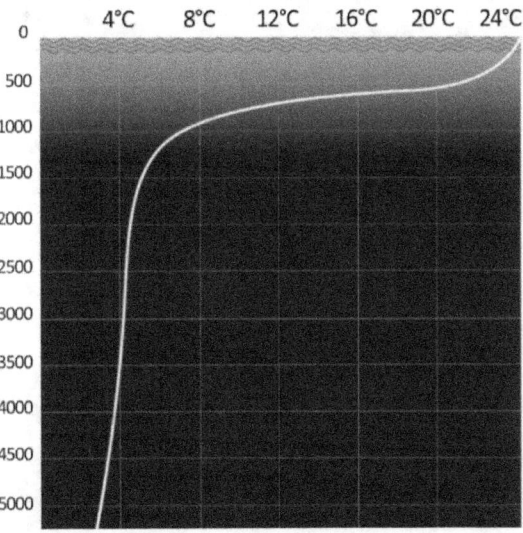

Thermocline depth (meters) vs. temperature (°C)

The ocean below the thermocline has its circulation patterns, which depend on salinity and the temperature of the waters.

Vertical movements of water through and below the thermocline allow heat to be stored in deep ocean areas and later released back into the atmosphere when recycled to the surface.

Thermocline water temperature decreases with depths

Oceans affect weather and the atmosphere by storing enormous amounts of moisture and heat. A tropical storm may form over a warm ocean, supplying the energy necessary for typhoons and hurricanes to grow powerful and destructive. For example, winter storms carrying precipitation to the western United States begin forming in the North Pacific Ocean.

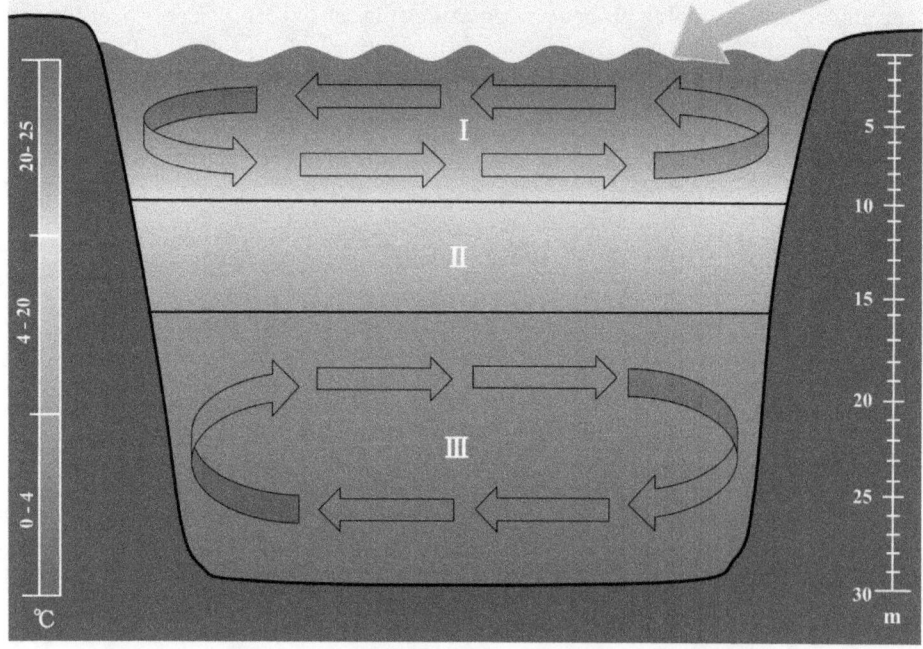

Water is stratified into three sections with temp in °C and distance in meters

Surface wind turnover in the *epilimnion* (or upper layer) and *hypolimnion* (or lower layer).

Hurricanes

A *hurricane* is a tropical cyclone that forms over tropical or subtropical waters.

A *tropical cyclone* is a rotating low-pressure system with no front (i.e., the boundary separating two air masses of different densities) but has organized thunderstorms.

Mild tropical cyclones with a maximum sustained wind speed of less than 39 mph are called *tropical depressions*. A tropical cyclone with a maximum sustained wind of 39 mph and higher is called a tropical storm.

Hurricanes are storms with a sustained wind speed of 74 mph and above and can be destructive.

The *Cheniere Caminada Hurricane* was a devastating hurricane that struck the island of Cheniere Caminada in southeastern Louisiana at 135 mph. Winds in early October of 1893. The island's main town had only 1,500 residents and lost 779 of them. In total, the hurricane claimed the lives of about 2,000 people and inflicted an estimated $5 million ($135 million in 2020 dollars) in property damage. Many ships and vessels throughout coastal Louisiana and Mississippi were sunk, and the orange and rice crops of the region were utterly devastated.

Galveston Hurricane of 1900 started as a tropical storm that hit some islands in the Caribbean and intensified into a category four hurricane that made landfall on September 8, just south of Houston, Texas. It continued northeastward as an extratropical storm throughout the Midwest, New England, and eastern Canada before it finally re-entered the North Atlantic. It included hurricane-force winds, lightning and thunderstorms, storm surge, and flooding.

Although it has been more than 100 years since the Galveston Hurricane, it remains the deadliest natural disaster in U.S. history, with estimated fatalities between 6,000 and 12,000 lives. Official estimates place the property damage between $28 and $35.4 million (as much as $142.7 billion in 2020 dollars).

Okeechobee Hurricane landed on September 6, 1928, on the east coast of Florida as a category five hurricane. It claimed the lives of 2,500 people in the United States and hundreds of lives on the nearby islands of Guadalupe, Puerto Rico, Martinique, Montserrat, and St. Nevis (4,112 lives in total). It resulted in an estimated $100 million ($1.5 billion in 2020) worth of property damage, and many people were displaced. Well-constructed homes with strong shutters did not suffer nearly the devastation that other homes did. As a result, state and city building codes improved.

Saffir-Simpson Hurricane Wind Scale

Saffir-Simpson Hurricane Wind Scale classifies hurricanes from 1 to 5 based on their maximum sustained wind speed and estimated potential property damage.

While hurricane categories 4-5 are *major hurricanes* with dangerous hurricane-force winds, category 1 and 2 storms are dangerous and require preventative measures to prepare for them.

Category 1 hurricanes have sustained winds of 74 – 95 mph (64 – 82 kt or 119 – 153 km/hr.). Very dangerous, with winds potentially damaging roofs, vinyl siding, gutters, and shingles. Large branches of trees will snap, and shallowly rooted trees may be toppled. Extensive damage to power lines and poles will likely result in power outages that could last several days. Large branches may snap, and trees may topple. Irene (1999), *Katrina* (2005), and several others were Category 1 hurricanes at landfall in South Florida.

Category 2 hurricanes have sustained winds of 96 – 110 mph (83 – 95 kt or 154 – 177 km/hr.). Extremely dangerous, with hazardous winds causing extensive damage. Major roof and siding damage is possible. Large branches snap, and trees will fall, blocking roads. Near-total power loss is expected with outages for several days to weeks. *Frances* (2004) was Category 2 when it hit just north of Palm Beach County, along with at least 10 other hurricanes that have struck South Florida since 1894.

Category 3 hurricanes have sustained winds of 111 – 129 mph (96 – 112 kt or 178 – 208 km/hr.). Devastating damage to well-built framed homes with damage or removal of roof decking and gable ends. Many trees will snap or uproot, blocking roads. Electricity and water will be unavailable for several days to weeks. Unnamed hurricanes of 1909, 1910, 1929, 1933, 1945, and 1949 were Category 3 storms when they struck South Florida, as were *King* (1950), *Betsy* (1965), *Jeanne* (2004), and *Irma* (2017). Category 3 hurricanes have a potential loss of life and damage.

Category 4 hurricanes have sustained winds of 130 – 156 mph (113 – 136 kt or 209 – 251 km/hr.). Catastrophic damage, including severe damage to homes, potentially losing roofs and exterior walls. Most trees will be snapped or uprooted, and power poles will be downed. Power outages may last weeks or months. Most of the area could be uninhabitable for weeks or months. The 1888, 1900, 1919, 1926 Great Miami (1928), *Lake Okeechobee/Palm Beach* (1947), and *Donna* (1960) made landfall in South Florida as Category 4 hurricanes.

Category 5 hurricanes have sustained winds of > 157 mph (> 137 kt or > 252 km/hr.). Catastrophic damage, with many framed homes destroyed by total roof failure or wall collapse. Fallen trees and power poles will isolate residential areas, and power outages will last weeks or months. Most of the area will be uninhabitable for weeks or months. The *Keys Hurricane* (1935) and *Andrew* (1992) landed in South Florida as Category 5 hurricanes.

Tides

Tides are very long-period waves that move through the ocean in response to the forces exerted by the Moon and Sun. Tides originate in the ocean and progress toward the coastlines, where they appear as the regular rise and fall of the sea surface.

Relative distances and positions of the Sun, Moon, and Earth affect the size and magnitude of Earth's two tidal bulges. The shape of the shoreline strongly influences the magnitude of tides.

Local wind and weather patterns affect tides. Strong offshore winds move water away from coastlines, exaggerating low tide exposures.

Onshore winds may pile water onto the shoreline, virtually eliminating low tide exposures.

High–pressure systems depress sea levels, leading to clear sunny days with shallow tides.

Low-pressure systems contributing to cloudy, rainy conditions are typically associated with much higher tides than predicted.

Tidal forcing temperature generates extreme tides and increases the vertical mixing of seawater, thereby causing episodic cooling near the sea surface.

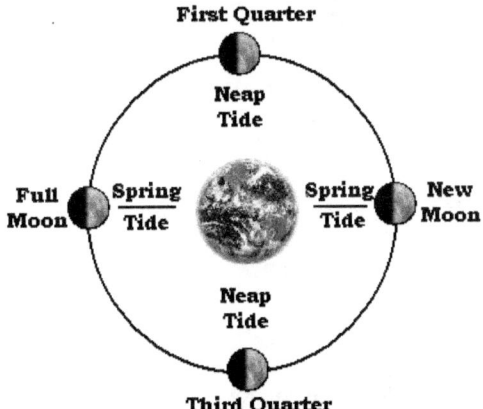

Tides and currents, National Oceanic and Atmospheric Administration

ENSO

El Niño-Southern Oscillation (ENSO) is the natural year-to-year changes in the atmosphere and waters of the tropical Pacific and is among Earth's longest-studied phenomena.

El Niño (or *the boy child*) was named because it typically occurs in December around the celebration of the birth of Jesus Christ. Even before 1900, scientists studied ENSO events. In the 1600s, Peruvian fisherman observed the warming of ocean waters off the coast of South America and the resultant impact it had on their fisheries.

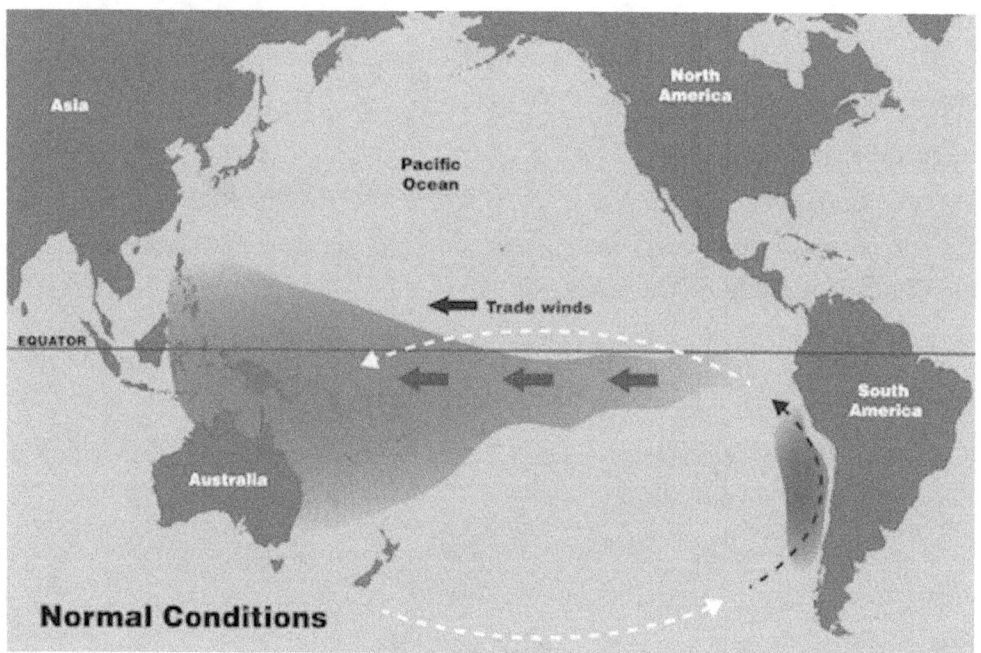

Typical trade winds patterns

El Niño can significantly change sea-surface temperatures, sea-level pressure, winds, and precipitation (not just in the tropics but globally). El Niño occurs when the eastern and central equatorial Pacific Sea surface temperatures are much warmer than usual.

El Niño typically results in much milder winters in North America.

La Niña

La Niña, a part of the ENSO cycle, is the contrary pattern and occurs when eastern and central equatorial Pacific Ocean waters are cooler than average.

Though not always, a La Niña event typically follows El Niño.

La Niña and El Niño last roughly eight to twelve months, but longer durations occur.

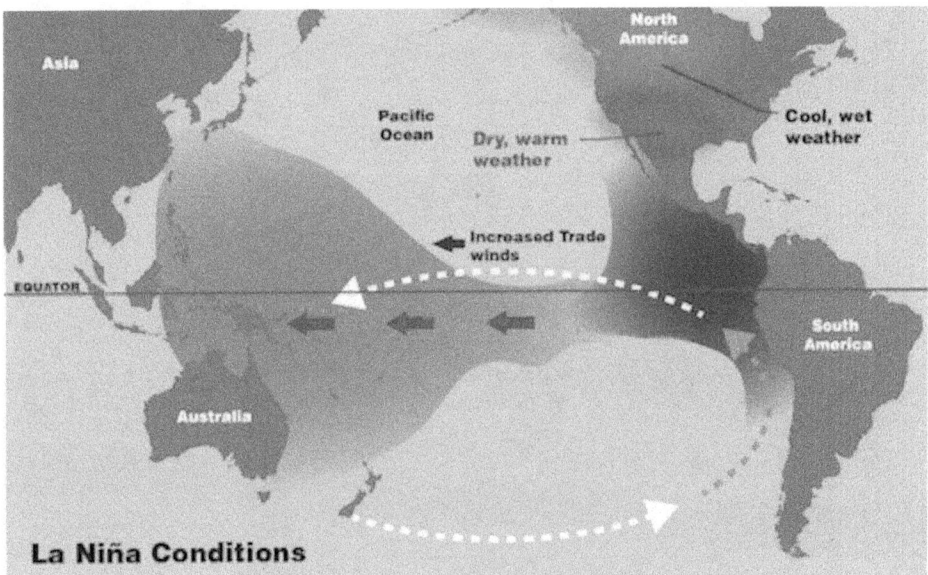

La Nina conditions produce increased trade winds

El Niño, temperature anomaly

Pacific Ocean receives more sunlight than any other area on Earth. Much of the sunlight energy is stored in ocean waters as heat. Typically, the Pacific trade winds blow east to west, pulling the warm surface waters westward, where they accumulate and pool to the east of Indonesia.

Colder waters from the deep Pacific Ocean rise to the surface, creating an east-to-west temperature gradient along the equator, a *thermocline tilt*.

Tradewinds often lose strength with the beginning of springtime in the Northern Hemisphere. As a result, less water is forced westward, and water in the eastern and central Pacific begins to heat by several degrees Celsius, causing the thermocline tilt to diminish.

Balance is again maintained when the summer monsoon in Asia replenishes the trade winds. In some instances, for reasons not fully understood, the trade winds will not replenish, or there is a reversed direction of wind current that travels west to east.

When this occurs, the ocean may respond in many ways. Warm surface waters that had pooled near the coast of Indonesia moved eastward. Beneath the ocean's surface, the steep thermocline along the equator flattens as warm surface waters prevent the cool, deeper waters from upwelling, warming the large central and eastern Pacific regions into an El Niño.

El Niño waters, on average, warm by 3 to 5 °F but by more than 10 °F in some areas. As temperatures increase, easterly water expands, causing sea levels to rise a few inches to as much as one foot. In the western Pacific, sea levels drop as warm surface water begins flowing east. During El Niño in 1983, the drop in sea level caused coral exposure and destruction.

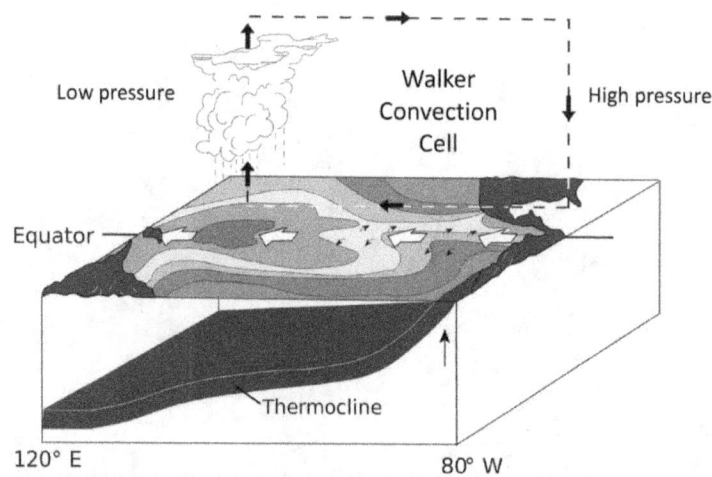

Normal conditions with convection cells moving from low to high pressure

Walker circulation (or convection cell) models troposphere (lower atmosphere) airflow in the tropics. Parcels of air follow a closed circulation in zonal and vertical directions.

Walker circulation is a model of tropics airflow in the lower atmosphere (or *troposphere*).

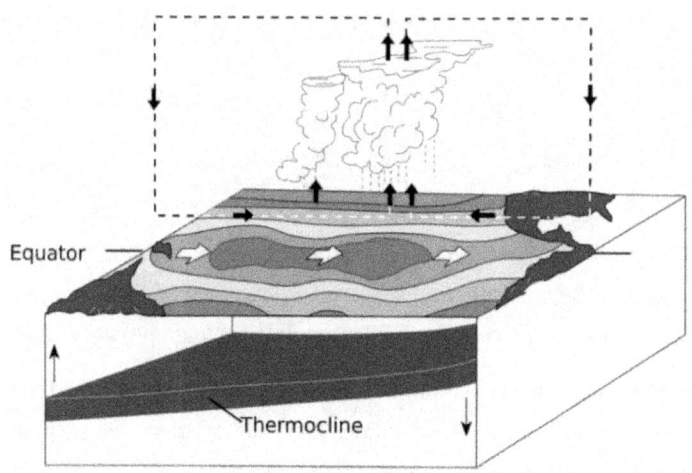

El Nino warms the water and disrupts Walker convection cell

During El Niño, Walker circulation is diminished. Increased precipitation and abnormally warm water occur in the central Pacific during El Niño (or ENSO warm phase).

Changing weather patterns have a cascading effect on weather patterns worldwide.

Ocean Circulations

Surface ocean currents

Ocean circulation is the large-scale movement of water in the ocean basins and is a key regulator of Earth's climate because ocean waters store heat, carbon, and nutrients.

Ocean currents are due to the horizontal movement of seawater.

Wind circulating above surface waters drives currents, interacting with evaporated water and the *Coriolis Effect* (from Earth's rotation). Stress between oceans and wind causes water to circulate in the same direction as the wind.

Currents can be temporary, affecting only regional pockets. Others can be permanent and extend horizontally over large distances. Large ocean currents are contained within landmasses bordering the ocean basins. These continental borders force currents to form in a circular pattern, producing a gyre.

Gyres

Gyres consist of four types of currents joining together: two *east-west currents* (which form the top and bottom borders of the gyre) and two *boundary currents that orient north and south*.

Each ocean basin contains a gyre, and the currents within these gyres are driven by atmospheric flow produced by subtropical pressure systems. The direction of flow within these gyre currents is due to wind circulation manipulated by the Coriolis Effect.

Boundary currents play an important role in redistributing *global heat*.

Existing only within the Atlantic and Pacific basins in the Northern Hemisphere, *polar gyres* are pushed by counterclockwise winds. *Westward-flowing currents* forming the *southern border* of the polar gyres are the obverse of the *eastward-flowing currents* forming the *northern border* of subtropical gyres.

Surface currents of subtropical gyres

Ocean basins have two west-flowing currents: The North and South Equatorial Currents.

These currents can penetrate 100-200 meters below the ocean's surface and flow between 3 and 6 kilometers daily.

Equatorial Countercurrent flows to the east, which consists partly of a return of the water carried west by the North and South Equatorial Currents. During El Niño, this current strengthens in force in the Pacific Ocean.

Western boundary currents flow from the equator to high altitudes and are warm water currents with location names: Gulf Stream (North Atlantic), Kuroshio (North Pacific), Brazil (South Atlantic), Eastern Australia (South Pacific), and Agulhas (Indian Ocean).

These currents are typically narrow and flow jet-like between 40-120 kilometers daily. The western boundary currents are the deepest of the ocean surface flows and penetrate 1,000 meters below the ocean's surface.

Eastern boundary currents flow from high latitudes to the equator. These are cold water currents, which have names associated with their location: Canary (North Atlantic), California (North Pacific), Benguela (South Atlantic), Peru (South Pacific), and Western Australia (Indian Ocean). These currents are typically broader than the western boundary currents and travel between 3 and 7 kilometers daily.

The eastward-flowing North Pacific Current and North Atlantic Drift of the Northern Hemisphere propel western boundary waters to the beginning point of the eastern boundary currents. In the Southern Hemisphere, the South Pacific Current, the South Indian Current, and the South Atlantic Current function at the same capacity.

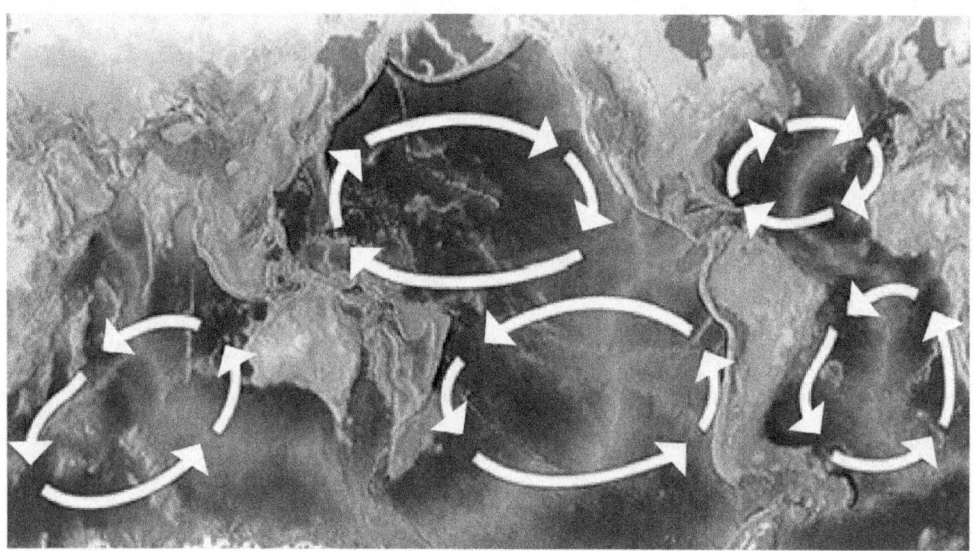

Map of the flow pattern of the five major ocean-wide gyres

Existing only within the Atlantic and Pacific basins in the Northern Hemisphere, the *polar gyres* (also known as *subpolar gyres*) are pushed by counterclockwise winds driven by wind and the Coriolis effect. Westward-flowing currents forming the southern border of the polar gyres are the obverse of the eastward-flowing currents forming the northern border of subtropical gyres. These large-scale circular currents typically form at above 60 degrees latitude.

Subsurface currents

Currents flow beneath the ocean's surface. These subsurface currents are much slower compared to surface currents and are driven by differences in seawater density, which differs due to salinity and temperature.

Currents near the ocean's surface begin to travel deeper in the North Atlantic. This downward propulsion is due to high evaporation levels that cool and increase seawater salinity.

Cold, dense saline water sinks; this action occurs between Northern Europe and Greenland. This water moves south along the coast of North and South America until it hits Antarctica.

Cold and dense water travels east, joining another deep current created by evaporation and sinking between Antarctica and the southern edge of South America. During this eastward movement, the flow splits into two currents, one moving northward.

In the North Pacific and the Northern Indian Ocean, these two split currents are drawn up from the ocean floor. The water warms up at the surface, forming another current that continues to flow at the surface (eventually returning to the starting point of the North Atlantic) or creating a shallower flow that encircles Antarctica.

Seawater takes about one millennium (a thousand years) to complete its circuit.

Relationship matrix

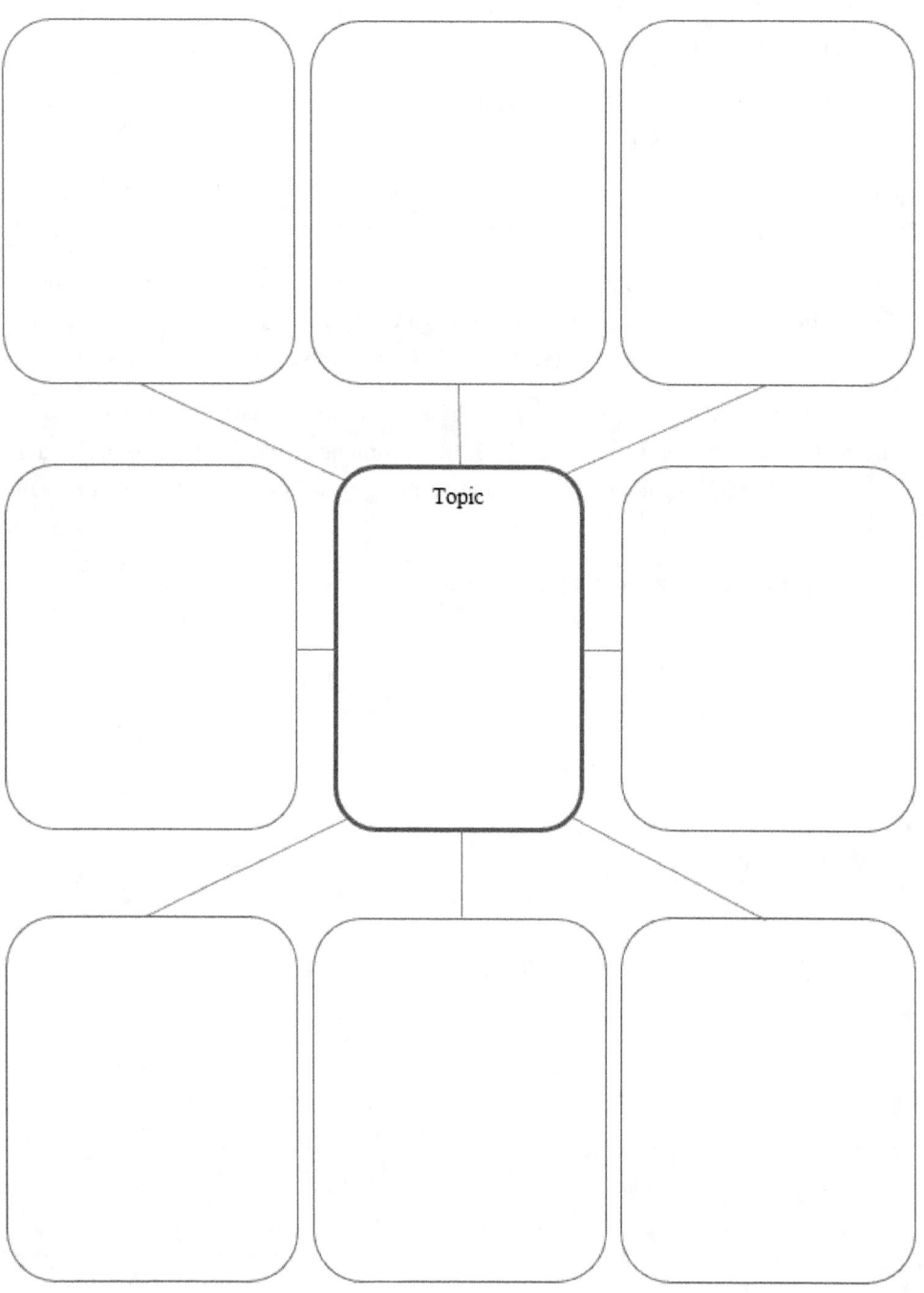

Questions: Weather & Climate

1. A cyclone is centered around a:

   A. region of high-pressure
   B. region of low-pressure
   C. cold front
   D. occluded front

2. Fog is a component of the:

   A. hydrosphere
   B. biosphere
   C. atmosphere
   D. lithosphere

3. Generally, temperatures along an ocean coastline vary less than temperatures 100 miles inland. This moderation of temperatures along the coastlines is because:

   A. as the oceans evaporate, it cools off the coastlines
   B. the sun shines more intensely away from the ocean coastlines
   C. ocean temperatures change more quickly than air temperatures
   D. ocean temperatures do not change as quickly as air temperatures

4. Humidity is highest when relative humidity is:

   A. high at low temperatures
   B. high at high temperatures
   C. low at high temperatures
   D. low at low temperatures

5. If a cold front moves into a moist region:

   A. humidity will likely decrease
   B. the chances of precipitation will increase
   C. evaporation will increase
   D. photosynthesis will increase

6. Examining the flight plans for a trip from Boston to Seattle, Washington, and back, the total time in the air for the flight to Seattle is much longer than the flight back to Boston. This is because:

   A. the jet stream
   B. several weather fronts along the way
   C. the mixing of the troposphere and stratosphere
   D. changes in time zones flown between the east and the west

7. As a cold front moves into an area of warm, moist air, we would expect to see cloud formation as:

   A. the warm air rises and condenses
   B. the cold air rises and condenses
   C. evaporation and transpiration increase
   D. high altitude air masses fall and condense

8. Winds we experience in our daily lives are mainly the result of:

   A. the rotation of the Earth
   B. changes in the direction of ocean currents and tides
   C. jet streams produced by Hadley cells
   D. the movement of air between lower-pressure and higher-pressure regions

9. Hadley cells at the equator consist of:

   A. rising, moist air that produces precipitation and rain forests, and falling dry air associated with deserts
   B. rising, dry air associated with deserts and falling moist air that produces precipitation and rainforests
   C. warm, moist air rising up the sides of mountains and cool, dry air descending on the leeward sides
   D. cool, dry air rising up the sides of mountains and warm, moist air descending on the leeward sides

10. The jet streams in the United States generally flow from west to east because of:

    A. ocean currents off the Pacific and Atlantic coastlines
    B. convection currents between the troposphere and stratosphere
    C. rotation of the Earth
    D. high-pressure systems generated by the Sun striking the North American continent

11. Most of the weather worldwide is based upon changes in the moisture, pressure, and/or temperature of the:

    A. mesosphere   C. stratosphere
    B. thermosphere   D. troposphere

12. London is farther north than Toronto, yet average temperatures in January are higher in London than in Toronto. London tends to be warmer in January because:

   A. Toronto gets more snow in January
   B. warm ocean currents flow past London
   C. people in London burn more fossil fuels
   D. it gets more sunshine than in Toronto in January

13. When water vapor in the atmosphere condenses to liquid water:

   A. a cloud forms
   B. it rains or snows
   C. dew falls to the ground
   D. All the above

14. Natural climate variability ranging from months to decades is primarily the result of:

   A. intense global warming
   B. ocean-atmospheric interactions, especially the La Niña/El Niño southern oscillation (ENSO)
   C. variations in the intensity of the Sun and the Milankovitch cycle
   D. changes in the lunar orbit around the Earth

15. A warm front forms when:

   A. a cold air mass displaces warmer air
   B. masses of cold air and warm air move past one another in opposite directions
   C. the Sun warms a stationary cold air mass
   D. a warm air mass advances over a mass of cooler air

Notes for active learning

CHAPTER 3

The Living World

Ecosystem Structure

Interactions Among Populations

Ecosystem Diversity

Energy Flow

Natural Biochemical Cycles

Ecosystem Change

Page intentionally left blank

Ecosystem Structure

Ecosystems

Ecosystems are communities of living and nonliving components functioning as a single system. This system works collectively to maintain life throughout the entire system.

Ecosystems take many forms with differing levels of complexity depending on living (*biotic*) and nonliving (*abiotic*) components within the system. This integrated network of interactions is an *ecosystem structure*.

At its simplest, an ecosystem includes one living organism in a non-living environment. An ecosystem is a plant inside a terrarium with adequate nutrients, water, and sunlight.

Ecosystems have complicated structures, with Earth being the most complicated — full of living organisms and nonliving components that sustain life, such as water and sunlight.

Ecosystem structure with complexity with Earth shown from space in a photograph of the Earth taken on December 7, 1972, by the crew of the Apollo 17 spacecraft at about 29,400 km (18,300 mi). It shows Africa, Antarctica, and the Arabian Peninsula.

Ecosystems have a basic structure, which includes *primary producers* using sunlight to create energy (i.e., ATP by photosynthesis) and organic compounds (e.g., glucose) necessary for life.

For example, the green fern is a primary producer that grows out of soil and uses sunlight to synthesize organic compounds (e.g., glucose and fructose) via photosynthesis.

Consumers eat primary producers of energy (e.g., glucose) and organic compounds. Consumers degrade organic components into their inorganic parts, which primary producers can use to repeat the cycle.

For example, a deer eats ferns with organic compounds synthesized via photosynthesis.

Terrestrial biomes

Biomes are distinct regions within a plant or animal community. Many terrestrial and aquatic biomes are vital for species adaptations and ecological communities.

Terrestrial biomes are on land. Mountains, forests, rainforests, and deserts are common terrestrial biomes, as definable regions with specific plant and animal communities.

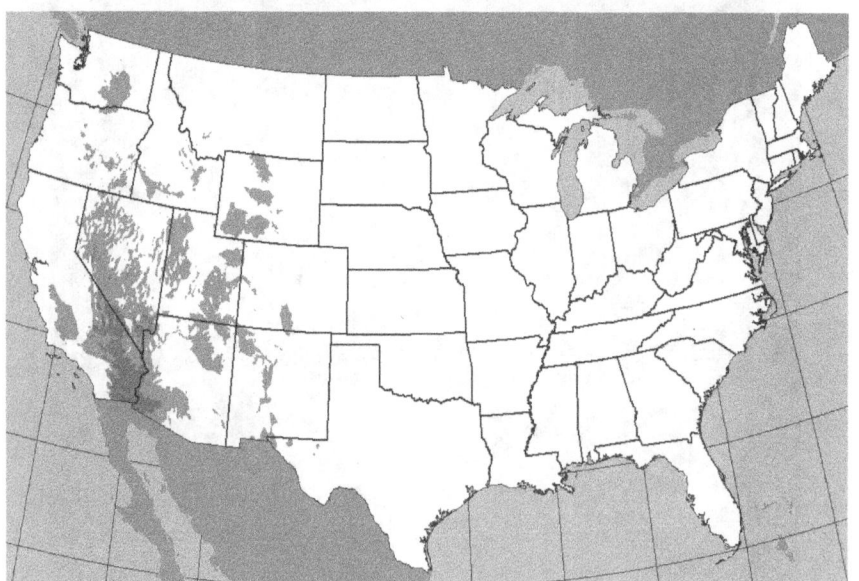

Deserts have annual rainfall of less than 10 inches. Temperature is irrelevant, and there are deserts in Alaska (northern AK) and Hawaii (the NW portion of the big island). Orange signifies less than 10 inches, with red for less than 5 inches of annual rain.

Tundra is a high-latitude biome often covered in permafrost and populated with only low, shrub-like vegetation.

Taiga is a coniferous forest that occurs at high latitudes.

Savanna lies between grasslands and deserts, which are grasslands with some scattered trees.

*Chaparral*s are between 30° and 40° latitude, mainly near the Mediterranean Sea, and include thorny shrubbery with hard and waxy evergreen leaves as a plant feature.

Scrub forest is a response to drought. It has small trees and thorns with a long dry season.

Ice caps are massive bodies of ice and snow that build up over time.

Aquatic biomes

Aquatic biomes occur in water, which covers about 71% of Earth's surface. Oceans, seas, lakes, ponds, rivers, streams, marshes, and swamps are typical aquatic biomes.

Oceans are the largest and deepest bodies of water, making up about 70 percent of the Earth's surface area and reaching depths of more than 36,000 feet. Oceans are easy to differentiate because there are only five of them — Pacific, Atlantic, Indian, Arctic, and Southern — and they are so massive that it is hard to mistake them for anything else. *Seas* are also large bodies of water. To be considered a sea, a body of water must be made of saltwater, connected to the ocean, and located at sea level. Seas are typically much larger and deeper than lakes.

In some cases, though, bodies of water are named seas but are lakes. For instance, the Dead Sea is technically a lake because it is landlocked and located below sea level. The Caspian Sea is also landlocked and is not connected to the ocean, but it is so big that it earned the title of "sea" anyway. It is technically the world's largest lake.

Gulf is a body of water surrounded by land, much like a bay. Gulfs and bays share the same basic definition, but the two have some slight nuances. The main difference between a gulf and a bay is size. Gulfs are typically (though not always) much larger than bays. Small openings and round bodies also characterize them. The Gulf of America (formerly the Gulf of Mexico) is the largest in the world.

Bay is also as a body of water surrounded by land. Bays are generally smaller than gulfs, but that is not always true. The world's largest bay, the Bay of Bengal in India, is bigger than the world's largest gulf. Typically, bays have a wider opening than gulfs compared to the rest of the body of water.

Lagoon is a shallow body of water separated from larger bodies of water by a natural barrier such as a sandbar or coral reef. They can be considered "leaky" if uninhibited water flows between the ocean and the lagoon or "choked" if a narrow channel hinders the connection. Lagoons receive most of their water from the ocean instead of from rivers or springs.

Pelagic biome is a far open ocean, excluding the ocean floor.

Benthic biome is a deep-sea habitat, often with little light and heavy pressure from the miles of water above.

Reef is a structure created by coral polyp skeletons that houses hundreds of fish species.

Oceanic vent biome is where hot sulfurous water is pumped from seafloor cracks where continental plates are pushed apart. These biomes house some highly specialized species able to tolerate such adverse conditions.

Temporary pools are water bodies that exist for part of the year before draining and drying for the remainder of the year, forcing species to tolerate the lack of water for extended periods.

Abyssal biome is the true deep sea, often with the absolute absence of light and intense pressure from the water above.

Brackish water is a mix of freshwater and saltwater, typically found in transitional zones (e.g., estuaries). It has a higher salinity than freshwater but not as high as seawater.

Tides churn material in oceans, allowing coastal ecosystems to thrive. Animals in these environments (e.g., crabs, mussels, starfish, snails) survive on tides. Tides influence the shoreline environment through the advance and retreat of marine water due to changes in the gravitational effects of the Moon as the Earth rotates each day.

Ecologists may focus on the tidal mixing of near-shore waters, where pollutants are removed and nutrients are recirculated. Tidal currents move animals and plants from breeding areas in estuaries to deeper waters. Not having a healthy coastal ecosystem can result in mass extinctions of land and sea animals.

Lakes are slow-moving or standing bodies of water, just like ponds. They are generally considered the larger of the two, and while there are no official standards to determine the difference between a lake and a pond, there are some unofficial ones. The following three conditions may help determine if a body of water is a lake:

- Light does not reach the bottom at the deepest point
- It can make waves up to one foot in height
- Temperature varies throughout

If all three are true, then the body of water is most likely a lake.

Lakes and ponds often get confused because they share many characteristics, like gulfs and bays. Ponds and lakes are standing or slow-moving bodies of water. Beyond that, there is no official difference between the two. Lakes are typically larger than ponds, but "larger" is subjective. Areas that do not have much standing water might consider one body of water a lake, while in a wetter area, it would be considered a pond.

The Great Pond in Maine, for example, is one of the largest ponds in the world at more than 13 square miles, much larger than many lakes. Maine has many ponds and lakes, so 13 square miles for the people who live there is not that big.

Wetlands are land areas saturated with water, either permanently or seasonally. Wetlands create a distinct ecosystem of aquatic plants, such as mangroves and eelgrass. Forested swamps and marshes, dominated by herbaceous, non-woody plant species, are the main types of wetlands.

Bogs are wetlands wrapped around the body of water where plant life flourishes. Wetlands provide an ecosystem for aquatic plants not found elsewhere. Environment degradation is more prevalent in wetlands than in any other ecosystem on Earth. The largest wetland near urban areas is Laguna de Rocha, Esteban Echeverria Partido, Argentina.

Biological populations and communities

Biological populations are groups of species living within the same region concurrently. Populations can be described based on the entire group instead of individuals.

Populations can have unique growth rates, mortality rates, age, and gender ratios. Populations change over time, increasing or decreasing due to births, deaths, or migrations. For example, during a drought, many populations suffer significant decreases; conversely, when resources are plentiful, populations may increase quickly.

Dry creek bed at Quivira National Wildlife Refuge due to severe drought in Kansas

Biological communities are the total of different populations interacting in a shared location. For example, moss, fern, and insect populations living underneath the same tree constitute a single biological community.

Biotic potential

Biotic potential is a population's ability to increase under ideal circumstances. If a population had ideal weather, constant and nourishing food and water supply, ample shelter, and without predators, the extent to which the population could grow would be its biotic potential.

Factors hindering population growth include climate, food availability, and predation. When factors such as predators, limited food and water supply, inclement weather, or disease are considered, a more realistic population size can be determined.

Carrying capacity is the realistic population size that a particular habitat can support, given its environment's positive and negative attributes.

Biological populations depend on their response to environmental capacity.

Ecological niches

As people have niches (e.g., students, family members, or teammates), species have niches.

Ecological niche is a species' role within its environment and includes how it gets food and shelter, how it reproduces, and what it does to survive.

It includes how a species, through its interactions with biotic and abiotic factors, helps the ecosystem function. It is suitable for a species to have its unique niche to reduce competition with other species in the ecosystem.

Organisms sharing niches must compete for limited resources and opportunities, creating greater challenges to survival and success.

Defining a species' ecological niche depends on the factors considered.

Grinnellian niche considers a species' behavior within its habitat. It emphasizes the environmental factors that determine where a species can survive and reproduce, including behavioral adaptations within that habitat.

For example, mole breeding, feeding, and protection occur underground. Therefore, moles fill a niche as underground dwellers and impact the ecosystem from underground.

Eltonian niche considers a species' behavior about its food preferences. It focuses on a species' functional role and impact on other organisms and the environment, including its trophic interactions (e.g., what it eats and what eats it).

For example, a niche of flying birds of prey that eat ground animals, such as mice, would have its Eltonian niche. Another example would be just for animals that eat antelopes, as they help regulate the antelope population.

Hutchinsonian niche is more complicated. It considers a species' behavior in response to its environment (i.e., the resources and conditions required for the species to survive).

For example, monarch butterflies lay their eggs on milkweed plants, and the caterpillars feed on milkweed plants once they have hatched.

Fundamental niches

A perfect niche, where a species can use the resources, it needs to survive without competition, is a *fundamental niche*. For example, monarch butterflies have a fundamental niche with complete access to plenty of milkweeds; no other organism ate or destroyed it.

However, organisms typically must live alongside other organisms and, therefore, must compete with them for access to resources necessary to survive in their ecological niche. The monarchs must compete with other animals that eat milkweed and humans that destroy milkweed during farming. This competition has led species to develop the ability to adapt.

Hutchinsonian niche with purple-throated Carib's bill fitting the flower's shape

Realized niche is the environmental niche to which a species is most closely adapted.

Adaptive zone is how much a species can adapt to its environment.

For example, Monarch butterflies cannot adapt to lay eggs on different plants, so using other plants is currently outside their adaptive zone. However, they may be able to adapt to life in captivity, which would then be inside their adaptive zone.

It is essential to understand that no two species can simultaneously be in the same ecological niche, and both succeed. This would create unsustainable competition for resources.

Species adjust and adapt their ecological niches in response to organisms within the ecosystem. For example, monarchs move to locate milkweed after a farmer plows milkweed patches.

Interactions Among Populations

Species diversity

Species diversity is the number of species within an ecological community.

Two factors define species diversity:

>*species richness* and *species evenness.*

Species richness is the numerical count of total species in the ecological community.

Species evenness is the comparative proportion and level of equality in the community.

For example, species richness would be 500 squirrels in each ecological community. In comparison, species evenness would be those 500 squirrels compared to the number of chipmunks and other small rodents in the same ecological community.

Species diversity depends on the specifics considered; areas of an ecological community may have varying species densities depending on resources, species, etc. It is imperative to define the boundaries of ecological communities when determining species diversity.

Keystone species

Keystone species have a disproportionally substantial impact on its ecosystem, considering the actual biological population of that species. These species play critical roles in the success of the ecosystem and the survival of other species within the ecosystem.

If the keystone species suffers a loss, other species suffer due to losing important biological niches that the keystone species can no longer fill. Therefore, understanding what species are "keystone" within an ecosystem is vital for considering specific impacts on ecosystems. Keystone species may develop such status because of their position in various roles.

For example, species can become keystone species based on their predation roles. A particular predator may eat enough of an invasive species to prevent it from overtaking the rest of the area's vegetation, dramatically changing the ecosystem landscape. This is evident in birds, which limits mosquito populations.

Another example is when there are so many specific predators that they must eat a significant number of other species, diminishing that food source and preventing other species from using it as prey. Removing these species would change the balanced ecosystem, impacting every other organism in a watershed effect.

For example, suppose a virus decimated birds that eat mosquitoes. In that case, the mosquito population might increase exponentially and introduce mosquito-borne diseases to other organisms at a greater rate, harming population levels.

Keystone species do not always need to be predators or even apex predators. They can be *mutualists*, performing tasks that benefit both themselves and other species. One example would be flowers that feed other species with their nectar to have their pollen spread for procreation.

Jaguar is a keystone species

Keystone species may be *engineers* who create and modify their shelters, providing opportunities for other species.

For example, Bisons prefer to eat land plants that prairie dogs have previously excavated. Additionally, when beavers build dams in streams, they create entirely new ecosystems.

Altogether, the smallest species may become a keystone species simply by how they fill their biological niche and how other organisms depend on them to fill that biological niche.

Species interactions

Biological species within an ecosystem must interact. Interactions can take many forms, and they are crucial to the ecosystem's success and the survival of the specific species. These interactions can be between members of the same species or different species.

Competition is a primary interaction between species in pursuing resources (e.g., food, water, mates, and territory). Competition most frequently occurs between members of different species; however, it can be between members of the same species, as when multiple males in a mountain goat herd compete for access to females.

Populations interact with each other in different ways.

For example, populations eating only plants are *herbivores*. *Predators* eat organisms, and their size depends on available prey.

Antagonism is when a black walnut tree's roots release a chemical harming nearby plants

Amensalism is a biological interaction in which a species harms another without receiving benefit. For example, when a buffalo herd tramples its environment during migration, it demonstrates amensalism.

Antagonism is an interaction with one benefiting at the expense of another. This often includes predation between species (e.g., deer consuming grass or lion killing and eating antelope).

Symbiosis

Some populations can interact in less violent ways. A *symbiotic relationship* is a close, long-term interaction between two different species. Based on the harm-benefit analysis, there are three main types of symbiotic relationships: mutualism, commensalism, and parasitism.

Mutualism is when both organisms benefit. An example of mutualism is beneficial bacteria within a human's intestines that aid digestion.

Commensalism is when one species benefits while another is neither helped nor harmed. An example of commensalism is barnacles growing on a whale.

Parasitism is when one organism benefits at the expense of the other. An example of a parasite is fleas on a dog.

Interactions between species and their impact on biological populations are vital in evolution via *natural selection*. When species interact, one often comes out "on top" because of superior adaptations to the environment.

Certain individual organisms may succeed in their interactions with others more than other organisms due to their adaptation. Interactions are essential for the "*survival of the fittest*" and propagating genes by mating.

Trophic interactions

Trophic interactions are interactions between producers and the organisms that eat them. When an organism eats a plant, a trophic interaction occurs.

Food chain is a trophic interaction; energy is transferred from abiotic (nonliving) sources to primary producers to consumers and back again.

Food chains transfer chemical compounds and sunlight to primary producers (e.g., grass) that use photosynthesis to make organic compounds, which are transferred to consumers of primary producers (e.g., a moose eating grass) and the consumers of the primary producers (e.g., a bear eating the moose).

Most ecosystems are complicated, with many abiotic and biotic components interacting to sustain life.

Edge effects

Edges are places where these unique ecological communities come into contact. *Edge effects* are changes that occur to the populations in these specific edge areas. Many ecological variables change at these edges, including temperature and moisture levels.

For example, certain plants grow at the edge between forests and suburban backyards (because of the specific moisture and sunlight levels present), and those plants are especially appealing to deer. The populations within these edges react and adapt to suit the area, such as when more deer come to an edge to feed.

Many edges and edge effects are humanmade. For example, the border between cleared farmland and walking trails, both human-made, creates edges to which the ecological communities on either side must adapt. When a hiking path is cut in a forest, more light and water can reach the ground in that area, changing the structure and niche of the ecological communities there.

The resulting increase in light and water may allow plant life to thrive, attracting different animals to feed there than had initially frequented the area. This can create a trickle-down effect based on the change in the predator-prey structures within the community. This may affect species diversity within a given ecological community, separating community members and changing the basic makeup of the species totals in the area.

Ecosystem Diversity

Evolution and origin of species

Evolution is changes in populations' heritable traits over time. It changes species' observable traits when combined with natural selection, sometimes until they become a new species.

Evolution does not explain the creation of life but describes how species adapt until they change visibly in response to their environments.

These visible changes eventually accumulate to create branching species and increased biodiversity, which explains the vast planet's biodiversity and predicts that biodiversity will continue increasing.

In *Origin of Species,* Darwin was the first to propose a theory to explain Earth's biodiversity. He proposed that natural selection ensures that genetically superior organisms survive to reproduce and pass along their superior genes, even though gene changes to create such superiority must come from DNA replication mistakes.

Charles Darwin, English naturalist and geologist

Some "mistakes" benefit organisms; those "mistakes" become more prevalent *via* natural selection and begin to transition species in new directions. Due to reduced breeding pairs, the same DNA changes tend to become more prevalent in smaller populations.

To confirm the theory of evolution, scientists search for fossilized remains of species that show a transition from one form to today's visible form of a similar animal. Many fossilized organisms are "intermediaries" along the evolution chain. These intermediaries show how animals looked before they successfully made it to the next state after the change. Many transitional forms existed before humans evolved into *Homo sapiens*, exemplified by changes in skeletal structure for upright walking, etc.

Vestigial structures support evolution, are structures with no known purpose, and may be carryovers from previous organisms. The human appendix is a vestigial structure, as it serves no currently known purpose, and a human can survive without it.

Embryology is the study of embryonic stages embryos during development to find similarities between organisms in an evolutionary context. Many organisms that are different at birth share similar characteristics in embryonic stages, such as webbed hands, tails, or even gills.

Scientists consider structures, bones, and other things shared across species. For example, arms and fingers share a remarkable similarity to the wings of particular species, and scientists attempt to map evolutionary pathways between animals with wings and those with arms with similar bone structures.

Shells and fossils

Regardless of a person's stance on evolution, species change over time in response to their environments, and genetically superior individuals will have a better chance of reproducing. This can drastically alter biodiversity now and in the years to come.

Natural selection

Natural selection is the underpinning of Darwin's theory of evolution, with organisms challenged by adversity.

Natural selection proposes that certain individual genetic variations within organisms facilitate survival. Individuals with certain traits may have a better chance of surviving and reproducing, thus passing along their "superior genes."

For example, animals with longer necks have an easier time reaching food, and genes for long necks in giraffes were passed on to the next generation.

Over time, these genes become more prevalent in species through increased offspring and the possibility that individuals with less successful genes are more likely to die before passing on their genes.

Species may begin to develop specializations for their specific niches, such as developing plumage that allows them to camouflage in their environment.

Over time, specializations develop so that organisms possessing them become new species. Animals with better plumage, for instance, may have found survival easier than those without it and may become so genetically separate from the original species that they form a distinct species over time. That is the *natural selection theory of biodiversity*.

Positive and negative selection

Positive selection is natural selection that increases the presence of a specific genetic allele in the gene pool. For example, increasing the prevalence of a gene that provides immunity to mumps would be a positive selection.

Negative selection reduces the presence of deficient genetic alleles in the gene pool. An example would be the death of those individuals without immunity to mumps during a mumps outbreak, thereby reducing the existence of their "deficient" genetic alleles in the gene pool.

Changes can be classified based on the part of an organism's lifecycle that the variation impacts, such as survival versus fertility. Changes that increase survival include neck growth in giraffes and immunity to mumps. However, fertility changes include natural selection for individuals with increased fertile windows, allowing for greater reproduction opportunities.

Over time, the species may increase their fertile windows by allowing individuals with longer fertility windows greater opportunity to procreate than those without them.

A well-known example of natural selection is antibiotic resistance of bacteria when some bacteria survive antibiotic assault because of genetic mutations. If they do, they can reproduce to create a colony of bacteria (i.e., clones of the original) no longer susceptible to the antibiotic while susceptible bacteria die.

Natural selection contrasts artificial selection, such as breeding for specific traits for dogs and horses. Natural selection occurs due to the impact of genetic diversity on overall survival and reproduction, while changes due to artificial selection are controlled externally.

Diversity

Ecosystem diversity (or *ecological diversity*) describes the ecosystems within a region and applies to the planet's various ecosystems. Ecosystem diversity considers trophic levels, system complexity, niches, and environmental differences within diverse ecosystems.

As the largest scale observing life's diversity, ecosystems are divided into subcategories.

Types of diversity are as numerous as observed across the planet: *biodiversity*, *species diversity*, and *ecosystem diversity*, but many others exist. The many biomes, ecological communities, and other aspects of ecosystems are considered.

Evolution and natural selection explain the existence and development of incredible organismal *biodiversity*.

Biodiversity is the incredible variety of life and considers all species within an area; it is the number of species in an ecosystem.

Species are organisms that breed to produce fertile (i.e., able to reproduce) offspring.

For example, elephants are a species that breed with each other. In contrast, elephants and crocodiles may live within the same ecosystem but are not the same species because they cannot breed successfully.

Biodiversity is most incredible in warmer, wetter climates with species. In such areas, the variety of species has been increasing over time.

Biodiversity is such a vast concept that several approaches narrow it into subcategories. One is *genetic biodiversity*, or the many variations of genes that can exist within the same species. This includes hair colors, eye colors, face shapes, and harmful genetic mutations.

Therefore, breeds within a single species can show genetic diversity (e.g., canines are the same as they can breed). However, they have a range of genetic diversity from Chihuahuas to Great Danes. Another subcategory of biodiversity is *ecosystem variation,* or the many varieties of plants comprising biomes where organisms live. Marine (water) and terrestrial (land) biodiversity exist.

Biodiversity is responsible for tremendous genetic variation, supporting survival and change. Without much genetic diversity, inheritable diseases become more prevalent, as demonstrated by the high rates of genetic disorders in closed communities like the Amish.

Genetic variation allows species to adapt by letting the stronger, better-adapted organisms survive, reproduce, and pass their successful genes on to the next generation.

However, many factors threaten to limit biodiversity. Habitat destruction, poaching, pollution, and climate change potentially limit biodiversity drastically.

Each time a species becomes extinct, much diversity that cannot be recovered is lost. That is why conserving the vast biodiversity for future generations is so important.

Ecosystem services

Ecosystem services are how people benefit from their environments. Organisms derive many benefits from their environments, as they are the source of support organisms need to survive.

These environmental services interrelate to create niches, support biodiversity, and support evolution and natural selection. Studying environmental services offered allows scientists to observe ecosystems and how they function to support overall life.

Ecosystem services include four categories:

>*provisioning* services for the creation of products for use

>*regulating* services that regulate ecosystem processes

>*supporting* services are required for other services to function

>*cultural* services such as religion and spirituality

Provisioning services include ecosystem food and water, supporting plant life and streams.

Regulating services include pest control, such as seasons killing mosquitoes during winter.

Supporting services include water cycles and purification.

Examples of cultural services include a beautiful part of a reservation used for Native American religious ceremonies and a whitewater rapid providing recreational opportunities for people to kayak and raft.

Other examples of ecosystem services include minerals and crop pollination via bees and other insects. Any benefit that humans receive directly from the environment that they did not engineer themselves is an ecosystem service, and even a brief overview of these services shows how much humans receive from the planet's natural resources.

Ecosystem services offer significant economic benefits to humans by addressing issues that would be incredibly expensive or impossible to replicate. This makes it extremely important for humans to support and preserve ecosystem services for present and future generations.

There are presumed to be ecosystem redundancies built into these services, meaning that several species or systems may provide the same ecosystem service. However, even so, it is vital to support and protect these ecosystem services.

By protecting the species and systems that create ecosystem services, the continued ecosystem balance of Earth is protected.

Energy Flow

Ecological energy flow

Ecological energy flow is the transfer of energy through the various levels of the food chain. Energy sources on Earth originate from the Sun's light energy, which is transferred to primary producers that synthesize glucose (i.e., CO_2 and water) combined with soil chemicals and the Sun's light energy (i.e., photosynthesis).

During photosynthesis, grass uses light energy to make glucose (i.e., a 6-carbon sugar).

Energy is (hypothetically) absorbed by subsequent food chain levels (*primary consumers*) who eat plants (*primary producers*). For example, rabbits eating grass absorb grass glucose.

Photosynthesis and *cellular respiration* are critical to energy flow because they initiate energy absorption (i.e., photosynthesis) to initiate energy flow in living organisms. These two steps occur in primary producers (plants with *chlorophyll*) to transfer light energy and nutrients found in soil into energy usable by plants and, eventually, the entire food chain.

Secondary consumers

Secondary consumers eat primary consumers, hypothetically transferring the original energy. An example would be a fox eating a rabbit. There may be other consumers after the secondary consumers, but generally, there are no more than tertiary consumers for the reasons discussed.

Secondary consumers eventually die, and as their bodies decompose, nutrients are transferred back into the soil and water. After the fox dies, its body is decomposed by flies and maggots, eventually returning to the soil as chemicals.

Primary producers use these nutrients with the Sun's light energy (i.e., photosynthesis) to create transferable energy (e.g., glucose), completing an energy flow cycle.

Energy transfer

Every time energy is transferred from one level of the food chain to another via consumption (e.g., each time the original energy goes from the grass to the rabbit to the fox), approximately 90% of it is rendered unusable because it is either expended through heat or indigestible food.

Ninety percent of the energy stored in glucose molecules is unusable, lost as heat during the transfer, or found inside food that the animal cannot consume (e.g., bones). Therefore, each consumer only gets 10% of the energy the previous consumer obtained. That is why there are rarely more than tertiary consumers in an energy flow chain; beyond secondary consumers, the amount of energy obtained by eating is not enough to meet a consumer's energy requirements.

Various processes are included in this energy flow. Each process works together to transfer energy across species within ecological communities. In this way, energy is not lost but transferred and eventually rendered unusable (i.e., energy dissipates) along the chain.

Photosynthesis

Photosynthesis is the first step in this two-step process. Photosynthesis creates a sugar molecule from carbon dioxide, water, and energy. CO_2 from the air and water from the ground are combined with *chloroplast* cells, or cells containing green chlorophyll pigment.

Light energy is then applied to the chemical reaction, which converts the carbon dioxide and water into a six-carbon sugar and oxygen gas to excrete into the atmosphere. This six-carbon sugar molecule is *glucose*, necessary for biological life as an energy source.

Energy is contained within the chemical bonds between the six-carbon molecules in glucose. It is stored in chemical bonds until the organism uses it as an energy source; at this point, the carbon bonds must be broken to release the stored energy. This process is *cellular respiration* and requires oxygen.

$$\begin{array}{c} H\diagdown_{}^{1}\!\!\diagup O \\ C \\ | \\ H-\overset{2}{C}-OH \\ | \\ HO-\overset{3}{C}-H \\ | \\ H-\overset{4}{C}-OH \\ | \\ H-\overset{5}{C}-OH \\ | \\ \overset{6}{C}H_2OH \end{array}$$

Glucose is a six-carbon alcohol

Cellular respiration

Cellular respiration is a chemical reaction that occurs after successful photosynthesis, and it occurs not only in chlorophyll-containing organisms. Organisms use cellular respiration to change glucose into usable energy. Once glucose has been created by photosynthesis, it can be transferred by consuming organisms containing glucose by a consumer organism.

Molecular bonds in glucose break and release energy within the mitochondria of living cells.

Cellular respiration is an overall name for several processes that convert glucose to energy. The process used depends on whether oxygen is present during the reaction.

Aerobic respiration processes require oxygen, and *anaerobic respiration* processes do not.

Aerobic respiration occurs in the mitochondria of cells by combining glucose and oxygen to obtain roughly thirty-six ATP (adenosine triphosphate).

Aerobic respiration involves a sequence of biochemical reactions, including *glycolysis, citric acid cycle,* and *Krebs cycle*.

Aerobic respiration converts glucose (i.e., six-carbon sugar) and oxygen into (depending on the organism) thirty-two to thirty-eight ATP (adenosine triphosphate) used for cellular energy.

Anaerobic energy uses glucose without oxygen to create a net two ADP and lactic acid in animals (or carbon dioxide and ethanol in plants) via proton pumps in cellular membranes.

Food webs and trophic levels

Food webs illustrate natural predation for organisms within an ecological population. Food webs show how energy is transferred from soil to the final predator and decomposed into soil.

Food webs show the interrelated connections created by feeding patterns and trace the transfer and energy loss across *trophic levels*.

For example, food webs may include pictorial representations of light energy (i.e., sunshine) transferred from grass to rabbit to fox and back to grass through decomposition.

Trophic levels are the positions animals occupy in the food chain and, therefore, on the food web. They can be used to categorize animals based on their positioning into three groups:

> *autotrophs* (e.g., plants and algae) do not eat other organisms but transfer nutrients from the environment into the food they make (i.e., photosynthesis);
>
> *heterotrophs* do not make their food but instead, obtain energy by eating autotrophs and other heterotrophs;
>
> *decomposers* degrade dead plants and animals and return their nutrients to the soil.

Examples of *heterotrophs* are cats, bears, and snakes, as these animals cannot produce their food and instead eat others for energy.

An example of a *decomposer* would be a fly, particularly its maggot larvae, as they feed on animal carcasses and return nutrients to the soil through their excrement.

Animals are categorized into trophic levels based on their *location within the food chains*.

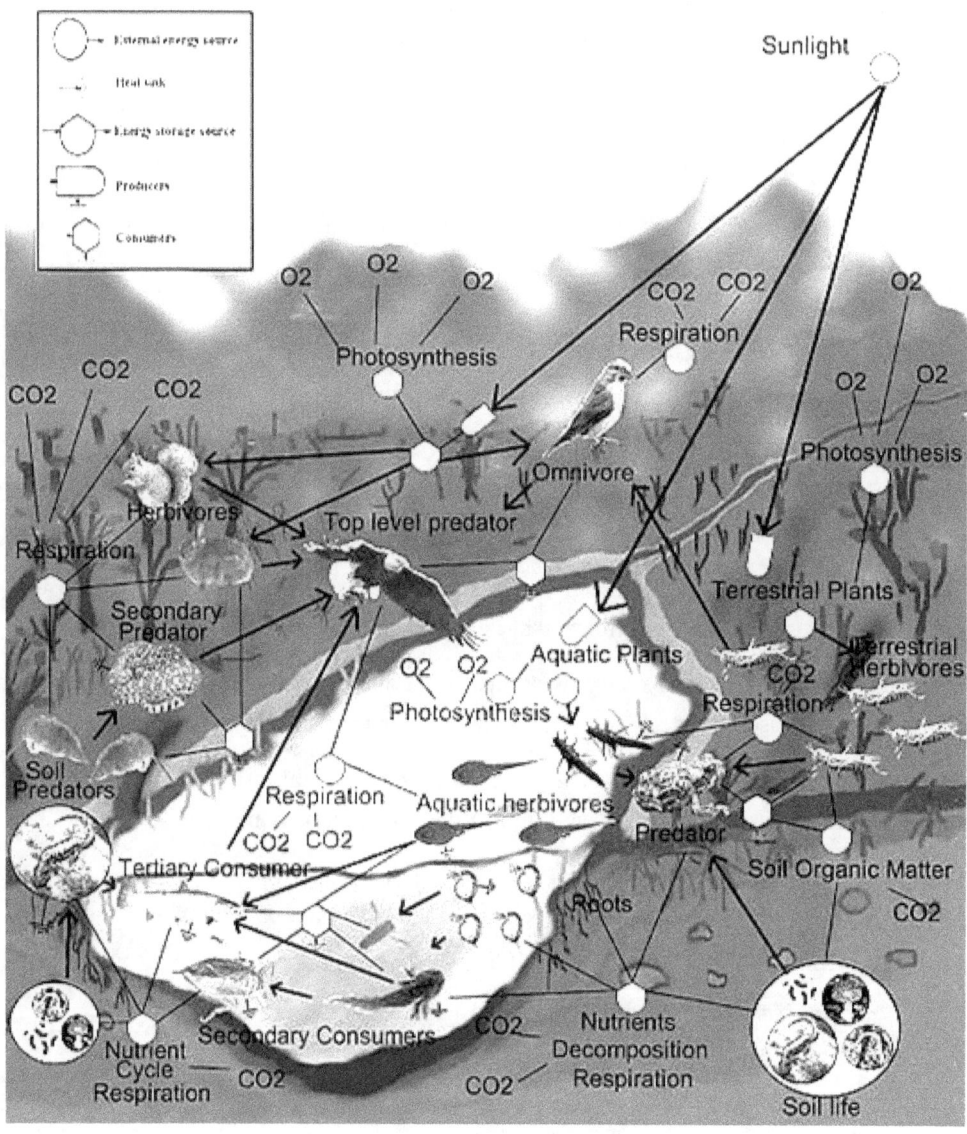

Freshwater aquatic and terrestrial food web

Trophic levels are numbered:

    Level 1, primary producers: plants and algae making their food;

    Level 2, primary consumers: herbivores that eat the plants and algae;

    Level 3, secondary consumers: predators that eat the herbivores;

    Level 4, tertiary consumers: predators that eat other predators and

    Level 5, apex predators: predators without predators (*top of the food chain*).

Hypothetically, this could be exemplified by a level 1 shrub, followed by a level 2 antelope that eats the shrub, a level 3 hyena that eats the antelope, a level 4 crocodile that eats the hyena, and a level 5 leopard that eats the crocodile. The leopard would be considered the apex predator in this food web and occupy trophic level 5.

Biomass

Decomposers feed on dead bodies of trophic-level organisms, returning them to the nutrients that primary producers can use to start the process over again.

Energy is transferred along with various levels of the food chain and is *biomass*. Biomass is a descriptive term covering the amount of energy available by consuming a trophic level, a ratio of energy available when considering the size of the organism consumed.

Biomass levels may seem skewed when considering animals with many inedible parts (e.g., tusks or hooves). Biomass indirectly measures energy flow across trophic levels.

Ecological pyramids

Ecological pyramids represent levels within an ecological community. Ecological pyramid pictorial representation depends on what facet of the ecological community is considered.

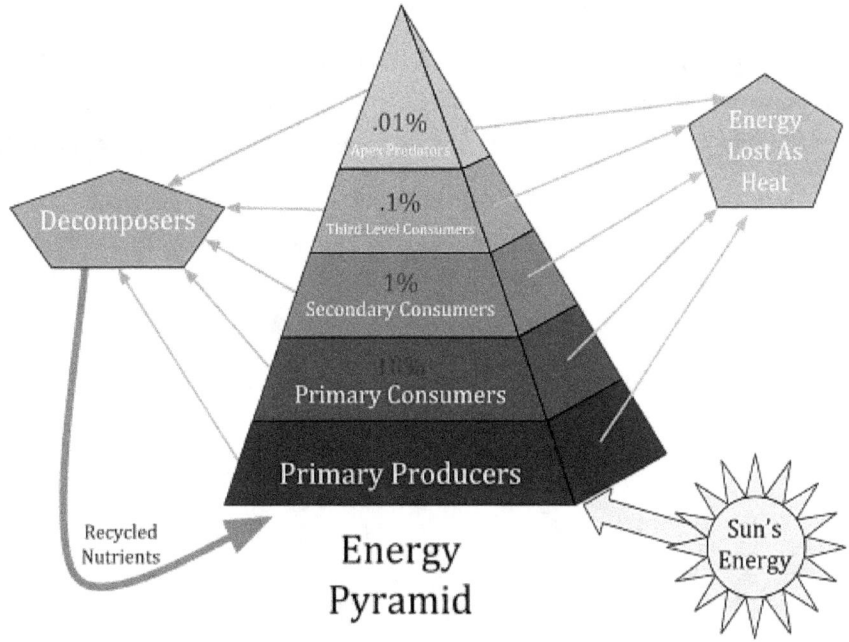

Energy pyramid with energy flow from primary producers to apex predators

Energy pyramids vertically stack five trophic levels to quantify energy transfer percentages. It begins with the producers on the bottom and follows energy transfer upward through the trophic levels. It allows a scientist to examine the approximate available energy in an ecological community at any time.

There can never be an inverted energy pyramid, as there must always be more energy at the lower levels than higher ones for enough energy to make the ecosystem viable.

Whether the ecosystem is a forest ecosystem or a desert ecosystem, there will always be more initial energy available at the primary producer level than at the apex predator level.

Energy pyramids of biomass

Energy pyramids of biomass track biomass within an ecological community. Each pyramidal layer represents the percentages of available biomass.

For example, in a stream ecosystem, the level of the primary producers for the ecosystem (i.e., water plants) will be smaller than the primary consumer level, as there is vastly more "mass" associated with the insects and fish in the stream.

Biomass energy pyramids can be deceiving because, at higher energy levels, particular species may have more mass. These species, such as birds, have a greater mass ratio to the energy available at that level, making their biomass ratios skew.

Numerical ecological pyramids show the ratios of species at each trophic level. This type of pyramid can be made in many shapes depending on the ratios of species. One example of this is if an ecological community has more primary consumers than it does primary producers.

For example, in a community with only five or six species of plankton and algae but upwards of ten species of fish and birds, there would be a larger level for the primary consumers (fish and birds) versus the primary producers (plankton and algae).

Ecological pyramids monitor energy transfer within an ecosystem in multiple ways. This allows them to understand the delicate balance between species and niches within an ecosystem and what would happen if any species were diminished.

Ecological pyramids help scientists gain a greater understanding of an ecosystem.

Natural Biogeochemical Cycles

Conservation of matter

Law of conservation of matter states that matter is *never created nor destroyed* in reactions.

Organic compounds are not created through biochemical cycles but through reactions and matter states.

The number of chemicals present at the beginning of Earth (3.7 billion years) continues; elements may be in a different form or compound, but the ratios of elements remain. Elements are converted into compounds and may be regenerated in a subsequent process.

Conservation of matter allows experimental scientists to quantify the transfer of compounds across chemical reactions.

Russian scientist Mikhail Lomonosov developed the law of mass conservation in 1756

Conservation of matter is observed from balanced chemical equations with equal transfer of molecules across the entire reaction (i.e., starting reactants and final products). It is possible to account for all matter entering the reaction through what is resolved in chemical reactions.

For example, if four water molecules are reactants, there will be the same number of hydrogen and oxygen atoms at the end, even if they are in subsequent molecules. This understanding allows people to see the balance in the world's biogeochemical cycles and know that they can rebalance these cycles for the betterment of the planet.

Biochemical cycles

Biogeochemical cycles are processes by which chemicals cycle across the Earth and become accessible at various levels. These levels include the water system (*hydrosphere*), the soil (*lithosphere*), and layers of the atmosphere.

Vital chemicals are passed among organisms via biogeochemical cycles necessary for life.

A predominant example of a biogeochemical cycle is the water cycle, which transitions H_2O through various states in the atmosphere cyclically. However, other chemicals are involved in biogeochemical cycles as well. These biogeochemical cycles recycle and continuously move chemicals throughout the environment to make them available for all organisms.

There are several biogeochemical cycles, depending on the chemical being transported and the locations to which it cycles.

Carbon cycle

Carbon cycle is necessary to sustain life on Earth, and it is the process by which carbon is exchanged across Earth's atmosphere. Carbon (C) is an organic compound in every living organism on Earth. Many levels of the "carbon cycle" depend on location, such as carbon cycling above the ocean and over land or the geological carbon cycle within rocks.

These cycles combine into the overall carbon cycle, which — along with the water and oxygen cycles — makes life on Earth possible.

The carbon cycle is generally described based on where it occurs. Carbon dioxide (CO_2) leaves the atmosphere through plants via photosynthesis and enters terrestrial and oceanic biospheres. It can enter the water cycle by dissolving into precipitation as carbonic acid, a key component of "acid rain."

In terrestrial biospheres, carbon is passed through various organic compounds when organisms consume each other and when they decompose upon death. It can quickly return to the atmosphere when organisms exhale carbon dioxide back into the air.

Carbon can be used during ocean photosynthesis or become part of calcium carbonate in shells or sediments. A significant amount of carbon is stored in Earth's lithosphere, or rocks (mainly limestone). It can be held there indefinitely or shed via runoff, weathering, or extraction (as in mining operations).

Humans significantly impact the amount of carbon available in the carbon cycle. For example, deforestation reduces the number of trees able to pull carbon from the atmosphere during photosynthesis. Air pollution introduces additional carbon into the atmosphere that would not naturally be present, which can overwhelm plants' ability to filter it out.

The increasing prevalence of fossil fuel, exhaust, and fertilizer adds carbon to the atmosphere and water runoff, forcing the rest of the carbon cycle to compensate to maintain carbon balance. These problems have an enormous negative impact on the climate, as this increase in carbon is changing the structure of Earth's atmosphere and allowing it to warm on the surface, impacting all living things.

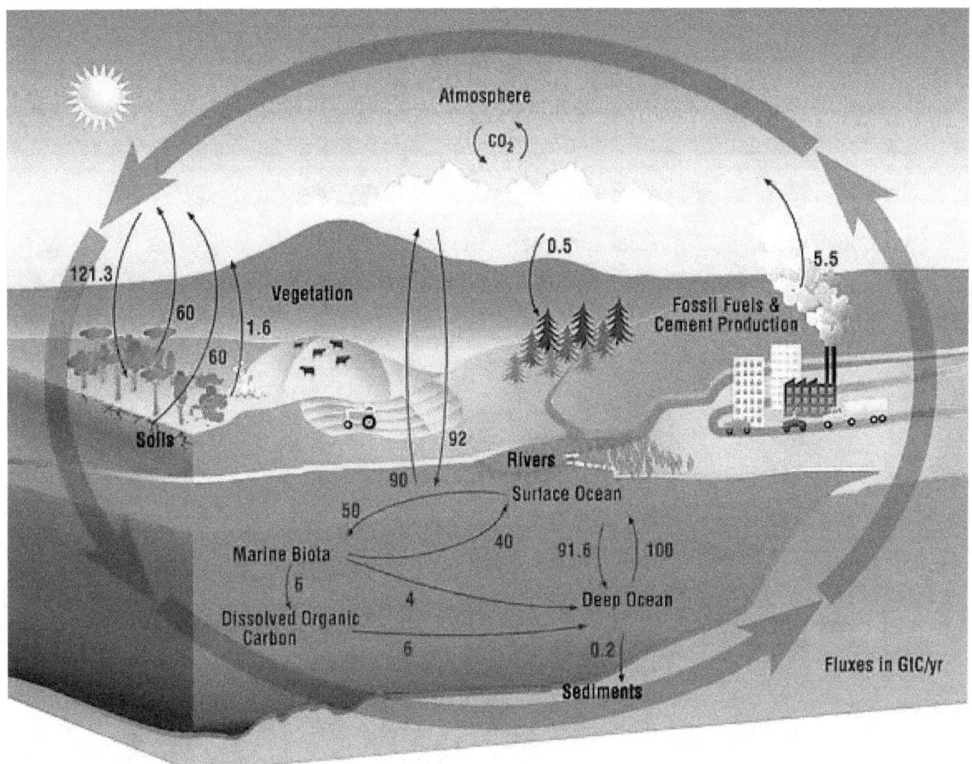

Carbon cycle

Nitrogen cycle

Nitrogen (N) is essential for life. The atmosphere contains and is a component of all amino acids (i.e., monomers of proteins) and nucleic acids (i.e., components of nucleic acids, DNA, and RNA). Therefore, nitrogen is needed for all living cells. Living organisms must have access to nitrogen to produce and use vital amino acids and proteins.

Nitrogen fixation, assimilation, ammonification, nitrification, and denitrification cycles generate several forms of nitrogen for living organisms.

Nitrogen fixation converts atmospheric nitrogen into a form that plants can use via symbiotic bacteria that transfer atmospheric nitrogen into ammonia and carbohydrates.

Assimilation is the process by which plants can absorb nitrogen from the soil, which is transferred to animals that consume the plants.

Ammonification is when a dead organism's decomposition returns organic nitrogen to soil.

Nitrification is a way to convert ammonia into nitrates via bacteria. This process sustains plant life because ammonia created during nitrogen fixation is hazardous to plants.

Denitrification turns these nitrates back into nitrogen gas in the atmosphere.

These processes transfer nitrogen from the atmosphere to plants and the soil and back again. Chemical fertilizers and the cultivation of certain crops, such as soybeans and alfalfa, have made more nitrogen available to live organisms via these processes.

Nitrogen makes atmospheric ozone destruction occur faster, and nitrous oxide is one of the three leading greenhouse gases contributing to global warming. While nitrogen is vital for life on Earth, it can potentially damage life. Understanding these processes and how they can potentially be used to limit atmospheric nitrogen is essential.

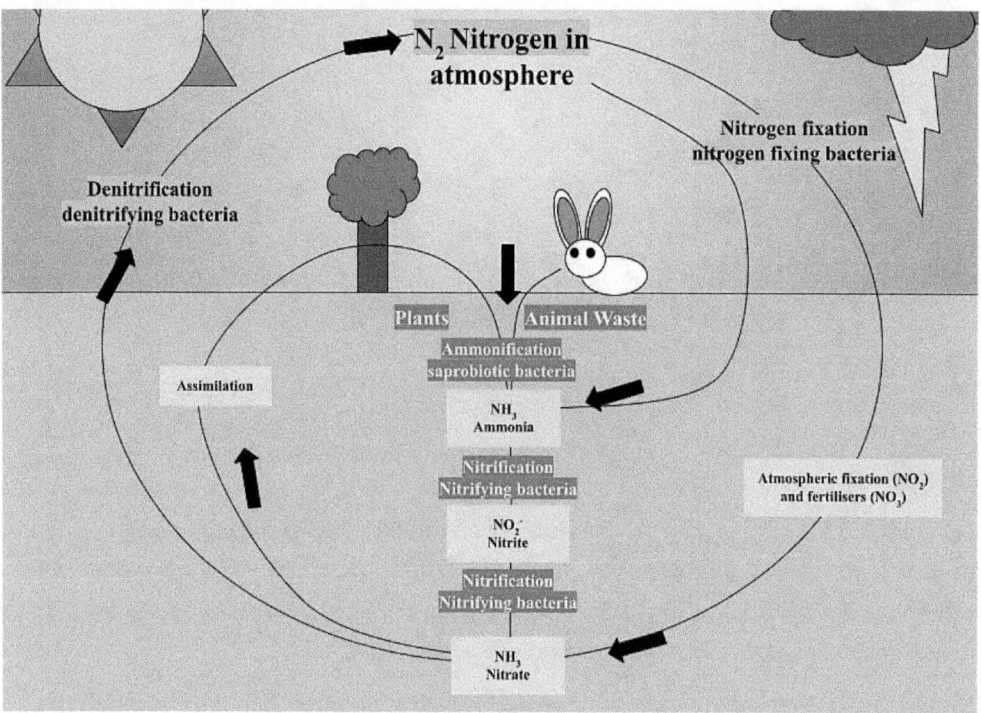

Nitrogen cycle

Phosphorus cycle

Phosphorus cycle moves phosphorus (P) through the lower atmosphere. Phosphorus is an essential building block of DNA molecules; every living organism requires phosphorus to survive. It is one of the three major components of agricultural commercial fertilizer.

Phosphorus is not present in appreciable quantities in the atmosphere because it is a solid at ambient temperatures, so it is primarily a terrestrial and lithospheric biogeochemical.

Much of the planet's phosphorus is in rocks that release phosphate into the soil, where plants absorb it, and animals eat it. After animals die, phosphorus in their bodies returns to the soil, and the process continues. Phosphorus is excreted as phosphates in animal manure and enters water streams, returns to the ocean, sinks, and reforms rocks.

Humans are responsible for a significant increase in soil phosphorus. Fertilizers and animal manure add phosphorus to the soil. Since phosphorus is vital to plant growth, using moderate amounts to fertilize crops is beneficial, but significant increases in phosphorous use can overwhelm water ecosystems by eutrophication.

Eutrophication is when vegetation overgrows in response to increased nutrients and decreases water oxygen levels available to other organisms. This can suffocate other water organisms and has been a significant pollution problem.

Therefore, how phosphorus is cycled through biospheres is essential in regulating and protecting ecological communities.

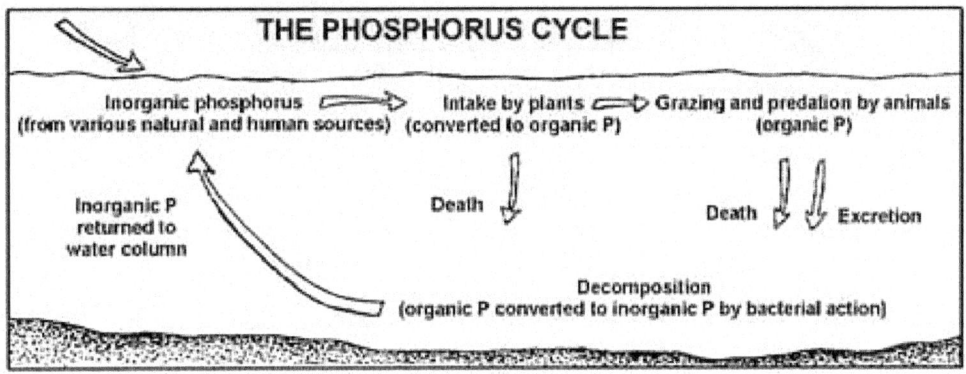

Phosphorus cycle

Sulfur cycle

Sulfur (S) is an element required for life. It has earned this designation through its presence in two primary amino acids used to make proteins: methionine and cysteine. It is in several proteins and polypeptides. Therefore, it is a significant component of the proteins that help build a structure in living cells.

Sulfur is in Earth's crust as rock or salt domes. Organisms may obtain the sulfur they require from the water runoff from rocks, but that does not necessarily mean that it will be in a form that the organisms can use. That is why the sulfur cycle is vital to life on Earth; organisms need to modify sulfur into several forms to be used by the organism. These modifications require a series of chemical reactions.

Sulfur formations in White Island, New Zealand

Sulfur cycle moves sulfur from minerals into living organisms and back again. Organic sulfur from living organisms is mineralized into compounds, such as hydrogen sulfide, which may be oxidized into sulfates. Plants absorb these, and they enter the food chain. Upon an organism's death, sulfide returns to the ground and is reduced to sulfate, reentering the sulfur cycle to continue the process.

Sulfur is released into the atmosphere by volcanoes or through sediment runoff and rains onto Earth and absorbed into water and the ground.

Sulfur is released into the atmosphere when fossil fuels are burned, especially coal, which has a high sulfur concentration. Significant increases in atmospheric sulfur have contributed to *acid rain* precipitation, which includes sulfuric acid. It is responsible for significant rock and concrete erosion worldwide. Therefore, maintaining sulfur cycle equilibrium is essential, as too much atmospheric sulfur negatively affects the planet.

Water cycle

Water cycle is one of the most important cycles, as water is necessary for life and must be recycled to be available for living organisms. Water (H_2O) is a significant component of all organisms, a carrier of nutrients, and a significant part of the environment. Water starts the cycle by falling as precipitation (rain, ice, snow, sleet, hail, etc.) onto the Earth, absorbed into lakes, streams, rivers, the ground, and groundwater.

Evaporation from water bodies returns water to the atmosphere. Water condenses within clouds in the atmosphere, turning into water droplets that return to Earth as precipitation. Air currents move condensed water in clouds until the water becomes precipitation.

Water is released through cracks in Earth's crust, mainly on ocean floors, where superheated water jets erupt. Water continuously cycles through the atmosphere and Earth, so water today may be in a different form tomorrow. It is distributed across the planet, allowing many life forms to exist.

Water remains unchanged during ecological processes as different physical molecular forms. Water cycling contributes to other biogeochemical cycles. It is instrumental in dissolving minerals from rocks into larger bodies of water and supporting those chemicals' cycles.

Water is necessary to cool temperatures on Earth because it removes heat as it evaporates (i.e., high specific heat), so environments warm less when water dissipates heat. The water cycle is crucial to maintain life and ecosystem status.

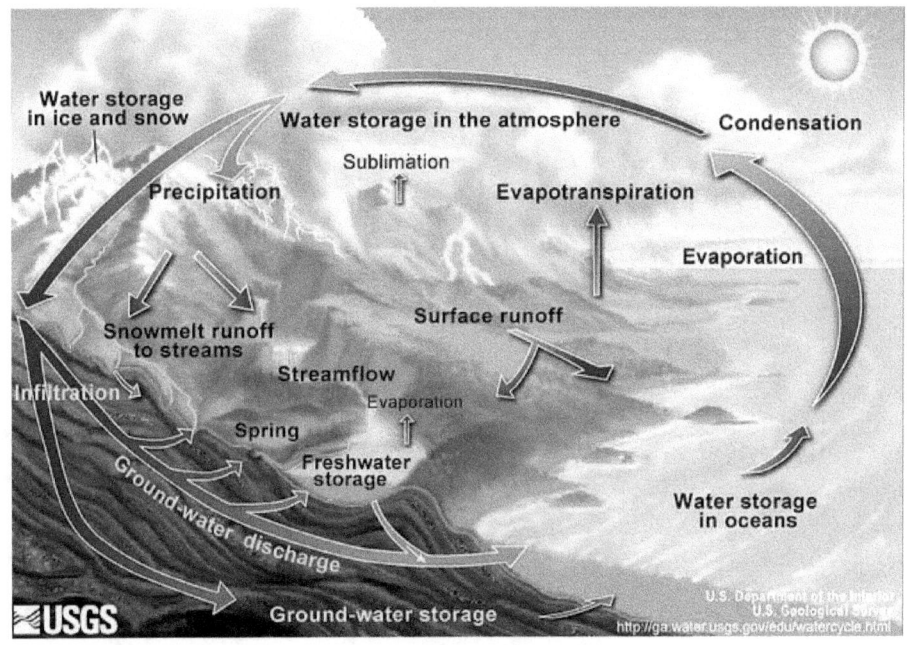

Water cycle

Notes for active learning

Ecosystem Change

Climate shifts

Ecosystems change over time in response to various factors, just as organisms change in response to their environments and external forces. However, the pressures that force ecosystems to change are not as simple and widely understood as the processes that force organisms to change.

There is significant research on how humans have positively and negatively impacted all levels of ecosystem change by affecting ecosystem services. There are natural processes that have a significant impact on how ecosystems change over time.

Climate shifts are changes in weather patterns for extended periods. Therefore, short-term weather shifts, such as a frigid winter or rainy season, do not indicate climate change; instead, the weather pattern shift must be sustained over a long period — decades or more — to qualify as actual climate change.

Various factors, not all human-made, cause climate change. Potential causes include changes in solar radiation levels, shifting plate tectonics, volcanic eruptions, space debris impact, and various actions caused by living organisms on Earth.

Each of these things has the potential to cause catastrophic cooling, as in the case of ash remaining in the atmosphere for long periods, or catastrophic heating, as in increased solar radiation due to the ongoing loss of the protective ozone layer. Such catastrophic heating or cooling could cascade effects on plants and animals by impacting environments, including significantly changing water levels worldwide or increasing the severity of weather systems, such as hurricanes and typhoons.

Earth has historically undergone stages of climate change caused by different factors. Climate change has been balanced in each case, allowing life to flourish. For example, the Ice Ages resulted from past climate changes.

Each climate shift can drastically change ecosystems by increasing or decreasing water tables, changing vegetation, altering the structural landscape, or causing mass extinctions that change how the ecosystem is maintained.

Species movement

Species must adapt to survival in new habitats when environments change. Some shifts are not challenging, and organisms quickly adapt to the unfamiliar environment. At times, species find their environment no longer suitable for survival and use *species movement* to find an environment where they can survive.

Species movement can be routine and necessary *migration* between environments. Animal migrations are predictable in response to environmental changes such as weather or temperature changes, the need for better breeding locations, or changes in food availability.

For example, Canadian geese migrate south for winter, while bald eagles migrate north for their preferred temperature ranges. Species' migrations are typical responses to regular environmental change and do not indicate unique environmental changes.

Environmental disruptions

In contrast, a forced and abrupt move can be disastrous for the species. Species may not have any preparation for an unfamiliar environment if their original environment is destroyed by an unexpected disruption (e.g., volcanic eruption, wildfire, logging).

Species may be so highly specialized that no other location would fully support their survival, such as marine animals that must live underwater and cannot move elsewhere if their current water becomes polluted or too warm to survive. Other species may lose competitive advantages in the new climate.

If another species can better adapt to adversity and utilize resources, they will be more successful in surviving. As a result, these species must either adapt to the changes in their current environment or risk extinction. In some cases, this is the natural process of change in ecosystems. However, it can indicate negative climate shifts killing off essential species, including keystone species, due to the disruptive changes in the animals' environments.

For example, the polar bear population is declining due to a decrease in ice cover, the increase in water tables resulting from melting glaciers, and a reduction in the presence of prey. These changes mean fewer predators in these ecosystems, fundamentally changing the environment's energy pyramid and having long-reaching consequences on the ecological community.

The changes contributing to the loss of polar bears, a significant organism in a major ecosystem, have the potential to impact other ecological communities negatively in a trickle-down effect. Humans need to be aware of the causes of species movement and how it relates to climate change and other unintended — often negative — consequences.

Ecological succession

Ecological succession is the observable change in the species present in an ecological community over time as it responds to environmental changes. Ecological communities start with a few plants and animals that increase and adapt over time until the ecological community grows strong and stable with varied populations.

These populations begin to respond to each other as they interact and grow, creating an interrelated ecosystem. Succession can describe the process environments undertake to "bounce back" from disasters, such as volcanic eruptions, earthquakes, and forest fires.

There are several types of ecological succession.

Primary succession is the first ecological *succession*, creating a community in a previously uninhabited area. This happens infrequently, as it is rare to find uninhabited locations for species to inhabit.

Secondary succession is the growth of a community in a location after traumatic events (e.g., forest fires, volcanism).

Cyclical succession follows predictable patterns based on routine climate and environmental change, like the ecological bounce back that occurs every spring after a severe winter.

Autogenic succession is based on soil changes brought about by adding plant species that allow additional species to join the community. An example of autogenic succession would be if a shrub that fertilized the surrounding area was introduced and nearby plants flourished in response to the positive change that that shrub brought to the community.

Allogenic succession is caused by external impacts and not by surrounding organisms. An example of allogenic succession would be if an area's soil improved due to water runoff from a nearby stream, changing the soil makeup and improving conditions for the area's vegetation to thrive.

Succession ends when the ecosystem has reached an equilibrium between the environment and the organisms. This is the *climax*. Ecological communities grow first with a strong emphasis on r-selected species that reproduce quickly but are eventually replaced by K-selected species that live longer and reproduce infrequently, stabilizing the community until it reaches the balancing climax.

However, a climax is nearly impossible to attain, as there is almost always some disruption in every ecological community. These disruptions are followed by a "bounce back" in one form or another, so the ecological community is never fully balanced.

Additions and removals to the ecological community force communities to be in a near-constant state of flux; even if the disruption is not severe, a perfect climax is nearly impossible.

Patterns and time frames for ecological succession are essential for scientists to observe in response to ecosystem loss and today's shifting climate. This information allows scientists to understand what would be required for a community to rebuild following significant damage.

Relationship matrix

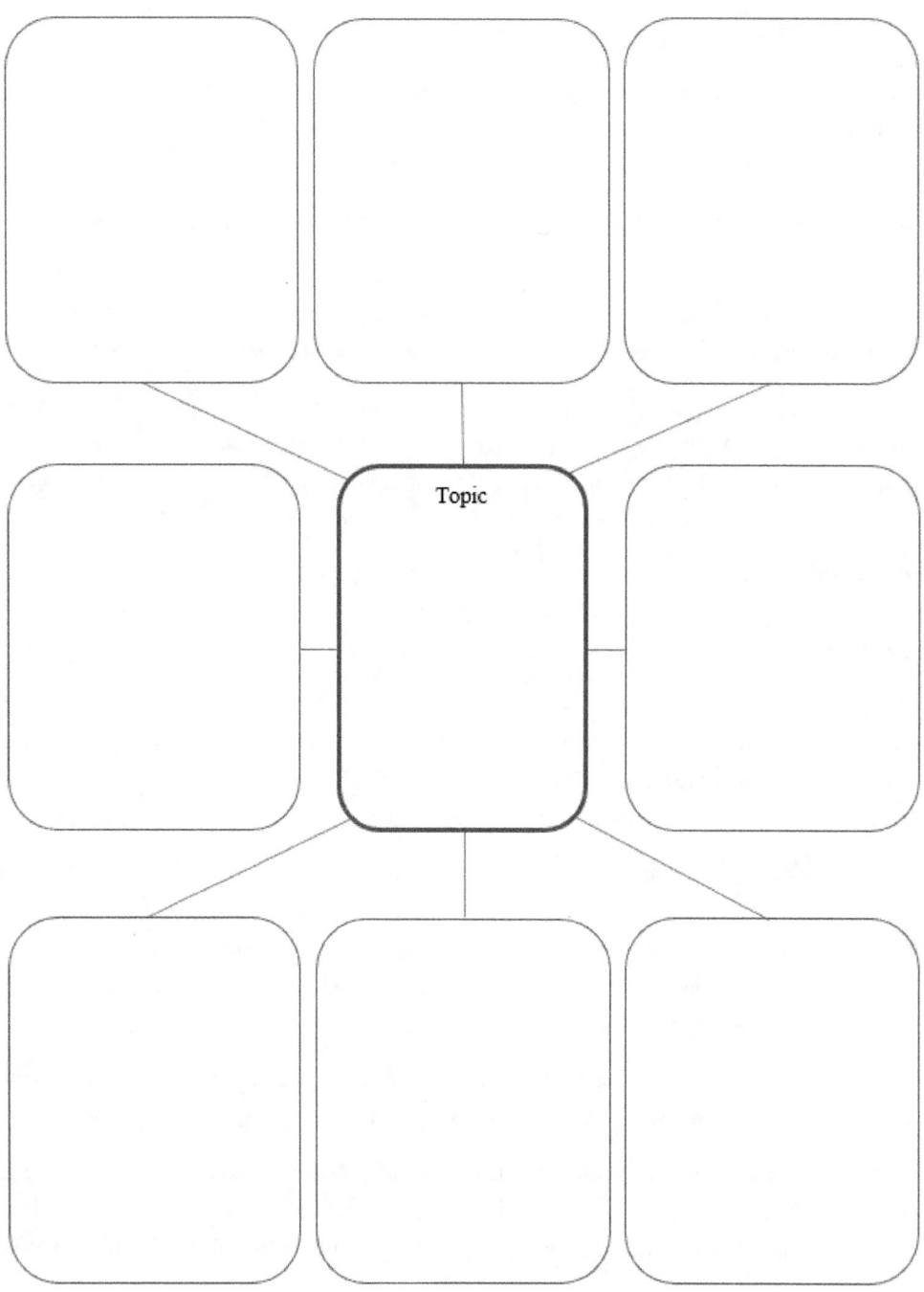

Questions: The Living World

1. Wild plants often have greater resistance to parasites than domesticated plants because wild plants experience:

   A. natural selection, while domesticated plants experience artificial selection
   B. natural selection, while domesticated plants do not experience any selection
   C. artificial selection, while domesticated plants experience natural selection
   D. artificial selection, while domesticated plants do not experience any selection

2. Biodiversity is important because:

   A. it is necessary to maintain the stability of ecosystems
   B. humans can use new sources of food
   C. If species decline, photosynthesis may not be possible
   D. If species decline, there would be too much oxygen in the atmosphere

3. Biogeochemical cycles involve:

   A. only biological processes
   B. heat loss from both respiration and photosynthesis
   C. only geological and chemical processes
   D. the cyclic movement of materials through ecosystems

4. A single ecosystem will include:

   A. an interactive complex of communities but not the abiotic environment
   B. the abiotic environment but not an interactive complex of communities
   C. many species of living organisms and may include humans
   D. either a plant community or an animal community, but not both

5. The best way to sustainably manage natural environments is to:

   A. maintain the interactions between the members of the ecosystem
   B. stop hunting animals and harvesting the fruits of the plants in the ecosystem
   C. minimize the impact of natural disasters, such as fires and storms
   D. carefully limit the growth of the major carnivores and herbivores in the ecosystem

6. Plants grow as new organic molecules are formed by plant cells. Most of the carbon in the newly created organic molecules of these plants ultimately came from:

   A. carbon dioxide in the air
   B. carbon dioxide released during the production of plant sugars
   C. proteins and carbohydrates absorbed by the roots of the plants
   D. carbon compounds absorbed from water

7. Which of the following statements of the sulfur cycle is not true?

   A. Most sulfur is found in rocks and minerals
   B. Unlike nitrogen and carbon, organisms do not require or contain sulfur
   C. Atmospheric sulfur dioxide is contributed when humans burn fossil fuels
   D. a natural source of sulfate in soil is the weathering of rocks

8. A keystone species:

   A. has a disproportionately large impact on the stability of an ecosystem
   B. typically reduces the overall biodiversity of an ecosystem
   C. is typically an herbivore
   D. is an example of amensalism

9. Which of the following represents an abiotic component of a forest community?

   A. the oak and hickory trees
   B. the mushrooms growing on and around rotting logs
   C. water trickling in a small stream
   D. bacteria in the soil

10. Consumers who eat plants rely upon:

    A. chemical energy stored in organic molecules produced by photosynthesis
    B. kinetic energy stored in organic molecules produced by photosynthesis
    C. photosynthesis to convert potential energy to kinetic energy
    D. entropy to generate heat to drive kinetic processes in their bodies

11. Dung beetles live in regions where cattle graze, quickly burying and recycling cattle droppings. Because of the dung beetle's activities, breeding habitats and resources for disease-carrying flies are reduced, and the plants upon which cattle feed are nourished and reduced. The relationship between the dung beetles and the cattle is a type of:

   A. mutualism
   B. parasitism
   C. intraspecific competition
   D. interspecific competition

12. Which of the following statements is accurate?

   A. food chains consist of many interrelated food webs
   B. food chains are interconnected to form food webs
   C. food webs consist of either consumers or producers
   D. food webs usually consist of 8-10 trophic levels

13. Many predator-prey relationships do not result in the elimination of the prey because:

   A. predators cannot catch all the healthy adults
   B. the predator population is limited by the availability of territorial space
   C. the prey does not provide enough nutrition
   D. the prey populations are always far below carrying capacity

14. Most ecosystems:

   A. are sharply divided from other ecosystems
   B. consist of two or more distinct landscapes
   C. grade into other ecosystems in regions called ecotones
   D. are clustered with other ecosystems to form communities

15. Biomes characterize regions with similar types of:

   A. vegetation and climatic conditions
   B. animals and plants
   C. soil, water systems, and animals
   D. rocks, soil, minerals, and water

Notes for active learning

CHAPTER 4

Population

Population Biology and Ecology

Population Dynamics

Reproductive Strategies and Survivorship Models

Human Population Dynamics

Human Population Growth

Population Demographics

Population Policies

Population and Environment

Population Biology and Ecology

Ecological hierarchy

Humans have been studying the natural world for hundreds of years, but the term *ecology* was coined in the 19th century by the German zoologist Ernst Haeckel (1834-1919).

Ecology studies organisms' distribution, abundance, and interactions with one another and the environment.

Widespread acceptance of the theory of evolution significantly advanced the field.

Evolution allowed scientists to understand how ecological pressures such as natural selection shape the environment.

Ecology has modernized with rigorous, comprehensive studies and sophisticated statistics. Modern ecology includes several fields (e.g., conservation, agriculture, and social science).

Ecology is hierarchical and is studied at many levels, from cellular to *biosphere,* the entire region of Earth in which organisms reside. Ecologists often study *organismal levels*.

Habitats and community

Habitat is an organism's physical and biological surroundings, including nearby organisms.

Species members live in groups called *populations,* which occupy the same region.

Community includes the populations of all species in each locale.

For example, a freshwater lake is a community of algae, plants, fish, and microorganisms.

Organisms and their interactions are *biotic factors.*

Population biology and ecology

Population biology is the study of organism populations (groups of organisms of a species that interbreed and live in the same place simultaneously). Population biology focuses on population size regulation, life-history traits (e.g., clutch size), and extinction.

Population biology and *population ecology* are occasionally used synonymously.

Population biology is the standard choice when studying diseases, viruses, and microbes. When studying plants and animals is central, population ecology is appropriate.

Population ecology studies growth, abundance, and distribution.

Population size is denoted as N, the total number of individuals.

Population size concerns *population density* or the number of individuals per given area unit.

Population dispersal is how density is patterned over a range.

Populations may be spread uniformly, randomly, or clumped.

Ecologists often study the changes in population distribution across space or time.

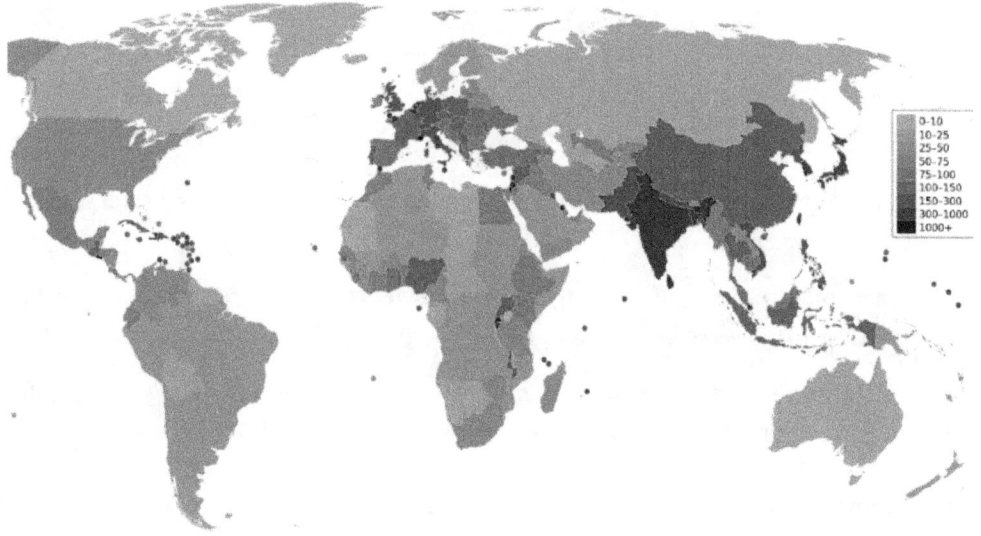

World map indicating the average population density per square kilometer

Physiological stressors

Generally, the population is densest near the center of its range and sparsest at the very edge.

Zone of physiological stress is the boundary with suboptimal conditions for the species.

Physiological stressors include extreme temperatures, inadequate water supply, or pollution.

Zone of intolerance is beyond the *zone of physiological stress* and where no individuals of the species survive.

Species theoretical range is determined by tolerable physiological stressors. However, other species may restrict this range due to *biological stressors* (e.g., competition and predation).

Limiting factors are stressors and conditions limiting a population's growth or abundance.

Density-independent factors do not depend on the number of organisms in a population and include changes in weather or seasons, which affect light availability and precipitation.

Density-dependent factors include competition, disease, parasites, food scarcity, and number of mating pairs, and they become more severe as population density increases. They typically fluctuate and drive a *population cycle,* a cyclic change in the population size.

Both categories of factors serve to limit biological populations.

Environmental resistance

Biotic and *abiotic resources* are often in limited supply, and the environment can only support some organisms in *carrying capacity* (K).

Populations approaching carrying capacity and depleted resources encounter *environmental resistance,* and growth slows.

Environmental resistance is density-dependent, becoming *restricted as growth increases.*

Stable populations do not maximize biotic potential but remain under carrying capacity.

Notes for active learning

Population Dynamics

Population cycle

Population cycle is a cyclic change in the population size, usually driven by density-dependent limiting factors.

Population size (N) over time can be predicted by:

natality (birth rate) and

mortality (death rate).

Together, natality and mortality calculate the *intrinsic rate of natural increase* (r).

$$r = \frac{(\text{birth rate} - \text{death rate})}{N}$$

However, population increase is usually subject to many factors.

For example, population ecologists must consider the *immigration* of individuals into or the *emigration* of others out of the population.

Population growth

Population growth typically exhibits one of two patterns.

Discrete growth (or *discrete breeding* and *discrete reproduction*) is when organisms breed at once at a time of year.

> *Semelparous* species may breed only once in their lifetime.

> *Iteroparous species* reproduce each year.

Semelparous species produce *discrete generations* in which adult generations reproduce and soon die, leaving behind the next generation, resulting in a population with only one generation at any given time.

Iteroparity species produce *overlapping generations* in which an elderly generation lives simultaneously as a reproductive generation and a sexually immature generation; at any time, at least two generations can be observed in the population.

Continuous growth is when organisms reproduce continuously without an established breeding season. Populations exhibiting continuous growth are iteroparous with overlapping generations.

Most organisms do not fit into one pattern and instead exhibit a combination. For example, plants may reproduce sexually at a specific time annually and asexually at any time.

Exponential growth often occurs in iteroparous populations with overlapping generations and a J-shaped (*exponential growth*) growth curve.

Lag phase is the curve's first phase when growth is slow because the population is small.

At a specific critical size, the population enters the *exponential growth phase*, during which growth accelerates rapidly.

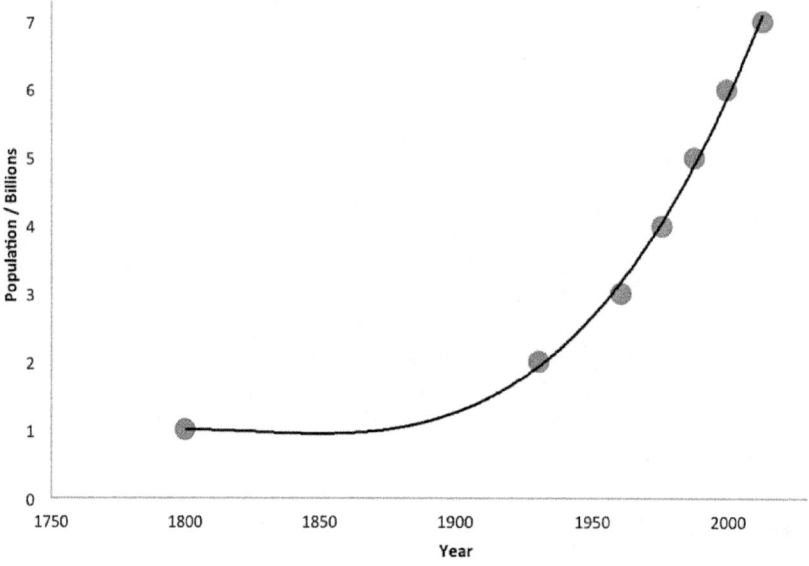

Line graph plotting human exponential population growth between 1800 and 2000

Growth curves

Populations experiencing maximum growth fulfill their biotic potential without hindrance from limiting factors. Biotic potential includes the number of offspring produced by each reproductive event (i.e., *clutch size*), the frequency and total number of reproductive events, the offspring survival rate, and the age at which an individual reaches sexual maturity.

Populations only reach biotic potential with ample space and resources and without predation. However, these factors are often in limited supply, and the environment can only support so many organisms according to their *carrying capacity* (K).

Populations approaching carrying capacity deplete resources and encounter *environmental resistance* with slowed growth.

Logistic growth curves are S-shaped graphs representing growth under environmental resistance. The first portion is *exponential*, with subsequent lag and exponential phases.

However, the population eventually reaches a *transitional* (or *deceleration*) *phase* when the birth rate falls below the death rate due to resource competition, predation, disease, and other density-dependent factors. At that time, growth begins to slow, and the graph plateaus.

Population enters a stable equilibrium phase at carrying capacity with minimal growth.

Stable equilibrium is when natality and mortality rates are roughly equal.

Logistic growth curve is calculated by:

$$\frac{\Delta N}{\Delta t} = rN\left(\frac{K-N}{K}\right)$$

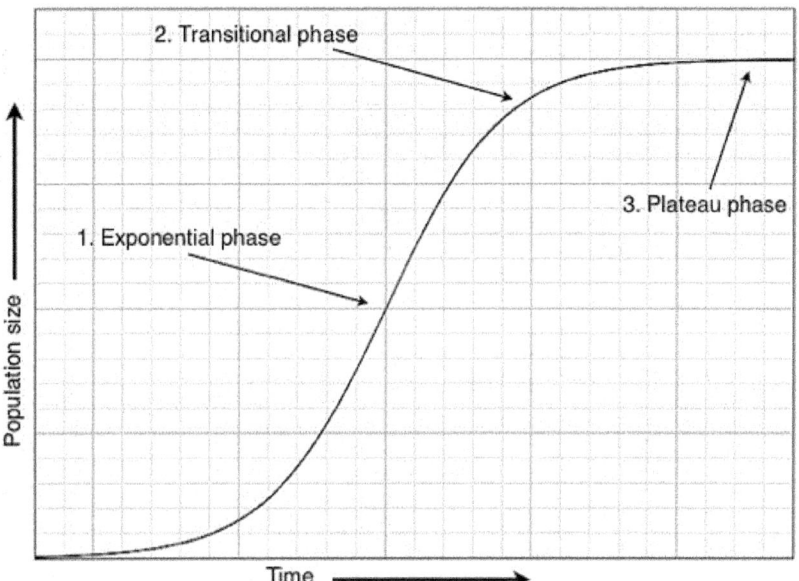

Sigmoid graph of exponential population growth

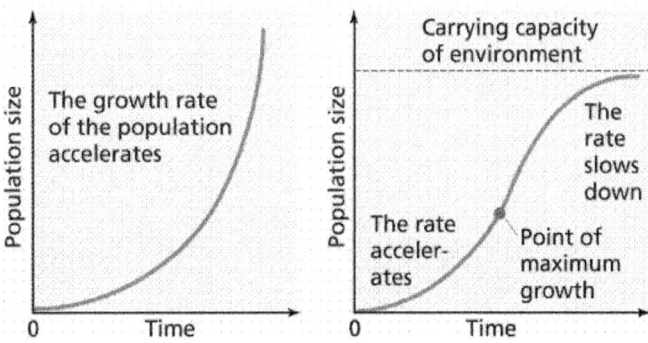

Graph showing unrestricted vs. restricted population growth

Carrying capacity

Carrying capacity is determined by the availability of water, space, food, light, and other factors. It is density-dependent, becoming more restricted as growth increases.

Stable populations do not attempt to maximize biotic potential but remain just under carrying capacity. However, overshooting carrying capacity can be beneficial, provided the population can produce individuals before it exceeds resource availability.

Carrying capacity is a vital population size regulator and powerful evolution driver.

Populations commonly respond to carrying capacity by expanding their range or evolving adaptations, which relieve them of some carrying capacity restrictions. However, no population can indefinitely evade carrying capacity; if it is overshot, high mortality will follow.

Reproductive Strategies and Survivorship Models

Reproductive strategies

Population biologists divide organisms' reproductive strategies into *r-selection* and *K-selection*.

Most species are not strictly r-strategists or K-strategists; it is more common for a species to exhibit characteristics of both and may shift strategies in response to environmental factors.

Population sizes of both r-selected and K-selected species depend on many factors that can be divided into two categories.

r-selection

R-selected species increase rapidly and continue expanding to fill available environments. Populations of these species maintain their size by having numerous young, shorter life spans, early sexual maturation, and little competition for resources.

r-selected species attempt to maximize their rate of natural increase and typically overshoot carrying capacity, causing sudden population crashes. Therefore, their population growth may experience severe fluctuations.

Typically categorized as *opportunistic species*, r-strategists rapidly seize opportunities to proliferate. They are often the first to colonize a habitat and do well in unstable environments subject to density-independent factors. Common examples of r-selected species include most insects and bacteria.

This is because r-strategists reproduce quickly and reach sexual maturity at an early age, maximizing the opportunity for reproduction before they die. They may get the chance only once, making semelparity (when an organism invests all its energy and resources into a single reproductive event, typically followed by death) a common characteristic of r-strategists. The trade-off is that they must produce many offspring simultaneously because they cannot protect them from infant mortality. To survive, r-selected organisms adapt quickly to the environment.

K-selection

K-selected species attempt to maintain their rate of natural increase sustainably. They exist near the carrying capacity at a state of equilibrium, making them *an equilibrium species*.

Unlike r-strategists, K-strategists tend to be specializers uniquely suited to their environment. This makes them very successful but also vulnerable to disturbances. They typically enter a habitat after r-strategists have already colonized it.

To maintain their existence, K-selected species are typically large and invest considerable energy in caring for their offspring, of which they often produce only one at a time. *K-selected species* increase over time under good conditions but level off once they reach their carrying capacity.

These species maintain their population size by having fewer young, competing for resources, having longer life spans, and taking a long time to mature sexually. They can reproduce several times throughout their lifespan, making them *iteroparous*. Examples of K-selected species are humans, whales, and elephants.

Mortality patterns

Predictions can be made in demography to ascertain an individual's death probability before their upcoming birthday based on age.

Life tables (or mortality and *actuarial tables*) are used to make predictions. This data ultimately signifies the survivorship of specific age-based populations.

In actuarial science, two varieties of life tables are used.

Period tables represent mortality rates during set periods for a specified population.

Cohort is a group of individuals born concurrently and aging simultaneously.

Life tables track cohorts over their lifetime and show how cohort members die at various ages.

Cohort life tables (*generation life tables*) represent a population's overall mortality rates.

Region	1990	1995	2000	2005	2010	2012	MDG target 2015	Decline (percent) 1990–2012	Annual rate of reduction (percent)		
									1990–2012	1990–2000	2000–2012
Developed regions	15	11	10	8	7	6	5	57	3.8	3.9	3.8
Developing regions	99	93	83	69	57	53	33	47	2.9	1.8	3.8
Northern Africa	73	57	43	31	24	22	24	69	5.4	5.3	5.5
Sub-Saharan Africa	177	170	155	130	106	98	59	45	2.7	1.4	3.8
Latin America and the Caribbean	54	43	32	25	23	19	18	65	4.7	5.1	4.4
Caucasus and Central Asia	73	73	62	49	39	36	24	50	3.2	1.6	4.5
Eastern Asia	53	46	37	24	16	14	18	74	6.1	3.7	8.0
Excluding China	27	33	31	20	17	15	9	45	2.7	-1.2	5.9
Southern Asia	126	109	92	76	63	58	42	54	3.5	3.1	3.9
Excluding India	125	109	93	78	66	61	42	51	3.3	3.0	3.5
South-eastern Asia	71	58	48	38	33	30	24	57	3.9	3.9	3.8
Western Asia	65	54	42	34	26	25	22	62	4.4	4.4	4.5
Oceania	74	70	67	64	58	55	25	26	1.4	1.0	1.7
World	90	85	75	63	52	48	30	47	2.9	1.7	3.8

Levels and trends in mortality rate for children under five, 1990-2012 (deaths per 1,000 live births). By Millenium Development Goal region, United Nations.

Survivorship curves

Survivorship refers to how many individuals *remain alive* at a given point.

Type I survivorship curve (i.e., long curve with a relatively short-end decline) is when most individuals survive until old age (e.g., human population).

Type II survivorship curve (i.e., negative linear slope) is when individuals die constantly over a theoretical lifespan (e.g., some birds and lizards).

Type III survivorship curve (i.e., negative linear slope) is when most individuals die early. Survivors tend to live relatively long (e.g., many invertebrates, plants, and fish); essentially, the opposite Type I curves.

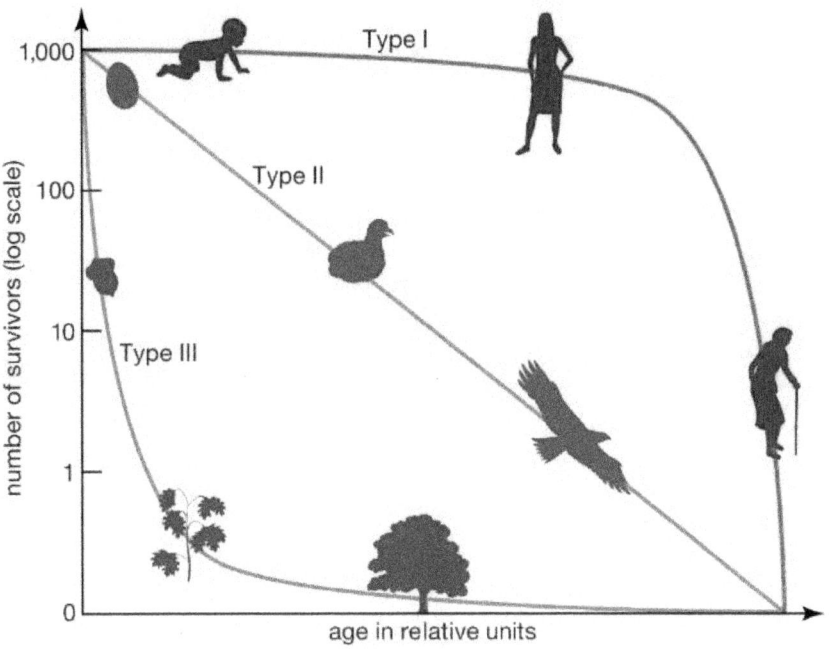

Survivorship curves

Notes for active learning

Human Population Dynamics

Historical population sizes

Human population is now in the exponential phase of a J-shaped growth curve.

The global population is increasing by about 80 million people annually. Technological advances, increased food supply, disease reduction, and habitat expansion have fueled this tremendous growth.

The world population signifies the total number of people alive, and 7.4 billion was the tally made in March 2016.

Estimates predict the world population will plateau at 8-10 billion people this century, but some predict that this number is a vast underestimation; the human population may reach 14 billion by the end of the 21st century.

In the mid-20th century, the most developed countries had a significant decline in mortality rate, soon followed by a decline in the birth rate.

The growth rate in first-world nations is 0.1%, with stable age structures; some countries exhibit declining populations.

Family planning

Nearly all human population growth will be in less developed countries, especially Africa, Asia, and Latin America. Even so, the growth rate in these countries is lower than at its peak of 2.5% in the 1960s.

Effective ways to curtail explosive population growth are family planning, birth control, and encouraging families with fewer children.

However, due to cultural attitudes and a high infant mortality rate in developing nations, convincing people to have fewer children or delay childbearing is difficult.

With 6.5 million residents, London was the most populous city at the turn of the 20th century

Distribution

The growing populations of less developed countries and the high consumption among more developed countries stress the environment.

Ecological footprint of those in the United States and first-world nations is unsustainable. The ecological footprint is determined by the amount of land required to sustain an individual's lifestyle, including the area in which they live, the farmland required to produce food, the factories required to produce material goods, and the distances these products must travel to reach the individual.

An average American family is comparable to thirty people in India in terms of consumption and waste production. Developed countries account for one-fourth of the world population but provide 90% of the hazardous waste production.

Intense resource consumption affects the cycling of chemicals and contributes to pollution and extinction. Without drastic reductions in the collective ecological footprint, humans will soon overshoot carrying capacity and possibly experience catastrophic disease, famine, and other density-dependent catastrophes.

Chapter 4: Population

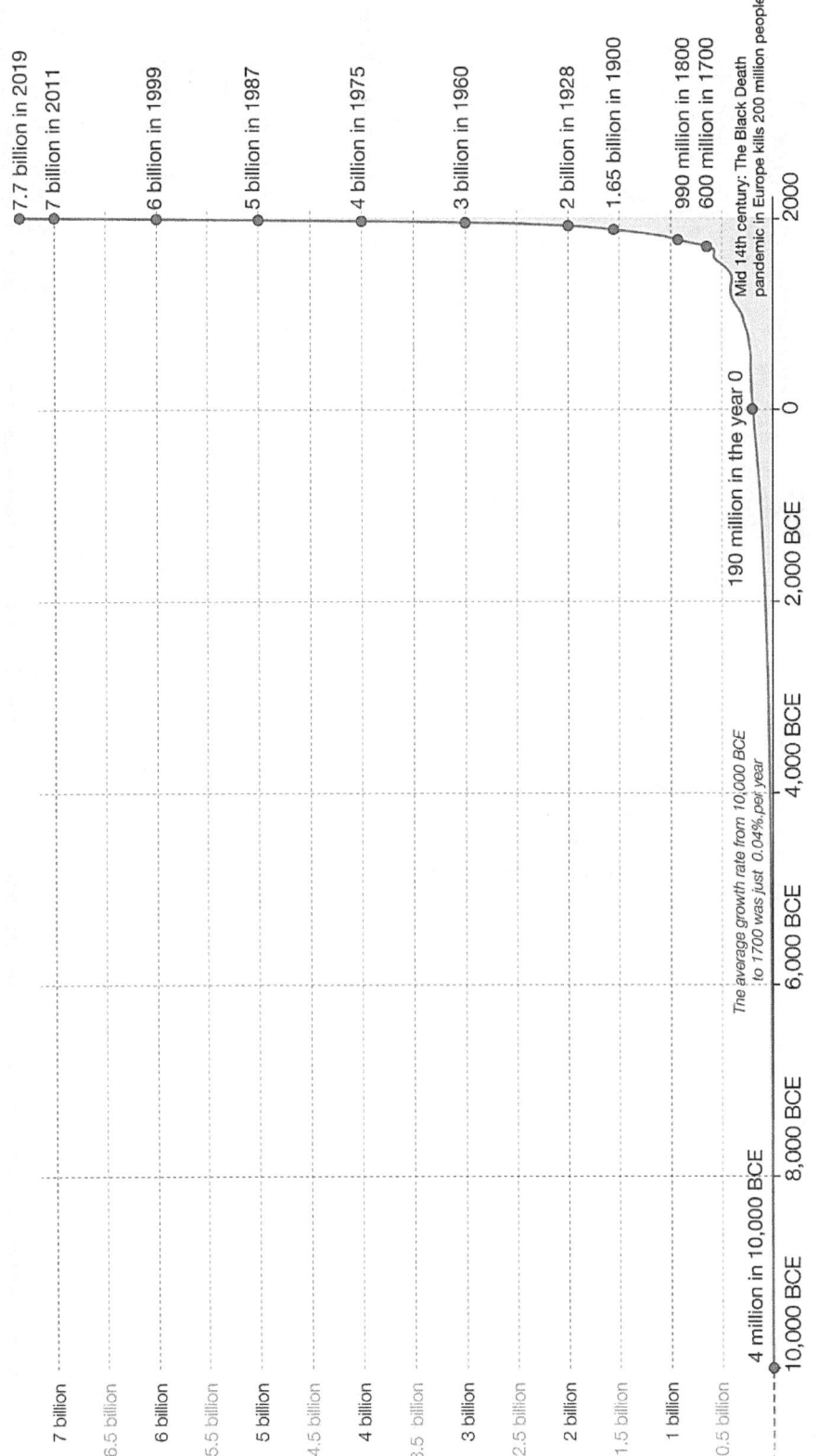

The size of the world population over the last 12,000 years

Notes for active learning

Human Population Growth

Fertility rates

Total fertility rate (TFR) is the average number of children a woman will have. *Replacement level fertility* is the number of children each woman needs to have to keep the population the same. In most developed countries, this number is close to exactly 2. Each couple needs to have two children to replace themselves. In some developing countries where more people in the fecundity range die young, then the replacement rate may often be 3 or higher.

Total fertility rate predicts the average number of children for a woman if:

    1) experiences precise, age-specific fertility rates throughout life; and

    2) survives childbirth during her reproductive life.

The single-year, age-specific rates at a given time are summed to find the *total fertility rate*.

TFR is a contrived rate not based on specific fertility rates (measurements until post-childbearing). It is not based on summing up the group of women's total lifetime number of children born.

Age-specific fertility rates of women in the 15–44 or 15–49 age range is what TFR is based upon instead. These two age ranges reflect conventional international statistical usage.

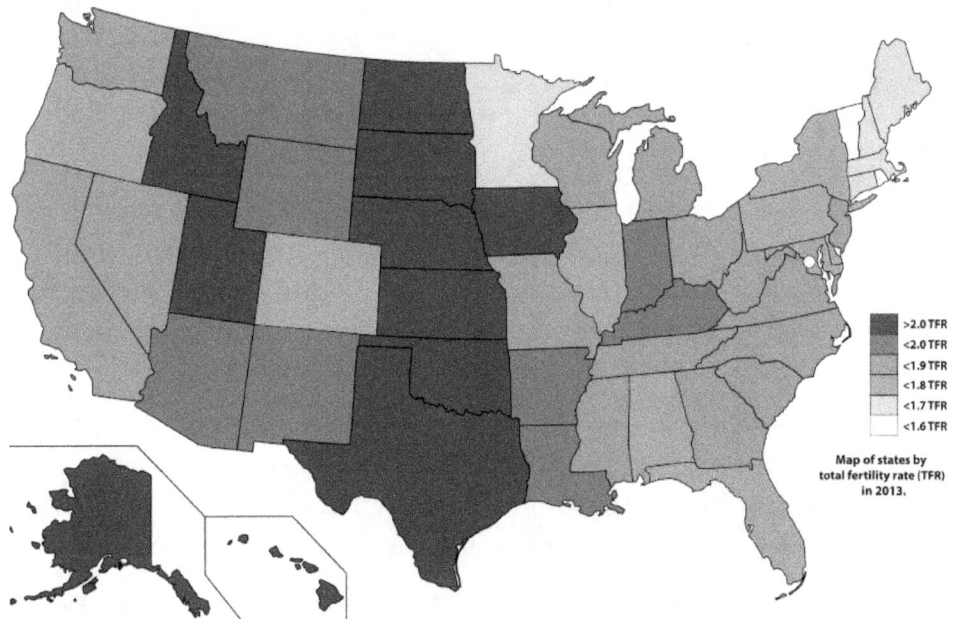

United States map indicates total fertility rates by state

Total fertility rate is a demographic measurement centered around an imaginary woman. As she passes (and survives) through her reproductive years, this woman is subject to all age 15-49 fertility rates recorded for a given population in a particular year.

So, under the premise that this woman (in a fast-forward manner) passes through reproductive years, subject to age-specific fertility rate calculations, the resultant TFR represents the average number of children this woman would have.

Net reproduction rate

Net reproduction rate (NRR) is an alternative fertility measurement. NRR, operating under the premise that a woman is subject to a given year's age-specific fertility and mortality rates, calculates the total number of daughters she would give birth to during her lifetime.

Net reproduction rate has been phased out (e.g., United Nations, 1998); it is relevant and used for countries experiencing high gender imbalance ratios (e.g., China and India). NRR is the *gross reproduction rate* (GRR), and unlike NNR, it ignores life expectancy.

A more accurate index of fertility rates uses TFR or TPFR instead of relying only on crude birth rates (annual number of births per thousand population). This accuracy stems from TFR and TPFR's independence from the population's age structure. However, this independence has negative effects and provides a less precise estimate of family size.

Total cohort fertility rate is preferred since it signifies the sum of applicable age-specific fertility rates to each cohort. Another deficiency of the TFR is that it does not account for generational differences in birth rates (e.g., women of younger generations having fewer children than women from older generations).

Replacement fertility rate

Replacement fertility rate is the minimum fertility rate needed to sustain a certain population level (i.e., zero growth rate). Hypothetically, if mothers had no childbirth deaths during reproductive years (improbable), replacement fertility rate is 2.0 (i.e., two children per woman). In the U.K., an industrialized nation where people generally have easy access to enough healthcare services, the replacement fertility rate is 2.075.

Developing nations with higher mortality rates have replacement fertility rates of 2.5 to 3.3. Currently, the global replacement fertility rate is 2.3, which means if each woman has an average of 2.3 children, the population will remain steady. It is essential to note that this is the average; many people will not have children, while others will have more than two.

Log transformation of data provides an alternative view of the relationship between population economy and reproduction rate. Every 1% *Gross Domestic Product* (GDP) gained has TFR reduced by 0.26%.

Birth rates

Birth rate is the number of live births per 1,000 people yearly. Typically, census data or registration systems for births, deaths, and marriages are used to calculate birth rates.

Combined with mortality and migration rates (immigration and emigration), the birth rate is used to calculate *population growth*.

Birth rate signifies the increase in the number of individuals for a specified period is the *population growth rate*, expressed as a fraction (or percentage):

$$Population\ growth\ rate = \frac{P(t_2) - P(t_1)}{P(t_1)(t_2 - t_1)}$$

Population growth rate showing a population gain indicates a growth rate; rates showing a population reduction indicate a negative growth rate.

Population growth rates of zero indicate neither a gain nor loss in the number of individuals.

Population growth rate is less meaningful without accounting for changes in birth, death, migration rates, and age distribution over time.

Wide-scale loss of life due to disease, calamity, and physiological and physical conflict can affect population growth rates.

Net reproduction rate

Net reproduction rate is a measurement premised on the absence of migration in interpreting the meaning of the net reproduction rate.

> values > 1 signifies an increase in the female population.

> values < 1 signifies a decrease in the female population (sub-replacement fertility).

Zero population growth (ZPG) or *replacement level of fertility*) is when the number of individuals neither increases nor decreases.

Zero population growth estimates include fluctuations in migration, births, and deaths.

According to some, ZPG is desirable for achieving long-term environmental sustainability, considering contemporary concerns about overpopulation.

Populations doubling times

Doubling time is the amount of time needed for a quantity to double.

Doubling time's fundamental properties are:

1. Larger rates of growth correspond with quicker doubling times;

2. Growth rates for organisms vary, especially when size is considered. Generally, smaller organisms (e.g., bacteria) grow and reproduce faster than larger organisms (e.g., elephants), and

3. There is a limit to population size. Natural resource constraints and disease contribute to reigning in the size of populations. The growth that accounts for the influence of resource availability and disease is *logistic growth*.

Doubling time is evident in the human population.

Increasing from 500 million people to one billion in 1804 took 300 years.

Increasing from 1 billion people to 2 billion in 1927 took 123 years.

Increasing from 2 billion to 4 billion in 1974 took 47 years.

According to UN projections, the world population is expected to reach 8.5 billion by 2030.

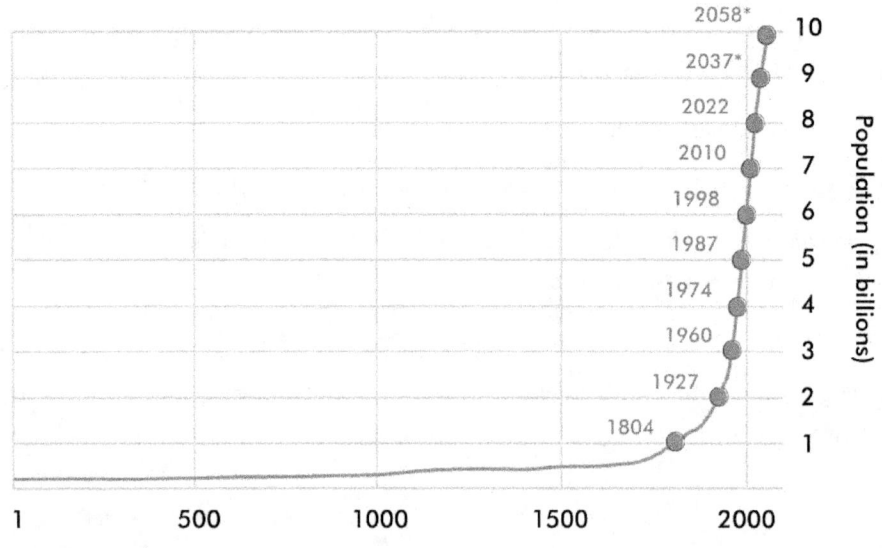

World population from 1 AD to 2058

For a simple calculation of a doubling time of something that grows at a constant rate (e.g., population), the Rule of 70 can be used to estimate. The doubling time of a variable that is growing at a constant rate. To use this rule, divide 70 by the annual growth rate to arrive at an approximate number of years for the variable to double.

For example, if the population grows by 5% yearly, divide 70 by the percentage increase to obtain the time (in years) for the population to double.

    70 / % growth = doubling time

    70 / doubling time = % growth

    70 / 5% = 14 years for the population to double at 5% growth rate

Growth Rate (% per year)	Approximate Doubling Time (years)
0.1	720
0.5	144
1.0	72
2.0	36
3.0	24
4.0	18
5.0	14
6.0	12
7.0	10
10.0	7

Growth rates and doubling times in years, using the Rule of 70

Population estimates

When a human population without high mortality or emigration rates sustains a 3.8 TFR for a protracted period, its doubling time is 32 years. Populations that maintain zero growth rates and are not subject to mass immigration experience an overall population drop over time.

Since it will take several generations for equilibrium in age distributions, it takes a similar amount of time for changes to appear in the total fertility rate, even when abruptly dropping below the replacement-level fertility rate. For example, a population will continue to grow due to many young couples (produced by the previously high fertility rate) now entering their reproductive years.

Over generations, *population inertia, population momentum,* or *population-lag effect* result.

Population inertia is a population's tendency to maintain density by resisting changes.

Population momentum is when national population levels grow even if childbearing levels decline to replacement levels.

Population lag is the rapid population growth when a total fertility rate of at least 3.8 is sustained for an extended time without an associated rise in death or emigration rates.

Exponential growth is when growth increases constantly proportionally, resulting in many environmental strains on society. Due to Earth's finite resources, exponential growth has resulted in climate change, biodiversity loss, and deforestation.

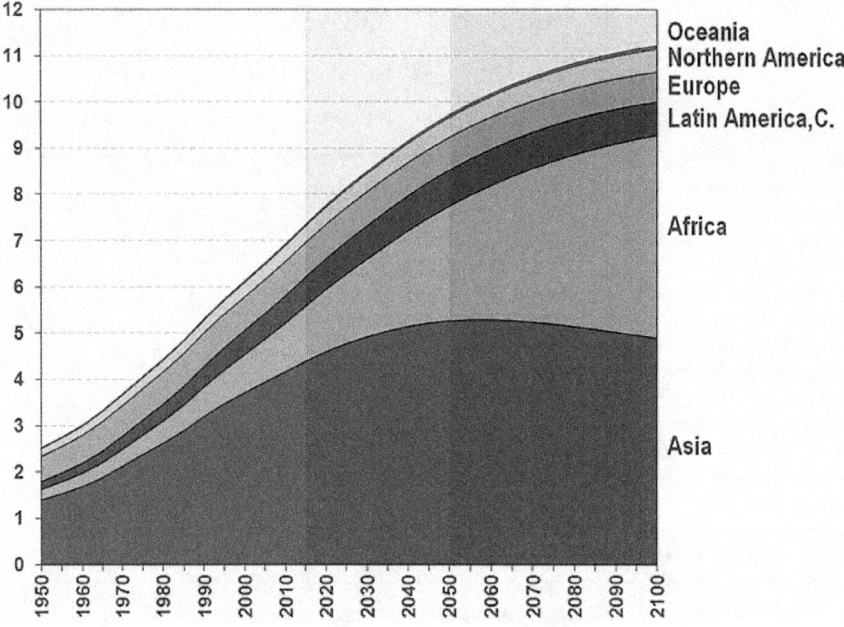

Relative population estimates from 1950 to 2100

Population Demographics

Demographic transition model

As a nation transforms from pre-industrialization to an industrialized economic system, the commonly resulting transition from high birth and death rates to low birth and death rates is a *demographic transition* (DT), demonstrated by a corresponding *demographic transition model* (DTM).

American demographer Warren Thompson (1887–1973) provided the basis for this theory through his 1929 interpretation of demographic history, noting birth and death rate changes over the previous 200 years in industrialized countries.

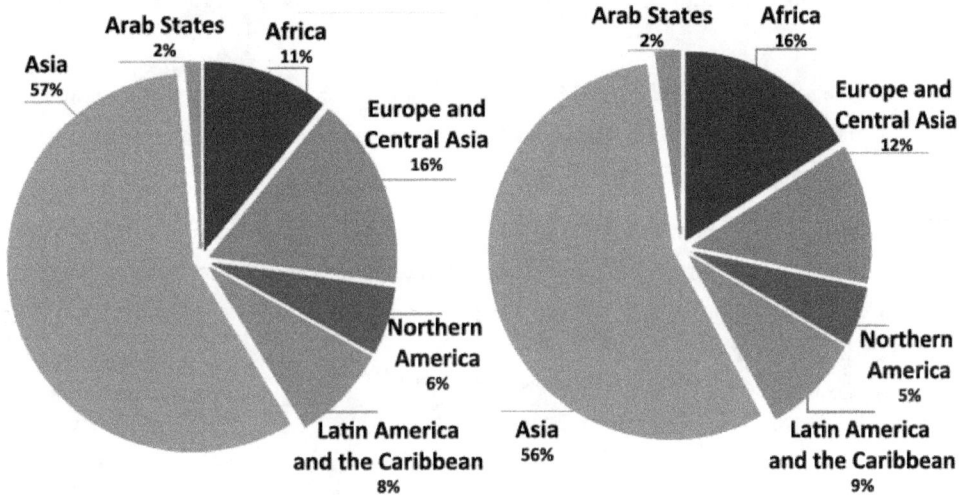

Worldwide demographic transition from 2000 (left) to 2030 (right)

Demographic transition stages

Demographic transition is composed of four (possibly five) stages:

Stage 1: Before the late 18th century in Western Europe, as indicated by research conducted on the history of human populations, pre-industrialized nations had high death rates and high birth rates — nearly a state of equilibrium.

Between the First Agricultural Revolution of 10,000 B.C.E. and the onset of industrialization in the mid-19th century, growth rates were at 0.05% or below, signifying prolonged growth rates due mainly to a lack of the food production required to sustain more rapid reproduction.

Stage 2: An industrializing nation, benefitting from the resultant improvements in food supply (e.g., selective breeding practices, crop rotation), sanitation, medicine, prolonged lifespans, access to technology, and expanded access to healthcare and education, typically experiences a rapid decline in death rates.

Death rates decline with fundamental improvements in public health (e.g., food handling, water supply, sewage, personal hygiene), and mortality rates (especially childhood ones) notably decrease. This trend could result in a large population increase if a drop in birth rates does not accompany it.

Stage 3: Access to contraception, wage gains, urbanization, the decline of subsistence agriculture, women's gains in both social status and education access, the disappearance of child labor, the bolstering of child education, and other fertility factors cause birth rates to fall. A leveling off in population growth manifests, as evidenced by the 19th-century trends in Northern Europe.

Stage 4: Populations experience low birth rates and low death rates. A dwindling population results if birth rates plummet too far under the replacement level, threatening industries that rely on positive population growth.

Aging of the population born during industrialization (stage 2) and their associated care needs cause a significant economic burden for the shrinking population (e.g., contemporary Japan's aging population situation).

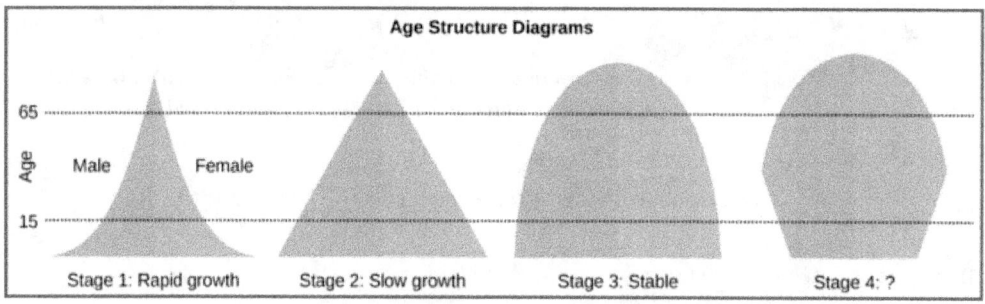

Ages structure diagrams with relative growth for stages 1 to 4

Negative behaviors and lifestyle choices (e.g., lack of physical activity and overeating) may increase disease. Birth and death rates leveled off in developed nations by the late 20th century.

Despite data recently indicating fertility rates resume rising after a certain development point, demographic transition models continue to predict decreasing fertility rates.

Despite establishing a demographic transition correlation, it remains uncertain whether diminished populations result from *industrialization and higher incomes* or vice versa.

While exceedingly impoverished African and Asian nations have yet to reach complete industrialization levels, most nations have reached stages 2 or 3, with many world populations at stages 3 or 4.

Age-structure diagrams

Populations with overlapping generations typically exhibit:

pre-reproductive,

reproductive,

post-reproductive generations.

Age structure diagrams indicate the abundance of each gender and population age group. Horizontal bars represent the number of individuals in each age group.

Pyramid-shaped diagrams indicate an expanding population (i.e., high birth rate and exponential growth). Pre-reproductive generation is the largest because offspring are rapidly reproduced, while the reproductive generation is intermediate.

Post-reproductive generation is the smallest as the elderly die off.

Bell-shaped diagrams indicate a stable population with equal pre-reproductive and reproductive generations, and the post-reproductive generation is slightly smaller.

Urn-shaped diagrams indicate declining populations, with the post-reproductive generation being the largest because few individuals are produced.

Individuals from the reproductive generation rapidly enter the post-reproductive generation and continually die off, while the pre-reproductive generation is too small to sustain growth.

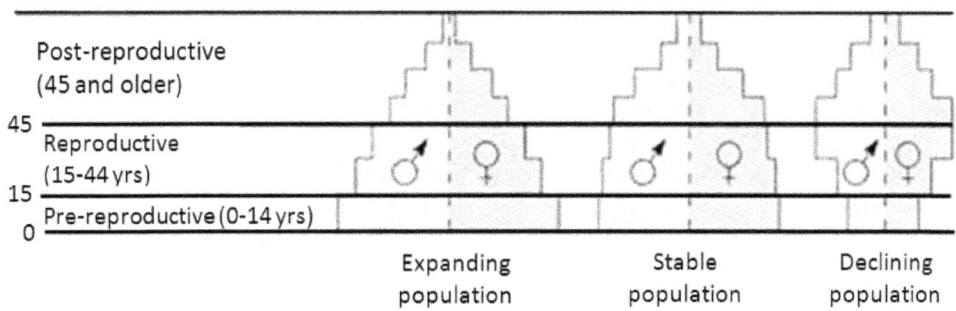

Age structure diagrams: pyramid for expanding (left), bell-shaped for stable (center), urn-shaped for declining populations (right)

Notes for active learning

Population Policies

Sustainability

According to United Nations statistical data, the world population grew by 30% between 1990 and 2010, resulting in approximately 1.6 billion more people. India was the nation that grew the most rapidly (at a 350 million increase), with China in second place (with an increase of 196 million). According to percentages of population increase, the United Arab Emirates (315%) and Qatar (271%) experienced the greatest positive change.

A powerful teaching tool – exponential population growth – presents its potential when considering how it affects environmental system health. The implications are stark: the greater the human population on Earth, the greater its strain on the environment.

The United Nations Population Fund (UNFPA) cites population growth and economic growth as two major environmental quality problems.

Population growth and its negative implications can be addressed in several ways. This notably includes promoting voluntary family planning (e.g., offering sex education, easy access to birth control and contraceptives) and ensuring women's fundamental rights (e.g., healthcare, education, and economic opportunity).

These approaches help mitigate the burden of overpopulation via empowerment, not coercion.

Fastest-growing populations are typically in *less economically developed countries* (LEDC).

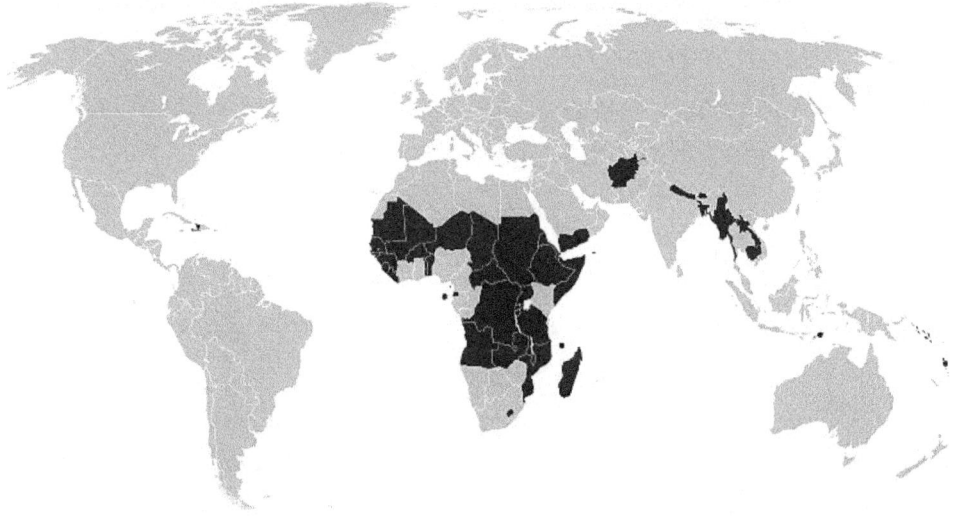

ECOSOC world map highlights LEDCs

In the demographic transition model, most of these countries have reached stages 2 or 3, with birth rates increasingly outpacing death rates and resulting in a population boom.

Death rates are declining due to improvements in healthcare and sanitation.

Several reasons help explain the high birth rates:

1. Inadequate access to contraceptives and family planning education.
2. Rural and urban demand for child labor in agricultural and informal sectors is deemed necessary by families struggling to make ends meet.
3. High levels of infant mortality lead women to have more children.
4. Religious and cultural norms that forbid the use of contraceptives.

More economically developed countries (MEDCs) typically have stabilized population growth with birth and death rates. Problematic situations, however, are not absent.

For example, the death rate in Germany is higher than the birth rate, meaning their population is steadily declining –0.1%. This contributes to an increasingly aging population, and when combined with increased longevity due to healthcare, diet, and lifestyle improvements, Germans face a future filled with an increased number of elderly dependents.

The U.K., facing a similar situation, seems likely to address the financial demands of an aging population by increasing taxes to fund pensions and healthcare needs.

Environmentally sustainable trajectory

Aligning the human population with an environmentally sustainable trajectory can be accomplished by several proposed strategies.

Providing parents access to safe and effective contraceptive options. Redressing the lack of adequate family planning services and access, as evidenced by the ratio of two out of five pregnancies reported as unplanned, could close the assurance gap that each child conceived is wanted and welcomed.

Secondary education for all children. In surveyed cultures, women who have attained a secondary school education tend to have fewer children in general, and those they do have are born later in the mother's life compared to the reproductive behaviors of less educated women.

Eradicating gender biases in law, economic opportunity, health, and culture. Postponing childbearing and limiting the number of children is more commonplace among women not deprived of the rights to own, inherit, and manage property, obtain credit, and participate in civic and political affairs as men.

Universal provision of age-appropriate sex education. Comprehensive programs on sex, sexual development, sexuality (sexual orientation), and reproductive health, as indicated in data gained in the United States, can ameliorate the rate of unwanted pregnancies and lower birth rates.

Elimination of child-birth incentives. Taxes (or other financial benefits) can be preserved or even increased by governments to assist parents based on parenthood status, as opposed to incentives based on the number of children born to a family.

Integrating population, environment, and development lessons at multiple levels into school curricula. Schools must provide knowledge for students to make well-informed decisions (e.g., whether to have children or not and when) on navigating and managing their comprehensive effect on the environment.

Pricing of environmental costs and impacts. Couples cognizant of the financial ramifications of childbearing can forecast the incentives and disincentives attached to the size of a family. Calculating taxes, the cost of food, clothing, and other associated costs incurred per child, as well as having an awareness of available government rebates, could impact the number of children couples would desire.

Refrain from encouraging childbirth through government incentives and programs instead of adjusting to an aging population. Societal adjustments (e.g., increased labor participation) must be implemented to manage an aging population responsibly.

Promoting leaders to adopt policies to stabilize population growth via human rights and human development. Policymakers can address problems associated with the population ethically and effectively by educating themselves on rights-based population policies and encouraging women to make informed reproductive choices through empowerment.

Policies that respect parents' reproductive goals promote women's health and are sensitive to supporting an educationally and economically active society are evidenced worldwide.

Many nations continue to halt progress through cultural resistance and political infeasibility, even though these implemented policies have proven inexpensive.

India's population

India has one of the highest growth rates and approximately 1.4 billion people (as of 2023). For example, in the last ten years, 181 million people (approximately the combined populations of neighboring Bangladesh and Sri Lanka) were added to India's population.

India surpassed China as the world's most populous country in 2023, when it reached 1.429 billion people, overtaking China for the first time.

Global growth rates are slowing, particularly in India's southern Kerala.

There, initiatives to reduce population growth have been implemented, including:

1. Women's education raised Kerala's female literacy rates to 85% (national average of ~50%), helping lower infant mortality rates due to mothers' increased abilities, which lowered birth rates (couples not having children in anticipation of infant mortality);

2. Increased access to contraceptives; and

3. Improving women's status in a society where they are viewed as an asset, not a burden (i.e., Kerala shifted marriage custom where the bridegroom's family pays dowry instead of the bride's family).

China's population

From at least 1950, when the United Nations began recording world population rankings, China has remained the world's most populous nation, reaching 1.4 billion in 2022.

China implemented a *One Child Policy* in 1979 to curb the nation's growth rate by incentivizing families with free education, healthcare, pensions, and other benefits if they limited themselves to having only a single child.

Under this policy, births in China needed prior governmental approval from family planning officials. Families ignoring the *One Child Policy* with unapproved children had governmental benefits removed and penalties levied.

Under China's *One-Child Policy*, its population growth rate declined, preventing an additional 320 million children from being born (about the size of the United States). This policy was not without its negative or problematic consequences.

Since traditional Chinese Confucian beliefs often result in male children being more valued than females (to carry on the family name), female infant and child abandonment became a severe issue. Additionally, due in large part to this policy, approximately 90% of the fetuses aborted during the height of the *One-Child Policy* were female.

China's *One-Child Policy* ended in 2016, when government allowed families to have up to two children. In May 2021, the Chinese government permitted women to have up to three children, prompted by the declining birth rate.

Population and Environment

Planetary boundaries

Human activity crossed planet boundaries (responsible societal and governmental stewardship of Earth to ensure its continuing habitability) in four critical areas in a study published in Science (January 2015).

Four transgressed planetary boundaries are:

climate change (e.g., atmospheric CO_2 concentrations),

biosphere integrity loss (i.e., species mass extinction),

land-system change (e.g., deforestation), and

biogeochemical cycles (e.g., phosphorus and nitrogen flows).

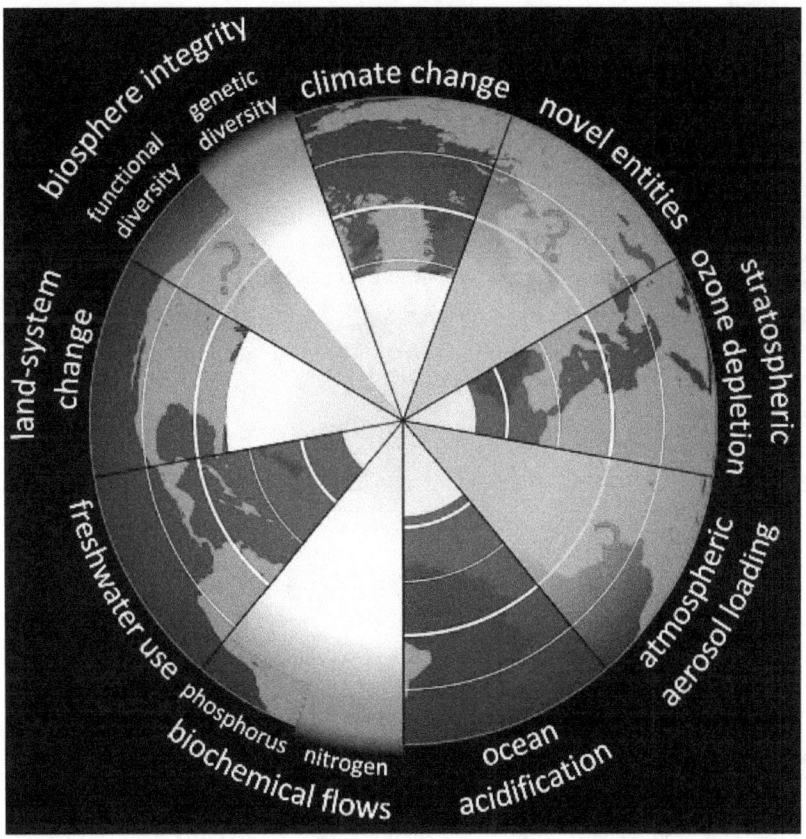

Planetary boundary integrity: The length of wedges from the center indicates risk from humans; the silver wedge from the center indicates a greater safety margin, with the periphery indicating greater danger.

The relationship between population and climate change warrants closer examination. Carbon dioxide emissions have significantly increased since the Industrial Revolution (and its associated boom in population size).

In 2011, CO_2 emissions were 150 times higher than in 1850, a drastic atmosphere alteration.

By 2014, the highest levels of CO_2 concentration on Earth in millions of years were recorded at 400 parts per million (PPM). Over time, population growth and CO_2 emissions reveal a strong positive correlation, indicating that inextricable links exist between population dynamics, consumption patterns, and climate change.

Hunger

No noticeable correlation exists between hunger and population density when assessing the world's food. In Bangladesh, a densely populated nation, hunger exists. Hunger exists in Nigeria, Brazil, and Bolivia, nations with significant per capita food resources. The Netherlands is a small, densely crowded nation where hunger has been eliminated, and it is a significant exporter of food.

World population growth shows a correlation between rapid population growth and hunger.

The fastest-growing nations in Asia, Africa, and Latin America also experience a lack of food resources. However, causation has not been proven. Understanding whether hunger is caused by rapid population growth or coincides with the same societal realities is crucial.

Remarkable insight was gained through Cornell University's 1989 study of 93 developing countries' population growth, food consumption, and other variables. Statistical analysis suggests that the rapid growth of populations does not cause hunger.

Income

People have less to eat in poorer countries, notably the poorest 20% of people earning the smallest share of total national income. Poverty, not population growth rates, causes hunger.

The 11.3% population increase between 2000 and 2009 increased the number of people from 6.085 to 6.775 billion. This was not uniform growth as developing nations (i.e., low per capita income) had the highest rates and essentially the same nations with hunger and malnutrition.

According to data, childhood malnutrition appears to increase with the world population. However, World Bank data reports that children under five experienced a malnutrition rate decrease of over 3% (24.6% in 2000, 21.3% in 2009). As the world population grew, the proportion of malnourished children declined. There is no strong relationship between overpopulation and world hunger.

Disease

Humanity will respond and likely change how disease epidemic prevention and treatment are handled due to increased international trade and travel, population growth, and humans' ever-increasing interactions with animals and ecosystems.

The second half of the last century's 2.5 billion to 6 billion population growth has likely influenced how infectious diseases emerge and spread.

When analyzing outbreaks from the mid-20th century until now, the rate of pathogen-caused emergent diseases has increased notably. This applies even when controlling improvements in diagnostic techniques and monitoring. This could result in the false perception that diseases were on the rise.

A study found that between 1940 and 2004, more than 300 infectious diseases emerged.

Pathogen migration among species accounts for some emerging diseases (e.g., West Nile virus, SARS coronavirus, and HIV), while other diseases are drug-resistant variants of existing pathogens (e.g., tuberculosis and malaria).

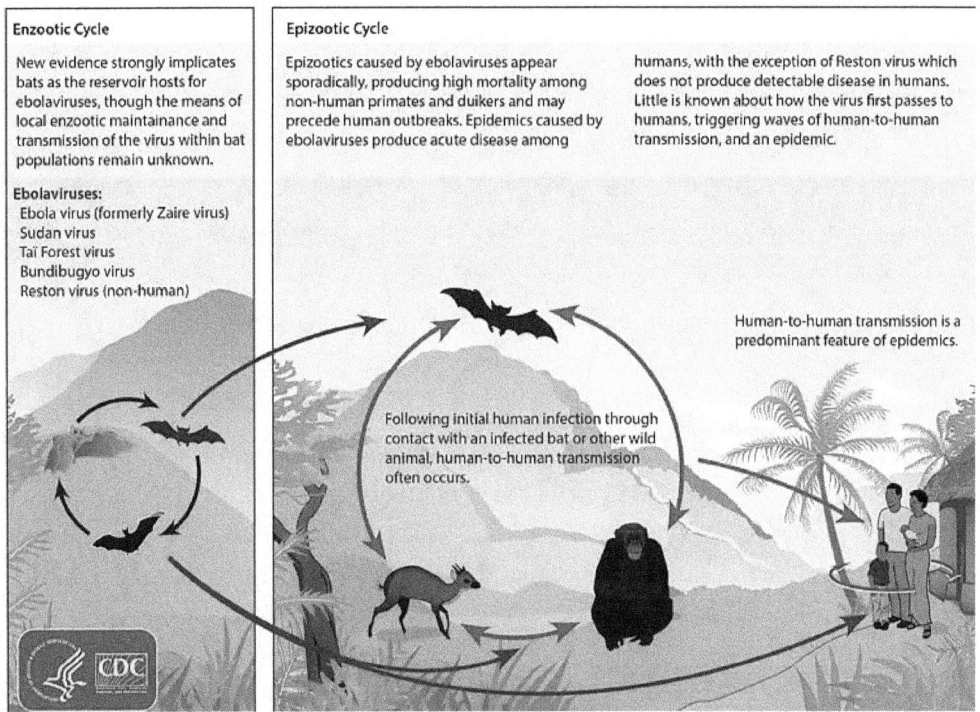

Ebola animal-animal and animal-human transmission cycle

Human interactions

Increased prevalence of certain diseases (e.g., bacterial-caused and deer-carried Lyme disease) suggests causation by patterns of human interactions with disease-carrying animals.

Parts of Earth (e.g., tropical Africa, Latin America, and Asia) are more likely to produce novel viruses; experts refer to them as *hotspots*.

A rise in human interactions with environments supporting high biodiversity is a probable cause for viral transmissions from animals. Given the globalization of modern times, these illnesses can quickly spread anywhere globally.

Sea and ground travel that previously would have required months can now be accomplished in a few hours by flight. While this has been beneficial on many levels, it does promote the spread of diseases to and from far-flung places.

For example, an asymptomatic passenger from Miami, Florida arriving in Shanghai can quickly introduce pathogens to that region. Considering Earth's projected population growth will result in more global travelers, it is likely that contagions will spread more quickly, contributing to extended epidemics.

In response to humanity's continued growth, health authorities are advocating for more robust public health organizations and increasing the distribution of resources to protect systems that serve the public.

For vaccine development, researchers are exploring methods for quickening viral identification. Scientists attempt to gain deeper insights into complicated human-ecosystem interactions to identify emergent disease hotspots.

Hopefully, these efforts will ameliorate pandemics by introducing creative solutions.

Overpopulation

Colloquial use of the term "overpopulation" suggests that full employment and guaranteed access to a decent standard of living might be unattainable due to more people in the economy than can be supported, but a more nuanced understanding is that an economy's capability to employ is dependent on a base of capital needs requiring people for its operation. Capital assets are lacking in overpopulated economies.

One method to increase the rate of capital asset acquisition – installing industries in the economy – is hindered because the associated savings rate is low. Such an economy risks lowering per capita income and reducing the savings percentage of people since more people consume the total production than are required to generate it.

The need for more goods to sustain a population is *overpopulation*, a state without enough resources (e.g., goods, supplies, water) to share per person.

Overpopulation strains education systems since more pupils can reduce a school's available funding. Classroom overcrowding and the associated decrease in one-on-one teacher-student time foster a reduction in education quality. Like classroom overcrowding, overpopulation can negatively affect people's access to housing.

Thirty-two children in a small classroom near Nagar, Pakistan

Relationship matrix

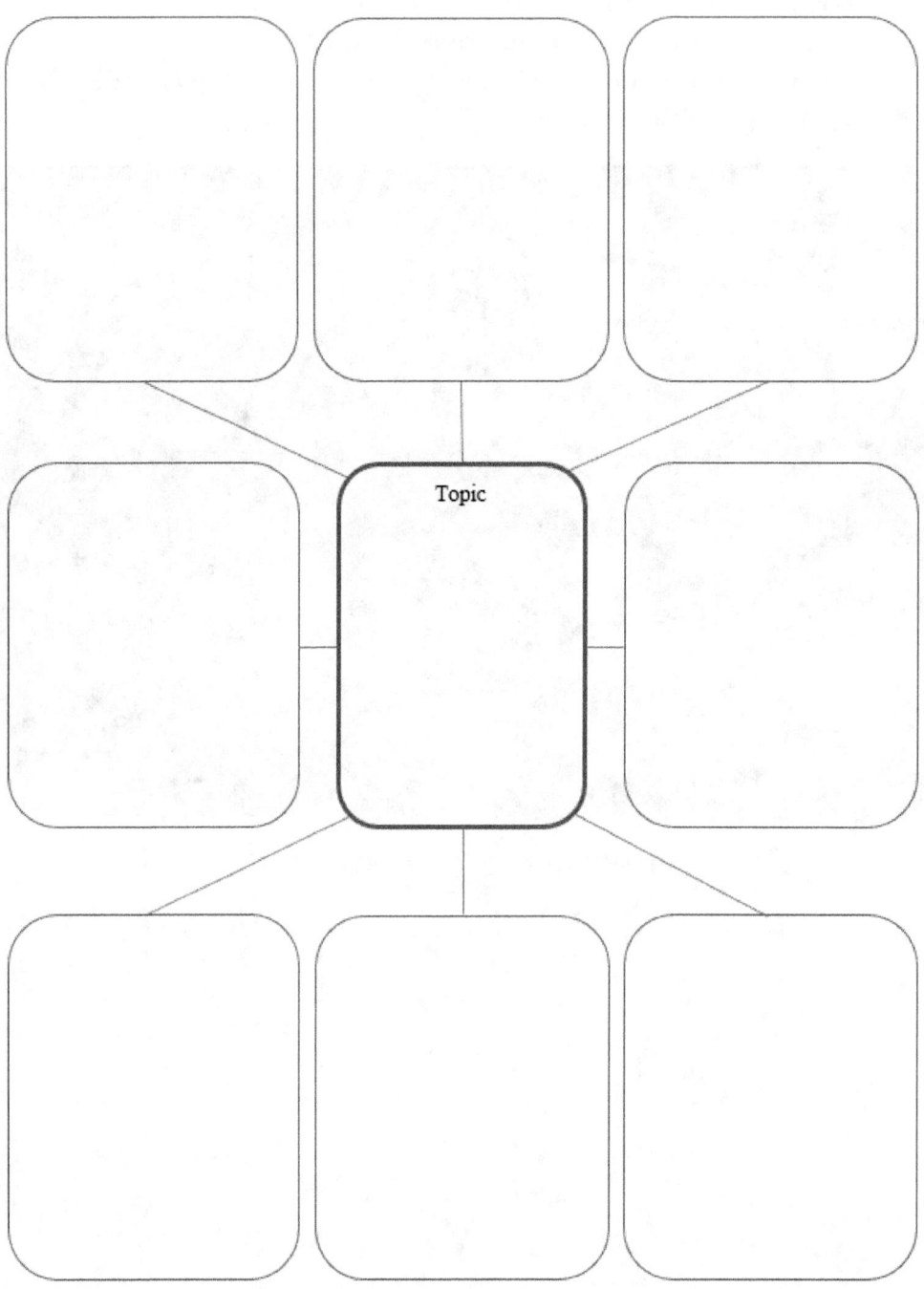

Questions: Population

1. Density-independent factors such as earthquakes and hurricanes are:

   A. abiotic factors that maintain a population near equilibrium
   B. biotic factors that maintain a population near equilibrium
   C. abiotic factors not involved in maintaining a population near its equilibrium
   D. biotic factors that are not involved in maintaining a population near its equilibrium

2. A group of frogs in a rainforest represents a population of frogs:

   A. live in the same region and can potentially reproduce with each other
   B. look similar and seem to be well adapted to the same region
   C. are preyed upon by the same group of predators and seem to be camouflaged
   D. live in the same region and feed on about the same types of food

3. A squirrel population in an oak forest in Indiana is limited by hawk predators, the number of acorns produced annually, nesting sites in the trees, and cold winter temperatures. Which of the following is an abiotic factor limiting this squirrel population?

   A. the hawks in the region
   B. the number of acorns produced annually
   C. the stress of cold winter temperatures
   D. the number of available nesting sites

4. A stable population would remain at equilibrium if:

   A. the birth rate increased as the death rate decreased
   B. emigration rates and death rates increased equally
   C. births and immigration increased by the same number of organisms
   D. births and deaths increased by the same number of organisms

5. A country that has undergone a complete demographic transition has:

   A. a lower birth rate and a higher death rate
   B. a higher birth rate and a lower death rate
   C. a higher birth rate and a lower death rate, and is about to undergo industrialization
   D. a lower birth rate, a lower death rate, and undergone industrialization

6. In general, K-strategists have a:

   A. type I survivorship pattern and r-strategists have a type III survivorship pattern
   B. type II survivorship pattern and r-strategists have a type I survivorship pattern
   C. type II survivorship pattern and r-strategists have a type III survivorship pattern
   D. type III survivorship pattern, and r-strategists have a type II survivorship pattern

7. Along the shoreline of a pond, Canadian geese, American toads, and grass frogs search for food, while bluegill and bass prey on small fish in the shallow water. These species, living and feeding in this location, represent one:

   A. species
   B. population
   C. community
   D. ecosystem

8. The growing human population:

   A. is best addressed by the conversion of ecosystems to more direct human uses
   B. requires the management of ecosystems to serve the needs of humans better
   C. will increase the need for ecosystem services
   D. will require an increase in forests and a decrease in agricultural land

9. What are the current limiting factors for future human population growth?

   A. pollution and land for agriculture
   B. availability of oxygen and water
   C. fossil fuels and carbon dioxide production
   D. oxygen levels in the atmosphere and availability of sodium chloride

10. Population growth and fertility rates are lowest in:

    A. upper-income countries
    B. upper- and middle-income countries
    C. middle- and low-income countries
    D. lower-income countries

11. Which of the following will reduce global population growth?

    A. Encouraging women to reproduce earlier
    B. Changing the total global fertility rate to 3
    C. Decreasing infant mortality in all countries of the world
    D. None of the above

12. Sustainable populations:

    A. are often near their carrying capacity
    B. have exceeded their biotic potential
    C. have grown beyond all types of environmental resistance
    D. are characterized by high emigration and low recruitment

13. What does the replacement-level fertility rate include that is not part of total fertility rate?

    A. nutrition of the family
    B. infant and childhood mortality
    C. availability of mates
    D. use of birth control

14. Although people living in the highest-density populations in urban areas generally live long, healthy lives, global overpopulation remains a problem because:

    A. environmental impacts are not always experienced where resources are consumed
    B. the greatest environmental problems are concentrated in these high-density populations
    C. people in these regions have the highest fertility rates
    D. the destruction of the ozone layer has affected agricultural output

15. In general, fertility rates:

    A. decrease as per capita income increases
    B. decrease as per capita income decreases
    C. increase as per capita income increases
    D. are unrelated to per capita income

Notes for active learning

CHAPTER 5

Land & Water Use

Human Impact on Global Resources

Water Resources

Forests

Rangelands

Agriculture

Land Conservation

Land Use

Transportation Infrastructure

Mineral Resources and Mining

Fishing

Global Economics

Globalization

Page intentionally left blank

Human Impact on Global Resources

Resource consumption rate

Millennium Ecosystem Assessment was a four-year research effort involving 1,360 leading scientists to measure valuable natural resources; it concluded that:

"the structure of the world's ecosystems changed more rapidly in the second half of the twentieth century than at any time in recorded human history, and virtually all of Earth's ecosystems have now been significantly transformed through human actions."

Humans absorb:

    42% of terrestrial net primary productivity,

    30% of marine net primary productivity

    50% freshwater

    40% of land allocated to food production

    50% of land developed for human overpopulation dominates Earth's physical, chemical, and biological conditions.

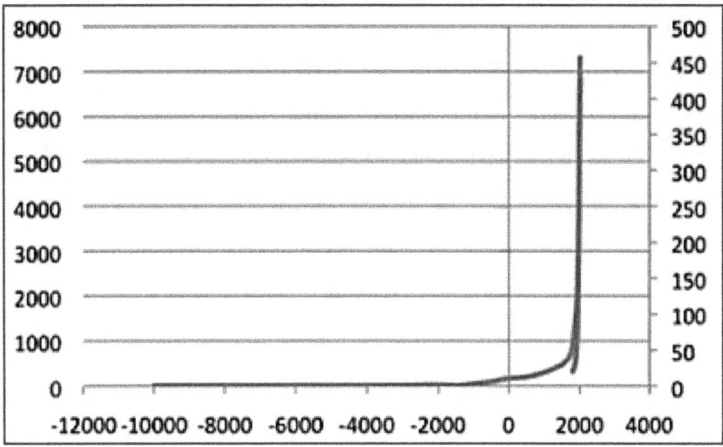

World population (in millions) vs. fossil fuels (joules) consumed, U.S. Census Bureau

Environmental impacts

Historically, the impact of land and water use on ecosystems has been underestimated and ignored. However, in recent years, it has become a growing concern. Some land-use practices can degrade the quality of soil, waterways, air, and other natural resources.

One issue that often arises in discussions of human use of natural resources is the "carbon footprint" created by the increased production of food, materials, and energy. Global authorities, industries, and individuals use ecosystem impact assessments to determine how land and water use has affected the environment.

The outpacing population growth compared to the availability of critically needed non-renewable and renewable resources over the past several decades, despite technological advances, resources per person are in decline. The extinction of species, the destruction of rainforests, desertification, the advance of urban sprawl, growing water shortages, toxic waste, oil spills, and air and water pollution evidence declining resources.

Finite resources (e.g., fossil fuels, fresh water, arable land, coral reefs, frontier forests) continue diminishing as humanity breaks population records yearly. This encourages increasing competition for vital resources, diminishing the quality of life.

Involving 1,400 scientists and five years of efforts, *the United Nations Environment Program* (UNEP) Global Environment Outlook study concluded that human consumption rates outweighed resource availability. Scaling this down to a micro perspective, each currently in existence requires one-third more land than the planet can supply to meet its resource needs.

Extinction events

Humanity is proposed as the cause of Earth's greatest mass loss of species since the extinction of dinosaurs 65 million years ago.

This human-made extinction rate is 1,000 to 10,000 times faster than average.

International Union for Conservation of Nature's (IUCN's) *Red List of Threatened Species* (2012 update) indicates that 19,817 of the 63,837 species examined (nearly a third) are threatened with extinction.

Scientists caution that if trends continue, at least 50% of Earth's plant and animal species will become extinct within a few decades.

Extinction records indicate that the average (not human-made) extinction rate was one species lost per million species per year.

The present-day loss of 30,000 species per year (or three per hour) indicates a rate that outpaced nature's rate of adding species through evolution.

Leading causes of extinction are:

    acidifying oceans

    climate change

    habitat loss

    human overpopulation

    invasive species

    natural resource exploitation

    overfishing and poaching

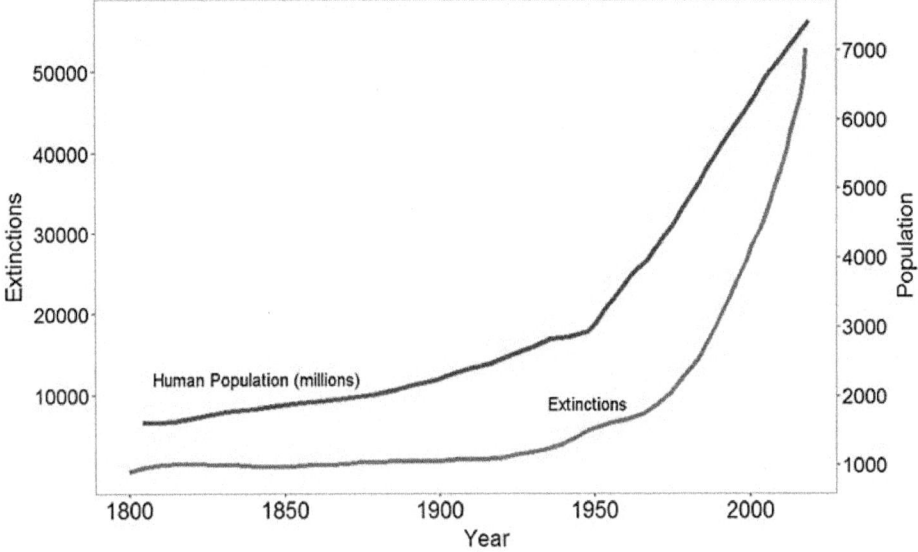

Correlation between human population levels and the number of species lost to extinction

Habitat destruction

The extensive loss of rainforests, coral reefs, wetlands, and Arctic ice, among other ecosystems, can be attributed mainly to human overpopulation. Once covering roughly 14% of the planet's land area, the rainforest has been reduced to 6% and could disappear in the next 40 to 84 years if deforestation rates continue increasing.

Due to warming temperatures and increasing ocean acidity and pollution, coral reefs could be decimated by the century's end. By 1980, nearly 30% of reefs disappeared, which includes 90% destruction of the Philippine reefs and 50% destruction of the Caribbean reefs.

The 11.5% per decade of permanent ice cover loss relative to averages from 1979 to 2000. In 4 to 30 years, this sustained loss rate could result in ice-free Arctic summers. Humanity's footprint reduces wetlands worldwide on interconnected, ecological infrastructures.

In the United States, about 47% of the original wetlands remain, a loss of about 104 million acres. In Europe, 30-40% of wetlands remain. As the world's population continues to grow, so will its footprint on the ecosystems.

Water Resources

Global water resources

Discussions of global resources and their use often begin by assessing the amount of water on Earth, such as glaciers, oceans, lakes, rivers, and groundwater. However, focusing on water inventories and reserves is askew because, unlike fossil fuels, water is a renewable resource. Water from rivers and streams is continually replaced through the *hydrologic cycle*.

To achieve global water sustainability, emphasis must be placed on the flows and fluxes of water. Knowing the amount of water in a lake or aquifer is valuable but not sustainable for humans if it is not replenished or if consumption exceeds the replenishment rate.

Water resources are not evenly distributed worldwide, nor are the people who use them.

United Nations Environment Program assessed human activities over two decades and found:

> *Freshwater global resources* are not evenly distributed, and much of the water resources are far from human populations. Several of the globe's largest river basins run through areas with minimal population.
>
> *Agricultural uses* of water account for 70% of the total global water consumption, mainly through crop irrigation. Industrial users account for 20%, while 10% is consumer use.
>
> *Groundwater accounts* for nearly 90% of the world's available freshwater resources, and approximately 1.5 billion people depend on groundwater as their primary source of drinking water.
>
> *Water-stressed areas* will affect two in three people worldwide by 2025. About 450 million people in 29 countries suffer from water shortages.
>
> *Sanitation and clean water* are major issues in many locations worldwide, with 20% of the world's population without access to clean water.
>
> *Water-borne diseases* from unsanitary drinking water (e.g., fecal matter) cause significant illness and death in developing countries.
>
> *Polluted water* affects 1.2 billion people's health globally and contributes to 15 million child mortalities yearly.

Freshwater and saltwater

Icecaps and glaciers comprise 10% of the world's landmass, primarily in Greenland and Antarctica. They contain around 70% of the world's freshwater but are far from human populations and not a readily available resource for human use.

United States Geological Survey (USGS) estimates that 96% of frozen freshwater is at the North and South poles, with 4% creating over 550,000 km of glaciers and mountain ice caps.

Groundwater is the most readily available and abundant source of freshwater on Earth, followed by reservoirs, lakes, wetlands, and rivers. Most freshwater lakes are in areas of high altitude, with about 50% of the planet's lakes located in Canada alone.

Many lakes, especially those in arid regions, become salty through evaporation. Reservoirs are human-made lakes created by constructing physical barriers that reroute water from large basins to pools and are used for various purposes. Wetlands include bogs, marshes, swamps, lagoons, and floodplains and range in depth from 0 to 2 meters.

Earth's total volume of water is estimated at 1.4 billion km^3. 30.8% of water is stored underground as groundwater. 97% of freshwater is available for human use and consumption. 2.5% of water volume is freshwater; three-quarters of this freshwater is frozen, covering most Arctic and Antarctic regions. Freshwater rivers and lakes comprise 0.3% of the world's freshwater supply. In comparison, humanity's total usable freshwater supply is less than 1% of freshwater and only 0.01% of the water on Earth.

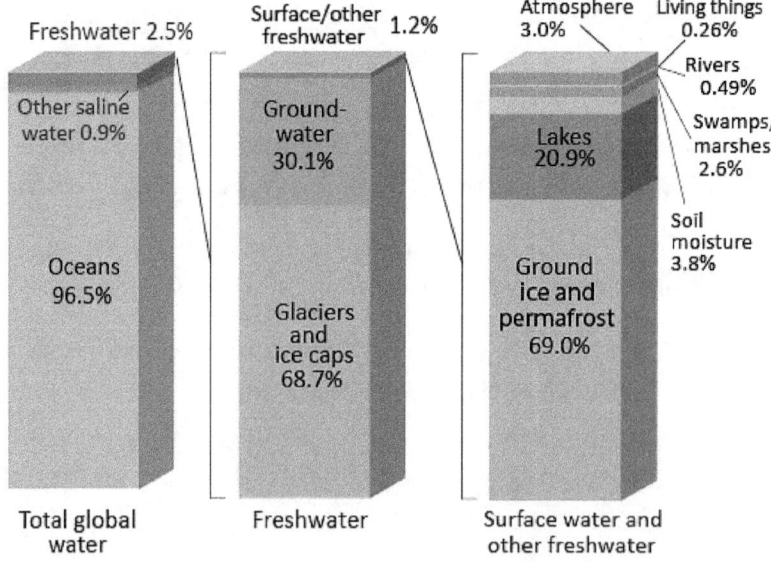

First column shows the division of Erath's fresh and saltwater. The second focuses on freshwater divisions, while the right reports surface water and other freshwater sources.

Ecosystem changes

Diverse populations in lakes, rivers, and wetlands (i.e., freshwater ecosystems accounting for 1% of Earth's surface) could live in some of the most endangered ecosystems. Research by the *International Union for Conservation of Nature* (IUCN, formerly the World Conservation Union), which tracks biodiversity threats, claims that 34% of freshwater fish species currently risk extinction.

Loss of a larger proportion of species and habitats than land or ocean-based ecosystems, freshwater ecosystems are vulnerable to irreparable damage, species endangerment, and extinction due to river damming, water pollution, overfishing, and other dangers.

Cultural eutrophication is an accelerated enrichment of water bodies with excess nutrients (e.g., nitrates and phosphates) due to human activities that involve sewage, detergents, and fertilizers. These added nutrients cause an overgrowth of algae, resulting in increased competition among other marine organisms for sunlight and oxygen. This decreases the water's dissolved oxygen, eventually killing other aquatic plants and animals.

Unlike natural eutrophication, which occurs over long periods, cultural eutrophication happens rapidly (within decades) and causes significant ecological problems. It can even cause the water to become unpotable.

Agricultural, industrial and domestic uses of water

70% of the water drawn from groundwater and rivers is used in irrigation, while 10% is used domestically and 20% in industry.

Industry and manufacturing, such as wood, metal, paper products, gasoline, oils, and chemicals, require water to function during production.

Water is used globally to produce electricity. Water may be rerouted from a river to power turbines that spin from the force of the onrushing water and produce electricity. Water is often recycled into the river once it runs through the hydroelectric system. Dams are used similarly to generate electricity.

Agriculture and food production consumes considerable amounts of water, requiring nearly 100 times more than is utilized for personal needs. Crops are grown worldwide but have requirements for food and water, no matter the location. Raising cattle for food requires water – six to twenty times as much as required to nourish cereal crops (grains).

Most water drawn for domestic use is returned to its sources, though wastewater is treated before being recycled.

Since the 1960s, farmers and scientists have considerably improved global nutrition by providing more food per capita at lower costs. This was achieved using high-yielding seeds, plant nutrition, and improved irrigation techniques.

Irrigation is how water is supplied to crops to thrive in areas with no water source or where water is inconsistent. Irrigation is practiced in many ways, such as through surface irrigation, localized irrigation, drip irrigation, sprinkler irrigation, and rotary irrigation.

Irrigation innovations allow for increased agriculture and crop growth and are essential to human development throughout history.

Spray irrigation is a modern technique that waters crops like a home sprinkler system (left); a low-pressure spray system conserves water by reducing water loss via evaporation (right)

Drip (or micro) irrigation effectively water crops using horizontal pipes that slowly drip water onto the soil. Micro-irrigation systems save water, increase crop yields, decrease fertilizer use, and decrease human labor demands.

Global water shortages

783 million people (about 11% of the world population) cannot access improved drinking water (e.g., public pipes, household connections, protected springs, or rainwater collections).

40% of these people without clean drinking water live in Sub-Saharan Africa.

A lack of clean drinking water, or water for any use associated with personal health and hygiene, causes many problems. Water-borne diseases from fecal matter contamination are prevalent, aggravated by the lack of good health care and medicine.

In 2010, the UN General Assembly proclaimed every person's right to access clean and sufficient water for domestic and personal use.

The General Assembly stated that this water must be acceptable, safe, and affordable (cost not exceeding 3% of household income) and be physically accessible (i.e., water source within 1,000 meters of the residence and total time for collection should not exceed 30 minutes).

Millennium Development Goals Report (2012) set specific goals for the need for clean drinking water, and it has met them several years ahead of schedule.

Millennium Development Goals include:

- Eradicate extreme poverty and hunger;
- Reduce child mortality and
- Ensure the sustainability of the environment.

Global Outlook for Water Resources report concluded that more than half of Earth's population will become water-vulnerable by 2025. Water demand will account for 70% of the available freshwater.

Another report, prepared by the 2030 Water Resources Group in 2009, proposes that by 2030, some developing areas worldwide will experience water demand exceeding the supply by 50%.

By 2030, a UN report commissioned by more than two dozen of its bodies claims that acute water shortages will affect nearly half of the world's population. Reports such as these provide the basis for the U.N.'s proclamation that Earth is experiencing a "*Global Water Crisis.*"

In North Africa, the Middle East, the Indian subcontinent, China, and the United States, freshwater is consumed ten times faster than the replenishment rate despite its vital, finite, and irreplaceable nature.

Water conservation

In 2015, California experienced some of the worst drought conditions in recorded history. North American Drought was the most catastrophic drought since the Dust Bowl of the 1930s and resulted in $53.25 billion of damage (as much as $116.4 billion in 2020 dollars).

During two years of the drought (1988-1989), severe droughts throughout 45% of the United States brought deadly heat waves, wildfires, and dust storms. Property damage, crop damage, and livestock casualties all occurred. Due to the near-nationwide crop damage, commodity prices experienced record increases.

Water conservation reduces waste, and using water efficiently ensures water for the future. Freshwater is a finite resource, and people must use water judiciously.

Xeriscape is a landscape design using low-water-use or drought-tolerant plants that require little to no supplemental irrigation.

Zeroscape is a landscape filled predominantly with gravel and dirt containing few or no plants. Several laws target water conservation.

Lifestyle changes to conserve water.

    Bathroom: (over half of domestic water used)

- Turn off the water while brushing teeth or shaving;
- Take short showers and avoid using substantial amounts of bath water. Restricting showers to five minutes saves over 1,000 gallons monthly;
- Wash hands with water off while lathering soap and
- Fix faucet leaks.

    Laundry:

- Wash only full loads, or use a washer that allows water levels to change according to load size and
- Invest in high-efficiency washers, saving over 50% water and energy.

    Kitchen:

- Wash only full loads of dishes in the dishwasher;
- Do not use running water to defrost foods; thaw them in the refrigerator;
- Compost food waste instead of disposing in trash or garbage disposal.

The government institutes rebate programs to upgrade water-consuming fixtures.

Forests

Importance of forests in the ecosystem

Forests are large areas of land covered with trees or other woody vegetation. Forests are valued for aesthetic beauty, cultural resources, and tourist attractions.

Forests are the dominant terrestrial ecosystem of Earth; they account for 75% of the gross primary productivity of Earth's biosphere and contain 80% of Earth's plant biomass.

Forests are important *carbon sinks* that extract carbon dioxide and pollutants from the air, contributing to biosphere stability and reducing the greenhouse effect. *Forest loss* from unsustainable human practices exacerbates climate change.

Greenhouse gases released by human activity, usually mitigated by trees absorbing CO_2 emissions, increasingly escape into the atmosphere as deforestation continues. Deforestation in tropical regions accounted for a 12% increase in greenhouse gas emissions (2000-2005).

Root systems stabilize stream banks and help slow erosion. Leaves and needles that fall into the water provide another food source (as they often carry small invertebrates) and help maintain water pH. Trees and branches fall into streams and provide shelter for young fish. Fallen trees are food sources with organic matter sustaining aquatic insect populations. Furthermore, they can direct and shape advantageous streamflow.

Forests at specific latitudes form distinctly different ecozones:

    Boreal forests near the poles consist of conifers.

    Tropical forests near the equator are distinct from *temperate forests* at mid-latitude.

Elevation and precipitation levels affect forest composition.

Old-growth forests

Old-growth forests largely contain trees over 30 inches in diameter that are often hundreds or thousands of years old and possess complex canopies. Much of the world's old-growth forests have been cleared; according to the *World Resources Institute* (WRI), 21% of the original old-growth forests remain.

Differences in the methods used to inventory remaining stands of *old-growth* forests can produce significant discrepancies. In 1991, the U.S. Forest Service and the nonprofit Wilderness Society each released their inventory of old-growth forests in the Pacific Northwest and Northern California.

Both classifications used the Forest Service's definition of *old-growth* based on the number, age, and density of large trees per acre, the characteristics of the forest canopy, etc.

However, because each agency used different remote sensing techniques to collect data, the Forest Service reported 4.3 million acres of old-growth. In comparison, the Wilderness Society found only 2 million acres.

National Commission on Science for Sustainable Forestry (NCSSF) concluded that 3.5 million acres (or 6%) of the region's 56.8 million forest acres are old-growth.

Yellow birch in the Allegheny National Forest, Pennsylvania

In the Northeast, less than 1% of forests are old-growth, though mature forests that will become old-growth in a few decades are more abundant there than elsewhere in the country.

The Southeast has fewer old-growth acreages; only 0.5% of the total forest area is considered old-growth, distributed between 425 sites across the region. The Southwest has only a few scattered pockets of old-growth, mostly Ponderosa pine, and is not known for its older trees. Old-growth forests are even scarcer in the Great Lakes region.

The protection of old-growth trees is vitally important. These forests provide critical habitat for salmon since they perform some functions that help foster salmon populations. Trees and vegetation that line freshwater streams give the shade needed for spawning streams.

Public lands

National, state, and local governments own 43% of U.S. forests; the remainder is owned by private landowners, including over 22 million family forest owners.

About 25% of U.S. forests are designed to protect soil and water and conserve biodiversity, including more than 100 million acres of reserves and roadless areas. The remaining 45% is designated for multiple uses as *working forests*.

Lands are cared for by public and private interests that balance their use as a source of income with the objectives of protecting wildlife, maintaining water quality, providing recreation, and maintaining the forests' aesthetic value.

The United States comprehensively assessed the regulatory programs for forest practice by state governments. Evaluations included an extensive review of information collected from program administrators in 50 states. The assessment determined that a wide range of forestry practices be implemented in private forests.

State agencies control forestry practices and related programs, especially stringent regulatory programs, in about 15 states. Administrators have suggested that regulatory programs would benefit from research on identifying forestry sectors requiring attention, determining appropriate enforcement regulations, evaluating program performance, and designing management systems to monitor regulatory programs.

National Forests

U.S. Forest Service oversees the protection of 155 National Forests, which contain almost 190 million acres (8.5%) of the total land in the United States.

National Forests east of the Great Plains are primarily re-acquired or replanted forests purchased from private owners by the U.S. government to create National Forests.

National Forests west of the Great Plains are held by the U.S. government (or donated).

Yellowstone Park Timber and Land Reserve was designated the first National Forest on March 30, 1891, following the *Forest Reserve Act* of 1891, which allowed the president to create forest reserves for public enjoyment.

Organic Act (1897) outlined more specific protection purposes for establishing forest reserves (e.g., securing water supplies and supplying timber). Natural resources are allowed, and sometimes encouraged, to be extracted from National Forests.

Forest reserves became part of the U.S. Department of Agriculture's recently established *Forest Service* under the *Transfer Act* (1905). As of September 2014, the Forest Service oversees 193,062,995 acres of land, most of which have been designated as National Forest.

Forty states have at least one National Forest. Alaska has the most National Forest land (21.9 million acres), followed by California (20.8 million acres) and Idaho (20.4 million acres).

Timber companies and environmentalists often disagree about using National Forest land. The disagreements center on endangered species protection, logging of old-growth forests, intensive logging, undervalued stumpage fees, mining laws, and road building.

Farles Prairie in Ocala National Forest

Forest management

Forestry has been a profession in North America for about 100 years. Over the past century, the field has evolved from practices focused on maximizing timber value to approaches deeply rooted in ecology, science, and sustainability.

Modern-day forestry includes rigorous college programs. Practitioners use continuing education, certification, and licensing to establish and maintain professional credentials.

Laws addressing safety and workers' rights also govern forestry activities.

Forest management concerns economic, legal, scientific, and social aspects, including aesthetics, recreation, water, wildlife, wood products, and genetic resources. Management includes conservation and economics using timber extraction, planting targeted flora, cutting roads and pathways through forests, and preventing fires.

U.S. forest management operates under layers of federal, state, and local regulations and guidelines that foresters and harvesting professionals must follow to protect water quality, wildlife habitat, soil, and other resources.

A forest on San Juan Island, Washington

For decades, net forest growth has outpaced the amount of wood harvested; this supports the idea that landowners economically dependent on wood have a strong incentive to continue sustainable management practices. This aligns with global forest data, which indicates that forest products and industrial round wood demands provide revenue and policy incentives to support sustainable forest management.

Due to urban development and increased demands from other interests vying for more land, it is important to ensure that landowners will continue to have reasons to prevent deforestation.

Production forests

30% of the forest area of the United States is *production forest*, where land is managed primarily to harvest forest products. Methods to manage and harvest trees include:

- *Even age management*: essentially, the practice of tree plantations;
- *Uneven-age management*: maintain a stand with trees of all ages, from seedling to mature;
- *Selective cutting*: specific trees in an area are chosen and cut;
- *High grading*: cutting and removing only the largest and best trees;
- *Shelterwood cutting*: most trees are removed except for scattered, seed-producing trees used to regenerate strands;

- *Clear-cutting*: trees in an area are cut at the same time (this technique is sometimes used to cultivate shade-intolerant tree species), and
- *Strip cutting*: clear-cutting a strip of trees that follows the land contour; the corridor is allowed to regenerate.

Planted trees

The Forest Stewardship Council's U.S. Forest Management Standard recognizes two categories of planted trees: *conventional plantations* and *Principle 10 Plantations*.

Conventional plantations account for most planting projects in the U.S. and are treated the same as natural and semi-natural forests under this standard.

Principle 10 Plantations are cultivated with blocks of trees lacking the traits of natural forests; this includes exotic trees (e.g., Eucalyptus) and cloned trees lacking genetic variation.

Principle 10 Plantations alleviate pressure on forests in producing commercial products but generally lack biodiversity or are unsuitable as wildlife habitats. FSC-US Standard aims to prevent further loss of natural and semi-natural forests to Principle 10 Plantations.

Disruptive management practices resulting in a *Principle 10 Plantation* tag include:

Harvest cycles are short to prevent stands from developing understory stages;

Steady use of chemical herbicides or frequent fertilization;

Promoting single species where occupied by multiple-species forests; and

Failing to leave a minimal number of trees or undisturbed spots for wildlife.

American Tree Farm System

American Tree Farm System (ATFS) is America's largest and oldest woodland certification system. It is one of three certification systems in the United States (the others include the FSC and the Sustainable Forestry Initiative).

American Tree Farm System specializes in private forests, primarily those held by individuals and families, certifying over 24 million acres of forestland. This network of over 90,000 woodland owners is organized through state committees and governed nationally.

Forty-five states have American Tree Farm System committees. With national coordination, ATFS strives to "*work on-the-ground with families . . . to promote stewardship and protect the nation's forest heritage.*"

According to the Standards of Certification for ATFS, woodland owners must own 10 or more acres and have a management plan that involves recognizing wildlife habitats, protecting water quality and threatened/endangered species, and practicing sustainable harvest. The minimum acreage to qualify for a tree farm refers to woodland.

Acreage that includes grazing or other non-wooded lands must have at least 10 acres of forest. Furthermore, programs supporting tree farming may require larger forested acreages and additional criteria.

For example, *The Forest Ag Program* in Colorado requires landowners:

> Perform forest management activities to produce tangible wood products (e.g., Christmas trees, firewood, and fence posts) for the primary purpose of obtaining a monetary profit;
>
> Must have at least 40 forested acres; and
>
> Submit a Colorado State Forest Service-approved management plan prepared by a professional forester or natural resources professional.

American Tree Farm System is a program of the *American Forest Foundation* (AFF) that focuses on America's forests' long-term ecological and economic sustainability.

American Forest Foundation's vision statement is: *"AFF is committed to creating a future where North American forests are sustained by a public that understands and values the social, economic, and environmental benefits they provide to our communities, nation, and the world."*

Forest fires

A wildfire is an uncontrollable fire that occurs in an area with combustible vegetation and outside ignition factors (e.g., humans, lack of moisture). A wildfire differs from other fires by its extensive size, speed at which it can spread from its source, potential to unexpectedly change direction, and ability to jump roads and rivers.

Four of the worst fires in U.S. history started in the Upper Midwest on October 8-14, 1871. The most prominent was the Great Chicago Fire, which left over 100,000 people homeless and caused massive economic disruption.

Simultaneously, the Great Michigan Fire ravaged the cities of Holland and Manistee, while another fire destroyed the city of Port Huron across the state. The Great Peshtigo Fire in Wisconsin may have been the most devastating of these fires. It killed over 1,500 people — the most fatalities of any fire in U.S. history. It is unclear whether these concurrent fires were simply coincidence or resulted from a natural phenomenon, such as a meteor shower or high winds moving through the region.

Devastating forest fires include:

> May 9-July 23, 2012, in Catron County, New Mexico. 297,845 acres of the Gila National Forest were burned;

> June 30, 2013, in Prescott, Arizona. The Yarnell Hill Fire killed 19 firefighters (the greatest single loss since 9/11) and burned 8,000 acres;

> July 14-August 7, 2014, in Washington. The largest wildfire in the state's history, started by lightning, burned 250,000 acres of land; and

> September 2015 in California. The Valley Fire burned 73,000 acres of land, the Butte Fire 70,000 acres, and the Rough Fire 14,000 acres.

The Brins Fire, Sedona, Arizona, 2006

While wildfires can devastate property and human life, fire is vital to many ecosystems, including prairies, savannas, and coniferous forests. Many plant species in these environments (e.g., Giant sequoias) require fire to germinate and thrive.

By suppressing naturally occurring fires in these habitats, humans threaten these plant species and the animals that depend on them. Suppression builds up flammable debris, which can result in even more destructive wildfires than normal.

Prescribed burning, a technique that utilizes smaller, controlled fires in the cooler months, can help to prevent these issues. Prescribed burns can reduce fuels, improve wildlife habitat, control competing vegetation, improve short-term forage for grazing, help control tree disease, and perpetuate fire-dependent species.

Types of forest fires

There are three basic types of forest fires:

ground, *surface*, and *crown*.

It is common to have all three types of fire during a wildfire. However, the proportion of each type can vary significantly from day to day or even minute to minute, depending on fuel, topography, and weather conditions.

Fuel, topography, and weather drive a fire's behavior, and changes to any of these may cause a ground fire to emerge as a surface fire or a surface fire to escalate into a crown fire, or vice versa.

Ground fires burn mostly in decayed roots below the ground and the duff layer. The duff layer comprises compacted, dead plant materials such as leaves, bark, needles, and twigs. Ground fires are sustained by glowing combustion (without flames) and can go undetected for a long time because they produce little to no smoke and spread slowly.

Surface fires burn loose needles, moss, lichen, herbaceous vegetation, shrubs, small trees, and saplings at or near the ground's surface, primarily by flaming combustion. Surface fires spreading in surface fuels dictate much of a fire's expansion. They can grow in intensity to scorch or even consume the forest canopy. This characteristic is seen in crown fires, depending on the amount of surface fuel (is high), fuel moisture content (is low), and slope. The speed (is high), the resultant surface flame length (is high), the height to the base of tree crowns (is small), and the density and compactness of tree crowns (is tight).

Crown fires burn forest canopy fuels, including live and dead foliage/branches, tree lichens, and tall shrubs that lie well above the surface. A surface fire usually ignites them. Crown fires can be passive or active.

Passive crown fires involve burning individual trees or small groups of trees (often called torching).

Active crown fires (also called running crown fires) present a solid wall of flame from the surface through the canopy fuel layers, as seen in the photo below. Active crown fires spread through the canopy from one tree crown to the next.

Deforestation

In 2006, forests covered 15 million square miles or 30% of the world's land area. Only 10,877 (thousands of sq. km) forests are present in North America, 1,779 (thousands per sq. km) in Central America, and 9,376 in South America.

The United States has 751 million acres of forest, about one-third of the country's total land area. The U.S. has about the same amount of forested land as it did 100 years ago despite a nearly three-fold increase in population (National Report on Sustainable Forests). This is a striking contrast to many countries where wide-scale deforestation remains a pressing concern. The United States and Canada contain 15.5% of the world's forests.

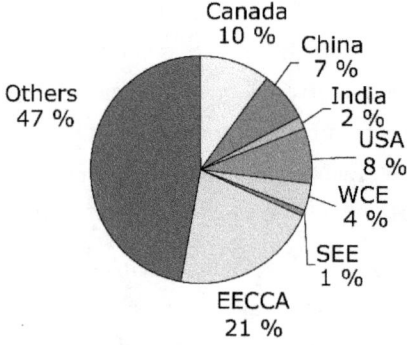

Worldwide forest share by country, 2005

Deforestation is the conversion of forested areas to non-forested areas. Natural factors like forest fires, volcanic eruptions, tsunamis, or glaciation can cause it.

Human-caused deforestation is tree-clearing within an area without replacement.

Human deforestation in rangelands occurs for two primary reasons:

    1) to create pastures and

    2) to convert rangeland to farmland.

These deforested areas become grasslands for grazing livestock, grain fields, mining, petroleum extraction, commercial logging, and urban sprawl.

Many organizations have stated that the primary reason for deforestation is subsistence farming and logging. Biofuel development, such as growing ethanol sugarcane and Jatropha plants for biodiesel, has led to deforestation.

As a result of deforestation, Central America has lost two-thirds of its tropical lowland forests, and South America has lost 70% of its rainforests. Brazil lost a vast portion of its rangelands, and, in some regions, cattle farming has brought about extensive destruction of rangelands. Brazil has declared deforestation a national emergency.

Deforestation results in a degraded environment with reduced biodiversity and fewer ecological services. It threatens species with specialized niches, reduces available habitats for migratory species of birds and butterflies, decreases soil fertility, and allows runoff into aquatic ecosystems.

It causes changes in local climate patterns and increases carbon dioxide released into the air from burning and tree decay. In addition to the direct effects of deforestation, indirect consequences caused by edge effects and habitat fragmentation can occur.

Deforestation alters the hydrologic cycle, increasing or decreasing the amount of water in the soil and groundwater. This affects aquifers' recharge and the atmosphere's moisture.

Deforestation contributes to decreased evaporation, which reduces atmospheric moisture and precipitation, affecting downwind precipitation as water is not recycled to downwind forests but, instead, is lost as runoff and returns directly to the oceans.

A lack of tree and plant roots interferes with soil cohesion and a landscape's ability to capture, retain, and transpire water. This reduces the landscape's capacity to intercept, retain, and transport precipitation. Instead of trapping precipitation, which percolates to groundwater systems, deforested areas become sources of surface water runoff, which moves much faster than subsurface flows. Faster surface water transport can lead to flash flooding and more extensive flooding than with the forest cover.

Destruction of plants results in the degradation of soil. As the soil loses its ability to infiltrate, it becomes unfit for the growth of plants, making the land sterile.

Deforestation of peat forest in Indragiri Hulu, Sumatra, Indonesia

Notes for active learning

Rangelands

Crop cultivation

Rangelands are extensive terrain areas with few trees, where native vegetation is predominantly grass, grass-like plants, forbs, or shrubs. Rangeland environments include tallgrass prairies, shortgrass steppes, grassland, savannas, shrub woodlands, chaparrals, and tundra.

Rangelands are generally unsuited for crop cultivation but are good for grazing by domestic and wild herbivores. The primary difference between rangeland and pasture is management; rangelands tend to have natural vegetation (along with a few introduced plant species) only managed by grazing, while pastures have forage adapted for livestock and managed by seeding, mowing, fertilization, and irrigation.

Rangeland of the Red Desert, Wyoming

The U.S. has about 770 million acres of rangelands; over half of this total is under private ownership. Nearly 43% of these rangelands belong to the federal government, and the rest are held by local and state governments (National Research Council, 1994).

Rangelands are good for grazing and produce various goods and services, including wildlife habitat, water, mineral resources, wood products, and recreation. Though the U.S. government has tried to preserve rangelands, their destruction persists for several reasons.

Overgrazing

Overgrazing is when livestock continuously eats grass without recovery periods, destroying 48% of rangelands.

Rangeland predominantly consists of perennial grasses, which can be renewable when not overexploited. Regular grazing allows the grass time to recover and regrow *via* the metabolic reserves in what remains of its blades and stems.

Overgrazed grass has stem damage and uses energy stored in roots for regrowth. Root dieback causes soil erosion and compaction, impeding regrowth. Overgrazing decreases desirable plants' growth rate, often up to 90%, and in harsh conditions, undesirable weeds thrive.

For example, New Mexico's South Chiflo Management Area has become bare due to overgrazing. The area flourished with lush green grasses and many small trees. Over 30,000 sheep grazed in the 1930s, and numerous bare patches remain because of overgrazing.

Sustainable grazing techniques enrich the soil, increase the growth of desirable plants, decrease invasive weeds, and yield thriving rangelands. However, private ownership makes it difficult for rangeland management to implement necessary measures to reduce overgrazing systematically.

Ranchers over-exploit public rangelands as grazing grounds for livestock. Cattle feeding has gained commercial importance in the United States, and cattle are fed vigorously on and off the rangelands as ranchers increase yield to increase income.

Desertification

Desertification occurs when dry (but productive) land becomes increasingly arid, resulting in the loss of plant life, animal life, and bodies of water. Dryland ecosystems cover half of Earth's land area, and because of the natural scarcity of water, they are especially vulnerable to desertification; 10 to 20% of drylands are already affected.

Dryland covers most of the western half of the continental U.S.; one-third is severely desertified, particularly in Arizona and on the Navajo reservation in New Mexico. In this region, the leading cause of desertification has been overgrazing and water erosion.

The increasing salinity of the Colorado River may lead to the eventual desertification of the surrounding area. The rangelands of Mexico and about 22% of South America have been severely desertified. UNESCO began efforts to prevent desertification in 1962.

Dried soil, Sonora, Mexico

Rangeland management

Rangeland management aims to implement improvement plans to conserve and protect rangelands. Governmental agencies have determined that brush control programs help protect rangelands and benefit the ecosystem.

Rangelands are one of the main ecosystems responsible for storing carbon. Their destruction releases carbon into the atmosphere; increased atmospheric carbon dioxide is a leading cause of climate change.

Management teams are increasing the density of shrubs in and around rangelands as their root systems help water retention and prevent erosion, which may be crucial to rangeland restoration. Officials have asked ranchers to reduce activities that cause soil erosion and decrease soil fertility on rangelands.

United Nations Convention to Combat Desertification (UNCCD) was established in 1994 to reverse the effects of desertification in rangelands.

Federal rangelands

Federal government manages 33 million acres of rangeland. These federal rangelands are managed so well that they provide pure water, produce renewable energy sources, and have become centers of recreation for the public.

In the western United States, livestock graze openly on federal land if the rancher pays fees. There is a set limit on the amount of grazing on federal rangelands; those who exceed it (or do not pay the fee) are subject to a fine or imprisonment.

U.S. government targets 39% of federal rangelands, risking desertification.

Federal Land Policy and Management Act (1976) allocates 50% of collected grazing fees toward rangeland rehabilitation, protection, and improvement. For example, Arizona has been declared a protected area due to its lack of rangelands. With rangeland management, ecosystems may be restored in some areas.

Agriculture

Nutritional requirements of a growing population

The world's population is expanding rapidly, and as a result, there is an ever greater need to devote resources to food security so that every human has the food they need to thrive.

The greatest challenge is producing nutritious food that is accessible to everyone. If estimates are correct, Earth's population will be 9.2 billion by 2050. Food production must increase by 70% to meet global needs. Steps are being taken to resolve this problem.

One method is creating a sustainable food production system, where methods of growing, processing, and disposing food are undertaken to yield the largest return while expending the fewest resources. This can involve using renewable resources like recycled waste for fertilizer.

Basic human nutritional requirements include carbohydrates, proteins, fats, vitamins, minerals, and water.

Carbohydrates include starch and dietary fibers, which provide the calories needed to fuel muscles and the brain. Carbohydrates are in insoluble fiber, whole grain bread, vegetables, fruit skins, etc.

Protein is in meat, fish, milk, eggs, and green vegetables and is broken down into amino acids by the digestive system. Amino acids make hormones and repair muscles, red blood cells, hair, and other tissues.

Fats are saturated or unsaturated and essential for hair, skin, and insulation.

Vitamins help regulate chemical reactions in the human body.

Minerals, such as calcium and magnesium, aid in creating and maintaining healthy bone and tissue structure and participate in countless other bodily processes. The mineral iron helps red blood cells transport oxygen.

Clean water is vital for maintaining life. The human body is 70% water, which helps control body temperature, carries nutrients cells, and eliminates waste.

Types of agriculture

Worldwide agricultural practices include:

Nomadic herding is when people of semi-arid and arid regions practice agriculture by herding animals into pastures. To find more nutritious and less exploited pastures for their animals to graze, those who practice nomadic herding move from place to place.

Livestock ranching (contrasted with nomadic herding) is when areas contain grazing animals.

Shifting cultivation is agriculture in rainy, tropical areas, and slash-and-burn techniques are used to create viable plots for farming. It is in decline due to harmful environmental impacts.

Commercial plantations are labor- and capital-intensive and developed to provide crops for U.S. markets. Major products cultivated are tea, coffee, rubber, bananas, and palm oil.

Sustainable agriculture is farming for crop production with minimal environmental impact. Sustainable agricultural practices utilize 30% less energy than industrialized agriculture.

Industrial agriculture and Green Revolution

Agriculture is a significant industry in the United States. The U.S. has been a leader in seed improvement, as evidenced by the creation of bioplastics and biofuels, which would have been impossible without the groundbreaking work of George Washington Carver.

Members of the U.S. agricultural sector have made significant contributions with the invention of such revolutionary products as John Deere's steel plow, Cyrus McCormick's mechanical reaper, Eli Whitney's cotton gin, and the Fordson tractor.

Cranberry harvest, New Jersey

"Green Revolution" was initially used by former *United States Agency for International Development* (USAID) director William Gaud in 1968 to label the implementation and spread of agricultural technologies.

Green Revolution refers to research and development initiatives from the 1930s through the late 1960s that increased worldwide agricultural production. These initiatives include:

New chemical fertilizers to increase crop yields;

Synthetic herbicides and pesticides to control weeds and insect destruction;

High-yielding varieties of cereal grains and other hybridized seeds;

Expansion of irrigation infrastructure; and

Modernization of management techniques.

Developing nations benefited most from the *Green Revolution*.

The "Father of the Green Revolution," Norman Borlaug (Nobel Peace Prize in 1970), saved over one billion people from starvation.

Genetic engineering

Genetically modified crops are engineered to target agricultural problems. The composition of an organism is altered by inserting, deleting, or changing specific pieces of DNA.

Genetic engineering can increase the productivity of crops by modifying them to prevent diseases; however, some diseases or insects that prey on crops can adapt to the genetic modifications designed to keep them away.

Genetically modified organisms (GMOs) cause concerns regarding safety for human health and broader ecosystems, and many consumer groups are calling for more independent research and stricter regulations for production and labeling.

Agricultural pests

Agricultural pests include various organisms that harm agricultural production by causing crop damage, reduced yields, and less marketable products. Farmers can have significant economic losses due to pest control and crop damage costs.

International Plant Protection Convention and Phytosanitary Measures Worldwide defines a pest as "any species, strain or biotype of plant, animal or pathogen injurious to plants."

Weeds are unwanted plant species that compete with crops for nutrient supply.

Pest insects damage crops, including caterpillars, aphids, beetles, grasshoppers, and flies.

Animals like snails, slugs, rodents, birds, and other vertebrates and invertebrates damage crops by eating seeds, fruit, and stems.

Some pests transmit m*icroorganisms* (e.g., bacteria and fungi) that cause plant diseases. Fungal, bacterial, and viral infections can weaken and kill plants.

Pest control regulates and manages unwanted species, which can cause detrimental impacts on livestock, disturb ecology, or adversely affect the economy.

Types of pesticides

*Pesticide*s are chemicals that control pests by killing or inhibiting growth (– *icide* means *to kill*). Pests have always been a problem for farmers; the quality and yield of crops can be enhanced by limiting the infestation of pests and the diseases they spread.

Pesticides target specific pests:

> *chemical pesticides* (synthetically derived chemicals) or
>
> b*iopesticides* (natural chemicals from plants or animals).

Insecticides kill insects (e.g., DDT, Gammexane, etc.)

Herbicide and *weedicide* prevent weed growth (e.g., Benzipram, Benzadox, etc.)

Miticides kill ticks and mites (e.g., Permethrin, organophosphates, etc.)

Fungicides kill and inhibit the growth of fungi that cause molds, rots, and diseases in plants (e.g., Thiram, Bordeaux mixture, etc.)

Rodenticides kill rats, mice, moles, and gophers (e.g., Aluminum phosphide, etc.)

Pheromones are biologically active chemicals that attract insects or disrupt mating behavior. Chemicals mimicking molecules insects produce to draw them into traps.

Benefits and harms of pesticide use

Pesticide production is a $32 billion industry; more than 5 billion pounds of pesticides a year are applied to crops worldwide, with 1 billion pounds in the U.S. Pesticides increase crop yields and greater profits for farmers (more products with lower labor costs).

However, these relatively short-term benefits have long-term consequences for human and environmental health, indirectly costing the U.S. at least $8 billion annually.

Many pesticides are proven *neurotoxins* and likely *carcinogens* and *endocrine disruptors*. Strong evidence links pesticide exposure to congenital disabilities and impaired fertility. Worldwide, 1 million human poisonings a year, with approximately 20,000 deaths.

Pesticide application, Yuma, Arizona

In the U.S., there are about 67,000 poisonings reported, most non-fatal; estimates indicate that this is considerably less than the total. These poisoning totals do not consider the long-term, low-dose exposure many humans receive by consuming produce treated with pesticides. Pesticides poison thousands of animals; meat, milk, and eggs are contaminated.

Pesticides can destroy natural predators and parasites and create secondary outbreaks of pests whose natural enemies were eliminated (leading to additional pesticide applications).

Pesticide use can create pesticide-resistant pests. Those pests naturally adapted to a control agent reproduce preferentially, changing the genetic composition of the pest population.

Genetic variation means some pests are naturally less vulnerable to specific control agents. They survive attempts at control while the vulnerable population is killed. Survivors reproduce in greater numbers and change the genetic makeup of the pest population by eliminating the susceptible genes from the population.

Pesticide contamination

Pesticides can contaminate groundwater and well water, where chemical residues remain for long periods. By seeping into aquatic ecosystems, pesticides can kill fish, fish eggs, and fish food; pesticides contaminating fish can render them unfit for human consumption. Birds are damaged by pesticide exposure.

DDT (dichlorodiphenyltrichloroethane) nearly eradicated bald eagles in the mid-20th century. While not lethal to adult eagles, DDT interfered with their fertility and calcium metabolism, producing eggs with thin, brittle eggshells unable to withstand their parent's weight.

The agricultural industry depends on bees to pollinate fruit and vegetable crops.

Most insecticides are toxic to bees and negatively impact their populations. It is estimated that 20% of losses of honeybee colonies are from pesticide exposure; some pesticides kill adult bees, while others weaken them or affect bee development.

Neonicotinoids and *coumaphos* target bees' brains and nervous systems, interfering with innate activities and increasing brood mortality.

Integrated pest management

Integrated pest management (IPM) minimizes pest infestation and long-term pest control by utilizing techniques that cause minimal harm to the existing ecosystem.

IPM focuses on identifying and controlling environmental factors for pest infestations.

Humidity, temperature, and waterlogging are essential factors for pest management. If these factors are closely monitored, pest infestations can be controlled with greater success, thereby preventing or reducing crop damage.

The University of California IPM issues statewide guidelines to minimize pest infestations.

*Integrated pest management program*s have five components:

1. Pest identification;
2. Monitoring and assessing pest numbers and damage;
3. Guidelines for when management action is needed;
4. Preventing pest problems; and
5. Using biological, physical, and chemical management tools.

Public awareness and relevant laws

The United States government works together with the *Center for Disease Control* (CDC) to implement effective IPM practices and ensure the safety of both consumers and agricultural workers. The CDC helps protect public well-being by providing information on crop health and potential disease outbreaks within animal populations.

Environmental Protection Agency (EPA) and pest management institutions provide public information and tools for addressing rodents, mites, and other pests, and they closely monitor the deleterious effect these organisms have on humans and the food they consume.

Many pesticides are banned in the U.S. due to health concerns. DDT was a famous harmful pesticide, widely used after World War II both agriculturally and to eradicate malaria.

DDT solution sprayed onto sheep for tick control in Benton County, Oregon, 1948

Concerns over DDT's adverse effects on humans, wildlife, and the environment came to a head in the 1960s, spurred by the publication of Rachel Carson's *Silent Spring*. After countless committees, lawsuits, hearings, and appeals, DDT was banned in 1972. However, the chemical has long-lasting effects, and DDT breakdown products can be in soil, crops, and human bloodstreams even today.

In 1985, the highly toxic insecticide *aldicarb* was responsible for over 2,000 poisonings in the U.S. (including six deaths and two stillbirths) due to contaminated melon. However, it took until 2010 for legislation to phase out aldicarb's production by 2015.

Notes for active learning

Land Conservation

Public and federal lands

Central or local governments hold or own public land in modern nations and states.

Federal lands are those in the United States that the U.S. federal government owns.

According to a survey by the Department of the Interior, out of the U.S.'s 2.27 billion acres of land, 28% is owned by the government.

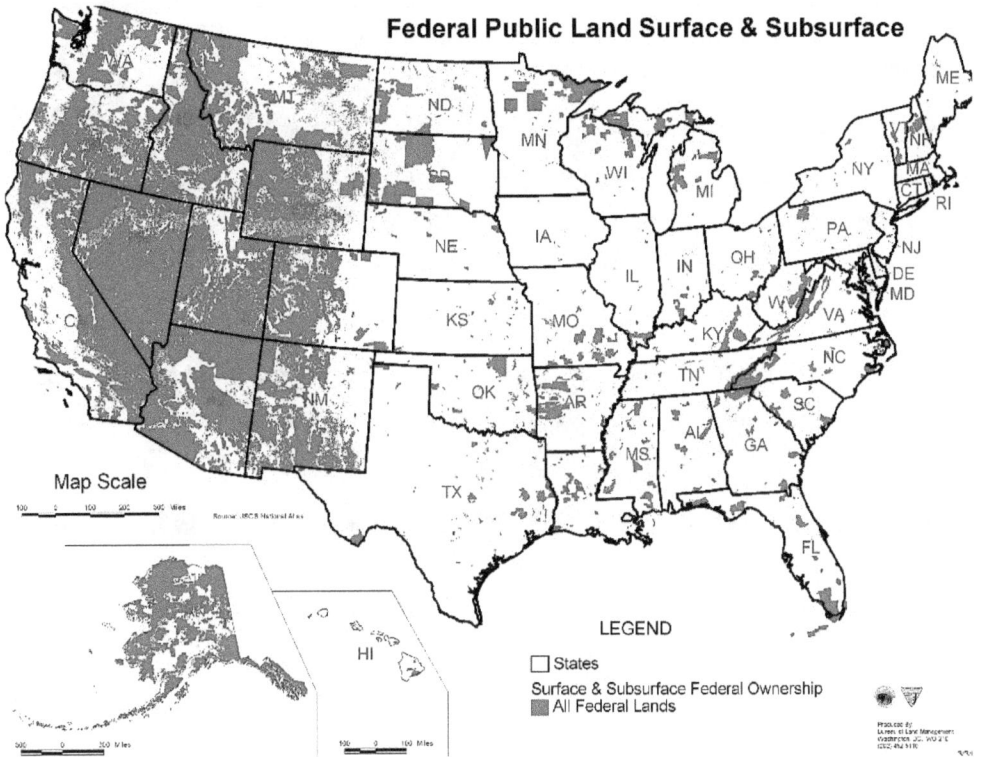

Federal Public Land, surface and subsurface, Bureau of Land Management

Federal Land Policy and Management Act (1976) established the management policy for public and federal lands. They established the concept of *multiple-use* land, defined as "*the management of public lands and their valuable resources so that they are used in such a manner that will best meet the present and future needs of the American people.*"

National Wilderness Preservation System of the U.S. protects and manages wilderness areas to preserve their natural and environmental conditions.

Wilderness is an area where nature exists unimpeded by human interruption.

Seven hundred sixty-two designated wilderness areas total nearly 109 million acres of land.

Wilderness areas include wildlife sanctuaries and refuges, national parks and forests.

As urbanization leads to the expansion of cities, it is crucial to consider the impact this growth has on wilderness areas and the animals and natural resources they contain.

National Parks

The U.S. has 63 protected *National Parks* operated by the *National Park Service* (NPS).

The National Park System has 423 sites; 63 **have "National Park" designations**.

The other sites have National Park System categories (e.g., National Historic Sites, National Monuments, National Seashores, and National Recreation Areas).

National Park Service was created

> *"to conserve the scenery and the natural and historic objects and wildlife therein and to provide for the enjoyment of the same in such manner and by such means as will leave them unimpaired for future generations."*

Yellowstone, the first National Park, was dedicated in 1872 by President Ulysses S. Grant.

Selection criteria for National Parks include natural beauty, unique geological features, unusual ecosystems, and recreational opportunities.

Approximately 51.9 million acres are protected by National Parks.

Twenty-seven states have National Parks, as do the territories of American Samoa and the United States Virgin Islands. California has the most (nine), followed by Alaska (eight), Utah (five) and Colorado (four). The four largest National Parks are in Alaska.

The biggest National Park is Wrangell-St–Elias. At over thirteen million acres, Elias is larger than each of the nine smallest states.

Hot Springs in Arkansas is the smallest National Park, less than 6,000 acres.

The most visited National Park is the *Great Smoky Mountains* in North Carolina and Tennessee, with over 12 million visitors annually.

Alaska's remote *Gates of the Arctic* is the least visited National Park, with 9,455 visitors. For comparison, the Grand Canyon is visited by 4.7 million people annually.

The International Union for Conservation of Nature's (IUCN) World Commission on Protected Areas (WCPA) has defined a *National Park* as a *Category II* protected area. According to IUCN, 6,555 national parks worldwide meet these criteria.

Chapter 5: Land & Water Use

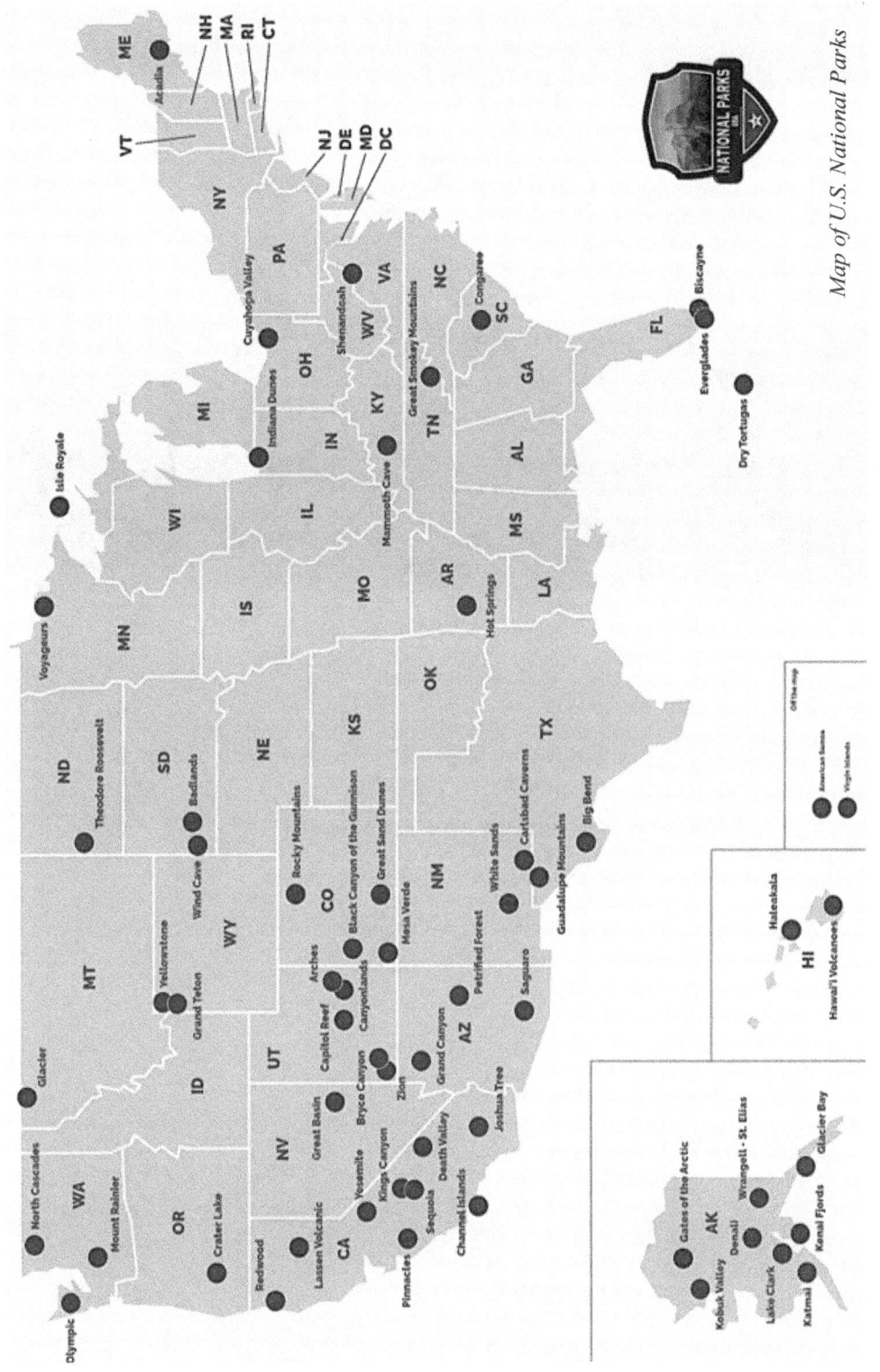

Map of U.S. National Parks

Mount Saint Elias, Wrangell-St. Elias National Park and Preserve, Alaska

Land conservation and preservation

Land conservation is when steps are taken to protect natural landscapes and return developed, disturbed areas to their natural state. Today, many people value their land's legacy values and natural beauty and often see it as crucial as financial concerns.

Understanding conservation options is essential in deciding the future of land use.

Land conservation often results in positive financial outcomes with income or tax savings.

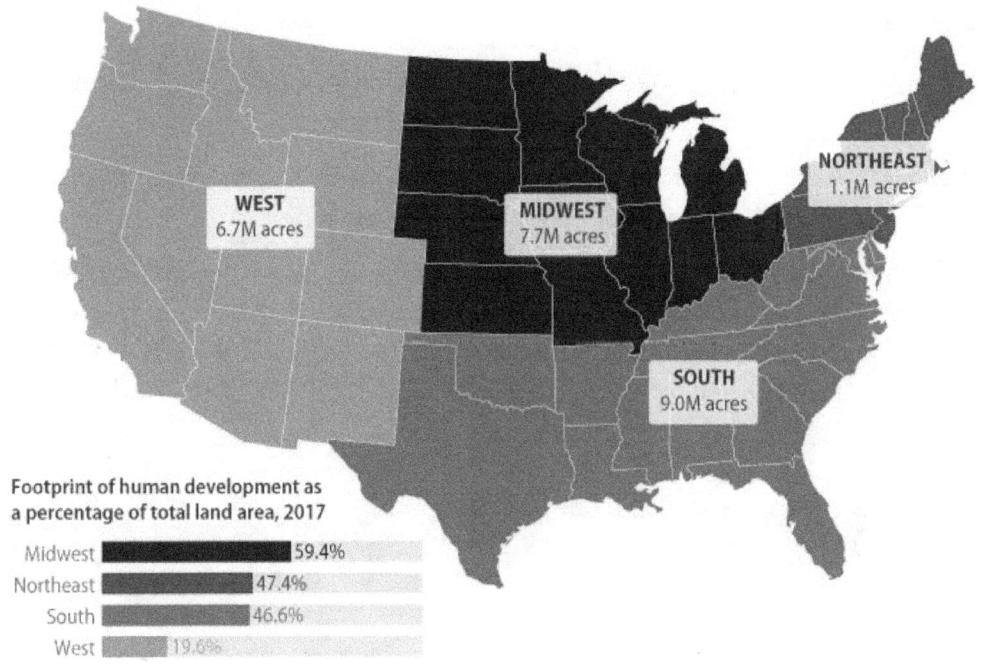

Natural area loss by region (2001-2017), Wilderness Society

Preservation is a process by which land and its natural resources are deemed protected from human intervention to maintain the land's pristine form. Preservation allows humans to access the land and enjoy its natural beauty and inspiration.

John Muir (1838-1914) was a land preservationist, a Scottish immigrant who founded the *Sierra Club* in 1892. He admired California's *Yosemite Valley* and wanted to protect the land and not plunder its natural resources so people could enjoy its pristine beauty. Muir's influence is evident through the continuing influence of his *Sierra Club* and the *Muir Woods National Monument*, a land preserve in Northern California with an ancient redwood forest.

Wildlife refuges are official territories created by the government or held by private owners designed to protect endangered animals.

Hunting, predation, and competition are restricted in protected areas.

Lake Merritt Wildlife Refuge in Oakland, California, was the first government-owned refuge in the Americas, established by then-mayor Samuel Merritt in 1870.

Today, some national and international organizations have taken responsibility for protecting the existing system of nonprofit wildlife refuges. The American Sanctuary Association plays an incredibly vital role in protecting wildlife animals by providing accreditation to facilities that follow high standards to ensure that the animals in their charge are well cared for.

Restoration

Restoration is the process of returning ecosystems and communities to their natural condition. However, to restore an ecosystem, the indigenous environment must be known.

Returning an area to its original state can be achieved by restoring waterways, reintroducing native plants and animals, and removing human-built infrastructure.

An ecosystem restoration project in Florida is the Everglades, which has rapidly dried over the years due to irrigation and flood management infrastructures. The project involves building dams and water control features to return the Everglades to its original habitat. If successful, it will allow wildlife to return and may increase ecotourism.

Land Use

Land use categories

Land use was defined by Albert Guttenberg in *A Multiple Land Use Classification System*, an article published in the *Journal of the American Planning Association* (1959):

> Land use is characterized by arrangements, activities, and inputs to produce, change, or maintain a specific land cover.

Land use includes near-surface water, and land area is often used for multiple objectives.

Land use modifies or converts natural environments into human-built environments.

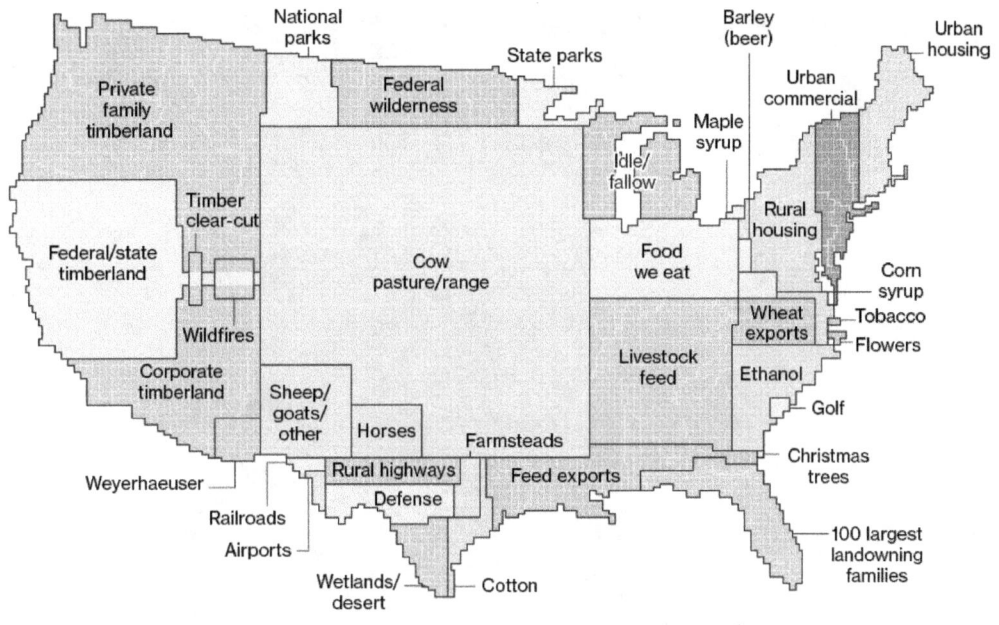

Major uses of land in each state

Half of the habitable land is used for agriculture, with 37% for forests, 11% as shrubs and grasslands, 1% as freshwater coverage, and the remaining 1% – a much smaller share is built-up urban areas, which include cities, towns, villages, roads, and human infrastructure.

Sustainable land use is a design reform movement that combines creating and enhancing land with the need to build high-performance infrastructures and buildings.

Components of sustainable land use implemented by cities and towns include open green space, walkability and connectivity, and sustainable water sources.

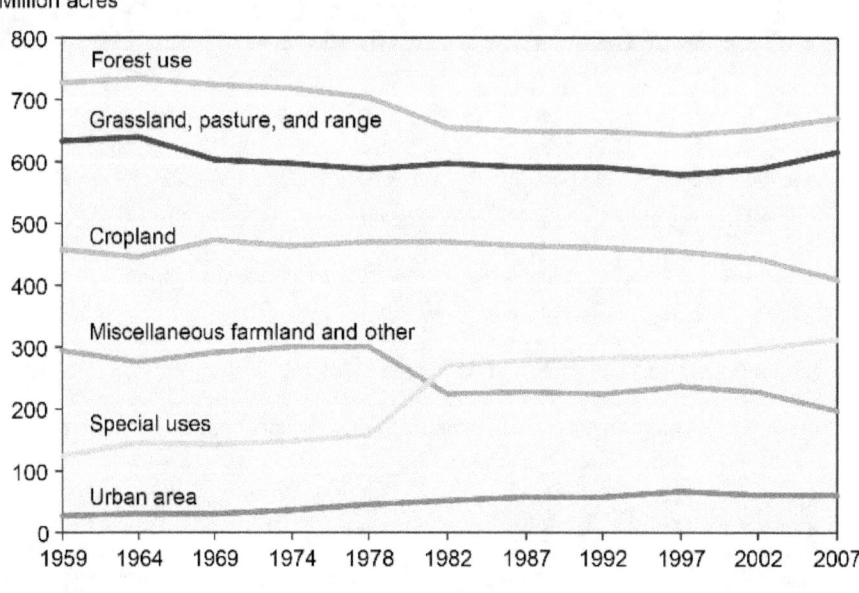

U.S. land uses, 1959-2007

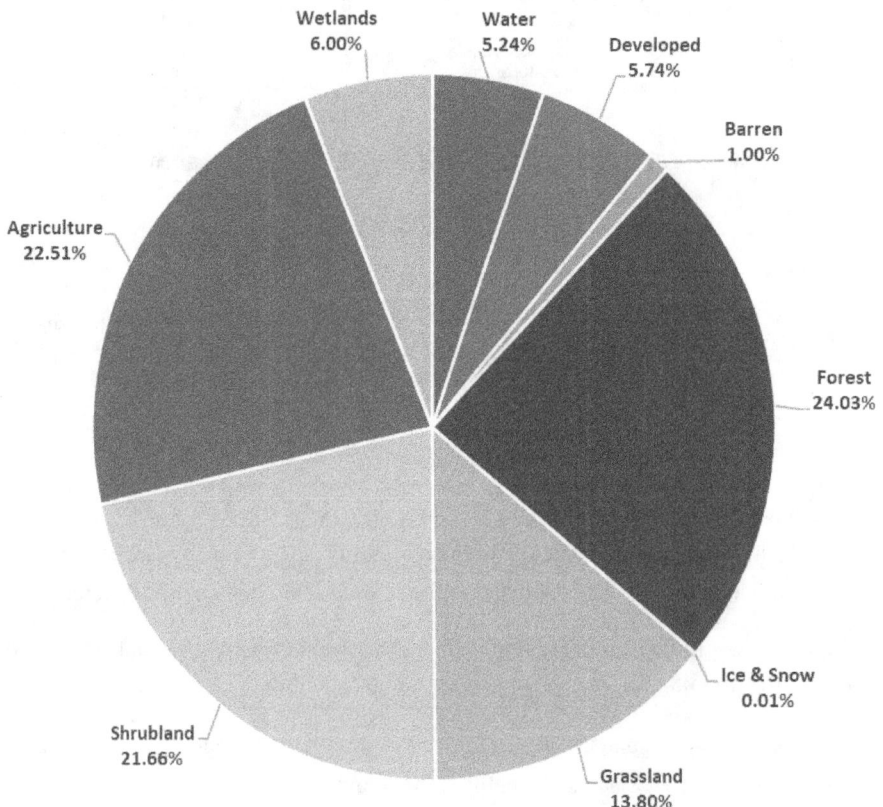

National Land Use for 2016, Multi-Resolution Characteristics Consortium (2019)

Urban land development

The increase in the proportion of people living in urban areas is a global phenomenon. Many cities struggle to cope with the challenges of urbanization, including increased poverty, slum growth, climate change, and resource scarcity.

Urban land use planning uses sustainable development principles, which require well-managed, well-planned initiatives.

Urban land development focuses on various issues, such as reducing the negative impacts of human-built environments on climate and natural resources, protecting built environments from unpredictable and volatile conditions, sensible use of energy resources, and making urban real estate more attractive, investment-wise.

Planned development of urban areas shows the incredible changes stemming from novel ideas and emergent technology, which can produce sustainable mega-infrastructures. Urban planning guides ensure the orderly development of local and satellite communication, which can communicate in and out of urban areas.

Urban planning encompasses architecture, landscape, civil structures, and public administration to achieve strategic, policy, and sustainability goals.

Urban development has become professionalized over the years. The Town and Country Planning Association was founded in 1899; it has grown along with the growth of urban centers.

Heat islands

Heat islands are created when hot air layers (or *temperature domes*) form over urban or industrial areas. Temperature domes are typically warmer by 5-7 °C than surrounding air, trapping air pollutants.

Heat islands are recognizable in the early mornings and late nights but disappear during the days because of the increased atmospheric temperature. Heat islands result from human activities through urbanization (e.g., converting natural land surfaces to asphalt or concrete). Unlike asphalt or concrete, native vegetation and soil absorb radiation.

Vegetation produces shade, intercepts radiation, and releases moisture into the atmosphere through evapotranspiration, which causes a cooling effect. Human-made surfaces lack this ability with water-resistant and non-reflective surfaces, causing surfaces to absorb radiation and release it as heat.

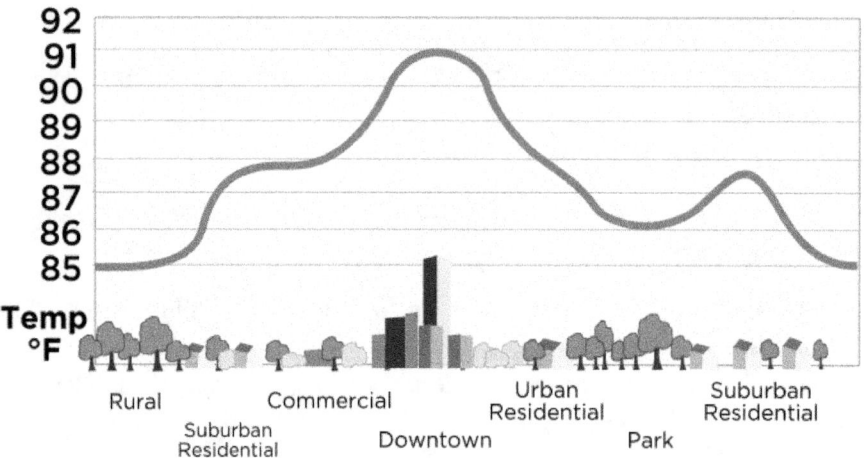

Urban heat island profile

Heat from energy usage (e.g., air conditioning systems, industrial processes, and refrigeration) contributes to temperature dome formation. Buildings obstruct the normal flow of air and lead to increased temperatures.

Temperature inversion is when cold air is trapped under a layer of warm air. This is an inversion as the average temperature decreases with height, "inverted" to an increase in temperature with height. This inversion impedes the convective overturning of air currents.

Air pollutants, typically dispersed over vast areas, become trapped below the inversion and affect weather patterns.

Suburban sprawl

University College London's Center for Advanced Spatial Analysis defines *suburban sprawl* (or *urban sprawl*) as "*uncoordinated growth; an indication of the expansion of community without concern for its consequences*."

It is the expansion of human populations from central urban areas into low-density, usually car-dependent bedroom communities, with commuters a large portion of the population.

Often, this leads to single-use development, where commercial, residential, and industrial areas are separated from one another to the extent that walking, public transit, and bicycles become impractical, requiring residents to own cars.

Urbanization

Urbanization is the gradual migration of people from rural to urban areas throughout history.

Components include geography, sociology, urban planning, economics, and public health.

Urbanization occurs at specific rates in countries. For example, the U.S. and the United Kingdom are more urbanized than India, Swaziland, and Niger.

Suburban sprawl, Rio Rancho, New Mexico

Notes for active learning

Transportation Infrastructure

Transportation

Transportation is the movement of people, animals, and goods using air, road, rail, or cable.

Transportation infrastructure consists of fixed installations that provide logistical support for transport. Examples include roads, railways, airways, waterways, canals, pipelines, and terminals such as airports, railway stations, and seaports.

Transport is essential to modern society; however, transportation consumes a lot of energy. Sustainable transportation is essential to humans' continued progress.

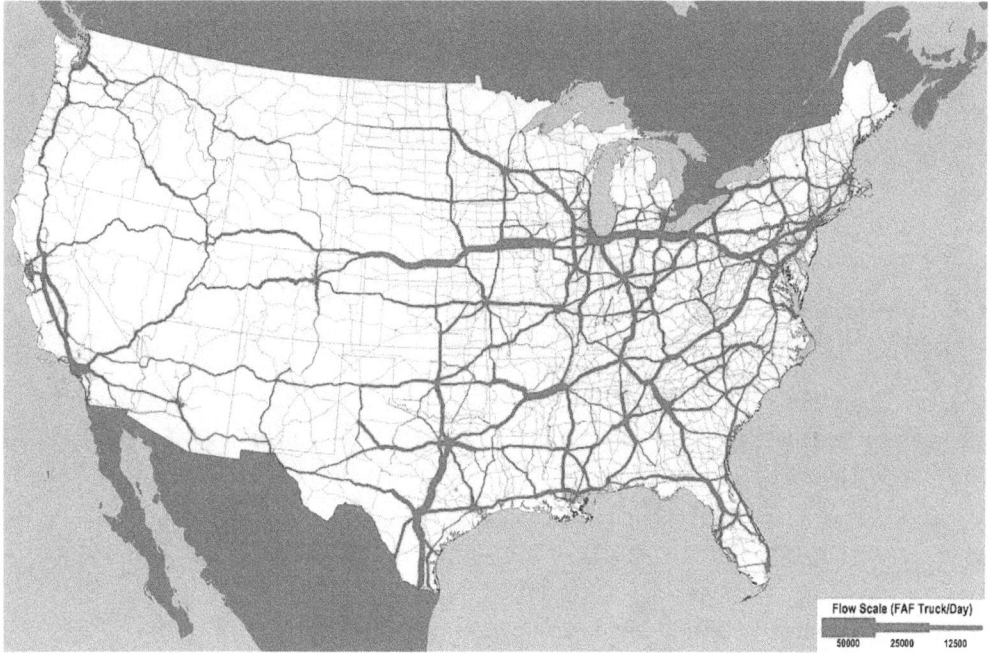

Freight routes with flow scales, U.S. Dept. of Transportation, 2017

Federal highway system

Federal-Aid Highway Act (1956), signed into law by President Eisenhower, created a 41,000-mile *"national system of interstate and defense highways"* to provide safe and rapid transcontinental travel and eliminate unsafe roads, traffic jams, and inefficient routes.

The federal government paid 90% of the expressway construction costs.

Federal-Aid Highway Act declared that expressways should be at least four lanes wide and designed for high-speed driving.

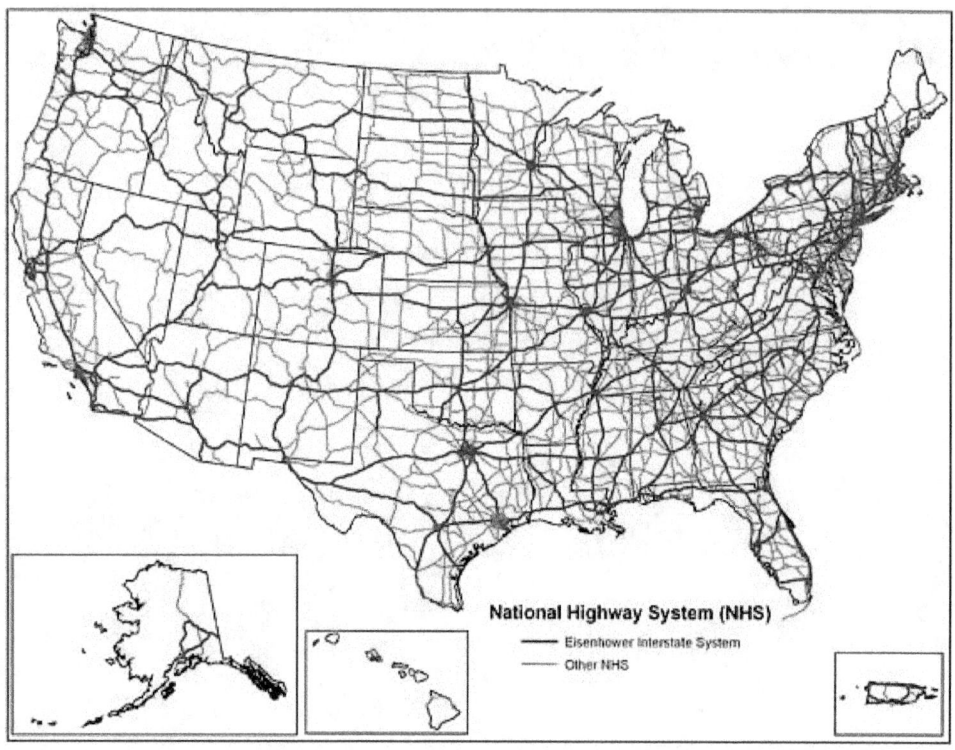

National Highway System expanded the Eisenhower Interstate System (1956)

Waterways

A *waterway* is a navigable body of water that can accommodate the passage of vessels, such as boats, ships, and other watercrafts. Waterways include rivers, canals, channels, lakes, and other water bodies wide and deep enough to accommodate vessels.

Waterways can be either natural or artificial.

Canals and channels are waterways controlling the flow of water.

Canals are manufactured waterways (e.g., Panama Canal, Suez Canal).

Channels (or straits) are natural waterways between landmasses (e.g., the *English Channel* and *Strait of Gibraltar*).

Navigation canals parallel a river and share part of discharge and drainage basins.

Water supply canals convey water for humans, industries, hydropower, and agriculture.

Canals are increasingly important, leading to new canals and expansion of existing ones.

Panama Canal connects the Pacific to the Atlantic Ocean in Panama.

Suez Canal connects the Mediterranean to the Red Sea through Egypt.

Chapter 5: Land & Water Use

USS America aircraft carrier passes through the Suez Canal, Egypt, 1981

Roadless areas

Access roads into wilderness habitats are convenient for industry and recreational activities (e.g., fishing, hunting, sightseeing) but may lead to adverse effects such as erosion, pollution, and biodiversity loss.

Building roads can lead to the further development of "splinter roads," causing fragmentation and environmental decay in ecologically delicate areas.

U.S. Forest Service, after three years of analysis, passed the *Forest Service Roadless Area Conservation Rule* (Roadless Rule, 2001), which preserves 58.5 million acres of pristine National Forests and Grasslands (one-third of NFS lands) from logging and road construction.

It advocated constructing roads to avoid harming the surrounding wilderness and wildlife. These areas provide critical habitat for more than 1,600 threatened, endangered, or sensitive plants and animal species.

Notes for active learning

Mineral Resources and Mining

Mineral resources

Minerals are naturally occurring elements or compounds, inorganic solids (except liquid mercury and a few organic minerals), defined by chemical composition and crystal structure. *Inorganic* means that an organism does not make the substance. For example, wood and pearls are made by organisms; thus, they are not minerals.

Minerals are made of chemical elements.

Elements are substances that have only one kind of atom.

By weight, 99.5% of minerals are formed from only 12 natural elements.

Minerals are solid, naturally occurring inorganic substances in the Earth's crust. They have unique chemical composition and crystal structure. *Solid* means it is not a liquid or a gas at standard temperature and pressure.

Minerals are naturally occurring inorganic elements (or compounds) with an orderly internal structure and characteristic chemical composition, crystal form, and physical properties.

Minerals may be metallic (e.g., gold) or non-metallic (e.g., talc).

Metals are elementary crystalline solids crystalline and naturally occur in minerals (e.g., gold, silver, and copper). Steel is not a mineral because it is an alloy produced by people.

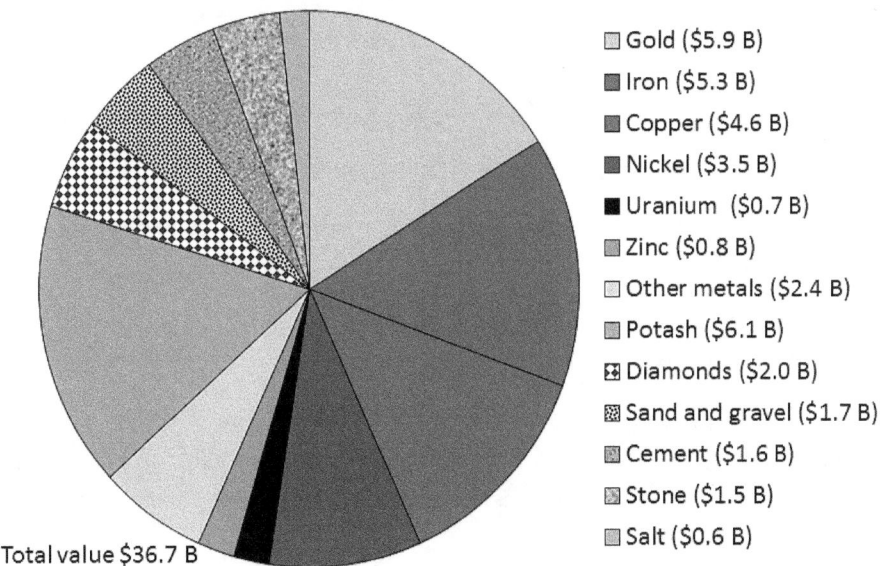

Canadian mining sector revenue (2013 Canadian dollars)

Mineral formation

Earth contains various minerals used for construction, electronics, jewelry, and fertilizers.

Some minerals are formed from saltwater when they evaporate from the Earth's surface and by the mixtures of water seeping through rocks far below the surface.

Many types of minerals form when molten rock mixtures cool by two methods:

> from *magma and lava* and
>
> through *chemical processes*.

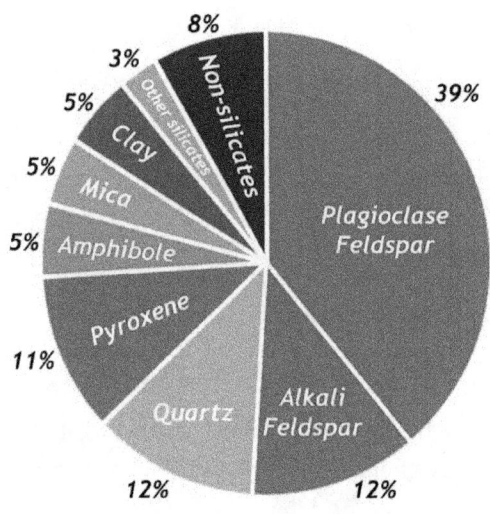

Minerals in Earth's crust

Many places beneath the Earth's surface have temperatures high enough to melt rock.

Magma is melted rock, which can reach temperatures above 1,000 °C.

Magma may not remain inside Earth; sometimes, it moves up to the surface through volcanoes, releasing *lava* (i.e., expelled magma).

Molten rock cools and produces minerals (e.g., quartz and feldspar). Magma cools slower than expelled lava, producing minerals with larger crystals than lava.

Most water contains dissolved minerals that are too small to be seen by the unaided eye (e.g., without microscopes) and difficult to remove even with filtration (e.g., carbon absorption); specialized methods (e.g., reverse osmosis) are used to remove mineral deposits from water.

Mineral formation from saltwater is a natural method of extracting minerals.

For example, *Mono Lake* in California and Utah's *Great Salt Lake* contain enough salt water to precipitate minerals from the water through evaporation. When the water evaporates, it leaves behind solid particles of minerals that do not evaporate.

Some minerals remain in the water. If the amount of minerals in the water is high, the minerals join to form mineral solids that remain underwater. In *Mono Lake*, the water has high calcium, so calcite deposits cause limestone "tufa" towers.

When magma flows, it heats nearby water, which moves through cracks inside Earth. Hot water dissolves more solid particles than cold water, making it saltier when it reacts with the rocks around it. This salty hot water flows through *veins* (or cracks) in rocks; solid particles are deposited into cracks in crystalline form.

For example, dolomite, galena, fluorite, and gypsum form this way.

Mining of minerals

Mining extracts intrinsically valuable minerals or geologically valuable materials from Earth.

Mining has been a part of the United States since the colonial era; however, drastic changes in the types of minerals mined and mining conditions have ensued. The first extensive U.S. mining was in North Carolina in 1799, the "Carolina Gold Rush."

United States mining occurs in Arizona, Colorado, Minnesota, Alaska, California, Michigan, and Nevada. The U.S. actively mines coal, gold, silver, uranium, and copper.

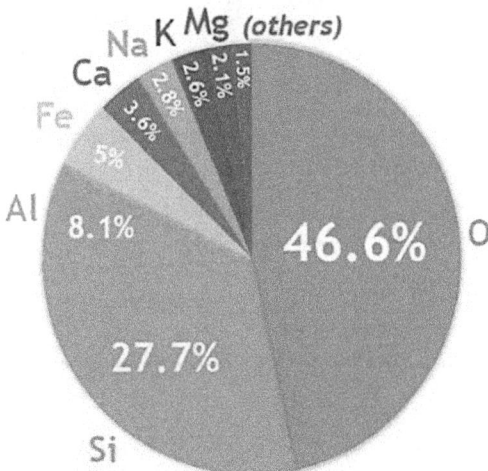

Elements in Earth's crust

Two primary mineral extraction methods are *underground mining* and *surface mining*.

Underground mining

Soft rock (e.g., coal) and *hard rock* (e.g., copper, lead) are minerals deep inside Earth.

Various methods are used to extract underground minerals depending on the minerals mined.

External factors (e.g., geological, economic, safety) affect the mining methods.

Hard rock mining blasts minerals from their deposits and dislodges waste rock. Ventilation is vital in hard rock mining. Toxic gases produced by blasting may become trapped in the mine and can prove harmful to miners or the structural integrity of the mine.

Many of these gases are highly combustible, and explosions are a risk.

It is essential that the walls and the opening of the underground mine be structurally sound so that sudden collapses that can trap, injure, or kill miners do not occur. After cost-effectively accessed minerals are removed from a mine, they are sealed off and intentionally collapsed or left to collapse spontaneously.

Longwall and room-and-pillar mining methods are most widely used in soft mining.

Automation and ventilation are provided for both methods. Room-and-pillar is a system in which the mined material is extracted across a horizontal plane, creating arrays of rooms and pillars. Pillars of untouched material support the roof overburden, and open areas (or rooms) are extracted. Automated equipment consists of a coal shearer mounted on a conveyor underneath a self-advancing hydraulic roof support.

Longwall method mines coal in large, single slices.

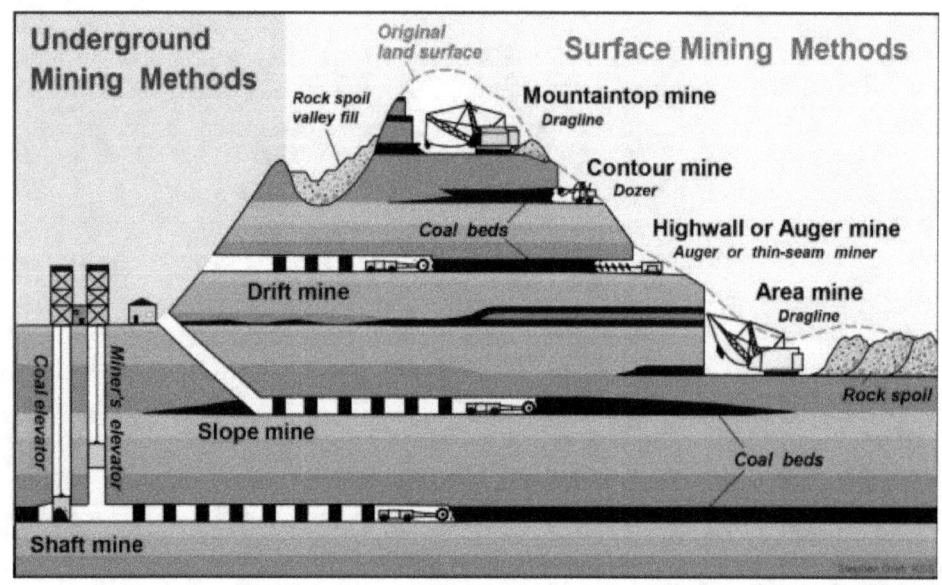

Mining methods

Surface mining

Surface mining extracts minerals on or near the exterior of the Earth by removing the topsoil layer (or overburden) to recover minerals.

Three types of *surface mining* are:

open-pit mining, strip mining, and *mountaintop removal.*

Surface mining is less dangerous than underground mining; however, it consumes vast land. It requires removing a massive amount of the top layer of earth and leads to erosion, dust pollution, and habitat loss.

The mining process can cause heavy metals to dissolve and seep into groundwater and surface water, contaminating drinking water sources and disrupting marine habitats.

Open-pit mining, Sunrise Dam Gold Mine, Australia

Depletion of global mineral reserves

Minerals are depleted when they become rare, expensive, and cannot be feasibly used.

The amount of mineral remaining in the ground and the difficulty of extraction will affect a mineral's price; as the price rises, another commodity will take the mineral's place.

For example, indium is a crucial mineral for manufacturing transparent conductive components in solar panels and LCD screens. As of 2025, the price of indium is four times higher than in 2000.

Extraction has remained constant at around 600 tons annually, even though developing technologies have increased demand.

U.S. Geological Survey states, "*Indium's recent price volatility and various supply concerns associated with the metal have accelerated the development of ITO (indium tin oxide) substitutes. Antimony tin oxide coatings, deposited by an ink-jetting process, have been developed as an alternative to ITO.*"

In general, the price of most metals has increased by about 400% since 1994, which suggests that demand is outpacing supply. The demand for minerals mainly comes from China, which now consumes over half of the world's supply of various metals.

Rare earth elements (REEs) comprise seventeen metallic elements, including fifteen of the lanthanide series (lanthanum through lutetium) and scandium and yttrium. REEs are desired for their unique magnetic, phosphorescent, and catalytic properties, making them critical for various technologies.

Demand for REEs is expected to double or triple in the coming years due to technological advancements and the shift towards clean energy. The use of magnets in electric vehicles, wind turbines, and other technologies is a major driver for REE demand.

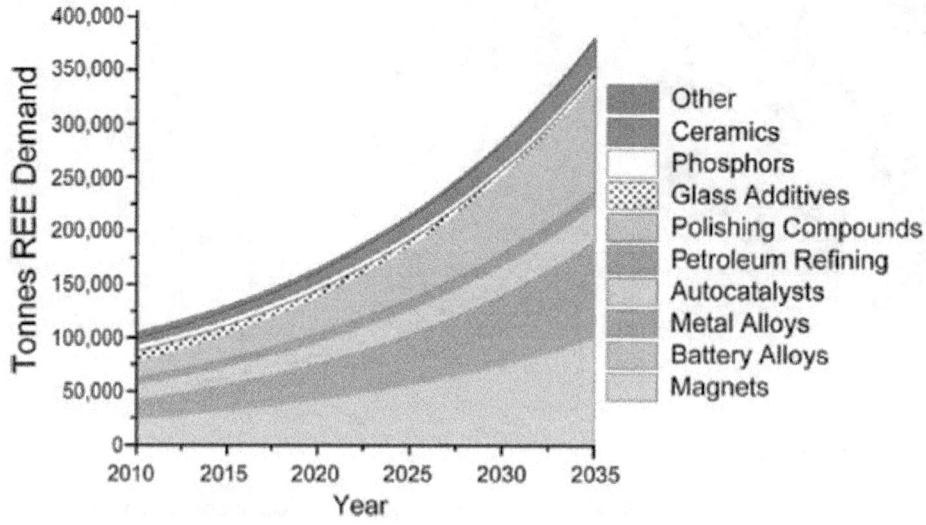

Projected total REE demand accounting for historical growth

The depletion of global mineral reserves is looming due to the decreasing availability of finite mineral resources. It is driven by unsustainable mining, overconsumption, and evergrowing demand for new technologies. While there have been many discoveries of new mineral reserves, there is a growing concern that the extraction rate of some critical minerals, including rare earth elements, outpaces new supplies.

Mining disasters

According to historical data on mining disasters, mining accidents claimed thousands of lives a year from 1880 to 1910, with over 3,200 deaths occurring in 1907 alone.

Monongah Mining Disaster (1907) was the worst mining accident in U.S. history when 362 people were killed in underground mines in an explosion in Monongah, West Virginia.

Farmington Mine disaster (5:30 a.m. on Nov 20, 1968) was an explosion at the Consol No. 9 coal mine north of Farmington and Mannington, West Virginia. The explosion was felt 12 miles away in Fairmont. At the time, 99 miners were inside.

In the 1950s, the death rate decreased to 450; in the 1990s, there were about 90 deaths yearly. However, that does not consider the thousands of people injured in mining accidents between 1991 and 1999.

A mining accident occurred in West Virginia in the Upper Big Branch mine (2010), where 29 miners died from an underground explosion.

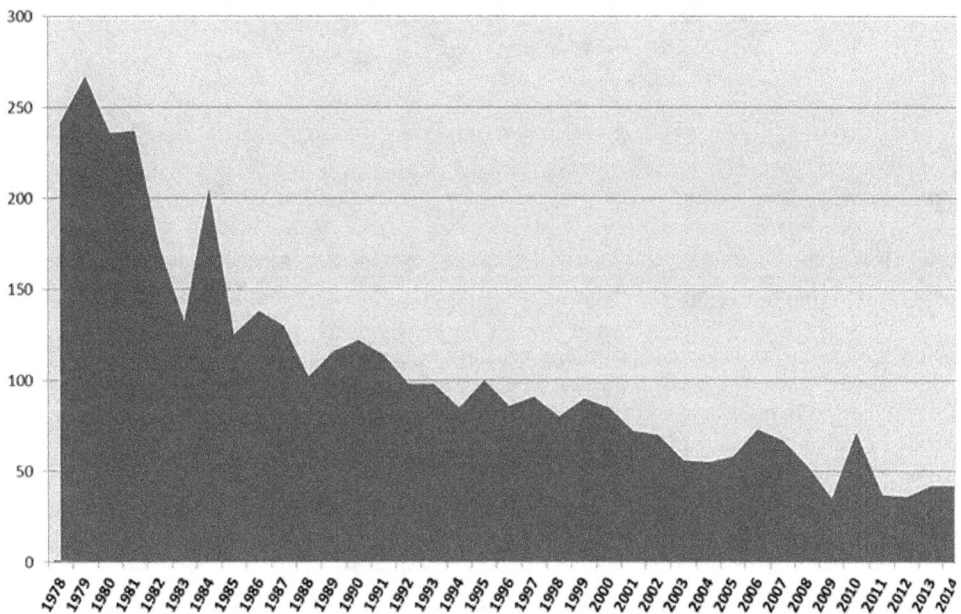

U.S. Mining Fatalities; U.S. Department of Labor, Mine Safety and Health Administration

Farmington Mine disaster, West Virginia (1968)

Relevant laws and treaties

Mining law in the United States is based on English common law, and the landowner owns raw materials to unlimited depth.

States retain rights to phosphate, nitrate, potassium salts, asphalt, coal, oil shale, and sulfur.

Department of the Interior has the rights to sand and gravel.

General Mining Act (1872) is a federal law authorizing and governing prospecting and mining for economically valuable minerals (e.g., gold, platinum, and silver) on federal public lands.

This law organized the informal system of acquiring and protecting mining claims on public land formed by prospectors in California and Nevada from the late 1840s to the 1860s during California's Gold Rush. It opened public domain federal land for prospecting and mining.

Federal Coal Mine Health and Safety Acts (1969 and 1977) were passed by the U.S. government, requiring multiple annual mine inspections.

U.S. Bureau of Mines (1910) was established for the safety of miners. It investigates accidents, advises the mining industry on best safety practices, and teaches courses in accident prevention for miners. Hence, they know how to react in the case of a mishap.

Hardrock Mining and Reclamation Act (2007) would have 1) permanently ended issuing patents for mining claims, 2) imposed a royalty of 4% of gross revenues on existing mining extractions from unpatented mining claims, and 3) imposed an 8% royalty on new mining operations. 70% of the royalty was allocated to a cleanup fund for abandoned mining operations and 30% to affected communities.

Opponents of the *Hardrock Mining and Reclamation Act* stated that U.S. mining operations have the highest effective worldwide tax rate, and further restrictions and royalties would force more domestic mining industry out of the country. The bill was not passed in the 110th Congress, and a 2009 version remained unsigned at the end of the 111th Congress.

International Labor Organizations governing mining in the U.S. are the Medical Examination of Young Persons Convention (or Underground Work) of 1965 and the Safety and Health in Mines Convention of 1995.

Notes or active learning

Chapter 5: Land & Water Use

Fishing

Commercial fishing

Fishing involves catching fish and other aquatic animals, such as echinoderms, crustaceans, mollusks, and cephalopods. Fishing does not refer to catching aquatic mammals, such as whales. Fishing can be done for commercial or recreational purposes.

Alaskan Fishermen, 1927

Commercial fishing sells their catches through a previously agreed-upon marketplace contract or to consumers. In recreational fishing, fish are caught for personal consumption or sport and are not sold in markets. Fishing industries are proliferating worldwide, leading to the growth of imports and exports.

There are various fish species in different regions of the world. The U.S. has an established position in the fishery industry, as it has abundant fishing and wildlife opportunities, with millions earning their livelihood from fishing.

U.S. Fish and Wildlife Services oversees and manages the *National Wildlife Refuge System* to protect wildlife and aquatic animals.

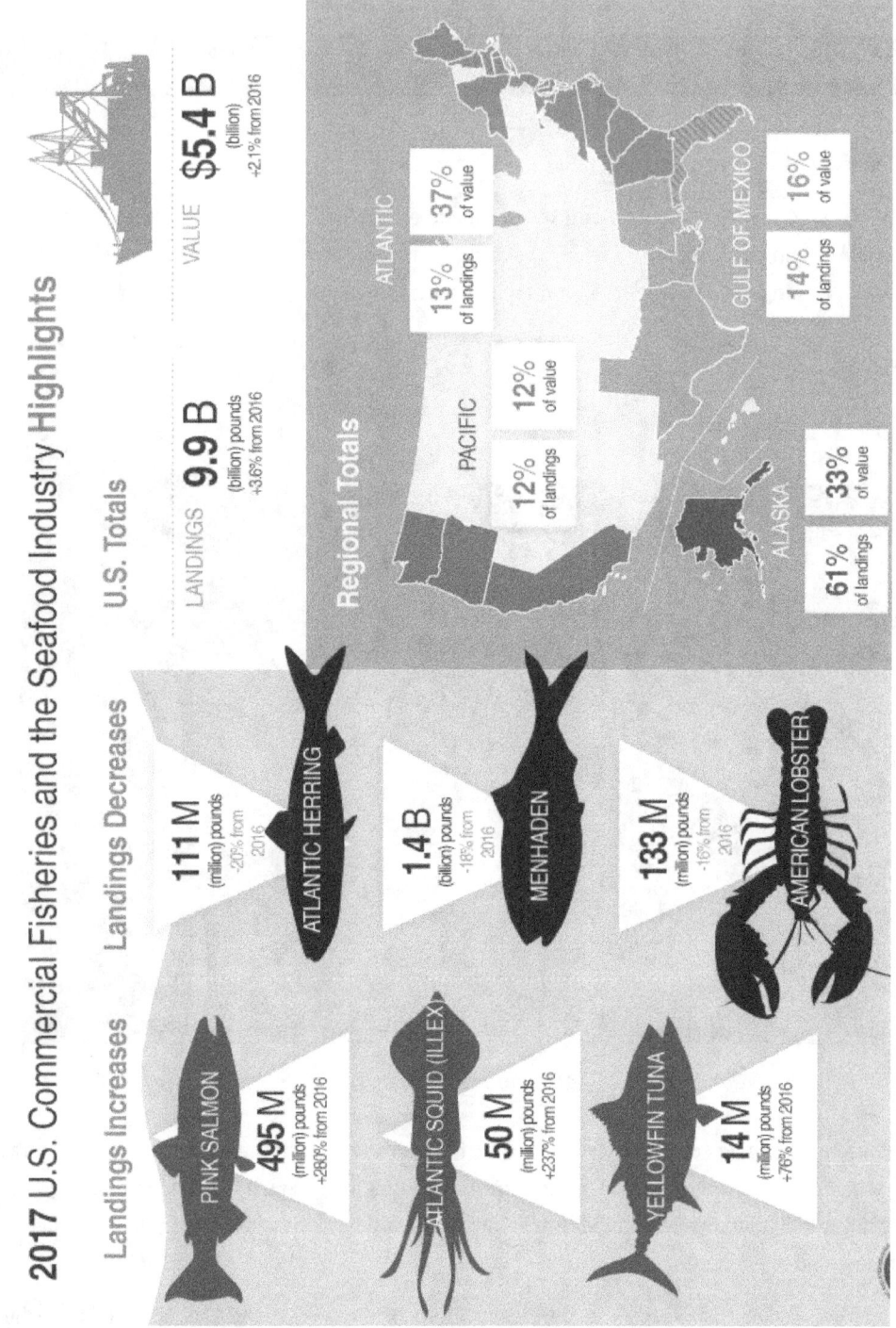

Commercial fisheries and seafood industry, U.S. 2017, NOAA Fisheries

Fishing methods

There are many methods of large and small-scale commercial fishing.

Pelagic trawling drags a cone-shaped net through the water to catch fish in their feeding area. It does not substantially impact the environment if practiced responsibly. However, deleterious environmental effects are evident in New Zealand and Australia.

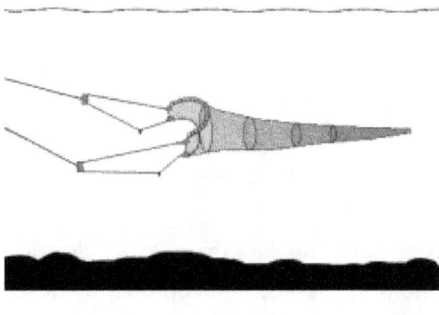

Pelagic trawling

Bottom trawling targets fish living and feeding on or near the seabed with *demersal trawling*, as nets are dragged through the *demersal zone* (i.e., water column near the seabed). Species caught include cod, haddock, sole, and whiting.

Otter trawling uses a wide-mouthed net dragged through the water with the net mouth by the boat's movement. This motion disorients fish which swim into the net's path. Once entangled, even attempting to swim, fish collect in the net's cod end, pinned by the force of the water.

Nets have mesh holes of assorted sizes, depending on the fish targeted. Often, the mesh is wide enough to allow immature, smaller fish to escape for sustainable harvests.

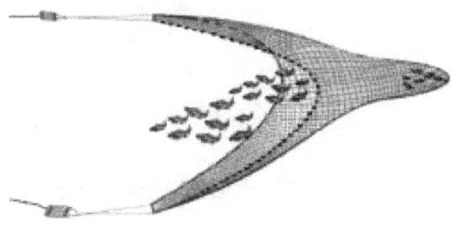

Otter trawling

Beam trawling catches fish burrowed under the seabed. A chain on the front of the net, which is lowered from a beam, strikes the ocean floor to scare fish from the safety of the seabed. When they emerge, they are swept up by the net.

Beam trawling is highly destructive to aquatic organisms and deleterious to the ecosystem by destroying swaths of the seabed on which many species depend. Each market pound of fish caught by beam trawling sacrifices sixteen pounds of marine life.

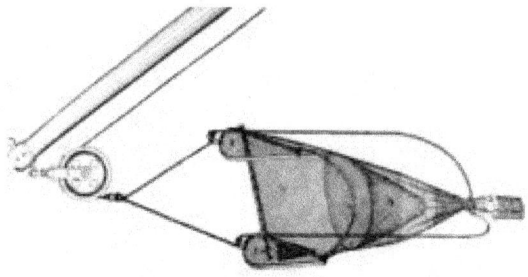

Beam trawling

Pulse trawling is a version of beam trawling that uses an electric current passed through the nets to stun fish liberated from the seabed and collected by nets. Fishermen claim it is less damaging than traditional beam trawling, but massive quantities of dead fish and devastation to the marine environment occur.

Pair trawling uses two boats pulling massive nets (e.g., the largest fits 10 Boeing 747 jets). This method is highly profitable, with a high fish yield ratio to cost expenditure. However, pair trawling's damaging environmental effects resulted in it being banned in many places worldwide. However, pair trawling is not banned in the United States.

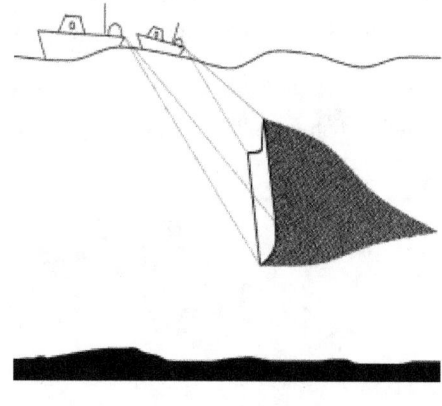

Pair trawling

Purse seining targets fish traveling in schools (e.g., herring, mackerel, sardines, and tuna). Purse seining uses large open-bottom nets pulled across the water. When target fish are within the net's radius, the bottom is closed to trap the fish, and the nets are pulled onboard.

Purse seining is not environmentally harmful if done sustainably; however, the scale is often unsustainable. Nets are thousands of square meters with hundreds of fish tons captured.

Purse seining often receives media attention because dolphin deaths may result.

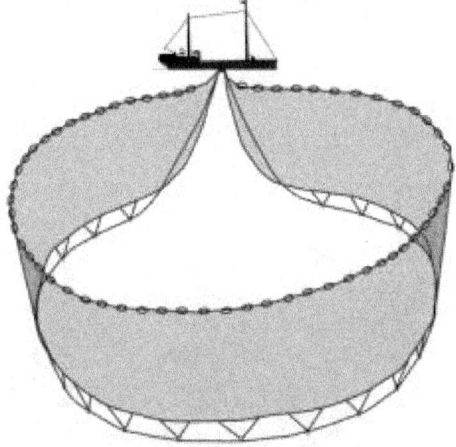

Purse seining

Dredging is used to catch shellfish living on the seabed. Nets are dragged behind a boat on the seafloor, with *teeth* (or water jets) on the front of the nets. The teeth dislodge shellfish from the seabed and force them into nets.

Dredging is highly destructive; one boat pass may destroy entire shellfish beds.

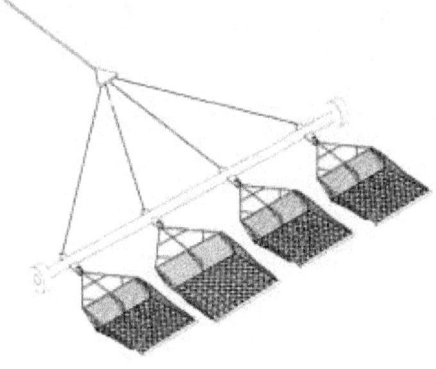

Dredging

Long-line fishing is used commercially to catch species such as marlin, tuna, and swordfish. This method uses a long line with thousands of baited hooks drifting behind the boat.

Long-line fishing is considered sustainable because it does not destroy seabed ecosystems.

However, endangered species from both the sea and air are often caught in long lines.

Controlling what species get caught is difficult, as some boats use lines 30 miles long.

Pots are used to catch lobsters and crabs. An open-mouth cage (i.e., pot) is filled with bait and lowered to the seabed. After a set period, the mouth closes, trapping organisms inside the pot.

This method is considered sustainable, as it targets the desired species. Further, if undesired species get trapped in the pot, they can be thrown back once the pot is taken to the surface. Due to the low-impact nature, intended and unintended species arrive alive on the ship's deck.

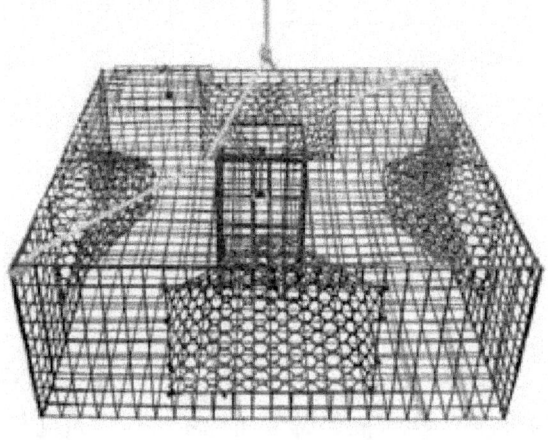

Pots

Overfishing

When the level of fishing taking place in an area is greater than the level of sustainable reproduction of the species in that area, a phenomenon known as *overfishing*.

Due to the competition in the fishing sector, there is a drive to catch the most fish in the shortest period; this results in overfishing, which is not conducive to a healthy ecosystem. It has a negative ecological impact on sea creatures and an adverse socioeconomic effect on local communities where such practices occur.

WWF has made several efforts to protect fish and aquatic life. It has created several regulations and laws to maintain balance. This helps wildlife and promotes sustainable fishing practices, which help fishermen. Due to its efforts, several national and international efforts have been made to control this activity.

In 2014, there was a declining rate of fishing in the U.S.; since 1997, fishing has been at an all-time low (NOAA). The U.S. is making respectable efforts to decrease the overfishing rate. It has made strides to restrict illegal fishing and overfishing. These efforts have helped safeguard the marine environment worldwide.

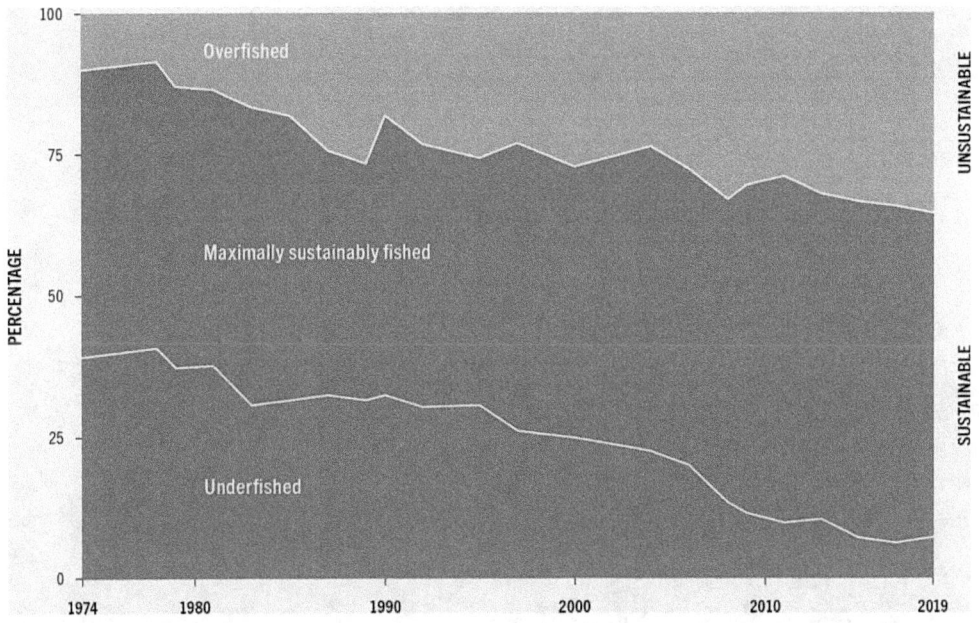

Fishery Resources Status, Food and Agriculture Organization

Aquaculture

Aquaculture is farming fish in segregated (or protected) areas and includes activities required for the proper growth of marine life, rearing, breeding, and harvesting of marine plants and animals in water bodies (oceans, ponds, lakes, rivers).

Aquaculture gives extra care to marine life so that they can flourish. Aquaculture components include farming of ornamental fish, crustaceans, mollusks, bait fish, sport fish, food fish, eggs, algae, and sea vegetables.

Marine aquaculture produces oysters, mussels, salmon, shrimp, cod, and barramundi.

Freshwater aquaculture produces Tilapia, trout, catfish, and bass.

The U.S. participates in both varieties of aquaculture.

Aquaculture in Luoyuan Bay, Fuzhou, China

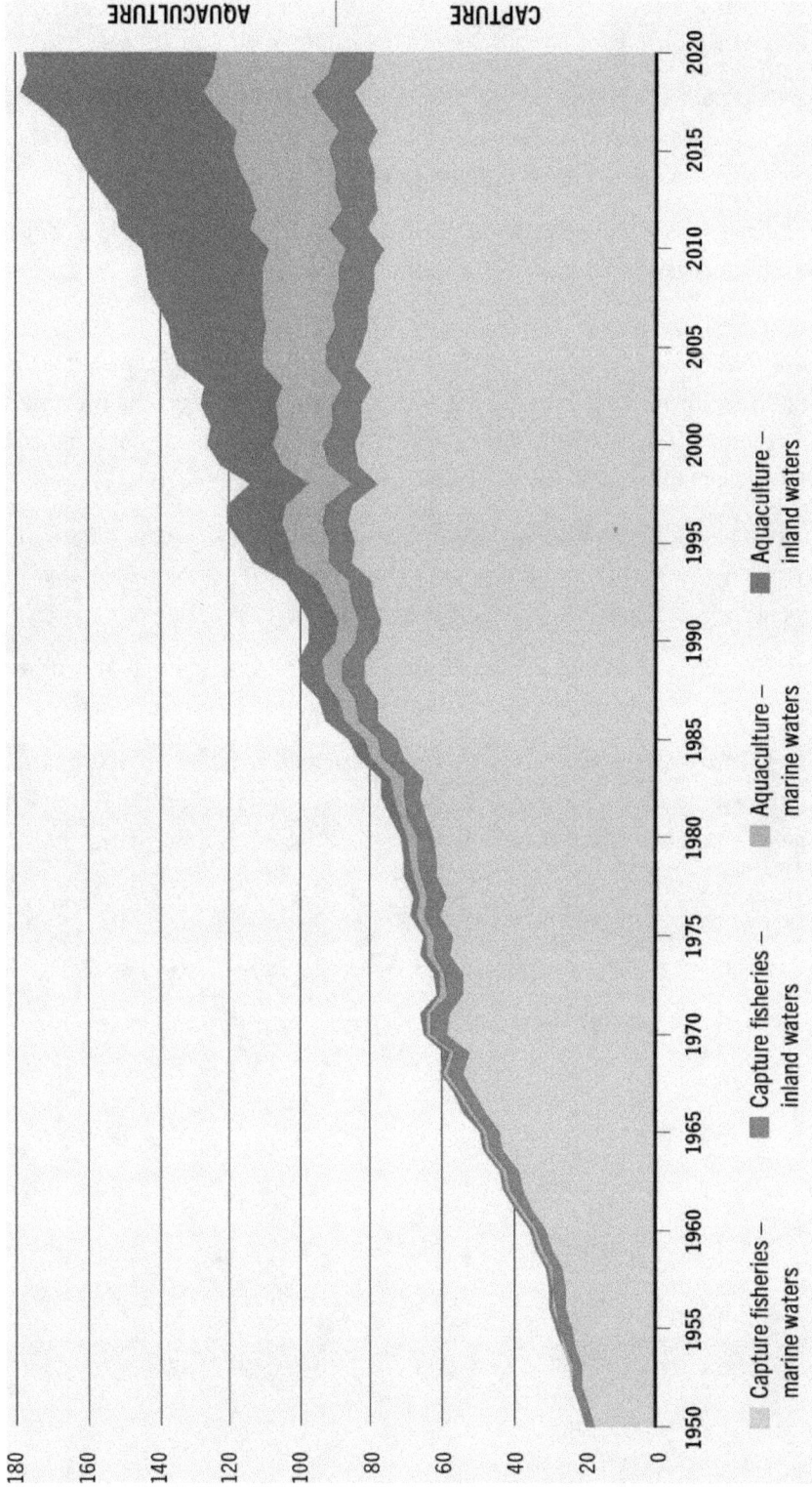

Global total capture vs. aquaculture harvest in millions of tons (Food and Agriculture Organization, UN)

Relevant laws and treaties

The basis for commercial fishing laws and policies in the United States is established on a federal level and enforced by the *U.S. Fish and Wildlife Service*. The federal government establishes how the nation interacts with other fishing nations.

Individual states dictate laws and policies within their waters, which extend three miles offshore. States must, however, abide by the minimum guidelines set forth by federal regulations.

Magnuson-Stevens Fishery Conservation and Management Act (1976) is the paramount federal law for fisheries management. It defined federal waters, restricting foreign countries from fishing near U.S. shores. It established eight regional fishery councils comprising state and federal representatives and fishing industry members.

Councils are under the jurisdiction of the federal *National Oceanic and Atmospheric Administration* (NOAA), the agency responsible for regulation and enforcement. Each council develops fishery management plans for its specific area.

Sustainable Fisheries Act (1996 amendment) conserved fish stocks, targeted overfished populations, bycatch, and habitats, and assisted traditional small-scale fishermen.

Magnuson-Stevens Fishery Conservation and Management Reauthorization Act (2006) took significant conservation measures to end overfishing with catch shares and sector allocation policies and requested increased global cooperation.

Global Economics

Global economy rankings

Global economy includes the annual international exchange of goods and services worldwide with countries ranked by nominal Gross Domestic Product (GDP). Gross Domestic Product is the primary indicator of economic performance. Rankings include financial and statistical estimates by institutions. Estimates are at market or governmental exchange rates.

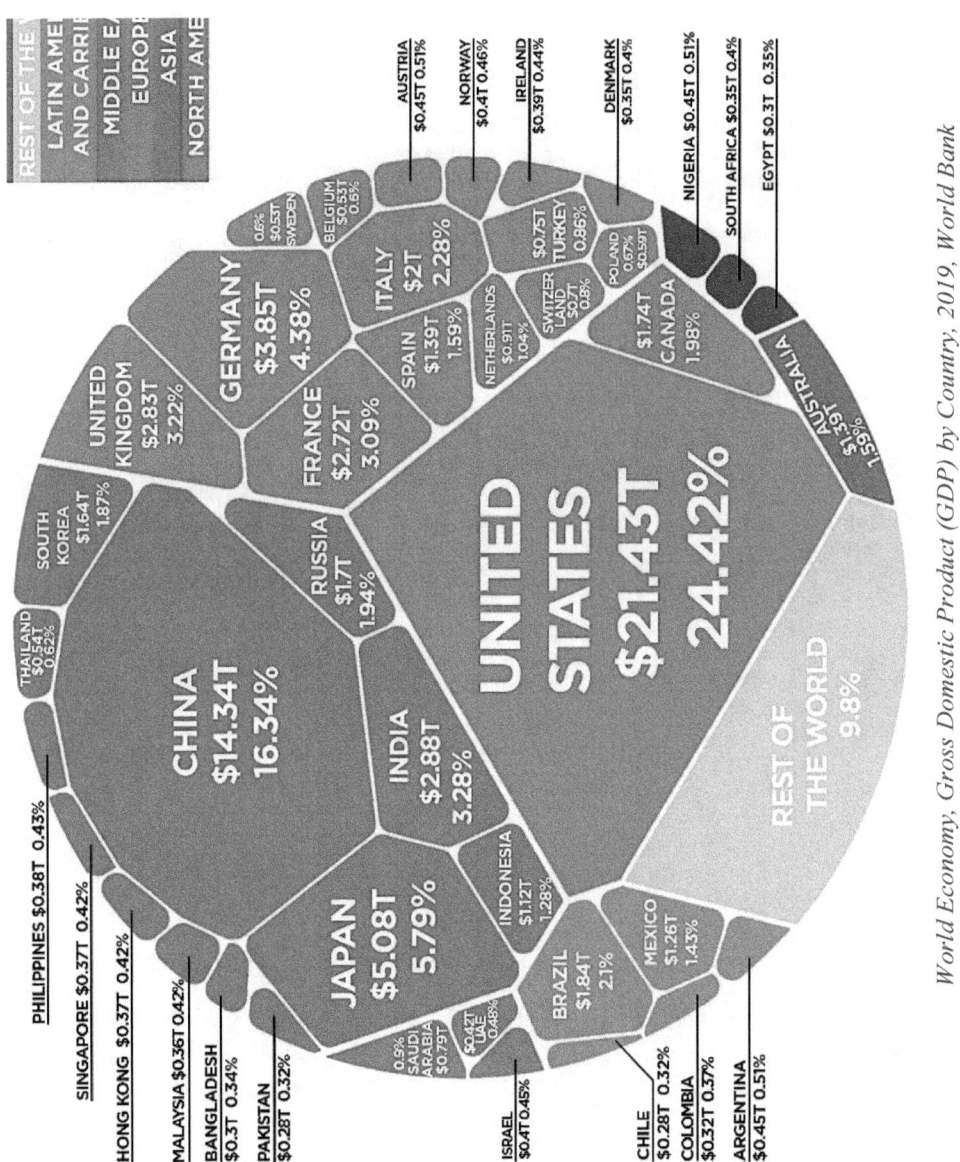

World Economy, Gross Domestic Product (GDP) by Country, 2019, World Bank

Nominal GDP does not include the country's cost of living and can vary widely based on exchange rate fluctuations of a country's currency. Fluctuations may change a country's ranking with imperceivable differences in the standard of living.

Advanced economies of countries worldwide contribute to the dynamics of world economies. The world economy is typically valued in monetary terms. Even trade of illicit services or goods generates economic growth rates in the global economy.

Within this sector, market valuations in local currency are converted to a single monetary unit using purchasing power, the method used for evaluating worldwide economic activity regarding U.S. dollars or euros.

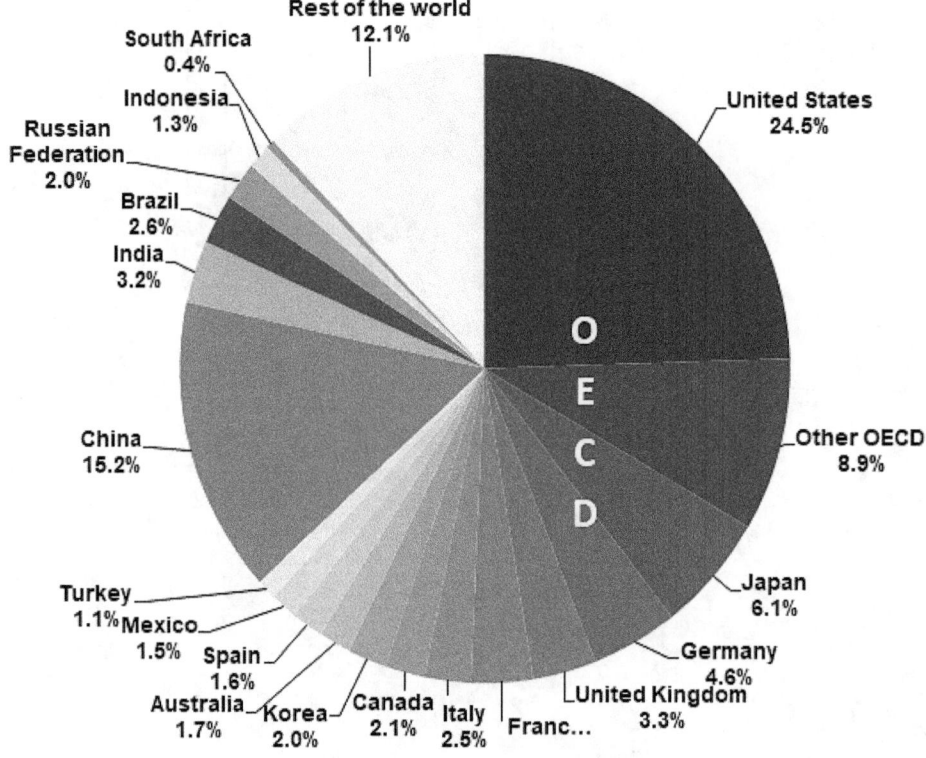

Gross Domestic Product (GDP) expressed in Purchasing Power Parities, OECD (2022)

Organization for Economic Cooperation and Development

The Organization for Economic Co-operation and Development (OECD) is a forum where the governments of 37 democracies with market-based economies collaborate to develop policy standards to promote sustainable economic growth.

OECD Countries and Year of Accession

Country	Year	Country	Year
Australia	1971	Austria	1961
Belgium	1961	Canada	1961
Chile	2010	Colombia	2020
Costa Rica	2021	Czech Republic	1995
Denmark	1961	Estonia	2010
Finland	1969	France	1961
Germany	1961	Greece	1961
Hungary	1996	Iceland	1961
Ireland	1961	Israel	2010
Italy	1962	Japan	1964
Korea	1996	Latvia	2016
Lithuania	2018	Luxembourg	1961
Mexico	1994	Netherlands	1961
New Zealand	1973	Norway	1961
Poland	1996	Portugal	1961
Slovak Republic	2000	Slovenia	2010
Spain	1961	Sweden	1961
Switzerland	1961	Türkiye	1961
United Kingdom	1961	United States	1961

Global economy metrics

The global economy is inexorably tied to natural resources. For example, in 2023, the annual oceanic fisheries revenue was $5.9 billion. However, catch rates continuously decline, with 75% of fish stocks worldwide depleted beyond sustainable limits.

Plant-derived pharmaceuticals are valued at $500 billion in industrialized countries. Forty to fifty percent of medicines are derived from natural products. Including oncology and anti-infection medicines, the total is over seventy percent.

Natural asset use and consumption are increasing with the global economy. Species and habitat loss are greater than the replenishment rate.

Gulf Coast with widespread flooding by Hurricane Katrina

Markets fail to capture most ecosystem service values. Existing prices only reflect value related to provisioning services like food, fuel, or water; prices may be distorted. Even these services often bypass markets when community-managed shared resources.

Ecosystem services generally do not reflect market value because they are *public goods* (i.e., *common goods*), often open access with no limits on consumption.

Private and public decisions affecting biodiversity rarely consider benefits beyond the immediate geographical area. Long-term benefits (e.g., ecological preservation) are ignored.

Systematic undervaluation of ecosystem services reflects implementation, monitoring, and enforcement of policy failures manifesting biodiversity crises.

Organization for Economic Co-operation and Development (OECD) is a forum where the governments of 38 democracies with market-based economies collaborate to develop policy standards to promote sustainable economic growth.

Globalization

Integration and assimilation

Globalization is the international integration and assimilation of products, ideas, and culture.

Globalization is an international network of economic systems.

Globalization predates the European Renaissance and the discovery of North America. Economic scholars placed it within the twentieth century and achieved scale in the late nineteenth century.

Globalization (as a term) emerged in the 1970s by scholars, journalists, editors, and librarians.

International Monetary Fund (IMF) designates four components of globalization:

    1) trade and transactions,

    2) capital and investments,

    3) migration, and

    4) knowledge diffusion.

Environmental impacts

Globalization uses a variety of actions such as building dams, linking roads between countries, technological innovations (e.g., communications), transporting goods and people, and automation.

Globalization involves resource utilization, leading to climate change, the greenhouse effect, water pollution, and ozone layer depletion.

Early Modern migration involved the forced transatlantic movement of 9-12 million enslaved people during the early to mid-19th century. This movement of people was comparable to the regional Arabic slave trade and European migration to North America during the Early Modern Period.

Most nations react to globalization. However, the United States, as the hegemon of the global economy, controls and regulates the pace and character of globalization.

Globalization has dramatically affected the United States and its citizens.

Globalization has spread American influence worldwide and opened commercial markets, allowing American companies to export and import more goods and services.

World Bank

World Bank is a financial organization with 189 member countries and a global partnership fighting poverty worldwide through sustainable solutions. The World Bank provides loans as purchasing capital to developing and underdeveloped countries for economic development.

World Bank is a *United Nations Development Group* with two institutions:

International Bank for Reconstruction and Development (IBRD) and

International Development Association (IDA).

World Bank is charged with easing poverty by promoting foreign investment and increasing international trade globally. It was created concurrently with the *International Monetary Fund* (IMF) at the Bretton Woods Conference (1944). Many nations attended, but the U.S. and the United Kingdom had the most influence and were the most powerful countries.

World Bank headquarters are in Washington, D.C., with traditionally American presidents.

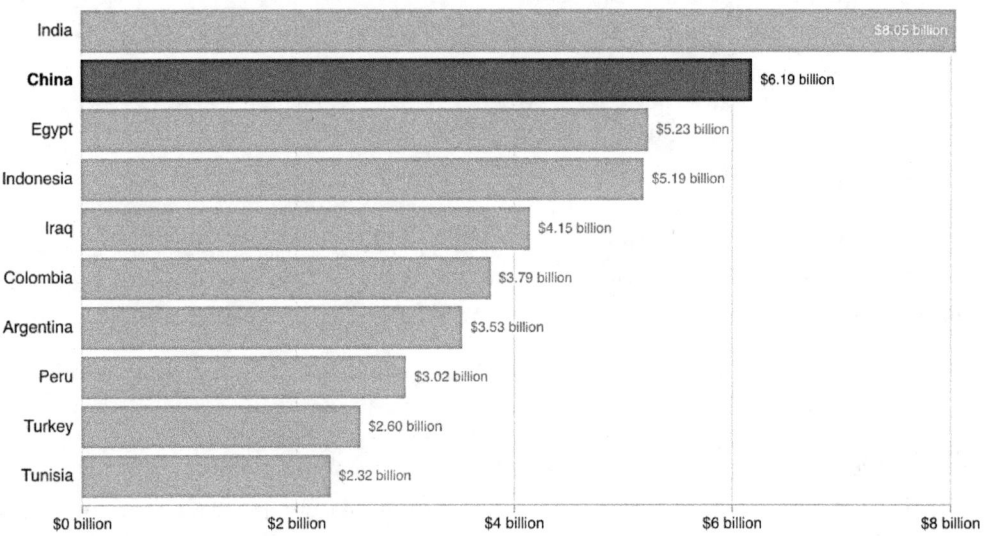

World Bank funding by countries, 2016-2018

France was the first country to receive a loan from the World Bank. Because the World Bank did not have sufficient funds initially, France received half the amount requested and with strict conditions. U.S. State Department asked the French government to remove communist members. Within hours of compliance, the World Bank approved France's loan.

World Bank faced competition when European countries received loans from other sources. Then, the World Bank focused on non-European countries.

From 1968 to 1980, the World Bank targeted the essential needs of developing countries. The size and number of loans increased since the focus shifted from improving infrastructure to small-scale ventures (e.g., social services).

In 1989, in response to harsh criticism from many, the Bank offered loans to environmental groups and non-government organizations (NGOs) in compensation for the effects of its prior development policies.

Per the Montreal Protocols, the World Bank worked to control the use of 95% of ozone-depleting chemicals by 2015. The Bank modified policies to protect the environment while facilitating development.

For example, in 1991, to protect against deforestation, the bank did not finance commercial logging or infrastructure projects that harm the environment.

To promote global public goods, the World Bank tries to control communicable diseases, such as malaria, by delivering vaccines to several parts of the world. In 2000, the Bank announced a "war on AIDS," in 2011, it joined the *Stop Tuberculosis Partnership*.

International Monetary Fund

The International Monetary Fund (IMF) is a major financial agency of the United Nations and an international financial institution funded by 190 member countries. It has headquarters in Washington, D.C. It is the global lender of last resort to national governments and a leading supporter of exchange-rate stability.

IMF's mission "fosters global monetary cooperation, secures financial stability, facilitates international trade, promotes high employment and sustainable economic growth, and reduces poverty around the world."

Established at the Bretton Woods Conference (December 27, 1945), primarily from the ideas of economists Harry White and John Maynard Keynes, it started with 29 member countries to reconstruct the international monetary system after World War II.

The International Monetary Fund is central to managing a country's balance of payments and international financial crises. Through a quota system, countries contribute funds to a pool from which countries can borrow if they experience balance of payments problems. As of 2016, the fund had US $667 billion.

Shared obligations and *Tragedy of the Commons*

Tragedy of the commons was initially coined in 1833 by English economist William Forster Lloyd to describe when individuals act in self-interests without regard for group welfare, eroding shared resources.

For example, Lloyd used cows grazing on a common where farmers graze one cow. By grazing one cow on the common, farmers lose nothing of the resource (i.e., grass consumed if the farmers put one cow). Each farmer gains a competitive advantage by acquiring more cows and grazing them on the commons. It is a rational act because adding one cow is not unsustainable. However, a problem arises if each farmer, acting from self-interest, adds cows to the commons. Collectively, their actions are unsustainable for the pasture.

Tragedy of the commons applies to the environment. No individual is responsible for much environmental degradation. However, actions of multiple individuals (over time and space) amalgamate and hurt the environment (e.g., soil erosion, ozone depletion, water pollution).

In 1968, Garrett Hardin published *The Tragedy of the Commons* in venerable *Science*. Hardin analyzed issues that were technically hard to solve. He focused on *"a change only in the techniques of the natural sciences, demanding little or nothing in the way of change in human values or notions of morality."*

Hardin highlighted the increased human population, the massive use of Earth's natural resources, and the welfare state. He proposed that if individuals considered their welfare alone and not society, the number of children each family had would decrease because parents realized they could not provide their children with ample resources without society's help.

Tragedy of the Commons applies to environmental problems like sustainability. The word "commons" connotes natural resources (e.g., atmosphere, oceans, rivers, fish stocks, energy) and shared resources not governmentally controlled or regulated.

"*Tragedy of the Commons*" denotes these resources' terrible and devastating plight due to human use and consumption without regard for future impact. The commons dilemma applies to resource issues (e.g., water, forests, fish, and non-renewable fuels). Excessive mining of coal and other minerals threatens the ecological balance of Earth.

Conditions provoking the tragedy of the commons include the overfishing and destruction of the Grand Banks, the destruction of salmon runs on rivers that have been dammed (e.g., the Columbia River in the Northwest United States), the devastation of the sturgeon fishery in modern Russia and the limited water available in arid regions.

Relevant laws and treaties

Everyone shares Earth's resources. Therefore, the foremost duty of world leaders is to regulate the usage of natural resources by implementing laws and treaties to protect the environment.

With a world population of over seven billion people, air and water pollution, resource allocation, habitat destruction, and burning fossil fuels are prevalent.

Resource consumption has reached unforeseen levels, leading to increased environmental policies and regulations worldwide. Environmental policy addresses human involvement with nature and determines regulations for resource utilization and pollution reduction.

Regulations are generally designed to contribute to human welfare and protect natural resources. Since environmental issues are not restricted to the state, country, or regional boundaries drawn by humans, international cooperation is often needed to address them. Many international laws and conventions have been formulated to support this cause.

John Day Dam and Fish Ladder, Columbia River

International Convention for the Regulation of Whaling (1946) is an environmental agreement signed to conserve whale stocks. It governs commercial, scientific, and aboriginal subsistence whaling practices of 59 member nations.

International Convention for the Prevention of Pollution from Ships (1973) was enacted to preserve the ocean from pollution caused by ships and other human activities.

Convention on Biological Diversity (1992) was created to develop international strategies for the conservation, share, and sustainable use of biodiversity.

International Tropical Timber Agreement (1994) *"promotes the expansion and diversification of international trade in tropical timber from sustainably managed and legally harvested forests and to promote the sustainable management of tropical timber-producing forests."*

International Commission for the Conservation of Atlantic Tunas (ICCAT) is an intergovernmental organization responsible for managing and conserving tuna and tuna-like species in the Atlantic Ocean and adjacent seas. Scientists have strongly criticized the organization for its repeated failure to conserve the sustainability of tuna fishing by consistently supporting overfishing.

ICCAT has adopted a strict recovery plan for Eastern Bluefin Tuna, which includes strict monitoring, reporting, and control measures and a reduction of allowable catches from 27,500 tons (2007) to 13,400 tons (2014).

Questions: Land & Water Use

1. About 40% of the land's primary production on Earth:

   A. has been appropriated to meet human needs
   B. has been destroyed by global climate change
   C. uses more oxygen than it produces
   D. has been lost to build enough homes for all the people on Earth

2. Which of the following is included in the concept of sustainable development?

   A. The needs of future generations
   B. Growth in profits from international trade
   C. The importance of developing the arts
   D. The fastest ways to economic prosperity

3. In developing countries, pressure to increase agricultural productivity has resulted in:

   A. increased yields
   B. more sustainable use of the land
   C. conversion of forests into agricultural fields
   D. reduced use of hybrid crops

4. To promote crop growth, a farmer is likely to apply fertilizers to the soil that contain:

   A. nitrogen
   B. nitrogen or phosphorus
   C. carbon or phosphorus
   D. carbon, nitrogen, or phosphorus

5. The frequency of crown fires will decrease if:

   A. forests are logged more frequently
   B. smaller forest fires are allowed to burn naturally
   C. deadwood is allowed to accumulate on the forest floors
   D. the environment experiences less precipitation

6. The mining company operations in the forest will likely lead to the loss of ecosystem services, such as:

    A. depletion of iron ore from the ground
    B. shift from logging to mining
    C. sources of freshwater
    D. construction of new roads

7. The amount of land and ocean needed to provide the resources for one person and absorb their waste defines the:

    A. carbon footprint
    B. demographic impression
    C. environmental footprint
    D. resource capacity

8. The removal of existing dams is motivated by:

    A. the need for more urban drinking water
    B. the need for more irrigation water
    C. restoration of scenic beauty of rivers and fisheries
    D. the need for more hydroelectric power stations

9. The largest reserves of fresh water on Earth are found in:

    A. lakes and wetlands
    B. rivers and groundwater
    C. aquifers
    D. polar ice caps and glaciers

10. How has converting forests to mostly paved urban areas changed the streams and rivers in the affected watersheds?

    A. Flooding has decreased
    B. Infiltration shifts to runoff
    C. Evaporation has increased
    D. Water flow and pollution decreased

11. Which of the following is true?

    A. Waste in water use and food production cancel each other out:
    B. Bottled water is cheaper than trying to move water by pumping it long distances
    C. Conservation of water resources, energy, and food production and distribution are linked
    D. The water needed to grow vegetables and grains is much greater than to produce beef

12. As a city moves toward sustainability and sustainable development typically:

    A. reduces the density of the resident population
    B. capitalizes on the natural resources in the region
    C. shifts the management of its waste to regions well beyond its borders
    D. focuses on the needs of the most abundant and most economically prosperous citizens

13. Urban sprawl typically results in:

    A. narrower highways
    B. increased commuting distances
    C. increased population densities
    D. decreased reliance on automobiles

14. When generally comparing life in suburban sprawl and life in the inner city, people living in the inner city:

    A. walk more and shop locally
    B. have larger homes and better city services
    C. experience lower crime rates
    D. enjoy lower-density residential living

15. Overgrazing by cattle primarily contributes to desertification by:

    A. promoting erosion and loss of rooted plant cover
    B. contaminating streams with cattle wastes
    C. cattle outcompeting natural herbivores
    D. spreading the growth of non-native species

Relationship matrix

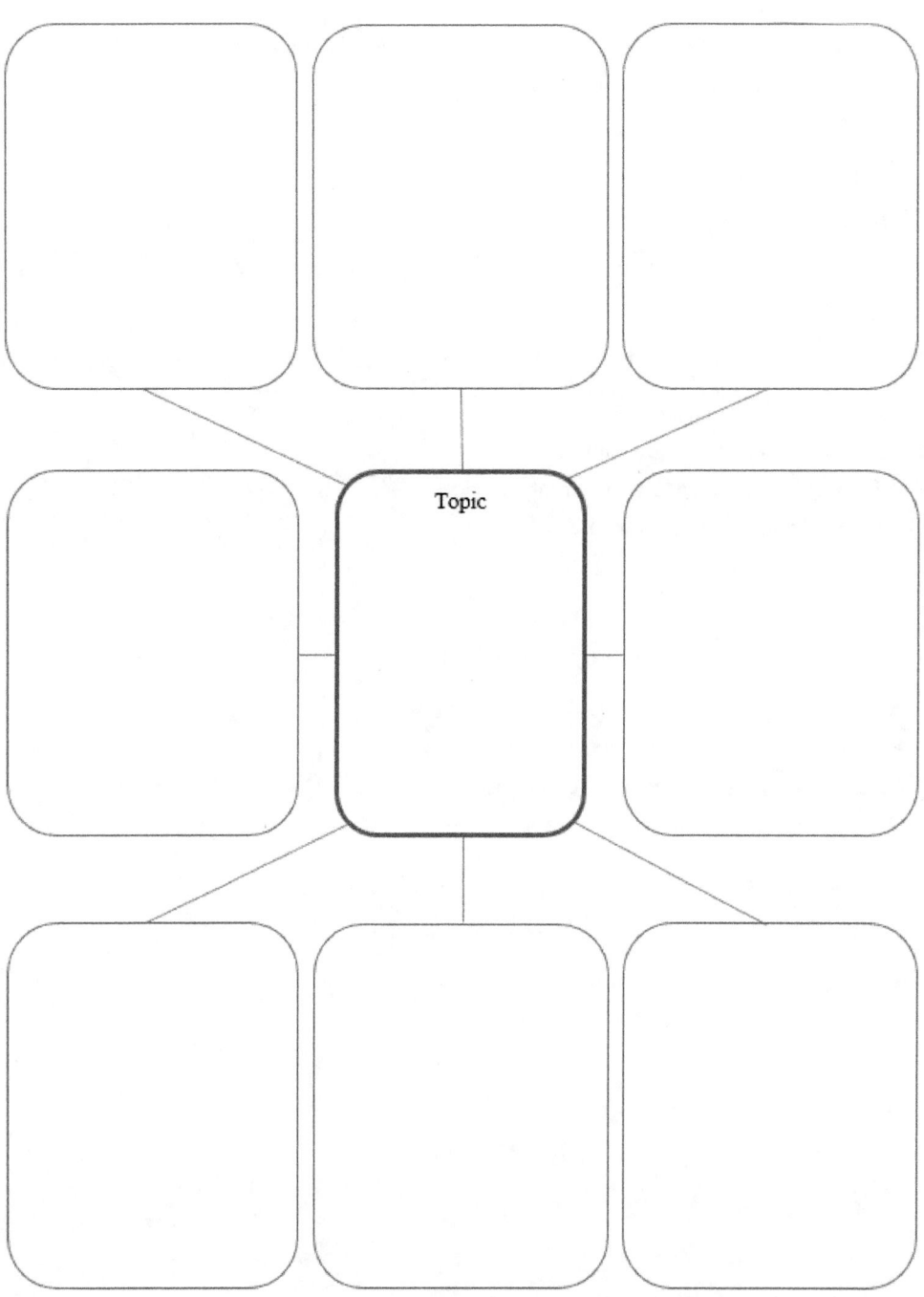

Notes for active learning

Notes for active learning

CHAPTER 6

Pollution

Air Pollution

Water Pollution

Waste Management

Pollution and Human Health

Economic Impacts

Page intentionally left blank

Air Pollution

Air pollution sources

Pollution is the contamination of an environment by introducing substances (i.e., *pollutants*) that hurt the environment's natural state. Pollution types include land pollution, air pollution, water pollution, noise pollution, light pollution, thermal pollution, and visual pollution.

Earth's atmosphere is made up of a mixture of complex gases that support life. The process by which harmful materials are introduced into the atmosphere, resulting in a threat to plant and animal health and natural ecosystems, is *air pollution*.

Air pollution has *natural* and *anthropogenic sources*.

Natural sources of air pollution include volcanic eruptions, which release significant amounts of pollutants (e.g., carbon monoxide, sulfur dioxide, and particulate matter) into the atmosphere, adversely affecting life, property, and the natural environment.

Anthropogenic sources of air pollution originate from human activities. For example, burning fossil fuels with motor vehicle exhaust releases toxic levels of SO_2 into the atmosphere.

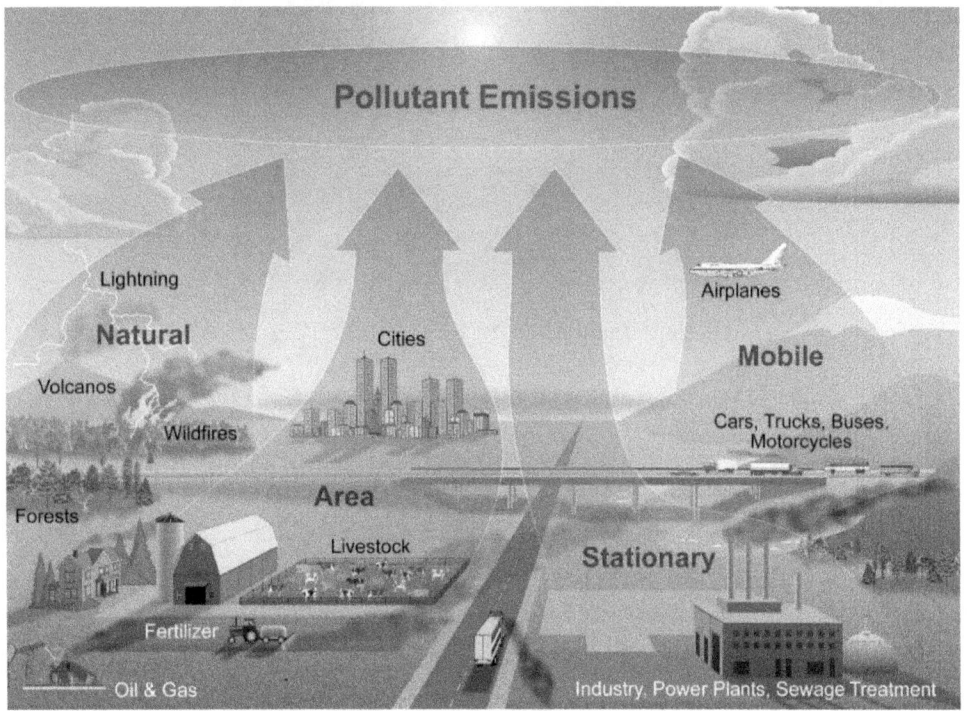

Air pollution sources, U.S. National Parks Service

Primary and secondary air pollutants

Pollutants are primary or secondary pollutants.

Primary air pollutants (e.g., carbon monoxide from vehicle exhaust) are emitted directly.

Secondary air pollutants are not directly emitted into the atmosphere but are formed chemically and physically interacting with atmospheric primary pollutants to form a different compound.

For example, ground-level ozone results from interactions of hydrocarbons (C_nH_{2n+2}) and nitrogen oxide (NO_2) in the presence of sunlight.

Exhaust from a diesel truck.

Carbon monoxide (CO) is a significant primary air pollutant. Carbon monoxide is a colorless, odorless toxic gas from *incomplete fossil fuel combustion*.

The primary source of carbon monoxide gas is vehicle exhaust. Carbon monoxide combines with blood hemoglobin to produce *carboxyhemoglobin*, reducing the amount of oxygen carried in the blood and reducing oxygen supplies in the body. Elevated levels of carbon monoxide in the blood can result in seizures, coma, and death.

Sulfur dioxide (SO_2) is a pungent poisonous gas. Volcanic activities, fossil fuel combustion, industrial processes, and electric utilities produce sulfur dioxide gas, adversely affecting health because it aggravates the respiratory system and can cause asthma and lung cancer.

Sulfur dioxide gas is the primary pollutant causing acid rain, which harms aquatic and terrestrial ecosystems. Atmospheric sulfur dioxide contributes to global warming and causes erratic weather patterns.

Nitrogen dioxide (NO_2) is a reddish-brown pollutant with a sharp, biting odor. It can be a primary or a secondary pollutant. While it is emitted from high-temperature fossil fuel combustions, particularly from vehicle exhaust, processing electric utilities, and industrial boilers, it can form through chemical reactions in the atmosphere when other pollutants react.

Nitrogen dioxide gas contributes to ground-level-ozone formation, eutrophication (i.e., vegetation overgrowth), and acid rain, harming aquatic, and terrestrial life. Nitrogen dioxide irritates the lungs, resulting in respiratory issues in children and adults.

Volatile organic compounds

Volatile organic compounds (VOC) are solids, liquids, or gases with primarily hydrogen (H) and carbon (C) that quickly evaporate (i.e., volatile) into the atmosphere.

VOCs are:

    1) *methane* (CH_4) or 2) *non-methane* (NMVOC) volatile organic compounds.

Volatile organic compound (VOC) sources include fossil fuel deposits, volcanic eruptions, vehicle exhaust emissions, household cleaning vapors, solvents, paints, and coatings.

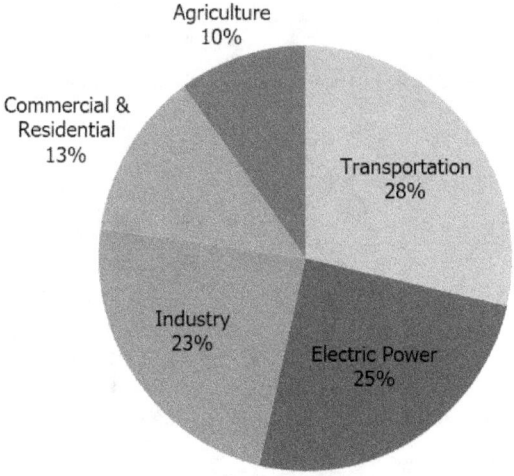

U.S. greenhouse gas emissions by economic sector, 2021, Environmental Protection Agency

Methane is a greenhouse gas that significantly contributes to global warming. Many ecological processes release CH_4 (e.g., wetlands and livestock).

Non-methane volatile organic compounds (NMVOC) such as toluene, xylene, and benzene are carcinogens (i.e., induce cancer).

Chlorofluorocarbons (CFCs) are volatile organic hydrocarbon derivatives with chlorine and fluorine from methane, ethane, and propane.

Chlorofluorocarbons (CFC) are human-made volatile organic compounds used in industrial manufacturing and refrigerants (i.e., Freon) before being banned (phased-in worldwide ban completed in 2010).

Chlorofluorocarbons were released from refrigerators, aerosol sprays, and solvents. They are a major contributor to ozone depletion, allowing harmful ultraviolet (UV) rays to reach Earth, damaging plants, and causing animal skin cancers.

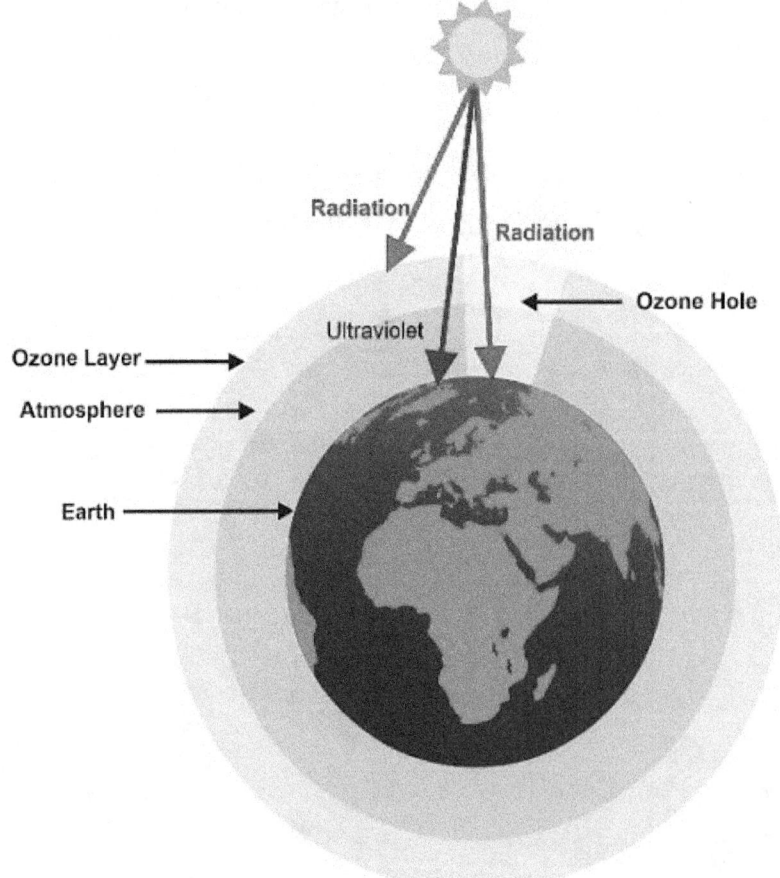

Ozone depletion permits harmful Sun rays to reach Earth

Ground-level ozone (O_3) is formed by sunlight when VOCs chemically react with nitrous oxides NO_x. Pollution sources are gasoline vapors, industrial emissions, motor vehicle exhaust, chemical solvents, and electric utilities.

The effects of these pollutants on humans are heart problems and respiratory symptoms, including lung diseases, asthma, shortness of breath, and coughing.

Ground-level ozone adversely affects sensitive vegetation and fragile ecosystems.

Acid deposition

Secondary air pollutants include *acidic atmospheric pollutants* (e.g., acidic precipitation).

Acid depositions are wet or dry and release acidic or acid-forming atmospheric pollutants.

> *Wet deposits* precipitate as rain, snow, sleet, mist, and fog.

> *Dry deposition* includes dust or smoke and falls to the ground as dry particles.

Sulfur dioxide and *nitrogen oxides* are the primary pollutants responsible for acid deposition. These are emitted from vehicle exhaust, electric utility, and power plants. These primary pollutants, once emitted, react with water and oxygen to produce *sulfuric acid* and *nitric acid*.

These acidic compounds dissolve readily in water and are carried long distances by wind, remaining airborne for extended periods before depositing on Earth's surface.

Acid deposition lowers the pH of the soil, which results in leaching of nutrients, affecting plants' health. For example, this occurred in New York in the Adirondacks, where widespread cations were leeched from the forest floor, resulting in increased levels of sulfur, nitrogen, and calcium deficiency in the soil. This led to a decrease in forest plant and animal diversity. Microorganisms are killed due to acid deposition, which leads to infertile soil.

Acid deposition can fall directly on water bodies or be introduced by terrestrial runoff. Acid deposits in water lower the pH of aquatic ecosystems, which is hostile to aquatic life, and animals and plants die. Long-term exposure to these chemical pollutants kills species within an ecosystem, reducing biodiversity and causing the area to become vulnerable to invasive and undesirable species.

The effect of acid deposition on forests is that trees become susceptible to diseases, and their growth becomes stunted. Severe forest damage due to acid deposits occurred in Europe, specifically Germany, Poland, and Switzerland.

Acid deposition erodes limestone (e.g., historic European buildings and settlements in the Northeast U.S.). Cars, bridges, and airplanes suffer corrosion and weakened structures.

Public health is affected by acid deposits (e.g., sulfur dioxide and nitrogen oxide gases), and particulates reduce visibility, causing accidents leading to injuries or deaths.

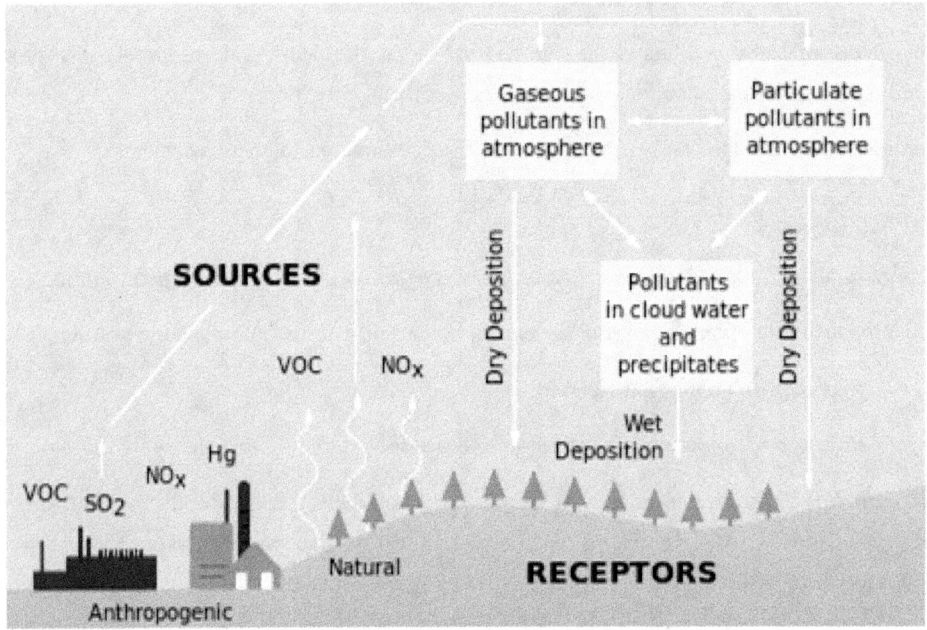

Anthropogenic sources of acid deposition

Acid rain is a form of precipitation with an acidic pH of 5.6 and below. It is caused by the reaction of rainfall (H_2O) to sulfur dioxide (SO_2) and nitrogen oxides (SO_2) to produce acids (i.e., substances with low pH).

Sulfur dioxide and nitrogen oxides are released from power plants, electric utility plants, and from burning fossil fuels.

Dilute *sulfuric acid* (H_2SO_4) is formed when precipitation meets sulfur dioxide in the air.

Carbon dioxide is the main greenhouse gas and is a primary pollutant when emitted by airplanes, cars, factories, and fossil fuel burning. Carbon dioxide reacts with water to form carbonic acid (HCO_3H).

Nitric oxide (NO), which contributes to the natural acidity of rainwater, is formed during lightning storms by reacting nitrogen and oxygen, two common atmospheric gases.

In air, NO is oxidized to nitrogen dioxide (NO_2), which reacts with water to produce *nitric acid* (HNO_3). This precipitation has a damaging effect on plants, animals, and infrastructure.

Industrial air pollution

Smog and particulate matter

Smog initially described the combination of human-made smoke and fog in 20th-century London. In contemporary vernacular, *smog* refers to pollution resulting from the excessive burning of coal or an excess of motor vehicle exhaust mixed with fog.

Smog forms when vehicle exhaust reacts with UV light in the atmosphere, forming secondary pollutants that combine with primary pollutants to form photochemical smog.

Industrial pollution and smog

Smog is typically produced through complex *photochemical reactions* between *volatile organic compounds* (VOC) and *nitrogen oxides* in sunlight. This reaction forms ground-level ozone and is an issue in industrialized cities.

Pollution sources include automobile exhausts, industrial emissions, hair spray, solvents, coal fires, and paint.

Primary pollutants in urban areas originate from vehicle emissions. This is very toxic to humans and causes coughing, difficulty breathing, asthma, colds, lung infections, choking, and eye irritation.

The effects on plant life are the restriction of plant growth and damage to forests and crops.

Particulate matter (PM) is suspended microscopic atmospheric solid or liquid particles.

Particulate matter includes a mixture of soot, dust, pollen, smoke, and water droplets that may originate from volcanic eruptions, dust storms, fossil fuel combustion, and ocean spray.

Particulate matter causes many respiratory diseases, including lung cancer.

Air quality measurements are typically reported in micrograms per cubic meter ($\mu g/m^3$) and parts per million (ppm) or parts per billion (ppb).

Particulate matter sizes are expressed in *microns* (or micrometers).

Indoor air pollution

Indoor air pollution is when gases and particles contaminate indoor air, concentrating more on pollutants than outdoor air. Indoor air pollution impacts developing countries more than developed ones. In developing countries, fuels (e.g., wood, oils, and charcoal) are burned inside homes for cooking and heating. Poor ventilation in homes prevents pollutants from escaping, causing occupants to breathe carbon monoxide and other dangerous contaminants.

Indoor fuel burning leads to human health problems such as pneumonia, bronchitis, cancer, heart disease, and asthma. Dangerous indoor air pollutants in developed countries are tobacco smoke, radon, and carbon monoxide. Second-hand smoke can cause lung cancer, emphysema, asthma, and heart disease.

Volatile organic compounds are common indoor pollutants in cologne, paint, plastic, solvents, pesticides, carpets, and furniture. VOC released indoors are more concentrated than when released into an open space.

Biological sources such as dust mites, pet dander, mold, mildew, and airborne bacteria are indoor pollutants that can irritate the human respiratory system.

Materials used in buildings, such as asbestos, lead, and formaldehyde, are indoor pollutants. Indoor pollution can be reduced by providing adequate ventilation in buildings and ridding the space of the source of the pollutants.

Radon is a carcinogen gas exuded from Earth in specific locations (e.g., Northeast U.S.) and trapped inside houses, businesses, and factories.

Chamber for measuring volatile organic compounds emitted from furnishings

Air pollution remediation

Air pollution remediation is the removal of air pollutants. Remediation is usually based on various regulatory requirements and assessment of human health and environmental risks where no legislated standards exist, or standards are merely advisory.

Commercial operations can reduce air pollution by using more sustainable forms of transportation such as electric, gas hybrid, clean fuel, or emissions-free vehicles.

Restaurants can use natural gas or electricity instead of open pit grills to prepare food.

Air pollution from the residential sector can be reduced by eliminating indoor fireplaces.

Environmentally friendly solvents and household cleaners are used instead of environmentally harmful ones. Sustainable transportation options include walking, carpooling, bike riding, or public transportation.

Efforts to reduce pollution for transportation include manufacturing hybrid vehicles, generating cleaner fuels, or using electric-powered vehicles.

Air pollution primarily results from burning fossil fuels (e.g., coal, gas, petroleum), which can be reduced by renewable energy sources (e.g., wind, solar, and hydropower).

Emission control devices (e.g., scrubbers) reduce air pollution from equipment by destroying or removing pollutants from exhaust streams before they are released into the atmosphere.

Air quality regulations

There are two types of air quality standards.

National Ambient Air Quality Standards sets maximum threshold limits for atmospheric concentrations of specific pollutants.

North American Air Quality Index uses a scale with thresholds to communicate the relative risk of outdoor activity; the scales may or may not distinguish between pollutants.

Air quality laws regulate the emission of air pollutants into the atmosphere and are specifically designed to protect human health by limiting airborne pollutants emitted. Some initiatives address ecological problems, such as reducing the emissions of chemicals that affect the ozone layer or acid rain.

Regulatory efforts include identifying and categorizing air pollutants, setting limits on acceptable standards, and suggesting mitigation strategies and technologies to implement.

Air Pollution Control Act (1955) was the first U.S. federal legislation related to air pollution. It provided funds for federal research on air pollution, identified air pollution as a national issue, and increased awareness of environmental hazards resulting from air pollution.

Clean Air Act (1963) is a federal law governing and regulating air pollution reductions. Environmental Protection Agency administers this law with state, local, and tribal (Native American) governments. The EPA sets standards for levels of pollutants in the air, such as ozone, particulates, and nitrogen oxides in smog, and requires companies to comply with the standards or pay fines. *Clean Air Act* has significantly reduced US air pollution.

Air Quality Act (1967) amended the *Clean Air Act* (1963). It enabled the federal government to investigate and enforce interstate air pollution transport and, for the first time, to perform ambient monitoring and stationary source inspections. It authorized expanded studies of air pollutant emission inventories, ambient monitoring, and control techniques.

Chapter 6: Pollution

President Lyndon B. Johnson signed the Clean Air Act in 1963

Each state is responsible for ensuring that *Clean Air Act* standards are met. Efforts to keep air-prescribed quality to standards include controlling emissions, such as changing gasoline composition, using alternative fuels such as natural gas and electricity, and banning charcoal barbecues and wood-burning stoves or fireplaces with high pollution levels.

State governments integrate traffic systems that encourage carpooling, manage traffic in congested areas, and improve access to public transportation systems. Some regulations encourage employers to contribute to employee mass transit costs, while others implement "smog fees" on cars in proportion to the distance traveled and vehicle emissions produced.

Notes for active learning

Water Pollution

Pollution of aquatic environments

Water pollution is the contamination of natural bodies of water (e.g., lakes, rivers, oceans, aquifers, and groundwater) by particles or chemicals from human activities.

Two primary sources of water pollution are *point* and *non-point sources*.

Point sources are pollutants that belong to a single source, such as factory emissions.

Non-point sources are pollutants emitted from multiple sources, such as water, that have traveled through several regions and picked up different contaminants.

Nutrient water pollution occurs when bodies of water become contaminated by wastewater, fertilizers, or sewage that contains high levels of nutrients. This contamination causes excessive weed and algae growth, making the water unpotable.

High levels of algae expend oxygen in bodies of water, starving other aquatic organisms.

Nutrient pollution: runoff of fertilizer during heavy rain

Oxygen depletion of water occurs when aerobic and anaerobic organisms feed on biodegradable material and cause it to accumulate in the water, encouraging microorganism growth and expending oxygen in water.

When oxygen is depleted, aerobic organisms die, and anaerobic organisms reproduce, producing harmful toxins such as ammonia and sulfides.

Microbiological water pollution is a natural pollution caused by numerous microorganisms, such as viruses, bacteria, and protozoa. This microorganism population can kill aquatic species of animals and plants and cause serious illness, including the transmission of water-borne diseases (i.e., cholera) to the humans who drink this water.

Suspended matter is a water pollutant characterized by chemicals and particles suspended in bodies of water that are insoluble or have a low solubility. Some suspended particulate matter may eventually settle under the water body, forming a layer of silt and endangering the aquatic life that lives on the floor of these bodies of water.

Chemical water pollution occurs when chemical runoff from farms and factories enter bodies of water, polluting them. These chemicals are poisonous to marine life and can infect the consumer if consumed by birds or humans.

Oil spills are water pollution from oil spilling into a body of water. These spills can spread across large areas and affect numerous wildlife. For example, oil spills kill fish and cause birds to lose their ability to fly as oil mats their feathers. When oil sticks to a bird's feathers, it **causes them to mat and separate, impairing waterproofing and exposing their sensitive skin to extremes in temperature**. This can result in hypothermia (i.e., birds become cold) or hyperthermia (i.e., overheating).

Surface water pollution

Surface water pollution contaminates natural surface water bodies, such as rivers, oceans, lakes, and lagoons.

Industrial waste, such as lead, mercury, sulfur, asbestos, nitrates, and other harmful chemicals, is produced as waste from industrial activities. Many industries do not practice proper waste management and drain their waste into water systems. This has the potential to cause eutrophication, damaging aquatic life.

Sewage and wastewater from homes are treated and released into the sea. Sewage water contains numerous pathogens that harm human health and the environment.

Marine debris on a Hawaii beach

Marine dumping occurs when garbage is disposed of in the sea, pollutes water, and harms marine plants and animals. Some materials take hundreds of years to decompose.

Oil spills can occur when a ship or train carrying oil containers crashes, or a pipeline ruptures. Any of these occurrences are cause for primary environmental concern due to the threat of oil spilling into the ocean or the water table. An oil spill may affect marine wildlife like fish, birds, and sea otters. The severity of the damage is dependent on the quantity and toxicity of the oil spill and the size of the body of water in which the spill occurred.

Farmers utilize chemical fertilizers and pesticides to protect crops from insects, weeds, and microorganisms such as bacteria. These chemicals may contact bodies of water due to rainwater runoff, posing a severe threat to aquatic animals. Animal waste can be washed into rivers through rainfall and mixed with other harmful chemicals. This can cause many water-borne diseases, such as cholera, diarrhea, jaundice, dysentery, and typhoid.

Nitrate and phosphate from fertilizer provide food for algae, resulting in algae blooming. When excess algae dies and decays, they use the existing dissolved oxygen and degrade the overall quality of the water. This oxygen deprivation kills other aquatic life.

Water pollution has a devastating effect on ecosystems, human health, and even tourism and recreational activities. This pollution affects sea creatures and accumulates in their bodies, the adverse effects of which are passed on to humans eating fish. Water pollution harms the environment on which humans depend on food, oxygen, and water.

Groundwater pollution

Groundwater pollution occurs when chemical contaminants, such as pesticides, are leached from soil and washed underground and into aquifers by rainwater. The pollutant creates a contaminant plume within an aquifer. Water currents quickly disperse the pollutant over a wide area. This pollutant can seep into springs and ground wells, contaminating the drinking water supply.

Contamination can result from naturally occurring elements (e.g., arsenic and fluoride) in soil. Drinking polluted groundwater may harm public health, plants, and animals through poisoning or spreading disease.

Groundwater pollution can occur from improperly maintained sanitation systems, landfills, effluent from wastewater treatment plants, leaking sewers, gas stations, air pollutants, or the overuse of fertilizers in agriculture.

Mining activities include extracting minerals, some containing harmful chemicals that can be released into groundwater supplies. This waste includes sulfides, which are toxic and may cause health problems.

Groundwater pollution: a pit latrine in Lusaka, Zambia, pollutes the nearby well

Landfills are massive, layered with piles of garbage. Rainwater percolates through a landfill and carries pollutants that may meet groundwater if the landfill is not properly lined. This will pollute the groundwater supply, affecting the public drinking water supply.

Industrial scrap yards are a source of groundwater pollution if not lined properly

While groundwater is used mainly for irrigation, over half of the people in the United States depend on groundwater for drinking. Drinking contaminated groundwater can have adverse health effects on humans and wildlife.

Hepatitis and dysentery are caused by consuming water contaminated with toxins leached from septic tank waste. Long-term effects include cancers linked to long or short-term exposure to polluted water.

Water quality and purification

Water is essential to life and environmental health. This valuable natural resource includes marine, estuarine, freshwater, and groundwater environments. Water has two attributes that are closely linked: *quantity* and *quality*.

Water quality refers to physical, chemical, biological, and aesthetic characteristics. A healthy environment supports water quality, supports a diverse community of organisms, and is safe for human consumption.

Water quality is vital because it assists in maintaining public health and ecosystems and is essential in industries such as farming, fishing, mining, and tourism.

Water quality is affected by public uses such as agricultural, urban, industrial, and recreational applications. Modification of the natural path of streams using dams and dikes may affect water quality. The weather can impact water quality, especially in dry seasons.

Water quality is measured by the level of contaminants and their characteristics. The chemistry of water can be affected by pH, dissolved oxygen, biological oxygen demand, minerals, and organic and inorganic compounds.

Biological characteristics of water include the level of microorganisms and algae.

Physical characteristics of water include temperature, turbidity and clarity, color, salinity, suspended solids, and dissolved solids.

Aesthetic qualities used to measure water quality are odor, taint, color, and floating matter.

Radioactive components of water include alpha, beta, and gamma radiation emitters. Closely monitoring these indicators is necessary to determine if the water is suitable for consumption.

Water quality can be improved by providing information to the public on the quality of water through programs and environmental reports. Public education is needed on the importance of maintaining water quality.

Pollution reduction programs and industrial and water quality management strategies help.

Water purification is the process by which chemical, biological, and suspended solid contaminants are removed from the water. This renders water suitable for specific uses, such as human, industrial, medical, pharmacological, and chemical applications.

This process removes bacteria, algae, viruses, fungi, lead, copper, and suspended particles. A small amount of disinfectant is usually left in the water at the end of the treatment process to reduce the risk of re-contamination once in the distribution system.

Boiling water is a simple procedure that can be used to treat water. Other physical methods to purify water include filtration, sedimentation, and distillation. Biological processes used for purification include slow sand filters or biologically active carbon. Chemical processes include flocculation, chlorination, and electromagnetic radiation, such as ultraviolet light.

A few states have accepted "zero tolerance" standards, where the maximum permissible level of sewage contaminants in drinking water is the same as in uncontaminated water. This sets the bar high; scientists are finding that even the best technology available today is incapable of thoroughly cleaning the groundwater from a site that has been contaminated.

Sewage treatment

Wastewater from flushing the toilet, bathing, and washing sinks goes down the drain into pipes, which join up with larger sewer pipes that lead to a treatment center.

Four stages of sewage treatment:

$$\text{screening} \rightarrow \text{primary treatment} \rightarrow \text{secondary treatment} \rightarrow \text{final treatment}$$

Screening is the first stage of the wastewater treatment process. This stage includes the removal of large objects such as plastics, rags, diapers, sanitary items, cotton buds, and face wipes that have the potential to block or damage equipment.

Primary treatment stage separates human waste from wastewater. Wastewater is moved into large settlement tanks where solids sink to the tank bottom and form sludge. Large scrapers at the bottom of circular tanks scrape the floor and push sludge toward the center, where it is pumped for further treatment. The remaining water is moved to secondary treatment.

Secondary treatment stage places water into *aeration lanes* (i.e., large rectangular tanks). Air is pumped into the water to facilitate bacteria breaking down the tiny bits of sludge that escaped the sludge scraping process.

Wastewater passes through a settlement tank in the *final treatment* stage. More sludge forms at the bottom of the tank through the settling of the bacterial action. The sludge is again scraped and collected for treatment. The water flows over a wall for further filtration through a bed of sand, removing additional particles. Filtered water is then released into the river.

Sewage treatment plant in Germany

Groundwater regulations

Before 1980, people believed soil and rock filtered unwanted elements from groundwater. The focus for groundwater was discovering more efficient ways to remove it from the Earth.

In 1978, those beliefs about groundwater drastically changed when President Carter declared that a small area near Niagara Falls in New York was under a federal emergency, as there were growing health issues associated with groundwater and contaminated soil. This area became known as the *Love Canal site* and was the first area where a federal emergency was implemented in response to a human-made environmental issue.

The U.S. population quickly realized that removing and treating groundwater before use was a serious concern, and doing so in the following decades became a large but necessary expense. The issue was even more complicated because very few scientists before 1980 were competent in these areas or knew about technologies capable of fixing the problem.

Threats to drinking water include improperly disposed chemicals, animal waste, pesticides, human waste, waste injected deep underground, and naturally occurring substances. Clean drinking water is vital to human health, as drinking improperly treated or distributed water poses severe health risks.

Three main laws regulate groundwater.

1) *Safe Drinking Water Act* (SDWA) was passed by Congress in 1974 as the primary federal law to protect public health by regulating public drinking water quality. It authorizes the Environmental Protection Agency (EPA) to set drinking water quality standards and oversee state, municipal, and commercial water suppliers. The EPA sets national health-based standards for drinking water to protect against naturally occurring and human-made contaminants in potable water.

Safe Drinking Water Act was amended (1986 and 1996) and now requires protecting drinking water sources (e.g., rivers, lakes, reservoirs, springs, and groundwater wells). However, the SDWA has no regulatory authority over the standards and use of private wells that service the needs of about 15% of the population.

2) *Federal Water Pollution Control Act* of 1972 was the federal law regulating water pollution in the United States. It aimed to maintain and restore the chemical, physical, and biological standards of the nation's water, including groundwater.

The Act gained significant prominence when it was amended in 1977 and became what is now known as *Clean Water Act* (CWA) of 1972. EPA administers the Clean Water Act in coordination with state governments. This law implements programs to control pollution, such as setting wastewater standards for industries at the federal and state levels.

3) *Resource Conservation and Recovery Act* (RCRA) was passed in 1976 to regulate the transportation, storage, treatment, and disposal of solid and hazardous wastes. The Act establishes a "cradle-to-grave" tracking system for hazardous waste to ensure proper management and disposal. RCRA aims to prevent contaminants from leaching into groundwater, which is a significant safety concern for groundwater quality.

Regulations aimed at protecting and remediating groundwater have focused mainly on hazardous pollutants. Chemicals commonly found in groundwater are widely used in many industrial processes, from treating lumber to manufacturing electronic equipment and producing plastics, fuels, food, cleaning supplies, etc.

Sewage from animals and humans in groundwater is becoming an increasing concern. States have adopted standards in the remediation and protection of groundwater, and most have legislated health guidelines with the permissible levels of sewage-based contaminants in drinking water (set by the EPA).

Surface water regulations

Clean Water Act (CWA) regulates surface water, the primary federal legislation dealing with quality and pollution. CWA aims to protect U.S. waters' chemical, physical, and biological integrity by regulating the release of pollutants into surface waters.

Clean Water Act sets surface water quality standards for contaminants and makes it illegal to discharge pollutants from any point source into navigable water without a permit.

Clean Water Act has three primary goals:

- Eliminate *discharges* of toxic contaminants (target is zero toxins);
- Eliminate *contaminants released* into navigable waters by 1985; and
- Protect and propagate wildlife, fish, shellfish, and recreation water sources so the water remains swimmable and fishable.

Environmental Protection Agency (EPA) has a *National Pollutant Discharge Elimination System* (NPDES) permit program controlling discharges. The agency sets and maintains pollution standards for surface waters using water-based technologies.

CWA includes civil, criminal, and administrative enforcement and allows citizen suits.

Surface water issues are also regulated by state laws that must meet standards set by CWA, and many states have formed independent agencies to enforce these standards.

Other regulations for surface water protection are:

- *Marine Protection Research and Sanctuaries Act* (MPRSA, also known as the Ocean Dumping Act) of 1972, which protects marine resources and ecosystems;

- *Coastal Wetlands Planning, Protection and Restoration Act* (CWPPRA) enacted in 1990 to restore and protect coastal wetlands;

- *Beaches Environmental Assessment and Coastal Health Act* (BEACH Act) of 2000 is an amendment to the Clean Water Act that focuses on improving public health at recreational coastal waters.

Waste Management

Solid and hazardous waste

Solid waste (or semisolid) is non-soluble discarded material and includes agricultural refuse, demolition, industrial, mining residues, garbage, sewage sludge, and food waste.

Types of solid waste are *municipal* (household), *industrial*, and *biomedical* (or hospital) waste.

Municipal solid waste mainly comprises garbage generated from residential households and commercial establishments. The municipal waste comprises household waste, construction and demolition debris, sanitation residue, and street waste. Generated waste is discarded into municipal waste collection receptacles, from whence it is collected by the area municipality to be further disposed of into landfills and dumps.

The increase in population has led to increased consumption of food and other items essential to everyday life. Increasing urbanization and lifestyle changes have resulted in an increased amount and composition of municipal solid waste. The packaging of products has changed as aluminum foil, plastics, cans, and other non-biodegradable materials are common.

Industrial waste is generated by many industries, including chemical, metal, and mineral processing facilities. These industries generate toxic waste from various processes involving metals, chemicals, paper, pesticides, dyes, refining, and rubber goods. Nuclear plants generate radioactive waste, thermal power plants produce fly ash, and chemical industries generate large quantities of hazardous and toxic material.

Biomedical waste is produced by hospitals, biotechnology companies, and medical research laboratories. It is generated during the diagnosis, treatment, or immunization of humans or animals in research activities and the production or testing of biologicals. Biomedical waste includes needles, syringes, swabs, bandages, cultures, discarded medicines, chemical waste, human tissue, body fluids, and excrement.

It is estimated that one in four kilograms of biomedical waste is infected. It is hazardous when contaminated by chemicals (e.g., formaldehyde and phenols) in disinfectants, mercury in thermometers, and blood pressure monitoring equipment. This type of waste is highly toxic and can severely damage human and wildlife health if not effectively managed in a scientifically correct manner.

Direct exposure to chemicals in *hazardous waste* (i.e., toxic to people and the environment), such as mercury and cyanide, can be fatal. While industrial and biomedical wastes are primary sources of hazardous waste, municipal waste can contain hazardous materials, such as batteries, paints, expired medications, shoe polish, and many other household items. These wastes can potentially be highly toxic to humans, animals, and plants due to their corrosive, flammable, explosive, and reactive properties.

Hazardous waste collection site

Landfills

Solid waste is disposed of using landfills, incineration, and composting.

Sanitary landfill is the most economical method of garbage disposal, and it is created by alternating layers of thin, compacted, and solid waste covered with clay or plastic foam. The bottom of the landfill is sealed with an impermeable material such as clay, plastic foam, and sand. This impermeable layer protects the groundwater from seepage from the landfill.

When the landfill is complete, it is covered with clay, sand, gravel, and topsoil to prevent water seepage. Areas close to the site are drilled and monitored to prevent groundwater contamination. In two to three years, the solid waste volume shrinks by 25-30%, and the land is returned to other uses for constructing roads, small buildings, and parks.

The advantages of using landfills to dispose of solid waste are easy and financial, and wastes need not be grouped based on similarity. Landfills use low-lying land and swamplands, which can be reclaimed and used for other purposes. Natural biodegradable waste returns to the soil and provides nutrients.

The disadvantage of using landfills to dispose of solid waste is the requirement for large land areas, which can be costly or unavailable in densely urbanized areas. Landfills require monitoring to prevent foul odors, groundwater seepage, and disease-carrying vectors such as mosquitoes, roaches, rats, and flies.

Landfills have the potential to ignite due to methane gas formation from decaying organic waste in wet weather conditions.

Incineration

Solid waste disposal uses *incineration* by burning solid, liquid, and gaseous waste until it is reduced to ashes. Incinerators are well-insulated furnaces that prevent the escape of excess heat and pollutants. It is a practical method of disposing of some types of hazardous waste materials, but there are concerns about the effects of incineration on air quality.

Garbage gets sorted into non-combustible and combustible matter. Non-combustible matter can be glass, porcelain, and metals separated and recycled or reused.

One of the main advantages of incineration is that it requires a small space, and the residue is much smaller than the original solid waste volume (about 20-30%). Residue or ashes from incineration require further disposal by sanitary landfill or other means. Heat generated during combustion is used as steam power to generate electricity through turbines. An incinerator disposing of 3,000 tons of garbage daily generates 3 megawatts of power.

Waste-to-energy incinerator plant in Saugus, MA, in service since 1975

Waste disposal by incineration has limitations, which include high capital and operating costs and the requirement of skilled personnel to operate the equipment. To prevent air pollution, smoke, dust, and ashes produced by incineration require management and further disposal.

Composting

Composting is prevalent in urban areas with a land shortage for landfills. Organic waste is naturally decomposed into fertilizer by microorganisms, especially bacteria and fungi. The main benefit of composting is recycling nutrients that are returned to the soil in a clean, inexpensive, and environmentally safe way.

Biodegradable waste is deposited in underground trenches in 1.5-meter layers covered with earth and left for decomposition. Decomposition forms *humus* with high nitrogen levels and is valuable in agriculture for plant growth to replace chemical fertilizers.

Vermicomposting uses worms added to compost piles to facilitate waste degradation with worm excreta (i.e., *vermicast* or *feces*) enriching the compost.

The New York City Department of Sanitation (DSNY) distributed brown bins in September 2017 for compostable food and yard waste.

Transport of hazardous waste

Hazardous waste generated at a site often requires transportation to an approved treatment, storage, or disposal facility. Because of the potential threat to public safety and the environment, governmental agencies give special attention to transport. Laws are enforced to ensure proper labeling, transporting, and tracking methods are used to dispose of hazardous waste.

Hazardous waste is transported in specially designed steel or aluminum alloy tanks, carried on trucks, or transported via ship or rail.

Manifest system monitors the transportation of hazardous waste from its source to disposal facilities. This system helps eliminate the "midnight dumping" issue when waste is left in secluded areas at night. It provides a way to determine the type and quantity of hazardous waste being generated and the recommended emergency procedures for an accidental spill.

A hazardous waste generator, such as a chemical manufacturer, must prepare a record-keeping document (i.e., manifest). The generator is responsible for the final disposal of the waste and is required to give the manifest, along with the waste itself, to a licensed waste transporter. The transporter must deliver a copy of the manifest to the waste recipient at an authorized disposal facility.

Every time waste changes from one person to another, a copy of the manifest must be signed. Copies of the manifest are kept by each party involved, and additional copies are sent to the appropriate environmental agencies. The transporter must notify local authorities and take other appropriate actions to reduce public and environmental effects in the event of a leak during transportation.

Treatment and disposal of hazardous waste

Hazardous waste management is the collection, treatment, and disposal of waste material that can cause substantial harm to human and environmental health when improperly handled. Hazardous waste can be solid, liquid, sludge, or gaseous.

Hazardous waste is generated by chemical production, manufacturing, and other industrial activities. Inadequate storage, transportation, treatment, or improper disposal can contaminate surface and groundwater.

Hazardous waste can be treated by chemical, thermal, biological, and physical methods.

Chemical methods of treating hazardous waste include ion exchange, oxidation and reduction, precipitation, and neutralization.

Thermal methods to treat hazardous waste include high-temperature incineration, which can detoxify organic waste. Thermal equipment such as a fluidized-bed incinerator, multiple-hearth furnace, rotary kiln, and liquid-injection incinerators are used to burn solid, liquid, or sludge waste. Thermal methods have the potential to pollute the atmosphere.

Biological methods treat organic waste, such as petroleum byproducts.

Landfarming is a biological method used to treat hazardous waste in which the waste is mixed with surface soil.

Fluor Fernald workers pneumatically remove hazardous waste

Bioremediation

Organisms are sometimes added to the mixture to assist in metabolizing the waste and to add nutrients, a process called *bioremediation*. Care is taken not to grow food or forage crops on the same site. These microbes can have a stabilizing effect on hazardous waste.

Unlike chemical, biological, and thermal methods that change the molecular structure of the waste, physical treatment methods concentrate, solidify, or reduce the volume of the waste. These processes include *evaporation, sedimentation, flotation, solidification*, and *filtration*.

Solidification is done by encompassing concrete, asphalt, or plastic waste.

Encapsulation produces a solid mass of material that is resistant to leaching. Waste can be mixed with lime, fly ash, and water to form a solid, cement-like product.

Hazardous waste must be disposed of, not destroyed by incineration or treated by various processes. Land disposal has proven to be the most suitable disposal site, as evidenced by landfilling and underground injection.

Temporary on-site waste storage facilities include open waste piles and ponds or lagoons. Waste piles must be carefully constructed over an impervious base and comply with regulatory requirements, such as landfills. Open pits or holding ponds (i.e., lagoons) are constructed with impervious clay soil and flexible membrane liners to protect groundwater.

Leachate collection systems should be installed along with groundwater monitoring wells.

Open lagoons provide no waste treatment except for some sedimentation, surface aeration, and evaporation of volatile organics. Accumulated sludge should be handled as hazardous and must be periodically removed.

Hazardous waste can be deposited in secure landfills with two impermeable liners and leachate collection systems. Leachate is collected and pumped into a treatment plant. An impermeable cap or cover is placed over a completed landfill to reduce the amount of leachate in the landfill and minimize the potential for environmental damage.

A groundwater monitoring system, which includes a series of deep wells drilled in and around the site, is implemented. These wells are routinely sampled, and the material is tested to detect leaks or groundwater contamination. If a leak occurs, the wells can be pumped to intersect the polluted water and bring it to the surface for treatment.

Deep well injections (see diagram) can be used to dispose of liquid hazardous waste. Liquid waste is pumped through a steel casing into a porous layer of limestone or sandstone. The liquid is pumped into rock pores and fissures using high pressures for permanent storage.

The injection zone must be below a layer of impermeable rock or clay. This method is inexpensive and requires little or no pre-treatment of the waste. Well injections, however, pose a danger of leaking hazardous waste and polluting subsurface water supplies.

Cleanup of contaminated sites

Many abandoned hazard disposal sites such as pits, ponds, or lagoons are unrestricted and unlined, posing a threat to human and environmental health. Depending on the level of risk these sites pose, remediation may be necessary.

Remediation may require removing waste material from the site and transporting it to another location for treatment and proper disposal. Alternatively, remediation can be done on-site to reduce leachate production and decrease the chance of groundwater contamination.

On-site remediation may include temporarily removing the hazardous waste, constructing a secure landfill on the same site, and adequately replacing the waste. Contaminated soil or groundwater may require treatment. Treated soil may be replaced on-site, and groundwater may be treated to the aquifer by deep-well injection.

Full containment of waste is a less costly method than on-site remediation. It involves placing an impermeable cover over disposal sites and blocking groundwater lateral flow by subsurface cutoff walls. These walls must be constructed around the site perimeter and be deep enough to penetrate the impervious layer. They can be excavated as trenches around the site, filled with bentonite clay slurry to prevent collapse during construction.

Trenches should be filled with soil and cement to form an impermeable barrier.

Cutoff walls are vertical barriers to water flow, and the impervious layer is a bottom barrier.

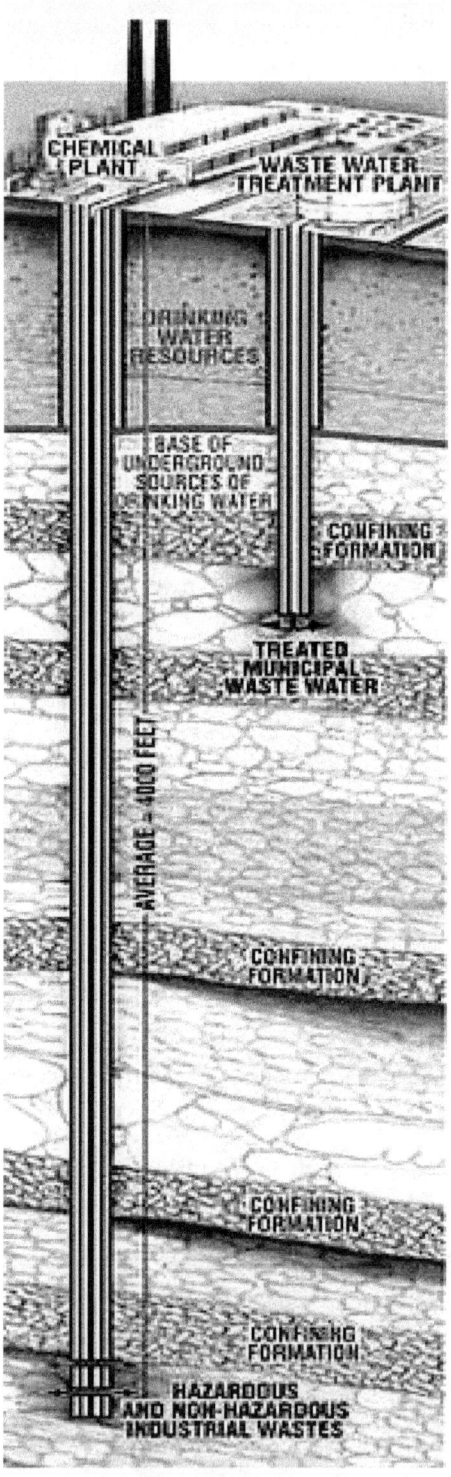

Deep well injection for disposal of hazardous, industrial, and municipal wastewater

Pollution and Human Health

Waste-related health hazards

Waste that is not managed correctly, especially excreta and other liquid and solid waste from households and the community, can have severe health and environmental effects. Municipalities sometimes lack resources or an inefficient infrastructure, leading to waste collection failure. Left unattended, standing waste may attract insects and vermin, which carry disease and contribute to poor living conditions.

Uncollected solid waste increases the risk of injury and infection. The main population at risk from waste build-up is people living in areas without proper waste disposal. Accumulated solid waste can also obstruct stormwater runoff, forming stagnant bodies of water that become breeding grounds for disease.

Dumping waste near a body of water or groundwater can cause contamination, affecting the human water supply. Dumping of untreated waste in rivers, seas, and lakes accumulates toxic substances in the food chain through plants and animals feeding on it. Populations living near waste dumps and those whose water supply has become contaminated due to either waste dumping or leakage from landfill sites are at risk.

Organic waste poses a serious threat because, as this waste decomposes, it creates conditions that encourage the survival and growth of microbial pathogens. Waste disposal workers are most vulnerable to infectious and chronic diseases from directly handling solid waste.

Disposing of industrial hazardous waste alongside municipal waste can expose people to hazardous chemicals and radioactive substances. Chemicals like cyanide, mercury, and polychlorinated biphenyls are highly toxic, and exposure can lead to diseases like cancer and death. People living near abandoned waste disposal sites may have a higher risk of affection.

Biomedical waste disposal requires special attention. Waste generated by medical facilities has a high potential for infections, toxic chemicals, and metals. Contact with infectious items may result in significant health hazards (such as Hepatitis B and C), particularly through wounds caused by discarded sharps.

Proper waste disposal methods will ensure that this practice does not affect the environment or cause health hazards to people near disposal sites. Improperly operated incineration plants cause air pollution, and improperly managed and designed landfills attract disease-carrying vectors. These sites should be a safe distance from human settlements. Landfill sites should be well-lined and solidly walled to prevent leakage into nearby groundwater sources.

Mercury waste from Brunswick Pulp and Paper Company destroyed marshland near the plant

Water pollution and health hazards

As water encounters decomposing solid waste, it dissolves with the soluble inorganic and organic wastes, producing a polluted liquid known as *leachate*. Solid waste affects water quality by releasing leachate from landfills into water sources.

Leachate becomes more concentrated as it seeps into deeper layers of the landfill; this contributes to the light brown/black color of leachate and its pungent odor. It has a high polluting potential impact due to the high concentrations of organic contaminants and ammonia nitrogen.

Leachate discharged into a body of water will have an acute and continuing impact. If toxic metals are present, this can lead to chronic toxin accumulation in organisms that depend on it, such as fish, and may consequently affect the humans who feed on these organisms.

Workers test a leachate collection system at the Savannah River Site

Environmental risk due to water pollution continues. Municipal wastewater systems are one of the largest sources of pollution to surface waters. Significant sources include residential and industrial discharges and agricultural runoff.

Chemicals from pesticides may contaminate bodies of water. Toxic releases from industrial plants and agricultural runoff into the environment have a long-term effect on water supplies. Air pollution and land pollution affect water quality. When chemicals contaminate a body of water, this can affect the surrounding wildlife, watershed, and residents. For instance, if chemicals find their way into a freshwater source that supplies people or animals, they may no longer be safe for use or consumption.

Air pollutants' impact on human health

The most significant human air pollutants are particles, acidic gases, aerosols, metals, and organic compounds resulting from incineration. Exposure to these particles has acute health effects, such as increased overall mortality and emergency hospital admissions.

Acidic gases such as SO_2 adversely affect lung functions, especially in asthmatics. Additionally, exposure to particulate matter increases cardiovascular and respiratory mortality and morbidity.

Metals from incinerator emissions, such as lead, cadmium, mercury, chromium, arsenic, and beryllium, have carcinogenic and non-carcinogenic health effects. The organic compounds derived from incineration, such as *dioxins* and *polychlorinated biphenyl*s (PCBs), have the potential to accumulate in the body—high levels of dioxin exposure in workplaces and after accidents have caused chloracne and increased cardiovascular disease.

Air pollutants cause asthma, a disease that affects the lungs. Repeated episodes of wheezing, breathlessness, chest tightness, and nighttime or early morning coughing characterize it. This disease can be controlled by medication and by avoiding the triggers that cause it.

Pollution has been linked to cancer clusters and larger-than-expected numbers of cancer cases occurring within a geographic area over time.

Infamous events occurred in the 1960s with mesothelioma, a rare cancer of the chest and abdomen lining. Studies traced the development of this cancer to exposure to asbestos.

Smog, created by automobile emissions, is the most extensive pollution threatening human health. Carbon monoxide is produced through the combustion of fossil fuels. This gas can cause sudden illness and death. This has been managed in the U.S. by raising awareness about carbon monoxide poisoning and monitoring the illnesses and deaths resulting from this gas.

Smoking and its risks

Cigarettes contain about 600 ingredients and, when burned, generate over 7,000 chemicals, including nicotine, tar, carbon monoxide, formaldehyde, ammonia, hydrogen cyanide, arsenic, and *dichlorodiphenyltrichloroethane* (DDT). Many chemicals are poisonous and sixty-nine carcinogenic, with ingredients in cigarettes, cigars, and tobacco smoked in pipes and hookahs.

National Cancer Institute reported that cigars have higher carcinogens, toxins, and tar than cigarettes. Centers for Disease Control and Prevention, the mortality rate for U.S. smokers is three times that of those who never smoked. Smoking harms most organs and organ systems and is a leading cause of preventable death.

Nicotine reaches the brain seconds after it is inhaled. It is a central nervous system stimulant with high habit-forming potential. Smoking increases the risk of macular degeneration, cataracts, and poor eyesight. It can weaken the senses, including taste and smell.

Inhaling smoke over time will damage the lungs, causing them to lose their ability to filter harmful chemicals. Coughing is not an adequate response to clear out the toxins, causing these toxins to become trapped in the lungs. This results in smokers having a higher risk of respiratory infections, colds, and flu.

Over time, smokers are at an increased risk of developing forms of chronic obstructive pulmonary disease (OPD), such as emphysema and chronic bronchitis. Emphysema is characterized by the air sacs in one's lungs being destroyed by harmful chemicals. In chronic bronchitis, the lining of the tubes of the lungs becomes inflamed. Long-term smokers are at an increased risk of lung cancer.

Smoking damages the cardiovascular system. Nicotine results in the tightening of blood vessels, which restricts blood flow. Smoking lowers the level of good cholesterol (LDL) in the blood.

It raises blood pressure, which can stretch arteries and accumulate bad cholesterol (HDL), leading to *atherosclerosis*.

Smoking increases the risk of blood clots, which, along with weakened brain blood vessels, increase stroke risk. The long-term effect is a greater risk for leukemia. Inhaling second-hand smoke increases stroke risk, heart attacks, and coronary heart disease, even in non-smokers.

More apparent consequences of smoking are its effects on the skin, including discoloration, wrinkles, and premature aging. Substances in tobacco smoke change skin structure. Fingernails and skin may develop yellow staining from holding cigarettes. Smokers usually develop yellow or brown stains on their teeth.

Smokers are at an increased risk of oral health problems with tobacco, causing gum disease, gingivitis, or infections such as periodontitis, which can develop into other issues, such as tooth decay, loss, and bad breath. Smoking increases the risk of developing mouth, throat, larynx, esophagus, kidney and pancreatic cancers.

Smoking increases the chance of developing insulin resistance, which makes it more likely for smokers to develop type 2 diabetes.

Smoking may affect sexuality and the reproductive system. Smokers have a higher risk of infertility, and women who smoke pre-menopause are at an increased risk of cervical cancer and are more likely to experience pregnancy complications (e.g., miscarriages and premature deliveries). Pregnant women who smoke may suffer complications at birth, and newborns inhaling second-hand smoke are susceptible to ill effects.

Noise pollution effects

Noise pollution is excessive noise or unpleasant sounds that disrupt the natural balance. Machines and transportation systems, motor vehicles, aircraft, and trains mainly cause outdoor noise sources. Urbanization contributes to noise pollution as industrial and residential buildings are nearby. Indoor noise pollution is caused by machines and equipment, especially in factories.

Hearing loss is a common health effect of high noise exposure levels (or long periods). Adverse effects include psychological issues, tinnitus, stress-related illnesses, high blood pressure, sleep disruption, cardiovascular diseases, and decreased productivity.

Preventing harmful effects from noise pollution includes wearing ear protection (e.g., acoustic earplugs or sound-dampening earmuffs) when areas with loud noise cannot be avoided (e.g., occupational settings).

Size and alteration of roadway surface texture, traffic controls to reduce vehicle speed, and noise barriers can help reduce noise. Residents who live close to airports benefit from aircraft with quieter engines and strategically chosen flight paths based on the time of day.

Dose-response relationships

Dose-response relationship (or exposure-response relationship) describes changes resulting from different levels of exposure to a stressor over a specified period.

Pollutants mainly enter humans through breathing. Pollutants are internalized by ingestion (e.g., children eating lead-contaminated soil) or absorbed through the skin. Once a pollutant such as asbestos enters the body, it stays in the lungs, is exhaled, or absorbed into the bloodstream through the lungs, stomach, or skin. In the bloodstream, it is transported to different areas.

Pollutants can undergo chemical changes as they are transported throughout the body, primarily through the liver. This mutation can cause the pollutants to decrease or increase in toxicity level. Pollutants can be excreted from the body through urination, bowel movements, breast milk, or perspiration. They can be stored in bones, fat, organs, or hair.

Toxic air pollutants affect normal body functions by changing chemical reactions within cells. These changes can destroy cells, damage cell function, or alter cell activity and result in impaired organs, congenital disabilities when the cells of an unborn child are damaged, or cancer that can develop when cells begin to grow uncontrolled.

The dose-response relationship for a specific pollutant refers to the relationship between exposure level and the corresponding health effect.

Environmental Protection Agency asserts that no exposures are "zero risk;" even significantly low exposure to carcinogenic pollutants can increase cancer risk. The EPA models the relationship between dose and response in a straight line; for each unit of increase in exposure, there is a corresponding increase in cancer response.

EPA has determined an exposure level at or below the minimum health effect level and asserts that this low exposure will not harm the body's natural protective mechanisms, which can repair any damage caused by a pollutant.

Dose-response relationships vary with pollutants, individual sensitivity, and health effects. Studies reveal that long-term exposure to low concentrations of particulate matter from combustion is associated with chronic health effects such as bronchitis, reduced lung function, shortened lifespan, lung cancer, and increased respiratory symptoms.

United States Environmental Protection Agency (EPA) logo

Biomagnification

Biological magnification is the increased concentration of toxic substances in animal tissues at successively higher levels of the food chain. This occurs when hazardous waste from industrial, agricultural, and human activities contaminates bodies of water, such as rivers, and is consumed by animals in the food chain.

As these animals consume more contaminated food, the toxins become more concentrated in the animal's tissues. These pollutants cause genetic mutation, diseases, congenital disabilities, reproductive difficulties, behavioral changes, and death in aquatic organisms.

Many of these toxins settle on the seafloor and are consumed by organisms that feed on food and sediments at the bottom of the ocean. These compounds are not digested and accumulate within the animals that consume them, becoming more concentrated as the compounds move along the food chain.

When the toxin reaches the top of the food chain, it is more concentrated and dangerous.

Humans, the species at the top of the food chain, eat contaminated animals and ingest the toxins within them, which can have a severe health impact.

In northwest Ontario, Canada, between 1962 and 1970, biomagnification occurred due to a paper plant dumping ten tons of mercury into a local river. The result was that approximately 100 residents developed Minamata disease or methylmercury poisoning, the symptoms of which include slurred speech, tunnel vision, and spasms and may lead to insanity and eventual death. The disease is named for its city of origin, Minamata, Japan, where residents started exhibiting such symptoms after a corporation dumped its mercury waste into a bay, contaminating the fish.

Hazardous environmental chemicals

Over the past century, humans have introduced many chemical substances into the environment. These wastes come from many sources, including industrial and agricultural processes. While some chemicals are beneficial, many are toxic, and their harmful effects on the environment and human health far outweigh their societal benefit.

The balance between human activity and environmental sustainability requires attention. Human activities have a multifaceted impact on the environment and create a chain of interconnecting reactions that may harm different ecosystems.

World Health Organization (WHO) study suggested that priority pollutants should be defined by toxicity, environmental persistence and mobility, bioaccumulation, and other hazards such as explosiveness.

Pollutants with the most significant potential to impact human health based on environmental persistence, bioaccumulation, the amount emitted, and toxic levels are cadmium, mercury, arsenic, chromium, nickel, dioxins, polychlorinated biphenyls (PCB), and sulfur dioxide.

Dioxins

Dioxins are some of the most toxic human-made organic chemicals; only radioactive waste is more toxic. They are a class of super-toxic chemicals formed by manufacturing, molding, or burning organic chemicals and plastics containing chlorine. These chemicals have serious health effects even at levels as low as a few parts per trillion.

Dioxins are practically indestructible and are excreted by the body exceptionally slowly. These compounds enter the body in food and accumulate in body fat. They bind to cell receptors and disrupt hormone functions, affecting the normal functioning of genes.

The human body is not designed to defend against dioxins, which may result in issues including cancers, reduced nervous system immunity, blood disorders, miscarriages, and congenital disabilities.

The effects vary in magnitude from very noticeable to subtle. The alteration of gene function can cause genetic diseases that may affect childhood development, resulting in attention deficit hyperactivity disorder (ADHD), diabetes, endometriosis, chronic fatigue syndrome, and rare nervous system or blood disorders.

Organochlorines

Organochlorines are a group of synthetic compounds that include organochlorine pesticides (OCBs) and polychlorinated biphenyls (PCBs). Organochlorines are dangerous chemicals developed as cooling agents for electric equipment. Millions of gallons of PCB oil leaked during the manufacture and disposal of PCB products.

The manufacture of PCBs ceased in the United States in the 1970s.

Despite being phased out of manufacturing, organochlorines remain in the environment. These chemicals, which are hard to detect and almost indestructible, accumulate in the food chain for decades and can be observed at high levels years after discontinued production.

The chemical is in marine species, especially mammals and seabirds. PCBs are carcinogenic, potentially damaging the liver, nervous, and reproductive systems.

Burning PCBs has resulted in the formation of dioxins, which are even more toxic.

A technician labels a PCB-containing transformer

Cadmium

Cadmium is a naturally occurring metallic element in Earth's crust. When combined with other elements, it forms compounds such as cadmium oxide, cadmium chloride, or cadmium sulfate, which are highly toxic.

Cadmium metal is used for its corrosion resistance to manufacture batteries, plastics, pigments, and metal coatings.

Cadmium enters the environment through landfills, poor waste disposal methods, and leaks at hazardous waste sites. It is a waste product of mining and other industrial activities.

Cadmium particles can enter the air from burning fossil fuels for energy and incineration of waste. The particles are small and can travel long distances before falling to the ground or into bodies of water. Cadmium enters the food chain by being discharged into the oceans, and animals and plants take cadmium from the soil.

Food contaminated with cadmium can potentially irritate human digestive systems, resulting in vomiting and diarrhea. If inhaled, it can damage the human respiratory system. Over time, cadmium accumulates in the body, even if the exposure is low, and it can be challenging to eliminate. Accumulated cadmium can cause kidney and bone disease.

Toxic Substances Control Act (TSCA)

Toxic Substances Control Act (TSCA) is a United States law passed by the United States Congress in 1976 and administered by the EPA. This law regulates the introduction of new or existing chemicals.

The main objectives of this Act are to assess and regulate

    1) commercial chemicals before entering the market,

    2) existing chemicals posing an adverse risk to health or the environment, and

    3) distribution and use of harmful chemicals.

Toxic Substances Control Act specifically regulates *polychlorinated biphenyl* (PCB) products.

TSCA does not separate chemicals into categories of toxic and non-toxic. The Act instead prohibits the manufacture or import of chemicals that are not on the TSCA.

Inventory manufacturers must submit a pre-manufacturing notification to the EPA before manufacturing or importing commercial chemicals.

The agency reviews notifications, and its use is banned if a proposed chemical is deemed potentially harmful to human health or the environment.

Chemical Safety Improvement Act (CSIA) was bipartisan legislation proposed in 2013. It was introduced to Congress to reform and modernize TSCA. The Act regulates the introduction of new or existing chemicals.

Economic Impacts

Pollution costs

Pollution becomes an expense when it costs money to solve problems caused by its effects. Industrial waste has been discarded into the environment for over 150 years without regard for the environment or economy. The initial view was that the environment had an infinite capacity to absorb pollutants. It was unknown that there are thresholds beyond which pollutant levels become lethal.

Debris and injured birds caused by water pollution

Biological damage is done before these thresholds are reached, and ecological costs that are not immediately observable are being incurred. These adverse effects will eventually be translated into economic costs once their effect becomes more readily apparent.

The recent enthusiastic interest in controlling pollution is due to many of these thresholds being reached and the beginning effect on the economy. Research has revealed that approximately 25% of respiratory diseases in the U.S. result from air pollution.

According to the *Organization for Economic Co-operation and Development* (OECD), the cost of air pollution in deaths and health effects of OECD countries, plus China and India, is 3.5 trillion dollars annually.

Remediation and mitigation

Remediation is fixing a contaminated area using relatively nondestructive methods to clean and restore the area while causing minimal disturbance, damage, or harm.

Remediation utilizes chemical, physical, and biological methods of removing contaminants.

Bioremediation is when naturally occurring or forcefully introduced organisms are used to degrade and alleviate pollutants. *Bioremediation* helped clean the Deepwater Horizon (2010) oil spill in the Gulf of Mexico. Naturally produced bacteria were used to clean; they could ingest and degrade the oil into less harmful substances.

Deepwater Horizon oil spill, Gulf of Mexico, 2010

Mitigation replaces a degraded site with a healthy site of equal ecological value in another location. Mitigation compensates for destroying one area by purchasing or creating areas of equal ecological value.

Mitigation is less desirable than other land conservation methods because it allows land to be destroyed, harmed, or damaged.

Externalities

Externality is a cost (or benefit) affecting a party who did not choose to incur it. If external costs (i.e., pollution) exist, the producer may choose to make more products than would be made if the producer were required to pay associated environmental costs.

Responsibility for the consequences of an action is not solely internal; an element of externalization is involved.

For example, a factory may pollute a river during production. If that river is used as a tourist attraction, revenue will be lost from contamination, and the city may have to absorb the cost to remediate damage. This is an external cost because the factory is not held accountable when producing goods.

If external benefits are to be gained, such as public safety, fewer goods may be made than if the producer had received payment for the external benefits to others. It can be deduced that the overall cost and benefit to society is the sum of the imputed monetary value of benefits and costs to all parties involved.

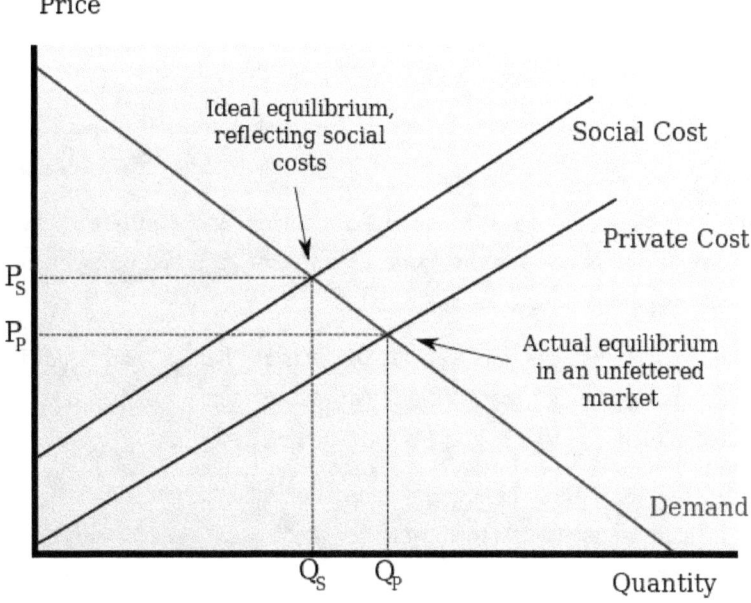

Demand curve showing the microeconomic concept of a negative externality

A voluntary exchange may reduce the well-being of society if external costs exist. The person affected by the negative externalities in the case of air pollution will see it as a lowered utility: either personal displeasure or the potential to incur costs, such as higher medical expenses. The externality may be a trespass on their lungs, which violates their property rights.

Therefore, an external cost has the potential to pose an ethical or political problem. Otherwise, it might be seen as a case of poorly defined property rights, such as the pollution of bodies of water that may belong to no one or are publicly owned.

Positive externalities increase the utility of third parties at no cost to them. Since collective societal welfare is improved, the providers have no way of monetizing the benefit; smaller quantities of the goodwill be made than would be optimal for society.

Cost-benefit analysis

Environmental economists use the concept of *scarcity* to perform cost-benefit analyses and recommend implementing pollution policies. This study assesses how people make decisions when faced with scarcity.

Humans have infinite wants but live with finite resources.

Scarcity implies that resources devoted to one end are unavailable to meet another. For instance, funds a municipality uses to modify its water treatment plant to remove trace amounts of arsenic cannot be used to improve local elementary education.

Scarcity demands compromises, so some consider total elimination of pollution undesirable and unnecessary. The subsequent response is to manage and eliminate *some* pollution.

Economists use cost-benefit analysis to decide the best options for eliminating pollution sources.

Cost-benefit analysis provides an organizational framework for identifying, quantifying, and comparing the costs and benefits in the monetary value of proposed policy action. The final decision is based on comparative costs and benefits.

Environmental regulations' benefits include decreasing human and wildlife mortality, improved water quality, species preservation, and greater recreation opportunities. Costs are usually reflected in higher consumer goods prices and taxes.

While it is easy to put a dollar value on the market effects, such as improving education, it proves more difficult to attach a cost to non-market effects, such as decreasing pollution and its effects on ecosystems.

This analytical tool shows how the interests, claims, and opinions of parties affected by a proposed regulation can be examined and compared. It demands specificity and practicality, which is necessary for making sound decisions.

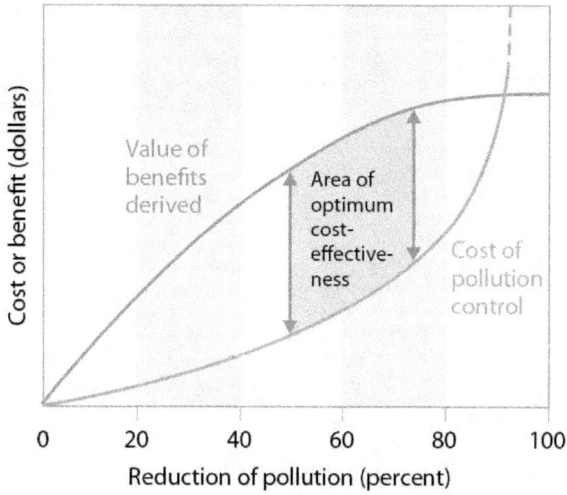
Sample cost-benefit analysis graph

Economic, social and environmental costs

There are several methods of improving overall social utility when externalities are involved. The market-driven approach to improving externalities is to "internalize" third-party costs and benefits (e.g., requiring a polluter to repair any damage caused).

However, in some instances, internalizing costs or benefits is impractical, especially if it is impossible to determine the actual monetary value.

Many negative externalities are related to the environmental consequences of production and use. Externalities of air pollution include economic, social, and environmental costs.

Economic costs include a variety of externalities, such as damage to property, structures, and infrastructure, as well as loss of productivity of people and crops. Acid deposition, smog, and ozone pollution alter the time-based scale during which investments in infrastructure can be remunerated and must be replaced.

For example, buildings usually amortized over 20-30 years may lose from 1-5 years of useful life, depending on the construction material. Aside from health costs, air pollution has a direct impact on labor force productivity. Productivity time decreases as time is lost from being in recovery.

Crops and timber products are directly affected by air pollutants, and losses may be calculated based on quantities produced per surface unit.

Smog-damaged plant at the statewide air pollution research center, University of California. The plant was damaged by fumigation with 1/2 part per million ozone for 3 hours

Social costs are related to pollution's physiological impact on humans, especially cardiovascular and respiratory systems. Some impacts are apparent, such as the effects of carbon monoxide.

Other effects, such as lead and VOCs, are less discernible and more malignant. It would be difficult to attribute a specific case of lung cancer to general air pollution or a smoking habit. Many people reside in urban areas and are constantly exposed to air pollution emissions.

Environmental costs encompass overall damage done to the ecosystem through the atmosphere, except for what may be considered economically valuable to human activities such as agriculture. Environmental costs are the most difficult to assess comprehensively. They can encompass various effects, such as biological diversity and sustainability, which may prove difficult to quantify.

Marginal costs

Marginal cost is an economic term referring to the change in total production cost brought about by producing an additional unit. For example, if a factory chooses to produce a new product line, the product's marginal cost includes additional costs (e.g., extra materials, added production, and additional work hours).

There is an optimum amount of pollution where the marginal benefit equals the marginal cost. To identify the optimum amount of pollution, determine the marginal cost, marginal abatement cost, and marginal benefit.

The economics of pollution suggests that there is an "ideal" amount of pollution where the well-being of society is at its peak, and the damage to the environment is at a sustainable level. Economists have argued that eliminating pollution is not economically or environmentally favorable because the cost of reducing pollution exceeds the benefits.

Aquatic environments and the atmosphere can naturally assimilate some pollutants without ill effects on the environment or humans. To disregard this, natural assimilative capacity would be wasteful. Furthermore, what one industry regards as a pollutant may be another industry's raw material.

The marginal cost for pollution involves an additional environmental cost from producing an additional unit. Therefore, an additional environmental cost may result in an increase in greenhouse gas emissions that arise from the production of the new product line.

Marginal abatement costs must be analyzed to assess optimum pollution levels. They are expenses incurred to remediate harmful occurrences. This cost is, therefore, associated with eliminating a unit of pollution.

For an example of *abatement costs*, consider a coal-burning power plant that produces toxic sulfur dioxide emissions, which have detrimental environmental effects. To reduce emissions, companies install smokestack scrubbers to remove pollutants. Costs associated with installing and using the scrubbers are abatement costs.

As pollution decreases, marginal abatement costs increase because more costly and advanced technologies are needed.

Society's well-being is at its optimum concerning environmental quality when the marginal cost of pollution abatement equals the marginal benefit from pollution abatement.

If the marginal benefit of reducing pollution exceeds the marginal cost, society would benefit from pollution reduction.

The benefit would equal the amount by which the marginal benefit of the cleanup exceeds the marginal costs of cleaning the environment.

However, if the marginal cost of pollution abatement exceeds the marginal benefit from the reduction, the benefit of cleaning the environment is not worth the expense; further attempts to clean the environment will result in a reduction in welfare.

Sustainability

Sustainability is the ability to support current needs without compromising future supply.

Environmental sustainability preserves the environment with long-term ecological balance. Pollution prevention is an integral part of sustainability and long-term planning.

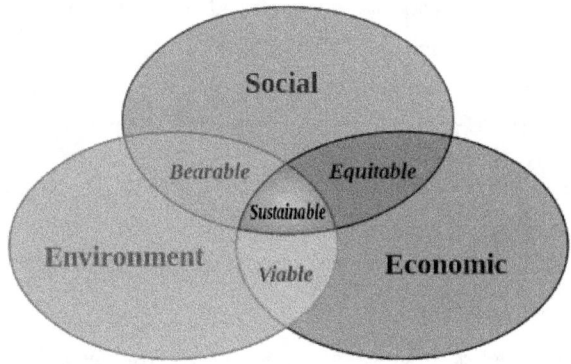

Sustainable development with economic, social, and environmental components

Sustainable Business Practices (SBPs) involve designing businesses to reduce or eliminate dependence on finite resources. This includes conserving areas around cities and using sustainable energy sources like solar, wind, geothermal, or biofuels instead of fossil fuels. It involves designing recyclable products and encouraging people to buy recycled products.

Sustainability principles apply to every aspect of business, such as construction, development, and production. Pollution prevention is the first step in achieving sustainability.

An understanding of how waste is generated and how it can be minimized is the first step to eliminating waste, increasing efficiency, and developing sustainable production methods.

Pollution prevention has economic and environmental benefits, including minimizing the energy and resources used to treat and dispose of waste. It ensures that waste produced can be reused or disposed of easily and without harming the environment. In this way, pollution prevention becomes essential to sustainability as the cost of extra raw materials, waste disposal, and waste treatment systems can be eliminated or substantially reduced.

Novel tools and processes are becoming more popular to prevent pollution at its source and institute sustainability practices. Companies' Business models can be reviewed to identify opportunities to incorporate pollution prevention practices.

Waste reduction strategies

Waste reduction is essential for environmental protection, conservation of natural resources, and economic sustainability. Reducing waste also reduces pollution, conserves valuable natural resources, and helps lower waste disposal and management expenses. Less waste translates into a reduced need for landfill space, less greenhouse gas emissions, and lower demand for resource extraction.

Individual households can achieve waste reduction by:

1) using reusable shopping bags;
2) choosing products with less or environmentally friendly packaging;
3) composting their kitchen waste;
4) reusing non-biodegradable items;
5) recycling as much as possible;
6) purchasing consumer goods manufactured from recycled products.

Relationship matrix

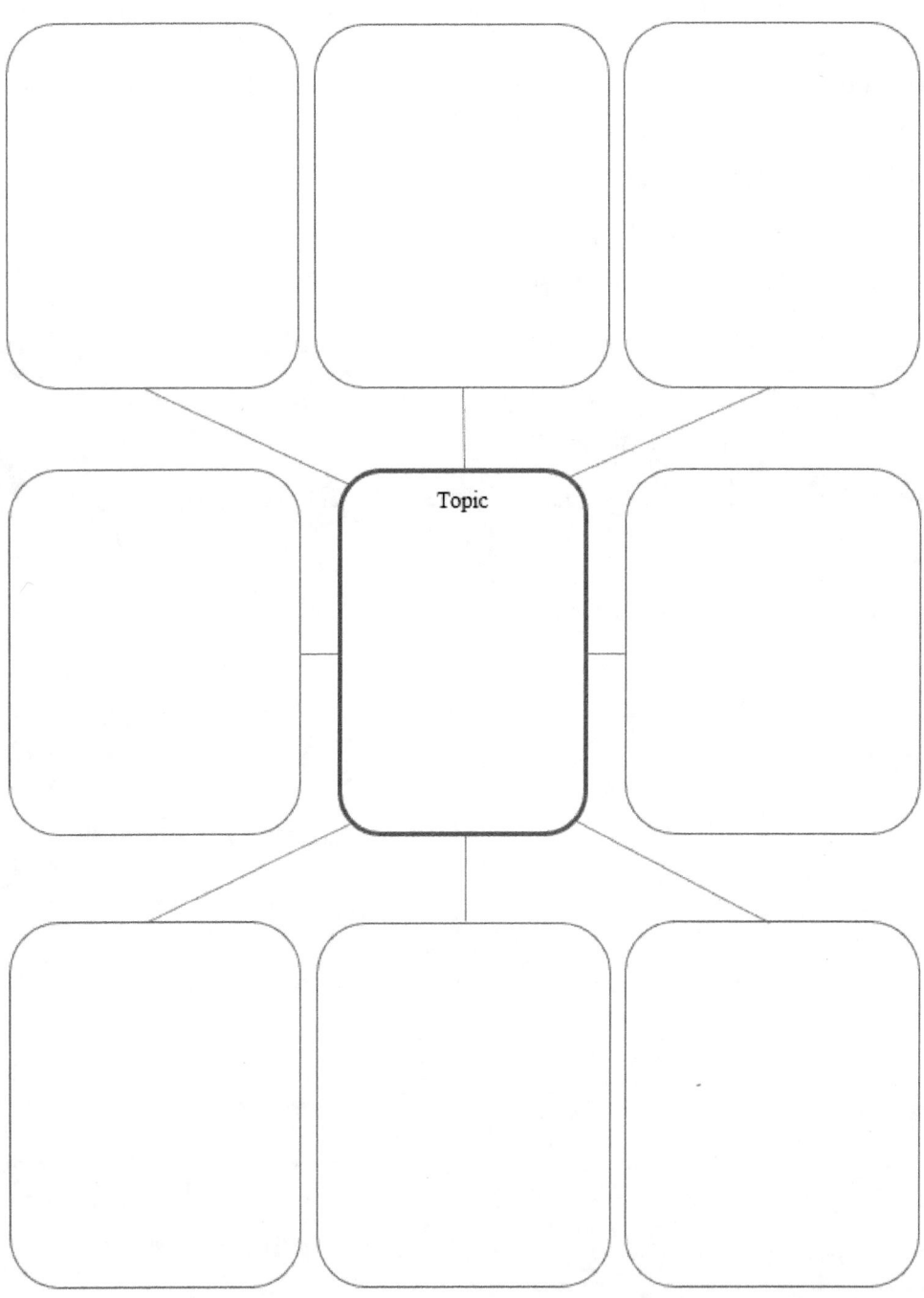

Questions: Pollution

1. In a community with mounting air and water pollution problems, the:

   A. economy of the region would decline
   B. unemployment rates would drop
   C. healthcare would become less important
   D. population would increase

2. Pollution control costs tend to:

   A. decrease over time because of initial investments in reductions and technologies
   B. decrease over time because regulations generally become less restrictive
   C. increase over time as levels of acceptable pollution become increasingly restrictive
   D. increase over time as new technologies require renewed investments

3. Being exposed to secondhand smoke by living with a person who smokes:

   A. only poses a health risk for those in the household who smoke
   B. has not been shown to increase the health risks to nonsmokers in the home
   C. increases the chances of cancer for everyone in the home
   D. increases the risk of cardiovascular disease but not cancer for household members

4. Many polluted ecosystems will recover if humans stop polluting them. This illustrates:

   A. loss of ecosystem capital
   B. the essential role of keystone species in ecosystems
   C. secondary succession
   D. the natural resilience of ecosystems

5. Secondary air pollutants are formed by:

   A. the evaporation of solvents and gasoline
   B. the incomplete combustion of fuels
   C. primary pollutants reacting with other compounds in the atmosphere
   D. radioactive substances such as radon reacting with primary pollutants

6. Contaminated water is responsible for more than 1.6 million deaths in developing countries. Contributing to this is the use of:

A. groundwater for consumption and the disposal of human sewage

B. groundwater for consumption and the disposal of human sewage in surface waters

C. surface waters for consumption and the disposal of human sewage

D. surface waters for consumption and the disposal of human sewage in groundwater

7. Which is a primary anthropogenic source of volatile organic compounds (VOCs)?

A. coal-fired electrical generating plants

B. agricultural fertilizers

C. incompletely combusted fossil fuels from vehicle exhaust

D. nuclear power plants

8. The best way to reduce the pollution of agricultural fertilizer runoff from farm fields is to:

A. treat the water before it reaches streams or rivers

B. reduce the amount of fertilizer leaving the farm fields through such techniques as no-till cultivation

C. add chemicals into the rivers and streams that neutralize the fertilizers

D. raise crops in the rivers and streams that use fertilizers

9. According to EPA requirements for landfills, leachate from the landfill must be:

A. collected by a system that intercepts percolation and treats it as necessary

B. collected into pools at the edge of the landfill where it can evaporate

C. absorbed by materials such as paper products added as the landfill is formed

D. contained within the landfill using a system of plastic liners that prevent its escape

10. Suspicious that their household drinking water from a well was being contaminated with gasoline, a family investigated possible sources of groundwater contamination. The underground storage tanks for gasoline at a nearby filling station were leaking. Promising to pay to fix the problem, the station owners sealed the gas tank and pumped out the contaminated groundwater. After several months of rain, the groundwater supplies were restored, and the water in the well was safe to drink. This is an example of:

A. reverse osmosis refinement

B. maximum containment remuneration

C. groundwater remediation

D. well-water containment

11. Industrial pollution from an oil refinery best represents a type of:

    A. biological environmental hazard
    B. cultural environmental hazard
    C. physical environmental hazard
    D. chemical environmental hazard

12. About one hundred years ago, cities began to address sewage disposal problems by dumping sewage into nearby rivers via stormwater drainage systems. One of the results of this strategy was that:

    A. cities no longer needed to treat drinking water drawn from nearby river systems
    B. the quality of the water in the local rivers and streams greatly improved
    C. people living upriver of these cities were more likely to experience contamination of their drinking water sources
    D. people living downriver of these cities were more likely to experience contamination of their drinking water sources

13. Biogas is mainly produced in landfills:

    A. by the anaerobic decomposition of organic materials
    B. by the release of compressed gases from aerosol containers
    C. by the evaporation of the liquids draining from the buried waste
    D. when solid materials melt into fluids and evaporate

14. The threshold level for harmful effects of toxic pollutants is most closely related to the:

    A. first appearance of chronic effects
    B. duration of exposure
    C. concentration of exposure
    D. concentration and duration of exposure

15. Deep-well injection of hazardous waste has the advantage that:

    A. it falls under the umbrella of the Superfund Cleanup (SARA)
    B. injected materials can easily be recovered for further treatment
    C. solids, liquids, and gases can be disposed of with this technology
    D. deep-injected liquids should not contaminate groundwater or surface ecosystems

Notes for active learning

CHAPTER 7

Energy Resources & Consumption

Foundational Concepts of Energy

Energy Consumption

Fossil Fuel Reserves and Use

Nuclear Energy

Hydroelectric Power

Energy Conservation and Renewable Energy

Page intentionally left blank

Foundational Concepts of Energy

Organisms require sunlight

Organisms rely on *electromagnetic radiant energy* from the Sun for survival.

Primary producers in a food chain (e.g., plants, algae, cyanobacteria) capture solar energy and initiate energy flow through a system.

Energy is the capacity to perform work.

Energy has several forms, which measure the ability of a system (or object) *to do work* on another system (or object).

Work is force applied over a distance ($W = F \times d$). Energy must be expended if work is done.

Over centuries, humans developed an in-depth understanding of energy, including methods to capture and utilize it for everyday activities.

Energy forms

Energy has many forms:

Thermal energy (or *heat energy*) is measured by temperature. Objects with higher temperatures have more thermal energy than colder objects.

For example, when a hot soup container is placed in a refrigerator, heat leaves the soup as it cools; particles lose thermal energy and slow. As particles slow (less kinetic energy), the temperature of the soup decreases. Thermometers measure thermal energy.

Chemical energy (or *bond energy*) is stored in chemical bonds, such as molecules and atoms. Bonds are broken when a chemical reaction occurs, and energy is often released as heat (i.e., exothermic reactions).

For example, gasoline has chemical energy that is used to power automobiles. As gasoline burns, small "explosions" (i.e., breaking of chemical bonds) release heat that moves pistons and the car.

Electrical energy is stored in electrons. It is generated when an electric field moves electrons along a conductor.

For example, storm clouds collect large amounts of electrical energy, released as lightning, when clouds bump.

Nuclear energy is in the atom's nucleus, holding protons and neutrons together. Nuclear energy is released during nuclear *fusion* (joining of nuclei) or *fission* (breaking of nuclei)

For example, nuclear power plants harness the atomic fission to produce electricity.

Potential energy (or *stored energy*) is based on an object's position (or condition) *rather than* motion. Potential energy examples include raised weight, battery, coiled spring, and boulder on top of a hill.

Kinetic energy (or *energy of motion*) is the movement of an object. The potential energy stored in an object becomes kinetic energy when the object moves. Examples of kinetic energy include a falling weight, a coiled spring being released, and a boulder rolling downhill.

Mechanical energy is the sum of potential and kinetic energy. Motion and position must be considered to determine the power. An object has mechanical energy when in motion and vertically above the ground. For example, when raised vertically from the ground, a wrecking ball has potential mechanical energy.

Electromagnetic energy (or *light energy*) is packets of *photons* (i.e., *light energy*). Photons are created when electrons transition from an excited state (i.e., *high energy orbital*) to a less excited state (ground state or lower energy orbital), releasing bursts of light energy.

Power

Power is the rate at which work is done or the energy consumed in a unit of time.

SI unit for power is the watt (W), equivalent to joules per second (J/s), and was named after James Watt, who developed the steam engine in the 18th century.

Power and work may sometimes seem like similar concepts, but they are different.

Work refers to an action involving a force and a movement in the direction of that force.

For example, a 10 Newton force pushes an object 2 ms; this action does 200 joules of work.

Power is the rate at which work is done.

For example, 200 joules of work is completed in one second; the power is 200 watts.

   Work = Force × Distance (N·m)

   Power = Work / Time (N·m)/s

Basic SI units

Dimension	Basic Unit	Symbol
Time	Second	s
Length	Meter	m
Mass	Kilogram	kg
Temperature	Kelvin	K
Electric Current	Ampere	A

Derived SI units

Dimension	Unit	Symbol
Power	Watt	W = (J/s)
Energy	Joule	J = N·m
Energy Flux	Watt per square meter	W/m^2
Speed	Meter per second	m/s
Acceleration	Meter per second squared	m/s^2
Force	Newton	N = kg·m/s^2
Area	Meter squared	m^2
Volume	Meter cubed	m^3
Pressure	Pascal	Pa = N/m
Voltage	Volt	V = W/A
Volume Flow	Cubic meter per second	m^3/s
Mass flow	Kilogram per second	kg/s
Calorific Value	Joule per kilogram	J/kg
Specific Heat	Joule per kilogram Kelvin	J/(kg·K)

Non-standard international units

Non-SI Unit for Energy	Symbol	Equivalence in SI-Units
Kilowatt-hour	kWh	3.60×10^6 J
Tera watt year	TWy	31.5×10^{18} J
British Thermal Unit	Btu	1.055×10^3 J
Horsepower-hour (metric)	hp·hr	2.646×10^6 J
Erg	erg	10^{-7} J
Foot pound force	ft·lbf	1.356 J
Kilogram-force meter	kgf·m	9.8 J
Calorie	cal	4.187 J

Laws of thermodynamics

Thermodynamics studies *energy*, *work*, and *heat* and focuses on *large-scale systems*.

Three *laws of thermodynamics* define properties (e.g., temperature, energy, and entropy) and predict how a system operates.

Entropy is the *degree of disorder* in a system. It is the unavailability of energy in a system to convert its thermal energy to mechanical work.

Zeroth Law of Thermodynamics states that two systems in thermal equilibrium with a third system will be in thermal equilibrium.

First Law of Thermodynamics (Conservation of Energy) states that energy cannot be created or destroyed. Total energy into a system equals energy out, though energy may change forms.

For example, plants receive solar energy converted to chemical energy by photosynthesis. No energy was lost; it simply changed forms from solar to chemical energy.

Second Law of Thermodynamics states that in cyclic systems, the entropy of that system either remains the same or increases. In closed systems, the initial total useful energy is greater than the useful energy at completion.

Energy "*wasted*" (e.g., heat, sounds, sparking) is not as valuable as thermal energy (heat). This does not violate the First Law as energy changes form.

Third Law of Thermodynamics states that the entropy of a system approaches a constant value as the temperature of that system approaches absolute zero (–273 °C).

Theoretically, systems at absolute zero have zero entropy (i.e., motion ceases).

Energy Consumption

Mastery of fire

Mastery of fire was a monumental advancement in human harnessing of energy. Early humans learned to use naturally occurring fires (e.g., a lightning strike) and create and control them. Burning fuel (wood in the case of early humans) has become a primary source of warmth, light, protection from predators, and a means to cook food, which is available for nutrients.

Later, burning biomasses led to the production of pottery and the refining of metals. Fire allowed our ancestors to work with new materials and develop more advanced tools and weapons. Fire was used for hunting, clearing land, and other purposes, allowing early civilizations to alter their environments.

In recent history, fire has been a vital component of essential inventions such as *steam engines*, which convert *chemical energy* stored in coal and wood into *kinetic energy* (i.e., energy of motion).

The coal-powered steam engine was a remarkable invention and mainspring of the Industrial Revolution. It was used to manufacture machinery to power locomotives, ships, and automobiles. Coal remained the largest fuel source until the mid-20th century when petroleum replaced it.

Industrial Revolution

Humankind began utilizing coal as an energy source as early as 1300 to cook food and provide warmth, but it was not until the 1800s that more uses for coal were discovered. A significant factor in this growing use of coal as an energy source was the Industrial Revolution of the late 17th and early 18th centuries.

It was not until the 1880s that coal provided electricity for homes and factories. As coal and fossil fuels came to be used to build factories and machines, power cars, and warm homes, the demand for fuel increased dramatically, as did drilling for resources.

This high demand and dependence on non-renewable energy sources have worried some scientists and economists, as they recognize that stores of fossil fuels are limited. If humans continue using fossil fuels at the same rate, stores may become depleted.

Industrial Revolution (1760 to 1840) was when Great Britain transitioned from hand production methods to machines. The period was marked by improved efficiency of water power, increased use of steam power, development of machine tools, and increased number of factories. Textile factories employed most people in this era, and the standard of living increased for the first time.

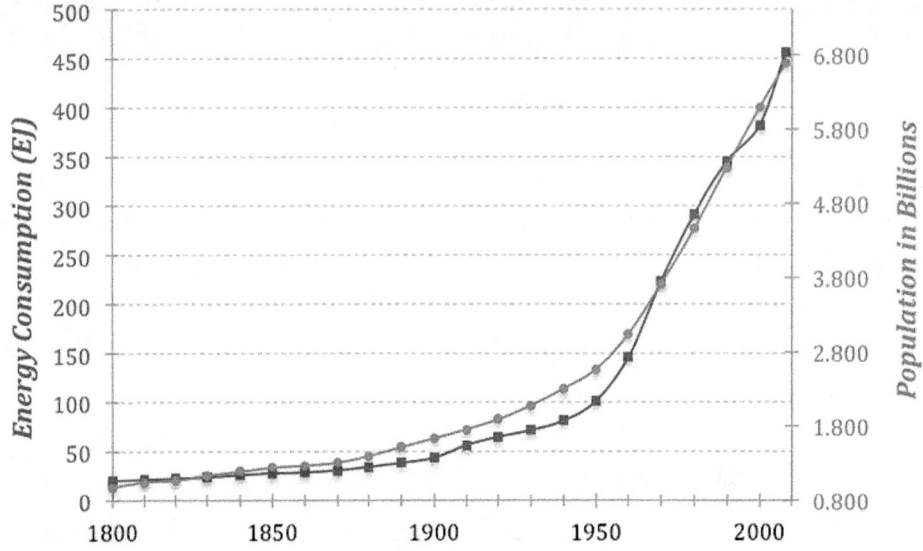

Global energy consumption and population, Penn State

Some of the most significant technological advancements and innovations occurred in the United Kingdom, including the Watt *steam engine*. The steam engine was named after James Watt, who perfected it in 1778. It was made of iron and fueled by coal.

Watt's improvements allowed greater steam engine efficiency to power other machines and factories. The earliest mills ran by waterpower, but the introduction of the steam engine allowed factories to be built anywhere, not just near water sources.

Global energy consumption

In 2022, the United States consumed an average of about 20.01 million barrels of petroleum daily, or about 20.01 billion barrels annually.

U.S. represents about 5% of the global population but consumes a quarter of the world's oil.

Global oil consumption is 11 billion tons annually. Crude oil reserves are used at 4 billion tons annually. If the trend continues, known oil deposits will be depleted by 2052.

Modern-day global energy use is undergoing a slow transition and diversification. Specifically, as more nations react to climate change, investments and innovations are increasingly made to seek sustainable alternatives to fossil fuels.

International Energy Agency (IEA), *European Environment Agency* (EEA), and *U.S. Energy Information Administration* (EIA) track consumption per source and published data.

In 2023, fossil fuel use (e.g., petroleum, coal, natural gas) accounted for 79%, nuclear power 8.0% and renewables 13%.

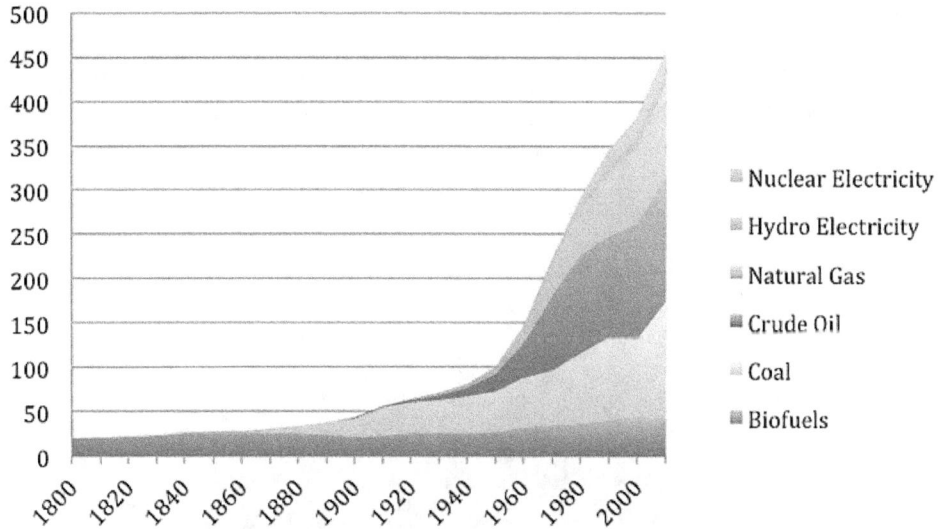

History of global energy consumption by source, Penn State

Nations adopting renewable energy (per Climate Council) are Germany, Sweden, Costa Rica, Nicaragua, Scotland, Uruguay, Denmark, China, Morocco, the United States, and Kenya.

A trend away from nuclear power continues as a sustained reaction to nuclear disasters (e.g., *Chornobyl*, 1986; *Three Mile Island*, 1979; *Fukushima Daiichi*, 2011).

Despite strategic pivoting toward cleaner energy, fossil fuels are overwhelmingly used.

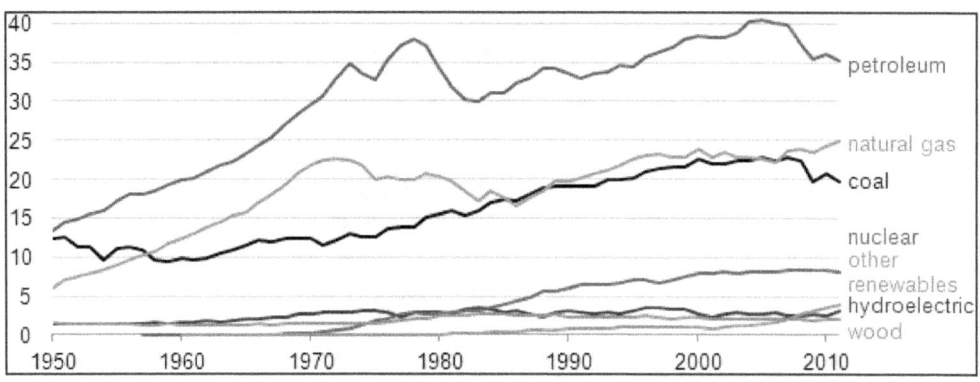

U.S. primary energy consumption by source (quadrillion Btu)

Petroleum, natural gas, and coal have been the primary energy sources for over 60 years. Not until the 1970s and 1980s did other fuel sources (e.g., nuclear and hydroelectric energy) become widely used.

Renewables being adopted include many sources:

> traditional biomass, bio-heat, ethanol, biodiesel, biopower generation, hydropower, wind, solar heating/cooling, solar PV, solar CSP, geothermal heat, geothermal electricity, and ocean power.

Unlike finite fossil fuels, renewable energy (e.g., solar power) is not depleted by use.

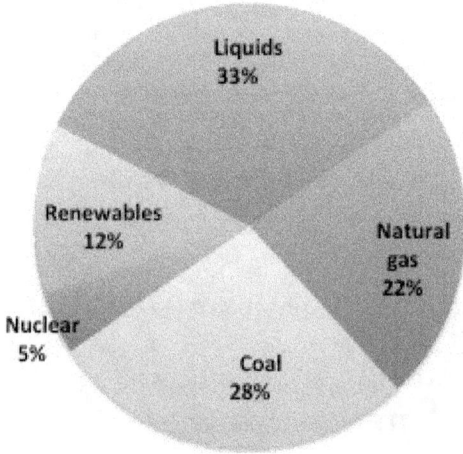

Global energy consumption by fuel type (576 quadrillion Btu, 2015)

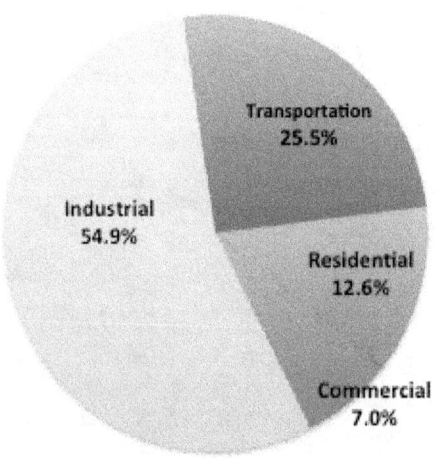

Global energy delivered by sector (433 quadrillion Btu, 2015)

Chapter 7: Energy Resources & Consumption

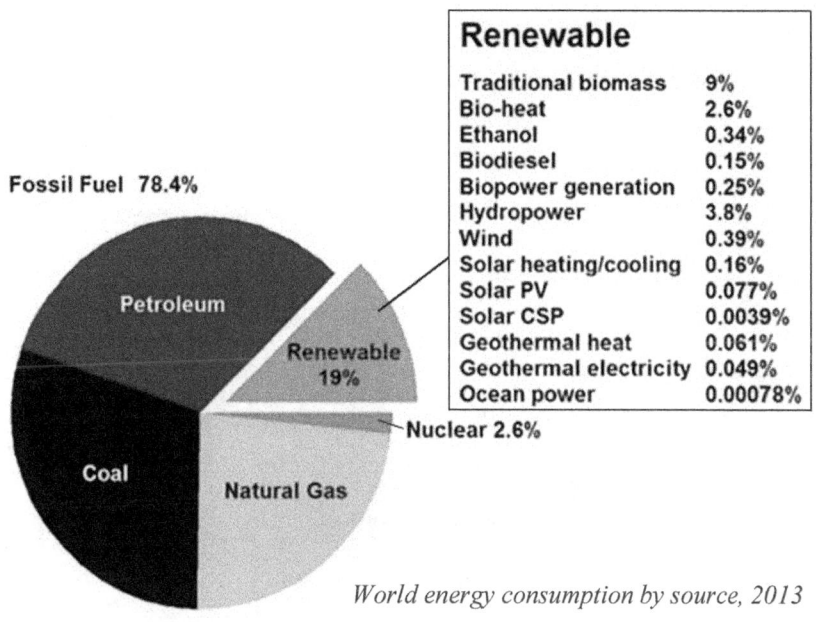

World energy consumption by source, 2013

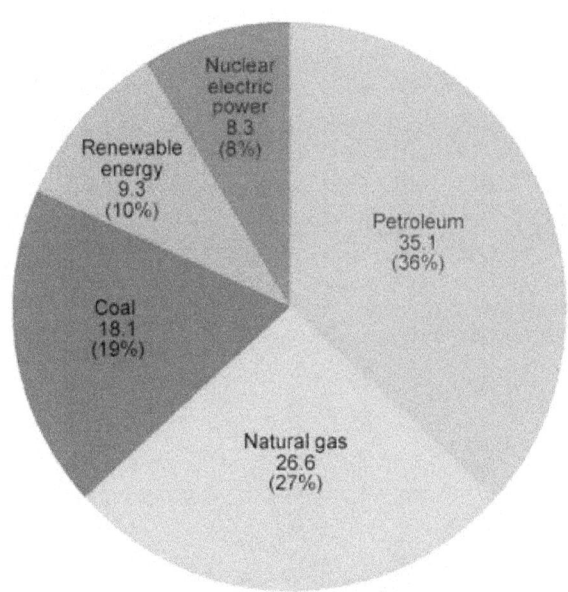

Primary energy source in the U.S. in 2013 (quadrillion Btu and percent). Total use was 97.5 quadrillion Btu. Fossil fuels (coal, oil, and natural gas) provided nearly 80% of energy used in the U.S., and 10% from renewable resources (wind, solar, and hydropower)

Future energy needs and global energy crisis

Over the last hundred years, the human population has doubled twice. Human energy consumption doubles *four times as fast* as the population, and the number of worldwide automobiles doubles *ten times* as fast.

Global reliance on relatively scarce fossil fuels creates concerns for future energy crises.

Oil, natural gas, and coal are *non-renewable energy sources*; once used, they are not replaced. As worldwide industrialization continues, fossil fuel demand exceeds supplies.

Natural gas and oil remain, but they will be depleted (2060) when used to fill the energy gap. If the world's population grows exponentially, fossil fuels will be depleted sooner.

Scientists refer to energy demands in periods: short-, medium- (2030), and long-term (2050).

Short-term key issues are prices and whether nations can tolerate depleting energy sources.

Medium-term, emergent risks must be addressed while additional supply sources are matured and utilized.

In 2050, the focus will be on resources beyond the current era of climate change and hydrocarbon concerns and instead on the ability to meet the energy needs of 9 billion people.

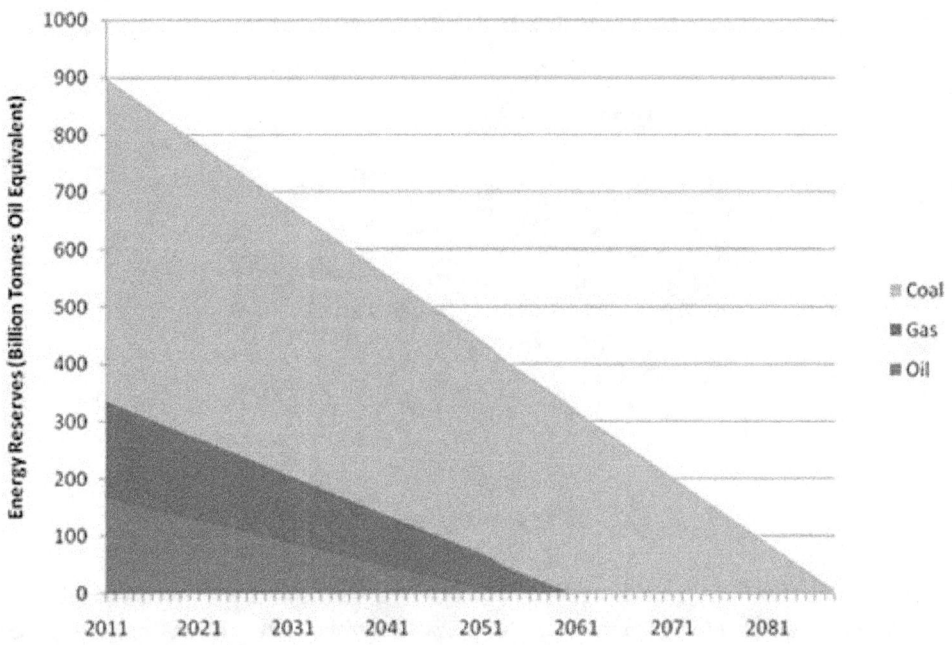

Proposed fossil fuels depletion projections, comparing oil, gas, and coal

Analyses of pressing present needs and what requires immediate action, scientists caution against protracted speculation about future "what ifs" and insufficient preventive actions.

Obstacles faced in the ongoing transition to renewable energy efforts are many and often reflect systemic political and economic barriers. Obstacles include:

> new technologies competing with mature technologies (commercialization barriers);
>
> existing subsidies and disproportionate tax burdens between renewables and fossil fuels/nuclear energy (price distortions);
>
> market failures to value public benefits gained through renewables;
>
> capital lack of access and split incentives (market barriers).

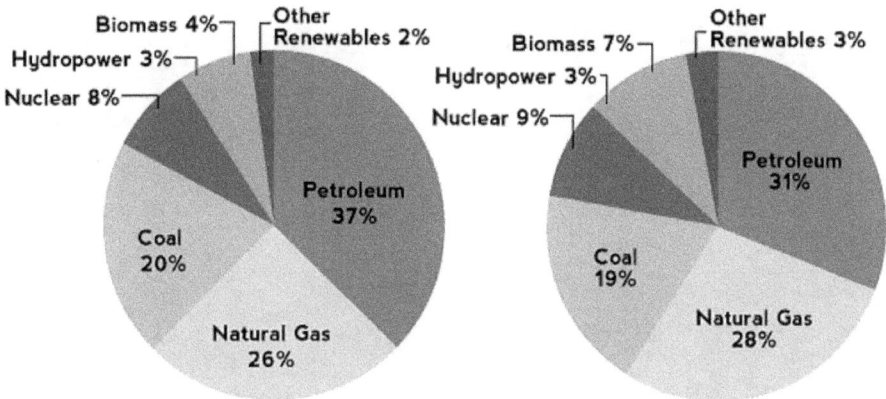

Energy source comparison for 2011 (left) and 2040 (right)

Notes for active learning

Fossil Fuel Reserves and Use

Fossil fuels

Fossil fuels are a non-renewable energy source naturally formed from the remains of prehistoric flora and fauna buried by layers of rock and sediment. The main types of fossil fuels are coal, oil, and natural gas.

Fossil fuels are a primary energy source for generating electricity and heat and powering machines, vehicles, aircraft, and vessels. Several countries worldwide produce oil and other products to meet global demand. Fossil fuels represent approximately 80% of energy sources used in the United States.

The United States both produces and imports oil. In 2020, the United States produced more barrels of oil domestically than imported from other countries for the first time since 1949. According to the *Energy Information Administration* (EIA), fossil fuels meet around 81% of the U.S. energy demand.

Coal is used primarily in the United States as an energy source to generate approximately 50% of the nation's energy. America has more coal than any other fossil fuel source and more coal reserves than any other country.

Coal, oil and natural gas formation

All fossil fuels were once-living organisms that lived hundreds of millions of years ago. As they died, they decomposed and became buried under sand, rocks, and mud layers. Thousands of feet of earth covered some areas, while others were flooded with waters that are now oceans.

Coal, oil, and natural gas form from organic matter under various time, temperature, and pressure conditions. For example, coal deposits were formed from the remains of dead trees, ferns, and other plants that lived up to 400 million years ago. In some areas of the eastern United States, coal was formed in swamps covered by seawater containing large amounts of sulfur. As the seas dried, sulfur deposits remained in the coal. Scientists are developing methods to extract sulfur, an air pollutant released into the atmosphere when coal is burned.

Oil and *natural gas* originate from organisms that lived in water. Over time, they decomposed and became buried in silt and sediment.

Extraction methods

Fossil fuels are extracted from the ground by drilling (for oil and gas) and mining (for coal) and are used for transportation, machinery, heating, and electricity.

Petroleum reserves must be located before oil and natural gas can be extracted.

Geophones are sensitive sound receivers set out in several lines on the ground. Scientists create small explosions (or vibrations) on the surface. Sound waves travel through mediums at different speeds, so material reflects waves under the surface differently when geophones receive reflected waves. Sound waves travel slowest through gas, faster through liquids, and the fastest through solids (i.e., strong molecular bonds).

If the material contains oil or natural gas, drilling begins. Rotary drilling rigs are used to reach the material deep in the Earth's surface. First, a large metal pipe containing a metal drilling bit in the center that rotates at high speeds is pushed into the Earth's surface, creating a hole lined with steel pipe casing that allows gas or oil to be pumped to the surface.

Over the years, methods have emerged for greater efficiency during drilling and pumping.

Hydraulic fracturing (or *fracking*) creates tiny cracks (or fissures) in the ground, allowing gas and oil to flow from solid shale rock.

Directional drilling uses a hole drilled straight but curves once it reaches deep underground. Often, oil is below the ocean floor. Large platforms are constructed out at sea, which anchors the drill and containers for the oil.

Coal (i.e., a solid fossil fuel) is extracted through surface and underground mining. Coal within 60 meters (197 feet) of the surface is extracted by surface mining.

Surface mining uses large machines (or explosives) to remove soil, animal remains, and plants on the coal seam. This method includes mountaintop removal and open-pit mining.

Processing

Extracted coal is moved to nearby processing plants and undergoes processing methods based on the type of deposits and location where it was mined.

Processing plants clean coal to remove contaminants and impurities (e.g., excess sulfur and mercury) and use a lot of water to wash the coal, which removes impurities.

After processing, coal is transported by railroad (or barge) for use. Some coal is taken to power plants, crushed, and burned (i.e., hydrocarbon combustion) to generate electricity.

Wastewater from coal processing is deposited into underground mines or retention ponds because it pollutes pristine water sources. An environmental issue is that retention ponds where wastewater is stored may leak, allowing contamination of surrounding water sources (e.g., aquifers and artesian wells).

Methane is the main compound in natural gas, but gases extracted from underground deposits contain components. Once extracted, the gas undergoes initial processing on-site. A pipeline transports it to a processing plant to separate methane from other compounds (e.g., butane, propane, water vapor, hydrogen sulfide, and carbon dioxide).

Some gas may be extracted for industrial use but must be purified and treated. For remote areas, purified gas is transported as liquid natural gas via tankers. For more local transport, the gas will remain in pipelines.

Global demand

Fossil fuels are currently meeting 80% of global energy demand.

Executive Summary of the International Energy Agency proposes countries must promptly address climate change as projections indicate global energy demand in 2035 will increase by 40% and fossil fuels will remain the primary source for 75% of global energy.

Economists propose that this spike in demand results from the increasing industrialization of countries such as India and China. Though fossil fuels will continue to meet the world's energy needs for the foreseeable future, there is concern about whether there will be enough resources to meet the continuing demand.

Fossil fuels worldwide are abundant, but most are resources, not reserves. Converting resources into reserves is critical for considering future energy needs.

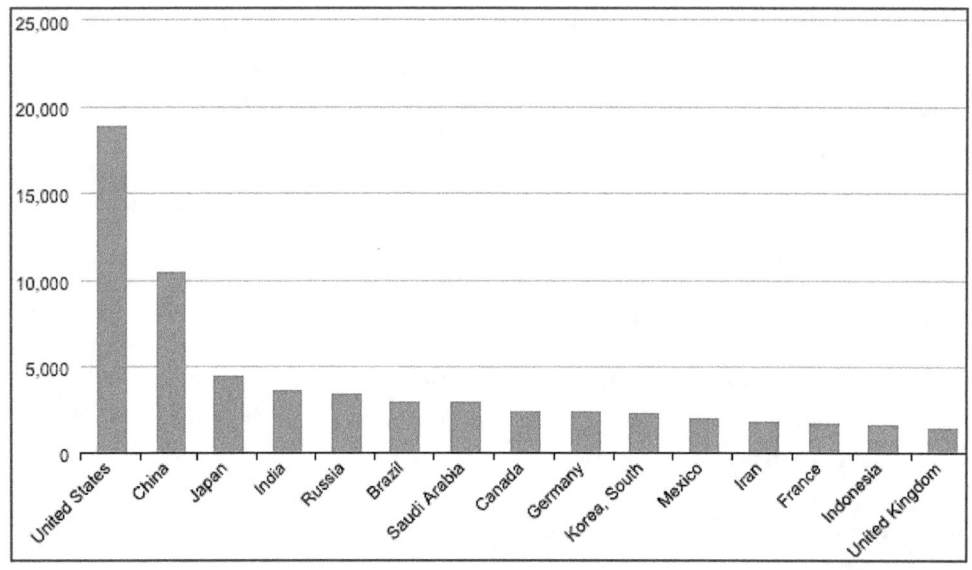

Global consumption of petroleum by country in 2013 (in thousands of barrels per day)

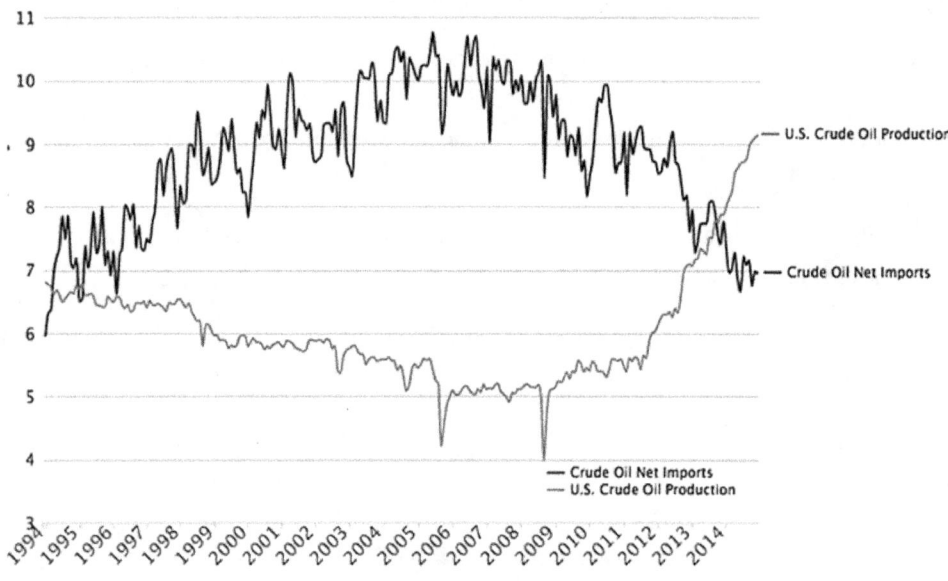

U.S. Oil production and imports (in millions of barrels per day)

Proven reserves

Proven oil reserves are 1.3 trillion barrels, with remaining resources (recoverable) at 2.7 trillion barrels. *Organization of the Petroleum Exporting Countries* (OPEC) reports 101 nations with notable oil reserves (e.g., Venezuela, Saudi Arabia, Canada, and Iran).

The largest producers of crude oil were the United States (13.9 million barrels per day; 2014), Saudi Arabia (11.6 million barrels per day), and Russia (10.8 million barrels per day).

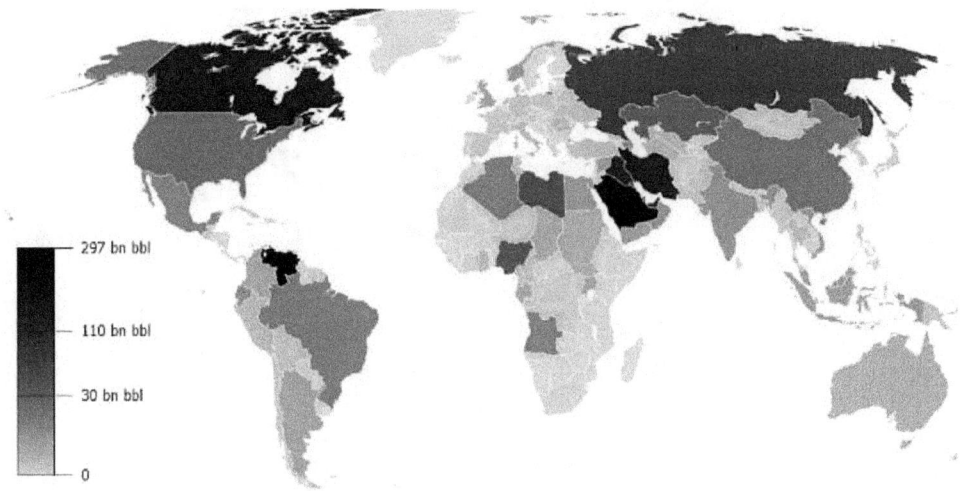

World Oil Reserves, 2013

Proven gas reserves are 220 trillion cubic meters (equivalent to 1.4 trillion barrels of oil), with recoverable resources at 3.2 trillion barrels. The largest natural gas producer is the U.S. (728 billion 200 million cubic meters, 2014), followed by Russia (578 billion 700 million cubic meters) and worldwide production of 3,460.6 trillion metric tons.

Leading energy company British Petroleum (BP) reports 102 nations with exploitable natural gas reserves (e.g., Russia, Iran, Qatar, and Turkmenistan).

Proven coal reserves are 730 gigatons (3.6 trillion barrels, 2014), with reserves at 18 trillion. The largest coal producer is China (3,874 million tons), followed by the U.S. (906.9 million tons). The estimate for worldwide production is 8,164.9 million tons.

Over 75 nations have significant coal deposits (e.g., ranked U.S., Russia, China, and Australia).

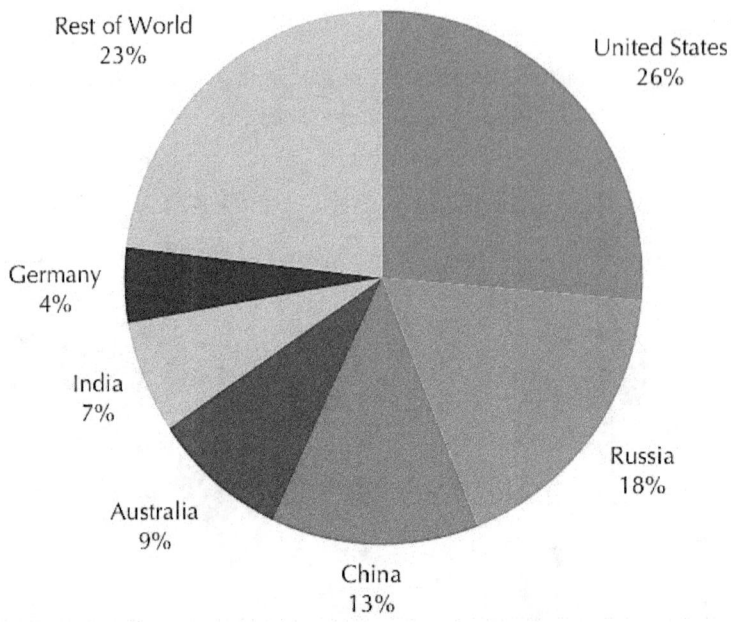

Recoverable Coal Reserves by Country, 2011

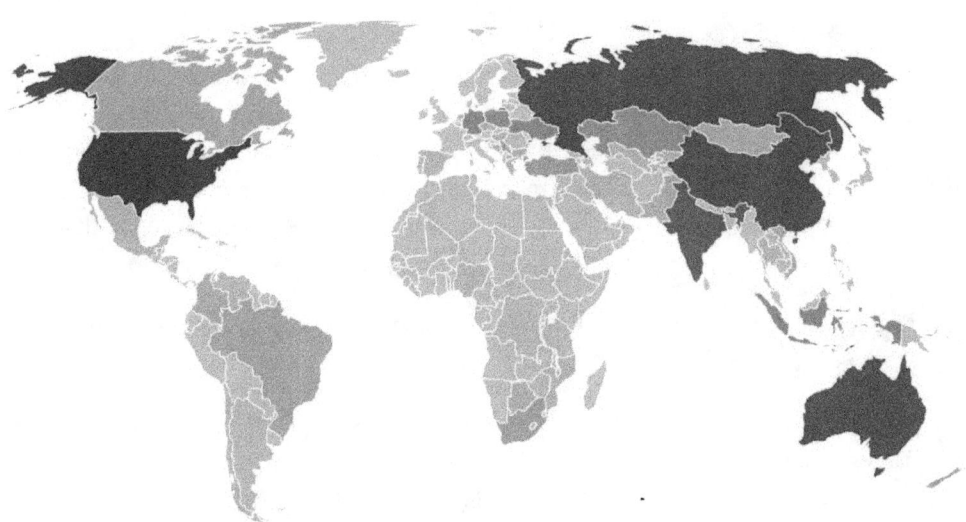

World coal reserves

Synfuels

Synthetic fuel (or synfuel) is a liquid or gaseous fuel obtained from syngas.

Syngas is a mixture of hydrogen and carbon monoxide derived from gasification of coal or biomass. Synthetic fuel is a liquid fuel obtained from natural gas or coal. Scientists have used non-food crops to make synfuel.

Plants utilize carbon dioxide in photosynthesis and using it to create fuel would drastically reduce CO_2 emissions (estimated at 50%).

Algae are promising as a future biofuel as they grow incredibly fast and readily available. Many believe synthetic fuel could meet future energy needs; it is not an effortless process.

For example, building a processing plant for converting algae into biofuel requires significant capital investment, and thousands of plants would have to be built nationwide to be a viable fuel supplier.

Some scientists, notably Christodoulos Floudas, a chemical and biological engineering professor at Princeton, estimate the United States needs 30 to 40 years to adopt a synthetic fuel system, and would cost over $1.1 trillion. Though this investment is steep, it would become profitable within a few years and provide less dependence on fossil fuels.

With rising oil prices and projected future prices, the availability of an equivalent synthetic fuel would provide an economic return to counter increasing fossil fuel prices.

Environmental advantages and disadvantages of fossil fuels

Fossil fuels offer several important advantages.

- Relative ease of locating them.
- Power plants worldwide are efficient with natural gas energy sources.
- Power plants are constructed where fuel is transported.
- Production of great amounts of electricity.
- Highly stable compared to other fuel substances.
- Easily transported through pipes.
- Least expensive type of fuel.

However, the use of fossil fuels has disadvantages.

- Pollution is the greatest disadvantage. When burned, fossil fuels release carbon dioxide (CO_2), which causes *greenhouse effects*. *Greenhouse effect* leads to *global warming* (i.e., increased global surface temperature), affecting weather, seasons, and sea levels.

- Burning coal produces CO_2 and sulfur dioxide, causing acid rain.

- Petroleum transportation poses environmental hazards (e.g., tanker oil spills and station leaks). For example, the Deepwater Horizon offshore drilling rig explosion in April 2010 killed 11 people and decimated thousands of sea life organisms in the Gulf region. Efforts continued for months to stop oil flowing from the rig. United States Coast Guard estimated that 4.9 million barrels (210 million gallons) of oil were lost before they capped the leak 89 days later.

- Fossil fuels are non-renewable, with projected severe shortage by 2080.

Nuclear Energy

Atomic nuclei

There is immense energy in the nucleus of an atom, which holds the nucleus together. Atoms make up all matter in the universe, from grass and rocks to pizza and soda; even air has these tiny, microscopic particles.

Nuclear energy is stored in an atom's nucleus (core of protons and neutrons).

Nuclear binding energy is required to disassemble a nucleus into protons and neutrons. Release or absorption of nuclear energy uses nuclear reactions or radioactive decay.

Italian-American physicist Enrico Fermi (Nobel prize in 1938) discovered the potential of splitting atoms (or *nuclear fission*) in 1934. Eight years later, Fermi created the first controlled nuclear reaction, using control rods and uranium. Using Fermi's technology, the production and testing of a nuclear bomb were only a few years away.

Country	Nuclear electricity generation capacity (million kilowatts)	Nuclear electricity generation (billion kilowatt-hours)	Nuclear share of country's total electricity generation
United States	95.49	778.15	19%
France	61.37	360.70	68%
China	53.26	407.52	5%
Russia	27.73	222.44	20%
South Korea	24.43	150.52	26%

Top five nuclear electric generation capacity countries, 2021,
U.S. Energy Information Administration, International Energy Statistics, August 2023

Nuclear power plants use nuclear fission, and most nuclear power plants use uranium atoms.

During nuclear fission, a neutron collides with a uranium atom and splits it, releasing much energy through heat and radiation.

Fission reactions

Fission and fusion are nuclear reactions that produce energy but through different processes. Fission splits a heavy, unstable nucleus into two lighter nuclei, and fusion is when two light nuclei combine, releasing vast amounts of energy.

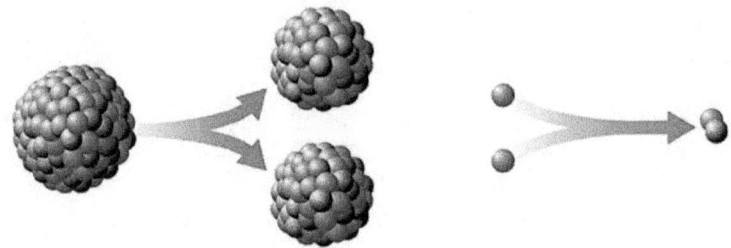

Fission splits nuclei (on the left) vs. fusion, which joins nuclei (on the right)

Nuclear fission is a nuclear reaction in which a large, unstable atom splits and releases energy.

Fission of heavy elements releases large amounts of energy, which is an exothermic reaction. It occurs in heavier elements when the electromagnetic force pulls atoms apart and dominates the nuclear force, which holds an atom together.

Fission reaction is initiated when a high-energy neutron collides with an atom, producing an *unstable isotope* that undergoes *fission* (i.e., atomic division).

This fission process produces additional neutrons, which initiate fission with other nuclei.

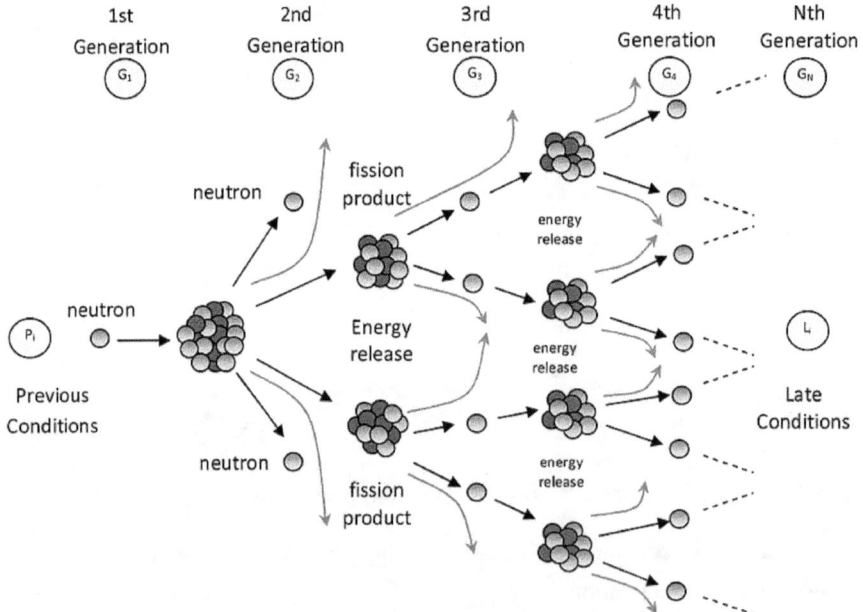

Nuclear fission splits atoms, releasing energy and propagating further reactions

Nuclear fusion is a reaction in which two or more nuclei collide at high speeds to join and form a new nucleus. During the process of nuclear fusion, energy is not conserved.

Some matter present during nuclei fusion is instead converted into *photons* (i.e., light energy). This release of light during fusion illuminates active stars in the night sky.

Energy is released when two nuclei with masses lower than iron-56 (^{56}Fe) undergo fusion.

Energy is generally absorbed when two nuclei heavier than iron-56 undergo fusion (the opposite is true for fission).

Lighter atoms (e.g., helium and hydrogen) are usually fusible, while heavier elements (e.g., plutonium and uranium) are fissionable.

Nuclear fusion is a reaction in which two or more atomic nuclei, usually deuterium and tritium, combine to form one or more different atomic nuclei and subatomic particles.

Mass differences between reactants and products either release or absorb energy.

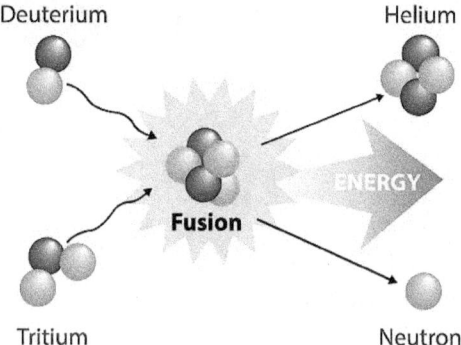

Nuclear fusion using the example of deuterium and tritium as atomic nuclei

Nuclear fuel

Commonly used fissile nuclear fuels are plutonium-239 (^{239}Pu) and uranium-235 (^{235}U).

*Nuclear fuel cycle*s include mining, refining, purifying, using, and disposing of nuclear fuel.

As a precursor to the nuclear fuel cycle, *uranium recovery* mines uranium ore from Earth and milling or concentrates it. This recovery process produces a *"yellowcake,"* which gets converted into uranium hexafluoride (UF$_6$). This compound undergoes enrichment, which increases uranium concentration in UF$_6$.

Reprocessing of *Mixed Oxide Fuel* (MOX) is not practiced in the U.S.

Yellowcake is moved to a fuel cycle facility and transformed into fuel. This nuclear fuel product is used in reactors to produce nuclear power, which generates electricity.

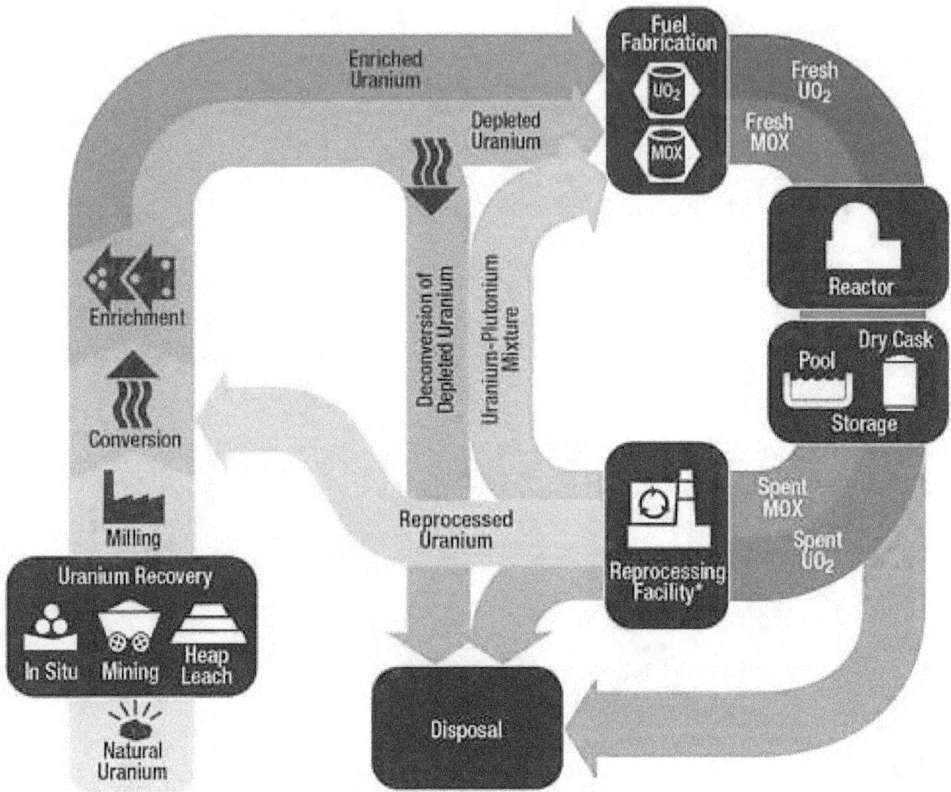

Nuclear fuel cycle for uranium recovery, enrichment, utilization, and disposal of uranium. Nuclear Regulatory Commission (NRC) has no regulatory role in mining uranium.

Electricity-producing nuclear reactors

The U.S. *Nuclear Regulatory Commission* (NRC) regulates power, research, and test reactors. Power reactors are those that generate electricity, and there are several types. Only two are in commercial operation in the United States: pressurized and boiling-water reactors.

The Nuclear Regulatory Commission oversees test reactors for training and research, testing materials, and producing neutrons and radioisotopes for industry and medicine. Test reactors are smaller than power reactors; many are on university campuses worldwide. They operate at lower temperatures and require less fuel.

Fission products that build up during fuel consumption are less than those in power reactors. Like power reactors, these testing facilities require cooling, but only high-powered test reactors need to use forced cooling, whereas power reactors require forced cooling. There are around 240 research and test reactors in operation in 56 countries.

Pressurized Water Reactors (PWRs) have a four-step process to produce electricity, which the *Nuclear Regulatory Commission* (NRC) is as follows:

1. The *core* inside the reactor vessel creates heat;

2. *Pressurized water* in a primary coolant loop brings heat to a steam generator;

3. Inside the steam generator, heat from the primary coolant loop vaporizes water in a secondary loop, producing steam and

4. Steam lines direct steam to the main turbine, causing it to turn the turbine generator, which produces electricity.

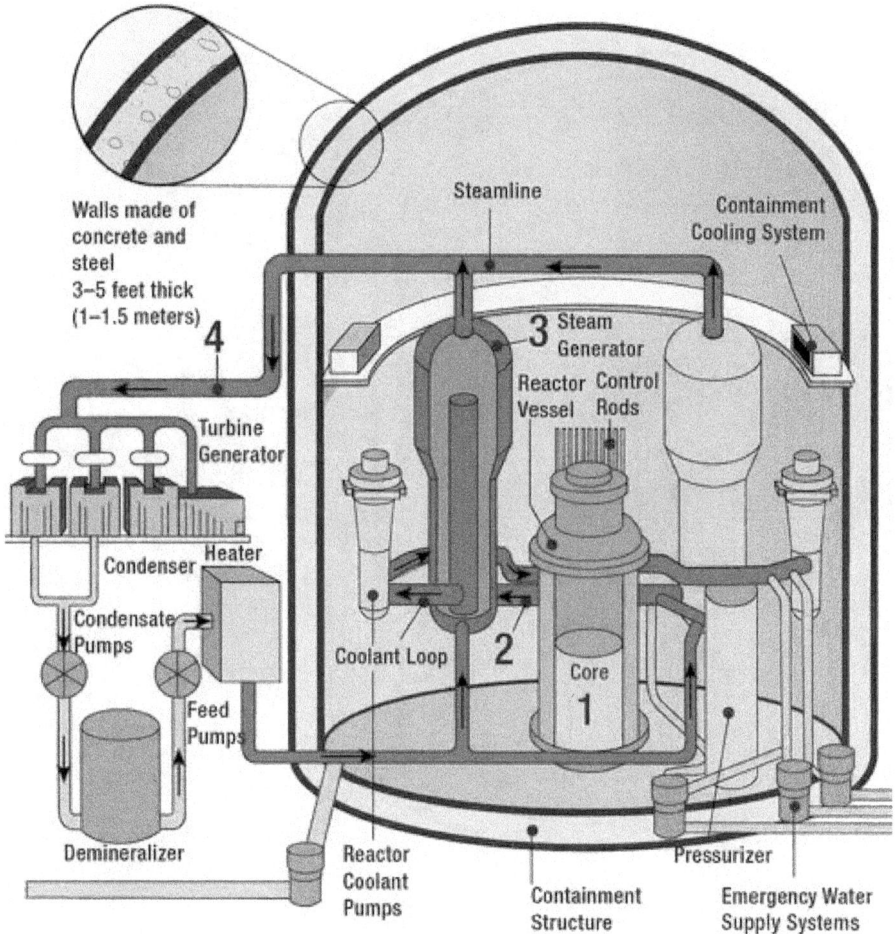

Pressurized water reactor, U.S. Nuclear Regulatory Commission

Boiling-water reactor (BWR) is the second type of power reactor:

1. The *core* inside the reactor vessel creates heat;

2. A *steam-water mixture* is produced when very pure water (reactor coolant) moves upward through the core, absorbing heat;

3. The steam-water mixture leaves the top of the core and enters the two stages of moisture separation, where water droplets are removed before the steam is allowed to enter the steam line and

4. Steam lines direct steam to the main turbine, causing the generator to rotate and produce electricity.

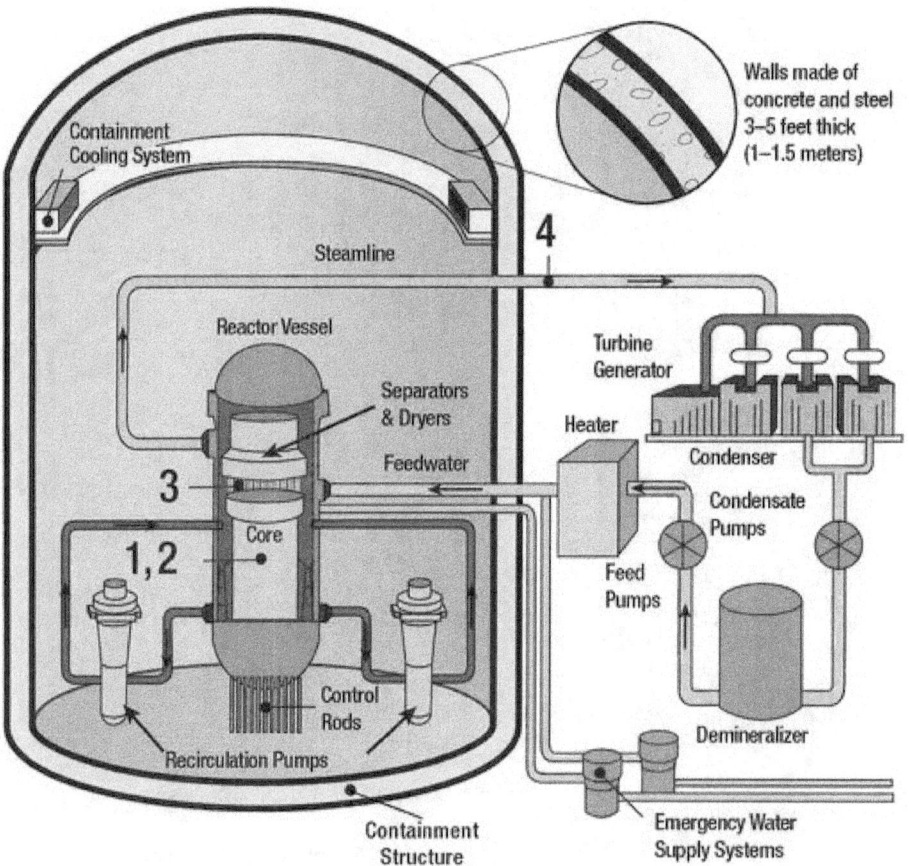

Boiling water reactor, U.S. Nuclear Regulatory Commission

Advantages of nuclear power

Nuclear energy potential is immense; 54 *nuclear power plants* in the U.S. produce about 20% of the nation's electricity. The U.S. has 92 *nuclear reactors.* The number peaked at 112, and their combined net summer electricity generation capacity was 99,624 megawatts.

The number of operating reactors declined to 104 in 1998 and remained there through 2013.

Advantages of using nuclear energy as a source of electricity in the U.S. include:

Low costs: Constructing nuclear power plants has a high cost (i.e., uranium enrichment) and economic advantages compared to generating electricity from natural gas, oil, and coal.

Base Load Energy: Nuclear power plants provide a stable energy base, and electricity production can be lowered when wind turbines and solar panels are available.

Thorium: Estimates report uranium reserves for 80 years. However, thorium (i.e., a "greener" alternative to uranium) is used in China, Russia, and India as nuclear reactor fuel.

Low pollution: The environmental effects of nuclear power are low compared to other energy sources, such as burning coal, oil, and natural gas.

High energy density: Energy released from nuclear fission is ten million times greater than fossil fuel combustion (i.e., burning).

Sustainability: Nuclear energy is not renewable but generates almost unlimited energy by controlling atomic fusion, the same reaction occurring in the Sun.

However, many obstacles and challenges must be addressed to make it a reality.

Disadvantages of nuclear power

Nuclear energy has downsides, including severe environmental and human health threats.

Radioactive waste: Nuclear power plants emit negligible amounts of CO_2, but the mining, enrichment, and waste management produce significant amounts of nuclear waste, an immediate and long-term concern (i.e., long half-lives for radioactive isotopes). Nuclear waste can have sudden yet long-lasting effects.

Accidents: Chornobyl (1986 incident) emitted radiation after an explosion and fire in a nuclear power reactor. Estimates of the disaster concluded that it was responsible for 15,000 to 30,000 deaths and over 2.5 million Ukrainians experienced health issues from high radiation exposure. Some of the greatest disaster effects were felt as far away as Wales from toxic atmospheric particles carried by jet streams and clouds throughout Europe.

There have always been safety concerns about the use of nuclear energy, specifically regarding the safety hazards of releasing radioactive materials. During the manufacturing of power plants, design and operation were taken very seriously to decrease the likelihood of an accident and avoid health consequences if something were to occur.

There have been three reactor accidents since nuclear power has been used:

Three Mile Island (1979), *Chernobyl* (1986), and *Fukushima* (2011).

Limited to these incidents, nuclear power has been used for over six decades and is a relatively safe method of generating electricity. For example, compare 7,500 deaths *mining* coal for electricity in the past six decades, according to the U.S. Department of Labor).

The overall risks associated with nuclear power are low and declining.

Ionizing radiation and human health

Ionizing radiation (or *nuclear radiation*) consists of subatomic particles (or electromagnetic waves) with sufficient energy to ionize atoms or molecules by detaching electrons.

Ionizing radiation can cause damage to cellular structures: direct or indirect radiation.

Direct radiation is when particles strike and damage cellular components (e.g., DNA).

Indirect radiation creates highly reactive free radicals (i.e., unpaired valence electrons) atoms or molecules that remove electrons from stable molecules and disrupt their function.

Radiation exposure includes:

Alpha particles, which are relatively slow and large, cannot penetrate the skin but may be inhaled or ingested. Due to their large size and high energy, alpha particles may cause more damage than other forms of radiation.

Beta particles, which are $1/2000^{th}$ the mass of alpha particles, penetrate the skin. However, their small size reduces the potential to cause harm.

Gamma rays have very high energy and no charge or mass. They can pass through small spaces between cells without notice but may damage the cellular structures they hit.

Humans are constantly exposed to radiation from natural and human-made sources. The risk associated with each source depends on how much radiation was absorbed, the time one was exposed to the dose, and the exposure pathway of the radiation.

Radiation dose is the amount of radiation absorbed by the human body, measured in *rems* (i.e., Roentgen equivalent man).

Dose equivalent (or *effective dose*) combines the amount of radiation absorbed and the medical effects of that type of radiation.

Beta and gamma radiation use a dose equivalent to the absorbed dose.

By contrast, the alpha and neutron radiation dose equivalent is larger than the absorbed dose because these radiation types are more damaging to human health.

Dose equivalent is the roentgen equivalent man (rem) and sievert (Sv).

Biological dose equivalents are measured in 1/1000th of a rem (i.e., millirem or mrem).

Practically, 1 R (exposure) = 1 rad (absorbed dose) = 1 rem or 1000 mrem (dose equivalent).

High doses of radiation are extremely harmful or fatal. Damage caused by exposure depends on the body part, type of radiation, and duration. The effects may manifest promptly (several months after exposure) or be delayed for several years.

Delayed effects include many diseases, such as cancer.

Radioactive waste

Radioactive waste is produced from radioactive materials (e.g., uranium for nuclear energy). It contains highly toxic chemicals, usually a byproduct of the generation of nuclear power, nuclear fission, and other nuclear technology (such as medicine and research).

Low-level waste (LLW) includes radioactively contaminated products, such as rags, medical tubes, tools, and protective clothing. Low-level waste disposal occurs at facilities licensed by either the Agreement States (37 states in agreement with NRC) or the NRC.

High-level waste is waste used in nuclear reactor fuel. Currently, the United States uses no single location to dispose of high-level waste. A site at Yucca Mountain in Nevada was developing as a high-level radioactive waste storage facility, but the government halted development in 2009. Many advocates want the repository to be utilized and are fighting for its completion.

High-level waste is mainly stored on-site at *nuclear weapons* and *nuclear power production* facilities, with a high risk of build-up and leakage. Nuclear waste must be disposed of carefully because it can have detrimental environmental implications.

Notes for active learning

Hydroelectric Power

Hydroelectricity

Hydroelectricity is electricity produced by *hydropower*, which generates electrical power by utilizing the energy of fast-running or falling water. It uses the energy of running water without reducing its quantity, so it is a renewable energy source.

Hydropower is among the oldest methods of producing electricity (e.g., the pre-Industrial Revolution mills).

Hydroelectricity contributes to the nation's drinking water. Power plants collect rainwater in their reservoirs, which can be used for irrigation or animal and human consumption.

Unlike natural gas and fuel, river water is not subject to price fluctuations.

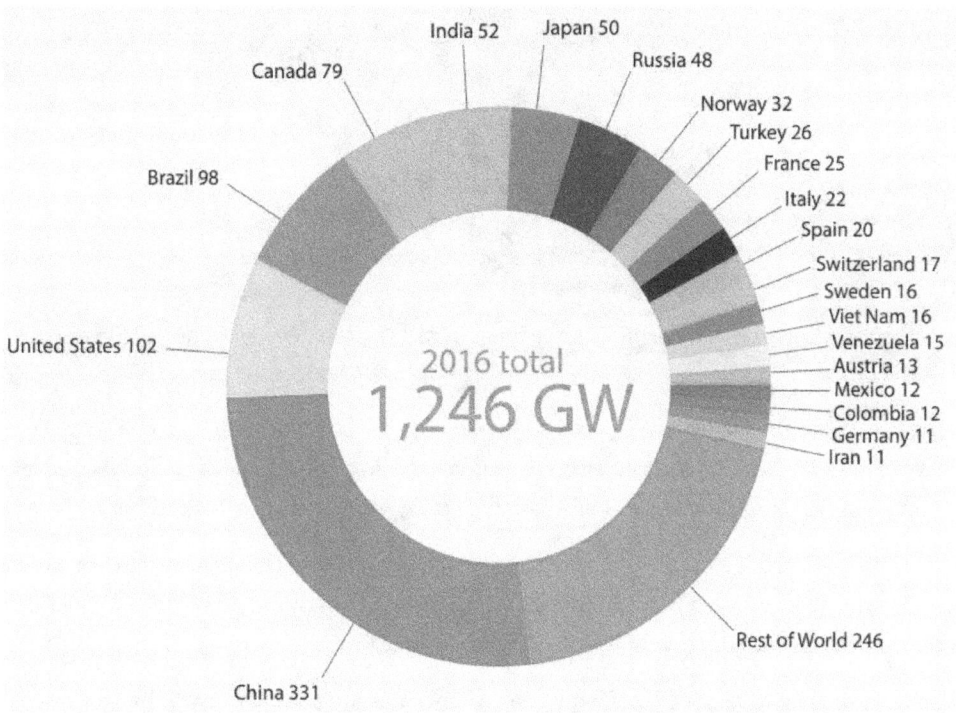

Global total hydropower capacity in 2016 (GW).

Hydroelectric power can be produced in various ways, from trapping it behind a dam and channeling a small amount to flow past a turbine to small-scale hydroelectric systems that produce electricity for individuals on their land.

China is the largest producer of hydroelectricity, followed by Canada, Brazil, and the U.S.

Hydropower is fueled by water and is a clean energy source because it does not produce high carbon emissions as for hydrocarbon-based sources (e.g., propane, butane, and petroleum).

Hydroelectric power is a domestic energy source, generating energy without relying on foreign fuel sources. Hydropower plants generate power immediately and provide backup power during electrical outages.

One advantage of hydroelectric power production and use is that hydroelectric cycles produce small amounts of greenhouse gases. Hydroelectric power is a green energy source that reduces pollution and greenhouse gas emissions into the atmosphere, acid rain, and smog.

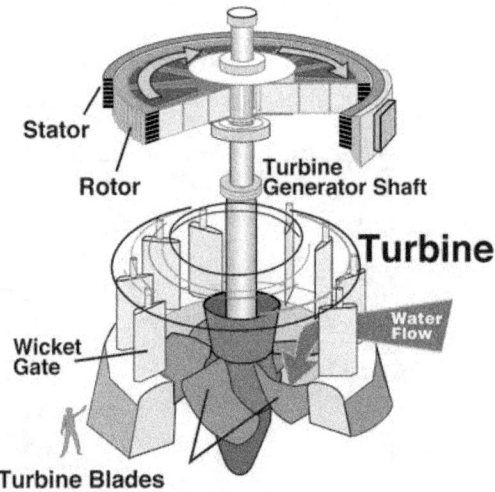

Hydroelectric generator with water driving turbine motion, U.S. Geological Survey

Dams and flood control

Dams are built on large rivers with steep elevations and store much water behind them. Near the bottom of the dam, an area takes in water, then travels down the penstock inside.

At the penstock's end is a turbine propelled by moving water. This turbine powers the generator above it, which sits inside a powerhouse and sends electricity through power lines. Water that passes through the turbine travels into an outflowing river.

Flood control lessens damage by floodwaters. Many dams are partially or wholly constructed to aid with controlling floodwaters. This design is slightly different from typical dam construction. The reservoir is often kept exceptionally low before an anticipated rainy season or storm, so there will be room for the water.

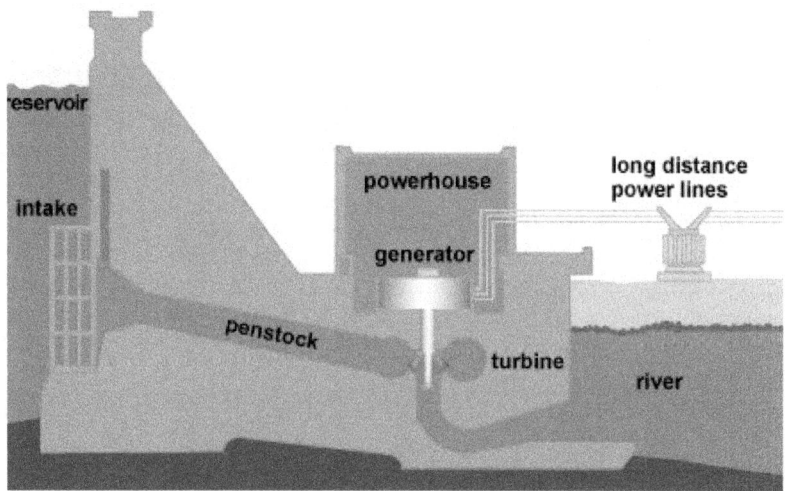

Hydroelectric dam with the route water moves to generate electricity, U.S. EIA

Dry dams serve the purpose of flood control. *Mountain Morris Dam* in NY and *Seven Oaks Dam* in California are two dry dams.

Habitat loss

While hydroelectric power is an essential energy source, the operation of hydropower facilities is one of the many contributing factors to the decline of salmon species throughout the Pacific Northwest. Dams block the passage of salmon between spawning (downstream) and rearing habitats (upstream), change river patterns, and raise water temperatures.

Over 55 percent of spawning and rearing habitats, once available to salmon, are permanently blocked by dams. Although dams were discovered to hurt salmon, few were removed.

For example, a dam across the Wallowa River in Oregon was the first to be destroyed in response to declining salmon populations. The hope was that the salmon would again thrive by opening the river. Unfortunately, regional salmon had adopted a migratory instinct around the construction of the dams and had become acclimated to the lake-like environment.

Dams keep adult fish from swimming back upriver and prevent juveniles from traveling downstream to lay their eggs. They must travel through the turbine, which spins at around 80 revolutions per minute. These high speeds usually kill or severely injure the juveniles, adding to the decline in salmon populations.

Dams may lead to an irreversible effect on salmon populations; others are less concerned, favoring economically produced and environmentally sustainable hydroelectric power (i.e., reduced greenhouse gases and resulting climate change) more than wildlife.

Silting

Siltation is water pollution by fine particles (e.g., silt or clay). It includes increased concentration of sediments suspended in water and particle accumulation on the bottom of a dam where they are not desired.

Though siltation is considered a minor issue for most dams, it may shorten their lifespan by decades. Siltation reduces the amount of storage for rainwater, may damage the turbines, and can even impact the river downstream.

Two main strategies are currently in use for reducing sediments entering a reservoir:

> 1) preventing erosion or
>
> 2) trapping the eroded sediment before it reaches the reservoir.

Some countries experience issues with sediment in dams. An efficient strategy was proposed to prevent it, in which upstream reservoirs act as sediment-retention structures.

Small-scale hydroelectricity

When most people imagine hydropower, they think of Hoover Dam, a gigantic facility that harnesses the power of the Colorado River behind it. However, hydropower facilities vary; some are large (e.g., Hoover Dam), and others are small, using small streams of running water.

Micro-hydropower systems allow small communities or individual landowners to control and produce electricity.

For a typical micro-hydropower system that uses a small river to generate power, a portion of the river's water is diverted to a section of land that includes a canal, forebay, a penstock, and a powerhouse. The water is delivered to a turbine or a waterwheel, which moves and spins a shaft. The motion of the shaft can be used to pump water or power a generator.

Micro-hydropower systems can be connected to an electrical grid or stand-alone. Stand-alone systems are used to power a home or small business.

Some generators are placed directly into streams, with water running slightly downhill. Intake at the top allows water to travel down to the powerhouse, where waterpower rotates a turbine.

Turbines power a generator, which produces electricity as a stand-alone system.

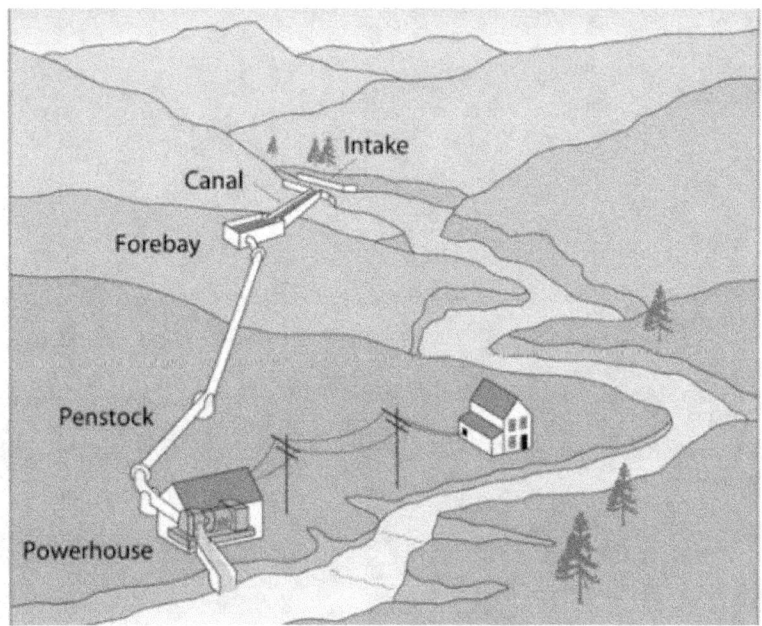

Small hydropower system on personal property with water is diverted into penstock.

Ocean waves and tidal energy

Tidal power is hydropower that converts energy from tidal waves into useful energy, like electricity (marine and hydrokinetic energy, MHK).

Tidal energy is promising as a future source of energy generation as tidal patterns are more predictable than either wind patterns or weather conditions obstructing direct sunlight for solar energy generation.

Oceans cover approximately three-fourths of Earth's surface and are one of the greatest potential renewable energy sources.

The United States Energy Department estimates that the maximum amount of electricity that could be generated by harnessing tidal wave power is 1,420 terawatt-hours, about one-third of the annual electricity usage.

In addition to harnessing tidal power, energy from ocean waves can generate electricity. Waves are caused by wind moving over the surface of ocean water.

Most ocean areas worldwide have predictable wind patterns, providing an opportunity to harvest energy through their constant movement.

Agucadoura Wave Farm off the shore of Portugal was one of the first tested and operated in 2008, three miles offshore. One of the four standard devices used for capturing wave energy.

Energy Conservation and Renewable Energy

Consumption

Energy conservation reduces energy consumption by using less energy or avoiding energy sources. For example, choosing to drive a car less is an example of conserving energy. Some countries charge an energy (or carbon) tax to get citizens to reduce the energy they expend, or the amount of carbon dioxide released into the atmosphere (i.e., *carbon footprint*).

Several industries have reduced energy expenditure, while consumers have become concerned about products impacting the environment. For example, *hybrid electric vehicles* (HEV) and *light-emitting diode* (LED) light bulbs aim to promote energy conservation.

United Nations has addressed climate change by establishing international agreements; unfortunately, the largest industrial polluting nations (i.e., the United States, China, and India) have rejected adopting agreements to limit emissions.

"Zero Energy Home" in New Paltz, NY, with average monthly energy bills of $47. Building homes with efficient energy devices, insulating extensively, and using energy-saving windows reduce energy consumption and carbon emissions.

Many governmental and non-governmental initiatives educate consumers on how they can do their part for energy conservation, such as:

1) borrowing/renting rarely used items instead of purchasing them;
2) using sustainable transportation (e.g., public transport, walking, bicycle);
3) choosing online periodicals, printing only what is necessary;
4) turning off lights and appliances that are not being used; and
5) turning off the faucet while brushing teeth and lathering in the shower.

Energy efficiency

Efficient energy use refers to consuming less energy for tasks. For example, driving a car the same distance but choosing one with better gas mileage. Actions include replacing appliances (e.g., computers or clothes dryers) with energy-efficient models using less energy, reducing greenhouse gas emissions, and decreasing energy consumption and costs.

Light-emitting diodes (LED) light bulbs provide 55-70 lumens per watt, compared to traditional incandescent bulbs with 13-18 lumens per watt. Homes are energy-efficient with wider framing lumber (more insulation and preventing air or moisture from penetrating) and high-efficiency water heaters and air conditioners.

It is estimated that gas and oil wells produce over 25 billion barrels of hot water yearly of oil and gas extraction. It is often discharged but can be treated and repurposed for different applications. For example, heat energy could provide the United States with over 3 gigawatts of clean energy.

CAFE standards

Corporate Average Fuel Economy (CAFE) standards are regulations Congress enacted to improve the average fuel economy of cars, vans, and trucks sold in the U.S.

Studies about car emissions and climate change encouraged car manufacturers to improve fuel efficiency and reduce carbon pollution. Manufacturers are fined (extending into millions of dollars) if they do not follow Congressional regulations.

Environmental Protection Agency (EPA) and *National Highway Traffic Safety Administration* (NHTSA) incentivize companies to adhere to CAFÉ standards.

CAFE's program saves operators money by decreasing the cost of transporting freight, upwards of $170 billion. If a customer is satisfied with an energy-efficient car and knows it is decreasing their carbon footprint, it is assumed that sales will rise. Additionally, the car dealers' image will be enhanced by complying with regulations.

Electric vehicles

Hybrid electric vehicles (HEV) combine conventional internal combustion engines with an electric propulsion system. The vehicle's electric powertrain produces better performance or fuel economy.

Hybrid electric vehicle prices are higher than conventional vehicles, but state and federal incentives and fuel savings offset some of this cost differential.

Electric cars are the most common type of HEV, although hybrid electric buses and trucks are available. Electric vehicles use technologies such as regenerative brakes, which convert the kinetic energy from the vehicle's motion into electrical energy to charge the battery.

Other HEVs use their internal combustion engine to spin an electrical generator that charges the car's battery or generates electricity to power the electric motor.

Plug-in hybrid electric vehicles (PHEVs) use a battery-powered electric motor and fuel source (e.g., gasoline) to power a propulsion source (e.g., internal combustion engine). PHEVs have larger batteries than combustion engine vehicles, driving between 220 and 400 miles on a fully charged battery.

All-electric vehicles (EVs) use only a battery to power the motor. EPA classifies these as zero-emissions vehicles because they produce no exhaust. EVs typically drive around 250-450 miles on a single battery charge.

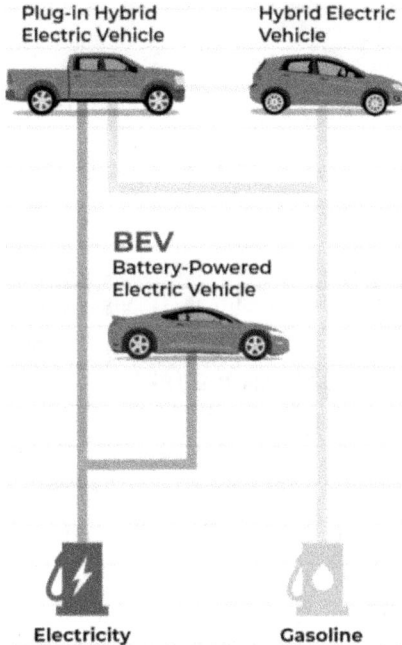

Plug-in Hybrid Electric Vehicle (top left) vs. Hybrid Electric Vehicle. Hybrid electric vehicles with an internal combustion engine and electric motor powered by fossil fuels.

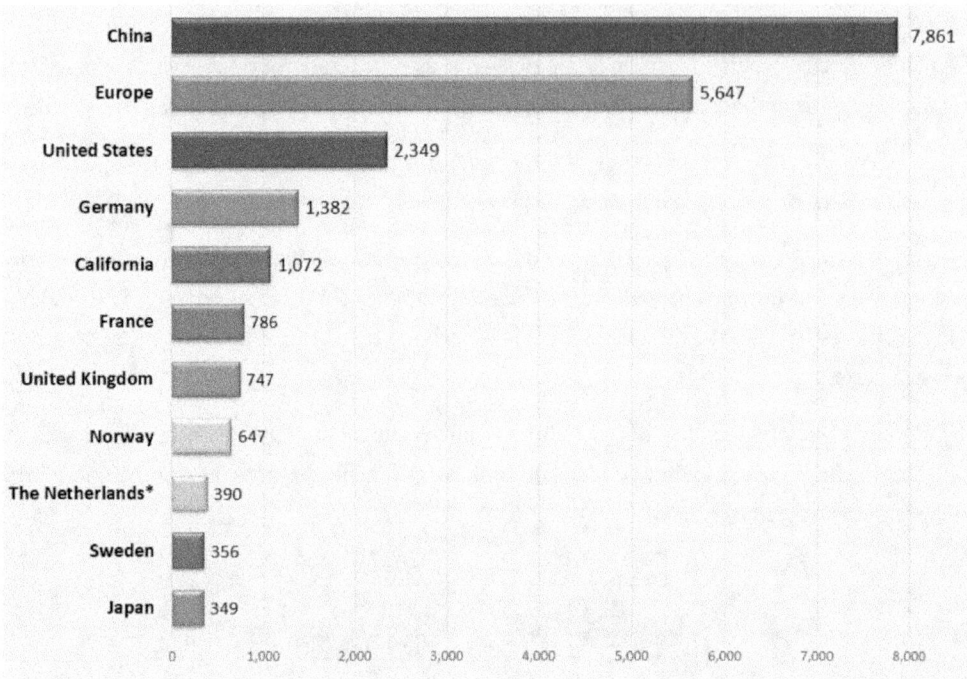

Top-selling consumer plug-in electric vehicles, 2021

Mass transit

In 2007, the Intergovernmental Panel on Climate Change report cited studies that concluded that to limit global temperature rise to no more than 2 °C, emissions of greenhouse gases must be reduced by 40-50% from the 2000 levels by 2050.

Nearly 28% of greenhouse gases emitted are due to burning fuel for transportation; with increased vehicles, the number of greenhouse gases released will increase.

Using public transportation reduces travel by individuals in their private vehicles. By riding mass transit vehicles such as buses, subways, and the metro, someone's carbon footprint can be significantly reduced. Public transportation saves a household an average of $6,251 annually and reduces carbon dioxide emissions by 37 million metric tons annually.

Drove alone	78%
Carpool	9%
Work at home (pre-COVID-19)	6%
Transit	5%
Other	2%

U.S. driving pattern while commuting to work, 2019

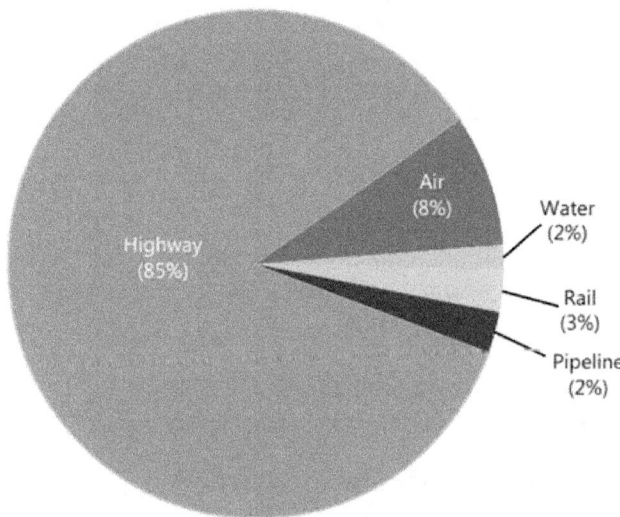

Greenhouse gases by transportation mode, 2014, Bureau of Transportation Statistics

Clean energy

Renewable energy (or *clean energy*) is from resources naturally replenished in a human time frame, as opposed to an earthly or universal one.

Clean energy includes sunlight, wind, waves, geothermal heat, rain, and tides.

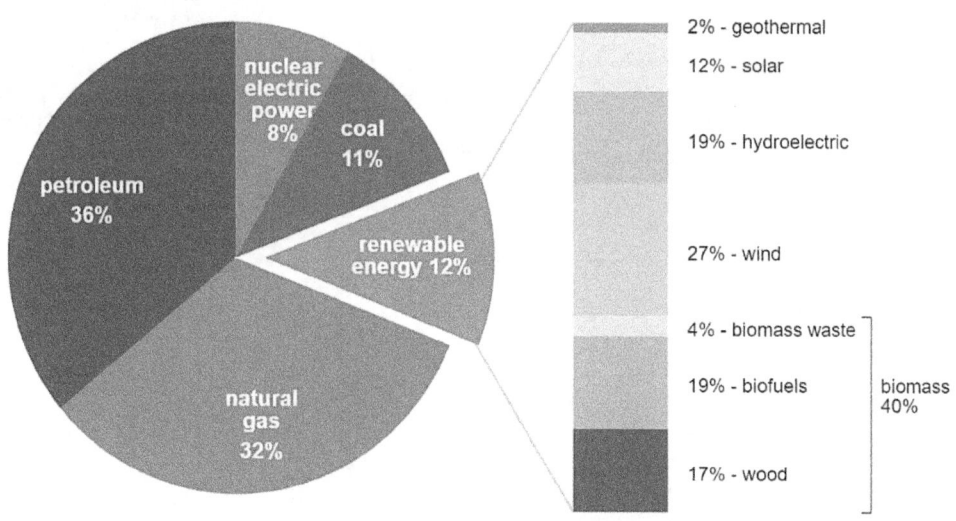

U.S. primary energy consumption by energy source, 2021.
Totals equal 97.33 quadrillion Btu with renewables at 12.16 quadrillion Btu.

Renewable energy has become prevalent in America in the past few decades as people have become aware of the need for less dependence on fossil fuels and the harm they are causing.

Creating products that run on clean energy is a billion-dollar industry, but only about 9% of energy in the United States comes from renewable resources.

Solar energy

Solar energy is heat and light from the Sun's energy harnessed for energy, including electricity generation, the cleanest and most abundant renewable energy source worldwide.

The United States is the most advanced country for solar energy, with modern technologies to capture sunlight and harness it for heating water and generating electricity.

The potential for solar energy to provide energy has yet to be fully developed, with emerging technologies increasing efficiencies and reducing costs.

International Energy Agency (IEA, 2011) stated:

> *Developing affordable, inexhaustible, clean solar energy technologies will have huge longer-term benefits. It will increase countries' energy security through reliance on an Indigenous, inexhaustible, and mostly import-independent resource, enhance sustainability, reduce pollution, lower the costs of mitigating global warming, and keep fossil fuel prices lower than otherwise. These advantages are global. Hence, the additional costs of the incentives for early deployment should be considered learning investments; they must be wisely spent and widely shared.*

30% of solar radiation that strikes Earth's upper atmosphere is reflected into outer space. Clouds, water sources, and land absorb the remaining radiation.

On average, Earth's surface receives 1,361 Watts of solar energy per square meter.

Hydropower	59%
Wind	21%
Solar	11%
Bioenergy	8%
Geothermal	1%

Renewable electricity generation by energy source, 2020

Solar power is produced by converting sunlight into electricity or heat and is expected to be the dominant energy source by 2050.

Photovoltaics (PV) and *concentrated solar power* (CSP) convert sunlight into electricity:

Photovoltaics uses solar cells to convert solar light directly into electricity using the photoelectric effect (i.e., emission of electrons). This method is increasingly popular, and solar panels are used in houses and businesses to generate electricity.

Concentrated solar power (CPS) uses lenses (or mirrors) tracking systems to concentrate light into a small beam. This concentrated beam produces heat that is used as a heat source.

Solar power is used in agriculture and transportation. Agriculture and horticulture seek to optimize solar energy capture to provide optimal conditions for plant productivity. Greenhouses have been constructed with roofs made of solar panels, which convert solar light to heat and allow year-round plant cultivation with optimal light and heat.

Solar-powered car development began in the 1980s. Some vehicles use solar panels to perform smaller electrical tasks than powering the vehicle, such as running the air conditioner, which reduces the amount of fuel consumption. A solar-powered boat crossed the Pacific Ocean in 1996 solely on sunlight-generated electricity.

Hydrogen fuel cells

Fuel cells convert chemical energy from a fuel source into electricity through a chemical reaction of oxygen (or another oxidizing agent) with positively charged hydrogen ions.

Fuel cells function like batteries, producing electricity and heat if fuel is supplied. Fuel cells consist of two electrodes (i.e., a negative electrode (or anode) and a positive electrode (or cathode) in an electrolyte (i.e., a solution with positive and negative ions). Electrolytes are necessary for electricity conduction.

Unlike batteries, fuel cells require a constant oxygen supply to maintain chemical reactions. They can supply constant electricity if a fuel source is present and has relatively long lifetimes.

Fuel cells require platinum and are expensive. They do not need to be recharged and do not become run-down easily. Fuel cells require a constant source of hydrogen to produce electricity. They are relatively durable, with stationary cells effective for roughly 40,000 operating hours.

Fuel cells have many applications, including backup power sources and transportation. They are more efficient than the standard combustion engine and have lower emissions because they only emit a byproduct of water. They are quiet during operations because they have no major moving parts.

Due to their lack of moving parts, a fuel cell can achieve up to 99.9999% reliability under perfect conditions. They are often used as power sources for spacecraft, research stations, remote weather stations, and military machinery.

Fuel cells produce water as a byproduct, zero pollution, in contrast to fossil fuels, which release carbon dioxide and greenhouse gases into the atmosphere.

Biofuels

Biofuels can be created from food, non-food sources, and biomass (e.g., algae). Biofuels are added to gasoline and power fuel cells.

Biomass power comes from plants such as corn, grass, trees, and even algae.

Biomass can be used directly to produce heat, such as through burning wood or another plant-based biomass, or indirectly after it has been converted to biofuel. To date, wood remains the largest source of biomass energy.

Biomass can be grown industrially to produce large quantities converted into biofuels, such as ethanol (made from corn) and butanol (produced by fermentation of biomass by bacteria).

Biofuels are classified into two categories based on the source of their biomass.

> *First-generation biofuels* are derived from biomass such as sugarcane and cornstarch. Bioethanol is produced from the fermentation of sugars and can be used as an additive to gasoline or to power a fuel cell directly.

> *Second-generation biofuels* utilize non-food source biomass such as waste products from agriculture and municipalities. These lignocellulosic biomasses are not edible and are considered non-valuable to waste industries. Alternative fuel sources from non-food biomass are preferred, but lignocellulosic material is rigid and difficult to work with during manufacturing.

First and second-generation biofuels take longer to produce than algal biofuel, as crops take longer to grow and harvest than algae.

The expense of creating enough stations for reliability dependent on algae biofuel is steep. Growing, processing, and converting algae to biofuel requires expensive equipment. The research seeks cost-effective alternatives for algae biofuels.

Recent research in biofuels is concentrated on *third-generation biofuels* or fuels produced from algae or algae-derived biomass. Due to the speed at which algae grow, algae-based biofuels can be produced up to 10 times faster than other biomass-based fuel sources (e.g., corn and soy).

The initial cost to create a plant capable of growing, harvesting, and creating biofuel from algae is steep, but estimates predict investment return within a few years. Algae are a natural, renewable resource harvested from the oceans or grown indefinitely (optimal conditions).

Wind energy

Wind power uses wind turbines (or sails) that move (e.g., rotate) from flowing air.

Wind turbines capture wind in Earth's atmosphere and convert it into mechanical energy and, later, electricity. When wind blows past a turbine, the blades capture the force and rotate. Rotation causes an internal shaft to spin, causing the gearbox to spin. The gearbox is connected to a generator to produce electricity.

Wind turbines are in high-wind areas (e.g., immense plains, hilltops, or sea) and connected to a power grid to provide energy.

Commercial wind farm 3.8 miles off the coast of Block Island, RI (Osborne, Smithsonian)

Three types of wind power:

>*Utility-scale wind* uses turbines larger than 100 kilowatts and delivers electricity to the power grid, routed to the end-user by a power system operator.

>*Distributed wind* (or *small wind*) uses turbines smaller than 100 kW and delivers power directly to consumers (e.g., houses, businesses, or farms) for their primary use.

>*Offshore wind* uses turbines on large bodies of water to capture blowing wind.

   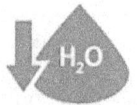

Carbon Dioxide reduced by **115,000,000** metric tonnes — Equivalent to CO₂ emissions from **270 million** barrels of oil

Sulfur Dioxide reduced by **157,000** metric tonnes — Equivalent to annual emissions of **12 uncontrolled coal plants**

Nitrogen Oxide reduced by **97,000** metric tonnes — Equivalent to annual emissions of **10 uncontrolled coal plants**

Water Consumption reduced by **36.5 billion** gallons — Equivalent to **116 gallons/person** in the U.S.

Emissions and water savings due to the energy generated by wind power in 2013. Wind generation provides environmental benefits. "Uncontrolled coal plants" have no emissions control technology. The U.S. ranks second worldwide for installed wind capacity. EPA

Geothermal energy

Geothermal energy is in the form of energy that uses the internal heat of the Earth, which can be converted to electricity. It reduces fossil fuel consumption, and many countries utilize geothermal energy to reduce *greenhouse gases* released into the atmosphere by burning fossil fuels.

Under Earth's crust is a layer of hot, flowing rock (or *magma*). Heat is produced by radioactive decay of materials (e.g., uranium (U)). The energy in magma is thousands of times more than in oil or natural gas. *Hotspots* have the highest underground temperatures and are where tectonic plates meet.

Geothermal energy has great potential, as even energy in underground rocks in communities can heat homes and businesses.

While large-scale geothermal projects require substantial initial investments, capturing Earth's natural heat as an energy source yields financial and environmental benefits.

Enhanced Geothermal Systems (EGS) technologies capture heat energy to produce electricity on a much larger scale.

Questions: Energy Resources & Consumption

1. Which of the following is accurate?

    A. coal is still the dominant fuel
    B. coal has largely been replaced by natural gas for energy supplies
    C. natural gas remains the dominant fuel in the United States
    D. coal and oil are the primary energy supply in the United States

2. Nuclear power plants in use today rely on:

    A. fission reactions to generate heat to boil water
    B. fission reactions to directly generate electricity
    C. fusion reactions to generate heat to boil water
    D. fusion reactions to directly generate electricity

3. Which of the following best illustrates sound science?

    A. asking voters to determine if wind turbines should be placed in their community
    B. measuring wind velocities to determine the cost-effectiveness of wind turbines
    C. selecting a source of energy based on profitability and yield of tax dollars
    D. lobbying government officials to increase drilling for offshore oil

4. Which of the following sources of energy is most sustainable?

    A. natural gas used to heat homes
    B. gasoline used to run cars
    C. hydroelectric dams
    D. a coal-fired electrical power plant

5. Which of the following is part of natural capital but not ecosystem capital?

    A. solar energy used to drive photosynthesis throughout the biosphere
    B. coal and oil reserves
    C. the production of electrical energy from wind turbines and dams
    D. the genetic diversity of all plants and animals used in modern agriculture

6. Burning fossil fuels, cutting down large forests, and not replanting the areas with trees:

   A. increases atmospheric concentrations of carbon dioxide
   B. decreases atmospheric concentrations of carbon dioxide
   C. increases the geological production of fossil fuels
   D. increases levels of nitrification and reduces acid rain

7. Potential environmental damage results from the harvesting of fossil fuels and:

   A. transportation and waste products generated by their use
   B. transportation and storage
   C. storage and waste products
   D. transportation, storage, and waste products generated by their use

8. The most cleanly burning fossil fuel available that produces the least pollutants is:

   A. coal, usually found in deposits deep within the Earth
   B. kerosene, found in deposits associated with oil wells
   C. natural gas, usually found in deposits associated with oil
   D. nuclear energy, produced from rocks and minerals within the Earth

9. Fossil fuels are considered non-renewable sources of energy because:

   A. their formation is so slow
   B. they release carbon dioxide when they are burned
   C. people are cutting down too many forests to allow trees to turn into coal
   D. carbon dioxide levels in the atmosphere are too low to allow fossil fuels to form

10. To meet the energy needs of all humans requires the capture of:

    A. all the Sun's energy striking the Earth
    B. all the Sun's energy reaching the outer atmosphere
    C. only about 1% of the Sun's energy striking the Earth
    D. only about 1/10,000 of the Sun's energy strikes the Earth

11. Compared to the generation of electricity using coal, nuclear power:

    A. contributes more to global climate change
    B. generates no sulfur dioxide or carbon dioxide emissions
    C. generates no sulfur dioxide but more carbon dioxide emissions
    D. will run out of fuel in about 40 years

12. Unlike fossil fuels, solar energy is considered non-polluting because of the chemical and radioactive products of fusion:

    A. stay near the Sun
    B. are destroyed in Earth's atmosphere
    C. would be produced on Earth anyway
    D. quickly break down when they strike the Earth's soil

13. Hydroelectric dams generate electricity without producing greenhouse gases, but:

    A. are short-lived structures that must be rebuilt about every 20 years
    B. are only able to contribute to about 5% of the electrical power throughout the world
    C. alter water control in ways that make it more challenging to irrigate crops
    D. eliminate farmland, wildlife habitats and, often, villages in the regions that are flooded

14. Enhanced geothermal systems:

    A. generate electricity using the heat of the Earth to make steam
    B. are routinely used in China to power automobiles
    C. use the energy of the Sun to boil water and generate electricity
    D. use gravity to propel large turbines, which generate electricity

15. Given the problems of inconsistent winds, the best place to position wind turbines is:

    A. along railroad tracks, where there are few trees
    B. along rivers and streams, where there is less human interference
    C. in offshore locations where winds are more consistent
    D. in deserts, where few manufactured structures are located

Relationship matrix

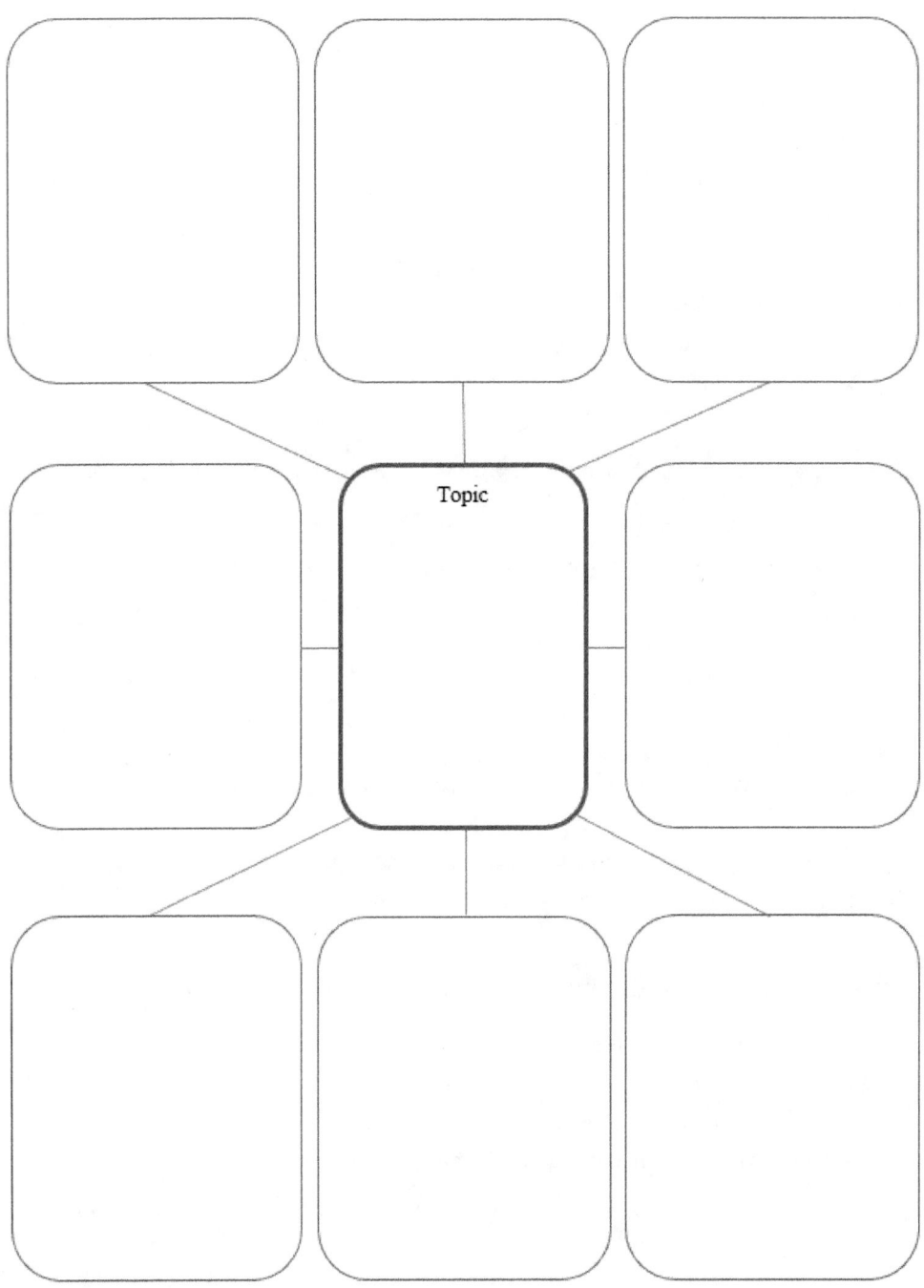

Notes for active learning

Notes for active learning

CHAPTER 8

Global Change

Stratospheric Ozone

Atmospheric Greenhouse Gases

Global Climate Change

Loss of Biodiversity

Page intentionally left blank

Stratospheric Ozone

Stratospheric ozone formation

Earth's stratospheric ozone layer contains approximately 90% of the ozone in the atmosphere. Ozone makes Earth habitable, as it absorbs the harmful ultraviolet radiation from solar rays before they can reach Earth's surface. UV radiation is harmful and causes sunburn and damage to cells, which can accelerate skin aging and lead to cancer.

Ozone is produced by stratospheric processes, absorbing about 99% of harmful UV rays. Ozone is produced near the Earth's surface in the troposphere layer, which can be harmful.

Stratospheric ozone formation occurs through the photolysis of O_2 (oxygen gas).

Photolysis of O_2 means "breaking" (lysis) by "light" (photo). This process does not occur in the troposphere because the ozone has wholly absorbed the intense UV rays that break oxygen gas molecules into smaller components in the stratosphere.

Breathing ozone causes many health problems (e.g., inflaming and damaging nasal passages, shortness of breath, and inhaling pain), making the lungs more susceptible to infection. Fortunately, most ozone layers are in the stratosphere and not inhaled by organisms.

Stratospheric ozone is formed naturally in the atmosphere by chemical reactions with oxygen (O_2) molecules and solar UV radiation (or sunlight). UV radiation breaks an oxygen gas molecule (O_2) into two oxygen atoms (2 O).

After oxygen gas splits, each oxygen atom is highly reactive and combines with oxygen gas (O_2) to form an ozone molecule (O_3). UV radiation in the stratosphere propagates reaction.

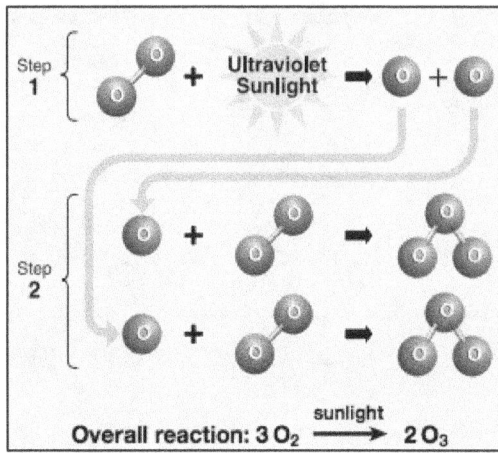

Ozone production from O_2 and sunlight

Ultraviolet radiation

Ultraviolet radiation (UV) comes from the Sun, and it has always been an essential aspect of human life with an important role in the environment.

UV radiation can occur at varying wavelengths, which have different effects. The beneficial effects of UV must be balanced with detrimental effects.

The longest UV radiation wavelengths are 320-400 nm and *UV-A* wavelengths. UV-A is essential for skin to form Vitamin D, but it is harmful as it causes eye cataracts and sunburn.

Another form of UV radiation is *UV-B,* with shorter wavelengths of light (290-320 nm). UV-B is harmful at the molecular level in cells, and it causes damage to the fundamental building blocks of life, deoxyribonucleic acid (DNA).

DNA readily absorbs UV radiation, which causes the shape of the DNA molecule to change. Shape changes prohibit protein-building enzymes from attaching to strands and correctly reading the genetic information in DNA molecules.

When DNA is not read correctly, distorted proteins may be created, or cells may die from the high level of dysfunction.

In one common damage event, adjacent bases bond with each other instead of across the strands to their complementary base. This creates a bulge in the DNA double helix, causing the DNA not to function correctly.

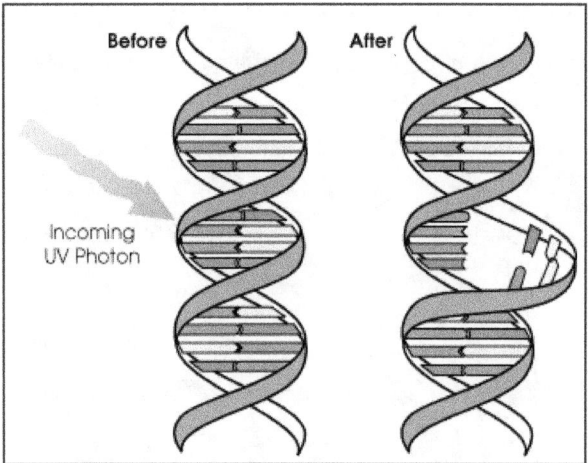

Ultraviolet (UV) photons harm the DNA molecules of living organisms

Ozone depletion causes

Scientific evidence shows that atmospheric chemicals containing bromine or chlorine deplete the stratospheric ozone. These *ozone-depleting substances*" (ODS) are stable, safe for the environment in the lower atmosphere, and generally not toxic. Their molecular stability allows them to float up into the atmosphere and interact with UV light rays, where they have broken apart and released bromine or chlorine.

Both elements deplete ozone astonishingly fast by stripping an oxygen atom from the ozone molecule. One bromine or chlorine can degrade thousands of stratospheric ozone molecules.

Ozone-depleting substances deplete ozone levels with a long half-life in the atmosphere; substances released by human activities 70-100 years ago remain in the stratosphere.

Main ODS causing ozone depletion are:

- *Chlorofluorocarbons* (CFCs) are the most widely used, accounting for over 75% of stratospheric ozone depletion. They were in freezers, air conditioners, refrigerators as coolants (e.g., Freon), and foam products that provided padding in shipping containers.
- *Halons* contain bromines and are in fire extinguishers.
- *Hydrofluorocarbons* substitute for ozone-depleting chlorofluorocarbons. Not as harmful to stratospheric ozone layers as chlorofluorocarbons, they cause ozone destruction.
- *Methyl chloroform* is used industrially to manufacture aerosols, adhesives, and various chemicals.
- *Carbon tetrachloride* is in fire extinguishers and industrial solvents.

Effects of ozone depletion

Stratospheric ozone functions as a filter, absorbing most shortwave UV radiation. If the ozone layer is depleted, more ultraviolet rays reach Earth. Exposure to high levels of UV radiation can harm humans, plants, and animals.

Human health is affected in several ways, including:

- Increased skin cancers, often caused by UV rays that burn the skin;
- Premature skin aging;
- Immunosuppression (i.e., weakened immune system) with UV radiation affects the efficacy of the immune system); and
- Blindness, cataracts, and other eye diseases are caused by UV radiation damaging the retina, cornea, lens, and conjunctiva.

Agriculture, ecosystems, and forests are affected because many crop species are harmed when exposed to increased UV radiation. This decreases the plants' overall growth and photosynthetic processes, decreasing crop production.

Species sensitive to UV radiation levels include corn, rice, oats, barley, wheat, tomatoes, cucumbers, carrots, peas, and broccoli.

Animals are affected; they, too, experience skin and eye cancer from high UV radiation.

In the Antarctic ozone hole, UV levels have already affected the developmental stages of various aquatic life forms.

Marine life experiences damage, in particular, plankton. Plankton are tiny life forms that reside in the first few meters under the ocean's surface and are the first step in many aquatic food chains. When the number of planktons decreases, the food chain is disrupted, and ocean biodiversity decreases, affecting humans who rely on aquatic life as a food source.

Wood, rubber, plastic, and fabrics are degraded by UV radiation. Protecting and replacing these materials would be a heavy financial burden.

Strategies for reducing ozone depletion

While the EPA and global agencies monitor and enforce laws to reduce the amount of ODS in the atmosphere, personal actions include:

> *Limit driving private vehicles.* Automobile emissions significantly add to atmospheric smog, a primary culprit in depleting the ozone layer. Alternatives to personal vehicles include public transportation, walking, riding a bicycle, and riding with a friend. Advances in personal transport in the past few decades, such as electric and hybrid vehicles, have helped reduce emissions.
>
> *Avoiding the use of pesticide-containing products.* Though they are an easy solution for ridding gardens of weeds, their effect on the atmosphere is long-lasting. Natural remedies for weed removal or removal by hand are two alternatives to using pesticides.
>
> *Using eco-friendly household cleaning.* Many cleaning products readily available for public use contain toxic chemicals that may harm health if not handled properly and expedite ozone depletion. Natural cleaning products are sold in supermarkets and health stores.

Relevant laws and treaties

Many strategies can be implemented to reduce ozone depletion in the atmosphere.

In 1987, 194 nations signed an agreement to end the production of chlorofluorocarbons, halons, and other substances known to deplete ozone (ODSs). This agreement is the *Montreal Protocol on Substances that Deplete the Ozone Layer*, in which countries agreed to reduce the production of ozone-depleting substances drastically.

This landmark global agreement to protect and restore the ozone layer achieved quantifiable results, and atmospheric levels of ODSs have been decreasing. Over the years, the agreement has been amended to help quicken the phase-out of ODSs.

Each country has undertaken to reduce ozone depletion. The *Environmental Protection Agency* (EPA) is the federal agency in the US primarily responsible for air quality management and protection of the atmosphere.

Clean Air Act created regulatory programs to address various problems, including:

- Ending the production of *ozone-depleting substances* (ODSs);
- Properly recycling refrigerants and halon fire extinguishing agents;
- Identifying effective alternatives to ozone-depleting substances;
- Banning the release of ozone-depleting refrigerants during service, maintenance, and disposal of air conditioners and other sources; and
- Requiring manufacturers to put warning labels on products containing or made with the most harmful ODSs.

In addition to enforcing the *Clean Air Act*, the *Environmental Protection Agency* works with other federal and international agencies to find methods to clean the stratosphere.

World Meteorological Organization and the *United Nations Environment Programme* gather scientific evidence for enacting laws.

To help protect people from harmful UV radiation exposure, the EPA has several educational services to inform the public of the dangers of unnecessary exposure to UV radiation. They partnered with the National Weather Service, so daily weather forecasts contain a UV Index, indicating UV radiation intensity.

EPA has the *SunWise School Program*, which educates children on the effects of overexposure to sunlight and practical steps for safety.

For example, combustion products during a spacecraft's trip into outer space harm the ozone layer. These products do not take tens or hundreds of years to reach the stratosphere, as spacecraft travel through it and expel ODS directly into the middle and upper layers.

While regulating rocket launches may not seem viable, scientific advances and EPA regulations are changing how NASA and other space programs operate.

Atmospheric Greenhouse Gases

Greenhouse effect

Greenhouse effect is when greenhouse gases trap infrared radiation before they escape into outer space. This warms the atmosphere and causes Earth's surface to warm.

It is named after a similar process in greenhouses, albeit on a smaller scale. A greenhouse is a structure made of glass that lets sunlight enter and prevents heat from escaping. Therefore, the inside of the greenhouse remains warm even though outside temperatures are too low to sustain specific plant life.

Scientists often agree that the cause of global warming is the greenhouse effect, which disrupts the stability of atmospheric layers through which infrared radiation (IR) passes. Greenhouse gases include fluorinated, nitrous oxide, carbon dioxide, and methane. These atmospheric gases block heat from escaping, which increases Earth's average temperature.

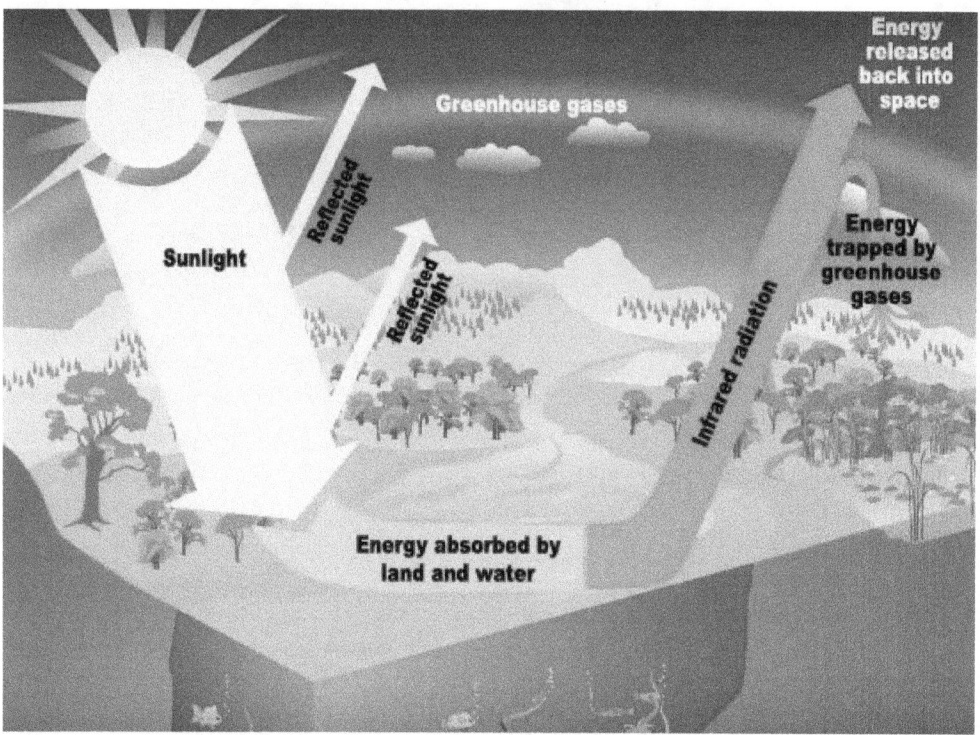

A condensed cycle outlining the greenhouse effect

Global Warming Potential (GWP) measures how much energy the emission of one metric ton of gas absorbs compared to one metric ton of carbon dioxide (CO_2) emissions. The greater the GWP, the more gas warms Earth compared to carbon dioxide.

Carbon dioxide has a GWP of 1 and is the reference gas. Nitrous oxide has a GWP of 265-298 times CO_2 over 100 years.

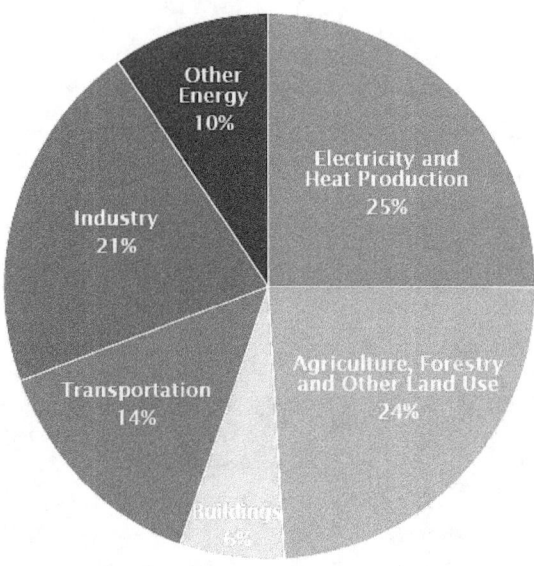

Worldwide greenhouse gas emissions by economic sector

Fluorinated gases

Fluorinated gases (or F-gases) only come from anthropogenic sources and have no natural source on Earth (unlike many other greenhouse gases). F-gases do not deplete the stratospheric ozone layer and are manufactured to replace ozone-depleting gases like chlorofluorocarbon (CFC) and hydrochlorofluorocarbon (HCFC). F-gases are ozone-friendly because they do not contain chlorine or bromine, causing ozone depletion. Substitution of F-gases for ozone-depleting substances accounts for 90% of F-gases emitted in the U.S.

Still, compared to other greenhouse gases, F-gases have a very high global warming potential (GWP), thousands to tens of thousands of times higher than carbon dioxide, so even small concentrations can have immense effects on the average global temperature. *Intergovernmental Panel on Climate Change* has stated that sulfur hexafluoride is the most potent greenhouse gas, with a GWP of 22,800.

F-gases have lifetimes in the atmosphere of up to several thousand years and can only be destroyed by solar radiation in the upper atmosphere.

Four main categories of F-gases are:

> nitrogen trifluoride (NF_3),
>
> sulfur hexafluoride (SF_6),
>
> perfluorocarbons (PFCs), and
>
> hydrofluorocarbons (HFCs).

These F-gases are released through many industrial processes, such as semiconductors and aluminum production.

Hydrofluorocarbons are used as fire retardants, refrigerants, laboratory solvents, and aerosol propellants. Electricity transmission and distribution uses sulfur hexafluoride in equipment such as circuit breakers.

Industrial processes produce perfluorocarbons (PFC) in aluminum and semiconductor manufacturing. Perfluorocarbons have a high GWP and long atmospheric lifetime, though not as potent as sulfur hexafluoride.

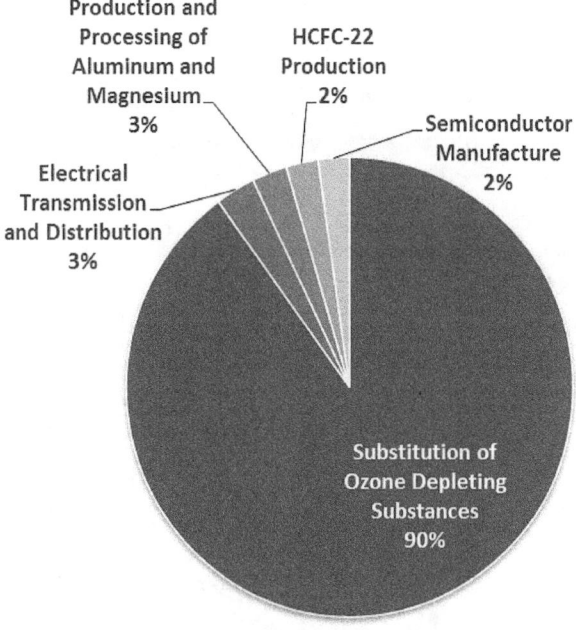

Fluorinated gas emissions in the United States, by source.
Estimates are from the Inventory Greenhouse Gas Emissions and Sinks: 1990-2013

Nitrous oxide

Nitrous oxide (N_2O) is 5% of greenhouse gas emissions from human activity in the U.S. It occurs commonly throughout nature, as in Earth's nitrogen cycle.

Nitrogen cycle is a natural circulation of nitrogen molecules among plants, animals, microorganisms, and the atmosphere. Nitrogen molecules can take on several forms, depending on their stage and how they are needed for a specific process. Bacteria degrade nitrogen in the ocean and soil, naturally releasing greenhouse gas nitrous oxide.

Nitrous oxide can be removed from the atmosphere through chemical reactions, UV radiation, and absorption by certain forms of bacteria. Nitrous oxide molecules remain in the atmosphere for 114 years before being destroyed through chemical reactions or removed by a *sink* (i.e., a reservoir that absorbs a compound during its natural cycle).

Nitrous oxide's atmospheric impact is enormous. Scientists estimate that the impact of one pound of N_2O on the warming of the atmosphere is nearly 300 times that of one pound of CO_2.

Human activity through agriculture, wastewater management, factories, and the combustion of fossil fuels has dramatically increased the amount of N_2O in the atmosphere.

Soil management in agriculture is the most significant contributor to N_2O emissions, accounting for 75% of U.S. nitrous oxide emissions in 2013. Soil management practice adds nitrogen to soil to produce nitrogen-rich fertilizers. This process emits nitrous oxide byproducts, which are absorbed into the atmosphere.

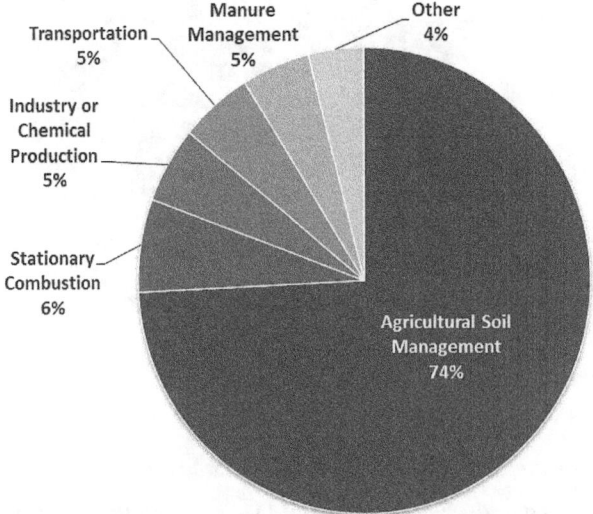

Nitrous Oxide (N_2O) emissions in the United States by source.
Estimates are from the Inventory Greenhouse Gas Emissions and Sinks: 1990-2013

Transportation adds to atmospheric nitrous oxide. Automobiles emit N_2O as a byproduct when fuel is burned. Motor vehicles (e.g., trucks and cars) produce the most nitrous oxide. As with carbon dioxide, the amount of N_2O released into the atmosphere depends on the type of fuel burned and the vehicle.

Industrial processes emit nitrous oxide into the atmosphere by producing nitric acid, an ingredient for commercial synthetic fertilizer. It is emitted in adipic acid production and used to make fibers such as nylon and synthetic products.

Carbon dioxide

Carbon dioxide (CO_2) accounts for 82% of greenhouse gas emissions in the U.S. and is the primary GHG emitted by anthropogenic forces. It is released through natural processes such as human (and animal) respiration, deforestation, volcanic eruptions, and burning fossil fuels.

Carbon dioxide constantly cycles through the ocean, atmosphere, and land surfaces because it is produced by plants, animals, and microorganisms (e.g., bacteria). Natural CO_2 production stabilizes atmospheric levels balanced in homeostasis.

Since the onset of the Industrial Revolution (1750s), human activity has increased atmospheric CO_2 concentration by one-third, which substantially affects climate change.

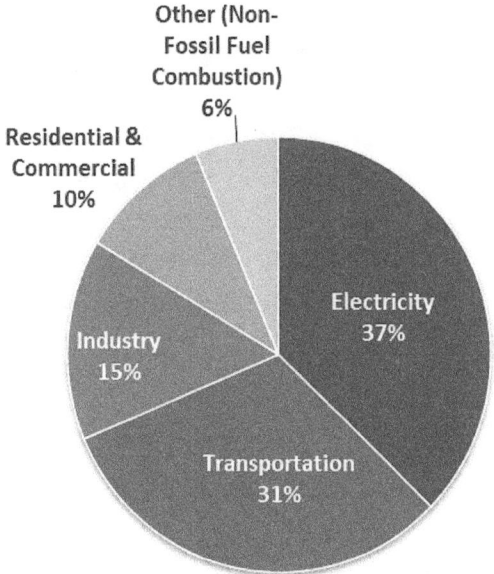

United States carbon dioxide (CO_2) emissions, by source.
Estimates are from the Inventory Greenhouse Gas Emissions and Sinks: 1990-2013

Human activities change carbon cycles by adding carbon dioxide into the air and changing the ability of forests to remove atmospheric CO_2 (deforestation decreases the number of trees available to absorb carbon dioxide during photosynthesis, leaving CO_2 in the atmosphere).

The main human activity that releases carbon dioxide into the atmosphere is fossil fuels combustion used to generate electricity and power automobiles, trucks, trains, and airplanes.

Transportation significantly contributes to carbon dioxide emissions; CO_2 is released by burning fossil fuels (e.g., natural gas, gasoline, and diesel). Contributing transportation methods include air travel, highway automobiles, railroads, and marine transportation (e.g., cargo and cruise ships).

Industrial processes such as the production and consumption of cement and metals (e.g., steel and iron) and chemicals emit carbon dioxide through the combustion of fossil fuels. Many industries require immense electrical power to operate and indirectly burn more fossil fuels due to burning hydrocarbons.

Electricity use and generation account for the largest CO_2 emissions in the U.S. Fossil fuels are combusted to produce electricity. Although other methods are used (e.g., hydro and wind energy), fossil fuels remain the primary energy source most countries use to generate electricity.

The amount of CO_2 released into the atmosphere depends on the combusted fossil fuel. For example, burning coal emits more CO_2 than burning natural gas or oil.

Methane

Methane (CH_4) accounts for 10% of greenhouse gases emitted in the U.S. by human action instead of natural processes. Methane does not persist in the atmosphere for very long (approximately 12 years), but it is more efficient at trapping infrared radiation than carbon dioxide. Natural processes during atmospheric chemical reactions remove methane from air.

Globally, methane emitted from human activities makes up 60% of methane emissions. It is released through agricultural practices, industrial practices, and waste management activities.

Agriculture is the largest source of global methane emissions, primarily due to increased livestock (e.g., cows, sheep, goats, poultry). Animals release methane as a byproduct of their digestion.

Industries contribute to methane emissions mainly through their natural gas and petroleum systems. Methane is the primary component of natural gas drilled underground and released during processing, production, storage, transportation, and distribution. Methane is often underground in crude oil reserves and in the extracted petroleum. During the processing and production of crude oil, methane is often released into the atmosphere.

Landfills are the third-largest contributor to CH_4 emissions in the U.S. As waste accumulates in landfills, it decomposes, releasing methane gas.

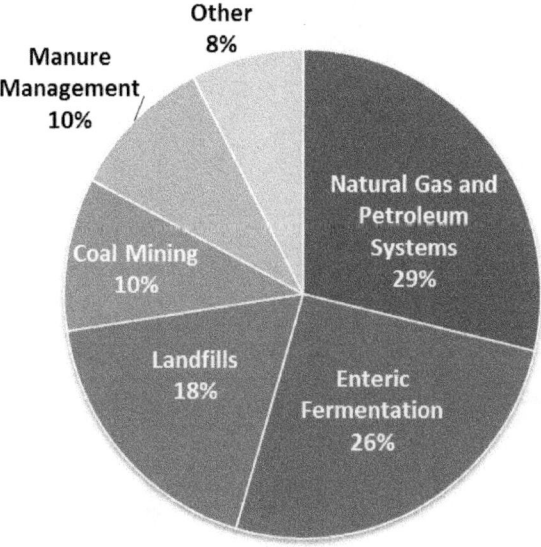

US methane (CH_4) emissions, Inventory Greenhouse Gas Emissions and Sinks: 1990-2013

Notes for active learning

Global Climate Change

Anthropogenic causes

Anthropogenic forces are occurrences due to human activity. Climate change is a controversial topic, mainly because of differing opinions. Climate change can occur because of both natural and human-made actions. Past global climate shifts have occurred without man-directed activity and permitted life to continue. It is crucial to understand how humans impact the climate.

Since the Industrial Revolution, the decrease in the ozone layer and increases in specific chemical concentrations in the air, water, and soil have significantly impacted the overall climate shift. It is essential to understand the human impact on the climate and mitigate what humans do to affect Earth's complicated ecosystem balances.

Scientists have studied past climate shifts to understand how they occurred and how they may be managed. These changes are studied by taking deep ice-core samples and reviewing sediment layers and past sea levels to observe changes over time.

Intergovernmental Panel on Climate Change (IPCC, 2014) stated that scientists are over 95% confident that increased anthropogenic greenhouse gases cause global warming. Scientists predict this change will permanently alter Earth's climate and consider it the greatest environmental threat.

During data analysis, scientists commonly use a 5% margin of error when how confident they are with their conclusion. Generally, scientists target a 95% confidence level (or higher) when concluding research findings to minimize error (i.e., 5 errors per 100 events). Therefore, when a researcher concludes with 95% confidence (i.e., 95 correct per 100 events) that actions cause a response (e.g., human activity causing global warming), there is a 5% chance (or less) that the conclusion is an error.

When scientists state that they are 95% certain that greenhouse gases and human activity are causing global warming, they assert that their research supports this statement.

Average temperature

Earth's temperatures are balanced by solar heat and thermal energy radiated back to space.

Infrared radiation is a form of energy Earth releases to cool from heat absorbed by solar energy.

Earth's surface absorbs and reflects solar energy (or sunlight).

Average surface temperature is Earth's average sea-surface and above-ground temperatures; the average water temperature is the first few feet below the ocean surface between Earth's surface and 1.5 meters above the surface.

Average surface temperature and *atmospheric temperatures* are used to analyze trends. Earth's average annual surface temperature is higher than when first recorded in the mid-to-late 1880s.

Why are seemingly minuscule changes and variations in temperatures concerning? Only Earth has known life forms requiring specific temperature ranges in our solar system. Oceans, plants, storms, the sea level, and the salt concentration in the oceans are influenced by Earth's surface temperature. Even the slightest variation has ramifications for ecosystems.

Climate change refers to increasing global temperature but also describes climate trends during Earth's history.

Global warming is a gradual increase in the average temperature of oceans and atmosphere. Over the past several decades, this increase has been exacerbated by emissions from automobiles, factories, and other machines. Global warming focuses on the current warming of Earth's climate.

Impacts and consequences of global warming

Climate change can have several effects on Earth, such as influencing crop yields, affecting human health, causing changes in rainfall, altering forests and ecosystems, and changing the available energy supply.

The impacts of global warming vary by region and ecosystems across the planet. For instance, a desert in Africa experiences a slight decrease in rainfall, which is different from the rainforests of South America.

Life on Earth is affected by global warming in many ways:

- *Energy* demands change with fluctuating temperatures, increased demands for cooling during summer, and increased need for heating during winter. Frequent and intense storms, along with rising sea levels, may disrupt extraction and transportation of fuels (e.g., drilling rigs on the ocean);

- *Agriculture* (e.g., crop yields) is affected by drought, flooding, and warming. While slight changes in atmospheric carbon dioxide levels help plants (i.e., reactants for plant physiology), high levels projected over several decades could be catastrophic;

- *Transportation* infrastructure is affected by higher temperatures, severe storms, and higher storm surges along the coasts;

- *Coasts* experience more stress during global warming. Increased ocean acidity and temperature will impact coastal and marine ecosystems;
- Climate change can *transform ecosystems* for species interactions.

For example, flooding in an area damages a species' habitat, causing relocation. Species instinctively look for new environments and may adapt to a less favorable habitat. This could fundamentally change aspects of that species over generations, from physiology to physical appearance. Introducing species could threaten Indigenous organisms (e.g., disturbing predator/prey balance).

Forests are negatively affected as warming temperatures change the frequency of wildfire and pestilent insect outbreaks. The productivity of forests (i.e., the amount of O_2 released) decreases due to changes in precipitation, temperature, and the amount of CO_2 in the air.

Temperature, precipitation, and changing sea levels alter water resource supply and quality. Water resources affect energy production, human health, and agriculture.

Society is affected, especially vulnerable impoverished young, sick, or older adults. Cities are sensitive to climate change because these changes affect a high concentration of people.

International impacts are profound, as developing countries are more susceptible to climate change than developed countries. These global changes affect trade, tourism, and energy production relationships.

Efforts to reduce climate change

Reducing carbon dioxide emissions has become a focal point among scientists and the public.

Environmental Protection Agency (EPA) has implemented laws and regulations to reduce carbon pollution emissions from power plants, automotive vehicles, and factories.

In the 1990s, carbon dioxide emissions increased by about 1.3% yearly and are expected to increase exponentially (estimated increases of 1.9-2.5% each year).

This increase in carbon dioxide emissions is partly due to the inability of *carbon sinks* (e.g., oceans, algae, and plants) to absorb carbon dioxide at the same rate as production. Before reducing carbon emissions can occur, reducing the increased emissions rate must be achieved.

Automobiles produce 30% of carbon emissions, so changing how transportation is used is a focus. Electric and hybrid cars emerged to decrease emissions by increasing automobile fuel efficiency (i.e., miles-per-gallon ratio).

Renewable energy sources such as hydroelectricity, wind power, and solar power have become dependable alternatives to fossil fuels.

Other ideas for reducing global warming include funding programs and supporting laws and treaties that reduce greenhouse gas emissions. Slowing the rate of deforestation is one way to ensure that excess carbon is naturally cycled and taken out of the atmosphere by plants.

Relevant laws and treaties

National Oceanic and Atmospheric Administration (NOAA) is a U.S. scientific agency focused on understanding atmospheric and oceanic conditions. They research dangerous or extreme weather and guide communities to protect coastal resources and oceans. They seek to improve the public's understanding of the environment.

Along with the *Clean Air Act* (1987) and Montreal Protocol (1987) discussed earlier, several protocols, treaties, and panels focus on anthropogenic forces damaging the planet's ecosystems. Their efforts include lowering carbon emissions, educating the public, and regulating industries.

Climate Action Network is a worldwide group of environmental organizations working with countries to solve global climate change issues. They work together to strike international negotiations, pressure governments to work more quickly on passing their legislation and contribute to developing the United Nations framework on climate change protocols.

Kyoto Protocol was signed a decade after the Montreal Protocol and aimed to get required industrialized countries (e.g., Europe, Canada, New Zealand, Japan, and others) to reduce carbon dioxide emissions and other greenhouse gases. Most industrialized countries agreed to the treaty except Australia and the United States.

While the US signed the protocol in 1998, the US Senate refused to ratify it because countries like China did not commit to these standards. The agreement was not binding for the US and ultimately withdrew from the protocol in 2001.

China ratified the protocol in 2002 and is a member of the United Nations Framework Convention on Climate Change (UNFCCC). The US maintains that complying with the agreement would have a negative economic impact without competitive assurances of universal commitments.

Loss of Biodiversity

Marine life

By 2050, climate change will threaten extinction for over one-quarter of land species.

Marine life and freshwater species risk extinction due to elevated water temperatures, especially those living in sensitive ecosystems (e.g., coral reefs). Over the past several millions of years, organisms have evolved and adapted to living in their environments.

When changes like temperature increase occur over a few short decades, evolving animals do not get enough time to adapt and may die out. Such events lead to the extinction of species and threaten species in the ecosystem, relying on the now-extinct organisms as a food source or as higher predators in the food chain. This "domino effect" is often irreversible and highly destructive to ecosystems.

Intergovernmental Panel on Climate Change (IPCC) predicted that by 2100, the surface of Earth will warm another 6 °C. This estimate is based on current trends of burning fossil fuels and toxic emissions. Scientists cannot predict precisely how each species and ecosystem will respond but forecast catastrophic effects.

During the last Ice Age, roughly 20,000 years ago, the global temperature was 6 °C cooler.

To put an average global temperature change of 6 °C in perspective, think of the changes over the last few decades that have been ascribed to global warming (e..g., glacial melting, extreme storms, flooding, droughts, heatwaves, coral reef bleaching and dying) have occurred when Earth's average global temperature changed by less than 1 °C.

Habitat loss

Species have evolved over millions of years to live and thrive in ecological *niches* with specific conditions (e.g., temperatures) and suitable plants and animals for consumption.

Some species are better capable of adapting to sudden changes, though most are not. For example, rats and cockroaches can live outside their ideal niche, while pandas must live where there is bamboo, or they will not survive.

Anthropogenic forces are causing rapid changes in global temperatures, disrupting the niches of organisms, and threatening the lives of those unable to migrate quickly to a suitable area.

Several studies have indicated that a rise in the average global temperature of about 1.8-2 °C would result in the threat of extinction for over a million species.

Unless greenhouse gas emissions are reduced drastically around the globe, habitat loss and the extinction of various organisms are inevitable.

For example, polar bears risk extinction due to the predicted disappearance of Arctic Sea ice over the 21st century. Polar bears are the world's largest land predators and can survive for months without eating because they store enough fat when food is unavailable.

Without sea ice, polar bears would not be the only species affected; much, if not all, of the Arctic ecosystem would collapse.

Polar bear families are living with the effects of climate change on habitat loss. Typically, this area is covered with glacial ice

Coral reefs are affected by coral bleaching, which occurs when rising temperatures or ocean acidity stresses coral. Under normal conditions, coral contains microscopic algae called zooxanthellae that provides the reef with food and gives the coral its vibrant colors.

When stressed, coral expels zooxanthellae and turns white. If the zooxanthella does not return to that coral, it will not receive food and eventually die. Changes in water temperature of 1 °C can stress coral from bleaching.

In 2002, 60% of the Great Barrier Reef in Australia was affected by bleaching.

Unless temperatures stop rising, much of this beautiful reef will be dead within decades, as will the hundreds of species that live on the reef and use it as a source of food and shelter.

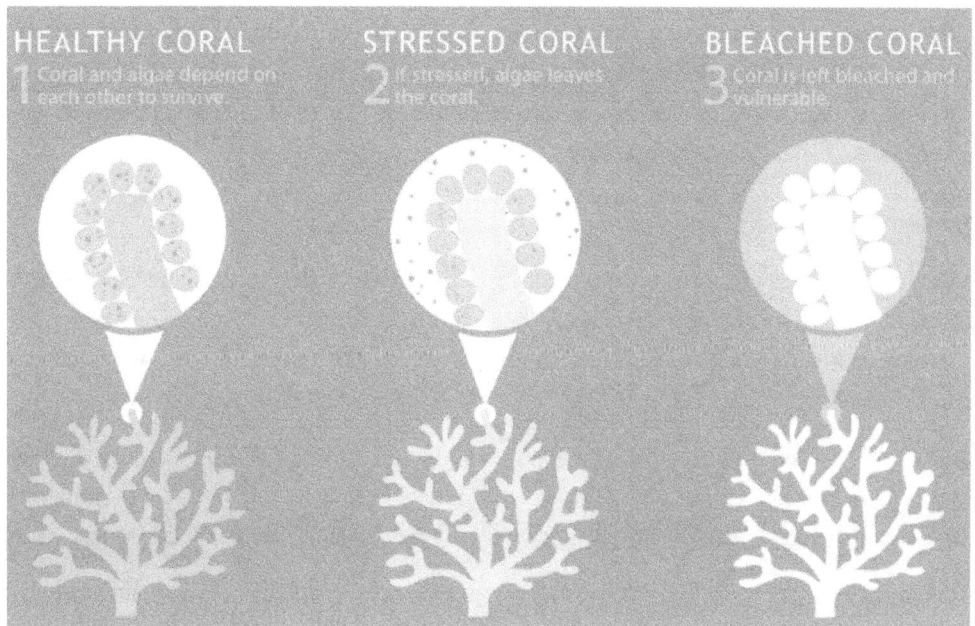

Coral bleaching occurs from stress and may recover when stress is removed

Like insects and animals, plants require a specific climate to grow and thrive. For example, silver maples will not grow next to the Saguaro Cactus; they are two very different species with specific physiological needs.

Changes in temperature and precipitation affect the ability of species to thrive. Unlike animals and insects, plants cannot move to a more suitable niche, and climate change may occur at a rate too rapid for adaptation by most plants.

Losing these plants affects the food chain significantly, as other organisms likely rely on that plant as a source of nutrition or shelter.

Overuse of species

Biodiversity loss occurs through overexploitation or overuse of species. One example is the overuse of marine species like invertebrates and fish. Overexploitation, including over-harvesting and overfishing, has depleted nearly 75% of marine species worldwide.

For example, anchovies off the coast of Peru and cod from Newfoundland are no longer viable food resources because their stock has been almost depleted.

As populations grow and the demand for food increases, humans have moved to other sources of marine life to meet their nutritional needs. Overexploitation of marine animals is wasteful, like the finning industry common to parts of Asia.

Dolphins and sharks are captured, and their fins are removed to make a delicacy called fin soup. The animals are either killed for their fins or released back into the ocean, often dying from blood loss and the inability to swim correctly. Finning has gained national attention in the past few years, and organizations have moved to end this practice.

Pollution

Although the effects of pollution on animals have not been as widely tested and measured as its effects on humans, it is safe to assume that animal life is affected by pollution just as much as humankind; holes in the ozone layer can allow harmful UV rays to reach Earth's surface, causing skin cancer in people, as well as damage to crops and other organisms.

Acid rain is a central phenomenon affecting biodiversity. Rain containing sulfuric acid and nitric acid is caused by fossil fuels burning as emissions are released into the air. Acidic water vapor travels into the atmosphere, forming clouds and returning as acidic rainfall.

Acid rain has a detrimental effect on streams and lakes as organisms are incompatible with acidic environments. It harms plants by damaging leaves and tree branches, slowing growth.

Exogenous species

Exogenous species are organisms not native to an area and introduced to an environment from the outside. Species may arrive by deliberate action or accidental transportation (e.g., North American tumbleweed).

Non-native species affect the local ecosystem in many ways; some have little or no impact, others have a negative impact, and others have a positive impact.

Some non-native species have been introduced to ecosystems as a method of biological pest control and are used as an alternative to chemical pesticides on crops.

For example, alfalfa weevil is a foraging pest substantially reduced by introducing predators.

Introduced species that become harmful or considered pests are *invasive species* and can cause significant harm to an ecosystem. They can proliferate and overcrowd areas in days. Ecologists are concerned that invasive species force native plants into extinction.

For example, Japanese stilt grass is an invasive species that was unintentionally introduced to the United States when used as packaging material for shipments from China. There is fear that the unstoppable growth of this grass, which grows in various habitats, will crowd out many native species.

Asian long-horned beetle was introduced to the U.S. unintentionally via cargo from Asia to New York. It is destructive to maple and other hardwoods. Another example is Burmese pythons, which were pets that were released or escaped into the wilderness of South Florida. They spread quickly and now threaten the existence of native species (e.g., Key Largo woodrat, deer, and indigo snakes) and disrupt the indigenous food chain balance.

Adult alfalfa weevils threatened the native species by foraging

Endangered and extinct species

Endangered species are plants or animals at significant risk for extinction (see table) and are "red-listed," meaning that efforts to conserve their species are of utmost importance.

An endangered species is the second most severe status for an organism after those deemed *critically endangered* (those with the highest risk of extinction in the wild).

The number of species on the list changes occasionally; some may be taken off if conservation efforts have been successful and they are no longer in danger of extinction. Despite worldwide efforts, species become extinct.

Natural extinction rate is how fast a species becomes extinct without human intervention. The current species loss is 1,000 to 10,000 times higher than the natural extinction rate. 0.01 to 0.1% of species will become extinct this year, and 10,000 to 100,000 species next year.

Mass extinction event is when a catastrophic event simultaneously decimates several species. For example, the cataclysmic impact of an enormous meteor striking Earth is hypothesized to have caused the extinction of dinosaurs 65 million years ago.

Group	United States			Foreign			Total Listings (U.S. + Foreign)	U.S. Listings with active recovery plans
	Endangered	Threatened	Total Listings	Endangered	Threatened	Total Listings		
Annelid worms	0	0	0	0	0	0	0	0
Flatworms and roundworms	0	0	0	0	0	0	0	0
Sponges	0	0	0	0	0	0	0	0
Corals	0	6	6	0	16	16	22	0
Snails	38	12	50	1	0	1	51	29
Amphibians	20	15	35	8	1	9	44	21
Reptiles	15	24	39	69	20	89	128	36
Mammals	75	25	100	254	20	274	374	64
Clams	75	13	88	2	0	2	90	71
Fishes	93	70	163	19	3	22	185	105
Arachnids	12	0	12	0	0	0	25	12
Insects	64	11	75	4	0	4	79	41
Crustaceans	22	3	25	0	0	0	25	18
Birds	79	21	100	217	17	234	334	86
Millipedes	0	0	0	0	0	0	0	0
Hydroids	0	0	0	0	0	0	0	0
Animal Totals	493	200	693	574	77	651	1344	483
Conifers & cycads	2	2	4	0	2	2	6	3
Flowering plants	700	161	861	1	0	1	862	646
Ferns and allies	29	2	31	0	0	0	31	26
Lichens	2	0	2	0	0	0	2	2
Plant Totals	733	165	898	1	2	3	901	677
Grand Totals	1226	365	1591	575	79	654	2245	1160

Organisms around the globe and the number of species endangered or threatened. Over 1226 plants and animals in the United States are endangered as of November 2015.

Maintenance through conservation

Earth's biodiversity results from billions of years of evolution. Unfortunately, humanity has over-exploited natural resources, resulting in disturbances in the natural environment. Scientists estimate that the extinction rate of species is between 1,000 and 10,000 times higher than it would be without any human interference.

Conserving biodiversity ensures that natural ecosystems are maintained and populations, species, genes, and interactions between them will survive and persist. Biodiversity conservation relies heavily on several disciplines of natural and biological sciences, law, public policy, and economics collaboratively. Conservation biology has grown as a scientific discipline and broadened our understanding of biodiversity and natural ecosystems.

Rainforest conservation is one method of preserving biodiversity. Rainforests are the biggest stores of the planet's biodiversity and are excellent climate change regulators. They filter pollution by absorbing substantial amounts of carbon dioxide from the atmosphere. Rainforests are rich in plant life, which requires CO_2 for photosynthesis. By removing excess atmospheric carbon dioxide, rainforests help keep the climate stable and functioning.

Biodiversity conservation methods include government incentives to private landowners to practice conservation and management practices on the part of local and state parks, sanctuaries, and wildlife services. These incentives may be monetary and offered as a part of the government's environmental protection programs.

Wildlife corridors are structures (e.g., bridges) crossing roadways and transportation routes. Before the bridge construction, wildlife crossed by road, risking danger or death. Motorists are harmed, with over two hundred annual deaths and thousands injured in animal collisions. Insurance companies estimate annual societal costs for injuries and deaths at $200 million.

Wildlife crossing over a busy highway allows for the safe crossing of deer, bears, reptiles, and other animals (left); an underground tunnel crossing for tortoises (right)

Seed banks

Seed banks foster plant conservation by storing dormant seeds in cold and dry conditions. Seeds are preserved and can propagate to future generations after prolonged storage. Seeds are collected and inventoried from thousands of plants for future use, including wild, ornamental, medicinal, and crop-based seeds.

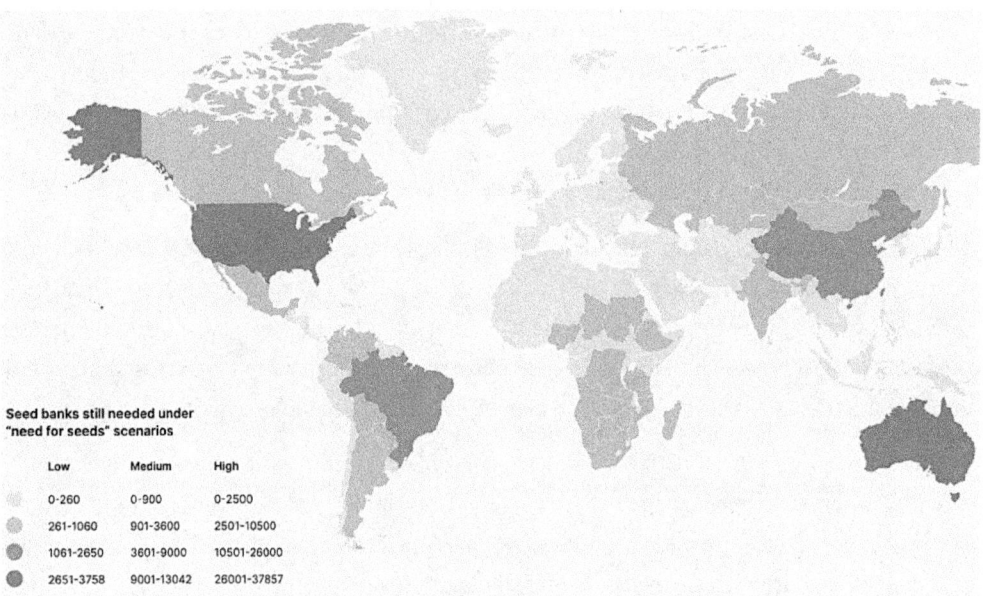

Seed banks needed per country based on low, medium, and high "need for seeds scenarios."

Millennium Seed Bank Project at *Royal Botanical Gardens* in Great Britain stores 10% of worldwide plant diversity. Seed banks provide ready access to plant samples, allowing scientists to evaluate nutritional, medicinal, and genetic attributes. In seed banks, they are protected from disease, predators, and factors endangering their species.

A recent example of a seed bank is in Svalbard, Norway, where there is a project to house seeds from known plants to preserve plant biodiversity in the event of a global cataclysm.

Recently, *cryopreservation* has become a more widely used process involving storing living tissue at extremely low temperatures (around -196 °C). This procedure is available for more than 150 species of plants, though, for each species, the method must be fine-tuned and empirically adapted. Seeds may remain viable for hundreds or even thousands of years when stored properly.

Cryopreservation includes using young zygotic embryos, adding retardants or inhibitors that slow down cell growth, an overlay of mineral oil after placement in a low-temperature storage facility, and reducing oxygen tension.

Cryopreservation has many uses:

- Conservation of endangered plant life through seed storage in seed banks;
- Plant pathogen conservation;
- Storing genetically altered tissues;
- Preservation and storage of plant tissue that has medicinal value;
- Conservation of plant germplasm; and
- Storage for use in genetic studies.

Laws and treaties

Endangered Species Act (1973) conserves threatened or endangered species in their ecosystems. In 1972, President Richard Nixon noted that the US did not meet suitable conservation efforts and must prevent human-induced species extinctions.

Congress passed the *Endangered Species Act* (ESA) to recognize that "*our rich natural heritage is of esthetic, ecological, educational, recreational and scientific value to our Nation and its people.*" Congress expressed great concern that native plants and animals were endangered. ESA lists threatened and endangered species and all species of animals and plants are eligible for inclusion.

Marine Mammal Protection Act (MMPA), enacted in 1972, extended protections to marine mammals. With certain exceptions, MMPA prohibits transporting marine mammals from U.S. waters or importation of marine mammals (or products) into the U.S. Congress passed the Act with a few embedded principles:

> Marine mammals may be endangered by human activity;
>
> Marine mammals are public resources for all nations;
>
> Species must not fall below optimum sustainable population levels; and
>
> Endangered species must be replenished

World Wildlife Foundation (WWF) advances policies to preserve resources, reduce emissions, and address climate change as people co-adapt to their environments.

Programs include *Adopt a Polar Bear*, *Adopt a Tiger*, *Adopt an Elephant*, or *Species at Risk*.

Relationship matrix

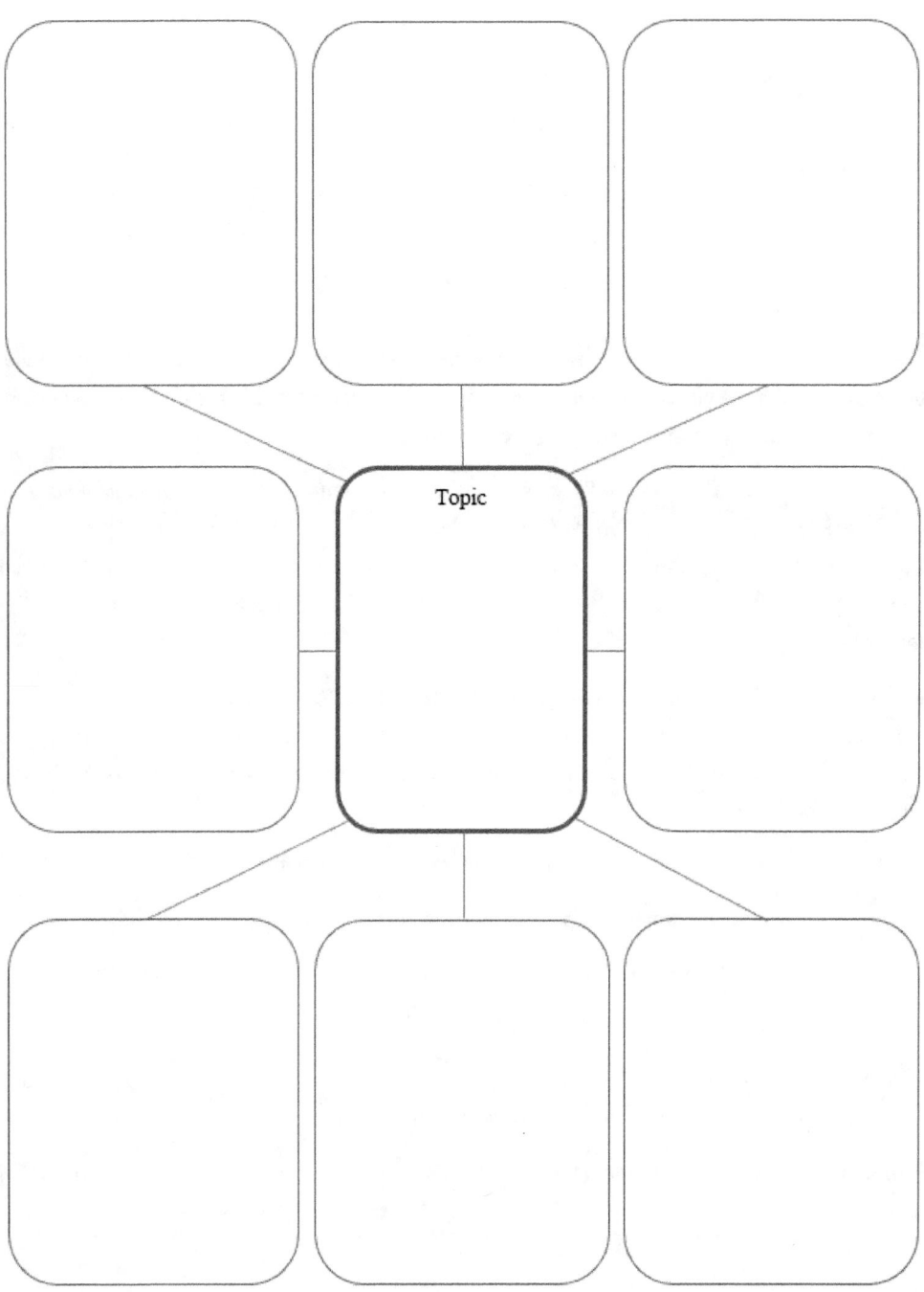

Questions: Global Change

1. Which of the following best illustrates a type of adaptation to global climate change?

    A. Increasing the use of public transportation systems in cities
    B. Building taller levees to hold back storm surges along ocean coastlines
    C. using solar and nuclear power to generate electricity instead of burning coal
    D. widening the Panama Canal to allow larger ships to move from China to Europe

2. Which of the following is a correlation that is causing widespread concern?

    A. As atmospheric oxygen levels decline, the ozone layer is being destroyed
    B. As atmospheric carbon dioxide levels decline, the ozone layer is being destroyed
    C. As levels of methane decline, average global temperatures are increasing
    D. As levels of carbon dioxide increase, average global temperatures are increasing

3. Which of the following best illustrates sustainability?

    A. constructing coal mines that do not require extensive surface excavations
    B. increasing our reliance upon renewable sources of energy
    C. upgrading or replacing computers every few years to improve performance
    D. converting automobiles from gasoline to natural gas as a new source of fuel

4. Globalization is primarily the result of:

    A. new forms of ground transportation
    B. worldwide electronic communication
    C. increased exploration into unpopulated regions of the world
    D. major discoveries of natural resources

5. The most important outcome of ecosystem management is:

    A. ecological sustainability
    B. economic productivity
    C. recreational use of managed regions
    D. opportunities to harvest natural resources

6. Which of the following global climate changes is most associated with increased hurricane activity?

    A. increased desertification in Africa   **C.** melting polar ice caps

    B. warmer oceans   **D.** melting glaciers in Alaska

7. Which of the following contributes the most to global climate change?

    A. the use of natural gas to heat homes

    B. planting forests to grow wood for lumber and paper pulp

    C. the generation of electricity from nuclear fuel

    D. eating a vegetarian diet

8. Using ice core samples and analyses, researchers have discovered that over the past 800,000 years:

    A. glaciers were greatest when greenhouse gases increased the most

    B. the Earth has gradually been warming, and sea levels have been rising

    C. there is a strong correlation between global temperatures and greenhouse gases

    D. atmospheric levels of methane and carbon dioxide have steadily been increasing

9. The greatest impact of globalization is seen in the:

    A. increased access to natural resources to poor developing nations

    B. economic reorganization and interdependency of the world

    C. move towards sustainable development throughout the world

    D. general shift in populations from cities to rural life

10. The acronym HIPPO identifies five major factors contributing to extinction. These are:

    A. humans, invasive species, periodic climate changes, pollution, and overexploitation

    B. hunting, immigration, people, population, and outsourcing

    C. housing, immigration, people, pollution, and overproduction

    D. habitat destruction, invasive species, pollution, population growth, and overexploitation

11. Introduced alien species that cause the most harm are those that:

    A. struggle to fit into new ecosystems and eventually die out

    B. eventually becomes naturalized

    C. become invasive

    D. become agricultural products

12. Destruction of the ozone layer primarily occurs in the:

    A. stratosphere   **C.** mesosphere

    B. thermosphere   **D.** troposphere

13. If climate change causes rain and temperature regional patterns to shift dramatically:

    A. plate tectonic action may dramatically change

    B. ocean levels could suddenly drop

    C. the region's biomes may shift to other types

    D. the region's biodiversity may suddenly increase

14. The most dramatic temperature shifts in the past few decades have been:

    A. in the north and south polar regions

    B. in the oceans near the equator

    C. on land near the equator

    D. in the innermost regions of the North American and African continents

15. Which activities have contributed the greatest amount of atmospheric carbon dioxide over the past 100 years?

    A. increased farming and production of grains

    B. increased reliance upon coal, oil, and natural gas

    C. deforestation of rainforests and other parts of the world

    D. volcanic eruptions and widespread forest fires

Notes for active learning

APPENDIX

Page intentionally left blank

Answer Keys

Chapter 1: Earth Systems & Resources

1: D	6: C	11: D
2: C	7: A	12: A
3: B	8: B	13: D
4: C	9: C	14: A
5: A	10: B	15: B

Chapter 2: Weather & Climate

1: B	6: A	11: D
2: C	7: A	12: B
3: D	8: D	13: A
4: B	9: A	14: B
5: B	10: C	15: D

Chapter 3: The Living World

1: A	6: A	11: A
2: A	7: B	12: B
3: D	8: A	13: A
4: C	9: C	14: C
5: A	10: A	15: A

Chapter 4: Population

1: C	6: A	11: D
2: A	7: C	12: A
3: C	8: C	13: B
4: D	9: A	14: A
5: D	10: A	15: A

Chapter 5: Land & Water Use

1: A	6: C	11: C
2: A	7: C	12: B
3: C	8: C	13: B
4: B	9: D	14: A
5: B	10: B	15: A

Chapter 6: Pollution

1: A	6: C	11: D
2: A	7: C	12: D
3: C	8: B	13: A
4: D	9: A	14: D
5: C	10: C	15: D

Chapter 7: Energy Resources & Consumption

1: D	6: A	11: B
2: A	7: D	12: A
3: B	8: C	13: D
4: C	9: A	14: A
5: B	10: D	15: C

Chapter 8: Global Change

1: B	6: B	11: C
2: D	7: A	12: A
3: B	8: C	13: C
4: B	9: B	14: A
5: A	10: D	15: B

Annotated Glossary of Environmental Science Terms

1–in–100 flood – a flood with 1 in 100-year chance (used as a safety requirement for the construction industry).

100-year flood – a flood or storm with a 1% probability of occurring in any given year. The 100-year flood zone is the extent of the area of a flood with a 1% chance of occurring or being exceeded in a given year.

100,000-year problem – discrepancy between climate response and forcing from incoming solar radiation.

20/30/10 standard – 20 mg/l Biochemical Oxygen Demand (BOD), 30 mg/l Suspended Solids (SS), 10 units of E. coli: the *water quality standard for greywater* use in toilets, laundry, and surface irrigation.

5Rs (*sustainability*) – reduce, remanufacture, reuse, recycle, recover.

A

A1B emissions scenario – a medium emissions scenario in which greenhouse gas emissions increase, with reductions in the rate of increase in emissions after 2070.

A2 emissions scenario – a high emissions scenario assuming continued increases in greenhouse gas emissions.

Abated – reduced by a degree or intensity, eliminating pollution.

Abiotic – non-living chemical and physical factors of the environment. See *biotic*.

Abiotic component – non-living chemical and physical parts of the environment affecting living organisms and the functioning of ecosystems. *Abiotic factors and associated phenomena underpin biology.*

Abiotic factor – a nonliving environmental factor, such as water, soil, temperature, or sunlight.

Abrupt climate change – significant, sudden (on the order of decades) changes in major climate system components, with rapid, widespread effects.

Absorption – one substance taking in another, either physically or chemically.

Absorption pit (or *soak away*) – a hole dug in the permeable ground filled with broken stones or granular material and usually covered with earth, allowing the collected water to soak into the ground.

Abundance – the number or amount of something.

Acclimation – the process of an organism adjusting to a chronic change in its environment.

Acids – substances that release hydrogen ions (H^+ or protons) in water.

Acid mine drainage – the outflow of acidic water from metal or coal mines.

Acid precipitation – acidic rain, snow, or dry particles deposited from the air due to increased acids released by anthropogenic or natural resources. See *acid rain*.

Acid rain – (liquid, snow, fog, dust particles) contains acids that form in the atmosphere when sulfur dioxide and nitrogen oxide from industrial emissions and automobile exhaust combine with water.

Active solar system – a mechanical system that collects, concentrates, and stores solar energy.

Acute – a short, short-term event. Contrast *chronic*.

Acute poverty – insufficient income or access to resources needed to provide the necessities for life, such as food, shelter, sanitation, clean water, medical care, and education.

Adapted – to become accustomed to the natural factors that are in each area and to be able to survive these factors; an organism can be either positively or negatively adapted.

Adaptation – 1. a characteristic of an organism favored by natural selection. 2. any adjustment in natural or human systems in response to a changed climate. *Adjustment or preparation of natural or human systems to a changing environment that moderates harm or exploits beneficial opportunities. Natural or human systems adjust to a new environment that exploits beneficial opportunities or moderates adverse effects.*

Adaptation science – integrated scientific research that directly contributes to enabling adjustments in natural or human systems to a new or changing environment in a way that exploits beneficial opportunities or moderates adverse effects.

Adaptive behavior (*behavioral ecology*) – behavior that contributes to an individual's reproductive success and is thus subject to the forces of natural selection.

Adaptive capacity – the ability of a system to adjust to climate change (including climate variability and extremes) to moderate potential damages, exploit opportunities, or cope with consequences. *The potential of a system to adjust to climate change (including climate variability and extremes) to moderate potential damage, take advantage of opportunities, and cope with the consequences.*

Adaptive management – a plan designed from the outset to "learn by doing" and actively test hypotheses and adjust treatments as information becomes available. *A structured process of flexible decision-making that incorporates learning from outcomes and scientific information. The process facilitates resource managers' decision-making in managing and responding to climate change impacts.*

Adaptive radiation – closely related species that look very different due to having adapted to widely different ecological niches.

Additionality (context of a project funded by carbon offsets) – the reduction in greenhouse gas emissions and what would have resulted in the absence of carbon offset funding.

Administrative courts – enforcement cases for agencies or consider appeals to agency rules.

Appendix: Annotated Glossary of Environmental Science Terms

Administrative law – executive orders, administrative rules and regulations, and enforcement decisions by administrative agencies and special administrative courts.

Adsorption – one substance taking up another at its surface.

Aerobic – requiring air or oxygen. *Decomposition processes in the presence of oxygen.*

Aerosol – solid or liquid particles suspended within the atmosphere. A suspension of solid or liquid particles within the air. Aerosols can cause cooling by scattering incoming radiation, affecting cloud cover, and causing warming by absorbing radiation. Some human-made aerosols (dust particles) in the atmosphere reflect solar radiation, cooling global temperatures; others absorb solar radiation (depending on the chemical's properties) to create a warming effect. *Depending on their composition, small particles or liquid droplets in the atmosphere can absorb or reflect sunlight.*

Aesthetic degradation – changes in environmental quality that offend aesthetic senses.

Affluenza (*affluence and influenza*; defined in the named book) – 1. the bloated, sluggish, and unfulfilled feeling resulting from efforts to keep up with the *Joneses*. 2. an epidemic of stress, overwork, waste, and indebtedness caused by the dogged pursuit of the Australian dream. 3. an unsustainable addiction to economic growth. *The traditional Western environmentally unfriendly high consumption lifestyle.* Compare *Froogle* and *freegan*.

Afforestation – planting forests on lands not recently forested.

Agroforestry (*sustainability*) – an ecologically based farming system that, through the integration of trees in farms, increases social, environmental, and economic benefits for land users.

Air pollution – the modification of natural atmospheric characteristics by a chemical, particulate matter, or biological agent.

Alaska Pipeline – built from April 1974 to June 1977, this above-ground pipeline through Alaska brings oil from the oil wells in northern Alaska to shipping ports in southern Alaska.

Albedo (or *reflectance*) – an index of "reflectiveness" of a surface; quantifies how much radiation is reflected. The ratio of light from the Sun is reflected by Earth's surface to the light it receives. Un-reflected light is converted to *infrared radiation* (i.e., heat), which causes atmospheric warming. Surfaces with a *high albedo* (e.g., snow and ice) generally contribute to *cooling*. Surfaces with a *low albedo* (e.g., forests) contribute to *warming*. *Land–use changes significantly alter land surface characteristics and can alter the albedo. Surfaces with low albedo (closer to 0) absorb most radiation directed toward them, and those with high albedo (closer to 1) reflect most of it.* See *radiative forcing*. Contrast *absorbed*.

Algae – any of the various chiefly aquatic, eukaryotic, photosynthetic organisms, ranging in size from single-celled forms to the giant kelp; once considered plants but now classified separately because they lack true roots, stems, leaves, and embryos.

Algal bloom – rapid and excessive algae growth, generally caused by high nutrient levels and favorable conditions. *For example, warmer surface waters or increased nutrient levels. Algal blooms may be toxic or harmful to humans and ecosystems. Blooms can deoxygenate the water, leading to the loss of wildlife.*

Alien species (or *introduced species* and *exotic species*) – living outside its native distributional range but arrived there by human activity, directly or indirectly, and deliberately or accidentally.

Allee effect (*population ecology*) – positive relationship between population size and growth.

Alloy – a composite of materials made under conditions. Metal alloys like brass and bronze are well known, but many plastic alloys exist.

Alternative fuels – ethanol and compressed natural gas produce fewer emissions than fossil fuels.

Alternative energy – derived from nontraditional sources (e.g., compressed natural gas, solar, hydroelectric, wind).

Alternative renewable energy – sources are replenished by natural processes at rates exceeding their use rate for human purposes, unlike fossil fuels that are not replenished at a useful rate, including solar, biomass, wind, geothermal, and hydropower.

Ambient air – the air immediately surrounding a location.

Amino acid – biological building block that makes peptide and protein molecules; it is an organic compound containing amino and carboxyl groups.

Ammonia (NH_3) – a pungent, colorless, gaseous alkaline compound of nitrogen (N) and hydrogen (H) that is soluble in water and can be condensed to a liquid by cold and pressure.

Anaerobic – not requiring air or oxygen; used for decomposition processes occurring without oxygen. See *anaerobic digestion* and *anaerobic respiration*.

Anaerobic digestion – the biological degradation of organic materials in the absence of oxygen to yield methane (CH_4) gas (which may be combusted to produce energy) and stabilized organic residues (e.g., a soil additive).

Anaerobic respiration – the incomplete intracellular breakdown of sugar or other organic compounds without oxygen that releases energy and produces organic acids or alcohol.

Ancient forest (or *old–growth forest*) – an area with great age and exhibits unique biological features.

Anemia – low levels of hemoglobin due to an iron deficiency or lack of red blood cells.

Animal behavior – the study of animal behavior. See *ethology*.

Annex I Countries (or *Annex I Parties*) – countries included in Annex I (as amended in 1998) to the U.N. Framework Convention on Climate Change, including developed countries in the Organization of Economic Co-operation and Development and economies in transition. By default, the other countries are non-Annex I countries. Under Articles 4.2 (a) and 4.2 (b) of the Convention, Annex I countries commit specifically to returning to their 1990 levels of greenhouse gas emissions by the year 2000.

Annual – a plant that lives for a single growing season.

Anomalies – deviation from the standard order or general rule.

Anoxic – with abnormally low levels of oxygen. See *euxinic*.

Anoxic event – when oceans are without oxygen below the surface layer.

Antarctic bottom water (ABW) – a type of water mass in the Southern Ocean surrounding Antarctica with temperatures ranging from −0.8 to 2 °C (35 °F) and salinities from 34.6 to 34.7 psu (i.e., *practical salinity units*). *As the densest water mass of the oceans, ABW is at depths below 4000 m of ocean basins connected to the Southern Ocean at that level.*

Antarctic oscillation (AAO) – a low-frequency mode of atmospheric variability of the Southern Hemisphere.

Anthropocentric – 1. a belief that humans hold a special place in nature; 2. being centered primarily on humans and human affairs.

Anthropogenic – created, caused, or strongly influenced by humans or human activities; manufactured. *Originating from or due to human activity* (i.e., human-made, not natural).

Anthropogenic climate change – with the presumption of human influence, usually warming.

Anthropogenic global warming (AGW) – global warming with presuming human influence.

Anthroposophy (*Rudolf Steiner*, 1861-1925) – spiritual philosophy and teachings that postulate the existence of an objective, intellectually comprehensible spiritual world accessible to direct experience through inner development – more specifically through cultivating a form of thinking independent of sensory experience conscientiously.

Anti-greenhouse effect – the cooling influences an atmosphere has on Earth's ambient temperature.

Application efficiency (*sustainability*) – watering efficiency after runoff, leaching, evaporation, wind losses, etc.

Applied ecology – uses ecological principles and insights to solve environment-related problems. *Applied ecology includes agroecology and conservation biology.*

Aposematism (or *warning coloration*) – a warning signal consisting of brightly colored or starkly contrasting patterns used by a prey species to advertise its unprofitability to potential predator species.

Appropriate technology – made at an affordable price by ordinary people using local materials to do valuable work in ways that do the least possible harm to humans and the environment.

Appropriated carrying capacity (or *ecological footprint*) – the imported ecological capacity of overseas goods.

Aquaculture – the cultivation of aquatic organisms under controlled conditions.

Aquatic plant – a vascular plant adapted to living in saltwater or freshwater aquatic environments. They are *hydrophytes* or *macrophytes* that distinguish algae from other *microphytes*. A macrophyte is a plant that grows in or near water and is either emergent, submergent, or floating.

Aqueduct – a pipe or channel designed to transport water from a remote source, usually by gravity. A bridge-like structure supporting a conduit or canal passing over a river or low ground.

Aquifer – a bed or layer yielding water for wells and springs; an underground geological formation capable of receiving, storing, and transmitting large quantities of water. Aquifer types include *confined* (sealed and possibly containing "fossil" water), *unconfined* (capable of receiving inflow), and *artesian* (an aquifer in which the hydraulic pressure causes water to rise above the upper confining layer).

Arable land – land used for growing crops.

Arbitration – a formal dispute resolution process in which there are stringent rules of evidence, cross-examining witnesses, and a legally binding decision the arbitrator makes that all parties must obey.

Area effect (*biogeographic*) – hypothesis that larger islands can support more species than smaller ones.

Arctic amplification – a positive feedback loop triggered by melting sea ice replaces high-albedo ice with low-albedo sea capable of absorbing more solar radiation, trapping more heat near the Earth's surface, and contributing to more ice melting.

Arctic oscillation (AO) – the dominant pattern of non-seasonal sea-level pressure (SLP) variations north of 20° N. It is characterized by SLP anomalies of one sign in the Arctic, and anomalies of the opposite sign centered about 37 to 45° N. See *North Atlantic oscillation*.

Arctic shrinkage – the observed decrease in sea ice in the Arctic Ocean and Greenland Ice Sheet melting in recent years.

Arithmetical growth – a pattern of growth that increases at a constant amount per unit of time (e.g., 1, 2, 3, 4 or 1, 3, 5, 7).

Artesian well (or *spring*) – the result of a pressurized aquifer intersecting the surface or being penetrated by a pipe or conduit, from which water gushes without being pumped.

Asbestos – a fibrous incombustible mineral known to cause fibrosis and scarring in the lungs; a known carcinogenic material that causes lung cancer and mesothelioma.

Ash – the grayish-white to black powdery residue left when something is burned.

Assisted migration – the intentional movement of individuals into areas assumed to be future habitats.

Asthma – a distressing disease with shortness of breath, wheezing, and bronchial muscle spasms.

Aswan High Dam – across Egypt's Nile River, which impounds one of the largest reservoirs in the world; the artificial lake created by the dam Lake Nasser inundated many villages along the Nile and submerged some of the pyramids; hydroelectric installations were added in 1960 to the Aswan Dam.

Atlantic Multidecadal Oscillation (AMO) – a model of natural variability occurring in the North Atlantic Ocean with its principal expression in the sea surface temperature (SST) field.

Atmosphere – Earth's atmosphere is composed of gases and water retained by Earth's gravity which helps retain heat and reflect UV radiation from the Sun. The layer of gases around a material body. Earth's atmosphere consists, from the ground up, of the *troposphere* (including the planetary boundary layer or *peplosphere*, the lowest layer), *stratosphere, mesosphere, ionosphere* (or *thermosphere*), *exosphere,* and *magnetosphere*. The dry atmosphere consists of nitrogen (78.1% volume mixing ratio) and oxygen (20.9% volume mixing ratio), with trace gases, such as argon (0.93% volume mixing ratio), helium, radiatively active greenhouse gases such as carbon dioxide (0.035% volume mixing ratio), and ozone. In addition, the atmosphere contains water vapor, whose amount is highly variable but typically has a 1% volume mixing ratio. The atmosphere contains clouds and aerosols.

Atmospheric deposition – sedimentation of solids, liquids, or gaseous materials from the air.

Atmospheric lifetime – the average time a molecule resides in the atmosphere before it is removed by chemical reaction or deposition. In general, if a compound is emitted into the atmosphere at a particular time, about 35 percent of that quantity will remain at the end of the compound's lifetime. This fraction will continue to decrease exponentially so that about 15 percent of the quantity remains at the end of two times the atmospheric lifetime. *Some compounds, notably CO_2, have a simple exponential equation that does not define more complex lifecycles and atmospheric lifetimes. Greenhouse gas lifetimes range from a few to a few thousand years.*

Atmospheric sciences – an umbrella term for studying the atmosphere, its processes, the effects other systems have, and the effects of the atmosphere on these other systems.

Atmospheric window – the parts of the electromagnetic spectrum not absorbed by Earth's atmosphere in its natural state.

Atom – the smallest unit of matter that has the characteristics of an element; consists of three main types of subatomic particles: protons, neutrons, and electrons.

Atomic number – the identifying characteristic number of protons per atom of an element.

Attribution of recent climate change – the study of the causes of climate change.

Autecology (or *population ecology*) – a major sub-field of ecology that studies the dynamics of populations and how they interact with the environment.

Auto emissions standards – regulate how much pollution is permissible by vehicles.

Autotroph – an organism that produces complex organic compounds from simple inorganic molecules using energy from light (i.e., photosynthesis) or inorganic chemical reactions.

Available energy (or *exergy*) – energy that can do work.

Available water capacity – that proportion of soil water that plant roots readily absorb.

Avoidance (*sustainability*) – the first step in the waste hierarchy where waste generation is prevented (avoided).

B

BOD: Biological oxygen demand

B1 emissions scenario – a lower emissions scenario in which emissions are reduced rapidly and substantially.

B2 emissions scenario – a low emissions scenario in which emissions are reduced substantially but not as rapidly as the B1 scenario.

Baby Boom – a sudden large increase in the birthrate over a period, specifically the 15 years after World War II.

Backflow – the movement of water back to the source (e.g., contaminated plumbing water).

Bacteria – any of a group (as kingdom *Prokaryotae*) of prokaryotic unicellular round, spiral, or rod-shaped single-celled microorganisms that are often aggregated into colonies or motile using flagella; live in soil, water, organic matter, or the bodies of plants and animals and are autotrophic, saprophytic, or parasitic in nutrition; important because of their biochemical effects and pathogenicity.

Baffle (*landscape design*) – an obstruction to trap debris in drainage water.

Ballast – anything that serves no purpose except to give bulk or weight to something or provide additional stability.

Bagasse – the fibrous residue of sugar cane milling used as a fuel to produce steam in sugar mills.

Barometric pressure – atmospheric pressure as indicated by a barometer.

Barrier islands – low, narrow, sandy islands that form offshore from a coastline.

Baseload – the steady and reliable supply of energy through the grid. This is punctuated by bursts of higher demand "peak–load." Supply companies must be able to respond instantly to extreme variations in demand and supply, especially during extreme conditions. *Gas generators react quickly, while coal is slow but provides a steady "baseload." Renewable energies are generally not available on demand.*

Bases – substances that bond readily with hydrogen ions.

Basin – a large, bowl-shaped depression on the surface of the land or on the ocean floor.

BAT – an acronym for *Best available, economically achievable technology*.

Batesian mimicry – evolution by a species to resemble the coloration, body shape, or behavior of another protected from predators by a venomous stinger, being inedible, or other defensive adaptation.

Batters (*landscape design*) – the slope of earthworks such as drainage channels.

Behavioral ecology – studies the ecological and evolutionary basis of animal behavior, mainly at the level of individual animals.

Benthos – the bottom of a sea or lake.

Best available, economically achievable technology (BAT) – the least pollution-causing technological solution; also known as *best available techniques*, *best practicable means*, or *best practicable environmental option*.

Best practical control technology (BPT) – the best technology for pollution control available at a reasonable cost and operable under normal conditions.

Best practice – a process or innovative use of technology, equipment, resources, or other measurable factors with a proven record of success.

Beta particles – high-energy electrons released by radioactive decay.

Bhopal, India (December 3, 1984) – a noxious methylisocyanate gas blanketed the city when water mixed with a tank containing 40 tons of MIC, setting off a chemical reaction; 1,754 died, with over 200,000 injured.

Bill – legislation introduced in Congress and intended to become law.

Bioaccumulation – accumulation of a substance (e.g., toxic chemical) in living tissue.

Biocapacity – a measure of the biological productivity of an area. *This may depend on natural conditions or human inputs like farming and forestry practices, the area needed to support the consumption of a defined population.*

Biocoenosis (or *biocoenose*) – interacting organisms living in a habitat (or biotope).

Biocentric preservation – a philosophy that emphasizes living organisms' fundamental right to exist and pursue their goods.

Biocentrism – the belief that creatures have rights and values centered on nature rather than humans.

Biocide – a broad-spectrum poison that kills a wide range of organisms.

Biodegradable – capable of decomposing through organisms' actions, especially bacteria.

Biodegradable plastics – plastics that microorganisms decompose.

Biodiversity – the variety of life in all forms, levels, and combinations, including ecosystem, species, and genetic diversity. *Variety among and within plant and animal species in each environment.*

Bioelement – an element required by a living organism. *Atoms that make up living organisms consist of six chemical elements: carbon (C), oxygen (O), hydrogen (H), nitrogen (N), phosphorus (P), and sulfur (S). These elements constitute more than 99% of the matter found in living things.*

Bioenergy – 1. narrowly, a synonym for biofuel, fuel derived from biological sources. 2. broadly, it encompasses biomass, the biological material used as a biofuel, and the social, economic, scientific, and technical fields associated with using biological sources for energy. *For example, energy is produced using plant or animal matter such as corn or manure.*

Biofuel – the fuel (or energy source) produced by biomass's chemical or biological processing (i.e., organic mass). Biofuel is solid (e.g., charcoal), liquid (e.g., ethanol), or gas (e.g., methane). *Gas or liquid fuel made from plant material. Includes wood, wood waste, wood liquors, peat, railroad ties, wood sludge, spent sulfite liquors, agricultural waste, straw, tires, fish oils, tall oil, sludge waste, waste alcohol, municipal solid waste, landfill gases, other, and ethanol blended into motor gasoline.*

Biogas (or *biomass gas*) – landfill and sewage gas.

Biogeochemistry – studies the effects of biota on global chemistry and the cycles of matter and energy that transport Earth's chemical components in time and space.

Biogeochemical cycle – 1. a pathway by which a chemical element or molecule moves through biotic (*bio-*) and abiotic (*geo-*) parts of an ecosystem, the atmosphere, hydrosphere, lithosphere, and biosphere. 2. movement of matter within or between ecosystems caused by living organisms, geological forces, or chemical reactions (e.g., the cycling of nitrogen, carbon, sulfur, oxygen, phosphorus, and water). *Movements through Earth's system of key chemical constituents essential to life, including carbon, nitrogen, oxygen, and phosphorus.*

Biogeographic realm (or *ecozone*) – an area with characteristics of natural origin such as climate, terrain, and vegetation; the largest division of Earth's surface, filled with living organisms.

Biogeographical area – a self-contained natural ecosystem and its associated land, water, air, and wildlife resources.

Biogeography – the study of the geographic distribution of species on Earth.

Bio-invader – a non-native species.

Biological community – the populations of plants, animals, and microorganisms living and interacting in a particular area at a given time.

Biological controls – use of natural predators, pathogens, or competitors to regulate pest populations.

Biological dispersal – the movement of organisms from birth to breeding sites or between breeding sites.

Biological factors (or *biotic factors*) – organisms and products of organisms that are part of the environment and potentially affect the lives of other organisms.

Biological magnification – the increase in the concentration of a chemical substance in the tissues of organisms comprising successively higher levels in a food chain.

Biological oxygen demand (BOD) – a chemical procedure for determining how fast biological organisms use oxygen in a body of water.

Biological pest control – a method of controlling pests (including insects, mites, weeds, and plant diseases) that relies on predation, parasitism, herbivory, or other natural mechanisms.

Biological pests – organisms reducing the availability, quality, or value of resources helpful to humans.

Biological productivity (or *bioproductivity*) – the capacity of an area to produce biomass; ecosystems (i.e., pasture, forest) have different levels of bioproductivity. Biological productivity is determined by dividing the biological production (how much is grown and living) by the area available.

Biological resources – the plants and animals necessary for the services provided.

Biologically productive land – fertile soil to support forests, agriculture, or animals. Biologically productive lands comprise their biological capacity. *Arable land is typically the most productive area.*

Biomagnification – an increase in the concentration of certain stable chemicals (e.g., heavy metals or fat-soluble pesticides) in a successively higher food chain or web trophic level.

Biomass – 1. materials derived from photosynthesis (fossilized materials may be included) such as forest, crops, wood and wood wastes, animal wastes, livestock operation residues, aquatic plants, and municipal and industrial wastes; 2. the quantity of organic material present in a unit area at a particular time, mostly expressed as tons of dry matter per unit area; 3. organic matter used as fuel. *Biological materials, including organic material (both living and dead) from above and below ground, for example, trees, crops, grasses, tree litter, roots, and animal and animal waste.*

Biomass fuel – organic material produced by plants, animals, or microorganisms burned directly as a heat source or converted into a gaseous or liquid fuel.

Biomass gas (or *biogas*) – landfill gas and sewage gas.

Biomass pyramid (or *ecological pyramid*) – a graph that illustrates the productivity within a trophic level. *Diagram illustrating the relationship between biomass amounts at different trophic levels.*

Biome (or *ecosystems*) – biotic communities occupying and characterizing a particular area. Climatic and geographically defined ecologically similar communities of plants, animals, and soil organisms.

Biophysical – the living and non-living components and ecosphere processes. *Biophysical measurements quantify the ecosphere in physical units such as cubic meters, kilograms, or joules.*

Bioregion (*ecoregion*) – an area with a natural ecological community bounded by natural borders.

Bioremediation – using organisms to remove or neutralize contaminants (e.g., petroleum), mainly in soil or water.

Biosolids – nutrient-rich organic materials derived from *wastewater solids* (or *sewage sludge*) stabilized through processing.

Biosphere – 1. the zone of air, land, and water at the surface of Earth occupied by living organisms; 2. the combination of ecosystems on Earth maintained by the energy of the Sun; 3. the interface between the hydrosphere, the geosphere, and the atmosphere. *The global sum of ecosystems on Earth. Earth's system comprises ecosystems and living organisms in the atmosphere, on land (terrestrial biosphere), or in the oceans (marine biosphere), including derived dead organic matter, such as litter, soil organic matter, and oceanic detritus.*

Biosphere reserves – world heritage sites the *International Union for the Conservation of Nature* (IUCN) identified them as worthy of national park or wildlife refuge status because of their high biological diversity and unique ecological features.

Biota – the total of organisms belonging to a particular geographic region or extent during a particular time. *Organisms in a given area.*

Biotic – relating to, produced by, or caused by living organisms. Compare *abiotic*.

Biotic factors (or *biological factors*) – organisms and products of organisms that are part of the environment and potentially affect the lives of other organisms.

Biotic potential – the maximum reproductive capacity of a population under optimum environmental conditions. Compare *environmental resistance*.

Birth control – 1. any method used to reduce births, including celibacy, delayed marriage, and contraception; 2. devices or medication intended to prevent the implantation of fertilized zygotes.

Birth rate – the number of people born as a percentage of the total population in any given period, expressed in the number of live births per 1,000 people.

Black carbon – soot produced from coal burning, diesel engines, cooking fires, wildfires, and other combustion sources. These particles absorb solar energy and have a warming influence on the climate.

Black carbon (BC) aerosol – the most strongly light-absorbing *particulate matter* (PM) component and is formed by the incomplete combustion of fossil fuels, biofuels, and biomass. It is emitted directly into the atmosphere as fine particles ($PM_{2.5}$).

Black lung disease – inflammation and fibrosis caused by coal dust accumulation in lungs or airways.

Blackwater – household wastewater that contains solid waste (i.e., toilet discharge) that cannot be reused without purification.

Blue-green algae (*Cyanobacteria* or *Cyanophyta*) – a phylum of bacteria obtaining energy through photosynthesis.

Blue revolution – fishing farming techniques that may contribute as much to human nutrition as miracle cereal grains but may create social and environmental problems.

Bluewater – collectible water from rainfall; the water that falls on roofs and hard surfaces usually flows into rivers and the sea and recharges the groundwater. The average global proportion of rainfall in blue water is about 40%. Bluewater productivity in gardens is increased by improving irrigation techniques, soil water storage, moderating the climate, using garden design and water-conserving plantings, and safe use of *grey water*.

Bog – an area of waterlogged soil that tends to be peaty, fed mainly by precipitation; low productivity; some bogs are acidic.

Boreal – 1. of the north or northern areas; 2. refers to the cold temperate Northern Hemisphere forests of birch, poplar, or conifers that grow where there is a mean annual temperature < 0 °C.

Boreal forest (or *taiga* in Siberia) – forest areas of the northern temperate zone, mainly consisting of conifers. *A broadband of mixed coniferous and deciduous trees that stretches across northern North America (and Europe and Asia), its northernmost edge, the taiga, intergrades with the arctic tundra.*

Borehole – any exploratory hole drilled into the Earth or ice to gather geophysical data. *Climate researchers often take ice core samples, a type of borehole, to predict atmospheric composition in earlier years.* See *ice core*.

BPT (best practicable control technology) – the best technology available for pollution control at a reasonable cost and operable under normal conditions.

Brackish water – fresh and saltwater combined.

Breeder reactor – 1. a nuclear reactor that produces more fuel than it consumes; this type of reactor is used mainly to produce plutonium; 2. a nuclear reactor that produces fuel by bombarding isotopes of uranium and thorium with high-energy neutrons that convert inert atoms to fissionable ones.

Breeding – a group of organisms with common ancestors and certain distinguishable characteristics, especially a group within a species developed by artificial selection and maintained by controlled propagation.

Broad-acre farm – commercial farm covering a large area; usually, it is a mixed farm in dryland conditions.

Brownfields – describes land previously used for industrial or commercial purposes with known or suspected pollution, including soil contamination due to hazardous waste. *Abandoned or underused urban areas with redevelopments blocked by liability or financing issues related to toxic contamination.*

Brundtland Commission Report (UN, 1987) *Our Common Future* addresses sustainable development and policies to achieve it, which the report characterizes as "*development that meets the needs of the present without compromising the ability of future generations to meet their own needs.*"

C

C_2F_6 (hexafluoroethane) – the perfluorocarbon counterpart to the hydrocarbon ethane, a non-flammable gas that is negligibly soluble in water and slightly soluble in alcohol. It is a highly potent and long-lived greenhouse gas. *Due to the high energy of C-F bonds, hexafluoroethane is inert and thus is a highly stable greenhouse gas, with an atmospheric lifetime of 10,000 years. It has a global warming potential (GWP) of 9200 and an ozone depletion potential (ODP) of 0. Hexafluoroethane is included in the IPCC list of greenhouse gases.*

C3 plants – comprise 95% of plants, photosynthesize to form 3 carbon molecules, and increase photosynthesis as CO_2 levels increase. Compare *C4 plants*.

C4 plants – comprise about 5% of plants, are abundant in hot and arid conditions, and include crops like sugar cane and soybeans. During photosynthesis, C4 plants form molecules with 4-carbon atoms and saturate at the given level of CO_2. Compare *C3 plants*.

Calendar effect (1938) – the theory linking rising atmospheric carbon dioxide (CO_2) concentrations to global temperatures. In 1938, Guy Calendar was among the first to show that the land temperature of Earth had risen over the previous 50 years. Svante Arrhenius earlier proposed this theory. *Calendar thought this warming was beneficial, delaying the return of deadly glaciers.*

Calorie – a basic measure of energy that the SI unit, the *joule*, has replaced; in physics, it approximates the energy needed to increase the temperature of 1 gram of water by 1 °C, which is about 4.184 joules. *Calories in food ratings (with capital C) and nutrition are 'capital C Calories or kcal.*

Calorific value – the energy content of a fuel measured as heat released on complete combustion.

Camouflage – an inconspicuous appearance adopted by an organism to deceive possible predators or prey.

Cancer – a group of diseases in which cells are aggressive (grow and divide without respect to normal limits), invasive (invade and destroy adjacent tissues) and sometimes metastatic (spread to other locations in the body).

Cap and trade – a system that limits aggregate emissions from a group of emitters by setting a "cap" on maximum emissions. It is a market-based policy to reduce emissions of pollutants and encourage business investment in fossil fuel alternatives and energy efficiency. See *emissions trading*.

Caprock – the last layer of material on top of a geological formation such as the Canadian Shield.

Capillary action (or *wicking*) – water drawn through a medium by surface tension.

Capillary water – droplets clinging in small pores, cracks, and spaces against the pull of gravity (e.g., the water retained in a sponge).

Capital – any wealth, resources, or knowledge available to produce more wealth.

Captive breeding – raising plants or animals in zoos or other controlled conditions to produce stock for subsequent release into the wild.

Carbohydrate – an organic compound consisting of a ring or chain of carbon atoms with hydrogen and oxygen attached (e.g., sugars, starches, cellulose, and glycogen).

Carbon budget – measures carbon inputs and outputs for a particular activity.

Carbon capture and sequestration (CCS) – technologies that significantly reduce carbon dioxide (CO_2) emissions from new and existing coal - and gas-fired power plants, industrial processes, and other stationary sources of carbon dioxide. *It is a three-step process that includes the capture of carbon dioxide from power plants or industrial sources; transport of the captured and compressed carbon dioxide (usually in pipelines); and underground injection and geologic sequestration, or permanent storage, of that carbon dioxide in rock formations that contain tiny openings or pores that trap and hold the carbon dioxide.*

Carbon capture and storage – the process of capturing carbon dioxide (CO_2) and injecting it into geologic formations underground for long-term storage.

Carbon credit – a market-driven way of reducing the impact of greenhouse gas emissions; it allows an agent to benefit financially from an emission reduction. Two forms of carbon credit are part of national and international trade and those that individuals purchase.

Kyoto Protocol sets caps (or limits) on participating countries' emissions are established. Countries set 'caps' (credits: 1 convertible and transferable credit = 1 metric ton of CO_2 emissions) for operators. Operators who meet the agreed caps can sell unused credits to operators who exceed 'caps.' Operators can choose cost-effective ways of reducing emissions. Individual carbon credits operate similarly.

Carbon cycle (*biogeochemical cycle*) – the biogeochemical cycle exchanging carbon between Earth's biosphere, geosphere, hydrosphere, and atmosphere with carbon exchanged between biosphere, geosphere, hydrosphere in Earth's atmosphere. Circulation of carbon atoms through Earth's systems because of the photosynthetic conversion of carbon dioxide into complex organic compounds by plants, consumed by other organisms, and return of the carbon to the atmosphere as carbon dioxide (CO_2) because of respiration, decay of organisms, and combustion of fossil fuels. *Includes photosynthesis, decomposition, and respiration (e.g., carbon dioxide is taken from the atmosphere by photosynthesizing plants and returned by the respiration of plants and animals and by the combustion of fossil fuels).*

Carbon diet – reducing the output of CO_2 to reduce environmental impact.

Carbon dioxide (CO_2) – the most abundant *greenhouse gas* emitted from fossil fuels. A naturally occurring gas and by-product of burning fossil fuels and biomass, land-use changes, and other industrial processes. *Carbon dioxide is the principal human-caused greenhouse gas affecting Earth's radiative balance. It is the reference gas against which other greenhouse gases are measured and has a Global Warming Potential of 1.* See *climate change* and *global warming*.

Carbon dioxide equivalent (CO_2e) – the unit used to measure the impacts of releasing (or avoiding the release of) the seven greenhouse gases; it is obtained by multiplying the mass of the greenhouse gas by its global warming potential. *For example, this would be 21 for methane and 310 for nitrous oxide.* A metric measure comparing the emissions from various greenhouse gases based on their *global warming potential* (GWP). Carbon dioxide equivalents are "million metric tons of *carbon dioxide equivalents* ($MMTCO_2Eq$)." The carbon dioxide equivalent for a gas is derived by multiplying the tons of the gas by the associated GWP. $MMTCO_2Eq$ = (million metric tons of a gas) * (GWP of the gas). See *greenhouse gas*, *global warming potential*, and *metric tons*.

Carbon dioxide fertilization – enhances the growth of plants because of increased atmospheric CO_2 concentration. *Depending on their photosynthesis mechanism, certain plants are more sensitive to changes in atmospheric CO_2 concentration.*

Carbon dioxide removal (CDR; or *carbon removal, greenhouse gas removal* (GGR) or *negative emissions*) – a process in which carbon dioxide gas (CO_2) is removed from the atmosphere by deliberate human activities and durably stored in geological, terrestrial, or ocean reservoirs, or products. *CDR is increasingly integrated into climate policy as a climate change mitigation strategy. CDR methods include afforestation, reforestation, agricultural practices that sequester carbon in soils (carbon farming), wetland restoration and blue carbon approaches, bioenergy with carbon capture and storage (BECCS), ocean fertilization, ocean alkalinity enhancement, and direct air capture with storage.*

Carbon equivalent (C-e) – obtained by multiplying the CO_2-e by the factor 12/44.

Carbon footprint – the greenhouse gas emissions caused by an organization, event, or product. *A measure of the carbon emissions emitted over a product or service lifecycle, usually expressed as grams of CO_2-e. A person's carbon footprint includes greenhouse gas emissions from fuel that an individual burns directly, such as by heating a home or riding in a car. It includes greenhouse gases from producing the goods or services the individual uses, including emissions from power plants that make electricity, factories that make products, and landfills where trash gets sent.*

Carbon labeling – product labels displaying greenhouse emissions associated with goods.

Carbon management – storing CO_2 or using it to prevent its release into the air.

Carbon monoxide (CO) – colorless, odorless, nonirritating, but highly toxic gas produced by incomplete combustion of fuel, incineration of biomass or solid waste, or partially anaerobic decomposition of organic material.

Carbon neutral – activities where net carbon inputs and outputs are the same. *For example, assuming a constant amount of vegetation, burning wood adds atmospheric carbon in the short term, but this carbon will cycle back into plant growth.*

Carbon offset – a mechanism for individuals and businesses to neutralize rather than reduce their greenhouse gas emissions by purchasing the right to claim someone else's reductions as their own.

Carbon pool – a storage reservoir of carbon.

Carbon sequestration – carbon storage in biomass or deep geological formations through natural or technological processes. Proposals for removing CO_2 from the atmosphere or preventing CO_2 from fossil fuel combustion from reaching the atmosphere. *Terrestrial or biological carbon sequestration is how trees and plants absorb carbon dioxide, release oxygen, and store carbon. Geologic sequestration is one step in carbon capture and sequestration (CCS) and involves injecting carbon dioxide deep underground, where it stays permanently.*

Carbon sinks – a natural or artificial reservoir accumulating and storing carbon-containing chemical compounds. Any carbon storage system that causes a net removal of greenhouse gases from the atmosphere. Places of carbon accumulation, such as large forests (*organic compounds*) or ocean sediments (*calcium carbonate*), remove carbon from the carbon cycle for moderately long to very long periods. Contrast *carbon sources*.

Carbon source – a net carbon source for the atmosphere. *Cellular respiration and combustion are the originating points of carbon that reenters the carbon cycle.* Contrast *carbon sink*.

Carbon stocks – the quantity of carbon held within a carbon pool at a specified time.

Carbon tax – a governmental charge on energy sources emitting carbon dioxide (CO_2).

Carbon taxes – a surcharge on fossil fuels to reduce carbon dioxide emissions.

Carbon tetrafluoride (or *tetrafluoromethane*) – the perfluorinated counterpart to the hydrocarbon methane. It can be classified as a haloalkane or halomethane. *Tetrafluoromethane is a useful refrigerant but a potent greenhouse gas. It has high bond strength due to the nature of the carbon-fluorine bond.*

Carbon trading (or *emissions trading*) – a system by which states and institutions receive permits to produce a specified amount of carbon dioxide (CO_2) and other greenhouse gases, which they may trade with others.

Carcinogen – a substance, radionuclide, or radiation that is an agent directly involved in promoting cancer or facilitating its propagation.

Carnivores – an organism that eats only or primarily the meat of other organisms.

Carpooling – when people ride in cars together to help reduce emissions and traffic.

Carrying capacity – the maximum number of individuals a given environment's resources can support, including the food and water available for that environment. *The maximum population that an ecosystem can sustain.*

Case law – precedents from both civil and criminal court cases.

Cash crops – crops that are sold rather than consumed or bartered.

Casks – barrels that are used to store spent fuels.

Catalytic converter – a reaction chamber typically containing a finely-divided platinum-iridium catalyst into which exhaust gases from an automotive engine are passed with excess air to oxidize carbon monoxide and hydrocarbon pollutants to carbon dioxide and water.

Catastrophic systems – 1. dynamic systems that jump abruptly from one seemingly steady state to another without any immediate changes; 2. the detrimental effect that something, perhaps a natural disaster, has on the environment, destroying the ecosystem and surrounding living conditions.

Catchment area – the source of water for a water supply, whether a dam or rainwater tank.

CDM (Clean Development Mechanism) – an arrangement under the *Kyoto Protocol* allowing industrialized countries with a greenhouse gas reduction commitment (called *Annex 1 countries*) to invest in projects that reduce emissions in developing countries as an alternative to more expensive emission reductions in their own countries.

Cell (*biology*) – the structural and functional unit of known living organisms and is the smallest unit of an organism classified as living.

Cellular respiration – the process by which a cell breaks down sugar or other organic compounds to release energy used for cellular work; it may be anaerobic or aerobic, depending on oxygen availability.

CERCLA (Comprehensive Environmental Response, Compensation, and Liability Act of 1980; Superfund) – an established fund to clean up abandoned hazardous waste sites; establishes strict liability, where individuals or corporations associated with the site can be held liable for the cleanup cost, regardless of contribution to the pollution; sets guidelines on how to clean up sites.

CFC (chlorofluorocarbons) – a series of hydrocarbons containing chlorine and fluorine; have been used as refrigerants, blowing agents, cleaning fluids, solvents, and fire extinguishing agents. These gases cause stratospheric ozone depletion and have been banned for many uses. Potent greenhouse gases, which the Kyoto Protocol does not regulate since the *Montreal Protocol* covers them.

CH_4 (or *methane*) – a gas emitted while producing and transporting coal, natural gas, and oil. Methane emissions result from livestock, agricultural practices, and decay of organic waste in municipal solid waste landfills.

Chain reaction – a self-sustaining reaction in which the fission of nuclei produces subatomic particles that cause the fission of other nuclei.

Channelization – to straighten using a channel.

Chaotic systems – systems that exhibit variability, which may not necessarily be "random," but whose complex patterns are not discernible over a typical human timescale.

Charismatic megafauna – a large animal species with widespread popular appeal that environmental activists use to achieve conservation goals beyond just those species. Examples include the giant panda, the Bengal tiger, and the blue whale. Compare *flagship species*.

Chemical bond – the force that holds atoms together in molecules and compounds.

Chemical ecology – studies the use of naturally occurring chemical compounds by organisms for various purposes (e.g., in defense against predators).

Chemical energy – potential energy in chemical bonds of molecules that chemical reactions release.

Chemoorganotroph (or *heterotroph*) – 1 an organism requiring organic substrates to obtain carbon for growth and development. 2. an organism incapable of synthesizing its food must feed upon other organisms' organic compounds.

Chornobyl – a city in Ukraine where a nuclear power plant suffered a meltdown in 1986 due to poor decisions made by power plant workers; the resulting explosions killed workers and leaked radioactive particles into the atmosphere.

Clathrate gun hypothesis – the proposal that melting methane clathrates could trigger runaway or severe global warming.

Clean Development Mechanism (CDM) – an arrangement under the *Kyoto Protocol* allowing industrialized countries with a greenhouse gas reduction commitment (called *Annex 1 countries*) to invest in projects that reduce emissions in developing countries as an alternative to more expensive emission reductions in their own countries.

Chlorinated hydrocarbon (or *organochloride, organochlorine compound,* and *chlorocarbon*) – an organic compound in which chlorine atoms have replaced most hydrogen atoms.

Chlorine (Cl) – a halogen element isolated as a heavy greenish-yellow gas of pungent odor; used primarily as a bleach, oxidizing agent, and disinfectant in water purification.

Chlorofluorocarbons (CFC) – widely known families of *haloalkanes*; gases used for refrigeration, air conditioning, packaging, insulation, solvents, or aerosol propellants. Since they are not destroyed in the lower atmosphere, CFCs drift into the upper atmosphere, where, given suitable conditions, they break down ozone layers. These gases are being replaced by other compounds: hydrochlorofluorocarbons, an interim replacement for CFCs covered under the *Montreal Protocol*, and hydrofluorocarbons, which are covered under the *Kyoto Protocol*. These substances are greenhouse gases.

Chlorophyll – any group of green pigments essential in photosynthesis.

Chloroplasts – chlorophyll-containing organelles in eukaryotic organisms; sites of photosynthesis.

Chronic – a continuous, low-level, long-term event. Contrast *acute*.

Chronic effects – long-lasting results of exposure to a toxin; can be a permanent change caused by a single, acute exposure or, over time, by continuous, low-level exposure.

Chronic food shortages – long-term undernutrition and malnutrition, usually caused by people's lack of money to buy food or lack of opportunity to grow it themselves.

Circular metabolism – a system in which wastes, especially water and materials, are reused and recycled. Compare *linear metabolism*.

CITES Treaty (Convention on International Trade in Endangered Species) – agreement among 167 governments aiming to ensure that cross-border trade in wild animals and plants does not threaten their survival; in 1989, participating countries agreed to ban the ivory trade.

Citizen science – trained volunteers work with scientific researchers to answer real-world questions.

City – a differentiated community with enough population and resource base to allow residents to specialize in arts, crafts, services, and professional occupations.

Civil law – a body of laws regulating relations between individuals or individuals and corporations concerning property rights, personal dignity and freedom, and personal injury.

Class A pan (*water management*) – an open pan used as a standard for measuring water evaporation.

Classical economics – modern Western economic theories of the effects of resource scarcity, monetary policy, and competition on the supply of and demand for goods and services in the marketplace; the basis for the capitalist market system.

Clay – a fine-grained, firm, earthy material that is plastic when wet and hardens when heated, consisting primarily of hydrated silicates of aluminum; widely used in making bricks, tiles, and pottery, as well as liners in landfills because it is *Impervious*.

Clean Air Act – long-standing federal legislation that is the legal basis for the national clean air programs; last amended in 1990.

Cleaner production – the continual effort to prevent pollution, reduce the use of energy, water, and material resources, and minimize waste – without reducing production capacity.

Clearcutting (or *clear-cut*) – a forestry or logging practice in which trees in a forest sector are *felled*. Cutting every tree in an area, regardless of species or size, is an appropriate harvest method for some species, but it can be destructive if not carefully controlled.

Climate – the average weather variations in a region over an extended period. Variations of weather in a region over a lengthy period (i.e., the "average weather"). 1. in a narrow sense, the average weather. 2. more rigorously, the statistical description of the mean and variability of relevant quantities ranges from months to thousands of years. The classical period is 3 decades, as defined by the World Meteorological Organization (WMO). These quantities are often surface variables such as *temperature*, *precipitation*, and *wind*. In a broader sense, climate is the state of the climate system, including a statistical description. See *weather*.

Climate change – refers to any notable change in the measures of climate lasting for an extended period. In other words, climate change includes significant changes in temperature, precipitation, or wind patterns, among others, which occur over decades or longer. A change in weather over time or region, usually relating to changes in temperature, wind patterns, and rainfall. Change in the details of a particular climate, such as cloud cover, wind, speed, temperature, rainfall, or humidity in a specific region. Includes global warming and its effects, such as changes in precipitation, rising sea levels, and impacts that differ by region. However, it may be natural or anthropogenic; everyday discourse asserts that climate change is anthropogenic (i.e., human-made).

Climate change feedback – a natural phenomenon of increasing or decreasing warming resulting from a change in radiative forcing.

Climate change refugia – areas buffered from contemporary climate change will likely increase species or ecosystem persistence.

Climate commitment – how much future warming is *"pre-determined,"* even if greenhouse gas levels do not rise, due to thermal inertia, mainly of the oceans.

Climate cycle – any recurring cyclical oscillation within global or regional climates. *They are quasiperiodic (not perfectly periodic), so a Fourier analysis of the data does not have sharp peaks in the spectrum. Many oscillations on different time scales have been found or hypothesized.* See c*limate oscillation.*

Climate ethics – an area of research focusing on the ethical dimensions of climate change.

Climate feedback – a process that amplifies or reduces direct warming or cooling effects.

Climate forcing – an energy imbalance imposed on the climate system externally or by human activities.

Climate justice – viewing climate change as an ethical issue and considering how its causes and effects relate to social and political concepts of justice.

Climate lag – delay occurs in climate change because some factors change slowly. For example, the effects of releasing more carbon dioxide (CO_2) into the atmosphere gradually because the ocean takes a long time to warm in response to a change in radiation. See *climate* and *climate change*.

Climate legislation – laws regulating greenhouse gas emissions.

Climate model – a quantitative way of representing the interactions of the atmosphere, oceans, land surface, and ice. *Models range from simple to quite comprehensive.* See *general circulation model*.

Climate oscillation – any recurring cyclical oscillation within global or regional climates. *They are quasiperiodic (not perfectly periodic), so a Fourier data analysis does not have sharp spectrum peaks. Oscillations on different time scales have been found or hypothesized.* See *climate cycle*.

Climate resilience – the capacity for a socio-ecological system to 1. absorb stresses and maintain function despite external stresses imposed by climate change and 2. adapt, reorganize, and evolve into desirable configurations to improve system sustainability, leaving it better prepared for climate impacts while benefiting from it now.

Climate sensitivity – responsiveness of climate temperature to changes in radiative forcing. Temperature change in °C from doubling atmospheric CO_2 levels (i.e., the most crucial factor of radiative forcing). Intergovernmental Panel on Climate Change (IPCC) reports that equilibrium climate sensitivity refers to the equilibrium change in global mean surface temperature following a doubling of the atmospheric (equivalent) CO_2 concentration. More generally, equilibrium climate sensitivity refers to the equilibrium change in surface air temperature following a unit change in radiative forcing (degrees Celsius, per watts per square meter, (C/Wm-2). One equilibrium climate sensitivity evaluation requires long simulations with Coupled General Circulation Models (Climate model). Effective climate sensitivity is a related measure that circumvents this requirement. It is evaluated from model output for evolving non-equilibrium conditions. It measures the strengths of feedback at a particular time and may vary with forcing history and climate state. See *climate* and *radiative forcing*.

Climate science (or *climatology*) – study of climate, defined as weather conditions averaged over time.

Climate system (or *Earth system*) – the five physical components (atmosphere, hydrosphere, cryosphere, lithosphere, and biosphere) are responsible for the climate and its variations.

Climate variability (or *natural variability*) – climate change with no presumption of cause. Natural climate changes within the observed range of extremes for a particular region, as measured by temperature, precipitation, and frequency of events. *Drivers of climate variability include the El Niño Southern Oscillation and other phenomena.*

Climatology (or *climate science*) – the study of climate, defined as weather conditions averaged over a long period.

Climax community – a relatively stable, long-lasting community arrived at through succession, usually determined by climate and soil type. *Species best adapted to average conditions in each area.*

Closed canopy – a forest where tree crowns spread over 20 percent of the ground; has the potential for commercial timber harvests.

Cloud forests – high mountain forests where temperatures are uniformly cool, and fog or mist keeps vegetation always wet.

CO_2 (carbon dioxide) – the most abundant *greenhouse gas* emitted from fossil fuels. A naturally occurring gas and by-product of burning fossil fuels and biomass, land-use changes, and other industrial processes. *Carbon dioxide is the principal human-caused greenhouse gas affecting Earth's radiative balance. It is the reference gas against which other greenhouse gases are measured and has a Global Warming Potential of 1.* See *climate change* and *global warming*.

Coal gasification – the heating and partial combustion of coal releasing volatile gases (e.g., methane, carbon monoxide); after pollutants are washed out, these gases become efficient, clean-burning fuel.

Coal liquefaction – a chemical process by which solid coal is converted to liquid; it is referred to as a "synfuel" or "synthetic fuel."

Coalbed methane – contained in coal seams and is called virgin coalbed methane or coal seam gas.

Coal mine methane – the subset of coalbed methane released from the coal seams during coal mining.

Coal washing – coal technology that involves crushing coal and washing out soluble sulfur compounds with water or other solvents.

Coastal Zone Management Act (1972) – legislation appropriating federal money to 30 seacoasts and Great Lakes states for development and restoration projects.

Co-benefit – policies implemented simultaneously, including climate change mitigation, acknowledge that most policies designed to address greenhouse gas mitigation have other, often at least equally important, rationales (e.g., related to development objectives, sustainability, and equity).

Co-composting – microbial decomposition of organic materials in solid waste into useful soil additives and fertilizer; often, extra organic material in the form of sewer sludge, animal manure, leaves, and grass clippings are added to solid waste to speed the process and make the product more useful.

Coevolution – the process in which species exert selective pressure on each other and gradually evolve features or behaviors due to those pressures.

Cogeneration – simultaneous electricity production and useful heat from combustion of the same fuel source. *A power generation process that increases efficiency by harnessing the heat that would otherwise be wasted in fuel combustion and using it to generate electricity, warm buildings, or other purposes.*

Cohousing – clusters of houses with shared dining halls and other spaces, encouraging stronger social ties while reducing the material and energy needs of the community.

Coir – the fiber of a coconut.

Cold front – a moving boundary of cooler air displacing warmer air.

Cold wave – a period of abnormally cold weather lasting days to weeks.

Coliform bacteria – bacteria that live in the intestines (including the colon) of humans and other animals; used to measure the presence of feces in water or soil.

Combustion – a chemical change, especially oxidation, accompanied by heat and light production.

Command and control – require polluters to meet specific emission-reduction targets and often requires the installation and use of specific types of equipment to reduce emissions.

Commensalism – a symbiotic relationship in which one member benefits and the other is neither harmed nor benefited.

Commercial and industrial waste (*waste management*) – solid waste generated by the business sector and created by State and Federal government, schools, and tertiary institutions. *Does not include that from the construction and demolition industry.*

Commercial breeding – commercial propagating animals or plants, such as breeding dogs.

Commercial harvesting – the harvesting of animals or cash crops for commercial reasons.

Commingled materials (*waste management*) – materials mixed, such as plastic, glass, and metal containers. *Commingled recyclable materials require sorting after collection before being recycled.*

Common law – court decisions constituting a working definition of individual rights and responsibilities where no statutes (i.e., legislation) define these issues.

Communal resource management systems – resources directed for long-term sustainability.

Community – a group of various populations in each area. *An assemblage of various organisms living in the same environment.*

Community ecology (*or synecology*) – studies the interactions between the species comprising an ecological community.

Comparative risk assessment – a methodology that uses science, policy, economic analysis, and stakeholder participation to identify and address areas of greatest environmental risk; it is a method for assessing environmental management priorities. *The U.S. EPA offers free software containing the history and methodology of comparative risk and many case studies.*

Compensation point – where the amount of energy produced by photosynthesis equals the amount of energy released by respiration.

Competition – organisms from the same or different species compete for food, living space, reproduction, or limited resources. *The most adapted individuals prosper, survive, and reproduce.*

Competitive exclusion principle (or *Gause's law*) – states that two species cannot coexist in the same environment if competing for precisely the same resource, often summarized as "*complete competitors cannot coexist.*" The theory that no two populations of species can occupy the same niche and compete for the same resources in the same habitat for a very long time.

Complex system – composed of many components that may interact with each other.

Complexity (*ecological*) – the number of species at each trophic level and the number of trophic levels in a community.

Compost – the aerobically decomposed remnants of organic matter.

Composting – the biological decomposition of organic materials in the presence of oxygen that yields carbon dioxide (CO_2), heat, and stabilized organic residues that may be used as a soil additive.

Compound – a molecule of two or more atoms held together by chemical bonds.

Comprehensive Environmental Response, Compensation, and Liability Act of 1980 (CERCLA, Superfund) – established a fund to clean up abandoned hazardous waste sites; establishes strict liability, where any individual or corporation associated with the site can be liable for the cleanup cost, regardless of their contribution to the site's pollution; sets guidelines for cleanup sites.

Concentration – the amount of a chemical in a particular volume or weight of air, water, soil, or another medium. See *parts per billion* and *parts per million*.

Condensation – 1. the change of state from a gas to a liquid (e.g., when water vapor in the air changes to liquid as it cools); 2. the aggregation of water molecules changing from vapor to liquid or solid when the saturation concentration is exceeded.

Condensation nuclei – tiny particles floating in air that facilitate condensation.

Conference of the Parties (COP) – the supreme body of the United Nations Framework Convention on Climate Change (UNFCCC). *More than 180 nations have ratified the Convention. Its first session was held in Berlin, Germany, in 1995, and is expected to continue meeting yearly. COP's role is to promote and review the implementation of the Convention. It will periodically review existing commitments considering the Convention's objective, scientific findings, and the effectiveness of national climate change programs.* See *United Nations Framework Convention on Climate Change*.

Confined aquifer – with a water table above their upper boundary and typically found below unconfined aquifers.

Conifer – needle-bearing trees that produce seeds in cones.

Coniferous forest – one of the primary terrestrial biomes, culminating in the taiga.

Conservation biology – the study of Earth's biodiversity to protect and conserve natural habitats and plant and animal species.

Conservation development – consideration of landscape history, human culture, topography, and ecological values in subdivision design; using cluster housing, zoning, covenants, and other design features, at least half of a subdivision can be preserved as open space, farmland, or natural areas.

Conservation of matter – in chemical reactions, matter changes form; it is not created nor destroyed.

Conspicuous consumption – the lavish spending on goods and services acquired mainly to display wealth rather than satisfy basic needs. *A term coined by economist and social critic Thorstein Veblen.*

Construction and demolition waste (*waste management*) – includes waste from residential, civil, and commercial construction and demolition activities, such as fill material (e.g., soil), asphalt, bricks, and timber. C&D waste excludes construction waste, which is included in the municipal waste stream. C&D waste does not generally include commercial and industrial waste stream waste.

Consumer – 1. an organism that obtains energy and nutrients by feeding on other organisms or their remains; see *heterotroph*; 2. an industry that maintains itself by transforming a high–quality energy source into a lower one. Compare *primary producers* and *heterotrophs*.

Consumer democracy – using the economic capacity to promote values.

Consumption – the fraction of withdrawn water lost in transmission or evaporated, absorbed, chemically transformed, or otherwise made unavailable for other purposes due to human use.

Consumption (*ecology*) – the use of resources by a living system, the inflow and degradation of energy used for system activity.

Consumption (*economics*) – part of disposable income (income after taxes paid and payments received) that is not saved, essentially the goods and services used by households; this includes purchased commodities at the household level (such as food, clothing, and utilities), the goods and services paid for by the government (e.g., defense, education, social services, and health care), and the resources consumed by businesses to increase their assets (e.g., business equipment and housing).

Consumptive – pertaining to consumption; having the quality of consuming or dissipating; consumptive uses of water include pumping water for irrigation or municipal uses and *evapotranspiration*.

Containment building – reinforced concrete structure for nuclear reactors designed to contain explosions.

Contaminants – something that makes a place or substance no longer suitable for use.

Continental – characteristic of a continent (one of Earth's large landmasses).

Contour plowing (or *contour farming*) – the farming practice of plowing across a slope following its contours. The rows formed have the effect of slowing water runoff during rainstorms so that the soil is not washed away and allows the water to percolate into the soil.

Control rods – neutron-absorbing material inserted into spaces between fuel assemblies in nuclear reactors to regulate fission reactions.

Controlled burning – used in forest management, farming, prairie restoration, or greenhouse gas abatement.

Convection cell – the transfer of heat or other atmospheric properties by massive motion within the atmosphere, especially by such motion directed upward.

Convection currents – rising or sinking air currents that stir the atmosphere and transport heat from one area to another; they occur in water. See *spring overturn*.

Convention on the International Trade in Endangered Species (CITES) – an international agreement among 167 governments aiming to ensure that cross–border trade in wild animals and plants does not threaten their survival. *The species covered by CITES are listed in three Appendices according to the degree of protection they need.*

Conventional energy – energy from sources, such as fossil fuels, that are widely used.

Convert – to express a quantity in alternative units.

Cool deserts – characterized by cold winters and sagebrush (e.g., the American Great Basin).

Cooperation – the process by which organisms work together for mutual benefit.

Coral bleaching – the process in which a coral colony, under environmental stress, expels the microscopic algae (zooxanthellae) that live in symbiosis with their host organisms (polyps). The affected coral colony appears whitened.

Coral reefs – an underwater ecosystem characterized by reef-building corals. Reefs are formed of colonies of coral polyps held together by calcium carbonate. Most coral reefs are built from stony corals, whose polyps cluster in groups. *Prominent oceanic features composed of hard, lime skeletons produced by coral animals, usually formed along the edges of shallow, submerged ocean banks or shelves in warm, shallow tropical seas.*

Core – the dense, intensely hot mass of molten metal, mostly iron and nickel, that is thousands of kilometers in diameter at Earth's center.

Core region – the primary industrial region of a country, usually located around the capital or largest port; has both the greatest population density and the greatest economic activity of the country.

Coriolis effect – the observed effect of the Coriolis force, especially the inertial force caused by Earth's rotation in deflecting an object moving above Earth, rightward in the northern hemisphere, leftward in the southern hemisphere.

Cornucopian fallacy – the belief that nature is limitless in its abundance and that perpetual growth is not only possible but essential.

Corporate Social Responsibility – integration of social and environmental policies into day-to-day corporate business.

Corridor – a strip of natural habitat that connects two adjacent nature preserves to allow migration of organisms from one place to another.

Corrosive – 1. causing damage to metal during chemical processes; 2. causing something to become weak; gradually destructive; steadily harmful.

Cost-benefit analysis – evaluates large-scale public projects by comparing the costs and benefits they will accrue.

Courtship display – ritual, social behavior between possible mates.

Covenants – formal agreements or contracts, often between government and industry sectors. *The national packaging covenant and sustainability covenants are voluntary covenants with a regulatory underpinning. Land covenants protect land for wildlife in the future.*

Cover crops – plants (e.g., rye, alfalfa, or clover) planted immediately after a harvest to hold and protect the soil.

Cracking – the breaking of the long carbon chains found in the hydrocarbons in crude oil by heating them at high temperatures to form smaller molecules that are more useful.

Criminal law – a body of court decisions based on federal and state statutes concerning wrongs against persons or society.

Criteria pollutants – the 1970 amendments to the *Clean Air Act* required the EPA to set *National Ambient Air Quality Standards* for certain pollutants known to be hazardous to human health; the EPA has identified six criteria pollutants: sulfur dioxide, carbon monoxide, lead, nitrogen oxides, ozone, and particulate matter.

Critical factor – the single environmental factor closest to the tolerance limit for a given species at a given time. See *limiting factors*.

Critical thinking – an ability to systematically, purposefully, and efficiently evaluate information.

Crop coefficient (Kc) (*water management*) – a variable to calculate the *evapotranspiration* of a plant crop based on that of a reference crop.

Crop evapotranspiration (ETc) (*water management*) – crop water use as the daily water withdrawal.

Crop rotation (or *crop sequencing*) – the practice of growing a series of different crops in the same space in sequential seasons for numerous benefits, such as avoiding the buildup of pathogens and pests that often occur when one species is continuously cropped.

Croplands – land that is suitable for growing crops.

Crude death rate (or *crude mortality rate*) – annual deaths per thousand persons.

Crude mortality rate (or *crude death rate*) – annual deaths per thousand persons.

Crude oil – a naturally occurring mixture (e.g., butane, octane) of hydrocarbons (i.e., molecules with carbon and hydrogen) under average temperature and pressure.

Crust – the cool, lightweight, outermost layer of Earth's surface floating on soft, pliable underlying layers.

Cryosphere – the combined portions of Earth's surface where water is frozen solid as ice, including sea ice, lake ice, river ice, snow, glaciers, ice caps, ice sheets, and frozen ground such as permafrost. One interrelated component of Earth's system, the cryosphere, is frozen water in the form of snow, permanently frozen ground (permafrost), floating ice, and glaciers. *Fluctuations in the volume of the cryosphere cause changes in ocean sea level, directly impacting the atmosphere and biosphere. There is a significant overlap with the hydrosphere.*

Curbside collection – a collection of household recyclable materials (separated or co-mingled) left at the curbside for collection by local government services.

Cullet – crushed glass that is suitable for recycling by glass manufacturers.

Cultural eutrophication – an increase in biological productivity and ecosystem succession caused by human activities. *The process that speeds up natural eutrophication because of human activity.*

Cultural services – the non-material benefits of ecosystems, including refreshment, spiritual enrichment, knowledge, and artistic satisfaction.

Culture jamming – altering existing mass media to criticize itself (e.g., defacing advertisements with an alternative message). *Public activism opposing commercialism is little more than propaganda for established interests and an attempt to find alternative expressions.*

Culvert – drain that passes under a road or pathway, maybe a pipe or other conduit.

Curbside collection – household recyclable materials (separated or co-mingled) left at the curbside for collection by local council services.

Cut and fill – mechanically removing earth from one place to another.

Cyanobacteria (*Cyanophyta* or *blue-green algae*) – a phylum of bacteria obtaining energy through photosynthesis.

Cyclones – intense low–pressure weather systems; mid-latitude cyclones are atmospheric circulations that rotate clockwise in the Southern Hemisphere and anticlockwise in the Northern Hemisphere and are generally associated with stronger winds, unsettled conditions, cloudiness, and rainfall. Tropical *cyclones* (called *hurricanes* in the Northern Hemisphere) cause storm surges in coastal areas.

D

Daughter – a material formed from the parent material after a given process, such as nuclear decay or movement through the rock cycle.

DDT (dichlorodiphenyltrichloroethane) – a chlorinated hydrocarbon used as a pesticide and a persistent organic pollutant. *A colorless, odorless water-insoluble crystalline insecticide $C_{14}H_9Cl_5$ that accumulates in ecosystems and has toxic effects on many vertebrates; became the most widely used pesticide from WWII to the 1950s; implicated in illnesses and environmental problems; now banned in the U.S.*

Debt-for-nature swap – a financial transaction in which a portion of a developing nation's foreign debt is forgiven in exchange for local investments in conservation measures.

Deciduous – trees and shrubs that shed their leaves at the end of the growing season.

Deciduous broadleaf forest – any tree-canopied area in a temperate zone whose trees shed their leaves during the cold season.

Deciduous forest – a tree-canopied area with trees that drop their leaves seasonally.

Decline spiral – a catastrophic deterioration of a species, community, or whole ecosystem; accelerates as functions are disrupted or lost in a downward cascade.

Decomposers – 1. any organism that breaks down decomposing bits of organic matter. 2. consumers, primarily microbial, change dead organic matter into minerals and heat.

Decomposition – the process by which tissues of dead organisms break down into simpler forms of organic matter, thereby clearing the limited space in a biome.

Deductive reasoning – deriving testable predictions about specific cases from general principles.

Deep ecology – a philosophy that calls for a profound shift in attitudes and behavior based on voluntary simplicity, rejection of anthropocentric attitudes, intimate contact with nature, decentralization of power, support for cultural and biological diversity, a belief in the sacredness of nature, and direct personal action to protect nature, improve the environment and bring about fundamental societal change.

Deep-sea community – organisms linked by a shared habitat in the deep sea.

Deforestation – the conversion of forested areas to non-forest land for agriculture, urban use, development, or wasteland. The removal of a forest or stand of trees from land converted to non-forest use. *Deforestation contributes to increasing carbon dioxide concentrations by 1) the burning or decomposition of wood releases CO_2, and 2) trees that remove carbon dioxide from the atmosphere in photosynthesis are no longer present. Deforestation can involve the conversion of forest land to farms, ranches, or urban use. The most concentrated deforestation occurs in tropical rainforests. About 31% of Earth's land surface is covered by forests.*

Degradation (*water resource*) – deterioration in water quality due to contamination or pollution; makes the water unsuitable for other desirable purposes.

Delaney Clause – an amendment to the *Federal Food, Drug, and Cosmetic Act* added in 1958 prohibiting the addition of any known cancer-causing agent to processed foods, drugs, or cosmetics.

Delivered energy – energy delivered to and used by a household, usually gas and electricity.

Delta – fan-shaped sediment deposit found at the mouth of a river.

Demand – the amount of a product that consumers are willing and able to buy at various possible prices, assuming they are free to express their preferences.

Demanufacturing – disassembly of products so components can be reused or recycled.

Dematerialization – decreasing the consumption of materials and resources while maintaining the quality of life.

Demographic transition – 1. a change in the make-up of a human population or group from one set of characteristics to another; 2. a pattern of falling death rates and, often, birthrates in response to improved living conditions; could be reversed in deteriorating conditions.

Demographics – the characteristics of a human population, especially its size, growth, density, distribution, and statistics regarding birth rate, marriage, the incidence of disease, and death rate.

Demography – 1. vital statistics about people: births, marriages, deaths, etc.; 2. the statistical study of human populations relating to growth rate, age structure, geographic distribution, etc., and their effects on social, economic, and environmental conditions.

Denitrification – the breakdown of nitrates (mainly in the soil) by anaerobic bacteria into their constituent chemical elements: nitrogen and oxygen.

Denitrifying bacteria – soil bacteria that convert nitrates to gaseous nitrogen and nitrous oxide.

Density – the quantity of something per unit measure, especially per unit length, area, or volume; it is the mass per unit volume of a substance under specified pressure and temperature conditions.

Density dependence – dependence of the growth rate of a population of a given species on density.

Dependency ratio – the number of non-working members compared to working members.

Depository or repository – a place where something is kept for safekeeping or storage, such as a warehouse or store for furniture or valuables. *Yucca Mountain in New Mexico is being studied as a potential depository for spent nuclear fuel.*

Desalination – producing potable (i.e., drinking water) or recyclable water by removing salts from salty or brackish water. Three methods do this: 1. distillation or freezing, 2. reverse osmosis using membranes, electrodialysis, and 3. ion exchange. At present, these methods are *energy-intensive*.

Desert – an area with an average annual precipitation of less than 250 mm (9.8 in) or where more water is lost than falls as precipitation.

Desert ecology – the sum of the interactions between biotic and abiotic factors in a desert biome, including interactions between plant, animal, and bacterial populations in a desert community.

Desertification – 1. a process by which areas become desert-like wastelands with lower and different biodiversity. 2. land degradation in arid, semi-arid, and dry sub-humid areas resulting from climatic variations, primarily human activities. Denuding and degrading a once-fertile land, initiating a desert-producing cycle that feeds on itself and causes long-term changes in an area's soil, climate, and *biota*. Land degradation in arid, semi-arid, and dry sub-humid areas results from various factors, including climatic variations and human activities. UNCCD (United Nations Convention to Combat Desertification) defines land degradation as a loss, in arid, semi-arid, and dry sub-humid areas, of the biological or economic productivity and complexity of rain-fed cropland, irrigated cropland, or range, pasture, forest, and woodlands resulting from land uses or a process or combination of processes, including processes arising from human activities and habitation patterns, such as (i) soil erosion caused by wind or water; (ii) deterioration of the physical, chemical and biological or economic properties of soil; and (iii) long-term loss of natural vegetation. Conversion of forest to non-forest.

Design for assembly/disassembly (dfX) – reuse and recycling.

Design for the environment (dfE) – considers cradle-to-grave costs and benefits of material acquisition, manufacture, use, and disposal.

Design for manufacturing (dfM) – designing products to make manufacturing easy.

Design for sustainability (dfS) – an integrated design approach aiming to achieve environmental quality and economic efficiency through redesigning industrial systems.

Detrital food web – a food web depicting the energy flow from photoautotrophs through detritivores and decomposers.

Detritivores (*detritus feeder*) – heterotrophs that consume decomposing bits of organic matter, such as plant litter. *Animals and plants that consume detritus (decomposing organic material) and, in doing so, contribute to the decomposition and the recycling of nutrients.*

Detritus – non-living particulate organic material (as opposed to dissolved organic material).

Detritus feeders – organisms that obtain their nutrients and energy by breaking down dead materials and organic compounds in an ecosystem.

Developing countries – have continuous economic growth and a relatively high standard of living. *The term is value-laden and prescriptive, implying a natural transition from "undeveloped" to "developed" when such transitions can be imposed instead. Although poverty and physical deprivation are undesirable, it does not follow that "undeveloped" economies should move towards affluent Western-style "developed" free market economies.*

Developing countries – development of a country is measured using a mix of economic factors (income per capita, GDP, degree of modern infrastructure, degree of industrialization, the proportion of economy devoted to agriculture and natural resource extraction) and social factors (life expectancy, the rate of literacy, poverty). The UN-produced *Human Development Index* (HDI) is a compound indicator of the statistics. *A strong correlation exists between low-income and high population growth within and between countries. Developing countries have low per capita income, widespread poverty, and low capital formation.*

Dewpoint – temperature at which condensation occurs for a given water vapor concentration in the air.

Deoxyribonucleic acid (DNA) – the long, double-helix molecule in the nucleus of cells that contains the genetic code and directs the development and functioning of cells.

Dichlorodiphenyltrichloroethane (DDT) – a chlorinated hydrocarbon used as a pesticide, a persistent organic pollutant. A colorless, odorless, water-insoluble crystalline insecticide $C_{14}H_9Cl_5$ that accumulates in ecosystems with toxic effects on vertebrates; became the most widely used pesticide from WWII to the 1950s; implicated in illnesses and environmental problems; now banned in the U.S.

Dieback (*arboriculture*) – 1. a condition in trees or woody plants in which peripheral parts are killed, either by parasites or due to conditions such as acid rain. 2. a sudden population decline. See *population crash*.

Diesel – 1. fuel made of 16 carbon hydrocarbons; 2. a high-compression internal combustion engine.

Dietary energy supply – food available for human consumption, usually in kilocalories per person per day (kg/person/day).

Diminishing returns – a condition in which unrestrained population growth causes the standard of living to decrease to a subsistence level where poverty, misery, vice, and starvation make life miserable; this dreary prophecy has led economics to be called "the dismal science."

Dioxin – chemical compounds that are persistent organic pollutants and carcinogenic.

Direct action – civil disobedience, guerrilla street theater, picketing, protest marches, road blockades, demonstrations, and other techniques borrowed from the civil rights movement and applied to environmental protection.

Direct energy – used mainly at home (delivered energy) and for fuels used for transport.

Disability-adjusted life years (DALY) – a measure of premature deaths and losses due to the onset of illnesses and disabilities in a population.

Discharge – the amount of water that passes a fixed point in a given time, usually expressed as liters or cubic feet of water per second.

Discharge rate – the amount of water that passes a fixed point in a given time, usually expressed as liters or cubic feet of water per second.

Disclimax community (or *equilibrium community*) – a community subject to periodic disruptions, usually by fire, that prevent it from reaching a climax stage.

Disease – a deleterious change in the body's condition in response to destabilizing factors, such as nutrition, chemicals, or biological agents.

Disinfection – to make free from infection by destroying harmful microorganisms.

Dispersal – the movement of organisms from their birth or breeding sites to another location.

Dissemination – to become widely scattered (seeds).

Dissolved Oxygen (DO) content – the amount of oxygen dissolved in a given volume of water at a given temperature and atmospheric pressure, usually expressed in parts per million.

Distillation – 1. the extraction of volatile components of a mixture by the condensation and collection of the vapors that are produced as the mixture is heated; 2. a process of desalinization in which water is evaporated and re-condensed.

Distributed water (*water management*) – purchased water supplied to a user, usually through a reticulated mains system, pipes and open channels, and irrigation systems supplied to farms.

Diversion rate (*waste disposal*) – the proportion of a potentially recyclable diverted from the waste disposal stream and, therefore, not directed to a landfill.

Diversity (or *species diversity* or *biological diversity*) – the number of species present in a community (species richness) and the relative abundance of each species.

Divertible resource (or *water management*) – the proportion of accessible water runoff and recharge.

DNA (deoxyribonucleic acid) – the long, double-helix molecule in the nucleus of cells that contains the genetic code and directs the development and functioning of cells.

Dominance hierarchy – the organization of individual organisms into groups with a social structure.

Dominance species – characterizes and dominates an ecological community as measured by its primary productivity or biomass.

Dominant – 1. an organism that behaves in such a way as to be in a position over others of the same species; 2. the allele of a gene that requires only one copy to be present in an individual for that trait to be present.

Dominant plants – those plant species in a community that provide the food base for most of the community; they usually occupy the most space and have the largest biomass.

Dose threshold level – the maximum level of a substance before toxic levels are reached.

Downbursts – sudden, powerful downdrafts of cold air with an advancing storm front.

Downcycling (*waste management*) – recycling with diminished item quality with each recycling.

Downstream – the processes occurring after a particular activity (e.g., transporting a manufactured product from a factory to the wholesale or retail outlet). Compare *upstream*.

Drainage (*water management*) – irrigation or rainfall that runs off an area or lost to deep percolation.

Drawdown (*water management*) – drop in water level, generally applied to wells or bores.

Dredging (*water management*) – the repositioning of soil from an aquatic environment using specialized equipment to initiate infrastructural or ecological improvements.

Drift net – a fishing net used in oceans, coastal seas, and freshwater lakes.

Drinking water (or *potable water*) – water fit for human consumption by the *World Health Organization* (WHO) guidelines.

Drip irrigation (*water management*) – a drip hose is placed near the plant roots to minimize deep percolation and evaporation. *Using pipe or tubing perforated with tiny holes to deliver water one drop at a time directly to the soil around each plant; conserves water, prevents soil waterlogging, and reduces the salt content.*

Driver (*ecology*) – any natural or human-induced factor that directly or indirectly causes a change in an ecosystem. *A direct driver unequivocally influences ecosystem processes and can be measured.*

Drop-off center (*waste management*) – where discarded materials can be left for recycling.

Drought – a period of abnormally dry weather marked by little or no rain that lasts long enough to cause water shortage for people and natural systems. *An acute water shortage relative to availability, supply, and demand in a region. An extended period of months or years when a region has a deficient water supply. Generally, this occurs when a region receives consistently below–average precipitation.*

Drought cycle – temporary, repetitive phases of dry conditions in an otherwise hospitable environment.

Dry alkali injection – spraying dry sodium bicarbonate into flue gas to absorb and neutralize acidic sulfur compounds. See *flue-gas scrubbing*.

Dryland farming – a technique that uses soil moisture conservation and seed selection to optimize production under dry conditions.

Dryland salinity (*water management*) – accumulation of salts in soils, soil water, and groundwater; may be natural or induced by land clearing.

Dry spell – a period with little or no rain. *Whether a dry spell becomes a drought depends on how long it lasts, expectations based on historical data and perceptions, and the water needs of people and natural systems.*

Dump (or *landfill*) – land waste disposal sites where waste is generally spread in thin layers, compacted, and regularly covered with fresh soil (e.g., daily). *It is a site for waste materials disposal by burial and is the oldest form of waste treatment. Solid waste disposal in which refuse is buried between soil layers. A method often used to reclaim low–lying ground. Landfill is sometimes used as a noun to refer to the waste itself.*

Dung – animal excrement (biomass) used as fuel for heating or cooking in many countries.

Dynamic state of equilibrium – a steady state in an ecosystem or a system where change is not observable because, even though there are changes in progress, they are being made at an equal rate with no net gain.

E

E-cycling – recycling electronic waste.

E–waste – electronic waste, especially mobile phones, televisions, and personal computers.

Earth's atmosphere – the layer of gases surrounding Earth retained by Earth's gravity.

Earth Charter – a set of principles for sustainable development, environmental protection, and social justice developed by a council appointed by the United Nations.

Earth science – includes fields of natural science related to Earth. This science focuses on the physical, chemical, and biological complex constitutions and synergistic linkages of Earth's four spheres: the biosphere, hydrosphere, atmosphere, and geosphere (or lithosphere). *Earth science is a branch of planetary science but has a much older history.*

Earthquakes – a sudden, violent movement of Earth's crust.

Earthshine – sunlight reflected from Earth and illuminating the dark side of the Moon, which helps determine Earth's albedo.

Eccentricity – the extent to which Earth's orbit around the Sun departs from a perfect circle.

Eco- – prefix indicating environmental considerations (e.g., eco-housing, eco-label, eco–material).

Eco-asset – a biological asset providing financial value to private landowners when maintained in or restored to their natural state.

Eco-efficiency – creating more goods and services with fewer resources, less waste and pollution.

Ecocentric (or *ecologically centered*) – a philosophy that claims moral values and rights for organisms and ecological systems and processes.

Ecofeminism – a pluralistic, nonhierarchical, relationship-oriented philosophy that suggests how humans could reconceive themselves and their relationships to nature in non-dominating ways (devised as an alternative to patriarchal systems of domination).

Ecojustice – justice in the social order and integrity in the natural order.

Ecolabel – notion indicating a product has met specific environmental or social standards.

***E. Coli* (*Escherichia coli*)** – a bacterium used to indicate fecal contamination and potential disease organisms in the water.

Ecological corridor – a habitat area connecting wildlife populations separated by human activities.

Ecological deficit – of a country or region; measures the amount by which its *Ecological Footprint* exceeds the ecological capacity of that region.

Ecological development – a gradual process of environmental modification by organisms.

Ecological economics – application of ecological insights to economic analysis in a holistic, contextual, value-sensitive, eco-centric manner.

Ecological equivalents – species occupying similar ecological niches in similar ecosystems worldwide.

Ecological footprint (or *eco-footprint*, or *footprint*) – a measure of the area of biologically productive land and water needed to produce the resources and absorb the waste of a population using the prevailing technology and resource management schemes. *A measure of the consumption of renewable natural resources by a human population, be it that of a country, a region, or the whole world, given as the area of productive land or sea required to produce the crops, meat, seafood, wood, and fiber it consumes, to sustain its energy consumption and to give space for its infrastructure.*

Ecological literacy – the ability to understand the natural systems that make life on Earth possible.

Ecological niche – 1. the habitat of a species or population within its ecosystem; 2. the functional role and position of a species (population) within a community or ecosystem, including what resources it uses, how and when it uses the resources and how it interacts with other populations. The match of a species to a specific environmental condition. It describes how an organism or population responds to the distribution of resources and competitors. See *niche*.

Ecological pyramid (or *biomass pyramid*) – illustrates productivity within a trophic level.

Ecological recycling (or *nutrient cycle*) – the movement and exchange of organic and inorganic matter back into the production of living matter.

Ecological selection – ecological processes that operate on a species' inherited traits without reference to mating or secondary sex characteristics.

Ecological succession – 1. the process by which organisms occupy a site and gradually change environmental conditions so other species replace the original inhabitants; 2. the predictable and orderly changes in the composition or structure of an ecological community over time. The change in the species structure of an ecological community over time.

Ecological sustainability – the capacity of ecosystems to maintain essential processes and functions and retain their biological diversity without impoverishment.

Ecologically sustainable development – using, conserving, and enhancing community resources so that ecological processes on which life depends can be maintained and enriched into the future.

Ecology – 1. the scientific study of living organisms and their relationships to one another; concerned with the life histories, distribution, and behavior of individual species as well as the structure and function of natural systems at the level of populations, communities, and ecosystems; 2. the scientific study of the processes regulating the distribution and abundance of organisms. *The study of the design of ecosystem structure and function.*

Ecology of fear – a framework describing the psychological impact that predator-induced stress experienced by animals has on populations and ecosystems.

Economic development – a rise in real income per person, usually associated with new technology that increases productivity or resources.

Economic globalization – the emerging international economy characterized by free trade in goods and services, unrestricted capital flows, and more limited national powers to control domestic economies.

Economic growth – an increase in the total wealth of a nation; if the population grows faster than the economy, there may be macroeconomic growth, but the share per person may decline.

Economic thresholds – in pest management, the point at which the cost of pest damage exceeds the costs of pest control.

Ecophagy – the destruction of an ecosystem.

Ecophysiology – the study of the interaction of the physiological traits of an organism with its abiotic environment.

Ecopoiesis – hypothetical shaping of a sustainable ecosystem by humans on a lifeless, sterile planet.

Ecoregion (*bioregion*) – 1. a region defined by its geography and ecology 2. the next smallest ecologically and geographically defined area beneath the *biogeographic realm* or *ecozone*, which are divisions of Earth's surface defined by the distribution of organisms. See *bioregion*.

Ecosynthesis – the use of introduced species to fill niches in a disrupted environment to increase the speed of ecological restoration.

Ecosystem – a dynamic complex of plant, animal, and microorganism communities and their non-living environment, interacting as a functional unit. *The total interacting organisms (biocoenosis) and non-living things (biotopes) in a specific environment. Any natural unit or entity, including living and non-living factors, interacts to produce a stable system through the cyclic exchange of materials.*

Ecosystem boundary – the spatial delimitation usually based on discontinuities of organisms and physical environment.

Ecosystem ecology – studies how energy and matter flow interact with ecosystems' biotic elements. See *nutrient cycle efficiency*.

Ecosystem management – integration of ecological, economic, and social goals in a unified systems approach to resource management.

Ecosystem modeling – using mathematics, computer programs, and models to understand and predict ecosystem behavior.

Ecosystem restoration – reinstate a community of organisms to as near natural conditions as possible.

Ecosystem services – 1. resources and processes provided in an ecosystem and beneficial organisms. 2. humans benefit from many resources and processes supplied by natural ecosystems. 3. the benefits produced by ecosystems on which people depend. For example, fisheries, drinking water, fertile soils for growing crops, climate regulation, and aesthetic and cultural value. The role organisms play without charge in creating a healthy human environment, from oxygen production to soil formation, maintenance of water quality, and more. *These services are divided into four groups: supporting, provisioning, regulating, and cultural.*

Ecotage – direct action (e.g., guerrilla warfare) or sabotage to defend nature. See *monkeywrenching*.

Ecotax – a fiscal policy introducing taxes intended to promote ecologically sustainable activities via economic incentives.

Ecotone – a boundary between two types of ecological communities. *A transition area between two adjacent but different landscape patches.*

Ecotope – the smallest ecologically distinct landscape features in a landscape mapping and classification system.

Ecotourism – combines native adventure travel, cultural exploration, and nature appreciation.

Ecotoxicology – the study of toxic chemicals' ecological role (often pollutants or natural compounds).

Ecozone (or *biographic realm*) – an area with natural origins such as climate, terrain, and vegetation; the largest division of Earth's surface, filled with living organisms.

E-cycling – electronic recycling waste.

Edge effects – a change in species composition, physical conditions, or other ecological factors at the boundary between two ecosystems.

Effective rainfall – the volume of rainfall passing into the soil; that part of rainfall available for plants after runoff, leaching, evaporation, and foliage interception.

Effluent – a discharge or emission of liquid, gas, or other waste product.

Effluent sewerage – a low-cost alternative sewage treatment for cities in developing countries that combines some features of septic systems and centralized municipal treatment systems.

El Niño – a band of anomalously warm ocean water temperatures that occasionally develops off the coast of South America and causes climatic changes across the Pacific Ocean. A warm water current periodically flows southwards along the coast of Ecuador and Peru in South America, replacing the usually cold northwards flowing current. *It occurs every five to seven years, usually during Christmas (the name refers to the Christ child).* The opposite phase is a *La Niña*.

El Niño Southern Oscillation (ENSO) – a set of specific interacting parts of a single global system of coupled ocean-atmosphere climate fluctuations resulting from oceanic and atmospheric circulations. The formation of an El Niño is linked with the cycling of a Pacific Ocean circulation pattern known as the *southern oscillation*; in a typical year, a surface low pressure develops in the region of northern Australia and Indonesia, and a high-pressure system over the coast of Peru.

Pacific Ocean trade winds move strongly from east to west; the easterly flow of the trade winds carries warm surface waters westward, bringing convective storms to Indonesia and coastal Australia; along the coast of Peru, cold bottom water wells up to the surface to replace the warm water that is pulled west.

Electron – a negatively charged subatomic particle orbiting the atom's nucleus (protons and neutrons).

Electrostatic – of or relating to electric charges at rest or produced or caused by such charges.

Electrostatic precipitators – the most common particulate controls in power plants; fly ash particles pick up an electrostatic surface charge as they pass between large electrodes in the effluent stream, causing particles to migrate to the oppositely charged plate.

Element – a molecule composed of one atom, not broken into simpler units by chemical reactions.

Embodied energy – 1. the energy expended over the lifecycle of a good or service; 2. the energy involved in the extraction of basic materials, processing/manufacture, transport, and disposal of a product; 3. the energy required to provide a good or service.

Embodied water – the hidden flow accompanying goods trade. See *virtual water*.

Emergent diseases – a disease that has been absent for at least 20 years.

Emergent properties – not evident in the individual components of an object or system. Characteristics of a complex system (or group) that arise from the interactions among the individual parts or changing membership of a larger system are not possible when individual parts of the system act alone.

Emergy (short for *energy memory*) – the available energy used in making a product directly and indirectly, expressed in units of one type of available energy (the work previously done to provide a product or service); the energy of one type required to make energy of another.

Emigration – 1. the movement of members from a population. 2. an organism leaving its native community for another.

Emission – substances, such as gases or particles, discharged into the atmosphere due to natural processes of human activities, including those from chimneys, elevated point sources, and tailpipes of motor vehicles.

Emissions – quantitative illustrations of how releasing different amounts of climate-altering gases and particles into the atmosphere from human and natural sources will produce future climate conditions. Scenarios are developed using various assumptions about population growth, economic and technological development, and other factors.

Emissions factor – value for scaling emissions to activity data in terms of a standard emissions rate per unit of activity (e.g., grams of carbon dioxide emitted per barrel of fossil fuel consumed or per pound of product produced).

Emission intensity – the average emission rate of a given pollutant from a given source relative to the intensity of a specific activity. *For example, grams of carbon dioxide released per megajoule of energy produced or the ratio of greenhouse gas emissions produced to gross domestic product (GDP).*

Emission standard – a level of emissions that, under law, may not be exceeded.

Emission standards – requirements set specific limits to the number of pollutants released into the environment. *Regulations for restricting air pollutants released from specific point sources.*

Emissions intensity – emissions expressed as quantity per monetary unit.

Emissions trading (or *carbon trading*) – a system by which states and institutions receive permits to produce a specified amount of carbon dioxide (CO_2) and other greenhouse gases, which they may trade with others. *A system that limits aggregate emissions from a group of emitters by setting a "cap" on maximum emissions. It is a market-based policy to reduce emissions of pollutants and encourage business investment in fossil fuel alternatives and energy efficiency.* See *cap and trade*.

Endangered species – the imminent risk of becoming extinct; at risk of becoming extinct because they are either few or threatened by changing environmental or predation parameters.

Endemism – a state in which species are restricted to a region.

Energetics – the study of how energy flows within an ecosystem: the routes it takes, flow rates, where it is stored, and how it is used.

Energy – 1. the capacity to do work (i.e., to change the physical state or motion of an object); 2. a property of systems that can be turned into heat and measured in heat units.

> *Atomic energy* (or *nuclear energy*) – released by reactions within atomic nuclei, as in nuclear fission or fusion.
>
> *Available energy* – with the potential to do work (energy).
>
> *Delivered energy* – delivered to and used by a household, usually gas and electricity.
>
> *Direct energy* – used mainly at home (delivered energy), and fuels used mainly for transport.
>
> *Embodied energy* – expended over the lifecycle of a good or service *or* energy involved in the extraction of basic materials, processing/manufacture, transport, and disposal of a product *or* energy required to provide a good or service.
>
> *Geothermal energy* – heat emitted from within Earth's crust as hot water or steam and used to generate electricity after transformation.
>
> *Hydro energy* – *potential* (stored) and *kinetic* (motion) water energy to generate electricity.
>
> *Indirect energy* – generated in and accounted for by broader economy of actions or demands.
>
> *Kinetic energy* – possessed by a body because of its motion.
>
> *Nuclear energy* (or *atomic energy*) – released by reactions within atomic nuclei, as in nuclear fission or fusion.
>
> *Operational energy* – used in carrying out a particular operation.
>
> *Potential energy* – possessed by a body because of its position or condition (e.g., coiled springs and charged batteries have potential energy).
>
> *Primary energy* – obtained directly from nature, the energy in raw fuels (electricity from the grid is not primary), used primarily on energy statistics when compiling energy balances.
>
> *Solar energy* – solar radiation used for hot water production and electricity generation (does not include passive solar energy to heat and cool buildings, etc.).
>
> *Secondary energy* – primary energies are transformed in energy conversion processes to more convenient secondary forms such as electrical energy and cleaner fuels.
>
> *Stationary energy* – other than transport fuels and fugitive emissions, is used mainly to produce electricity but also for manufacturing and processing, agriculture, fisheries, etc.
>
> *Tidal/ocean/wave energy* – mechanical energy from water movement to generate electricity.
>
> *Useful energy* – available to increase system production and efficiency.
>
> *Wind energy* – kinetic energy of wind used for electricity generation using turbines.

Energy accounting – measuring value by energy input required for goods or services. *Accounting builds on measuring human impact on nature (rather than being restricted to human-based items).*

Energy audit – a systematic gathering and analysis of energy use for energy efficiency improvements. Energy Audits define three levels for consistency: *basic*, *detailed*, and *precision energy audits*.

Energy crisis – a significant rise in price due to scarcity of energy supplies within an economy.

Energy cycle – how energy is cycled through the biosphere (e.g., when the Sun's energy is taken up by plants, from plants to animals, and from animals to other animals through ingestion).

Energy efficiency – using less energy to provide the same level of energy service. *A measure of energy produced compared to the energy consumed.*

Energy footprint – the area required to provide or absorb the waste from coal, oil, gas, fuelwood, nuclear energy, and hydropower. *Fossil Fuel Footprint* is required to sequester the emitted CO_2, considering CO_2 absorption by the sea, etc.

Energy-for-land ratio – the amount of energy produced per hectare of ecologically productive land. The units used are gigajoules per hectare and year (GJ/ha/yr). For fossil fuel (calculated as CO_2 assimilation), the ratio is 100 GJ/ha/yr.

Energy management – a program of well-planned actions to reduce energy use, recurrent energy costs, and harmful greenhouse gas emissions.

Energy pyramid – represents the loss of valuable energy at each step in a food chain. A graphical representation showing the biomass or biomass productivity at each trophic level in each ecosystem.

Energy recovery – 1. incineration of solid waste to produce valuable energy; 2. the productive extraction of energy, usually electricity or heat, from waste or materials that otherwise go to a landfill.

ENERGY STAR – U.S. Environmental Protection Agency voluntary program that helps businesses and individuals save money and protect climate through superior energy efficiency.

Energy systems – the infrastructure and systems of electricity production, transport, storage, and consumption.

Enhanced greenhouse effect – the increase in natural greenhouse effect from increased atmospheric concentrations of greenhouse gases due to emissions from human activities. *The natural greenhouse effect has been enhanced by increased atmospheric concentrations of greenhouse gases (e.g., CO_2 and methane) emitted by human activities. These added greenhouse gases cause the Earth to warm.*

Enriched uranium – uranium (U) ore occurs naturally in a state that cannot be used in most reactors or to make nuclear weapons. Enrichment makes it easier to use in reactors; the enrichment process increases the amount of the fissionable ^{235}U isotope; uranium enriched to contain less than 20% ^{235}U is low-enriched uranium; uranium enriched to contain 20%, or greater ^{235}U is highly-enriched uranium that can be directly used to make nuclear weapons.

ENSO (El Niño–Southern Oscillation) – events occurring during El Niño; at one extreme of the cycle, when the central Pacific Ocean is warm, and the atmospheric pressure over Australia is relatively high, the ENSO causes drought conditions over eastern Australia. Compare *El Niño* and *Southern Oscillation*.

Enteric fermentation – anaerobic metabolism in the digestive systems of ruminant animals. *Enteric fermentation is a cause of methane (CH_4) emissions. Livestock, especially cattle, produces methane during digestion, representing one-third of emissions from agriculture.*

Entropy – for a closed thermodynamic system, a quantitative measure of the amount of thermal energy not available to do work; the symbol is S.

Evapotranspiration – evaporation of water from soil and plant leaves.

Environment – 1. the external conditions, resources, stimuli, etc., with which an organism interacts. 2. the conditions surrounding an organism (or group of organisms) and the complex social or cultural conditions affecting an individual or community. *The biotic and abiotic surroundings of an organism or population and the chemical interactions between these factors influence their survival, development, and evolution. An environment can vary in scale from microscopic to global.*

Environmental backlash (or *greenlash*) – dramatic changes in ecosystems' structure and dynamic behavior.

Environmental crime – a crime against environmental legislation subject to prosecution.

Environmental ethics – 1. decisions humans make concerning the environment. 2. a search for moral values and ethical principles in human relations with the natural world.

Environmental flows – river or creek water flow allocated to maintain the waterway ecosystems.

Environmental hormones – chemical pollutants that, come to substitute for or interfere with naturally occurring hormones; these chemicals may trigger reproductive failure, developmental abnormalities, or tumor promotion.

Environmental impact statement (EIS) – an analysis, required by the *National Environmental Policy Act* of 1970, of the effects of any major program a federal agency plans to undertake.

Environmental indicator – 1. physical, chemical, biological, or socio-economic measures used to assess natural resources and environmental quality. 2. organisms with these characteristics are "bioindicators."

Environmental justice – a recognition that access to a clean, healthy environment is a fundamental human right. *The fair treatment and meaningful involvement of people, regardless of race, color, national origin, or income, in developing, implementing, and enforcing environmental laws, regulations, and policies.*

Environmental law – the special body of official rules, decisions, and actions concerning environmental quality, natural resources, and ecological sustainability.

Environmental literacy – fluency in the principles of ecology that gives us a working knowledge of the basic grammar and underlying syntax of environmental wisdom.

Environmental migrant – a displaced person caused by climate-induced environmental disasters.

Environmental movement (or *environmentalism*) – conservation and green movements; a diverse scientific, social, and political movement. *The movement is centered around ecology, health, and human rights in recognizing humanity as an ecosystem participant. Environmentalists generally advocate sustainable management of resources and stewardship of the natural environment through changes in public policy and individual behavior.*

Environmental noise (or *noise pollution*) – displeasing human or machine-created sound that disrupts the activity or happiness of human or animal life.

Environmental policy – the environmental rules or regulations adopted, implemented, and enforced by some governmental agency.

Environmental racism – decisions that restrict certain groups of people to polluted or degraded environments by race.

Environmental resistance – the limiting factors that tend to reduce population growth rates and set the maximum allowable population size or ecosystem carrying capacity. Compare *biotic potential*.

Environmental resources – anything an organism needs that the environment can provide.

Environmental restoration – undoing the damage caused to an area by human activity or natural disasters.

Environmental science – the study of interactions among the environment's physical, chemical, and biological components and human role in them.

Environmentalism – 1. active participation in attempts to solve environmental pollution and resource problems. 2. conservation and green movements: a diverse scientific, social, and political movement. *The movement is centered around ecology, health, and human rights in recognizing humanity as an ecosystem participant. Environmentalists generally advocate sustainable management of resources and stewardship of the natural environment through changes in public policy and individual behavior.*

Enzymes – molecules, usually proteins or nucleic acids, acting as catalysts (i.e., increase reaction rates) in biochemical reactions.

Ephemerality – the concept of things being transitory, existing only briefly.

Epidemiology – the study of factors affecting the health and illness of populations. *It serves as the foundation and logic of interventions made in public health and preventive medicine.*

Epiphyte – a plant that grows on a substrate other than soil, such as the surface of another organism.

Equilibrium community (or *disclimax community*) – a community subject to periodic disruptions, usually by fire, that prevent it from reaching a climax stage.

Erosion – displacement of solids, such as sediment, soil, rock, and other particles, usually by the agents of currents such as wind, water, or ice by downward or down-slope movement in response to gravity or by living organisms. *Removal of vegetation and trees can increase erosion of topsoil.*

***Escherichia coli* (*E. Coli*)** – a bacterium used to indicate fecal contamination and potential disease organisms in the water.

Estimated reserves – reserves of resources whose quantities are not known for certain.

Estuary – 1. the broad lower course of a river where the tide flows in, causing fresh and saltwater to mix; 2. a semi-enclosed coastal body of water with one or more rivers or streams flowing into it and with a free connection to the open sea.

Ethical consumerism – buying things that are made ethically (i.e., without harm to or exploitation of humans, animals, or the natural environment); *generally, it entails favoring products and businesses that take account of the greater good in their operations.*

Ethical living – adopting lifestyles, consumption, and shopping habits that minimize negative impacts and maximize positive impacts on people, the environment, and the economy. See *consumer democracy*.

Ethology – the study of animal behavior. See *animal behavior*.

Eukaryotic cell – a cell containing a membrane-bounded nucleus and membrane-bounded organelles.

Eutectic fluid – eutectic salts (salts that melt at low temperatures) are phase-changing chemicals used in active solar heating to store solar energy; heating melts these materials and cools them to the original phase.

Eutrophic [*eu* = well and *trophic* = nutritious] – rivers and lakes rich in organisms and organic material, often due to runoff from land.

Eutrophication – the enrichment of water bodies with nutrients, primarily nitrogen and phosphorus, stimulates aquatic organisms' growth. An increase in natural or chemical nutrients in an ecosystem. This nutrient increase typically stimulates the growth of aggressive plant species and hampers that of others, thereby harming biodiversity. *In aquatic ecosystems, it may result in hypoxia.*

Euxinic – with insufficient oxygen. See *anoxic*.

Evaporation – 1. water converted to water vapor. 2. changing liquid into vapor (the gas phase) due to increased temperature or pressure. 3. the slow vaporization of water from soil or surface water.

Evapotranspiration (ET) – 1. the water evaporating from the soil and transpired by plants. 2. the sum of water evaporation and plant transpiration. *The combined process of evaporation from Earth's surface and transpiration from vegetation. Actual evapotranspiration can never be greater than precipitation and will usually be less because some water will run off in rivers and flow to the oceans.*

Evergreen – coniferous trees and broad-leaved plants that retain their leaves year-round.

Evolution – 1. change in heritable characteristics over successive generations. 2. how random changes in genetics (DNA) and competition for scarce resources cause species to change gradually.

Evolutionary ecology – changes occurring to an organism within its population or the wider community.

E-waste – electronic waste, especially mobile phones, televisions, and personal computers.

Exhaustible resources – generally considered Earth's geologic endowment: minerals, non-mineral resources, fossil fuels, and other materials present in finite amounts in the environment.

Existence value – an economic value in which the benefit of knowing that a particular species, organism, or resource exists is appraised.

Exotic organisms – alien species introduced by the human agency into biological communities where they would not naturally occur.

Exotic species – an introduced species not native or endemic to a habitat.

Exponential curve – describes growth at a constant rate of increase per unit of time; it can be expressed as a constant fraction or exponent.

Exponential growth – growth at a constant rate of increase per unit of time; it can be expressed as a constant fraction or exponent. See *geometric growth*.

Extended producer responsibility (EPR) (or *product take-back*) – a requirement (often in law) that producers take back and accept responsibility for the responsible disposal of their products; this encourages the design of products easily repaired, recycled, reused, or upgraded.

External costs – monetary or otherwise expenses borne by someone other than those using a resource.

External water footprint – embodied water of imported goods. Compare *internal water footprints*.

Externality (*environmental economics*) – a cost or benefit not borne by the producer or supplier of a good or service. In many situations, environmental deterioration may be caused by a few while the community bears the cost. *For example, overfishing, pollution (e.g., production of greenhouse emissions that are not compensated for by taxes, etc.), and the environmental cost of land clearing.*

By-products of activities that affect the well-being of people or damage the environment, where those impacts are not reflected in market prices; the costs or benefits associated with externalities do not enter standard cost accounting schemes; in many environmental situations, environmental deterioration may be caused by a few while the cost is borne by the community (e.g., overfishing, the production of greenhouse emissions not compensated for by taxes); the environment is often cited as a negatively affected externality of the economy.

Extinction – 1. the cessation of a species or group of taxa, reducing biodiversity. 2. the irrevocable elimination of species; it can be a normal process of the natural world as species out-compete or kill off others or as environmental conditions change, causing a reduction in biodiversity. 3. the termination of an organism or a taxon, usually a species, occurs when the last individual organism dies. Compare *functional extinction*.

Extinction event (or *mass extinction, extinction-level event,* or ELE) – a sharp decrease in species in a relatively short period.

Extirpate – to eradicate a species; extinction by direct human action, such as hunting, trapping, etc.

Extreme events (or *extreme weather*) – a weather event that is rare at a particular place and time of year, including, for example, heat waves, cold waves, heavy rains, periods of drought and flooding, and severe storms. *Extreme is a statistical concept that varies depending on the historical record's location, season, and length.*

Extreme environment – an environment in which few living organisms can survive.

Extreme points of Earth – the geographical locations that differ relative to other land masses, continents, or countries.

Extreme precipitation (*events*) – an abnormally high rain or snow episode. *Extreme is a statistical concept that varies depending on the historical record's location, season, and length.*

Extremophile – an organism that thrives in physically or geochemically extreme conditions.

Eye – the center of a hurricane, where no storm activity occurs.

Eye wall – the area between the eye and the storm.

F

Fair trade – a guarantee that a fair price is paid to producers of goods or services; it includes a range of other social and environmental standards, including safety standards and the right to form unions.

Fall overturn – the mixing (or *turning over*) of lake water occurs in autumn, facilitating its re-oxygenation.

Family planning – controlling reproduction; planning the timing and number of births.

Famines – acute food shortages characterized by large-scale loss of life, social disruption, and economic chaos.

Fauna – animals in a region.

Feces – food waste discharged from the bowels after it has been digested.

Fecundity – the physical ability to reproduce.

Feedback – flow from outputs back to interact with the action. An amplification (i.e., *positive feedback*) or a reduction (i.e., *negative feedback*) of the rate of global warming caused by its effects.

Feedback mechanisms – factors that increase (*positive feedback*) or decrease (*negative feedback*) the rate of a process. *An example of positive climatic feedback is ice-albedo feedback. The process through which a system is controlled, changed, or modulated in response to its output. Positive feedback results in the amplification of the system's output; negative feedback reduces the output of a system.*

Feedlot (or *feed yard*) – a type of *Confined Animal Feeding Operation* (CAFO, or *factory farming*) used for finishing livestock, notably beef cattle, before slaughter.

Fen – waterlogged soil that tends to be peaty; fed mainly by upwelling water; low productivity.

Feral – 1. in a natural, wild state; 2. a once domestic animal that has taken up a wild existence.

Fermentation – any of a group of chemical reactions induced by living or nonliving ferments that split complex organic compounds into relatively simple substances, especially the anaerobic conversion of sugar to carbon dioxide and alcohol by yeast.

Fertigate – applying fertilizer through an irrigation system.

Fertility – a measurement of the number of offspring produced through sexual reproduction; it is usually based on the number of offspring of females since paternity can be difficult to determine.

Fertility rate – number of live births per 1,000 women aged 15 to 44. Compare *mortality rates*.

Fertilization – the union of two gametes (e.g., egg and sperm) whereby the somatic (or *body cell*) chromosome number is restored, and the development of a new individual is initiated; the addition of materials to the soil to increase the available nutrient content.

Fertilizers – compounds given to plants to promote growth; they are usually applied either through the soil for uptake by plant roots or by foliar feeding for uptake through leaves.

Fetal alcohol syndrome – a tragic set of permanent physical, mental, and behavioral congenital disabilities that can result when the mother drinks alcohol during pregnancy.

Fibrosis – the general name for accumulating scar tissue in the lung.

Fidelity – a principle that forbids misleading or deceiving any creature capable of being misled or deceived.

Filters – a porous mesh of cotton cloth, spun glass fibers, or asbestos-cellulose that allows air or liquid to pass through but holds back solid particles.

Fire-climax community – an equilibrium community maintained by periodic fires (e.g., grasslands, chaparral shrubland, and some pine forests).

Fire ecology – a branch of ecology that studies the ecological role of naturally occurring wildfires.

First law of thermodynamics – energy is conserved; energy is neither created nor destroyed; it is only changed to a different state (e.g., from chemical energy, such as gasoline, into mechanical energy to power an engine and heat from friction).

Fitness – an individual organism's reproductive success.

Fixed action pattern (*ethology*) – an instinctive behavioral pattern.

Flagship species – representative of an environmental cause, such as an ecosystem needing conservation.

Flood control devices – measures to protect areas that are easily flooded by either reducing flood flows or confining the flow; devices include building dams or levees or modifying the river or stream channel.

Flood Disaster Protection Act of 1973 – this law signaled a shift in federal policy from reducing floods through structural controls to reducing damages by limiting the development in flood-prone areas by making federally subsidized flood insurance available to property owners in flood-prone areas only in those communities which adopted *floodplain* zoning.

Floodplains – lowlands along riverbanks, lakes, and coastlines subjected to periodic inundation.

Flora – plants in a given region.

Fluorinated gases – powerful synthetic greenhouse gases such as hydrofluorocarbons, perfluorocarbons, and sulfur hexafluoride are emitted from various industrial processes. Fluorinated gases sometimes substitute stratospheric ozone-depleting substances (e.g., chlorofluorocarbons, hydrochlorofluorocarbons, and halons). *They are used in coolants, foaming agents, fire extinguishers, solvents, pesticides, and aerosol propellants. These gases are emitted in small quantities compared to carbon dioxide (CO_2), methane (CH_4), or nitrous oxide (N_2O). However, because they are potent greenhouse gases, they are High Global Warming Potential gases (High GWP gases).*

Fluorocarbons – carbon-fluorine compounds often contain other elements such as hydrogen, chlorine, or bromine. Common fluorocarbons include chlorofluorocarbons (CFCs), hydrochlorofluorocarbons (HCFCs), hydrofluorocarbons (HFCs), and perfluorocarbons (PFCs). See *chlorofluorocarbons, hydrochlorofluorocarbons, hydrofluorocarbons,* and *ozone-depleting substances*.

Fluctuations – rising and falling, such as population numbers; a variant.

Flue-gas scrubbing – treating combustion exhaust gases with chemical agents to remove pollutants; spraying crushed limestone and water into the exhaust gas stream to remove sulfur is a common scrubbing technique.

Fluidized bed combustion – high-pressure air is forced through a mixture of crushed coal and limestone particles, lifting the burning fuel and causing it to move like a boiling fluid.

Flyway – flight paths during bird migration. *Flyways generally span over continents and often oceans.*

Food aid – financial assistance intended to boost less-developed countries' living standards.

Food chain (*food webs, food networks,* or *trophic networks*) – the feeding relationships between species within an ecosystem. *The sequence of organisms through which energy and materials are transferred, in the form of food, from one trophic level to another. A group of organisms interrelated because each member feeds upon the one below it.*

Food density – the amount of food available within a given *ecotope.* (i.e., distinct landscape).

Food miles – emissions produced and resources needed to transport food and drink around the globe.

Food network (*food chain, food webs,* or *trophic networks*) – the feeding relationships between species within an ecosystem. *The sequence of organisms through which energy and materials are transferred, in the form of food, from one trophic level to another.*

Food security – enough to meet the complete requirements of all people (i.e., total global food supply equals total global demand). Food security always has components of production, access, and utilization. *For households, the ability to purchase or produce the food needed for a healthy and active life (disposable income is crucial). For national food security, the focus is on sufficient food for people in a nation, and it entails a combination of national production, imports, and exports.*

Food surpluses – excess food supplies.

Food webs (*food chain, food networks*, or *trophic networks*) – feeding relationships between species within an ecosystem. A set of interconnected food chains by which energy and nutrients circulate within an ecosystem. *A complex, interlocking series of individual food chains in an ecosystem.*

Footprint (or *ecological footprint*) – in a general environmental sense, *footprint* measures environmental impact. However, this is usually expressed as an area of productive land (*footprint*) needed to counteract the impact. *A measure of the consumption of renewable natural resources by a human population, be it that of a country, a region, or the whole world given as the area of productive land or sea required to produce the crops, meat, seafood, wood, and fiber it consumes, to sustain its energy consumption and to give space for its infrastructure.*

Forage – the plant material (mainly plant leaves) eaten by grazing animals.

Forcing – factors that affect Earth's climate. *For example, natural factors such as volcanoes and human factors such as the emission of heat-trapping gases and particles through fossil fuel combustion.*

Forcing mechanism – a process altering a climate system's energy balance (i.e., the relative balance between incoming solar radiation and outgoing infrared radiation from Earth). *Such mechanisms include changes in solar irradiance, volcanic eruptions, and enhancement of the natural greenhouse effect by emissions of greenhouse gases.* See *radiation, infrared radiation,* and *radiative forcing.*

Forest – land with a canopy cover greater than 30%.

Forest ecology – studies the interrelated patterns, processes, flora, fauna, and ecosystems within forests.

Forest management – scientific planning and administration of forest resources for sustainable harvest, multiple uses, regeneration, and maintenance of a healthy biological community.

Formula for photosynthesis – CO_2 (from air) + H_2O + Sun's energy (light) * $C_6H_{12}O_6$ (glucose) + O_2

Fossil fuel – a general term for organic materials formed from decayed plants and animals that have been converted to crude oil, coal, natural gas, or heavy oils by exposure to heat and pressure in Earth's crust over hundreds of millions of years. *Hydrocarbons are within the top layer of Earth's crust. Any hydrocarbon deposit burned for heat or power, such as coal, oil, and natural gas (produces carbon dioxide when burnt); fuels formed from once–living organisms that have become fossilized over geological time. (e.g., petroleum, natural gas, coal).*

Fossil water – groundwater that has remained in an aquifer for thousands or millions of years; when geologic changes seal the aquifer, preventing further replenishment, the water becomes trapped inside and is *fossil water. Fossil water is a limited resource and can only be used once.*

Foundation species – a dominant primary producer in its ecosystem in terms of abundance and influence on other organisms and the environment.

Founder effect – the accumulation of random genetic changes in an isolated population.

Fourth World – a political/economic category describing very developing nations with neither market economies nor central planning and either not developing or developing very slowly; also used to describe poor indigenous communities within wealthier nations.

Freegan – a person using alternative strategies for living based on limited participation in the conventional economy and minimal consumption of resources. Freegans embrace community, generosity, social concern, freedom, cooperation, and sharing – contrary to materialism, moral apathy, competition, conformity, and greed. The most notorious freegan strategy is "urban foraging" or "dumpster diving." This technique involves rummaging through the garbage of retailers, residences, offices, and other facilities for useful goods. Freegan is compounded from "free" and "vegan." Compare *affluenza, Froogle*.

Freezing condensation – a process that occurs in clouds when ice crystals trap water vapor; as the ice crystals become larger and heavier, they begin to fall as rain or snow.

Freon – DuPont's trade name for odorless, colorless, nonflammable, noncorrosive chlorofluorocarbon and hydrochlorofluorocarbon refrigerants used in air conditioning and refrigeration.

Freshwater – 1. water containing no significant amounts of salt. 2. water other than seawater covers only 2% of Earth's surface, including streams, rivers, lakes, ponds, and water associated with several kinds of wetlands. Compare *potable water*.

Freshwater ecosystems – where fresh water from streams, rivers, ponds, or lakes plays a defining role.

Friction – the rubbing of two objects against each other when one or both are moving; a significant percentage of the energy produced by an automobile engine is dissipated in friction, reducing the system's overall efficiency.

Front (*weather*) – the boundary between warm (*high-pressure*) and cold (*low-pressure*) air masses.

Frontline communities – those communities that experience climate change first and often feel the worst effects. They are communities with higher exposures, are more sensitive, and are less able to adapt to climate change impacts for various reasons.

Froogle – a play on the word frugal; people who lead low–consumption lifestyles: a person who is part of a movement towards self–sufficiency and waste reduction achieved by bartering goods and services mainly through the internet, making their products, soap, clothes, and breeding chickens and goats, growing their food, baking bread, harvesting water and energy, and helping to develop a sense of community. Sometimes, it refers to people who have resolved to buy essentials for a particular period. Compare *freegan, affluenza*.

Frost-free season – the time between the last occurrence of an air temperature of 32 °F in spring and the first occurrence of 32 °F in the subsequent fall.

Fuel assembly – hollow metal rods containing uranium oxide pellets used to fuel a nuclear reactor.

Fuel cell – an electrochemical device with no moving parts that converts the chemical energy of a fuel, such as hydrogen, and an oxidant, such as oxygen, directly into electricity; clean, quiet, and highly efficient sources of electricity.

Fuel-switching – generally, this is substituting one fuel type for another. *In the climate-change discussion, it is implicit that the substituted fuel produces lower carbon emissions per unit of energy produced than the original fuel (e.g., natural gas for coal).*

Fuelwood – branches, twigs, logs, wood chips, and other wood products harvested for use as fuel.

Fugitive emissions – 1. in the context of the *National Greenhouse Gas Inventory*, these are greenhouse gases emitted from fuel production itself, including processing, transmission, storage, and distribution processes, and including emissions from oil and natural gas exploration, venting and flaring, as well as the mining of black coal; 2. substances that enter the air without going through a smokestack, such as dust from soil erosion, strip mining, rock crushing, construction, and building demolition.

Fujita Scale – measures the intensity of a tornado based on its wind speed, diameter, and the amount of damage caused.

Full-cost pricing – the cost of commercial goods, such as electric power, that includes the private costs of inputs and the costs of the externalities required by their production and use. See *externality*.

Functional ecology – a branch of ecology that studies the roles or functions that species (or groups of species) play in an ecosystem.

Functional extinction – the effective extinction of a species or other taxon such that reports of its existence cease, the reduced population no longer plays a significant role in ecosystem function, or the population is no longer viable because it is unable to sustain healthy reproduction, even if the last individual organism of the species has not yet died.

Functional response – the intake rate of a consumer as a function of food density.

Fungi or Fungus – one of the five kingdom classifications: non-photosynthetic, eukaryotic organisms with cell walls, filamentous bodies, and absorptive nutrition. *Bacteria and fungi are primary decomposers in terrestrial (and some aquatic) ecosystems and play a crucial role in nutrient cycles.*

Fungicide – a chemical that kills *fungi*.

G

G8 (Group of Eight) – an international forum for the world's major industrialized democracies that emerged following the 1973 oil crisis and subsequent global recession. It includes Canada, France, Germany, Italy, Japan, Russia, the UK, and the US, representing about 65% of the world economy.

Gaia's hypothesis – proposes that living and nonliving parts of Earth are complex interacting systems thought of as single organisms, named after the Greek Earth mother goddess Gaia.

Gamma rays – very short wavelength forms of the electromagnetic spectrum.

Gap analysis – a biogeographical technique of mapping biological diversity and endemic species to find gaps between protected areas that leave endangered habitats vulnerable to disruption.

Garden city – a town designed with special emphasis on landscaping and rural ambiance.

Garden organics – organics derived from garden sources (e.g., prunings, grass clippings).

Gasohol – a mixture of gasoline and ethyl alcohol; used in the internal combustion engine.

Gasoline – a volatile, flammable liquid made from petroleum and used as fuel in internal combustion engines; it is made up of hydrocarbons made of 8 carbon chains.

Gause's law (or *competitive exclusion principle*) – states that two species cannot coexist in the same environment if competing for precisely the same resource, often memorably summarized as "complete competitors cannot coexist."

Gene – 1. a unit of heredity; a segment of the DNA nucleus of the cell that contains information for the synthesis of a specific protein, such as an enzyme. 2. a locatable region of a genomic sequence corresponding to a unit of inheritance associated with regulatory regions, transcribed regions, or other functional sequence regions.

Gene banks – storage for seed varieties for future breeding experiments.

Gene pool – 1. collective genetic information within a population of sexually reproducing organisms. 2. the complete set of unique alleles in a species or population.

General circulation mode (**GCM** or *global climate model*) – a computer model of the world's climate system, including the atmosphere and oceans. A global, three-dimensional computer model of the climate system that can be used to simulate human-induced climate change. *GCMs are highly complex and represent the effects of such factors as reflective and absorptive properties of atmospheric water vapor, greenhouse gas concentrations, clouds, annual and daily solar heating, ocean temperatures, and ice boundaries. The most recent GCMs include global representations of the atmosphere, oceans, and land surface.* See *climate modeling*.

General fertility rate – the crude birthrate multiplied by the percentage of women of reproductive age.

Generalist species – organisms that thrive in environmental conditions with various resources.

Appendix: Annotated Glossary of Environmental Science Terms

Genetic assimilation – the disappearance of a species as its genes are diluted through crossbreeding with a closely related species.

Genetic bottleneck – an evolutionary event in which a significant percentage of a population or species is killed or prevented from reproducing.

Genetic diversity – one of three levels of biodiversity, refers to the number of genetic characteristics.

Genetic engineering – 1. the use of various experimental techniques to produce molecules of DNA containing novel genes or combinations of genes, usually for insertion into a host cell for cloning; 2. the technology of preparing recombinant DNA in vitro by cutting up DNA molecules and splicing together fragments from more than one organism; 3. the laboratory modification of genetic material that would otherwise be subject to the forces of nature only; 4. laboratory manipulation of genetic material using molecular biology techniques to create desired characteristics in organisms.

Genetic rescue – a conservation tool used to increase the fitness of a small, imperiled population by adding genetic variation through a small number of immigrants.

Genetically modified organisms (GMO) – any organism whose genetic material has been altered using genetic engineering techniques.

Genome – the total genetic composition of an organism.

Geoengineering – intentional modifications of Earth's system (e.g., reducing climate change).

Geometric growth – a geometric pattern of increase (e.g., 2, 4, 8, 16, etc). See *exponential growth*.

Geosphere – the solid part of Earth, the main divisions being the crust, the mantle, and the liquid core. The *lithosphere* is the geosphere's part, which consists of the crust and the upper mantle.

Geothermal energy – derived from Earth's natural heat through geysers, fumaroles, hot springs, or other natural geothermal features or deep wells that pump heated groundwater. *It is used to generate electricity after transformation.*

Germplasm – genetic material that may be preserved for future agricultural, commercial, and ecological values (plant seeds or parts or animal eggs, sperm, and embryos).

Glacial earthquake – a large-scale temblor occurs in glaciated areas where glaciers move faster than one kilometer yearly.

Glacier – a multi-year surplus accumulation of snowfall above snowmelt on land resulted in a mass of ice at least 0.1 km^2 in an area showing some evidence of movement in response to gravity. *A glacier may terminate on land or in water. Glacier ice is the largest reservoir of fresh water on Earth, second only to the oceans as the largest reservoir of water. Glaciers are on every continent except Australia.*

Global acres – acres/hectares adjusted according to world average biomass productivity to be compared meaningfully across regions; 1 global acre is 1 acre of biologically productive space with average world productivity. See *global hectares*.

Global average temperature – an estimate of Earth's mean surface air temperature.

Global change – differences in the global environment may alter the capacity of Earth to sustain life. Global change encompasses climate change but includes other critical drivers of environmental change interacting with climate change, such as land use change, the alteration of the water cycle, changes in biogeochemical cycles, and biodiversity loss. See *climate change*.

Global climate model (GCM) (or *general circulation model*) – a computer model of the world's climate system, including the atmosphere and oceans.

Global cooling – a concern during the 1970s of imminent cooling of Earth's surface and atmosphere and a posited glaciation commencement.

Global dimming – the observed decrease in surface insolation that may have recently reversed. *A reduction in the amount of direct solar radiation reaching Earth's surface due to light diffusion because of air pollution and increasing levels of cloud. A phenomenon of the last 30–50 years.*

Global ecology (or *macroecology*) – studies relationships between organisms and their environment at large spatial scales to characterize and explain statistical patterns of abundance, distribution, and diversity.

Global ecophagy – the destruction of Earth's ecosystems.

Global environmentalism – a concern for and action to help solve global environmental problems.

Global hectares – acres/hectares adjusted according to world average biomass productivity so they can be compared meaningfully across regions; 1 global hectare is 1 hectare of biologically productive space with average world productivity. See *global acres*.

Global temperature record (or *historical temperature record*) – the temperature fluctuations of the atmosphere and oceans through various periods.

Global warming (GW) – average temperature increases of Earth's near-surface atmosphere and oceans. The increase in global temperatures mainly caused by human-induced enhanced greenhouse effect trapping the Sun's heat in Earth's atmosphere; Earth's average temperature has risen and fallen over millions of years, such as during the Ice Ages. *Any period in which the temperature of Earth's atmosphere increases; the theory of such changes. The concern is that the increase in greenhouse gases generated by humans, particularly carbon dioxide emissions from fossil fuels, will contribute to global warming; the preferred term is "global climate change" because changes in average temperatures have effects on other aspects of weather and climate, including the amount of rainfall.*

Global warming controversy – socio-political issues surrounding the theory of global warming.

Global warming period – any period in which the temperature of Earth's atmosphere increases.

Global warming potential – a system of multipliers devised to enable the warming effects of different gases to be compared. *Measures how much a given mass of greenhouse gas is estimated to contribute to global warming. A measure of the energy that a gas absorbs over a particular period (usually 100 years), compared to carbon dioxide.*

Globalization – 1. the expansion of interactions to a global or worldwide scale; 2. the increasing interdependence, integration, and interaction among people and organizations worldwide; 3. a mix of economic, social, technological, cultural, and political interrelationships.

Glyphosate – a nonselective herbicide particularly effective against perennial weeds. The active ingredient in the herbicide *Roundup*™.

Governance – the decision-making procedure; who makes decisions, how they are made, and with what information; and the structures and processes for collective decision-making involving governmental and non-governmental actors.

Grasslands – an area where grasses dominate the vegetation. *A biome dominated by grasses and associated herbaceous plants.*

Green (*sustainability*) – indicates environmental consideration (e.g., green plumbers, green purchasing, etc.). *Sometimes used as nouns* (e.g., the Greens, green plumbers, green purchasing, etc.).

Green architecture – building design that moves towards self-sufficient sustainability by adopting *circular metabolism*.

Green design – 1. environmentally sustainable design. 2. designing objects, services, and buildings to achieve environmental sustainability.

Green manure – a cover crop grown primarily to add nutrients and organic matter to the soil.

Great Pacific garbage patch – a gyre of marine debris particles discovered in the central North Pacific Ocean between 1985 and 1988. *The patch is characterized by exceptionally high relative pelagic concentrations of plastic, chemical sludge, and other debris that the currents of the North Pacific Gyre have trapped.*

Green plans – integrated national environmental plans for reducing pollution and resource consumption while achieving sustainable development and environmental restoration.

Green political parties – political organizations promoting environmental protection, participatory democracy, grassroots organization, and sustainable development.

Green power – electricity generated from clean, renewable energy sources (such as solar, wind, biomass, or hydropower) and supplied through the grid.

Green products and services – have a reduced effect on health and the environment compared with competing products or services. *Green products or services contain recycled content, reduce waste, conserve energy or water, use less packaging, and reduce the number of toxins disposed of or consumed.*

Green purchasing – purchasing goods and services that minimize environmental impacts and are socially just.

Green Revolution – the ongoing transformation of agriculture that led in some places to significant increases in agricultural production between the 1940s and 1960s. *It usually requires high inputs of water, plant nutrients, and pesticides.*

Green Star – a voluntary rating system for buildings for green design, covering nine impact categories. *The highest rating is six stars, which equals a world leader in sustainability.*

Green waste – plant material discarded as non-putrescible waste – includes tree and shrub cuttings and pruning, grass clippings, leaves, natural (untreated) timber waste, and weeds (noxious or otherwise).

Greenhouse debt – the measure to which a person, incorporated association, business enterprise, government instrumentality, or geographic community exceeds its permitted greenhouse footprint and emits greenhouse gases contributing to global warming and climate change.

Greenhouse effect – 1. the insulating effect of atmospheric greenhouse gases (e.g., water vapor, carbon dioxide, methane) that keeps Earth's temperature about 60 °F (16 °C) warmer than otherwise. 2. the process in which the emission of infrared radiation by the atmosphere warms a planet's surface. *The warming of Earth's climate caused by solar irradiance trapped in the atmosphere.*

The phenomenon is caused by atmospheric gases, which allow the Sun's energy to reach Earth's surface but subsequently absorb heat that is radiated back from the warmed surface. Trapping and build-up of heat in the atmosphere (troposphere) near Earth's surface. Some heat flowing back toward space from Earth's surface is absorbed by water vapor, carbon dioxide, ozone, and other atmospheric gases and reradiated toward Earth's surface. *If greenhouse gases' atmospheric concentrations rise, the lower atmosphere's average temperature will gradually increase.* See *greenhouse gas, anthropogenic, climate,* and *global warming.* Compare *enhanced greenhouse effect.*

Greenhouse gas (GHG) – 1. any gas that absorbs infrared radiation (i.e., greenhouse effect) and traps heat in the atmosphere. 2. contributes to the greenhouse effect; gaseous atmospheric constituents, both natural and from human activity, absorb and re–emit infrared radiation. Greenhouse gases include carbon dioxide, methane, nitrous oxide, ozone, chlorofluorocarbons, hydrochlorofluorocarbons, hydrofluorocarbons, perfluorocarbons, and sulfur hexafluoride.

Greenhouse gases are a natural part of the atmosphere, including carbon dioxide (CO_2), methane (CH_4, persisting 9–15 years with a greenhouse warming potential (GWP) 22 times CO_2), nitrous oxide (N_2O persists 120 years with a GWP of 310), ozone (O_3), hydrofluorocarbons, perfluorocarbons, and sulfur hexafluoride. *Water vapor (H_2O) is the most abundant greenhouse gas.*

>   Carbon dioxide (CO_2) – a gas entering the atmosphere through burning fossil fuels (coal, natural gas, and oil), solid waste, trees, and wood products, and because of specific chemical reactions (e.g., manufacture of cement). Carbon dioxide is removed from the atmosphere (or *sequestered*) when plants absorb it as part of the biological carbon cycle during photosynthesis.
>
>   Methane (CH_4) – a gas emitted while producing and transporting coal, natural gas, and oil. Methane emissions also result from livestock and other agricultural practices and the decay of organic waste in municipal solid waste landfills.

Appendix: Annotated Glossary of Environmental Science Terms

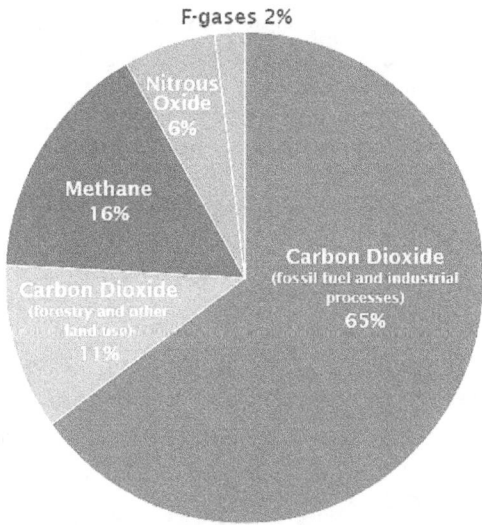

Global greenhouse gases by gas emitted, EPA, 2014

Nitrous oxide (N_2O) – a gas emitted during agricultural and industrial activities and during the combustion of fossil fuels and solid waste.

Fluorinated gases – hydrofluorocarbons, perfluorocarbons, sulfur hexafluoride, and nitrogen trifluoride are synthetic, potent greenhouse gases emitted from various industrial processes. Fluorinated gases sometimes substitute stratospheric ozone-depleting substances (e.g., chlorofluorocarbons, hydrochlorofluorocarbons, and halons). These gases are typically emitted in smaller quantities, but because they are potent greenhouse gases, they are High Global Warming Potential gases (*High GWP gases*).

Greenhouse gas inventory – a type of emission inventory that includes greenhouse gas emissions from source categories and removal by carbon sinks.

Greenlash (or *environmental backlash*) – dramatic changes in ecosystems' structure and behavior.

Greenwashing – companies that portray themselves as environmentally friendly when their business practices do not back this up. *Generally, this applies to excessive use of green marketing and packaging when this does not consider the total ecological footprint.*

Greenwater – water replenishing soil moisture, evaporating from soil, plants, and other surfaces, and transpired by plants. In nature, the global average amount of rainfall becoming green water is about 60%. Of the green water, about 55% falls on forests, 25% on grasslands, and 20% on crops. *Green water productivity increases through rainwater harvesting, infiltration, and runoff collection. Green water cannot be piped or drunk (cannot be sold) and is generally ignored by water management authorities. However, it is crucial to plants and agriculture and needs careful management as an essential part of the global water cycle.*

Greywater – household wastewater that has not encountered toilet waste; includes water from baths, showers, bathrooms, washing machines, laundry, and kitchen sinks. *It can be reused without purification for some purpose.*

Gross domestic product (GDP) – the economic activity within national boundaries.

Gross national product (GNP) – goods and services produced in a national economy; *Gross domestic product* (GDP) distinguishes economic activity within a country from offshore corporations.

Gross primary productivity – total carbon assimilation.

Ground cover – any plant growing in an area of ground, protecting topsoil from erosion and drought.

Groundwater – 1. water found below the surface – usually in porous rocks, soil, or underground aquifers. 2. water beneath the ground surface in soil pore spaces and the fractures of lithologic formation. *It does not include water or crystallization held by chemical bonds in rocks or moisture in upper soil layers.*

Group of Eight (G8) – an international forum for the world's major industrialized democracies that emerged following the 1973 oil crisis and subsequent global recession. It includes Canada, France, Germany, Italy, Japan, Russia, the UK, and the US, representing about 65% of the world economy.

Growth – increase in size, weight, power, etc.

Guest – a generic term for parasitic, mutualistic, and commensalist symbionts.

Gulf Stream – a powerful, warm, and swift Atlantic Ocean current originating in the Gulf of Mexico, exits through the Strait of Florida and follows U.S. eastern coastlines and Newfoundland before crossing the Atlantic Ocean.

Gully erosion – removal of soil layers, creating channels or ravines too large to be removed by normal tillage operations.

H

Habitat – an ecological or environmental area that is inhabited by a species. A specific ecological area inhabited by specific plant and animal species.

Habitat conservation plans – agreements under which property owners are allowed to harvest resources or develop the land if habitats are conserved or replaced to benefit resident endangered or threatened species; *some incidental "taking" or loss of endangered species is generally allowed in such plans.*

Habitat fragmentation – the discontinuation of a species' habitat caused by environmental change. *A process during which larger habitat areas are broken into several smaller patches of smaller total area, isolated by a matrix of habitats, unlike the original habitat.*

Hadley cells – circulation patterns of atmospheric convection currents sinking and rising in several intermediate bands.

Halocarbons – compounds containing chlorine, bromine, fluorine, and carbon. Such compounds are potent atmospheric greenhouse gases. *Chlorine and bromine-containing halocarbons are involved in the depletion of the ozone layer.*

Halophyte – a *salt-loving* plant.

Halophile – a *salt-loving* organism.

Hard waste (or *municipal solid waste*) – household trash (or rubbish) not generally accepted into garbage bins (e.g., old stoves, mattresses). Generally, *garbage* means food waste, while *rubbish* or *trash* refers to other solid, nonhazardous waste.

Hard water – water with high mineral content.

Hazardous chemicals – dangerous chemicals, including flammables, explosives, irritants, sensitizers, acids, and caustics; many are hazardous in high concentrations but harmless when diluted.

Hazardous waste – any discarded material containing substances known to be toxic, mutagenic, carcinogenic, or teratogenic to humans or other life forms; ignitable, corrosive, explosive, or highly reactive alone or with other materials.

Health – a state of physical and emotional well-being; the absence of disease or ailment.

Heap-leach extraction – a technique for separating gold from highly low-grade ores; crushed ore is piled in massive heaps and sprayed with a dilute alkaline-cyanide solution, which percolates through the pile to extract the gold, which is separated from the effluent in a processing plant; this process has a high potential for water pollution.

Heat – energy derived from the motion of molecules; *it is a form of energy into which other forms of energy may be degraded.*

Heat capacity – the amount of heat energy that must be added or subtracted to change the temperature of a body; water has a high heat capacity.

Heat island (or *urban heat island*) – an urban area with temperatures higher than the surrounding non-urban area. *As urban areas develop, buildings, roads, and other infrastructure replace open land and vegetation. These surfaces absorb more solar energy, creating higher temperatures in urban areas.*

Heat of vaporization – the heat energy required to convert water from a liquid to a gas.

Heat stress – the negative health impacts, such as heat stroke or heat exhaustion, caused by exposure to extreme heat or long periods in hot environments.

Heat tax – a tax imposed on the use of energy supplies.

Heat waves – prolonged excessive heat, often combined with excessive humidity. *A period of abnormally hot weather lasting days to weeks.*

Heath – low-growing woody vegetation found on free-draining acidic soils.

Heavy metals – mercury, lead, cadmium, and nickel- are highly toxic in tiny quantities and can be fatal and accumulate in the environment with long-term cumulative effects on humans.

Heavy precipitation events – an episode of abnormally high rain or snow. *Extreme is a statistical concept that varies depending on the historical record's location, season, and length.*

Heiligendamm process – an initiative to institutionalize high-level dialogue between the G8 countries and the five crucial emerging economies, known as Outreach 5 (O 5), consisting of China, Mexico, India, Brazil, and South Africa.

Hemoglobin – the iron-containing respiratory pigment in red blood cells of vertebrates, consisting of about 6 percent heme and 94 percent globin.

Herbicide – a chemical that kills or inhibits plant growth.

Herbivore – an organism that eats only plants.

Herbivory – predation in which an organism known as an *herbivore* primarily consumes autotrophs such as plants, algae, and photosynthesizing bacteria.

Heterarchy – a way of organizing that does not include rank (i.e., each element possesses the same level of importance or authority). Compare *hierarchy*.

Heterotroph (or *chemoorganotroph*) – 1. an organism requiring organic substrates to obtain carbon for growth and development. 2. an organism incapable of synthesizing its food must feed upon other organisms' organic compounds.

Hexafluoroethane (C_2F_6) – the perfluorocarbon counterpart to the hydrocarbon ethane; a non-flammable gas negligibly soluble in water and slightly soluble in alcohol. It is a highly potent and long-lived greenhouse gas. *Due to the high energy of C-F bonds, hexafluoroethane is inert and thus is a highly stable greenhouse gas, with an atmospheric lifetime of 10,000 years. It has a global warming potential (GWP) of 9200 and an ozone depletion potential (ODP) of 0. Hexafluoroethane is included in the IPCC list of greenhouse gases.*

Hidden energy – energy within a system that one is not aware of.

Hierarchy – an organization of parts in which control from the top (generally with few parts) proceeds through a series of levels (ranks) to the bottom (generally consisting of many parts). Compare *heterarchy*.

High-density polyethylene (HDPE) – a polyethylene plastic used to make products such as milk bottles, pipes, and shopping bags. *HDPE may be colored or opaque.*

High-level wastes – highly radioactive wastes.

High-level waste repository – where intensely radioactive wastes are buried and kept unexposed to groundwater and earthquakes for tens of thousands of years.

High-quality energy – intense, concentrated, and high-temperature is considered high-quality because of its usefulness in performing work.

Histogram – a statistical graph of a frequency distribution in which vertical rectangles of heights are proportionate to corresponding frequencies; used to graph distributions of populations, such as the population percentage in distinct age groups.

Historical temperature record (or *global temperature record*) – the fluctuations of the temperature of the atmosphere and the oceans through various periods.

Hockey stick graph – reconstructions of the Northern Hemisphere or *global mean temperature* changes during the past 600 to 11,300 years, a name coined by Mann, Bradley, and Hughes in 1999.

Holistic science – the study of integrated systems rather than isolated parts; often takes a descriptive or interpretive approach.

Holocene – a geological period that began approximately 11,550 calendar years BP (before present; about 9600 BC) and continued to the Anthropocene.

Holocene Climatic Optimum – a warm period during 9,000 to 5,000 years AD.

Home energy audits – analyzing the energy expenditure in a home, including the loss of energy.

Homeostasis – a system that regulates its internal environment and maintains a constant and stable condition (e.g., endothermic animals maintain a constant body temperature). *The property of an open or closed system, especially a living organism. Regulating the internal environment to maintain a stable, constant condition.*

Homestead Act – a U.S. legislation passed in 1862 allowing any citizen or applicant for citizenship over 21 years old and the head of a family to acquire 160 acres of public land by living on it and cultivating it for five years.

Homoclime – a region with the same weather patterns (i.e., climate) as the one under investigation.

Horsepower (hp) – a power unit in physics equal to 550 foot-pounds/sec or 745.7 watts.

Horton overland flow – the tendency of water to flow horizontally across land surfaces when rainfall has exceeded infiltration capacity and depression storage capacity.

Host – an organism that harbors a parasitic, mutualistic, or commensal symbiont.

Host organism – an organism that provides lodging for a parasite.

Hot deserts – deserts of the American Southwest and Mexico, characterized by extreme summer heat and cacti.

House energy rating – an assessment of the energy efficiency of a residential house or unit design using a 5-star scale.

Household metabolism – the passage of food, energy, water, goods, and waste through the household unit, like the metabolic activity of an organism. Compare *industrial metabolism*.

Human ecology – the study of the interactions of humans with the environment. *A branch of ecology that studies the relationships between humans and their natural, social, and built environments.*

Human equivalent (He) – the approximate human daily energy requirement of 12,500 kJ or its approximate energy generating capacity at a basal metabolic rate, which is equivalent to about 80 watts or 3.47222 kWh per day; a 100-watt light bulb, therefore, runs at 1.25 He.

Human resources – human wisdom, experience, skill, labor, and enterprise.

Humus – 1. organic material in soil lending it a dark brown or black coloration. 2. semi-persistent organic matter in the soil that can no longer be recognized as tissue. 3. sticky, brown, insoluble residue from the bodies of dead plants and animals. *Humus gives soil its structure, coating mineral particles and holding them together; it is a significant source of plant nutrients.*

Hurricanes – large cyclonic oceanic storms with heavy rain and winds exceeding 119 km/hr. (74 mph). Intense, low–pressure weather systems; mid-latitude cyclones are atmospheric circulations that rotate clockwise in the Southern Hemisphere and anticlockwise in the Northern Hemisphere and are generally associated with stronger winds, unsettled conditions, cloudiness, and rainfall. Tropical *cyclones* (called *hurricanes* in the Northern Hemisphere) cause storm surges in coastal areas.

Hurricane Nor'easter – a hurricane that generates from the northeast and moves southwest.

Hybrid gas-electric motor – automobiles run on electric power and small gasoline or diesel engines.

Hydro energy – potential and kinetic energy of water used to generate electricity.

Hydrocarbons – carbon and hydrogen molecules in petroleum, coal, and natural gas as well as derived products such as plastics. An organic chemical compound containing only hydrogen and carbon atoms, arranged in rows or rings or both, and connected by single, double, or triple bonds; constitute an extensive group, including alkanes, alkenes, and alkynes (e.g., petroleum, coal, methane).

Hydrochlorofluorocarbons (HCFCs) – compounds containing hydrogen, fluorine, chlorine, and carbon atoms. However, ozone-depleting substances are less potent at destroying stratospheric ozone than chlorofluorocarbons (CFCs). They have been introduced as temporary replacements for CFCs and are also greenhouse gases. See *ozone-depleting substances*.

Hydroelectric power – the electrical power generated using the power of falling water.

Hydrofluorocarbons (HFCs) – compounds containing only hydrogen, fluorine, and carbon atoms. They were introduced as alternatives to ozone-depleting substances for industrial, commercial, and personal needs. HFCs are emitted as by-products of industrial processes and used in manufacturing. They do not significantly deplete the stratospheric ozone layer but are powerful greenhouse gases with global warming potential ranging from 140 (HFC-152a) to 11,700 (HFC-23).

Hydrologic cycle (or *water cycle*) – the cyclic process of evaporation and condensation of water and its distribution across Earth as driven by solar energy. *The natural cycle of water from evaporation, transpiration in the atmosphere, condensation (rain and snow), and flows back to the ocean (e.g., rivers). Evaporation involves the vertical and horizontal transport of vapor, condensation, precipitation, and water flow from continents to oceans. It is a major factor in determining climate through its influence on surface vegetation, clouds, snow and ice, and soil moisture. The hydrologic cycle is responsible for 25 to 30% of the mid-latitude heat transport from the equatorial to polar regions.*

Hydrophyte (or *aquatic plants*) – plants adapted to aquatic environments. *They are hydrophytes or macrophytes, distinguishing them from algae and other microphytes. Macrophytes are plants that grow in or near water and are emergent, submergent, or floating.*

Hydrosphere – the combined mass of water found on, under, and above Earth's surface. Earth's water, including water in the sea, streams, lakes, waterbodies, soil, groundwater, and air.

Hydrothermal vent – an underwater steaming fissure that has a unique ecosystem.

Hydroxyl radical (·OH) – the monovalent group ·OH in such compounds as bases and some acids and alcohols; this radical is characteristic of hydroxides, oxygen acids, alcohols, glycols, phenols, and hemiacetals.

Hyperalimentation (or *overnutrition*) – when the amount of nutrients ingested exceeds what is needed for average growth, metabolism, and development.

Hypothesis – a tentative explanation that accounts for facts and can be tested for further investigation.

Hypoxia – reduced oxygen content of air or a body of water detrimental to aerobic organisms.

I

Ice age – a long-term reduction in the temperature of Earth's climate, resulting in expansions of continental ice sheets, polar ice sheets, and alpine glaciers. *A cylindrical section of ice removed from a glacier or ice sheet to study past climate patterns. By performing chemical analyses on air trapped in ice, scientists estimate the percentage of carbon dioxide and trace gases in the atmosphere at a given time. Analysis of the ice itself can give indications of historic temperatures.*

Ice core – a sample from snow and ice accumulation over many years that have re-crystallized and trapped air bubbles from previous periods.

Igneous rocks – crystalline minerals solidified from molten magma deep in Earth's interior (e.g., basalt, rhyolite, andesite, lava, and granite).

Illegitimate receiver – an organism that intercepts a signal intended for another organism to the fitness detriment of either the signaler or the legitimate signal receiver.

Impervious – incapable of being penetrated.

Inaccessible – not available.

Inbreeding depression – in a small population, an accumulation of harmful genetic traits (through random mutations and natural selection) that lowers the viability and reproductive success of enough individuals to affect the whole population.

Incineration – combustion (i.e., *chemical oxidation*) of waste to treat or dispose of that material.

Incinerator – an apparatus, such as a furnace, for burning waste.

Indicators – 1. quantitative markers for monitoring progress towards desired goals. 2. an observation or calculation allows scientists, analysts, decision-makers, and others to track environmental trends, understand key factors influencing the environment, and identify effects on ecosystems and society.

Indicator species – any biological species that defines a trait or characteristic of the environment. *Any species that defines a characteristic of its environment. The presence or abundance of organisms of these species indicates the health of a given ecosystem.*

Indigenous knowledge – refers to Indigenous peoples' systems of observing, monitoring, researching, recording, communicating, and learning that is required, as for any group, to support survival and flourishing in an ecosystem and the socially adaptive capacity to adjust to or prepare for changes.

Indirect emissions – release of greenhouse gases resulting from generating electricity used in a building, home, or business. These emissions are "indirect" because the actual emissions occur at the power plant that generates electricity, not at the building using electricity.

Indirect energy – the energy generated in and accounted for by the broader economy as a consequence of an agent's actions or demands.

Inductive reasoning – inferring general principles from specific examples.

Industrial agriculture – a form of modern farming involving industrialized production of livestock, poultry, fish, or crops.

Industrial ecology (the term originated by Harry Zvi Evan, 1973) – 1. a period in the late 18th and early 19th centuries when significant changes in agriculture, manufacturing, and transportation profoundly affected socioeconomic and cultural conditions. 2. the observation that nature produces no waste provides an example of sustainable waste management. Natural Capitalism espouses industrial ecology as one of its four pillars: energy conservation, material conservation, redefinition of commodity markets, and product stewardship in a service economy.

Industrial metabolism – the processes to which materials and components are subjected in industrial ecosystems. It is analogous to the metabolic processes occurring with food and nutrients in biological systems. Like biological metabolism, industrial metabolism may be addressed at several levels. Compare *household metabolism*.

Industrial Revolution – a period in the late 18th and early 19th centuries when significant changes in agriculture, manufacturing, and transportation profoundly affected socioeconomic and cultural conditions. *A period of rapid industrial growth with far-reaching social and economic consequences, beginning in England during the second half of the 18th century and spreading to Europe and later to other countries, including the United States. The Industrial Revolution marked the beginning of a strong increase in the combustion of fossil fuels and related emissions of carbon dioxide.*

Industrial timber (or *roundwood*) – trees used for lumber, plywood, veneer, particleboard, chipboard, and paper.

Inertial confinement – a nuclear fusion process in which a small pellet of nuclear fuel is bombarded with extremely high-intensity laser light.

Infrared radiation – light whose wavelength is longer than the red color in the visible spectrum but shorter than microwave radiation. Infrared radiation can be perceived as heat. Earth's surface, atmosphere, and clouds emit infrared radiation, terrestrial or long-wave radiation. In contrast, solar radiation is mainly short-wave radiation because of the temperature of the Sun.
See *radiation, greenhouse effect, enhanced greenhouse effect*, and *global warming*.

Infiltration – 1. water movement below topsoil to the plant roots and below. 2. the process by which water on the ground surface enters the soil. 3. the act or process of infiltrating water into a porous substance or fluid into the cells of an organ or part of the body.

Informal economy – small-scale individual or family businesses in temporary locations outside the control of normal regulatory agencies.

Inherent value – ethical values or rights that exist as an intrinsic or essential characteristic of a particular thing or class of things simply by their existence.

Inholdings – private lands within public parks, forests, or wildlife refuges.

Insecticide – a pesticide used to control insects in developmental forms.

Insolation – incoming solar radiation. The amount of solar radiation reaching the surface of Earth. The amount of solar energy reaching Earth is 70 percent. Earth's surface absorbs 51 % of insolation. Water vapor and dust account for 16 % of the energy absorbed.

Instinctive behavior – the inherent inclination of an organism towards a particular complex behavior.

In-stream – using freshwater where it occurs, usually a river or stream. *Hydroelectricity, recreation, tourism, scientific and cultural uses, ecosystem maintenance, and waste dilution.*

Instrumental temperature record – the fluctuations of the temperature of the atmosphere and the oceans as measured by temperature sensors. *The longest-running quasi-global record started in 1850.*

Instrumental value – value (or worth) of objects satisfying the needs and wants of moral agents; objects that can be used for some desirable end.

Insular biogeography – the study of the distributions of biological communities on islands.

Intangible resources – factors that cannot be contained or measured, such as open space, beauty, serenity, wisdom, diversity, and satisfaction.

Intergovernmental Panel on Climate Change (IPCC) (1988) – jointly by the UN Environment Program and the World Meteorological Organization. IPCC assesses scientific and technical literature related to significant components of climate change. *Leading experts on climate change and environmental, social, and economic sciences from 60 nations have helped the IPCC to prepare periodic assessments of the scientific underpinnings for understanding global climate change and its consequences. With its capacity for reporting on climate change, its consequences, and the viability of adaptation and mitigation measures, the IPCC is considered the official advisory body to the world's governments on the state of the science of the climate change issue. For example, the IPCC developed internationally accepted methods for conducting national greenhouse gas emission inventories.*

Integrated pest management (IPM) – a pest control strategy using several complementary methods. For example, natural predators and parasites, pest–resistant varieties, cultural practices, biological controls, physical techniques, and strategic use of pesticides. *An ecologically-based pest-control strategy that relies on natural mortality factors, such as natural enemies, weather, cultural control methods, and carefully applied doses of pesticides. Minimizes chemical use by combining pest control options. IPM does not eliminate pests but reduces pest populations to acceptable levels, an ecologically based pest control strategy relying on natural mortality and control tactics that minimally disrupt these factors.*

Integrated product life-cycle management – managing all phases of goods and services to be environmentally friendly and sustainable.

Intercropping – the agricultural practice of cultivating crops simultaneously in the same space.

Interdecadal Pacific Oscillation (IPO) – a 15 to 30-year cycle between warm or cool waters in the north and the south Pacific Ocean.

Intergenerational equity – intention of leaving the world in the best condition for future generations.

Intergovernmental Panel on Climate Change (IPCC, 1988) – established by the World Meteorological Organization and the UN Environment Program to provide the scientific and technical foundation for the United Nations Framework Convention on Climate Change (UNFCCC), primarily through periodic assessment reports.

Intermediate disturbance hypothesis – predicting how species diversity will change with varying levels of disturbance.

Intermittent – any phenomenon that stops and starts at intervals.

Internal costs – the monetary or otherwise expenses borne by those who use a resource.

Internal water footprint – the water embodied in goods produced within a country (although these may be subsequently exported). Compare *external water footprints*.

Internalizing costs – those who reap the benefits of resource use will bear the external costs.

Interplanting – the system of planting two or more crops, either mixed or in alternating rows, in the same field; protects the soil and makes more efficient land use.

Interpretive science – an explanation based on observation and description of objects or systems rather than isolated parts.

Interspecific competition – competition for resources between members of species in a community. *A form of competition between individuals of species (e.g., when species use the same resources in an environment).* Contrast *intraspecific competition*.

Intertidal zone – a coastal area periodically submerged underwater by tides.

Intraspecific competition – a form of competition between individuals of the same species, e.g., when members of the same species compete for territories or access to mates. Compare *interspecific competitions*.

Intrinsic value – the value of something independent of its utility.

Introduced species (*alien species* or *exotic species*) – organisms living outside its native distributional range but which have arrived there by human activity, directly or indirectly, and either deliberately or accidentally. *A non-native species brought to an area either by accident or intentionally. An introduced species may prey upon or compete more successfully with one or more species that are native to the community and thereby alter the nature of the community.*

Inundation – the submergence of land by water, particularly in a coastal setting.

Invasive species – any non-native, introduced species that adversely affects the habitats and bioregions it invades economically, environmentally, or ecologically. *A non-native species whose introduction to an area causes economic, environmental, or harm to human health.*

Ion exchange – a reversible chemical reaction where ions with the same charge are switched. *This principle is used in the purification of wastewater.*

Ionizing radiation – high-energy electromagnetic radiation or energetic subatomic particles released by nuclear decay.

Ionosphere – the lower part of the thermosphere.

Ions – electrically charged atoms that have gained or lost electrons.

Iris hypothesis (Richard Lindzen et al., 2001) – increased sea surface temperature in the tropics would result in reduced cirrus clouds and, thus, more infrared radiation leakage from Earth's atmosphere.

Irradiance – the amount of electromagnetic radiation reaching a surface (watts per square meter).

Irrigation – 1. watering of plants, no matter what system is used. 2. an essential component of agriculture developed across cultures.

Irrigation index (Ii) – an efficiency indicator showing the degree of match between water supplied and water used. Ideal rating = 1 with an Ii of 1.5 for a 50% oversupply of water.

Irrigation scheduling – watering plants according to their needs.

Irruptive growth – an expansion in population followed by a dramatic decrease in population. See *Malthusian growth*.

Island biogeography – the study of colonization rates and species extinction rates on islands or other isolated areas based on size, shape, and distance from other inhabited regions.

ISO 14001 (1996) – an international standard for companies seeking to certify their environmental management system. The International Organization for Standardization (ISO) specifies the requirements for environmental management systems in companies and institutions to minimize harmful environmental effects and the goal of continually improving environmental performance.

Isobars (or *isopiestic*) – lines on a weather map connecting points of equal atmospheric pressure.

Isolated – a population separated from other populations of the species (as on an island).

Isotopes – forming a single element differing in atomic mass due to the number of neutrons in nucleus.

J

J curve (or *J-shaped curve*) – a growth curve that depicts exponential growth; called a J curve because of its shape; it looks like a "J."

Jet stream – a high-speed, meandering wind current, generally moving from a westerly direction at altitudes of 10 to 15 miles and speeds often exceeding 250 miles per hour, like oceanic currents in extent and effect on climate.

Joule (J) – the basic unit of energy; the equivalent of 1 watt of power radiated or dissipated for 1 second; natural gas consumption is measured in megajoules (MJ), where 1 MJ = 1,000,000 J. On large scales, it may be measured in gigajoules (GJ), where 1 GJ = 1,000,000,000 J.

Jungle – a dense, wet, humid forest, often tropical, which supports many wild plant and animal species.

K

k-selected species – a species that forms a group of strong competitors in a crowded environment and has fewer but stronger offspring. Contrast *r-selected species*.

Karst – an area of irregular limestone in which erosion has produced fissures, sinkholes, underground streams, and caverns.

Keeling Curve – a graph showing variations in atmospheric carbon dioxide concentration since 1958.

Kerosene – a colorless, flammable oil distilled from petroleum and used as a fuel for jet engines, heating, cooking, and lighting.

Keystone species – an organism with a disproportionate environmental effect relative to its abundance, affecting many other organisms in an ecosystem and determining the types and numbers of other species in a *community*.

Kinetic energy (KE) – energy contained in a body because of its motion; equal to one-half the mass of the body times the square of its speed (e.g., a rock rolling down a hill, the wind blowing through the trees, water flowing over a dam).

Known resources – those that have been located and are not mapped but are likely to become economical in the foreseeable future.

Kwashiorkor – a widespread human protein deficiency disease resulting from a starchy diet low in protein and essential amino acids.

Kyoto Protocol (1997) – an international agreement adopted in Kyoto, Japan, sets binding emission targets for developed countries to reduce emissions by 5.2 percent below 1990 levels. A UN Framework Convention on Climate Change modification. *See post–Kyoto Protocol negotiations on greenhouse gas emissions.*

Kyoto unit (or *Removal unit*) – a tradable carbon credit represents an allowance to emit one metric ton of greenhouse gases absorbed by a removal or carbon sink activity in an Annex I country.

L

Lake – an inland body of water localized in a basin and often fed by a river.

Lake effect snow – lake-generated snow squalls form when cold air passes for long distances over relatively warm waters of a large lake, gathering moisture and heat from the lake and depositing the moisture in the form of snow upon reaching the downwind shore.

Land cover – the physical characteristics of the land surface, such as crops, trees, or concrete.

Land reform – democratic redistribution of land ownership to recognize the rights of those who work the land to a fair share of the products of their labor.

Land use – activities taking place on land, such as growing food, cutting trees, or building cities.

Land use, land-use change, and forestry (LULUCF) – land uses and land–use changes can act as sinks or emission sources. The *Kyoto Protocol* allows parties to receive emissions credit for certain LULUCF activities to reduce net emissions. *An estimated one–fifth of global emissions result from LULUCF activities.*

Land use planning – a branch of public policy encompassing various disciplines that seek to order and regulate land use efficiently and ethically.

Landfill (or *dump*) – land waste disposal sites where waste is generally spread in thin layers, compacted, and regularly covered with fresh soil (e.g., daily). *It is a site for waste materials disposal by burial and is the oldest form of waste treatment. Solid waste disposal in which refuse is buried between soil layers. A method often used to reclaim low–lying ground. Landfill is used as a noun to refer to waste itself.*

Landfill gas – emissions from biodegrading waste in landfills, including CO_2, CH_4, and small amounts of nitrogen and oxygen with traces of toluene, benzene, and vinyl chloride. The gas emissions from biodegrading waste in a landfill include carbon dioxide (CO_2), methane (CH_4), and small amounts of nitrogen (N) and oxygen (O) with traces of toluene, benzene, and vinyl chloride.

Landfill levy – 1. taxes applied (at differential rates) to municipal, commercial, and industrial waste and prescribed wastes disposed to licensed landfills; 2. taxes to foster the environmentally sustainable use of resources and best practices in waste management.

Landfill prohibition – banning a particular material or product type from disposal to landfills. *It occurs occasionally, for example, when a preferable waste management option is available.*

Landscape ecology – the study of the reciprocal effects of spatial patterns on ecological processes (i.e., how landscape history shapes the features of the land and the organisms that inhabit it, as well as reaction to and interpretation of the land). *An interdisciplinary branch of ecology combining aspects of ecology, botany, biogeography, physical geography, and environmental planning.*

Landslide – the sudden fall of earth from a hill or cliff, often triggered by an earthquake or heavy rain.

La Niña – is a coupled ocean-atmosphere phenomenon that is the colder counterpart of El Niño, as part of the broader El Niño–Southern Oscillation climate pattern. La Niña [*the little girl*] is analogous to El Niño [*the little boy*]. During La Niña, the sea surface temperature across the equatorial Eastern Central Pacific Ocean is below average by 5.4 to 9 °F (3 to 5 °C). La Niña persists for at least five months and has effects on the weather across the globe.

Large marine ecosystems – 64 global extensive coastal sea areas by the National Oceanic and Atmospheric Administration, where primary production and biomass are higher than in the open ocean.

Latitude – 1. the angular distance north or south of the equator, measured in degrees along a meridian, as on a map or globe; 2. a region of Earth considered with its distance from the equator (e.g., the temperate latitudes). 3. north or south of the equator, designated 0°. Lines of latitude are parallel to the equator and circle the globe. North and South poles are at 90° North and South latitude.

Lava (or *magma*) – magma spewing from an erupting volcano. Magma is the molten rock beneath the Earth's surface (or *terrestrial planets*; Mercury, Venus, Earth, and Mars with compact rocky surfaces and innermost four planets) and collects in a magma chamber and *lava* when ejected by volcanoes.

Law of the minimum – the concept that the growth or survival of a population is directly related to the life requirement in the least supply and not to a combination of factors.

Leachate (*waste*) – the mixture of water and dissolved solids (possibly toxic) that accumulates as water passes through waste and collects at the bottom of a landfill site.

Leaching – the movement of a chemical from the upper layers of soil into the lower layers of groundwater by being dissolved in water.

Lead – a soft, malleable, ductile, bluish-white, dense metallic element, extracted chiefly from galena and used in containers and pipes for corrosives, solder and type metal, bullets, radiation shielding, paints, and antiknock compounds (atomic number 82; atomic weight 207.19; melting point 327.5 °C; boiling point 1,744 °C; specific gravity 11.35; valence 2, 4).

Leaf area index (LAI) – the ratio of photosynthetic leaf area to the ground area covered (optimal for photosynthesis = 3–5). *Shifts in leaf angles, a form of solar tracking, often optimize LAI.*

Least developed country – low indicators of socioeconomic development and human resources, as well as economic vulnerability, as determined by the United Nations.

Lee – the side or part sheltered or turned away from the wind, such as with a mountain.

Legionnaires Disease – an acute bacterial respiratory illness caused by the gram-negative bacterium *Legionella pneumophila*, a member of the family *Legionellaceae*; the bacteria have been found in water systems and can survive in the air conditioning systems of large buildings; risk factors for infection include smoking, Chronic Obstructive Pulmonary Disease (COPD), renal failure, cancer, diabetes, and alcoholism.

Lek mating – an animal mating system in which an aggregation of male animals gathers to engage in competitive displays to entice females during the breeding season.

Less-developed countries (LDC) – non-industrialized nations characterized by low per capita income, high birth and death rates, high population growth rates, and low levels of technological development.

Lethal dose (LD50) – a chemical dose lethal to 50 percent of a test population. *The amount of material given at once causes the death of 50% (one-half) of test animals.*

Leukemia – malignant neoplasm of blood-forming tissues characterized by abnormal proliferation of leukocytes; one of the four major types of cancer.

Level (scale, context, or framework) – a context, frame of reference, or degree of organization within an integrated system; may or may not be spatially delimited.

Lichen – a composite organism that results from a symbiosis between algae or cyanobacteria and the hyphae of a fungus. Combined lichens have properties different from their component organisms.

Lifecycle (*of a product*) – stages of product development, from its raw materials and manufacturing process to its consumption and ultimate disposal.

Life-Cycle Assessment (LCA) – an objective process to evaluate the environmental impacts of a product, process, or activity. *Measures the material and energy inputs and outputs at each stage of a product's manufacture, use, and disposal, identifying resource use and waste released to the environment and assessing management options.*

Life expectancy – the average age a newborn infant can expect to live in a particular time and place.

Life form – an entity or being that is living.

Life history – the sequence of events experienced by an organism, from birth to reproduction to death.

Lifespan – the most prolonged period of life reached by a type of organism.

Life support systems (World Conservation Union (IUCN)) – the biophysical processes "*that sustain the productivity, adaptability, and capacity for renewal of lands, waters, or the biosphere as a whole.*"

Lilac water – recycled water unsuitable for drinking.

Limiting factor – any essential resource in short supply in each environment and therefore limits the possibilities for change in other aspects of the same environment. Chemical or physical factors that limit an organism's existence, growth, abundance, or distribution. See *tolerance limits*.

Limnology – the study of inland waters, regarded as forming part of ecology or environmental science.

Linear low-density polyethylene – a polyolefin plastic; a strong and flexible plastic usually used in film for packaging, bags, and industrial products such as pressure pipes.

Linear metabolism – direct conversion of resources into wastes often sent directly to landfills.

Lipid – a non-polar organic compound that is insoluble in water but soluble in solvents, such as alcohol and ether; includes fats, oils, steroids, phospholipids, and carotenoids.

Liquid metal fast breeder – a nuclear power plant that converts ^{238}U (uranium 238) to ^{239}Pu (plutonium 239). *The breeder creates more nuclear fuel than it consumes; because of its core's extreme heat and density, the breeder uses liquid sodium as a coolant.*

Lithosphere – the solid outermost shell of a rocky planet. *It is considered ideal for gardening and agricultural uses.*

Little Ice Age – a historical period of cooling that followed a warmer period known as the Medieval climate optimum.

Loam – a soil composed of sand, silt, and clay in even concentration (40–40–20% respectively).

Locally existing capacity – the ecological production within a country's territories. It is usually expressed in hectares based on average world productivity.

Lobbying – using personal contacts, public pressure, or political action to persuade legislators to vote in a particular manner.

Locally Unwanted Land Uses (LULU) – an acronym for toxic waste dumps, incinerators, smelters, airports, freeways, and other environmental, economic, or social degradation sources.

Logistic curve – an S-shaped curve representing the population growth of a given species.

Logistic growth – growth rates regulated by internal and external factors that establish an equilibrium with environmental resources. See *S curve*.

Longevity – the length or duration of life.

Long-wave radiation – emitted in the spectral wavelength greater than 4 micrometers, corresponds to the radiation emitted from the Earth and atmosphere, sometimes called *terrestrial* or *infrared radiation*, although somewhat imprecise. See *infrared radiation*.

Lotka–Volterra equation – a mathematical expression for predator-prey interactions between species.

Love Canal – an area in Niagara Falls, New York, where seepage from buried toxic wastes contaminates local soil and water. *In 1968, President Carter relocated almost all the residents of Love Canal, the impetus for the 1980 Superfund legislation.*

Lovelock Retreats (or *polar city*) – a proposed human refuge in northern Earth regions and Tasmania, New Zealand, and Antarctica, where people might live to survive global warming events.

Low-density polyethylene – a flexible polyolefin plastic used as a film for packaging or as bags.

Low entropy energy – carriers with the lowest entropy (i.e., highest quality) transformed into mechanical energy at efficiency rates well above 90%. *In contrast, fossil fuel chemical energy can be converted into mechanical energy at a typical efficiency rate of 25% (for cars) to 50 percent (for modern power plants). The chemical energy of biomass is lower.*

Low-head hydropower – small-scale hydro technology that can extract energy from small headwater dams causes much less ecological damage.

Low-level wastes – wastes that are not highly radioactive.

Low-quality energy – diffuse, dispersed energy at a low temperature that is difficult to gather and use for productive purposes.

LULU (Locally Unwanted Land Uses) – an acronym for toxic waste dumps, incinerators, smelters, airports, freeways, and other environmental, economic, or social degradation sources.

M

Macroecology (or *global ecology*) – studies the relationships between organisms and their environment at large spatial scales to characterize and explain statistical patterns of abundance, distribution, and diversity. *A branch of ecology examining ecological phenomena at the largest scale.* Compare *microecology*.

Macrophyte (or *aquatic plants*) – a plant that grows in or near water and is either emergent, submergent, or floating. Plants that have adapted to living in aquatic environments. *They are hydrophytes or macrophytes, distinguishing them from algae and other microphytes.*

Magma (or *lava*) – molten rock that sometimes forms beneath the surface of Earth (or terrestrial planet) that often collects in a magma chamber and is ejected by volcanoes; *lava* when it spews from an erupting volcano.

Magnetosphere – the region around an astronomical object in which phenomena are dominated or organized by its magnetic field.

Magnetic confinement – a technique for enclosing a nuclear fusion reaction in a powerful magnetic field inside a vacuum chamber.

Malignant tumor – a mass of cancerous cells that have left their site of origin, migrated through the body, invaded normal tissues, and grown out of control.

Malnourishment – a nutritional imbalance caused by a lack of specific dietary components or an inability to absorb or utilize essential nutrients.

Malthusian growth – a population explosion followed by a population crash. See *irruptive growth*.

Man and Biosphere (MAB) program – a design for nature preserves that divides protected areas into zones for different purposes. *A highly protected core is surrounded by a buffer zone and peripheral regions where multiple-use resource harvesting is permitted.*

Mangrove wetland – shrubs or small trees that grow in coastal saline or brackish water in the tropics and provide a habitat to many marine organisms.

Mantle – a hot, pliable rock layer surrounding Earth's core and underlying the cool outer crust.

Manure – organic matter used as fertilizer in agriculture.

Marasmus – a widespread human protein deficiency disease caused by a diet low in calories and protein or imbalanced in essential amino acids.

Marginal costs (*economics*) – the cost to produce one additional unit of a good or service.

Marine – living in or on the sea.

Marine climate – as its name suggests, west coast marine climates (Cfb) are generally found on the western sides of continents in the belt of the westerly winds between roughly 40° to 60° latitude; this location produces a humid climate, often quite rainy, with mild temperatures considering the relatively high latitudes. *This is the effect of having large bodies of water windward; water is a great modifier of temperatures because it heats and cools slowly. The proximity of water to windward leads to much milder winter temperatures and somewhat cooler summer temperatures that are experienced at continental locations at the same latitudes (some consider Cfb climates to be gloomy climates because they are the world's cloudiest climates; distinctive biological community adapted to those conditions).*

Marine ecosystem – an aquatic ecosystem dominated and defined by saline water.

Marine snow – tiny particles, including dead organic matter from the ocean's upper layers, sinking deep into the ocean.

Mark and recapture – an observational methodology used to estimate variables of a population under study, including population density, survival rates, movement, and growth.

Market benefits – climate policy can be measured in terms of avoided market impacts such as changes in resource productivity (e.g., lower agricultural yields, scarcer water resources) and damages to the human-built environment (e.g., coastal flooding due to sea–level rise).

Market equilibrium – the dynamic balance between supply and demand under a given set of conditions in a "free" market (where there are no monopolies or government interventions).

Marsh – a wetland dominated by herbaceous rather than woody plant species and often found at the edges of lakes and streams, where it forms a transition between the aquatic and terrestrial ecosystems. *Wetland without trees; in North America, this type of land is characterized by cattails and rushes.*

Mass burn – incineration of unsorted solid waste.

Mass extinction (or *extinction event, extinction–level event, ELE*) – a sharp decrease in species in a relatively short period.

Material flow – the cycling of materials driven by the flow of energy.

Material identification – words, numbers, or symbols used to designate the composition of a product or packaging components. *Note: a material identification symbol does not indicate whether an item can be recycled.*

Materials recovery facility (MRF) – a center for receiving and transferring materials recovered from the waste stream. MRF sorts materials by type and treatment (e.g., cleaned, compressed).

Matter – anything that takes up space and has mass.

Mauna Loa – home to the longest instrumental CO_2 record.

Mauna Loa record (1958) – the measurements of atmospheric CO_2 concentrations taken at Mauna Loa Observatory, Mauna Loa, Hawaii. The record shows the continuing increase in average annual atmospheric CO_2 concentrations.

Maunder Minimum – a historical period from 1645 to 1715 when sunspots became exceedingly rare, as noted by solar observers of the time.

Maximum soil water deficit – the amount of water stored in the soil readily available to plants.

Meander – a turning or winding of a stream.

Mediation – an informal dispute resolution process in which parties discuss issues but in which decisions are reached by consensus, and any participant can withdraw at any time.

Mediterranean climate areas – specialized landscapes with warm, dry summers, cool, wet winters, many unique plants and animal adaptations, and many levels of endemism.

Medieval Warm Period – a warm historical period from about the 10th century to the 14th century.

Megacity (or *megacity* and *super city*) – a large city, typically with a population over ten million.

Megadiverse countries – 17 countries home to the largest fraction of wild species (e.g., Australia).

Megalopolis (or *megacity* and *super city*) – an urban area with more than 10 million inhabitants.

Megawatt (MW) – a unit of electrical power equal to 1,000 kilowatts or 1 million watts.

Mesosphere – the atmospheric layer above the stratosphere and below the thermosphere; the middle layer; temperatures are usually very low.

Mesopredators – a predator that occupies a mid-ranking trophic level in a food web. *There is no standard definition of a mesopredator, but they are usually called medium-sized, compared to the apex predator and the prey in the food web. Mesopredators typically prey on smaller animals.*

Mesopredator release hypothesis – as the top predators dwindle in an ecosystem, different populations of mesopredators occur.

Metabolic theory of ecology – explains the relationship between an organism's body mass and metabolic rate.

Metabolism – energy and matter exchanges within a living cell or organism; collectively, life processes.

Metalimnion – a layer within a lake where the temperature changes rapidly with depth.

Metamorphic rock – igneous and sedimentary rocks modified by heat, pressure, and chemical reactions.

Meteorology – the interdisciplinary scientific study of the atmosphere and weather processes, focusing on weather forecasting.

Methane (CH_4) – a greenhouse gas released by enteric fermentation in livestock, rice production, and fossil fuel extraction. A hydrocarbon greenhouse gas with global warming potential has recently been estimated at 25 times that of carbon dioxide (CO_2). Methane is produced through anaerobic (i.e., without oxygen) decomposition of waste in landfills, animal digestion, decomposition of animal wastes, production and distribution of natural gas and petroleum, coal production, and incomplete fossil fuel combustion. GWP is from the IPCC's Fourth Assessment Report (AR4).

Methane hydrate – tiny bubbles or individual molecules of methane (CH_4: natural gas) trapped in a crystalline matrix of frozen water.

Metric ton – common international measurement for the quantity of greenhouse gas emissions. A metric ton is equal to 2205 lbs. or 1.1 short tons. See *short ton*.

Microbial ecology – studies microorganisms.

Micro-climate – a local set of atmospheric conditions that differ from surrounding areas.

Microecology – studies ecological phenomena at tiny scales, a large field that includes many topics such as evolution, biodiversity, exobiology, ecology, bioremediation, recycling, and food microbiology. *In humans, gut microecology is the study of the microbial ecology of the human gut, including its composition, metabolic activity, and interactions between the microbiota, host, and environment.* Contrast *macroecology*.

Micro-hydro generators – small power generators that can be used in low-level rivers to provide economical power for four to six homes, freeing them from dependence on large utilities and foreign energy supplies.

Microorganism – an organism visible only through a microscope.

Microwave – a high-frequency electromagnetic wave, one millimeter to one meter in wavelength, intermediate between the infrared and short-wave radio wavelengths.

Middle East – a region in western Asia and northeast Africa including 15 countries, including Bahrain, Islamic Rep. Iran, Iraq, Israel, Jordan, Kuwait, Lebanon, Oman, Qatar, Saudi Arabia, Syria, United Arab Emirates, and Yemen.

15 countries: Bahrain, Islamic Republic of Iran, Iraq, Israel, Jordan, Kuwait, Lebanon, Oman, Qatar, Saudi Arabia, Syria, the United Arab Emirates, and Yemen.

Migration – moving one species or group of species from one area to another.

Milankovitch cycles – periodic variations in the tilt, eccentricity, and wobble of Earth's orbit; Milutin Milankovitch suggested they are responsible for cyclic weather changes.

Milpa agriculture – an ancient farming system in which small patches of tropical forests are cleared and perennial polyculture (growing many crops in the same space) agriculture is practiced, followed by many years of fallow to restore the soil. See *Swidden agriculture*.

Mineral – a naturally occurring, inorganic, crystalline solid with a definite chemical composition and characteristic physical properties.

Mimicry – an adaption of one species to another that protects one or both species from predators.

Mitigation – repairing or rehabilitating a damaged ecosystem or compensating for damage by providing a substitute area. *Measures to reduce the amount and speed of climate change by reducing emissions of heat-trapping gases or removing carbon dioxide from the atmosphere. Human intervention to reduce the human impact on the climate system includes strategies to reduce greenhouse gas sources and emissions and enhance greenhouse gas sinks.*

Mitigation of global warming – any procedure involving reducing greenhouse gas emissions and enhancing sinks to reduce the degree of global warming.

Mixed perennial polyculture – growing a mixture of perennial crop species (where the same plant persists for more than one year) together in the same plot.

Mobile garbage bin – a wheeled curbside container for collecting garbage or other materials.

Mode of variability – a pattern of climate change, usually oscillatory, with specific regional effects.

Moderators – a substance, for example, graphite or beryllium, that slows neutrons in a nuclear reactor so that they can bring about the fission of uranium.

Molecule – a combination of two or more atoms.

Molecular ecology – applies molecular population genetics, molecular phylogenetics, and genomics to traditional ecological questions. It is essentially the same as ecological genetics.

Monitored, retrievable storage – holding wastes in underground mines or secure surface facilities such as dry casks where they can be watched and repackaged, if necessary.

Monkeywrenching – environmental sabotage, such as driving large spikes in trees to protect them from loggers, vandalizing construction equipment, pulling up survey stakes for unwanted developments, and destroying billboards. See *ecotage*.

Mono Lake – an oasis in the dry Great Basin in California and a vital habitat for millions of migrating and nesting birds.

Monoculture – producing or growing one crop over a wide area.

Monoculture agroforestry – intensive planting of a single species; an efficient wood production approach, but one that encourages pests and disease infestations and conflicts with wildlife habitat or recreation uses.

Monsoon – 1. a wind system that influences large climatic regions and reverses direction seasonally; 2. a wind from the southwest or south that brings heavy rainfall to southern Asia in the summer or the rain accompanying this wind. *The predictable occurrence of dramatic seasonal changes in atmospheric circulation and precipitation patterns.*

Montane coniferous forests – coniferous forests of mountains consisting of belts of forest communities along an altitudinal gradient.

Montreal Protocol (1987) – an international treaty to protect the ozone layer by phasing out the production of numerous substances responsible for ozone depletion, especially CFCs. *The treaty governs stratospheric ozone protection and research as well as the production and use of ozone-depleting substances. Provides for ending the production of ozone-depleting substances such as CFCs; under the Montreal Protocol, various research groups continue to assess the ozone layer. The Multilateral Fund provides resources to developing nations to promote their transition to ozone-safe technologies.*

Moral agents – beings capable of distinguishing between right and wrong and acting accordingly (i.e., those held responsible for their actions).

Moral extensionism – expansion of understanding of the inherent value or rights of people, organisms, or things that might not be considered worthy of value or rights under ethical philosophies.

Moral subjects – beings that are incapable of distinguishing between right and wrong or cannot act on moral principles and yet are capable of being wronged by others.

Morals – a set of ethical principles that guide actions and relationships.

Morbidity – describes how often a disease afflicts a certain area (e.g., "how many people have lung cancer in New York City").

More-developed countries (MDC) – industrialized nations characterized by high per capita incomes, low birth and death rates, low population growth rates, and high levels of industrialization and urbanization.

Mortality – 1. the death rate in a population; 2. the probability of dying.

Mortality rate – the number of deaths per 1,000 people of a given age group.

Mount Pinatubo – a volcano in the Philippine Islands that erupted in 1991. The eruption of Mount Pinatubo ejected enough particulate and sulfate aerosol matter into the atmosphere to block some incoming solar radiation from reaching Earth's atmosphere. *This effectively cooled the planet from 1992 to 1994, masking the warming occurring for most of the 1980s and 1990s.*

Mullerian mimicry – the evolution of two noxious species who share common predators to resemble each other; the theory is that predators who associate the unique characteristics of one noxious species with danger will choose to ignore the mimicking species.

Mulch – any composted or non–composted organic material, excluding plastic, suitable for placing on soil surfaces to restrict moisture loss from the soil and provide a source of nutrients to the soil.

Multiple uses – many coincidences. Used in forest management; limited to mutually compatible uses.

Municipal sewage – the wastewater from households, offices, and other buildings in a city; can be sanitary sewage only or sanitary sewage and stormwater. *Collected at treatment plants where solids are removed by "primary sewage treatment" and treated by other methods, including aerobic bacteria to remove organic wastes in "secondary treatment" and advanced or "tertiary treatment" with chemical and physical processes.*

Municipal solid waste (MSW) – residential solid waste (i.e., garbage and hard waste) and some non-hazardous commercial, institutional, and industrial wastes such as street sweeping litter, tree lopping, waste dropped at transfer stations, and construction waste from owner/occupier renovations. *This material is generally sent to municipal landfills for disposal.* See *landfill*.

Mutagens – agents, such as chemicals or radiation, that alter cellular genetic material (DNA).

Mutation – a change, either spontaneous or by external factors, in a cell's genetic material; future generations of organisms can inherit mutations in the gametes (egg or sperm cells).

Mutualism – a symbiotic relationship between individuals of two species in which both species benefit from the association. *Both individual organisms derive a fitness benefit.*

N

NF_3 – Nitrogen trifluoride

N_2O – Nitrous oxide

NAAQS (*National Ambient Air Quality Standard*) federal standards specifying maximum allowable levels (averaged over specific periods) for regulated pollutants in *Ambient air*.

Natality – the production of individuals by birth, hatching, germination, or cloning.

National ambient air quality standards – health-based pollutant concentration limits established by the EPA that apply to the outside air.

National Packaging Covenant – a self–regulatory agreement between packaging and government.

National Priority List (NPL) – established by the EPA as part of the *Superfund* program; locates and sets priorities for cleaning up hazardous waste sites.

Native species – species that are initially in a specific area.

Natural – the existing air, water, land, and energy resources from which resources derive. Primary functions include resource production (such as fish, timber, or cereals), waste assimilation (such as CO_2 absorption and sewage decomposition), and life support services (UV protection, biodiversity, water cleansing, and climate stability). *Environmental services must be maintained so that human development can be sustainable.*

Natural capital – natural resources and ecological processes equivalent to financial capital.

Natural gas – underground deposits of gases consist of 50 to 90 percent methane (CH_4) and small amounts of heavier gaseous hydrocarbon compounds such as propane (C_3H_8) and butane (C_4H_{10}).

Natural history – the study of where and how organisms carry out their lifecycles.

Natural increase – the crude death rate subtracted from the crude birth rate.

Appendix: Annotated Glossary of Environmental Science Terms

Natural resources – naturally occurring substances valuable in their relatively unmodified (i.e., natural) form. *Natural biotic and abiotic resources combined.*

Natural selection – the process by which favorable heritable traits become more common in successive generations of reproducing organisms, and unfavorable heritable traits become less common.

Natural variability (or *climate variability*) – variations in the mean state and other statistics (such as standard deviations or statistics of extremes) of the climate on all time and space scales beyond that of individual weather events. *Natural variations in climate over time are caused by internal processes of the climate system, such as El Niño, as well as changes in external influences, such as volcanic activity and variations in the Sun's output.*

Negative feedback loop – a process in which the effects of a change in a system act to reduce or counteract the change. Negative feedback loops promote stability and settle to equilibrium, reducing the effects of perturbations in the system. Contrast *positive feedback loop*.

Neighborhood environment improvement plan – developed by a local community, including residents, special interest groups, local government, local industry, and government agencies.

Nematocide – a chemical that kills nematodes (e.g., roundworms and threadworms).

Neutralism – changes in evolution are caused by random mutation rather than by natural selection.

Neo-classical economics – a branch of economics that attempts to apply the principles of modern science to economic analysis in a mathematically rigorous, non-contextual, abstract, predictive manner.

Neo-Luddites – people who reject technology, believing it is the cause of environmental degradation and social disruption; named after the followers of Ned Ludd, who tried to turn back the Industrial Revolution in England by wrecking factories.

Neo-Malthusian – a belief that the world is characterized by scarcity and competition in which too many people fight over too few resources, named for Thomas Malthus, predicted a dismal cycle of misery, vice, and starvation due to human overpopulation.

Net energy yield – useful energy produced during the lifetime of an energy system minus the energy used, lost, or wasted in making useful energy available.

Net primary production – the energy or biomass content of plant material accumulated in an ecosystem over time through photosynthesis. It is the amount of energy left after subtracting the respiration of primary producers (primarily plants) from the amount of solar energy fixed biologically: gross primary productivity minus respiratory losses (carbon gain).

Neurotoxins – toxic substances, such as lead or mercury, that poison nerve cells.

Neutron – a subatomic particle found in the atom's nucleus with no electromagnetic charge.

New towns – experimental urban environments combining best features of rural villages and cities.

Niche – a position or function of an organism in a community of related organisms. *A specific category that an organism fits into in an environment and its role in carrying out the processes in that ecosystem.*

Any duplication (copies, uploads, PDFs) is illegal.

Niche construction – when an organism alters its or another organism's ecological niche.

Niche differentiation – in a biological community, various populations share environmental resources through specialization, thereby reducing direct competition. See *resource partitioning*.

Nickel-cadmium batteries – typically used in appliances such as power tools and mobile phones. Cadmium is a heavy metal that risks human and ecosystem health.

Nihilists [Latin, nihil for nothing] – those who reject moral or religious beliefs, often concluding that the world and everything in it amounts to nothingness or is meaningless.

NIMBY – an acronym for "Not In My BackYard;" the rallying cry opposing *LULUs*.

Nitrates – 1. salt or ester of nitric acid; 2. sodium nitrate or potassium nitrate used as a fertilizer.

Nitrate-forming bacteria – combine ammonia with oxygen to form nitrites that green plants can use to build proteins.

Nitrification – the oxidation of ammonia with oxygen into nitrite.

Nitrogen cycle – the continuous cycle by which atmospheric nitrogen and compounded nitrogen are exchanged through the soil into substances taken up and used by green plants; the remainder returns to the atmosphere due to denitrification. The circulation and utilization of nitrogen in nature consist of a cycle of chemical reactions in which atmospheric nitrogen is compounded, dissolved in the rain, and deposited in the soil, where it is assimilated and metabolized by bacteria and plants, eventually returning to the atmosphere by bacterial decomposition of organic matter. *Specific principles include: N_2 is the most abundant gas in the atmosphere (78%), nitrogen-fixing bacteria convert it to NH_3, and nitrate-forming bacteria combine NH_3 with oxygen to form NO_2. Then NO_3, plants absorb and make NH_4, consumers eat plants, and nitrogen re-enters the environment when these organisms die, shed, urinate, and produce excrement, which de-nitrifying bacteria break down into N_2, and the process repeats.*

Nitrogen fixation – the conversion of nitrogen into nitrogen compounds (e.g., nitrate, nitrite) carried out naturally by certain bacteria and algae.

Nitrogen-fixing bacteria – bacteria that convert nitrogen from the atmosphere or soil solution into ammonia that can be converted to plant nutrients by nitrite- and nitrate-forming bacteria.

Nitrogen oxides (NOx) – highly reactive gases formed when nitrogen in fuel or combustion air is heated to over 650 °C (1,200 °F) in the presence of oxygen or when bacteria in soil or water oxidize nitrogen-containing compounds; often mentioned in discussions of nitrogen-based air pollution as a reference to both nitric oxide (NO) and nitrogen dioxide (NO_2). *In addition to particulates and sulfur dioxide, NOx, a major pollutant related to energy use, can transform into nitrates in the atmosphere.*

Nitrous oxide (N_2O) – a potent greenhouse gas with a global warming potential 298 times that of carbon dioxide (CO_2). *Major sources include soil cultivation practices, especially commercial and organic fertilizers, fossil fuel combustion, nitric acid production, and biomass burning. The global warming potential (GWP) is from the IPCC's Fourth Assessment Report (AR4). Natural emissions of N_2O are mainly from bacteria breaking down nitrogen in soils and the oceans. Nitrous oxide is mainly removed from the atmosphere through destruction in the stratosphere by ultraviolet radiation and associated chemical reactions. However, certain types of bacteria can be consumed in soils.*

Noise pollution (or *environmental noise*) – displeasing human or machine-created sound that disrupts the activity or happiness of human or animal life.

Non-criteria pollutants – not explicitly mentioned in NAAQS or the *Hazardous Air Pollutants* (HAPs) in the *Clean Air Act* (e.g., benzene, dioxins, pesticides). See *unconventional air pollutants*.

Nongovernmental organizations (NGO) – a not–for–profit or community–based organization. *Refer collectively to advocacy and research groups, advisory agencies, political parties, professional societies, and other groups concerned about environmental quality, resource use, and other issues.*

Non-ferrous metals – contain little or no iron (e.g., copper, brass, and bronze).

Non-Methane Volatile Organic Compounds (NMVOCs) – organic compounds other than methane participate in atmospheric photochemical reactions.

Nonpoint source pollution – affecting a water body from diffuse sources rather than a point source discharging to a water body at a single location.

Nonpoint sources – scattered, diffuse sources of pollutants, such as runoff from farm fields, golf courses, construction sites, etc.

Nonradiative forcing – a type of climate forcing that creates an energy imbalance that does not immediately involve radiation.

Nonrenewable resources – minerals, fossil fuels, and other materials present in essentially finite amounts (within human time scales) in our environment.

Nor'easter – a storm blowing from the northeast.

North/South division – describes that most of the world's wealthier countries tend to be in North America, Europe, and Japan, while the poorer countries tend to be closer to the equator.

North Atlantic Deep Water – one of the water masses of the ocean.

North Atlantic oscillation – an atmospheric climate model. See *arctic oscillation*.

No-till farming (or *zero tillage*) – a conservation tillage system. An agricultural technique for growing crops or pasture without disturbing the soil through tillage. *No-till farming decreases soil erosion tillage caused in certain soils, especially in sandy and dry soils on sloping terrain. Benefits include an increase in the amount of water infiltrating into the soil, soil retention of organic matter, and nutrient cycling.*

Nuclear energy (or *atomic energy*) – released atomic nuclei reactions, as in nuclear fission or fusion.

Nuclear fission – the radioactive decay in which isotopes split apart to create two smaller atoms.

Nuclear fusion – when two smaller atomic nuclei fuse into one larger nucleus and release energy; the power source is a hydrogen bomb.

Nucleic acids – large organic molecules made of nucleotides that transmit hereditary traits, protein synthesis, and control of cellular activities.

Nucleus – 1. the center of the atom, occupied by protons and neutrons; 2. in cells, the organelle that contains chromosomes (DNA).

Nuées ardentes – deadly, denser-than-air mixtures of hot gases and ash ejected from volcanoes.

Numbers pyramid – a diagram showing the relative population sizes at each trophic level in an ecosystem; usually corresponds to the biomass pyramid.

Numerical response – a change in predator density as a function of change in prey density.

Nutrients – chemicals required for the growth of organisms; chemicals (e.g., nitrogen and phosphorus) that plants and animals need to live and grow. At high concentrations, particularly in water, nutrients can become pollutants. *Phosphorus, nitrogen, and potassium are major plant nutrients. However, many trace elements are needed in small quantities for growing and developing animal and plant life.*

Nutrient cycle (or *ecological recycling*) – the movement and exchange of organic and inorganic matter back into the production of living matter.

Nutrient cycle efficiency – studies how energy and matter flow interact with ecosystems' biotic elements. See *ecosystem ecology*.

O

O_3 – (Tropospheric) Ozone

Ocean – a vast body of saltwater. Oceans cover almost 75% of Earth's surface.

Ocean acidification – reduced pH from increased carbon dioxide concentrations in seawater causes a measurable increase in acidity (i.e., a reduction in ocean pH). The process by which ocean waters have become more acidic is due to the absorption of human-produced carbon dioxide, which interacts with ocean water to form carbonic acid and lower the ocean's pH. *Acidity reduces the capacity of crucial plankton species and shelled animals to form and maintain shells. This may lead to reduced calcification rates of calcifying organisms such as corals, mollusks, algae, and crustaceans. It is caused by their uptake of anthropogenic carbon dioxide from the atmosphere.*

Ocean heat content (OHC) – the energy absorbed and stored by oceans. Ocean temperature measurements at many locations and depths are required to calculate ocean heat content. *Integrating the areal density of ocean heat over an ocean basin, or entire ocean, gives the ocean heat content.*

Ocean planet – the opposite concept of *Snowball Earth*.

Ocean shorelines – rocky coasts and sandy beaches along oceans; prosperous, stratified communities.

Ocean thermal electric conversion (OTEC) – energy derived from the temperature differential between warm ocean surface waters and cold, deep waters. *This temperature differential can be used to drive turbines attached to electric generators.*

Oceania – the southern, western, and central Pacific Ocean islands, including Melanesia, Micronesia, and Polynesia; in some definitions, Oceania encompasses Australia, New Zealand, and Maritime Southeast Asia.

Oceanic islands – islands formed by breaking away from a continental landmass, volcanic action, coral formation, or a combination of sources; support distinctive communities.

Offset – something that balances, counteracts, or compensates.

Offset allowances – a controversial component of air quality regulations that allows a polluter to avoid installation of control equipment on one source by an "offsetting" pollution reduction at another source.

Ogallala aquifer – the largest aquifer in North America, located under the Great Plains in the U.S.A.

Oil glut – when oil supply on the market dramatically exceeds demand, resulting in lower oil prices.

Oil shale – a fine-grained sedimentary rock rich in solid organic material called "kerogen;" when heated, the kerogen liquefies to produce a fluid petroleum fuel.

Old-growth forests (or *ancient forests*) – an area of great age that exhibits unique biological features. Forests without disturbances for long enough (generally 150 to 200 years) to have mature trees, ideal physical conditions, species diversity, and other characteristics of equilibrium ecosystems. *Dominated by mature trees with little evidence of disturbance, such as logging, ground clearing, and building.*

Oligotrophic [*oligo* = little; *trophic* = nutrition] – the condition of rivers and lakes with clear water and low biological productivity. *Oligotrophic waters are clear, cold, infertile headwater lakes and streams.*

Omnivore – a species of animal eating plants and animals as its primary food source.

OPEC (Organization of Petroleum Exporting Countries, 1960) – unify petroleum policies.

Open access system – a commonly held resource for which there are no management rules.

Open burning – uncontrolled fires in an open dump.

Open canopy – a forest where tree crowns cover less than 20 percent of the ground. See *woodland*.

Open-pit mining (or *opencast mining* and *open–cut mining*) – a method of extracting rock or minerals from the earth by removing them from an open pit or borrowing.

Open range – unfenced, natural grazing lands; includes woodland and grassland.

Open system – a system that exchanges energy and matter with its environment.

Operational energy – the energy used in carrying out a particular operation.

Optimum – the most favorable condition regarding an environmental factor.

Orbital – the space or path in which an electron orbits the nucleus of an atom.

Organic – derived from a living organism containing *carbon*.

Organic agriculture – a holistic production management system that avoids synthetic fertilizers, pesticides, and genetically modified organisms (GMO), minimizes air, soil, and water pollution, and optimizes the health and productivity of interdependent communities of plants, animals, and people.

Organic compounds – complex molecules organized around skeletons of carbon atoms arranged in rings or chains; includes biomolecules, molecules synthesized by living organisms.

Organic gardening – gardening that follows, in principle, the philosophy of organic agriculture.

Organic matter – compounds that contain carbon and hydrogen covalently bonded together in molecules; molecules from living matter; organic wastes in sewage and runoff from lawns and farms in freshwaters can cause oxygen depletion and degradation of water quality.

Organics – plant or animal matter originating from domestic or industrial sources (e.g., grass clippings, tree pruning, food waste).

Orographic effect (Chinook winds) – a moist wind blowing from sea on the Northwestern U.S. coast.

Overburden – overlying noncommercial sediment layers removed onto mineral or coal deposits.

Overdrawn – taking too much out or depleting resources (e.g., pumping water from an aquifer faster than it can be replenished or recharged by rainfall).

Overnutrition (or *hyperalimentation*) – when the amount of nutrients ingested exceeds what is needed for normal growth, metabolism, and development.

Overshoot – growth beyond an area's carrying capacity; ecological deficit occurs when human consumption and waste production exceed the capacity of Earth to create new resources and absorb waste. *Natural capital is being liquidated during overshot to support current use, so Earth's ability to support future life declines.*

Oxidation – the process of oxidizing (i.e., to change a compound by increasing the proportion of electronegative elements or charge (an element or ion) from a lower to a higher positive valence); removing one or more electrons from an atom, ion, or molecule to combine with oxygen.

Oxidize – to chemically transform a substance by combining it with oxygen.

Oxygen cycle – the circulation and utilization of oxygen in the biosphere.

Oxygen sag – oxygen decline downstream from a pollution source that introduces materials with high biological oxygen demands.

Ozone (O₃) – the triatomic form of oxygen, is a gaseous atmospheric constituent as an inorganic pale blue gas with a distinctively pungent smell. It is an allotrope of oxygen much less stable than the diatomic allotrope O_2, breaking down to O_2 (dioxygen) in the lower atmosphere. Ozone is formed from dioxygen by ultraviolet (UV) light and electrical discharges within Earth's atmosphere. *A colorless, highly reactive molecule containing three oxygen atoms; a dangerous pollutant in ambient air that is soluble in alkalis and cold water; in the stratosphere, ozone forms an ultraviolet absorbing shield that protects us from mutagenic radiation; a strong oxidizing agent and can be produced by electric discharge in oxygen or by the action of ultraviolet radiation on oxygen in the stratosphere.*

In the troposphere, ozone layers are created by photochemical reactions involving gases resulting from natural sources and human activities (photochemical smog). In high concentrations, tropospheric ozone can harm many living organisms. Tropospheric ozone acts as a greenhouse gas. In the stratosphere, ozone is created by the interaction between solar ultraviolet radiation and molecular oxygen (O_2). Stratospheric ozone plays a decisive role in the stratospheric radiative balance. Depleting stratospheric ozone due to chemical reactions that may be enhanced by climate change results in an increased ground-level flux of ultraviolet (UV-) B radiation. See *atmosphere* and *ultraviolet radiation*.

Ozone-depleting substance (ODS) – family of manufactured compounds that includes, but are not limited to, chlorofluorocarbons (CFCs), bromofluorocarbons (halons), methyl chloroform, carbon tetrachloride, methyl bromide, and hydrochlorofluorocarbons (HCFCs). These compounds have been shown to deplete stratospheric ozone and are typically ODSs. See *ozone*.

Ozone depletion – two related events observed since the late 1970s: a steady lowering of about four percent in the amount of ozone in Earth's atmosphere and a more significant springtime decrease in stratospheric ozone (i.e., the ozone layer) around Earth's polar regions; the *ozone hole*.

Ozone layer – begins approximately 15 km above Earth and thins to an almost negligible amount at about 50 km, shielding Earth from harmful ultraviolet radiation from the Sun. The highest natural ozone concentration (approximately 10 parts per million by volume) occurs in the stratosphere approximately 25 km above Earth. Stratospheric ozone concentrations change during the year as stratospheric circulation changes with seasons. Natural events such as volcanoes and solar flares can produce changes in ozone concentration, but manufactured changes are of the most significant concern.

A region of Earth's stratosphere that absorbs most of the Sun's ultraviolet radiation. It contains a high ozone concentration (O_3) in other parts of the atmosphere, although small compared to other gases in the stratosphere. The ozone layer contains less than 10 parts per million, while the average ozone concentration in Earth's atmosphere is about 0.3 parts per million. The ozone layer is mainly found in the lower portion of the stratosphere, from approximately 15 to 35 kilometers (9 to 22 mi) above Earth, although its thickness varies seasonally and geographically. See *stratosphere* and *ultraviolet radiation*.

Ozone precursors – chemical compounds, such as carbon monoxide, methane, non-methane hydrocarbons, and nitrogen oxides, in the presence of solar radiation, react with other chemical compounds to form ozone, mainly in the troposphere. See *troposphere*.

P

Pacific Decadal Oscillation (PDO) – a 23–30-year warm or cool water pattern in the north Pacific Ocean. A large pool of warm water moves north and south in the Pacific Ocean, dramatically affecting North America's climate.

Paleocene–Eocene Thermal Maximum (PETM) – a historical warming event that suddenly and fundamentally altered the geological and biological aspects of the planet.

Paleoclimate – the climate that existed during the period before modern record-keeping. Paleoclimate can be measured with "natural thermometers" such as ice cores or tree rings.

Paleoclimatology – the study of climate change taken on the scale of Earth's history.

Paleoecology – a branch of ecology that uses data from fossils to reconstruct past ecosystems.

Parabolic mirrors – curved mirrors that focus light from a large area onto a single central point, concentrating solar energy and producing high temperatures.

Paradigm – a model that provides a framework for interpreting observations.

Parasite – an organism that lives in or on another organism, deriving nourishment at the expense of its host, usually without killing it. An organism that depends on a symbiotic relationship with a host, which it does not usually kill directly but does negatively affect.

Parasitoid – an organism that is a parasite for most of its life and usually kills its host.

Parent – an original radioactive atom or any material.

Parsimony – the reluctance to use resources or spend money.

Particulate material (PM) – tiny pieces of solid or liquid matter such as particles of soot, dust, fumes, mist, or aerosols. *The physical characteristics of particles and how they combine with other particles are part of the feedback mechanisms of the atmosphere. Atmospheric aerosols, such as dust, ash, soot, lint, smoke, pollen, spores, algal cells, and other suspended materials; originally applied only to solid particles but are now extended to liquid droplets.* See *aerosols* and *sulfate aerosols*.

Parts per billion (ppb) – number of chemical parts in 1 billion parts of a gas, liquid, or solid mixture.

Parts per million (ppm) – number of chemical parts in 1 million parts of a gas, liquid, or solid mixture.

Parts per trillion (ppt) – number of chemical parts in 1 trillion parts of a gas, liquid, or solid mixture.

Passive heat absorption – using natural materials or absorptive structures without moving parts to gather and hold heat; the simplest and oldest use of solar energy.

Patchiness – within a larger ecosystem, the presence of smaller areas that differ in physical conditions and support somewhat different communities; a diversity-promoting phenomenon.

Pathogen – an organism that produces disease in a host organism, the disease being an alteration of one or more metabolic functions in response to the organism's presence.

Pathogenic – describes any microorganism capable of causing disease.

Patterns in nature – visible regularities of form found in the natural world.

Pay-by-weight systems – financial approaches to managing waste by charging according to the quantity of waste collected rather than a price per pick–up or fixed annual charge, as typical for households with curbside services. *Pay–by–weight systems may provide an incentive to reduce waste generation.*

Peat – deposits of moist, acidic, semi-decayed organic matter.

Pedosphere – the outermost layer of Earth composed of soil and subject to soil formation processes. *It exists at the lithosphere, atmosphere, hydrosphere, and biosphere interface.*

Pellagra – a disease characterized by lassitude, torpor, dermatitis, diarrhea, and sometimes dementia and death, brought about by a diet deficient in tryptophan and niacin.

Peptides – two or more amino acids linked by a peptide bond.

Per capita consumption – the average amount of commodity used per person.

Percolation – water slowly moving through soil and gravel into an aquifer.

Perennial species – plants that grow for more than two years.

Perfluorocarbons (PFCs) – a group of carbon and fluorine chemicals. These chemicals (predominantly CF_4 and C_2F_6) were introduced as alternatives, along with hydrofluorocarbons, to the ozone-depleting substances. In addition, PFCs are emitted as by-products of industrial processes and used in manufacturing. PFCs do not harm the stratospheric ozone layer but are powerful greenhouse gases. CF_4 has a global warming potential (GWP) of 7,390, and C_2F_6 has a GWP of 12,200. These chemicals are predominantly human-made, though they are a small natural source of CF_4. See *ozone-depleting substances.*

Permafrost – a permanently frozen layer of soil that underlies the arctic tundra; perennially (continually) frozen ground occurs where temperatures remain below 0 °C for years.

Permanent retrievable storage – placing waste storage containers in a secure building, salt mine, or bedrock cavern where they can be inspected periodically and retrieved, if necessary.

Persistent organic pollutants (POPs) – organic compounds resistant to environmental degradation through chemical, biological, and photolytic processes.

Pervious surface – penetrated by air and water.

Pest – any organism that reduces a useful resource's availability, quality, or value.

Pest resurgence – the rebound of pest populations due to acquired resistance to chemicals and nonspecific destruction of their natural predators and competitors by broad-scale pesticides.

Pesticide – any substance or mixture intended to prevent, destroy, or control any pest. *Includes substances intended for use as a plant growth regulator, defoliant, desiccant, or agent for thinning fruit or preventing the premature fall of fruit and substances applied to crops before or after harvest to protect the commodity from deterioration during storage and transport.*

Pesticide treadmill – a need for constantly increasing pesticide doses or new, more potent pesticides to prevent pest resurgence.

Petrochemicals – chemicals synthesized from oil.

pH – a value that indicates the acidity or alkalinity of a solution on a scale of 0 to 14, based on the proportion of H+ ions present.

pH scale – p(potential of) H(hydrogen); the logarithm of the reciprocal of hydrogen-ion concentration in gram atoms per liter. pH measures the acidity (pH < 7) or alkalinity (pH > 7) of a solution on a scale of 0 to 14 (where 7 is neutral).

Phenology – 1. the pattern of seasonal life cycle events in plants and animals, such as the timing of blooming, hibernation, and migration. 2. the study of periodic events in biological life cycles and how these are influenced by seasonal and interannual variations in climate and habitat factors (e.g., elevation). *The timing of natural events, such as flower blooms and animal migration, is influenced by changes in climate. Phenology is the study of such important seasonal events. Climate factors influence phenological events, including light, temperature, rainfall, and humidity.*

Phenotypic plasticity – the ability of an organism to change its behavior, physiology, or physical characteristics in response to its environment. *Therefore, this change occurs within an organism's lifetime and does not require genetic change.*

Pheromone – a chemical excreted into the environment as a signal, causes a natural behavioral response in members of the same population.

Phosphates – 1. a salt or ester of phosphoric acid. 2. the trivalent anion PO_{43}, derived from phosphoric acid H_3PO_4, an organic compound of phosphoric acid in which the acid group is bound to nitrogen or a carboxyl group in a way that permits valuable energy to be released (as in metabolism). 3. a phosphatic material used for fertilizers.

Phosphorous (phosphorus) cycle – the biogeochemical cycle that describes the movement of phosphorus through the environment. *The movement of phosphorus atoms from rocks and soil through the biosphere and hydrosphere and back to the soil.*

Photochemical oxidants – products of secondary atmospheric reactions. See *smog*.

Photodegradable plastics – materials that degrade from sunlight or a specific wavelength of light.

Photosynthesis – the transformation of radiant energy to chemical energy by plants; the manufacture by plants of carbohydrates from carbon dioxide and water. The capture of the Sun's energy (*primary production*) to power life on Earth (*consumption*). *The reaction is driven by energy from sunlight, catalyzed by chlorophyll, and releases oxygen as a byproduct. The process by which plants take CO_2 from the air (or bicarbonate in water) to build carbohydrates, releasing O_2. There are several pathways of photosynthesis with responses to atmospheric CO_2 concentrations.* See *carbon sequestration* and *carbon dioxide fertilization*.

Photosynthetic efficiency – the percentage of available sunlight captured by plants and used to make useful products.

Photovoltaic – the direct conversion of light into electricity.

Photovoltaic cell – an energy-conversion device that captures solar energy and directly converts it to electrical current.

Physical or abiotic factors – nonliving factors, such as temperature, light, water, minerals, and climate that influence an organism.

Phytophysiognomy – the appearance (i.e., physiognomy) and physical characteristics of a plant community.

Phytoplankton (or *plant plankton*) –microscopic, free-floating, autotrophic organisms that are producers in aquatic ecosystems. The autotrophic (i.e., self-feeding) components of the plankton community are a crucial part of ocean and freshwater ecosystems. *Phytoplankton obtain their energy through photosynthesis, like plants and trees on land. Phytoplankton must have sunlight, so they live in well-lit surface layers (euphotic zone) of oceans and lakes.* See *autotroph* and *plankton*.

Pioneer species – in primary succession on a terrestrial site, the plants, lichens, and microbes that first colonize the site. A species that is the first to inhabit a previously unoccupied environment or niche.

Plague – a disease that spreads rapidly, infecting many people and killing many of them. *It is an outbreak of such a disease.*

Plankton – mostly microscopic animal and plant life suspended in water and a valuable food source for fish and marine animals. See *phytoplankton*.

Plant litter – the layer of dead plant material on the ground providing habitat to plants, microorganisms, and animals. It plays a vital role in the nutrient cycle.

Plant quality – a standard of plant appearance or yield.

Plasma – a hot, electrically neutral gas of ions and free electrons.

Plastic – high–polymeric substances, including natural and synthetic products, excluding rubbers. *At some stage in its manufacture, every plastic can flow, under heat and pressure, if necessary, into the desired final shape.*

PM-10 – particulates less than 10 microns in diameter; present in the smoke created by burning wood.

Poachers – those who hunt wildlife illegally.

Point sources – specific locations of highly concentrated pollution discharge, such as factories, power plants, sewage treatment plants, underground coal mines, and oil wells.

Polar amplification – greater temperature increases in the *Arctic* than on Earth due to the collective effect of positive feedback loops and other processes. *Despite its name, polar amplification only applies to the Arctic, not the Antarctic, because the Southern Ocean acts as a heat sink.*

Polar City (or *Lovelock Retreats*) – a proposed human refuge in northern Earth regions and Tasmania, New Zealand, and Antarctica, where people might live to survive global warming events.

Policy – a societal plan or statement of intentions intended to accomplish some social good.

Policy cycle – the process of identifying and acting on problems in the public arena.

Political ecology – a branch of ecology that studies how political and economic power affects ecosystems and how environmental factors influence social activity.

Political economy – the branch of economics concerned with modes of production, distribution of benefits, social institutions, and class relationships.

Pollination – a type of fertilization when pollen grains are transported through air from a seed plant to the ovule-bearing organs of another. *Either wind, water, or animal assistance helps with this transport.*

Polluter Pays Principle (PPP) – pollution producers compensate others for their pollution.

Pollution – to make foul, unclean, or dirty; any physical, chemical, or biological change that adversely affects the health, survival, or regular activities of living organisms or alters the environment in undesirable ways.

Pollution charges – fees assessed per unit of pollution based on the *polluter pays principle*.

Polycentric complex – cities with several urban cores surrounding a once-dominant central core.

Polyethylene terephthalate (PET) – a clear, tough, light, and shatterproof plastic used to make products such as soft drink bottles, film packaging, and fabrics.

Polypropylene (PP) – a polyolefin plastic. PP is light, rigid, and glossy and is used to make products such as washing machine agitators, clear film packaging, carpet fibers, and housewares.

Polystyrene (PS) – a styrene plastic. *PS molds are easy to make for refrigerator and washing machine components. It can be foamed to make single-use packaging, such as cups, meat, and produce trays.*

Polyvinyl chloride (PVC) – a vinyl plastic. PVC can be clear, flexible, or rigid, making products like fruit juice bottles, credit cards, pipes, and hoses.

Population – a group of individuals of the same species occupying a given area.

Population crash – a sudden decline caused by predation, waste accumulation, or resource depletion. See *population dieback*.

Population density – the number of individuals of a species living in a defined area.

Population dieback – when the growth of a population slows due to some factor.

Population distribution (or *range*) – the prevalence of a species in the geographical area within which that species can be found.

Population ecology (or *autecology*) – a branch of ecology focused on the dynamics of populations within species and interactions of these populations with environmental factors.

Population explosion – the population growth at exponential rates to a size that exceeds environmental carrying capacity, usually followed by a *population crash*.

Population momentum – a potential for increased population growth as young members reach reproductive age.

Population size – the number of individuals of a species in a particular population.

Pore spaces – the amount of space available for groundwater due to the topography of the area.

Porosity – the ratio of the volume of the pores in a material to the whole volume.

Positive feedback loop – a process in which the effects of a slight change in a system include an increase in the magnitude of the change; "A produces more of B, which in turn produces more of A." Contrast *negative feedback loop*.

Postconsumer material or waste – refuse that served its intended purpose and has been discarded for disposal or recovery. *This includes returns of material from the distribution chain, waste collected and sorted after use, and curbside waste.* Compare *pre–consumer waste*.

Post-materialist values – a philosophy emphasizing quality of life over acquiring material goods.

Post-modernism – a philosophy that rejects and often mocks modern positivism's optimism and universal claims.

Potable water (or *drinking water*) – water that is safe to drink. Water fit for human consumption by *World Health Organization* (WHO) guidelines.

Potential energy – the energy of a particle or system of particles derived from its position or condition rather than motion (e.g., a raised weight, coiled spring, or charged battery).

Power – the rate at which work is done; electrically, power = current × voltage (P = I V)

Precautionary principle – where there are threats of severe irreversible environmental damage, lack of scientific certainty should not be used as a reason for introducing measures to prevent degradation (*Rio Declaration*).

Precedent – a decision used as an example in addressing subsequent similar situations.

Precession – the wobble over thousands of years of Earth's axis tilt for the plane of the solar system.

Precipitation (*weather*) – any liquid or solid water particles falling from the atmosphere to Earth's surface. Includes drizzle, rain, snow, snow, ice crystals, and ice pellets.

Precipitator – pollution control device that collects particles from an air stream.

Pre-consumer waste – material diverted to the waste stream during a manufacturing process, *waste from manufacture and production*.

Precycling – making environmentally sound decisions at the store and reducing waste.

Predation – the act of feeding by a *Predator*.

Predator – an organism that feeds directly on other organisms to survive; live-feeders, such as herbivores and carnivores.

Pre-industrial – referring to the time before industrialization (i.e., before the Industrial Revolution c. 1750-1850).

Preparedness – actions taken to build, apply, and sustain the capabilities necessary to prevent, protect against, and ameliorate adverse effects.

Prescribed waste and industrial waste (1998) – Environment Protection (*Prescribed Waste*) Regulation lists requirements under the industrial waste management policy. *Prescribed wastes carry special handling, storage, transport, and often licensing requirements, attracting substantially higher disposal levies than non-prescribed solid wastes.*

Prevention of significant deterioration – a clause of the *Clean Air Act* that prevents degradation of existing clean air; opposed by the industry as an unnecessary barrier to development.

Prey – an organism upon which a predator feeds.

Price elasticity – a situation in which the supply of and the demand for a commodity will fluctuate with price changes.

Primary energy – forms of energy obtained directly from nature; the energy in raw fuels (electricity from the grid is not primary) is used primarily on energy statistics when compiling energy balances.

Primary pollutants – chemicals released directly into the air in a harmful form.

Primary producers (or *producer*) – responsible for a substantial amount of the food for the rest of the food chain in an ecosystem. *An organism that produces food from inorganic material in the environment through photosynthesis or chemosynthesis in the deep sea. A plant that can produce its food from inorganic substances (energetics) is an organism or process that generates concentrated energy from sunlight beyond its own needs.*

Primary production – synthesis of organic compounds from carbon dioxide (CO_2) in Earth's atmosphere. *Life on Earth, directly or indirectly, depends on it.*

Primary productivity – 1. the fixation rate at which plants fix energy. 2. synthesizing organic materials (*biomass*) by green plants using the light energy captured in photosynthesis.

Primary (sewage) treatment – removes solids from sewage before it is discharged or treated further.

Primary standards – the 1970 *Clean Air Act* regulations intended to protect human health.

Primary succession – an ecological succession where no biotic community previously existed.

Principle of competitive exclusion – a result of natural selection whereby two similar species in a community occupy ecological niches, thereby reducing competition for food.

Producer (or *primary producer*) – an organism that produces food from inorganic material in the environment through photosynthesis or chemosynthesis in the deep sea. *A plant that can produce its food from inorganic substances (energetics) is an organism or process that generates concentrated energy from sunlight beyond its own needs.*

Producer responsibility – the legal responsibilities of manufacturers for their products' lives.

Product – 1. produced by labor; 2. items bought in shops; 3. in ecology, the photosynthesis results.

Product stewardship – shared responsibility by sectors involved in manufacturing, distributing, using, and disposing of products for the consequences of these activities. *Manufacturing responsibility extends to the product's life.*

Production frontier – the maximum output of two competing commodities at production levels.

Productivity (*ecology*) – the rate at which producers use radiant energy to form organic substances as food for consumers.

Prokaryotic – cells that do not have a membrane-bounded nucleus or membrane-bounded organelles.

Promethean environmentalism (or *technological optimists*) – those believing technology and human enterprise will find solutions for problems.

Promoters (or co-carcinogens) – not carcinogenic agents assisting tumor progression and spread.

Pronatalist pressures – influences that encourage people to have children.

Proteins – chains of amino acids linked by peptide bonds.

Protocooperation – a type of mutualism without necessity.

Proton – a positively charged subatomic particle in the nucleus of an atom.

Proven resources – those that have been thoroughly mapped and are economical to recover at current prices with available technology.

Provisioning services – one of the major ecosystem services: the products obtained from ecosystems (e.g., genetic resources, food, fiber, and freshwater).

Proximity – the state, quality, sense, or fact of being near or next to; closeness.

Proxy – a variable related to one of interest (e.g., tree rings can be proxies for temperature variations).

Public trust – a doctrine obligating the government to maintain public lands in a natural state as guardians of the public interest.

Pull factors – in urbanization, conditions attracting people from the country to cities.

Push factors – in urbanization, conditions forcing people from the country into cities.

Pyrolysis – advanced thermal technology involving the thermal decomposition of organic compounds in the complete absence of oxygen under pressure and at elevated temperatures.

Q

Quadrat (or *quad*) – a rectangular plot of land extensively studied for its ecology.

Qualitative – of or concerning a trait, characteristic, or property.

Quantitative – relating to or expressed as a specified or indefinite number or amount.

R

Radiation – energy transfer in the form of electromagnetic waves or particles that release energy when absorbed by an object. See *ultraviolet radiation, infrared radiation, solar radiation,* and *long-wave radiation*.

Radiative forcing – the change in energy flux in the atmosphere caused by natural or anthropogenic climate change factors as measured by watts / meter². A change in Earth's energy balance–atmosphere system in response to a change in factors such as greenhouse gases, land–use change, or solar radiation. *It is a scientific concept to quantify and compare the external drivers of change to Earth's energy balance. Positive radiative forcing increases the temperature of the lower atmosphere, which increases temperatures at Earth's surface. Harmful radiation cools the lower atmosphere. Radiative forcing is most measured in watts per square meter (W/m^2) units.*

Radiatively active gases – gases that occur naturally or are produced anthropogenically, affecting atmospheric radiation by absorption or emission.

Radioactive – an unstable isotope decays spontaneously and releases subatomic particles (or units of energy).

Radioactive decay – a change in the nuclei of radioactive isotopes that spontaneously emit high-energy electromagnetic radiation (or subatomic particles) while gradually changing into another isotope or a different element.

Radionuclides – isotopes that exhibit radioactive decay.

Radon – a radioactive gaseous element formed by the disintegration of radium, the heaviest of the inert gases; occurs naturally (especially in areas over granite) and is considered a health hazard.

Rain garden – an engineered area for collecting, infiltrating, and evapotranspiration rainwater runoff, mostly from impervious surfaces. *It reduces rain runoff by allowing stormwater to soak into the ground (as opposed to flowing into storm drains and surface waters, which can cause erosion, water pollution, flooding, and diminished groundwater). Rain gardens absorb water contaminants entering water bodies. Terminology arose in Maryland, USA, in the 1990s as a marketable expression for bioremediation.*

Rainshadow – an area with a consistently arid or semi-arid climate due to its position on the lee (i.e., sheltered side) of a mountain range. *A dry area on the downwind side of a mountain.*

Rainforest – a forest with high humidity, constant temperature, and abundant rainfall (generally over 150 inches per year); it can be tropical or temperate.

Rainwater harvesting (or *water harvesting*) – collecting rainwater either in storage or the soil mainly close to where it falls; the attempt to increase rainwater productivity by storing it in ponds, wetlands, etc., and helping to avoid the need for infrastructure to bring water from elsewhere. *Practiced on a large scale upstream, this reduces available water downstream.*

Range (or *population distribution*) – the prevalence of a species in the geographical area within which that species can be found.

Rangeland – grasslands and open woodlands suitable for livestock grazing.

Range shift – change in the area extent of a species or geographic limits for species.

Rational choice – public decision-making based on reason, logic, and science-based management.

Raw materials – ground materials extracted and processed (e.g., bauxite is processed into aluminum).

Reasonably Available Control Technology (RACT) – the lowest emissions limit that a source can meet by applying control technology that is reasonably available considering technological and economic feasibility.

Recharge zones – an area where water filters into aquifers.

Reclaimed water – water from a waste (effluent) stream and purified to a level suitable for further use.

Reclamation – chemical, biological, or physical cleanup and reconstruction of severely contaminated or degraded sites to return them to their original topography and vegetation.

Recoverable resources – those accessible with current technology but deemed not economical under current conditions.

Recovered material (*waste*) – material that would have otherwise been disposed of as waste or used for energy recovery but has instead been collected and recovered (reclaimed) as material input, thus avoiding using new primary materials.

Recovery rate (*waste*) – the percentage of materials consumed and recovered for recycling.

Re-creation – construction of a biological community to replace one destroyed on that or another site.

Recreational fishing – by the 1890s, most states in the U.S. had restrictions on fishing; today, a fishing license is needed to fish for recreation in lakes and inland bodies of water.

Recyclables – strictly, all materials may be recycled, including the recyclable containers and paper or cardboard components of curbside waste (excluding garden organics).

Recycled content – the mass proportion of recycled material in a product or packaging. *Only pre-consumer and post-consumer materials are considered recycled content.*

Recycled material – waste converted into usable forms, not necessarily in its original use. See *recovered material*.

Recycled water – treated stormwater, greywater, or blackwater suitable for toilet flushing, irrigation, industry, etc. *Non–drinking water is indicated using a lilac non–drinking label.*

Recycling – 1. includes collection, sorting, reprocessing, and manufacturing products into goods. 2. reprocessing discarded materials into new, valuable products; different from reusing materials for their original purpose, but the terms are often used interchangeably. Collecting and reprocessing a resource so it can be used again. *For example, collecting aluminum cans, melting them, and using them to make cans or aluminum products.*

Red tide – a population explosion (or *bloom*) of minute, single-celled *dinoflagellate* marine organisms. *Billions of cells accumulate in protected bays where toxins poison other marine life.*

Reduced tillage systems – such as minimum-till, conserve-till, and no-till preserve soil, save energy and water, and increase crop yields.

Reducing Emissions from Deforestation and Forest Degradation (REDD) – using market and financial incentives to reduce greenhouse gas emissions from deforestation and forest degradation.

Reflected – to return light rays from a surface so that the angle at which a given ray is returned equals the angle at which it strikes the surface.

Reflectivity – the ability of surface material to reflect sunlight, including the visible, infrared, and ultraviolet wavelengths.

Reforestation – 1. replanting of forests on lands that have recently been harvested; 2. the direct human conversion of non-forested land to forested land through planting, seeding, or promotion of natural seed sources on land that was once forested but now no longer. According to the *Kyoto Protocol*, for the first commitment period (2008–2012), reforestation activities were limited to reforestation occurring on lands without forests at the beginning of 1990.

Reformer – a device that strips hydrogen from fuels such as natural gas, methanol, ammonia, gasoline, or vegetable oil so they can be used in a fuel cell.

Refracted – to alter the course of a wave of energy that passes into something from another medium, as water does to light entering it from the air, caused by differences in wave speed.

Refuse-derived fuel – the processing of solid waste to remove metal, glass, and other unburnable materials; the organic residue is shredded, formed into pellets, and dried to make fuel for power plants.

Regenerative farming – farming techniques and land stewardship that restore the health and productivity of the soil by rotating crops, planting ground cover, protecting the surface with crop residue, and reducing synthetic chemical inputs and mechanical compaction.

Regional consequences – the impact of global climate change varies from one region to another; dry areas may become wetter, and another region may have less precipitation.

Regulating services (*sustainability*) – the benefits obtained from regulating ecosystem processes, including, for example, climate, water, or disease regulation.

Regulations – rules established by administrative agencies; that can be more important than *statutory law* in managing resources.

Rehabilitate land – a utilitarian program to make an area useful to humans.

Rehabilitation – to rebuild elements of structure or function in an ecological system without necessarily achieving complete restoration to its original condition.

Relative – the relation of one thing to another, expressed as the ratio of the specified quantity to the total magnitude (as the value of a measured quantity) or the mean of the quantities involved.

Relative humidity – at any given temperature, a comparison of the actual water content of the air with the amount of water that could be held at saturation.

Relative sea level rise – the increase in ocean water levels at a specific location considers global sea level rise and local factors, such as local subsidence and uplift. *Relative sea level rise is measured for a specified vertical datum relative to the land, which may change elevation over time.*

Relativists – those who believe moral principles are always dependent on the situation.

REM (*roentgen equivalent man*) – a unit in radiation protection to measure the amount of damage to human tissue from a dose of ionizing radiation. The amount of ionizing radiation required to produce the same biological effect as one "*rad*" of high-penetration X-rays. *An average American receives about 0.370 rems of radiation per year.*

Remediation – cleaning up chemical contaminants from a polluted area.

Removal unit (or *Kyoto unit*) – a tradable carbon credit represents an allowance to emit one metric ton of greenhouse gases absorbed by a removal or carbon sink activity in an Annex I country.

Renewable energy – any source of energy used without depleting its reserves. *These sources include sunlight (solar energy) and other sources such as wind, waves, biomass, geothermal, and hydro energy. Naturally replenishing energy such as biomass, hydro, geothermal, solar, wind, ocean thermal, wave action, and tidal action.*

Renewable energy certificates – Market trading mechanisms created through the *Renewable Energy (Electricity) Act 2000* in connection with the Canadian government's mandatory renewable energy target. *Provides a "premium" revenue stream for renewable sources.*

Renewable resources – resources typically replaced or replenished by natural processes; resources not depleted by moderate use (e.g., solar energy, biological resources such as forests and fisheries, biological organisms, and some biogeochemical cycles).

Renewable water supplies – annual freshwater surface runoff plus annual infiltration into underground freshwater aquifers that are accessible for human use.

Roentgen equivalent man (REM) – a unit in radiation protection to measure the amount of damage to human tissue from a dose of ionizing radiation. The amount of ionizing radiation required to produce the same biological effect as one "*rad*" of high-penetration X-rays. *An average American receives about 0.370 rems of radiation per year.*

Replacement level of fertility (or *zero population growth, ZPG*) – the number of births at which people are just replacing themselves.

Representative Concentration Pathways (RCP) – time series of emissions and concentrations of the suite of greenhouse gases, aerosols, and other chemically active gases, as well as land use/land cover. *The word "representative" signifies that each RCP provides only one of many possible scenarios leading to the specific radiative forcing characteristics. The term "pathway" emphasizes that not only the long-term concentration levels are of interest but also the trajectory taken over time to reach that outcome.*

Reprocessing (*waste*) – changing the physical structure and properties of waste that would otherwise have been sent to a landfill to add financial value to processed material; may involve a range of technologies, including composting, anaerobic digestion, and energy from waste technologies such as pyrolysis, gasification, and incineration.

Reservoir – a natural or artificial pond or lake for storing and regulating water.

Residence time – the time a component, such as an individual water molecule, will spend in a compartment or location before it moves on through a process or cycle. *The average time spent in a reservoir by an individual atom or molecule. For greenhouse gases, residence time refers to how long, on average, a particular molecule remains in the atmosphere. The residence time is approximately equal to the atmospheric lifetime for most gases other than methane and carbon dioxide.*

Residual waste – residue after separating recyclable materials (including *green waste*).

Residue – 1. material remaining; residues of contaminants may remain after clean-up; 2. the part of a molecule that remains after a portion of its constituents is removed.

Resilience – 1. the ability of a community or ecosystem to recover from disturbances. 2. a capability to anticipate, prepare for, respond to, and recover from significant multi-hazard threats with minimum damage to social well-being, the economy, and the environment. *A capability to anticipate, prepare for, respond to, and recover from significant multi-hazard threats with minimum damage to social well-being, the economy, and the environment.*

Resistant – the ability of an individual or community to resist change by potentially disruptive events.

Resource – 1. a substance or object in the environment required by an organism for normal growth, maintenance, and reproduction. 2. in economic terms, anything with potential to be used in creating wealth or giving satisfaction.

Resource Conservation and Recovery Act (RCRA) – regulates waste handling from *cradle to grave*. Establishes rules for handling such waste from its generation while being packaged, stored, transported, and how it is disposed of, as well as the disposal sites themselves.

Resource flow – the totality of changes in multiple resource stocks, or at least any pair of them, over a specified period

Resource intensity – the ratio of resource consumption relative to its economic or physical output; for example, liters of water used per dollar spent or liters of water used per ton of aluminum produced. *At the national level, energy intensity is the ratio of the country's primary energy consumption to either the gross domestic product or the physical output* (*total goods produced*).

Resource mismatch – decoupling a previously synchronized ecological relationship, such as changes in timing within a trophic (food-web) relationship.

Resource productivity – the output obtained for a given resource input.

Resource partitioning – in a biological community, various populations share environmental resources through specialization, thereby reducing direct competition. *The coexistence of two or more competing species that use the same natural resource differently.* See *ecological niche*.

Resource recovery (*waste*) – obtaining matter or energy from discarded materials.

Resource scarcity – a shortage or deficit in some *resource*.

Resource stock – the amount of a resource often related to resource flow (the number of resources harvested or used per unit of time). *Stocks are measured in mass, volume, or energy and flow in mass, volume, or energy per unit of time. The harvest must not exceed the net production to harvest a resource stock sustainably.*

Respiration (*biology*) – 1. uptake by a living organism of oxygen from the air (or water), which is used to oxidize organic matter or food; the outputs of this oxidation are usually CO_2 and H_2O. 2. the metabolic process by which organisms meet their internal energy needs and release CO_2.

Restoration – to bring something back to a former condition; ecological restoration involves active manipulation of nature to recreate the conditions that existed before human disturbance.

Restoration ecology – a branch of ecology targeting the ecological basis needed to restore impaired or damaged ecosystems. *Seeks to repair or reconstruct ecosystems damaged by human actions.*

Retail therapy – shopping to compensate for things psychologically and physically lacking.

Retrofit – to replace existing items with updated items.

Reuse – the second pillar of the waste hierarchy. Recovering value from a discarded resource without reprocessing or remanufacturing (e.g., clothes sold through opportunity shops represent a form of reuse *rather than recycling*).

Reverse osmosis – a process of desalinization where water is forced under pressure through a semipermeable membrane whose tiny pores allow water to pass but exclude most salts and minerals.

Riders – amendments attached to bills in the conference committee, often wholly unrelated to the bill to which they are added.

Rill erosion – the removal of thin layers of soil caused by little rivulets of running water cutting small channels in the soil.

Risk – 1. the probability that something undesirable happens due to hazard exposure. 2. threats to life, health and safety, the environment, economic well-being, and things of value. *Risks are often evaluated for how likely they will occur (probability) and damage resulting if they did happen (consequences).*

Risk assessment – evaluates short-term and long-term risks associated with an activity or hazard, usually compared to anticipated benefits in a cost-benefit analysis. Estimates the likelihood of specific events occurring and their potential positive or negative consequences.

Risk management – planning to manage the effects of climate change to increase positive and decrease negative impacts.

Risk perception – the psychological and emotional factors that affect people's behavior and beliefs about potential adverse hazards or consequences.

Risk-based framing – planning based on the pros and cons of a given set of possibilities includes assessment of a risk in terms of the likelihood of its occurrence and the magnitude of the impact associated with the risk.

RNA (Ribonucleic acid) – nucleic acid used to transcribe and translate the genetic code found on DNA (deoxyribonucleic acid) molecules.

Rock – a solid, cohesive aggregate of one or more crystalline minerals.

Rock cycle – the process whereby rocks are broken down by chemical and physical forces; sediments are moved by wind, water, and gravity, settle and reform into rock, and eventually are crushed, folded, melted, and re-crystallized into new forms.

Roundwood (or *industrial timber*) – trees used for lumber, plywood, veneer, particleboard, chipboard, and paper.

Routinely monitored – regular, periodic testing.

r-selected species – a species selected for superiority in variable or unpredictable environments. Contrast *k-selected species*.

Ruminant animals – cud-chewing animals, such as cattle, sheep, goats, and buffalo, have multi-chambered stomachs in which bacteria digest cellulose.

Runoff – the flow of water over land from rain, melting snow, or other sources. *The excess of precipitation over evaporation; water that the ground cannot absorb. The main source of surface water and, broadly, the water available for human use.*

Run-of-the-river flow – ordinary river flow not accelerated by dams, flumes, etc.; some small, modern, high-efficiency turbines can generate useful power using only run-of-the-river flow, with a current of only a few kilometers per hour.

Runaway greenhouse effect – an ill-defined term associated with irreversible temperature rises.

Rural area – where residents depend on agriculture or harvesting natural resources.

S

SF₆ – Sulfur hexafluoride

S curve (or *S-shaped curve*) – a curve that depicts logistic growth; called an S curve because of its shape. See *logistic growth*.

Saffir/Simpson – a scale to measure hurricanes based on wind speeds and air pressure.

Salinity (*ecology*) – 1. salt in water and soil, generally in the context of human activity such as clearing and planting for annual crops rather than perennial trees and shrubs. Can make soils infertile. 2. dissolved salts in water and soils, generally in the context of human activity such as clearing and planting for annual crops rather than perennial trees and shrubs, can make soils infertile.

Salinization – 1. the process by which land becomes salt-affected. 2. a process in which mineral salts accumulate in soil, killing plants. *Occurs when the soil in dry climates is irrigated profusely.*

Salt domes – a solid mass of salt that was once fluid but has flowed into fractures in surrounding rock and geologic structures.

Saltwater intrusion – the movement of saltwater into freshwater aquifers in coastal areas where groundwater is withdrawn faster than replenished. *Fresh or ground water is displaced by the advance of salt water due to its greater density, usually in coastal and estuarine areas.*

Sanitary landfills – a landfill where refuse and municipal waste are buried daily under enough soil or fill to eliminate odors, vermin, and litter.

Saturation point – the maximum concentration of water vapors in air at a given temperature.

Savanna – a tropical or subtropical grassland ecosystem with trees without a closed canopy.

Scale – the physical dimensions of phenomena or events in either space or time.

Scattered – few and far apart in distance or time.

Scavenger – an organism feeding on dead organisms.

Scenarios – 1. a plausible and often simplified description of how the future may develop based on a coherent and internally consistent set of assumptions about driving forces and key relationships. 2. sets of assumptions used to help understand potential future conditions such as population growth, land use, and sea level rise. *Scenarios are neither predictions nor forecasts but are used for planning purposes.*

Scientific method – a systematic, precise, objective study of a problem; generally, this requires observation, hypothesis development and testing, data gathering, and interpretation.

Scientific theory – an explanation supported by many tests that have come to be accepted by the consensus of scientists.

Scrubbers – an air pollution device that uses water spray, reactant, or a dry process to trap pollutants.

Sea surface temperature (SST) – the top several feet of ocean measured by ships, buoys, and drifters.

Second law of thermodynamics – states that with each successive energy transfer or transformation in a system, less energy is available to do work.

Secondary energy – primary energies transformed in energy conversion processes to more convenient secondary forms, such as electrical energy or cleaner fuels.

Secondary pollutants – chemicals modified to a hazardous form after entering the air or formed by chemical reactions as components of the air mix and interact.

Secondary recovery technique – pumping pressurized gas, steam, or chemical-containing water into a well to squeeze more oil from a reservoir.

Secondary standards – the 1972 *Clean Air Act* regulations intended to protect materials, crops, visibility, climate, and personal comfort.

Secondary succession – a stage of ecological succession that occurs after the original community has been destroyed or disturbed, as with a forest fire. *Succession on a site where an existing community has been disrupted.*

Secondary treatment – bacterial decomposition of suspended particulates and dissolved organic compounds that remain after primary sewage treatment.

Sectors (*economics*) – economic groupings to generalize patterns of expenditure and use.

Secure landfill – a solid waste disposal site lined and capped with impermeable barriers preventing leakage or *leaching*; drain tiles, sampling wells, and vents provide monitoring and pollution control.

Sediment (*ecology*) – soil or particles settling to the bottom of water bodies.

Sedimentary rock – deposited material that remains in place long enough or has been covered with enough material to compact into stone; examples include shale, sandstone, breccia, and conglomerates.

Sedimentation – the deposition of organic materials or minerals by chemical, physical, or biological processes.

Seed sourcing – seed sources are taken from areas where the climate is like the predicted future climate in the planting location to assist with climate adaptation.

Seismic activity – describes the size, type, and frequency of earthquakes in an area over time.

Selective cutting – harvesting only mature trees of particular species and size; usually more expensive than clear-cutting, but it is less disruptive for wildlife and often better for forest regeneration.

Selfish herd – individuals in a group acting together without planned direction.

Self-organization – the process by which systems use energy to develop structure and organization.

Self-regulating – an internal mechanism by which a system or organism controls its functions.

Sensitivity – the degree to which a system is affected, either adversely or beneficially, by climate variability or change. The effect may be direct (e.g., a change in crop yield in response to a change in the mean, range, or variability of temperature) or indirect (e.g., damages caused by increased coastal flooding due to sea level rise).

Sentinel indicator (*ecology*) – captures the essence of the change process affecting a broad area of interest and is easily communicated.

Septic sewage – sewage in which anaerobic respiration occurs. *Characterized by a blackish color and the smell of hydrogen sulfide*

Septic tank – a sedimentation tank in which the sludge is retained for organic content to undergo anaerobic digestion. *It is typically used for sewage from houses too isolated for sewer connections.*

Sequestration (*global warming*) – the removal of carbon dioxide from Earth's atmosphere and storage in a sink, as when trees absorb CO_2 in photosynthesis and store it in their tissues.

Seriously undernourished – those who receive less than 80 percent of their minimum daily caloric requirements.

Sessile – permanently attached or established; not free to move about.

Sewage – water and raw effluent disposed of through toilets, kitchens, and bathrooms. *Includes water-borne waste from domestic uses of water from households or similar uses in trade or industry.*

Sewer – a pipe conveying sewage.

Sewerage – a system of pipes and mechanical appliances for collecting and transporting domestic and industrial sewage.

Sewerage system (*infrastructure*) – the network of pipes, pumping stations, and treatment plants used to collect, transport, treat and discharge sewage.

Sewer-mining – tapping directly into a sewer (either before or after a sewage treatment plant) and extracting wastewater for treatment and use.

Sexual selection – a mode of natural selection in which members of one biological sex choose mates of the other sex to mate and compete with same-sex members for access to members of the opposite sex.

Shallow ecology – a critical term applied to superficial environmentalists who claim to be green but are quick to compromise and do little to bring about fundamental change.

Shantytowns – settlements created when people move onto undeveloped lands and build their shelter with cheap or discarded materials; some are illegal subdivisions where landowners rent land without city approval, and others are land invasions.

Sheet erosion –thin soil layers peel from land surfaces; accomplished primarily by wind and water.

Short ton – standard measurement for a ton in the United States. A short ton equals 2,000 lbs. or 0.907 metric tons. See *metric ton*.

Short-wave radiation (or *solar radiation*) – emitted by the Sun. Solar radiation has a distinctive range of wavelengths (i.e., electromagnetic spectrum) determined by the temperature of the Sun. See *ultraviolet radiation, infrared radiation*, and *radiation*.

Shredder flock – residue from shredded car bodies, white goods (i.e., large appliances), and the like.

Sick Building Syndrome – a building whose occupants experience acute health or comfort effects that appear to be linked to the time spent there but where no specific illness or cause can be identified. *Complaints may be localized or spread throughout the building.*

Sign stimulus – a fixed action pattern such as a mating dance.

Silent Spring (Rachel Carson, 1962) – an environmental science book that inspired the environmental movement and later led to the creation of the U.S. Environmental Protection Agency (EPA) in 1970.

Siltation – to become choked or obstructed with silt or mud.

Simple living – a lifestyle individuals pursue for various motivations, such as spirituality, health, or ecology. Some explicitly reject "Westernized values," while others live more simply for personal taste, a sense of fairness, or personal economy. Others may choose simple living for social justice or rejection of consumerism. Simple living as a concept is distinguished from the simple lifestyles of those living in conditions of poverty in that its proponents consciously choose not to focus on wealth directly tied to money or cash–based economics.

Sinkholes – large surface craters caused by the collapse of an underground channel or cavern; often triggered by groundwater withdrawal.

Sinks – 1. processes or places that remove or store gases, solutes, or solids; 2. any process, activity, or mechanism that results in the net removal of greenhouse gases, aerosols, or precursors of greenhouse gases from the atmosphere. *Any process, activity, or mechanism that removes greenhouse gases, an aerosol, or a precursor of a greenhouse gas or aerosol from the atmosphere. A natural or technological process that removes and stores carbon from the atmosphere.*

Slash and burn – a form of deforestation used to clear fields for agricultural use.

Slow Food – a movement founded in Italy in 1986 by Carlo Petrini to respond to the negative impact of international food industries. *Slow food is a counteracting force against fast food as it encourages local seasonal produce, restores time-honored production and preparation methods, and encourages food sharing at communal tables. It encourages environmentally sustainable production, ethical treatment of animals, and social justice. Slow Food members seek to defend biodiversity in the food supply, to appreciate better and improve understanding of the sensation of taste, and to celebrate the connection between plate and planet. Gatherings of Slow Food supporters are convivial.*

Sludge – 1. waste in a state between liquid and solid. 2. a semi-solid mixture of organic and inorganic materials that settle wastewater at a sewage treatment plant.

Slums – legal but inadequate multifamily tenements or rooming houses; some are custom-built for rent to poor people; others have been converted for some other use.

Smart growth – efficient use of land resources and existing urban infrastructure.

Smog – 1. (*photochemical*) air pollution produced by the action of sunlight on hydrocarbons, nitrogen oxides, and other pollutants; 2. (*industrial*) primarily a winter phenomenon that occurs when sulfur dioxide emissions and smoke particles react with water vapor; 3. describes the combination of industrial smoke (and automobile exhaust) and fog formerly in the stagnant air of London and the air of present-day Los Angeles.

Snowball Earth – a geohistorical hypothesis proposing one or more of Earth's icehouse climates, when the planet's surface becames frozen with no liquid oceanic or surface water exposed to the atmosphere.

Snowpack – a seasonal accumulation of slow-melting snow that accumulates over the winter and slowly melts to release water in spring and summer.

Snow water equivalent (SWE) – the amount of water held in a volume of snow, which depends on the density of the snow and other factors.

Soak away (or *absorption pit*) – a hole dug in permeable ground filled with broken stones or granular material and usually covered with earth, allowing collected water to soak into the ground.

Social behavior – the behavior of an individual organism towards members of the species population.

Social ecology – a socialist philosophy based on the communitarian anarchism of Russian geographer Peter Kropotkin; shares much with *Deep ecology* except that it is more humanist in its outlook.

Sociality – the degree to which animal population members associate in social groups and form cooperative societies.

Social justice – equitable access to resources and their benefits; a system that recognizes people's inalienable rights and adheres to what is fair, honest, and moral.

Sodicity (*ecology*) – measures the sodium content of soil. Sodic soils are dispersible and vulnerable to erosion. *An indicator of the suitability of water for use in agricultural irrigation, as determined from the concentrations of the main alkaline and earth alkaline cations present in the water.* See *sodium absorption ratio*.

Sodification – the build–up in soils of sodium relative to potassium and magnesium as exchangeable cations (i.e., *positively charged ions*) of clay fractions. *Sodic soils present challenges because they tend to have very poor structure, which limits or prevents water infiltration and drainage.*

Sodium absorption ratio (SA) – an indicator of the suitability of water for use in agricultural irrigation, as determined from the concentrations of the main alkaline and earth alkaline cations present in the water. See *sodicity*.

Soil – the naturally occurring, unconsolidated, or loose covering of Earth's surface; part of the pedosphere. *A complex mixture of weathered mineral materials from rocks, partially decomposed organic molecules, and a host of living organisms.*

Soil acidification – reduction in pH, usually in soil. *Acidification can result in poorly structured or hard-setting topsoil that cannot support sufficient vegetation to prevent erosion.*

Soil bulk density – the relative density of soil measured by dividing dry weight of soil by its volume.

Soil carbon – a major component of terrestrial biosphere pools in the carbon cycle. *The amount of carbon in soil is a function of historical vegetative cover and productivity, dependent on climatic variables.*

Soil compaction – the degree of compression of soil. *Heavy compaction impedes plant growth.*

Soil conditioner – any composted or non-composted material of organic origin produced for adding to soils; it includes *soil amendment*, *soil additive*, *soil improver*, and similar materials. However, it excludes polymers that do not biodegrade, such as plastics, rubbers, and coatings.

Soil ecology – a branch of ecology that studies the pedosphere (i.e., soil mantle).

Soil horizons – horizontal layers analyzed to reveal a soil's history, characteristics, and usefulness.

Soil moisture deficit – the volume of water needed to raise the soil water content of the root zone to *field capacity* (i.e., the amount of water held by soil after excess has drained).

Soil organic carbon (SOC) – the total organic carbon of a soil exclusive of carbon from undecayed plant and animal residue.

Soil organic matter (SOM) – the organic fraction of soil without undecayed plant and animal residues.

Soil structure – how soil particles collect into aggregates (or *crumbs*) needed for air and water passage.

Soil water storage – the amount of water stored in the soil in the plant root zone.

Solar energy – Sun's radiant energy, converted into other forms of energy (e.g., heat or electricity).

Solar power – electricity generated from solar radiation (Sun's rays).

Solar radiation (or *short-wave radiation*) – emitted by the Sun. Solar radiation has a distinctive range of wavelengths (i.e., electromagnetic spectrum) determined by the temperature of the Sun. See *ultraviolet radiation*, *infrared radiation*, and *radiation*.

Solar variation – changes in the amount of radiant energy emitted by the Sun.

Solar wind – the stream of charged particles ejected from the Sun's upper atmosphere.

Solid industrial waste – generated from commercial, industrial, or trade activities, including factories, offices, schools, universities, State and Federal government operations, and commercial construction and demolition work. *Excludes wastes prescribed under the Environment Protection Act (1970) and quarantine wastes.*

Solid inert waste – hard waste and dry vegetative material that has a negligible activity or effect on the environment, such as demolition material, concrete, bricks, plastic, glass, metals, and shredded tires.

Solid waste – non–hazardous, non-prescribed solid waste ranging from municipal garbage to industrial waste, generally domestic and municipal; commercial and industrial; construction and demolition.

Soluble – susceptible to being dissolved in a liquid, particularly in water.

Song system – discrete brain nuclei in songbirds used to learn and produce specific sequences.

Source separation (*waste*) – separation of recyclable material from other waste at the point and time the waste is generated (i.e., at its source). This includes the separation of recyclable material into its component categories, e.g., paper, glass, aluminum) Furthermore, it may include further separation within each category (e.g., paper into computer paper, office whites, and newsprint). The practice of segregating materials into discrete streams before collection by or delivery to reprocessing facilities.

Source-sink dynamics – a theoretical model used by ecologists to describe how variation in habitat quality may affect organisms' population growth or decline.

Southern pine forest – the United States coniferous forest ecosystem characterized by a warm, moist climate.

Special Report on Emissions Scenarios (SRES) – a set of emission scenarios from the IPCC Special Report on Emission Scenarios released in 2000 that describe a wide range of potential future socio-economic conditions and resulting emissions.

Specialist species – only thrive in a narrow range of environmental conditions or have a limited diet.

Speciation – the evolutionary process when biological species emerge from a common ancestor.

Species – a taxonomic category subordinate to a genus (or subgenus) and superior to a subspecies or variety, composed of individuals possessing common characteristics and that can reproduce sexually among themselves but cannot produce fertile offspring when mated with other species, distinguishing them from other categories of individuals of the same taxonomic level. *In taxonomic nomenclature, species are designated by the genus name followed by a Latin or Latinized adjective or noun.*

Species diversity – the number and relative abundance of species in a community.

Species recovery plan – restoring an endangered species through protection, habitat management, captive breeding, disease control, or other techniques that increase populations and encourage survival.

Specific heat capacity – the amount of energy needed to increase the temperature of 1 kg of a substance by 1 °C. *Measures resistance to temperature increase and is essential for energy transfer.*

Spectrum – an ordered array of the components of an emission or wave.

Spent fuel – the uranium cores taken out of the nuclear power plant.

Spillways – a passage permitting surplus water to run over or around an obstruction (such as a dam).

Spontaneous – 1. happening or arising without apparent external cause; self-generated; 2. arising from a natural inclination or impulse and not from any external incitement or constraint; 3. unconstrained and unstudied in manner or behavior; 4) plants growing without cultivation or human labor; indigenous.

Sport hunting – hunting animals, not just for food.

Sprawl – an unlimited outward extension of city boundaries that lowers population density, consumes open space, generates freeway congestion, and causes decay in central cities.

Spring overturn – 1. a springtime lake phenomenon that occurs when the surface ice melts, and the surface water temperature warms to its greatest density at 4 °C and sinks, creating a convection current displacing the nutrient-rich bottom waters. 2. the mixing of lake water through the melting of ice cover, warming surface waters, convection currents, and wind action occurring in spring.

Squatter towns – *Shantytowns* that occupy land without the owner's permission; some are highly organized movements in defiance of authorities; others grow gradually.

Stability – 1. in ecological terms, a dynamic equilibrium among the physical and biological factors in an ecosystem or a community; 2. relative homeostasis.

Stable runoff – the fraction of water available year-round. *Usually more important than total runoff when determining human uses.*

Stack emissions – emissions from a smokestack, including dioxin, furans, nitrogen oxides, and carbon.

Stakeholders – parties having an interest in a particular project or outcome. *An individual or group directly or indirectly affected by or interested in the outcomes of decisions.*

Standard Metropolitan Statistical Area (SMSA) – an urbanized region with at least 100,000 inhabitants with strong economic and social ties to a central city of at least 50,000 people.

Standing – the right to take part in legal proceedings.

State Environment Protection Policies – statutory instruments (e.g., legislation, rules) under the *Environment Protection Act* 1970 identifying beneficial uses of environmental protection, established environmental indicators and objectives, and attainment programs to implement policies.

State of Environment Reporting – a scientific assessment of environmental conditions focuses on human impacts, their significance, and social responses to the identified trends.

Stationary energy – that energy that is other than transport fuels and fugitive emissions; used mostly for producing electricity but also for manufacturing, processing and in, agriculture, fisheries, etc.

Statute law – formal documents or decrees enacted by the legislative branch of government.

Statutory law – rules passed by a state or national legislature.

Steady-state – a constant pattern; a balance of inflows and outflows.

Steady-state economy – characterized by low birth and death rates, use of renewable energy sources, recycling of materials, and emphasis on durability, efficiency, and stability.

Steppe – a dry, grassy plain occurring in temperate climates between the tropics and polar regions. *Temperate regions have distinct seasonal temperature changes, with cold winters and warm summers.*

Sterilization – 1. making an organism barren or infertile (unable to reproduce); 2. clearing an object of living organisms by heating it or applying chemicals.

Stewardship – the philosophy that humans are responsible for managing, caring for, and improving nature.

Storm surge – giant waves, often fifty miles wide and twenty-five feet or more high, that are caused by the force of a hurricane. An abnormal rise in sea level accompanying a hurricane or other intense storm, whose height is the difference between the observed sea surface level and the level that would have occurred without the cyclone. *For example, as the eye of the hurricane makes landfall, the wave comes sweeping across the coastline; aided by the hammering effect of the waves breaking, it acts like a giant bulldozer sweeping everything in its path.*

Stormwater – rainfall accumulating in natural or artificial systems after heavy rain; surface runoff or water sent to (stormwater) drains during heavy rain.

Stranded assets – assets that have suffered from unanticipated or premature write-downs, devaluations, or conversion to liabilities. A variety of environment-related risks can cause them.

Strategic Environmental Assessment (SEA) – a system of incorporating environmental considerations into policies, plans, and programs, especially in the European Union (EU).

Strategic Lawsuits Against Public Participation (SLAPP) – lawsuits that have no merit but are brought merely to intimidate and harass private citizens who act in the public interest.

Strategic metals and minerals – materials a country cannot produce but needs to use for essential materials or processes.

Stratification – the layering of water by temperature and density can occur in lakes or other bodies of water, often seasonally.

Stratosphere – the zone in the atmosphere extending from the tropopause to about 30 miles above Earth's surface; temperatures are stable or rise slightly with altitude; has very little water vapor but is rich in ozone; above the *troposphere* and below the *mesosphere*. A region of the atmosphere between the troposphere and mesosphere has a lower boundary of approximately 8 km at the poles to 15 km at the equator and an upper boundary of approximately 50 km. *Depending upon latitude and season, the temperature in the lower stratosphere can increase, be isothermal, or even decrease with altitude. However, the temperature in the upper stratosphere generally increases with height due to ozone's absorption of solar radiation.*

Stratospheric ozone – See *ozone layer*.

Stream – a flowing water ecosystem that starts as a freshwater spring or melting snow.

Streamflow – the volume of water moving over a designated point within a fixed period, often expressed as cubic feet per second (ft^3/sec).

Stressor – something that influences people and natural, managed, and socio-economic systems. Multiple stressors can have compounded effects, such as when economic or market stress combines with drought to impact farmers negatively.

Strip cutting – harvesting trees in strips narrow enough to minimize edge effects and allow natural forest regeneration.

Strip farming – planting different crops in alternating strips along land contours; when one crop is harvested, the other remains to protect the soil and prevent water from running straight down a hill.

Strip mining – removing surface layers over coal seams using giant earth-moving equipment; creating a vast open pit from which enormous surface-operated machines scoop coal and transport it by trucks; an alternative to deep mines.

Structure – in ecological terms, patterns of organization, both spatial and functional, in a community.

Sublimation – the process by which water can move between solid and gaseous states without ever becoming liquid.

Subsidence – a settling of the ground surface caused by the collapse of porous formations that result from the withdrawal of large amounts of groundwater, oil, or other underground materials.

Subsiding/Subsidence – the downward settling of Earth's crust relative to its surroundings.

Subsistence – 1. broadly refers to any human system that seeks to secure survival and flourish within ecosystems. 2. in legal and policy contexts, it is used more narrowly to refer to the provision of food that is a necessary part of a household's or a community's regular diet or legal entitlements to harvesting rights in particular situations. 3. the harvest or use of naturally produced renewable resources for direct personal or family consumption, such as food, shelter, fuel, clothing, tools, transportation, or production of handicrafts for customary and traditional trade, barter, or sharing.

Subsoil – a layer of soil beneath topsoil with lower organic content and higher concentrations of fine mineral particles. *Often contains soluble compounds and clay particles carried by percolating water.*

Sulfate aerosols – particulate matter consists of compounds of sulfur formed by the interaction of sulfur dioxide and sulfur trioxide with other compounds in the atmosphere. Sulfate aerosols are injected into the atmosphere from the combustion of fossil fuels and the eruption of volcanoes like Mt. Pinatubo. Sulfate aerosols can lower Earth's temperature by reflecting away solar radiation (negative radiative forcing). General Circulation Models, which incorporate the effects of sulfate aerosols, more accurately predict global temperature variations. See *particulate matter*, *aerosol*, and *general circulation models*.

Sulfur cycle – the chemical and physical reactions by which sulfur moves into or out of storage and through the environment.

Sulfur dioxide – a colorless, corrosive gas directly damaging plants and animals.

Sulfur hexafluoride (SF$_6$) – a colorless gas soluble in alcohol and ether and slightly soluble in water. A potent greenhouse gas used primarily in electrical transmission and distribution systems and as a dielectric in electronics. The global warming potential of SF$_6$ is 22,800. This GWP is from the IPCC's Fourth Assessment Report (AR4). See *global warming potential*.

Sulfur oxides – molecules formed by combining sulfur and oxygen (SOx).

Sullage – domestic wastewater from baths, showers, laundries, and kitchens (but *not* from toilets).

Sunspot – a region on the Sun's surface (i.e., photosphere) marked by a lower temperature than its surroundings. *It has intense magnetic activity, inhibiting convection and forming areas of low surface temperature.*

Supercity (or *megacity* and *megalopolis*) – an urban area with more than 10 million inhabitants.

Superfund (1980) – a U.S. federal program funds the cleanup of sites contaminated with hazardous substances and pollutants. It was established as the *Comprehensive Environmental Response, Compensation, and Liability Act* of 1980 (CERCLA).

Supply – the quantity of a product offered for sale at various prices, other things being equal.

Supporting services (*sustainability*) – ecosystem services necessary for producing other services. *For example, biomass production, production of atmospheric oxygen, soil formation, nutrients, and water cycling.*

Surface mining – when minerals are extracted from surface pits. See *strip mining*.

Surface runoff – rainfall passing out of an area into the drainage system.

Surface tension – when the water surface meets the air and acts as an elastic skin.

Survivorship – the percentage of a population reaching a given age or the proportion of the maximum lifespan of the species reached by any individual.

Survivorship curve – a graph showing the number or proportion of individuals surviving at each age for a given species.

Suspended particulate matter (SPM) (*aerosols*) – a suspension or dispersion of fine particles of a solid or liquid in a gas.

Suspended solids (SS) – solid particles suspended in water, an *indicator of water quality*.

Sustainability covenant (Section 49 of the *Environment Protection Act* of 1970) – a sustainability covenant is an agreement that a person or body undertakes to increase the resource use efficiency or reduce environmental impacts of activities, products, services, and production processes. *Parties can voluntarily enter into such agreements with the EPA or could be required to if they are declared by a Governor in Council (Canada), on the recommendation of the EPA, or have the potential for a significant impact on the environment.*

Sustainability science – the multidisciplinary scientific study of sustainability, focusing primarily on the quantitative dynamic interactions between nature and society. *Its objective is a deeper and more fundamental understanding of the rapidly growing interdependence of the nature-society system and the intention to make this sustainable. It critically examines the tools used by sustainability accounting and the methods of sustainability governance.*

Sustainability triangle – a graphic indication of the action needed to stabilize CO_2 levels below about 500 ppm. *It shows stabilization 'wedges' indicating yearly savings using a particular strategy.*

Sustainable – present needs without compromising the ability of future generations to meet their needs.

Sustainable agriculture – an ecologically sound, economically viable, socially just, and humane agricultural system; stewardship, soil conservation, and integrated pest management are essential for sustainability.

Sustainable consumption (or *sustainable resource use*) – a change to society's historical patterns of consumption and behavior enabling consumers to satisfy their needs with better–performing products or services using fewer resources, causing less pollution, and contributing to social progress worldwide.

Sustainable development – meets the needs of the present without compromising the ability of future generations to meet their own needs. *An increase in the well-being and standard of life for the average person maintained over the long term without degrading the environment or undermining the ability of future generations to meet their needs.*

Sustainable resource use (or *sustainable consumption*) – a change to society's historical patterns of consumption and behavior enabling consumers to satisfy their needs with better–performing products or services using fewer resources, causing less pollution, and contributing to social progress worldwide.

Sustained yield – utilization of a renewable resource at a rate that does not impair or damage its ability to be fully renewed long-term.

Swale – an open channel transporting surface run–off to a grassed drainage system. *Swales promote infiltration, the filtration of sediment by plants, and offer ornamental interest.*

Swamp – a wetland with trees, such as the extensive swamp forests of the southeastern United States, especially Florida and Louisiana.

Swidden agriculture – land cleared for cultivation, left to regenerate and repeated. See *Milpa agriculture*.

Symbiosis – the intimate living together of members of two species; *it includes mutualism, commensalism, and, in some classifications, parasitism.*

Synecology (or *community ecology*) – studies the interactions between the species comprising an ecological community.

Synergistic effects – when an injury caused by exposure to two environmental factors is together greater than the sum of exposure to each factor separately would be.

Synfuels – synthetic gas or synthetic oil made from coal or other sources.

System – a set of parts organized into a whole, usually processing energy flow. *A group of interacting, interrelated, or interdependent elements forming a complex whole.*

Systemic – a condition or process that affects the whole body; many metabolic poisons are systemic.

T

Taiga in Siberia (or *boreal forest*) – 1. forest areas of the northern temperate zone, mainly consisting of conifers. 2. the northernmost edge of the boreal forest, including species-poor woodland and peat deposits, intergrading with the arctic tundra.

Tailings – mining waste left after mechanical or chemical separation of minerals from crushed ore.

Take-back – a concept commonly associated with product stewardship, placing responsibility on brand–owners, retailers, manufacturers, or supply chain partners to accept products returned by consumers at the end of their useful life. *Products may be recycled, treated, or sent to landfills.*

Taking – unconstitutional confiscation of private property.

Tar sands – sand deposits containing petroleum or tar.

Tax incentive – reduction in taxes given to encourage specific behavior on the part of the recipient.

Technological optimists (or *Promethean environmentalism*) – those believing technology and human enterprise will find solutions for problems.

Technosphere – synthetic and composite components and materials formed by human activity. *True technosphere materials, like plastics, are not biodegradable.*

Tectonic plates – huge blocks of Earth's crust that slide slowly, pulling apart to open ocean basins or crashing ponderously into each other to create new, larger landmasses.

Temperate – with moderate temperatures, weather, or climate; neither hot nor cold. *A mean annual temperature between 0 and 20 °C.*

Temperature climate – characterized by relatively moderate mean annual temperatures, with average monthly temperatures above 10 °C in their warmest months and above −3 °C in colder months. *In geography, the temperate climates of Earth occur in the middle latitudes, which span between the tropics and the polar regions of Earth.*

Temperate deciduous forest – any forest in a temperate zone whose trees shed their leaves during the cold season. See *deciduous broadleaf forest*.

Temperate rainforest – the cool, dense rainforest of the northern Pacific coast, shrouded in fog often, dominated by large conifers many hundreds of years old.

Temperature – a measure of the speed of motion of molecules in a substance.

Temperature inversions – an atmospheric condition in which a layer of warm air traps cooler air near Earth's surface, preventing the standard rising of surface air.

Tennessee Valley Authority (TVA) – a federal corporation created by Congress in 1933 to operate Wilson Dam and develop the Tennessee River and its tributaries for navigation, flood control, and production and distribution of electricity; enactments include reforestation, industrial and community development, test-demonstration farming, the development of fertilizer and the establishment of recreational facilities; includes several dams for electricity and flood control.

Teragram – 1 trillion (10^{12}) grams = 1 million (10^6) metric tons.

Teratogens – chemicals or other factors that specifically cause abnormalities during embryonic growth and development.

Terracing – shaping the land to create level shelves of Earth to hold water and soil requires extensive hand labor or expensive machinery, enabling farmers to use steep hillsides.

Territoriality – an intense form of intraspecific competition in which organisms define as theirs an area surrounding their home site or nesting site and defend it, primarily against members of their species.

Territory – an area where individual organisms defend against competition from others.

Tertiary treatment – removing inorganic minerals and plant nutrients after primary and secondary sewage treatment.

Tetrafluoromethane (or *carbon tetrafluoride*) – the perfluorinated counterpart to the hydrocarbon methane. It can be classified as a haloalkane or halomethane. *Tetrafluoromethane is a useful refrigerant but a potent greenhouse gas. It has high bond strength due to the nature of the carbon-fluorine bond.*

TEX-86 – a paleothermometer based on the composition of membrane lipids of marine picoplankton.

Thermal ecology – the study of the relationship between temperature and organisms.

Thermal expansion – the increase in volume (and decrease in density) by warming water. Warming of the ocean leads to an expansion of the ocean volume, which leads to an increase in sea level.

Thermohaline circulation – large-scale density-driven circulation in oceans caused by differences in temperature and salinity. *In the North Atlantic, the thermohaline circulation consists of warm surface water flowing northward and cold deep water flowing southward, resulting in net poleward heat transport. The surface water sinks in highly restricted sinking regions located in high latitudes.*

Thermal mass (*architecture*) – any mass that can absorb and store heat and, therefore, be used to buffer temperature change. *Concrete, bricks, and tiles need a lot of heat energy to change their temperature and, therefore, have high thermal mass; timber has low thermal mass.*

Thermal plume – a plume of hot water discharged into a stream or lake by a heat source, such as a power plant.

Thermal pollution – industrial discharge of heated water into a river, lake, or another body of water, causing a temperature rise that endangers aquatic life.

Thermocline (or *metalimnion* for lakes) – a layer within a body of water or air where the temperature changes rapidly with depth. *In oceans and lakes, a distinctive temperature transition zone separates an upper layer mixed by the wind (the epilimnion) and a colder, deeper layer not mixed (the hypolimnion).*

Theoretical ecology – the development of ecological theory, usually with mathematical, statistical, or computer modeling tools.

Thermodynamics – a branch of physics focused on energy transfers and conversions.

> *First law of thermodynamics*: energy can be transformed and transferred but cannot be destroyed or created.

> *Second law of thermodynamics*: less energy is available for each successive energy transfer or transformation.

Thermohaline circulation – the global density-driven circulation of the oceans.

Thermosphere – the highest atmospheric zone; a region of hot, diluted gases above the mesosphere extending to about 1,000 miles from Earth's surface.

Third pipe system – a third pipe, in addition to the standard water supply pipe and sewer disposal pipe, which carries recycled water for irrigation purposes.

Third World – less-developed countries that are neither capitalistic and industrialized (the First World) nor centrally-planned socialist economies (the Second World).

Threat display – a signal used by organisms of certain species that the user intends to attack.

Threatened species – while it may be abundant in parts of its territorial range, a species that has declined significantly in numbers and may be on the verge of extinction in specific regions or localities.

Three Gorges Dam – near Yichang on the Yangtze River in China, helps control the flooding of the Yangtze River Valley; in addition, multiple river flows make the Three Gorges complex the largest electricity-generating facility in the world; a lake about 400 miles long was formed behind the dam, forcing the relocation of more than a million people and permanently submerging many historical sites.

Threshold (*ecology*) – a point that, when crossed, can bring rapid and sometimes unpredictable change in a trend. *An example would be the sudden altering of ocean currents due to ice melting at the poles.*

Tidal/ocean/wave energy – mechanical energy from water movement used to generate electricity.

Tidal station – a dam built across a narrow bay or estuary that traps tidewater in and out of the bay; water flowing through the dam spins turbines attached to electric generators.

Timberline – in the mountains, the highest-altitude edge of the forest that marks the beginning of the treeless alpine tundra.

Tipping fee – a fee for disposal of waste.

Tipping point (or *threshold*) – when a change in the climate triggers a significant environmental event, which may be permanent, such as widespread bleaching of corals or the melting of vast ice sheets.

Tipping points in the climate system – thresholds in the climate system that, when exceeded, can lead to significant changes in the system's state that are often irreversible.

Tolerance limits – maximum and minimum requirements in which an individual or system can maintain normal processes. See *limiting factors*.

Topography – a detailed map of the contours of surfaces of land.

Topsoil – 1. mostly fertile surface soil moved or introduced to top-dress gardens, road banks, lawns, etc. 2. usually, the uppermost 3 to 10 inches of soil. However, its thickness ranges from a meter or more under virgin prairie to zero in some deserts, a layer in which organic material is mixed with mineral particles. *Topsoil is critical for agriculture.*

Tornado – a rotating column of air usually accompanied by a funnel-shaped downward extension of a cumulonimbus cloud and having a vortex several hundred yards in diameter whirling destructively at speeds of up to 500 miles per hour.

Tort law – civil court cases that seek compensation for damages.

Total energy use – combined direct and indirect energy use.

Total equivalent warming impact (TEWI) – the sum of the direct emissions (chemical) and indirect emissions (energy use) of greenhouse gases.

Total fertility rate – the number of children, on average, a woman would have in her lifetime at present age-specific fertility rates. *Calculated as the average number of children born per woman of every given age in a particular year and totaled for all ages.*

Total growth rate – the net population growth rate from births, deaths, immigration, and emigration.

Total maximum daily loads (TMDL) – the amount of a pollutant that a water body can receive from point and non-point sources and meet water quality standards.

Total water use – in water accounting, the *distributed water* use plus *self-extracted water* use plus *reuse water*. Water consumption includes *direct* and *indirect* water use.

Town water – supplied by the government or privately as mains or reticulated water supply.

Toxic – poisonous; a substance that reacts with specific cellular components to kill cells.

Toxic colonialism – shipping toxic wastes to a weaker or poorer nation.

Toxic Release Inventory – a program created by the *Superfund Amendments and Reauthorization Act* (1984) requires manufacturing facilities, waste handling, and disposal sites to report annually on releases of more than 300 toxic materials.

Toxins – poisonous (i.e., harm or kill) chemicals that react with specific cellular components to kill cells or alter growth or development in undesirable ways; often harmful, even in dilute concentrations.

Appendix: Annotated Glossary of Environmental Science Terms

Trace gas – any one of the less common gases found in Earth's atmosphere. Nitrogen, oxygen, and argon comprise more than 99 percent of Earth's atmosphere. *Other gases, such as carbon dioxide, water vapor, methane, nitrogen oxides, ozone, and ammonia, are trace gases. Although relatively unimportant in terms of their absolute volume, they significantly affect Earth's weather and climate.*

Tradeable permits – pollution quotas or variances that can be bought or sold.

Traditional knowledge – information, practices, and beliefs handed down through generations.

Tragedy of the commons – an inexorable process of degradation of pooled resources due to the selfish self-interest of "free riders" who use or destroy more than their fair share of common property. See *open access system*.

Transfer station (*waste*) – allows drop–off and consolidation of refuse and a wide range of recyclable materials. *Transfer stations have become integral to municipal waste management, essential in materials recovery and improving transportation economics associated with municipal waste disposal.*

Transgenic plant – a plant with genetic material (e.g., DNA) transferred by genetic engineering.

Transitional zone – where populations from two or more adjacent communities meet and overlap.

Transparent – a substance capable of transmitting light so that objects or images are as clear as without the intervening material.

Transpiration – evaporation of water through plant leaves. *The process by which root systems of plants absorb water moves up through the plant and evaporates into the atmosphere as water vapor.*

Treeline – any delineation between habitats where trees can grow and not grow. *Tree lines are at the edges of habitats with suitable conditions for tree growth and development; trees cannot tolerate harsher environmental conditions beyond the tree line, usually because of frigid temperatures or insufficient moisture.*

Tributary – a small stream that empties into a bigger river.

Triple Bottom Line (*John Elkington, 1994*) – a form of sustainability accounting going beyond the financial 'bottom line' to consider *social, environmental, and economic consequences of an organization's activity.*

Trophic level – 1. a step in the movement of energy through an ecosystem; 2. an organism's position in the ecosystem's food chain. *Organism's position within a food chain: what it eats and what eats it.*

Trophic networks (*food chain, food webs,* or *food network*) – the feeding relationships between species within an ecosystem.

Trophic social network (or *food chain, food network,* or *web of life*) – the feeding relationships between species in each ecosystem.

Tropical – occurring in the tropics (the regions on *either side of the equator*); hot and humid with a mean annual temperature greater than 20 °C.

Tropical depression – hurricanes due to weather, climate, altitude, latitude, or direction changes.

Tropical rainforests – a biome characterized by regular, heavy rainfall, a humidity of at least 80 percent, and incredible biodiversity. *Forests in which rainfall is abundant (more than 80 inches per year), and temperatures are warm to hot year-round.*

Tropical seasonal forest – semi-evergreen or partly deciduous forests tending toward open woodlands and grassy savannas dotted with scattered, drought-resistant tree species; has distinct wet and dry seasons and is hot year-round.

Tropopause – the boundary between the troposphere and stratosphere.

Troposphere – the layer of air nearest to Earth's surface; temperature and pressure usually decrease with increasing altitude (depending on specific latitude). It ranges from the surface to about 10 km in altitude in mid-latitudes (ranging from 9 km in high latitudes to 16 km in the tropics on average), where clouds and "weather" phenomena occur. In the troposphere, temperatures generally decrease with height. See *ozone precursors*, *stratosphere*, and *atmosphere*.

Tropospheric ozone (O_3) – See *ozone*.

Tropospheric ozone precursors – See *ozone precursors*.

Tsunami – giant seismic sea swells moving rapidly from the center of an earthquake; can be 32-65 feet (10-20 meters) high when they reach shorelines hundreds or even thousands of miles from their origin.

Tundra – 1. a permanently frozen, treeless expanse between the Arctic region's ice cap and tree line. 2. treeless arctic or alpine biome characterized by cold, harsh winters, a short growing season, and potential for frost any month. *Vegetation includes low-growing perennial plants, mosses, and lichens. A treeless, level, or gently undulating plain characteristic of the Arctic and sub-Arctic regions characterized by low temperatures and short growing seasons.*

Turbine – a machine for converting heat energy in steam or high–temperature gas into mechanical energy. In *a turbine, a high–velocity flow of steam or gas passes through successive rows of radial blades fastened to a central shaft.* See tidal energy.

Turbulence – an eddying motion of the atmosphere that disrupts the normal flow of wind.

Typhoon – a tropical cyclone occurring in the western Pacific or Indian oceans.

U

U-238 – an isotope of uranium (U) used in nuclear power plants.

UHI – Urban heat island

Ultraviolet (UV) radiation – Sun's radiation that can be useful or harmful; UV rays from one part of the spectrum (UV-A) enhance plant life; UV rays from (UV-B) can cause skin cancer and tissue damage; the ozone layer in the atmosphere partly shields Earth from ultraviolet rays reaching Earth's surface. The energy range just beyond the violet end of the visible spectrum. *Although ultraviolet radiation constitutes only about 5 percent of the energy emitted from the Sun, it is the primary energy source for the stratosphere and mesosphere, playing a dominant role in energy balance and chemical composition. Most ultraviolet radiation is blocked by Earth's atmosphere, but some solar ultraviolet penetrates and aids in plant photosynthesis and helps produce vitamin D in humans. Too much ultraviolet radiation can burn the skin, cause skin cancer and cataracts, and damage vegetation.*

Umbrella species – a species selected for making conservation-related decisions because protecting it indirectly protects the many other species that make up the ecological community of its habitat. Compare *flagship species*.

Uncertainty – an expression of the degree to which future climate is unknown. *Uncertainty about the future climate arises from the complexity of the climate system and the ability of models to represent it, as well as the inability to predict society's decisions. There is uncertainty about how climate change and other stressors will affect people and natural systems.*

Uncontrolled – not under control, discipline, or governance.

Unconventional air pollutants – toxic or hazardous substances, such as asbestos, benzene, beryllium, mercury, polychlorinated biphenyls, and vinyl chloride, not listed in the original *Clean Air Act* because they were thought not to be released in large quantities. See *non-criteria pollutants*.

Unconventional oil – resources such as *shale oil* and *tar sands* liquefied and used as oil.

Undernourished – those who receive less than 90% of the minimum dietary intake over a long-term period; they lack energy for an active, productive life and are more susceptible to infectious diseases.

Underutilized – to utilize less than fully than or below its potential.

Undiscovered resources – speculative or inferred resources or those that have not yet been thought of.

United Nations (1945) – an international organization based in New York formed to promote international peace, security, and cooperation under a charter signed by 51 founding countries.

United Nations Framework Convention on Climate Change (UNFCCC; March 1994) – the Convention on Climate Change sets an overall framework for intergovernmental efforts to address the challenges posed by climate change. *It recognizes that the climate system is a shared resource whose stability can be affected by industrial and other carbon dioxide emissions and other greenhouse gases. The Convention has near universal membership, with 189 countries having ratified. Under the Convention, governments:* 1. report information on greenhouse gas emissions, national policies, and best practices. 2. launch national strategies for addressing greenhouse gas emissions and expected impacts, including providing financial and technological support to developing countries. 3. cooperate in preparing for adaptation to the impacts of climate change.

Universalists – those who believe that some fundamental ethical principles are universal and unchanging; to them, these principles are valid regardless of the context or situation.

Upstream – processes necessary before an activity is completed. *This is the extraction and transport of materials needed before manufacturing a product.* Compare *downstream*.

Upwelling – wind-driven motion of cooler nutrient-rich ocean water towards the ocean's surface, which stimulates the growth of phytoplankton. *The movement of nutrient-rich bottom water to the ocean's surface can occur far from shore but along certain steep coastal areas, where the surface layer of ocean water is pushed away from shore and replaced by cold, nutrient-rich bottom water.*

Urban area – where most people are not directly dependent on natural resource-based occupations.

Urban ecology – studies ecosystems in urban areas.

Urban heat island – any metropolitan area significantly warmer than its surroundings. Urban areas tend to have warmer air temperatures than the surrounding rural landscape due to the *low albedo* of streets, sidewalks, parking lots, and buildings. *These surfaces absorb solar radiation during the day and release it at night, resulting in higher temperatures. These surfaces absorb solar radiation during the day and release it at night, resulting in higher night temperatures; sparse vegetation and paved surfaces increase rain runoff, further reducing cooling effects; temperatures in cities are usually 3-5 °F hotter than the surrounding countryside.*

Urban heat island effect (or *heat island*) – the tendency for higher air temperatures to persist in urban areas because of heat absorbed and emitted by buildings and asphalt, tending to make cities warmer than the surrounding countryside.

Urban metabolism – the functional flow of materials and energy required by cities.

Urbanization – an increasing concentration of the population in cities and a transformation of land use to an urban pattern of organization.

Useful energy – available energy used to increase system production and efficiency.

Utilitarian conservation – a philosophy that resources should be used for the greatest good for the greatest number for the longest time.

Utilitarianism – a theory that states that the best moral action is often the most utilitarian one, meaning maximizing the well-being of others. See *utilitarian conservation*.

V

Validate – to establish or verify accuracy. *For example, measurements of temperature or precipitation can be used to determine the accuracy of climate model results.*

Values – 1. (*economics*) an estimation of worth; 2. a set of ethical beliefs that determine the sense of right and wrong; beliefs or ideals individuals or society hold about what is essential or desirable.

Vector (*disease*) – an organism, such as an insect, that transmits disease-causing microorganisms such as viruses or bacteria. Vector-borne diseases include, for example, malaria, dengue fever, and Lyme disease. See *vector-borne disease*.

Vegetation – ground cover provided by plants.

Vegetation formation – a concept used to classify vegetation communities.

Veloway – cycle track; cycleway. Contrast *freeway*.

Vertical stratification – the vertical distribution of specific subcommunities within a community.

Village – a collection of rural households linked by culture, custom, and association with land.

Vinyl – a plastic (usually PVC) used to make beverage bottles, credit cards, pipes, and hoses.

Virtual water (*J.A. Allan*, early 1990s) – the volume of water required to produce a commodity or service. First coined by Professor J.A. Allan of the University of London, it is now widely known as *embodied water*.

Virus – a microscopic obligate intracellular parasite that infects and replicates exclusively within the living cells of host organisms.

Viscous – having a relatively high resistance to flow.

Visible light – a portion of the electromagnetic spectrum with wavelengths used for photosynthesis.

Visual waste audit – observing and estimating waste streams and practices without physical weighing.

Vitamins – organic molecules essential for life that cannot be manufactured in the body but must be gotten from one's diet; they act as enzyme cofactors.

Volatile organic compounds (VOC) – molecules containing carbon and differing proportions of hydrogen, oxygen, fluorine, and chlorine. *With sunlight and heat, they form ground-level ozone.*

Volcanism – the eruption of molten rock (magma) onto the surface of Earth or a solid-surface planet or moon, where lava, pyroclastic, and volcanic gases erupt through a break in the surface is a vent. *It includes phenomena resulting from and causing magma within the crust or mantle of the body to rise through the crust and form volcanic rocks on the surface. Magmas that reach the surface and solidify form extrusive landforms.*

Volt or voltage (V) – the potential difference between two points. 1,000 volts equals 1 kilovolt (kV).

Voluntary simplicity – deliberately choosing to live at a lower level of consumption as a matter of personal and environmental health. See *simple living*.

Vortex – a spiral motion of fluid within a limited area, especially a whirling mass of water or air that sucks everything near it toward its center.

Vulnerability – the degree to which a system is susceptible to, or unable to compensate, adverse effects of climate change, including climate variability and extremes. *This is a function of the character, magnitude, and rate of the climate variation, the system's sensitivity, and adaptive capacity.*

Vulnerability assessment (or *vulnerability analysis*) – an analysis of the degree to which a system is susceptible to or unable to cope with the adverse effects of climate change.

Vulnerable species – naturally rare organisms or species whose numbers have been so reduced by human activities that they are susceptible to actions that could push them into a threatened or endangered status.

W

WMO – World Meteorological Organization

Warm front – a long, wedge-shaped boundary caused when a warmer advancing air mass slides over neighboring cooler air parcels.

Warning coloration (or *aposematism*) – a warning signal consisting of brightly colored or starkly contrasting patterns used by a prey species to advertise its unprofitability to potential predator species.

Waste – material (liquid, solid, or gaseous) produced by domestic households and commercial, institutional, municipal, or industrial organizations that cannot be collected and recycled for further use. *Solid waste involves materials currently entering landfills, even though some are potentially recyclable.*

Waste analysis – quantifying waste streams, recording and detailing it as a proportion of the total waste stream, determining its destination, and recording details of waste practices.

Waste assessment (or audit) – observing, measuring, and recording data and collecting and analyzing waste samples. *Some practitioners consider an assessment where observations are carried out visually, without sorting and measuring individual streams (see visual waste audit).* See *visual waste audit*.

Waste avoidance – the primary pillar of the waste hierarchy; avoidance works on the principle that the greatest gains result from efficiency–centered actions remove or reduce the need to consume materials in the first place but deliver the same outcome.

Waste factors (*round-wood calculations*) – the ratio of one cubic meter of round wood used per cubic meter (or ton) of product.

Waste generation – unwanted materials, including recyclables as well as garbage. Waste generation equals materials recycled plus waste to landfill; waste generation = materials recycled + waste to landfill.

Waste hierarchy (or *waste management hierarchy*) – promoting waste avoidance ahead of recycling and disposal, often referred to in community education campaigns as 'reduce, reuse, recycle.' The waste hierarchy is recognized in the *Environment Protection Act* (1970), promoting prioritized management of wastes: avoidance, reuse, recycling, energy recovery, treatment, containment, and disposal.

Waste lagoons – a blocked-off area used for the dumping of waste products.

Waste management – practices and procedures related to handling waste.

Waste minimization – 1. techniques to keep waste generation at a minimum level to divert materials from landfills and thereby reduce the requirement for waste collection, handling, and disposal to a landfill; 2. recycling and efforts to reduce waste going into the waste stream.

Waste reduction – measures to reduce the amount of waste generated by individuals or organizations.

Waste stream – materials of a particular type (e.g., timber waste stream) or produced by a particular source (e.g., C & I). *There is a steady flow of varied wastes, from domestic garbage and yard wastes to industrial, commercial, and construction refuse.*

Waste treatment – where some additional processing is undertaken of a waste; may be done to reduce its toxicity or increase its degradability or compostability.

Wastewater – used water, generally not suitable for drinking.

Water consumption – in water accounting: distributed water uses plus self–extracted water use plus reuse water use minus distributed water supplied to other users minus in–stream use (where applicable).

Water cycle (*hydrological cycle*) – 1. passage of water between oceans and water bodies, land, and atmosphere. 2. the recycling and utilization of water on Earth, including atmospheric, surface, and underground phases and biological and non-biological components. *The non-stop water circulation on, above, and below Earth's surface. Water changes states during the cycle: liquid, vapor, and ice.*

Water droplet coalescence – condensation in clouds too warm for ice crystal formation.

Water entitlement – the benefit defined in a statutory water plan to share water from a water source.

Water footprint – the volume of fresh water required in each period to perform a particular task or to produce the goods and services consumed at any level of the action hierarchy. *Country water footprint is a concept introduced by Hoekstra in 2002 as a consumption-based indicator of water use – the volume of water needed to produce the goods and services consumed by the inhabitants of a country.*

Water harvesting (or *rainwater harvesting*) – collecting rainwater either in storage or the soil mainly close to where it falls; the attempt to increase rainwater productivity by storing it in ponds, wetlands, etc., and helping to avoid the need for infrastructure to bring water from elsewhere. *Practiced on a large scale upstream, this reduces available water downstream.*

Water intensity – the volume of water used per unit of production or service delivery; generally further reduced to monetary unit return per given volume of water used. *Essentially, it is equivalent to water productivity.*

Water neutral – a scientifically based calculator for individuals to be extended to cover the construction industry, the food and beverage sector, and other corporations or organizations. *The water offset calculators aimed at businesses and other organizations are being developed and will be launched with the Individual Water Offset Calculator.*

Water productivity (WP) – the efficiency of outcomes for water used; the quantity required to produce a given outcome. WP–field relates to crop output (e.g., kg of wheat produced per m^3 of water). *WP–basin relates to water productivity in the widest possible sense, including crops, fishery yield, environmental services, etc. Increasing WP increases the value of available water.*

Water quality – the microbiological, biological, physical, and chemical characteristics.

Water resources – water in various forms, such as groundwater, surface water, snow, and ice, are present in the land phase of the hydrological cycle. *Some parts may be renewable seasonally, but others may be effectively mined.*

Water restrictions – mandatory restrictions on water use relative to water storage levels.

Water security – reliable availability of water in sufficient quantity and quality to sustain human health, livelihoods, and the environment.

Watershed – the land from which rain and melted snow drain downhill into a body of water (i.e., a river, lake, reservoir, estuary, wetland, sea, or ocean).

Water stress – when the demand for water by people and ecosystems exceeds the available supply. A situation when residents of a country or region do not have accessible enough high-quality water to meet their everyday needs.

Water table – upper level of water in saturated ground. The surface between the zone of saturation and the zone of aeration; water seeping down from rain-soaked surfaces will sink until it reaches an impermeable or water-tight layer of rock; the water will collect above this layer, filling the pores and cracks of the permeable portions; the top of this area of water is the water table.

Water trading – transactions involving water access entitlements or water allocations assigned to water access entitlements.

Water treatment – 1. converting raw, untreated water to a public water supply safe for human consumption can involve screening, initial disinfection, clarification, filtration, pH correction, and final disinfection. 2. where some additional processing is undertaken of a particular waste. This may be done to reduce its toxicity or increase its degradability or compostability.

Water vapor – the most abundant greenhouse gas is the water present in the atmosphere in gaseous form. Water (H_2O) vapor is integral to the natural greenhouse effect. *While humans are not significantly increasing their concentration through direct emissions, it contributes to the enhanced greenhouse effect because the warming influence of greenhouse gases leads to positive water vapor feedback. In addition to its role as a natural greenhouse gas, water vapor affects the planet's temperature because clouds form when excess atmospheric water vapor condenses to form ice, water droplets, and precipitation.* See *greenhouse gas*. The gaseous state of water. *Water vapor is a greenhouse gas because its presence in Earth's atmosphere contributes to the greenhouse effect.*

Waterlogging – water saturation of soil that fills air spaces and causes plant roots to die from lack of oxygen, often due to over-irrigation.

Watershed – a water catchment area (North America) or drainage divide (non–American usage). *The area of land that catches rain and snow and drains or seeps into a marsh, stream, river, lake, or groundwater; often contained in the area of land between two ridges of high land, which divide two areas that are drained by different river systems.*

Watt, Kilowatt – a unit of measure of electric power at a point in time as capacity or demand; 1 watt = 1 joule/second; 1 joule = energy spent in one second when a current of 1 amp flows through a resistance of 1 ohm; 1 kilowatt – 1000 watts.

Weather – the hourly/daily change in atmospheric conditions over a more extended period constitutes the climate of a region. 1. atmospheric conditions at any given time or place. It is measured in terms of wind, temperature, humidity, atmospheric pressure, cloudiness, and precipitation. In most places, weather can change from hour to hour, day to day, and season to season. 2. in a narrow sense, the climate is usually the "average weather" or, more rigorously, the statistical description regarding the mean and variability of relevant quantities over a period ranging from months to thousands or millions of years. The classical period is 30 years, as defined by the World Meteorological Organization (WMO). These quantities are often surface variables such as temperature, precipitation, and wind. 3. in a broader sense, the climate is the state of the climate system, including a statistical description. A simple way of remembering the difference is that *climate* is expected (e.g., cold winters), and *weather* is what results (e.g., a blizzard). See *climate*.

Weathering – 1. the degradation of rocks, soil, minerals, wood, and artificial materials through contact with Earth's atmosphere, water, and biological organisms. 2. changes in rocks by exposure to air, water, changing temperatures, and reactive chemical agents.

Web of life (or *food chain, food network, trophic social network*) – the feeding relationships between species in each ecosystem.

Weed – a plant growing where it is not wanted, often at a high dispersal rate.

Well-being – a context–dependent physical and mental condition determined by the presence of basic materials for a good life, freedom and choice, health, good social relations, and security.

Wetlands – areas of permanent or intermittent inundation, whether natural or artificial, with static or flowing water, fresh, brackish, or salt, including areas of marine water not exceeding 6 m at low tide. An ecosystem consisting of land permanently or seasonally saturated with water; the habitat of aquatic plants. *Engineered wetlands* are becoming more frequent, and so are *constructed wetlands*. In urban areas, wetlands are the *kidney of a city*.

Whitegoods – household electrical appliances like refrigerators, washing machines, and dishwashers.

Wicked problems – problems with no simple right or wrong answer where there is no single, generally agreed-on definition of or solution for the particular issue.

Wicking (or *capillary action*) – water drawn through a medium by surface tension.

Wilderness – an undeveloped land affected primarily by the forces of nature; *it is an area where humans are visitors who do not remain.*

Wilderness Act (1964) – legislation recognizing that leaving the land in its natural state may be the highest and best use of some areas.

Wildlife – plants, animals, and microbes that live independently of humans; plants, animals, and microbes that are not domesticated.

Wildlife corridor – a strip of land intended to facilitate the movement of wildlife species between separate areas of their habitat.

Wildlife refuges – areas set aside to shelter, feed, and protect wildlife; however, due to political and economic pressures, refuges often allow hunting, trapping, mineral exploitation, and other activities that threaten wildlife.

Wind – moving air, especially a natural and perceptible movement parallel to or along the ground.

Wind energy – the kinetic energy present in the motion of the wind. Wind energy can be converted to mechanical or electrical energy. *A traditional mechanical windmill can be used to pump water or grind grain. A modern electrical wind turbine converts the force of the wind to electrical energy for consumption on–site or export to the electricity grid.*

Wind farms – large numbers of wind turbines concentrated in a single area; usually owned by a utility or large-scale energy producer.

Wind turbines – a turbine with a large, fanned wheel that spins in the wind to generate electricity. See *wind energy*.

Windbreak – rows of trees or shrubs planted to block wind flow, reduce soil erosion, and protect sensitive crops from high winds.

Wise Use Groups – a coalition of ranchers, loggers, miners, industrialists, hunters, off-road vehicle users, land developers, and others who prefer unrestricted access to natural resources and public lands.

Withdrawal – a description of the amount of water taken from a lake, river, or aquifer.

Woodland – a low-density forest. A forest where tree crowns cover less than 20 percent of the ground. See *open canopy*.

Work – 1. physical or mental effort; 2. a force exerted for a distance; 3. an energy transformation process that results in a change of concentration or form of energy.

World conservation strategy – a proposal for maintaining essential ecological processes, preserving genetic diversity, and ensuring that utilization of species and ecosystems is sustainable.

World Trade Organization (WTO) – association of 135 nations that regulate international trade.

X

Xeric – extremely dry, as of a landscape or habitat.

Xeriscaping – landscaping with drought-resistant plants that need no watering.

Xerocole – an animal adapted to live in a desert. The main challenges xerocoles must overcome are lack of water and excessive heat.

Xerophyte – a plant adapted to dry conditions.

Xylophagous – feeding on wood, as of an organism.

X-ray – very short wavelength in the electromagnetic spectrum; can penetrate soft tissue; although it is useful in medical diagnosis, it damages tissue and causes mutations.

Y

Yellowcake – the concentrate of 70 to 90% uranium oxide extracted from crushed ore.

Yellow rain – a powdery, poisonous, yellow substance reported dropping from the air in the eastern parts of China and Asia and found to be the excrement of wild honeybees contaminated by a fungal toxin.

Yucca Mountain, Nevada – the U.S. Department of Energy's potential underground geological repository for spent nuclear fuel and high-level radioactive waste.

Z

Zebra mussel – a European and Asian freshwater mussel regarded as a nuisance in the Great Lakes and surrounding waterways, where it was accidentally introduced.

Zero population growth (ZPG) (or *replacement level of fertility*) – the number of births at which people are just replacing themselves.

Zero tillage (or *no-till farming*) – a conservation tillage system. An agricultural technique for growing crops or pasture without disturbing the soil through tillage. *Zero tillage farming decreases soil erosion tillage caused in certain soils, especially in sandy and dry soils on sloping terrain. Benefits include an increase in the amount of water infiltrating into the soil, soil retention of organic matter, and nutrient cycling.*

Zero waste – turning waste into a resource; redesigning resource–use so waste is reduced to zero; ensuring that by-products are used elsewhere and goods recycled, emulating cycling of natural wastes.

Zone of aeration – the area immediately below the ground surface within which pore spaces are partly filled with water and air.

Zone of leaching – the layer of soil just beneath the topsoil where water percolates, removing soluble nutrients that accumulate in the subsoil.

Zone of saturation – lower levels of soil where spaces are filled with water.

Zooplankton – the animal component of the planktonic community. Plankton are aquatic organisms that are unable to swim effectively against currents. Consequently, they drift or are carried along by ocean currents, seas, lakes, or rivers.

Homeschool study aids

STEM

- Physics
- Chemistry
- Organismal Biology
- Cell and Molecular Biology
- Anatomy & Physiology
- Environmental Science
- Psychology

Social Studies

- American History
- U.S. Government & Politics
- Comparative Government & Politics
- World History
- European History
- Human Geography
- Sociology

Visit our Amazon store

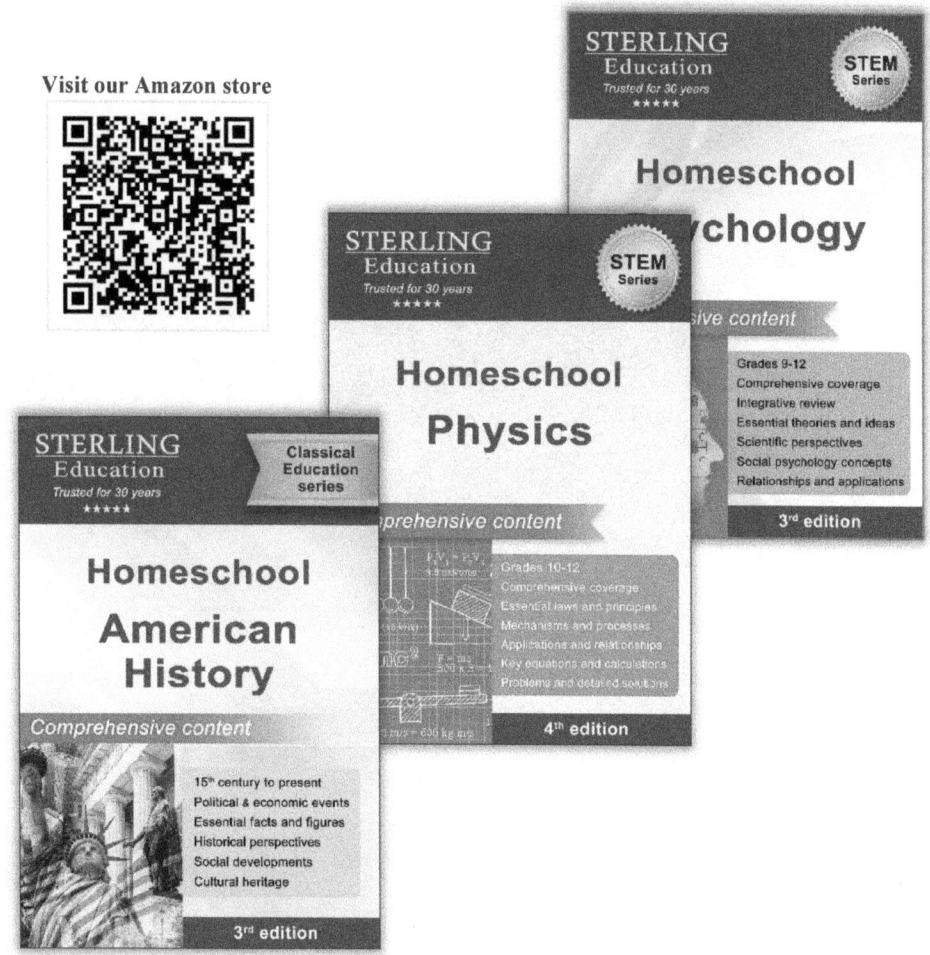

www.ingramcontent.com/pod-product-compliance
Lightning Source LLC
LaVergne TN
LVHW081344060526
838201LV00050B/1706